REFERENCE CHART FOR REVISION

4 MATERIALS
4a (72–76)   Dev
ADEQUATE DEVELOPMENT
4b (77–78) Sources
SOURCES FOR MATERIAL

7c (154–158)   Intro
INTRODUCTIONS
7d (161–164)   Conc
CONCLUSIONS

8 PARAGRAPHS
8a (173–177)   ¶
PARAGRAPHING
8b (184–185)   ¶, Di
DIALOGUE PARAGRAPHS

Directions for use of this chart and for correction symbols are in chapter 1, pp. 19–22. Numbers in parentheses refer to pages in the text. For an alphabetical list of correction symbols, see inside back cover. If an expression in a paper is circled without reference to this chart, look it up in the Glossary, chapter 27, or the index.

14 VARIATIONS
14a (277–280)   Expl
EXPLETIVE SENTENCES
14b (280–284)   Pass
PASSIVE SENTENCES

15 COORDINATION
15a (290–293)   Paral
PARALLEL STRUCTURE

15b (294–295)   Inc
INCOMPLETE CONSTRUCTION

15c (295–298)   Comp
COMPLETING COMPARISON

17 COHERENCE
17a (329–330) Conj C
COORDINATING CONJUNCTIONS
17b (330–331) Conj Adv
CONJUNCTIVE ADVERBS

17c (331–333) Conj S
SUBORDINATING CONJUNCTIONS
17d (333–334)   Prep
PREPOSITIONS

17e, f (334–340)   Ref,
PRONOUN,   W Ref
WORD REFERENCE
17g (342–344)   Agr
AGREEMENT

18 EMPHASIS
18a (356–357)   Em
EMPHASIS BY STRUCTURE
18b (362–364)   F Em
FALSE EMPHASIS

21 STYLE
21a (438–442)   Tone
APPROPRIATE TONE
21b (442–446)   PV
POINT OF VIEW

24 RESEARCH PAPER

24a (486–488) R Subj
RESEARCH SUBJECT

24b (493–495)   Fn
FOOTNOTE FORM
24c (505–507) Bibliog
BIBLIOGRAPHY FORM

RESEARCH WRITING

25d (539–541)   P4
PUNCTUATION IN SERIES

25e (541–544)   P5
PUNCTUATION OF NONRESTRICTIVE MODIFIERS

25f (545)   P6
PUNCTUATION AFTER INTRODUCTORY MODIFIERS

25g (546–547)   P7
PUNCTUATION OF STATISTICS

25k (553–555)   P11,
DASH   Dash

25l (555–556)   P12
PARENTHESES, BRACKETS

25m (556–558)   P13,
INAPPROPRIATE   No P
PUNCTUATION

26d (576–579)   Hy
HYPHENS

26e (579–581)   Pl,
PLURAL FORM   Sing

26f (581–582)   Num
NUMBERS

26g (582–584)   Apos,
APOSTROPHES,   Poss,
POSSESSIVES,   Cont
CONTRACTIONS

26k (588–589)   Div
DIVISION OF WORDS

27 (596–653)   Gloss
GLOSSARY
CHECK MARKED ITEMS AGAINST ALPHABETICAL LIST

27
USAGE

MODERN
ENGLISH
HANDBOOK

MODERN ENGLISH HANDBOOK

FIFTH EDITION

Robert M. Gorrell

University of Nevada

Charlton Laird

University of Nevada

PRENTICE-HALL, INC., ENGLEWOOD CLIFFS, NEW JERSEY

Library of Congress Catalog Card Number: 77–38291

ISBN: C   0–13–594200–4

Printed in the United States of America

10 9 8 7 6 5 4 3 2 1

Prentice-Hall International, Inc., *London*
Prentice-Hall of Australia, Pty. Ltd., *Sydney*
Prentice-Hall of Canada, Ltd., *Toronto*
Prentice-Hall of India Private Limited, *New Delhi*
Prentice-Hall of Japan, Inc., *Tokyo*

Acknowledgments

The authors are grateful for permission to quote from the following copyrighted works:

THE AMERICAN HERITAGE DICTIONARY OF THE ENGLISH LANGUAGE. Copyright © 1969, 1970, 1971 by American Heritage Publishing Co., Inc. Used with permission.

SHERWOOD ANDERSON, from *Winesburg, Ohio.* Copyright 1919 by B. W. Huebach, Inc., renewed 1947 by Eleanor Copenhaven Anderson. Used by permission of the publisher, The Viking Press, Inc., and Jonathan Cape Ltd.

PETER AXTHELM, "Introduction" in *The City Game.* Copyright © 1970 by Peter Axthelm. Used by permission of Harper & Row, Publishers and The Sterling Lord Agency.

ALBERT C. BAUGH, from *A History of the English Language,* 2nd ed. Copyright © 1957 by Appleton-Century-Crofts, Educational Division, Meredith Corporation. Used by permission of the publisher.

ROBERT BENCHLEY, from "Ladies Wild" in *Benchley or Else.* Copyright 1938 by Robert C. Benchley. Used by permission of Harper & Row, Publishers.

RUTH BENEDICT, from *Patterns of Culture.* Reprinted by permission of Houghton Mifflin Company and Routledge & Kegan Paul, Ltd.

FRANZ BOAS, from *The Mind of Primitive Man,* revised edition 1965, The Macmillan Company. Used by permission of the publisher.

VAN WYCK BROOKS, from *The World of Washington Irving.* Copyright 1944, 1950 by Van Wyck Brooks. Used by permission from E. P. Dutton & Co., Inc., and J. M. Dent & Sons Ltd.: Publishers.

MARGARET M. BRYANT, from *Current American Usage.* Used by permission of Thomas Y. Crowell Company.

RACHEL CARSON, from *The Sea Around Us,* copyright © 1950, 1951, and 1961 by Rachel L. Carson; and *Under the Sea Wind,* copyright 1941 by Rachel L. Carson, renewed 1969 by Roger Christie. Used by permission of Oxford University Press, Inc., and MacGibon and Kee.

JAMES BRYANT CONANT, "Force and Freedom," Copyright © 1949 by The Atlantic Monthly Company, Boston, Mass. Reprinted with permission from author and publisher.

NORMAN COUSINS, "History Is Made by Headlines" from *Saturday Review.* Used by permission of the publisher.

MICHAEL CRICHTON, from *The Andromeda Strain.* Copyright © 1969 by Centesis Corporation. Used by permission of Alfred A. Knopf, Inc., and Jonathan Cape, Ltd.

ROBERT M. ESTRICK and HANS SPERBER, from *Three Keys to Language.* Used by permission of the publisher, Holt, Rinehart & Winston, Inc.

BERGEN EVANS, from *The Natural History of Nonsense.* Copyright 1946 by Bergen Evans. Used by permission of the publisher, Alfred A. Knopf, Inc.

ROBERT FROST, "Stopping by Woods on a Snowy Evening," from *The Poetry of Robert Frost,* edited by Edward Connery Lathem. Copyright 1923 by Holt, Rinehart & Winston, Inc., 1951 by Robert Frost. Reprinted by permission of Holt, Rinehart & Winston, Inc., and Jonathan Cape Ltd.

FUNK & WAGNALLS *Standard College Dictionary.* Used by permission of Thomas Y. Crowell Company.

ROBERT GRAVES, from "Lars Porsena." Used with permission of Cassell & Company, Ltd.

ERNEST HEMINGWAY, from *A Moveable Feast,* copyright © 1964 by Ernest Hemingway Ltd., and from *The Old Man and the Sea,* copyright 1952 by Ernest Hemingway. Used by permission of the publisher, Charles Scribner's Sons and Jonathan Cape Ltd.

IRVING HOWE, from *Politics and the Novel.* Copyright © 1967 by Irving Howe. Reprinted with permission.

ROBERT A. HUME, from *Runaway Star: An Appreciation of Henry James.* Copyright © 1951 by Cornell University. Used by permission of Cornell University Press.

SIR ARTHUR KEITH, from *Man: A History of the Human Body.* Copyright © 1912 by Oxford University Press. Used by permission of Clarendon Press, Oxford.

JACK KEROUAC, from *On the Road.* Copyright © 1955, 1957 by Jack Kerouac. Reprinted by permission of The Viking Press, Inc., and Andre Deutsch, Ltd.

LOUIS KRONENBERGER, from *Company Manners.* Copyright © 1951, 1953, 1954 by Louis Kronenberger. Reprinted by special permission of the publishers, The Bobbs-Merrill Company, Inc., and the author.

JOSEPH WOOD KRUTCH, from *The Voice of the Desert.* Copyright © 1955 by William Sloane Associates. Used by permission of William Morrow & Company, Inc.

SUSANNE K. LANGER, from *Philosophy in a New Key: A Study in the Symbolism of Reason, Rite, and Art.* Copyright © 1942, 1951 by Harvard University Press. Used by permission of the publisher.

D. H. LAWRENCE, from "The Novel" in *The Later D. H. Lawrence.* Copyright 1952 by Alfred A. Knopf, Inc. Reprinted by permission of Alfred A. Knopf, Inc., and L. D. Pollinger, Ltd.

RUSSELL LYNES, from "Highbrow, Middlebrow, Lowbrow," from *Harper's Magazine,* February 1949. Used by permission of Harper's Magazine.

ARTHUR MACHEN, from *Hieroglyphics: A Note Upon Ecstasy in Literature.* Used by permission of the publisher, Alfred A. Knopf, Inc.

ARCHIBALD MACLEISH, from *What Is 'Realism' Doing to American History.* Used by permission of the publisher, Houghton Mifflin Company.

NORMAN MAILER, from *The Naked and the Dead.* Used by permission from Hellerstein, Rosier & Rembar.

MARYA MANNES, from "The 'Night of Horror' in Brooklyn," in *But Will It Sell?* Copyright © 1964 by Marya Mannes. Reprinted by permission of J. B. Lippincott Company and Victor Gollancz Ltd., London.

SOMERSET MAUGHAM, from "Rain" in *The Complete Short Stories* published by William Heinemann in the United Kingdom, and Doubleday & Company, Inc. Used by permission of the publishers and Literary Executor of W. Somerset Maugham.

MEET THE PRESS, NBC interview with Lord Kenneth Clark, Merkle Press, November 15, 1970. Reprinted with permission.

M L A STYLE SHEET. Used by permission of Modern Language Association of America.

THE OXFORD DICTIONARY OF ENGLISH ETYMOLOGY, edited by C. T. Onions 1966. By permission of the Clarendon Press, Oxford.

VERNON LOUIS PARRINGTON, from *Main Currents in American Thought.* Copyright 1927, 1930, by Harcourt Brace Jovanovich, Inc.; renewed, 1955, 1958, by Vernon Louis Parrington, Jr., Louise P. Tucker, Elizabeth P. Thomas. Reprinted by permission of the publisher.

THE RANDOM HOUSE DICTIONARY OF THE ENGLISH LANGUAGE—COLLEGE EDITION. Copyright © 1969, 1968 by Random House, Inc. Reprinted with permission.

KENNETH REXROTH, from "Le Morte D'Arthur." Used by permission of the author.

LEO ROSTEN, from "Handy-Dandy Plan to Save Our Colleges" in *Look* December 15, 1970. Reprinted by permission of the author.

CARL SANDBURG, from *Abraham Lincoln: The Prairie Years.* By permission of the publisher, Harcourt Brace Jovanovich, Inc.

EDWARD SAPIR, from *Language: An Introduction to the Study of Speech.* Copyright 1921 by Harcourt Brace Jovanovich, Inc.; renewed, 1949, by Jean Sapir. Reprinted by permission of the publisher.

RONALD SEARLE, cartoon with the caption, "Some little girl didn't hear me say 'unarmed combat'" from *The Female Approach.* Used with permission from Alfred A. Knopf, Inc., and A.P.I.A. of London.

THEODORE L. SHAW, cartoon with the caption "The Wall of Perfections; Tear It Down" from *That Obnoxious Fraud: The Art Critic.* Copyright © 1969 by Stuart Publications. Reprinted with permission.

PETER SHRAG, from "Decline of the Wasp" in *Harper's Magazine,* April, 1970. Used with permission of the author.

JOHN UPDIKE, from "On the Sidewalk" in *Assorted Prose.* Used by permission of the publisher, Alfred A. Knopf, Inc. Originally published in *The New Yorker,* Feb. 21, 1959.

ANDREW P. VAYDA, "On the Nutritional Value of Cannibalism," in *American Anthropologist,* Volume 72, Number 6, 1970, pp. 1462–1463. By permission of the author and American Anthropological Association.

JOSEPH WAMBAUGH, from *The New Centurions.* Used by permission of the publisher, Atlantic-Little Brown.

NESTA H. WEBSTER, from *The French Revolution.* Used by permission of the author.

WEBSTER'S SEVENTH NEW COLLEGIATE DICTIONARY. Copyright © 1971 by G. & C. Merriam Co., Publishers of the Merriam-Webster Dictionaries. Used with permission of the publisher.

E. B. WHITE, from "Sound" in *The Second Tree from the Corner,* pp. 113–114. Copyright 1948 by E. B. White. Originally appeared in *The New Yorker* and reprinted by permission of Harper & Row, Publishers, and Hamish Hamilton Ltd.

A. N. WHITEHEAD, from *Science and the Modern World*. Copyright 1925 by The Macmillan Company, renewed 1953 by Evelyn Whitehead. Used by permission of The Macmillan Company and Cambridge University Press.

PETER WINCH, from "Universities and the State," in *Universities Quarterly*, XII, November 1957. Used by permission of Turnstile Press Ltd.

THOMAS WOLFE, from *Of Time and the River*, copyright 1935 by Charles Scribner's Sons, renewal copyright © 1963 by Paul Gitlin, administrator, C.T.A., and from *The House of the Far and Lost*. Used by permission of the publisher, Charles Scribner's Sons.

TOM WOLFE, from "Pause Now and Consider Some Tentative Conclusions About the Meaning of this Mass Perversion Called Porno-Violence." First published in *Esquire*. Copyright © 1967 by Tom Wolfe. Reprinted by permission of Tom Wolfe c/o International Famous Agency.

TOM WOLFE, from *The Kandy-Kolored Tangerine-Flake Streamline Baby*. Reprinted with permission of Farrar, Straus & Giroux, Inc. and Tom Wolfe c/o International Famous Agency.

CHARLES LESLIE WRENN, *The English Language*. Copyright © 1952 by Methuen & Company, London. Reprinted by permission.

ART YOUNG, cartoon with the caption, "Chee, Annie, look at de stars . . ." from *The Best of Art Young*. Copyright 1963, 1964, by The Vanguard Press, Inc. Reprinted by permission of the publisher.

PREFACE

But easy writing's curst hard reading.
RICHARD BRINSLEY SHERIDAN

Writing is hard work, but this book assumes that it becomes easier and better with serious study. The book is based on the following beliefs:

1. Writing grows from expression and is intended to communicate; good writing says something, and develops from clear thinking.

2. Writing improves more readily through understanding than through correction. Some correction is essential, but many so-called errors diminish when the student learns to construct a sentence or a paragraph and to utilize the interactive process of prewriting, writing, and rewriting.

3. Basic principles can be discovered, learned, and applied — some by analyzing examples of successful prose, some by learning how language works.

4. Writing is educative in the best sense; by learning to write the student trains his use of the mind and provides himself with more of the materials that minds work with.

Because of these beliefs we have approached writing with two major emphases: rhetorical and linguistic. Rhetoric we have taken to be a study of how to develop ideas through language and how to choose among available means of expression, that is, how to build sentences and groups of sentences so that they will achieve the results the writer wants, whether in brief paragraphs or in extended compositions. We have accordingly offered the student writer information about available means of expression, about the varied devices for communication. We have also attempted to help him learn to distinguish among these by anticipating their effects, learning which tools will do which jobs.

Since the basic tool of writing is language, we have rested discussion upon it. The native language is obviously worthy of study for itself, but language study is also practically important for writing because it describes the tools with which the writer works. The book treats English grammar because grammatical principles show how words work together and thus define constructions available to the writer, but it limits grammatical discussions to problems having direct impact on writing and speaking. The book discusses usage differences as linguistic phenomena because the traditions of standard English influence the effect of any piece of writing. Words are the building blocks of writing, and accordingly we have given special attention to word choice, taking advantage of modern linguistic study. We have attempted through such approaches to make the book practical, to teach the essentials of linguistics and rhetoric while applying these to the modern student's daily writing needs.

In this fifth edition we have retained the principles of earlier versions, but we have tried to implement those principles more thoroughly, notably by expanding rhetorical discussions at all levels and by adding illustrations. We have added rhetorical chapters on writing examinations and other impromptu pieces (chapter 22) and on writing themes about literature (chapter 23). The discussion of documented papers has been adapted to the new MLA style sheet, and the treatment of scholarly writing at once enlarged and simplified. We have reorganized and expanded the discussions of development; see chapters 3 and 4. We have tried, also, to simplify portions of the book especially concerned with revision, continuing the "Guide for Revision" sections, but enclosing them in boxes and including them within the positive rhetorical discussion of the principles involved. A student given a revision symbol like 2a can interpret this as a reference to the boxed recommendation (see p. 29) for a brief suggestion, or if he feels uncertain about how to proceed he can take this symbol as reference to the rhetorical exposition, "Unity About a Theme or Thesis Idea," pp. 28–33. A student in need of "something to write about" may consult "Collecting Ideas for Writing," pp. 15–18, and before revising a theme he will do well to consult "Revising a Theme" and "Correcting a Theme," pp. 18–22.

For revisions embodied in this edition we are unusually indebted to William H. Oliver on the part of the publisher, who has been zealous in obtaining criticisms of the fourth edition. These analyses have been invaluable in our attempts to adapt the book to the needs of today's teachers and to a new generation of students. Through Mr. Oliver we are especially indebted to the following: Fred Tarpley, East Texas State University; Brenda Frank, Ashland College; Ronald Freeman, UCLA; Donald W. Good, Ohio State University; Fred C. Harrison, Portland State University; Frank Meriwether, University of Southwestern Louisiana; Gerald Pierre, Marquette University; Donald Rigg, Broward Junior College; Nelson Smith, Sacred Heart College; Robert Stellar, University of Minnesota; Dr. Vernon Torczon, Louisiana State University. Through Robb Reavill we have profited from uncommonly assiduous creative editing. We have had innumerable helpful suggestions from our colleagues at the University of Nevada, especially from some of the teaching assistants. From several generations of students we have gained good as well as horrible examples, but, more important, we have had evidence that teaching English is not entirely futile. To our wives, Johnnie Belle Gorrell and Helene Laird, we are grateful for patience and practical assistance; we had need of both.

ROBERT M. GORRELL
CHARLTON LAIRD

CONTENTS

25 THE WRITING SYSTEM: PUNCTUATION 528

MODERN
ENGLISH
HANDBOOK

THE TOPIC: PREWRITING AND REWRITING

CHAPTER 1

*Good writing animates a purpose, develops
from good prewriting.*

To write and to speak well is to think well and to use language so that thoughts become hearable, seeable, and graspable. Thought is our most precious and useful product, but it remains very slippery stuff until it is given form, clothed in some sort of reality, in maps, in graphs, in numbers. Of all the means that man has devised to reify his thoughts, language is the most useful. It is the means we know best; we start learning language at birth, and we never cease, so long as our minds work. We amass a body of knowledge about language that is never matched in any other medium, drawing pictures, for example, or juggling numbers, and we develop great skill in using it. It is more adaptable than any other medium. Painting reveals form and color well; it can express mood, feeling, character, and moral attitudes but not intellectual concepts as such. Language is itself a means of thinking; a committee meeting or a conference may get results, not only because people exchange ideas they already have, but because, by trying to express these ideas, they refine them, they add to them, they build them. Expressing oneself results from a continuous interplay of thinking and using language, each promoting the other.

Writing from Experience

Serious writing and speaking come from experience. Some of this experience may result from physical participation, climbing a mountain or learning to sail a boat into the wind. But reading, also, can be experience, or listening to a sonata, very exciting experience. Performing an experiment may be experience, as can a growing understanding, whether it comes from a sudden flash of insight or putting together notions that have been developing for a long time. Thus working with experience through thinking about it, and trying to formulate thoughts through language, becomes the employment of the whole man, the cultivation of the best in us. Writing or speaking well is not easy and cannot be learned quickly; but the study of rhetoric through the ages demonstrates that both writing and speaking can improve through study, especially the broad study of man, his mind, and his use of language.

Consider Fyodor Dostoevsky, one of the great writers of all time. While he was an engineering student he wrote and published a few pieces which attracted enough attention so that he became associated with a liberal group trying to gain more freedom for Russian peasants. He was accused of reading an inflammatory letter at a meeting; in all likelihood he did, since he would have considered the reading of a letter no crime, but he and his companions were arrested and condemned to be shot. They were facing the firing squad when, at the command of the Czar, the sentence was reduced to life imprisonment. Four years later Dostoevsky was, in effect, paroled to the army, and still later was discharged. Back from Siberia he collected various papers into a work which has been translated under several titles, most commonly *The House of the Dead,* but we shall prefer the more accurate title, *Notes from a Dead House,* used in the standard collection of Dostoevsky's works, since the word *notes* revealingly describes the contents. "Dead house" in Russian refers to what was formerly called a charnel house in English, the place where dead bodies were taken.

Now let us examine what had happened and what it led to. We start with experience. Dostoevsky had been deeply moved by the injustice he saw heaped upon innocent human beings. He protested in what must have seemed to him a gesture to help mankind, but he was brutally arrested, suffered the ignominy of a trial, and faced a firing squad. With this traumatic experience he became burningly aware of all he saw, and what he saw in prison was other prisoners dying and losing their minds. He fought for his life and his sanity, and when he was released but exiled in Siberia, he was still trying to make his peace with his life and the world he would have to live in.

For Dostoevsky imprisonment must have seemed mainly a hard time that he managed to live through. For us, it represents one of the steps in writing, what is sometimes called prewriting.

In prison he endured physical suffering and even terror, but he was also beginning to put his experience in some kind of order. After he got out of prison, he was able to write letters, and to prepare any documents he wished; he was now beginning to write, but he was still doing prewriting, since he could now reconceive his time in prison as he relived it. Back in European Russia, a free man, he compiled his *Notes from a Dead House*, partly his view of prison life as it must have been recorded in his mind at the time, partly documents he had then or later prepared, the whole now reworked, filled out with what he was recalling under the stimulus of writing. That is, he was now working at all three of the levels of the writing process; he was rewriting documents prepared before, writing fresh material to go with these rewritten pieces, and although he probably did not know this at the time, he was doing prewriting for works yet to come.

If Dostoevsky had been an ordinary person, or the engineer he set out to be, and nothing more than that, *Notes* might have remained an isolated work. He might, of course, have returned to the imitative pieces he was writing before he was arrested, or to something that sprung from them. So far as *Notes* was concerned, he had gone through the writing cycle; he had experienced events and had brought together his mental and written notes. He had written the book, going back to do rewriting as he did so, and when he had finished, he rewrote, revising for publication. Many a person has done just this. A woman living in Old Deerfield, Massachusetts, was ravished by Indians and later allowed to escape; a pioneer trapped in Death Valley found his way out and brought help to save his companions. Both of these people wrote accounts of their adventures, but neither of them ever wrote anything of consequence again. Dostoevsky was so much the writer, however—one should recall that he was beginning to publish before he was arrested—that he continued to repeat the interreliant activities of the writing process, preparing to write, writing, and rewriting.

A few years later he published a much more remarkable work, which for convenience we shall refer to as *Letters from the Underworld*, again preferring the official title to the more popular *Notes from Underground*. As this title suggests, Dostoevsky's Siberian imprisonment has now been transmuted into an epistolary novel; and as the title does not necessarily imply, *Letters* is much more concerned than is *Notes* with the fundamental nature of man as it is revealed in prison life. In the subsequent years, Dostoevsky had relived his life in Siberia; the experiences on which he was relying were the same, but by rethinking these events he was able to write more penetratingly, more revealingly about them. Good rewriting must grow from rethinking, so that the writing and the rewriting of *Notes* became the prewriting of *Letters.*

Nor was this the end. Dostoevsky now produced the great series of novels for which he is known, *Crime and Punishment, The Idiot, The Possessed, The Brothers Karamazov.* The germs of all of them can be found in the *Letters.* That is, as *Letters* can be thought of as a rewriting of *Notes,* works such as *Crime and Punishment* can be thought of as a rewriting of *Letters,* the rewriting embodying the thinking and emotional experience that Dostoevsky had gone through in subsequent years. Even to the year of his death, more than thirty years after he read the letter that precipitated his arrest, Dostoevsky was still publishing his *Diary of a Writer,* in which we can detect him reworking what his life as a prisoner had done to him. Thus, if we wish, we may think of Dostoevsky's life as a continued embodiment of the writing process: experience, prewriting based upon experience, writing based upon prewriting, more prewriting that grows in part from the experience of writing, rewriting on the basis of rethinking, experience reviewed and new prewriting and writing that has grown from the rewriting. And so, on and on.

Why did Dostoevsky become a writer the world knows? Doubtless for many reasons. He wrote from deeply moving experiences, but, superficially, others had similar experiences even more harrowing. His friends also faced the firing squad, and others stayed longer in the Siberian prison than did he and fared worse, even to death and dementia. But we must assume he lived more than did some others, because he experienced the same events intellectually and emotionally to a degree of which others were incapable. He had creative imagination and a remarkable command of language, and with long study and practice, he learned to write. Anyone who reads *The Brothers Karamazov*—his last novel and many would say his best—and compares it with *Notes from a Dead House* is likely to conclude that Dostoevsky had learned to plan his writing, had learned to persist in rewriting, as he could not when he was less experienced. No doubt he had native genius; we do not know very clearly what genius is, but we can be sure that genius alone will not produce a *Brothers Karamazov.* Whatever Dostoevsky was born with, he had to learn, and learn to practice, the writing process.

Most writing has nothing like the scope of *The Brothers Karamazov,* nor do prewriting, writing, and rewriting usually occupy a lifetime. But even a brief composition resembles in miniature writing as Dostoevsky knew it. It grows from experience—from the writer's physical participation in events, from observation, from reading, from conversation.

4

The old recipe for rabbit stew begins with the obvious— "first catch the rabbit"—but it begins wisely. The rabbit is essential, and the essential must not be overlooked just because it is obvious. Having something to say is essential to writing. Ideas are more elusive than rabbits, and writing is more complicated than rabbit stew. For the student writer facing the practical assignment of meeting a deadline, finding a topic is not always easy, even when a general subject has been specified. The problem is identifying the rabbit.

Occasionally, of course, a topic is dictated by an unusual experience. The parents of a murdered child produce a biography for the Sunday supplement or a World Series hero tells how he hit that home run. Most writers cannot expect to capitalize on their experiences as astronauts or winners of beauty contests. In fact, the student agonizing over blank paper is wasting his time if he thinks he can solve all his problems by finding a novel or sensational topic—the drug traffic in the Near East or piranha fish or the future of the jumbo jets. He can more profitably explore the relatively simple and familiar subjects all around him—in his past life, his conversation, his reading, his friends, his courses, or the library.

Usually a general subject for writing is in effect assigned. An instructor may require that a college theme illuminate a particular essay or report on a laboratory experiment; or he may specify how the paper should be constructed. An editor commissioning an article may designate the subject, and a newspaper reporter, given a beat, has in effect been assigned to write about whatever occurs on that beat. Circumstances dictate the subject of a legal brief, a report from a committee, or a directive to an office staff. But even within such restrictions, and in the many less restricted situations in which writing occurs, focusing on a particular, individualized topic is an important initial step of writing. The following guides are useful.

1. *Interest.* The topic should have some interest for the writer. Sometimes, an assigned subject may seem to offer the writer no topic that interests him. Often, however, further exploration will suggest some aspect of the general subject he wants to explore. An instructor might, for example, require a paper based on assigned reading for a class, an essay on the women's liberation movement of the 1970's. A student has no enthusiasm for the general topic, but as he re-examines the essay, he notices a passage on the status of women among migratory agricultural workers. He is interested generally in labor problems and particularly in

problems of fruit pickers in California, with whom he worked one summer. He can find within the assigned subject a topic that intrigues him: "The Status of Women Among Migratory Workers in California."

2. *Experience.* The topic should relate to the writer's experience, which may include the writer's reading and thinking as well as events in which he has participated. But writing must say something, and a topic should concern material the writer knows about or can find out about. The more familiar, more obvious topics are often the more successful, because the writer is able to invest them with the individuality of his first-hand knowledge.

3. *Limitation.* The topic should be so limited that it can be developed adequately in the space available. A paper is doomed from the outset if the writer tries in 500 words to discuss "The Culture of the Middle West," "America's Foreign Policy," or "University Education Today." These are worthy general subjects, but they are topics for books or series of books, not for short essays. The writer must limit himself, focusing on an aspect of his general subject to which he can make a personal contribution.

LIMITING THE TOPIC

1a

A topic tends to limit itself as a writer considers what he wants to say about it, turns the topic into an idea for writing. Frequently, however, a broad subject must be narrowed deliberately; one especially useful technique is analysis, breaking a subject into its parts. For example, a student starts with a broad subject like "The Culture of the Middle West" and limits it geographically, restricting his topic to the culture of one state or to the culture of a city or a section of a city. He might narrow the subject still more to various aspects of culture—the literature or the religion or the art of a restricted area. Religion could then be restricted to some attitude toward religion, and a possible working topic might be "Fundamentalism in Religion in Midtown, Michigan." Or a student might decide to write a paper taking advantage of his interest in extracurricular activities in college. Since he realizes that "Extracurricular Activities in College" is too broad for a 750-word paper, he decides to narrow the topic by considering one activity. He breaks the general subject into athletics, music, drama, social affairs, campus politics. He might, of course, have thought of more subtopics, but he knows something of campus politics. "Campus Politics," however, is not specific enough for a relatively short paper. The student considers various aspects of campus politics: graft in campus politics, relations of campus politics to academic work, methods for succeeding in campus politics, the

6

1a

Top

Revise the paper, narrowing the topic so that it can be developed in the space available, or select a new topic.

ORIGINAL	REVISION
Fishing	How To Tie a Fly
Interesting People I Have Known	My Temperamental Music Teacher
Athletics	How To Play First Base
Photography	Photographing Against the Sun
Newspapers in the United States	The Editorial Attitude of the *Daily News* Toward Expansion of the School System
War Between the States	A Problem in Tactics at the Battle of Gettysburg

The introduction can be used to reflect the analysis behind an adequately limited topic.

ORIGINAL

REVISION

The accomplished skier has many means of negotiating steep country. The beginner, of course, cannot hope to learn them all at once, and he does not need to, although they are all worth learning, and anyone who loves to ski will keep learning new ones. Some maneuvers are important for safety, even though they are not much used by experts interested in speed.

[*The writer has not broken the broad subject of skiing maneuvers into its parts and selected one to write about.*]

The accomplished skier learns many means of negotiating steep country, but for the beginner the snowplow is the most useful. With this simple skill even a novice can come down any slope without breaking his neck.

[*More or less consciously the writer has divided maneuvers into those suitable for experts and those for beginners, then divided the latter group again and selected the snowplow, thus restricting his topic.*]

value of campus politics. He decides on the last, but as he considers ways in which campus politics is valuable, he recognizes that political activity has more than one value, and he sees he must subdivide his topic. Re-examining his ideas, he finds that he considers campus politics valuable to the nation as training in democracy, valuable to the school, and valuable to the student. He sees that these subtopics partially overlap, but he also sees the advantage of separating them and selecting one for his paper. Because he feels he is best able to discuss the value of politics to the student, he works down to a topic specific enough so that he can hope to do something with it: "Campus Politics as Education." The process, then, whereby a specific topic can be drawn from a general subject is roughly pictured in the following chart:

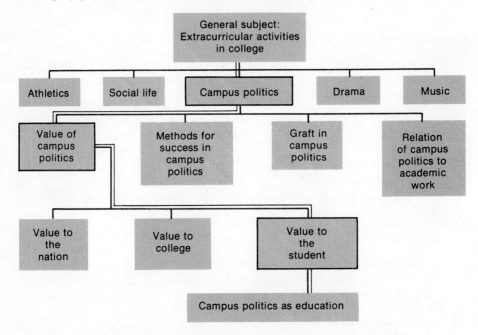

The process is essentially that of analysis (see chapter 5), breaking a subject into its parts in an orderly manner and then selecting a specific part to be discussed in detail.

Even when a subject is assigned, the writer can usually improve his paper by narrowing the topic. After class study of an essay on language, the instructor might ask for a paper recording some of the student's observations or attitudes on language, but the student would need to restrict the subject for his own purposes. He might ask himself questions and rule out large portions of the subject, such as the history of English, comparison of different languages, or changes in modern studies of grammar, as too complicated or outside his knowledge and interest; he might decide to write on some aspect of modern usage. Again he could think of various narrower possibilities: dialect peculiarities, modern "errors" in usage, current slang. He could pick any one of these and narrow it; modern "errors" in usage might be restricted to current attitudes toward *like* and *as* or *me* and *myself* as accusatives. Or current slang might be narrowed as the student remembers his experiences with a rock group, decides to write about musicians' slang, and then realizes that he can restrict still further and write about musicians' slang for naming instruments. With his topic restricted he can recall pertinent details from his experience, fill in by reading, and write an interesting paper. Or he might turn the assignment in a quite different way. He might recall that dictionaries provide exciting information and decide to do something on word history or word origins. He could then start working toward something specific and develop a good paper on meaning variations in a single word—"Rapping About *Rapping*," or "*Nice* Was Not Always Nice."

A final title may differ from the descriptive topic that a writer selects for his own guidance, but a writer can help himself by restricting his thinking to a topic narrow enough to be manageable and descriptive enough to serve as a guide. He need not, of course, proceed as formally as the chart above suggests, but he needs to ask himself questions until he can focus on a topic that interests him, that is familiar to him, and that can be developed in the space allotted.

Prewriting: An "Idea for a Theme"

A topic is necessary, but it is not enough to get writing started, even if it has been restricted. The writer must have some notion of why he selected the topic, what purpose he has in writing about it, what kind of audience he is addressing, how he will approach his material. He must have what students sometimes call an "idea for a theme."

An idea for writing must be more than a general inclination toward a topic: "I think I might write something about icebergs" or "The successors of rock music might be an interesting subject." The starting place for a composition, as for all communication in language, is a topic plus a comment about it, at its simplest a subject and a predicate. Usually, in fact, we select a topic in this way, because we have some idea about it. The motive for expression is an observation or thought about a topic, not just the topic. We do not say "Dogs smell" because we select the topic "Dogs" and then look for something to say about it. What we have noticed about the topic motivates the expression. "Dogs smell," if not an especially promising theme idea, is nearer a start than "Dogs," or even a more limited aspect of the topic such as "Weimaraners."

The idea for a theme may develop so naturally from an account of an experience that no conscious attention to a topic or approach is necessary. A student returned from the fighting in Vietnam, for example, thinks of developing an account of one of his experiences. As an adviser to some native troops, he found that one of the men he was working with had studied at an American college and was fluent in English. They talked about the native's experiences; he complained that as a student he had been discriminated against, that he could not rent a decent room, that girls would not date him, that some of the men would not eat with him. "But what burns me up," he concluded, "is that you guys think I'm a Vietnamese or one of those damned Montagnards. I'm not. I'm a Cambodian." The student did not need to decide that he would write on the broad problem of race relations, of human prejudices, of the fact that prejudice is deep-seated and not restricted to attitudes in the United States. He was aware of the implications of his story, and he told it because of its implications, but the idea for the theme was apparent the minute he remembered the story. Often, however, the idea comes less easily, and the writer has to search in his experience to discover a likely combination of topic and comment that will get his writing started.

Thinking About Experience

Thinking and writing are not totally separate activities; one does not sit down and think about a topic and then move to his typewriter and record the results. The processes proceed simultaneously, stimulating each other. And writing develops in various ways. Sometimes, a writer may have a vague notion and turn it about in his mind for days before writing a word. He may start by roughing out disorganized and undisciplined notions as they occur, using the writing to build his ideas. But he does think, and ideas for writing are most likely to emerge from orderly thinking. The practiced writer, of course, does not follow formulas for thinking, but he commands many sources for ideas and many ways of considering them.

The germ for an idea may appear in an object or person, in an event or incident, or in an opinion or feeling. A Grecian urn may become the subject of a notice in a museum catalog, a letter to a friend, a treatise on archaeology, or an ode by John Keats. A committee hearing on a student conduct case may produce an objective report for a newspaper, a new code of conduct, a character sketch of the committee chairman, or a personal essay on justice. A desire to promote the cause of peace may be focused into a discussion of a disarmament proposal, a satiric sketch of a military staff meeting, or a poem about a friend killed in battle.

Ideas for writing may emerge almost spontaneously when a writer thinks of an object or event or concept, or they may not.

The thinking that produces ideas for writing can be stimulated by a kind of question-and-answer dialogue between the writer and himself. Most ideas can be thought of as answers to questions like the following.

1. *What is it?* A butterfly or a hay baler, a wedding or a bombing raid, a passion for Siamese cats or a dislike for psychedelic posters may be considered as individual phenomena, each of which could lead to a definition or a description, provided the writer's audience might be interested in such knowledge. A description of a butterfly would be useful for a textbook in entomology; a description of a particular bicycle might appear in a mail-order catalog. Thinking about a person might produce an idea for a character sketch. The writer could ask himself about an event and decide to write a narrative account of the sort that might appear in a history or a newspaper. The process of analysis, discussed above, implies a supplementary question, "What are the parts or kinds of it?" A writer asking himself questions about an old house might decide to write a paper describing the junk in the attic. Examination of the thing itself might lead to a workable idea, but it might also lead to further questions.

2. *Where did it come from?* With this question the writer looking at an old house might see the possibilities of writing about its history. A look at a person might produce a biographical essay rather than a character description. In considering an event, the question is likely to become "What caused it?" As he considers a fist fight between two campus leaders, the writer proposes not to provide a blow-by-blow account but to present the reasons for the encounter. Consideration of a conviction that women should have equal rights on the campus might lead to a paper on the origins of the tradition that only men can enter the north room of the Union Building.

3. *What does it do? How does it work?* Among the most common types of writing that might emerge from these questions is the process paper, the recipe for making home-brewed beer or the step-by-step account of how a generator produces electricity. These questions, however, can produce ideas for broader kinds of writing—the effects of school segregation, the ways in which weather changes affect air pollution, how the presence of city police at campus functions affects student morale.

4. *What is it like? What does it remind me of?* Questions like these lead to generalizations, propositions, or theses, which are the ideas behind many expository and argumentative essays. For example, the person thinking about an old house relates it to others and proposes writing something about architectural styles in central Ohio in the late nineteenth century. But he still has only a

topic, not an idea, and as he compares further he decides to expound the proposition that these houses as a group are distinguished by their reliance on nonfunctional, conventionalized, and ugly decoration. Or a writer begins thinking about a minor incident, a blown fuse in the house where he is living. As he pokes around in the dark looking for a candle and an extra fuse, he remembers a four-hour power failure during a storm earlier in the year and recalls reading about a power blackout in the East a few years ago. He considers writing a paper to illustrate that our society is dangerously dependent on electricity. His idea is too broad; it needs refining and perhaps modification; but it is a start. Sometimes this sort of idea can be reached even more quickly by phrasing the question thus, "What is it an example of?" Such questions may promote a paper of comparison or contrast: the similarities between decoration on some Victorian houses and the artificial decorations used in a futile attempt to distinguish some modern tract houses from one another or, on a larger scale, a comparison between modern faith in electricity and medieval faith in religion.

5. *What is its significance? How is it important?* Any phenomenon exists not only independently but as part of the world around it. The writer thinking about his blown fuse arrived at his idea for writing by thinking of related events but also by thinking of their importance in the world, of the effects of a power blackout on transportation, on home freezers, on furnaces in steel mills, on hospital operating schedules. Many poems have developed as the writer explored the significance of a relatively common or ordinary event: Shelley looked at the west wind and developed a comment on the importance of ideas that change society; Wilfred Owen looked at the body of a fellow soldier and commented ironically on the romanticizing of war; Hopkins saw a windhover flying above him and wrote a poem on religion.

Interpreting Experience

An idea for writing, in other words, anticipates some way of interpreting experience to give a paper the distinctiveness of personal insight. It develops, may even change completely, as writing progresses, but it gives the writer a start. An idea may occur as a flash of insight, or it may grow from questions like those above, or from the many other questions possible. But it is likely to result from thinking that involves a combination of different sorts of questions. Consider, for example, possible approaches to an assignment suggesting a paper based on the cartoon opposite.

The question "What is it?" would yield an idea for an objective   **12**

"Some little girl didn't hear me say 'unarmed combat.'"

description. The scene is apparently the interior of the gymnasium in a girl's school. The girls are engaged in an exercise interestingly called "unarmed combat," and they are participating with considerable enthusiasm. A pair of legs and a hand protrude above a vaulting horse in the background. At least two girls are knotted in a confusion of arms and legs in the upper right corner, and in the foreground a little girl, with her lower lip stuck out, is plunging a dagger into the back of her opponent. The instructor, with an

13

admonishing finger and a raised eyebrow, is reminding the girls of the rules of the game.

Such a description might be helpful as part of something else, but it does not contribute much to an understanding of the cartoon, does not illuminate its irony, its "point." An idea for writing based on the cartoon probably requires more than a superficial view. It requires interpretation, which might be stimulated by other questions, relating the incident of the cartoon with other incidents and with affairs of the world. A writer might look at the cartoon as a comment on violence, as an ironic suggestion that human beings have a natural tendency to fight. Or he might find it commenting on the attitudes of society, perhaps more specifically of education, with the instructor seeming to approve most of the activity and offering only a gentle and understanding reproof of the girl whose zeal has become excessive. Or the writer might consider a belief accepted by many that aggressions and vindictiveness are so native in human beings that efforts to prevent war are useless. The writer might suggest that violence and war are the result of encouraging children in combat, even when it is unarmed. The cartoon might be related to crime in the streets, to student revolt, to methods of classroom discipline, or more broadly to law enforcement. Further questions might produce still other kinds of ideas.

As another way of looking at the development of ideas consider the possible origins of a completed composition such as "Sound," by E. B. White.

> The sound truck, or Free Speech on Wheels, won its first brush with the law by a close decision in the Supreme Court. We have an idea, however, that the theme of amplification is not dead and will recur in many variations. The Court found itself in a snarl; free speech became confused with free extension-of-speech, noise with ideas wrapped in noise. A sound truck, it seems to us, is not a man on a soapbox—it is Superman on a tower of suds. The distinction will eventually have to be drawn. Loud speaking is not the same thing as plain speaking; the loudspeaker piles decibel on decibel and not only is capable of disturbing the peace but through excess of volume can cause madness and death, whereas the human voice is a public nuisance only to the extent that it aggravates the normal human resentment against the whole principle of free speech. Amplified sound is already known among military men as a weapon of untried potency, and we will probably suffer from it if there is another war.
>
> Up till now, modern man has meekly accepted the miracle of his enlarged vocal cords. He has acquiesced in jumboism. A modern baby is born amplified, for even the nursery is wired for sound and the infant's earliest cries are carried over a private distress system

to the ears of its mother in the living room — along with street noises that drift in through the open nursery window. (Note to political candidates: Always park your sound truck under nursery windows and your remarks will be picked up by an interior network and carried to uneasy elders.) One wonders, though, how much longer the human race will string along with its own electrical gifts, and how long the right to speak can remain innocent of wattage. We have a feeling that only if this issue is met will the principle of free speech survive. There are always plenty of people who are eager to stifle opinion they don't admire, and if the opinion happens to be expressed in a volume of sound that is in itself insufferable, the number of people who will want to stifle both the sound *and* the fury will greatly increase. Amplification, therefore, is something like alcohol: it can heighten our meanings, but it can also destroy our reason.

This brief essay stemmed from a specific event, a decision of the Supreme Court on the legality of sound trucks. In developing his idea for writing White apparently skipped quickly over the question "What is it?" as he was interested not in the law involved or an explanation of the decision but rather in how the decision related to society. The significance of the court action leads him to focus on the relationship between freedom of speech and freedom to amplify speech, and White develops the idea that "loud speaking is not the same thing as plain speaking." Probably as he writes and explores the notion further, he emphasizes the importance of the issue by suggesting the fear that "free extension-of-speech" will aggravate resentment against the whole principle of freedom of speech. His interpretation derives from insight into the implications of the court decision.

Collecting Ideas for Writing: A Journal

H. G. Wells in his *Experiment in Autobiography* recalls that in his student days in London he "went on writing, indeed, as a toy-dog goes on barking. I yapped manuscript, threateningly, at an inattentive world." What Wells produced in these days he considers

copious rubbish, imitative of the worst stuff in the contemporary cheap magazine. There was not a spark of imagination or original observation about it. I made not the slightest use of the very considerable reservoir of scientific and general knowledge already accumulated in my brain. I don't know why. Perhaps I was then so vain that I believed I could write *down* to the public. Or so modest that I thought the better I imitated the better I should succeed.

As he looks back at his early compositions, he finds that

> The only writing of any quality at all is to be found in the extremely self-conscious letters I wrote to my friends. Here I really did try to amuse and express myself in my own fashion. . . . There is fun in them.

Wells's early efforts may have been less clearly "vacuous trash" than he judged, but his finding greater value in his informal writing is not unusual. As he learned writing from his letters, others have learned from similar informal compositions—from writing letters, from imitative exercises, from taking notes on reading, from keeping a journal.

A journal or notebook or diary may be a highly personal recording of heartaches and gossip—sometimes more valuable as psychological therapy for the writer than as literature—a jumbled miscellany of impressions of all sorts, or a rather carefully written series of comments, sometimes prepared by a writer with half an eye on future publication. Samuel Taylor Coleridge kept notebooks all his life; more than fifty survive. A typical volume contains notes on alligators from a travel book he was reading, two or three lines of verse he has composed, an account of an injury to his brother, thoughts that have occurred to him about poetry and pain and children and anger and materialism, a long list of possible topics and plans for future writing, a reminder of some needed reform in his behavior, and a recipe for stewed mutton.

Most of the diaries or journals we know much about contained enough interesting information or such skillful writing that they were published. We read the *Diary* of Samuel Pepys for its insight into seventeenth-century England—the plague, the great fire—and for its revelation of the writer. The *Diary* of Anne Frank shows us a sensitive girl maturing under the impact of the unnatural life of a family gone underground, and incidentally clarifies such events as the Nazi occupation of the Netherlands during World War II. A student journal may have value for similar reasons. If it develops fully enough and contains precise records of events, it may become an engaging commentary on student life or other affairs that interest the writer. But even when it does not make incisive and lasting comments, a journal can be useful for a student developing his own competence.

1. *Convenience for future reference.*   A journal provides a convenient place for jotting down ideas that seem worth exploring in the future: "The noise and confusion in the dining hall make conversation almost impossible; explore possibility of paper relating decline of conversational ability with increase of public sound,

canned music, dinner entertainment, floor shows, etc." If this kind of note gets recorded, it may be useful, but if it is not recorded, it will probably be forgotten. Milton was making notes on possible subjects for an epic years before he began *Paradise Lost.*

2. *Immediacy.* A journal entry may record detail with a freshness that could be lost if the idea or the event were not recorded rather soon. The following entry from Coleridge's notebook for March 16, 1805, shows the writer recording an idea:

> Seeing a nice bed of glowing embers with one junk of firewood well placed, like the remains of an old edifice, and another well-nigh mouldered one corresponding to it, I felt an impulse to put on three pieces of wood that exactly completed the perishable architecture, though it was eleven o'clock, though I was that instant going to bed, and there could be, in common ideas, no possible use in it. Hence I seem (for I write not having yet gone to bed) to suspect that this disease of totalising, of perfecting, may be the bottom impulse of many, many actions, in which it never is brought forward as an avowed or even agnized as a conscious motive.

And Coleridge adds to the entry a note for a possible writing project:

> Mem. — to collect facts for a comparison between a *wood* and a *coal* fire, as to sights and sounds and bodily feeling.

3. *Collection.* A journal can preserve scattered bits of information that may later illustrate ideas or combine with other bits to prompt new ideas. A student jotting down events of the day might recall his observations during his walk home and write, "I think I can detect three generations of style in architecture on the campus." Whether or not this sentence becomes the theme idea for a composition by itself, it may well enter into other thinking or writing involving related subjects. Coleridge's notebooks contain numerous notes on his reading that he ultimately transformed into images in his poetry. He combined notes on water snakes from a travel book, for example, and some observations from a book on optics to create the striking image in *The Rime of the Ancient Mariner* in which the water snakes

> moved in tracks of shining white,
> And when they reared, the elfish light
> Fell off in hoary flakes.

4. *Analysis.* Keeping a journal will promote sorting and evaluating ideas, sifting out the best ones, and remembering them. The mere process of reliving something in order to write it, of

17

laboring to express it adequately and to phrase it well, will give the writer a readier command of it.

5. *Practice.* Keeping a journal provides an opportunity for regular writing practice, for experimenting, for trying to use new words, for trying different ways of producing ideas. One student improved his writing by trying each day to put into his journal just one well-formed sentence that seemed to him to say something worthwhile. It was not an easy discipline.

Revising a Theme

A student learning composition is like a man thrown into midocean to learn how to swim. He has to write while learning to write. And while he is studying rhetorical principles in the early chapters of this book, he will need to apply principles discussed in later chapters. One partial solution to the problem is careful revision. Almost no writing takes its final form in a first draft, and almost any writing profits from some reworking.

The student writer can often improve a composition by working through it from a checklist of questions like the following:

1. Did the subject prove too big or too little or unsuitable?
2. Have you focused the material about a main idea?
3. Have you made your commitment clear and precise and have you filled your commitment?
4. Have you developed your subject adequately and logically?
5. Have you made each paragraph a developed unit?
6. Are style and tone appropriate and consistent?
7. Are sentences clear and direct? Could any profitably be revised from a passive or expletive pattern?
8. Is your predication exact; that is, can the verb you have chosen work with its subject?
9. Have you chosen words that mean what you want to say?
10. Have you corrected mechanics? Be sure of the spelling of each word, using a dictionary when necessary.

The example on page 19 suggests how a revision of a first draft might look.

When the draft has been thoroughly revised, it should be carefully and neatly copied, and then the final version should be checked for typographical errors or blunders introduced in the process of copying. This final proofreading is important; errors that are only typographical may look like mistakes in writing unless they are corrected in the final draft. And minor errors can be corrected without recopying the entire paper.

The ~~stock market~~ crash ~~,~~ *however,* ~~of 1929~~
was only the be~~gi~~*n*ining ~~of the great de-~~
~~pression;~~ in the summer of 1932 the depression reached its lowest point, both
economically and psychologically. The
first signifi*c*ant event ~~to start the~~
~~ball rolling for the epoch~~ of the great
depression was the stock market crash in
October,1929. ~~The clerks in Wall Street~~
~~brokers' offices worked late into the~~
~~night posting records of an unprecedented~~
~~volume of sales.~~ ~~Apples~~ began to ~~be sold~~ *sell apples*
on the street ~~by~~ (unemployed citizens.) In
New York, as well as in other cities,
bread lines appeared, displaying the
extreme poverty suffered by some people.

As early as January, 1932, ~~there was a~~
demonstration *ed* at the national capital .
~~conducted by~~ (10,000) unemployed men. When
destitute families lacked sufficient
funds even to buy a few pounds of coal,
~~they gave them~~ *a relief bureau had to provide* fuel. People began crowd-
ing into banks, fearing failures and hop-
ing to rescue any savings they had.

	The opening sentence is moved to improve continuity in the paragraph.
	Spelling errors are corrected.
	Unnecessary words are deleted.
	A comma is supplied.
	A sentence not relevant to the main idea of the paragraph is dropped.
	Word order is changed to make the sentence active.
	The sentence is shifted to regular actor-action order and moved to the end. where it provides a transition to the next paragraph. Round number spelled out.
	The sentence is revised to correct vague pronoun reference.

Correcting a Theme

Even though the student has carefully revised his theme, the instructor is likely to add corrections and suggestions. Inside the front cover of this book is a chart of key numbers and abbreviations that may be used in improving themes. An alphabetical list of the abbreviations will be found inside the back cover. To profit from his instructor's corrections, the student should revise his paper according to the following procedures:

1. If the instructor uses abbreviations to mark corrections, refer to the alphabetical list inside the back cover and find the number of the chapter to which each abbreviation refers.

2. If the instructor uses numbers as symbols, or after you have found numbers corresponding to his abbreviations, turn to the chapter of the book headed by each number indicated on the paper, locating chapters by the running heads at the tops of the pages.

3. Study the chapter of the book to which the instructor has referred you until you are sure you understand his suggestion. You will find that any given symbol, such as **2a** or **10b,** refers to an extended discussion and a brief, specific recommendation. If you already understand the subject, this brief statement, which is always in a box, may be sufficient to suggest the appropriate revision. If not, you should work through the longer discussion following the same number.

4. Then rewrite each passage as it should be written.

The student should note that profitable revision often requires more than rewriting misspelled words or changing punctuation. The writer derives the greatest benefit from carefully reworking sentences and paragraphs. A mark like *Con* or 7 in the margin of the paper, for instance, indicates to the student that the portion of his theme so marked lacks continuity; it tells him to strengthen ties between ideas, to devote special study to chapter 7 in the text, and to rewrite the passage so that it holds together. If the mark

W-Ref

agr

CF

Sp
Sp

Sub

```
          The public is fooled every day by a
  variety of people ranging from the glib
  medicine man to people working for high
  geared political machines.  The inteligence
  of these people vary widely.  The pcople
  they fool are often more inteligent than
  they, however, their skills are so great
  that they overcome even the inteligent
  man.  Inteligence is not acquired, but
  knowlege can be acquired, due to man's
  ability to learn.  Salesmen often state
  as fact information about their products.
  Often these are untrue.
```

Hy
Sp

Sp

Sp
Dev

Con

Sub or 16 appears in the margin of the paper, the student needs to devote special study to chapter 16, where he will find a discussion of methods for improving sentence structure through subordination; to achieve this improvement he may need to combine two or three sentences by reducing a clause to a phrase or a single word. The selection on page 20 has been marked with the abbreviations listed inside the back cover.

The opening for the theme is not promising, and frequent errors in structure and mechanics have been marked. To correct them, the student should check each abbreviation in the list inside the back cover. He will discover, for example, that *W Ref* indicates faulty word reference and is discussed under 17g in the text. He can find 17 quickly by using the running heads. *Hy*, the student will find, indicates faulty hyphenation and is discussed under 26c, and *Agr* refers to agreement of subject and verb and is discussed under 17. The fourth sentence is marked *Dev*, which refers to relevance of the development and is discussed under 4, but it contains an expression, *due to*, circled and not otherwise marked. Whenever no abbreviation or number is used with a marked passage, the student should look up the marked expression in the glossary or index, where he will find an explanation or a reference.

A theme may also be marked directly with the numbers that appear in the margins and in the running heads and that are summarized in the chart inside the front cover. The following selection from the theme begun above has been marked with numbers.

```
        Many methods are used to influence ⌉
people.  These methods include as one of
the most popular the use of propaganda. ⌡
Pamphlets, newspapers, magazines, books,
posters, billboards, radio, movies and
television are all mediums for the
spread of propaganda.  For example, know-
ing the kinds of things audiences want to
hear, many facts are distorted by radio
commentators.  There are many kinds of in-
formation which are distorted for propa-
ganda purposes.
```

The student can look up 16a and find a suggestion that the sentences be combined, with one subordinated to the other. The reference to 25d points out an omission of a comma in a series, and 16c marks a dangling modifier. The instructor has also suggested that the writer see 14b, which refers to overuse of passive sentences. The reference to 4 calls attention to a weakness that is apparent throughout the theme, overuse of general rather than specific development.

FOR STUDY AND WRITING

A Select one of the following subjects and divide it into at least five divisions. For example, if one were "Higher Education" you might divide it into the following: The Role of Higher Education in Modern Society, Purposes of Higher Education, Methods in Higher Education, Relevance of Higher Education, Higher Educational Institutions, A University as a Functioning Unit, and the like. Then you might select one of these and divide it again into at least five subdivisions. In the example above, if you selected the last, you might break it into the role of the governing body, the board of regents or trustees; the functions of administrators such as the president, controller, various deans, directors, and department heads; the influence of the public as expressed through the legislature, donors, and the like; the role of the faculty in administration, and the place of representatives of the student body in determining and implementing university policy. Again, if you choose the last for further subdivision, you might consider student participation in the meetings of university faculties, boards, and committees; student involvement in staff and curricular problems through colleges and departments; student control of their own funds; student direction of cooperative students ventures, such as a book store, a film program, an intramural sports program; student control of government and discipline; student direction of student publications, and a student system of faculty rating. You might select one of these and divide it again into at least five, and, if it is not now sufficiently restricted to be suitable for a paper of 750 words, restrict it further until it is.

Now select one of the following subjects, or one that your instructor may suggest, and divide it into subcategories again and again until you have a topic restricted enough for a paper of 500–1,000 words.

1. Advertising	**6.** College sports
2. Television	**7.** Snobs
3. Magazines	**8.** International tensions
4. Desserts	**9.** Pollution
5. Racial prejudices	**10.** Farming

B Keep a journal for a week. Record anything you think of that seems to you interesting. Let yourself go and just write. Do not hesitate to jumble facts and opinions, if this is the way the words come. Usually, one idea well developed will produce the most interesting writing. Pick something that attracts you, and recall all you can. But if you cannot happen on one good idea, use several and if you have any trouble thinking of some events or ideas to record, check back through this chapter for suggestions.

C Knowing that the more carefully you examine anything the more you are likely to see in it, look once again at the cartoon by Ronald Searle (page 13). Notice details and see what you can make of them. Is the cartoonist trying to say anything by scattering dumbbells around? Do you infer anything from the fact that the girl who is doing the stabbing looks rather like a crayfish, or some other low-browed, pop-eyed creature, whereas the girl being stabbed wears glasses? Look closely at the woman; she is what might be called a gym teacher in this country—the cartoon is British—and hence she may be the gymnastics trainer, the schoolmistress, the preceptress, or something of the sort. Who or what did Searle intend her to represent?

After studying the cartoon write a brief paper telling what you think it is about.

D Look back at an entry in your journal, rethinking the experience that led to it, and perhaps adding to it details you have observed along the same line since, or recalling earlier experiences suggested by it. What do you now conclude about this bit in your journal? Rewrite this material into a carefully prepared paper.

E You are no doubt familiar with Robert Frost's poem "Stopping by Woods on a Snowy Evening," but reread it, carefully.

Whose woods these are I think I know.
His house is in the village though;
He will not see me stopping here
To watch his woods fill up with snow.

My little horse must think it queer
To stop without a farmhouse near
Between the woods and frozen lake
The darkest evening of the year.

He gives his harness bells a shake
To ask if there is some mistake.
The only other sound's the sweep
Of easy wind and downy flake.

The woods are lovely, dark and deep.
But I have promises to keep,
And miles to go before I sleep,
And miles to go before I sleep.

Once again, superficially the subject of the piece is obvious. Some-body, presumably a man and presumably sitting in a cutter, has stopped far from any habitation and is watching snow fall in the woods. Such stoppings are apparently unusual; the horse drawing the sleigh seems puzzled, suggesting that it may be time to be moving on. The driver reminds himself that he has promises to keep.

This is one of the most widely admired of modern American poems, although nobody would guess it from the summary above. It must be about something that has been lost in the summary. What is it? One critic, apparently irked at people who try to discover far-fetched allegories, especially in modern poetry, suggested that the person in the sleigh is Santa Clause. Is it not the darkest night of the year, Christmas? If the driver is not supernatural, how could he see into a blizzard on a dark night? And who but Santa Claus has so many promises to keep in a village on Christmas—all those letters from little boys and girls. And the reindeer are ringing their bells—of course in the poem Donner and Blitzen appear as "my little horse," but that is only evidence of the beautiful simplicity of allegory.

You may not accept this interpretation. Some people did, and wrote the magazine that printed the purported explication, praising the critic for his acuity. The critic, somewhat embarrassed, explained that he just thought he was having fun, and the editor agreed that he had assumed that everybody would take the piece as a joke, but the writer of the letter objected. He insisted that whether the critic and the editor knew it or not, they had blundered onto the true explanation, the one the poet must have intended, or if he did not intend it, one that was clearly in his subconscious.

Whether you agree with the letter writer or not—and you can find more Santa-esque details in the poem if you hunt for them—write your own interpretation of the poem.

F Consider the cartoon opposite. It shows two young people, who, by the tracks in the snow, have just come out of the building to the right. We are told that the boy has just said, "Chee, Annie, look at de stars—thick as bed-bugs!" The dialect identifies the boy as living in what the cartoonist, Art Young, drawing in 1936 or before, would probably have called a slum, and we might call a ghetto—a rickety barrel opposite the steps suggests that the newly fallen snow covers other unsightly objects. There must be some kind of intimate relationship between the pair, whether Annie is the boy's girlfriend, his sister, or whatever. He speaks to her familiarly, and he seems to expect that she will share his feelings.

What is the cartoon about? Two young people are looking at a winter sky, brilliant with stars. Is the idea that modern society is cruel and stupid to allow children to grow up in such circumstances that, presented with the idea of multitude, even the infinity of stars, they can express their sense of wonder only by comparing galaxies to bedbugs? Is the idea that love so changes people that even a street gamin wonders at the stars, although he probably would not have, except that he was walking with Annie? Or what is the cartoon about? Ask yourself the most searching questions you can, and then write a short theme interpreting the cartoon.

"Chee, Annie, look at de stars—thick as bed-bugs!"

UNITY: TOPICAL DEVICES

CHAPTER 2

*Unity requires focus on a main idea; devices like a precise
topic statement can help.*

Unity in a composition helps the reader to focus on a main idea.
A sharp sense of the main idea helps the writer to provide unity.
Thus unity involves both selecting materials and handling them
once they are selected, and the writer, facing the practical problem
of unifying his composition, may find he works at least as much
with means as with matter. Several devices of composition benefit
both reader and writer.

Unity Through Focusing Devices

A physical object may provide one of the simplest and clearest
focusing devices. A motion picture cameraman photographing a
crowd faces a problem like the writer's. He attempts to present a
large number of details in such a way that they will make a unified
impression. He may provide views from a distance that give a general impression of the large scene, and then turn his camera to
details, to pictures of people and smaller scenes; and almost always
he helps his audience to keep these more concentrated scenes in
order by focusing attention on some central object. A tree or a
building or an important character becomes a focal point, and the
camera swings back to it and then away from it so that the audience can keep the great mass of details in order by relating them to
this point of focus.

26

Such a simple focusing device may be useful, also, in writing. In his famous essay "On a Piece of Chalk," Thomas Henry Huxley develops the main idea that the earth "has been the theatre of a series of changes," that physical characteristics and living inhabitants of the earth have been affected by evolution. The essay is unified around a specific example, the story of the changes embodied in a piece of chalk. Similarly, Esmé Wingfield Stratford labels a chapter of his *History of British Civilization* "Gothic Christianity." He wishes to describe the particular qualities of the growth of religious ardor in thirteenth-century England. To unify his chapter he relates his ideas to the development of Gothic architecture, which distinguishes English cathedrals built during the period. These cathedrals become a symbol for the thesis of the chapter.

Thus a focal object may serve complex purposes. While it relates details to one another, it may also become a symbol, revealing the main idea in various ways, including introduction and summary. The following paragraphs open Michael Crichton's novel *The Andromeda Strain.*

A man with binoculars. That is how it began: with a man standing by the side of the road, on a crest overlooking a small Arizona town, on a winter night.

Lieutenant Roger Shawn must have found the binoculars difficult. The metal would be cold, and he would be clumsy in his fur parka and heavy gloves. His breath, hissing out into the moonlit air, would have fogged the lenses. He would be forced to pause to wipe them frequently, using a stubby gloved finger.

He could not have known the futility of this action. Binoculars were worthless to see into that town and uncover its secrets. He would have been astonished to learn that the men who finally succeeded used instruments a million times more powerful than binoculars.

There is something sad, foolish, and human in the image of Shawn leaning against a boulder, propping his arms on it, and holding the binoculars to his eyes. Though cumbersome, the binoculars would at least feel comfortable and familiar in his hands. It would be one of the last familiar sensations before his death.

The novelist, like the cameraman, focuses the reader's attention, using field glasses as a point of reference to unify the passage, but the binoculars also have a more complex rhetorical function. Lieutenant Shawn in the science-fiction story is looking at a town where most of the inhabitants have been struck dead by a microscopic intruder from outer space, brought back by a man-made satellite and called the Andromeda strain. The opening paragraphs use the binoculars to anticipate this story, to introduce its theme, its main idea. In the first paragraph the binoculars are simply mentioned; the man has them. In the second they become part of the immediate practical problems of the lieutenant; the metal is cold and the lenses frost. In the third paragraph, however, the binoculars acquire significance in contrast to the electronic microscope with which in the novel scientists detect the Andromeda strain threatening mankind. In the fourth paragraph the binoculars suggest even more pointedly some basic topics of the novel: the ignorance of human beings about the universe, their helplessness when confronted with unknown sorts of disaster, the role of science in the modern world. At the end of the novel a character says, "That's the important thing. That we understand." This is perhaps as near as the novel comes to stating a thesis. The binoculars, of course, do not tell the reader all that the novel is about, but they serve as a unifying device in two ways: by providing a central point of reference for the description of the physical scene and by focusing attention on the kinds of ideas that will pervade the book.

UNITY ABOUT A THEME OR THESIS IDEA

2a

As we have seen, a writer of fiction may suggest the unity of his novel or short story through a symbol such as a pair of binoculars. A poet may rely even more heavily upon a symbol; Amy Lowell, in her poem "Patterns," relates the patterns in a formal garden to what she calls "a pattern called a war." But expository or argumentative prose usually deals more directly with ideas than do belles lettres, and thus although an external focusing device may have its uses, in most nonfiction prose a theme or thesis expressed in words provides the best unifying device.

A precise topic statement helps the writer to provide unity and helps the reader to see it. An early chapter in Henry M. Leicester's *Historical Background of Chemistry* begins as follows:

> Since it was from Mesopotamia and Egypt that the ideas of primitive science reached the Greeks, it is to Mesopotamia and Egypt that we must look for the earliest traces of our science of chemistry. The form of rational thinking assumed in these cultures explains much that we meet later in alchemy and chemistry.

2a

U

Revise, focusing the composition on a clear statement of the main idea.

ORIGINAL

There was an oval mirror on one wall with a heavy black frame containing fat angels carved into the wood. I have never much cared for representations of angels. The insipid ones on Sunday-school cards seemed to me dull even when I was a child, and fat ones are not very attractive, to say the least. There was a faint tinge of violet perfume hanging over the room. A bad print of a Rosa Bonheur picture was hanging on the wall over the high walnut bed. Faded lace curtains bordered the high, narrow windows, which contrasted with a mantel that had been recently dusted; they were rather dirty. Some books sat on the table.

[*Presumably the details are accurately recorded, but they produce no unified effect because they are set down one after the other with no apparent main idea controlling the selection.*]

REVISION

The contents of the room seemed to exhale the faint scent of violet that hung over it. The oval mirror, framed heavily with fat angels carved into blackened wood, the silver brush and comb on the massive walnut dresser, the faded lace curtains, the high walnut bed, the bad print of a Rosa Bonheur picture all seemed part of the odor of the mildly sickening perfume. A few volumes, propped between bookends painted with roses, were slim and gold-lettered; one sensed that they concerned well-dressed gentlemen, very properly courting demure but willing ladies in crinoline.

[*The writer has focused upon a main idea, supplying a topic sentence. He has furthered unity by rearranging his materials, removing the irrelevant comment on his personal reaction to angels, and, by closer observation, describing the details to show how they relate to the main idea.*]

The author isolates key characteristics of the rational thinking of these two cultures and unifies his chapter through details limited to the areas mentioned in the topic statement, details that objectify his announced purpose, to examine ideas influential in the development of chemistry.

The following sequence is somewhat more complex; taken from Irving Howe's *Politics and the Novel*, it concerns George Orwell's *1948*.

No other book has succeeded so completely in rendering the essential quality of totalitarianism. *1984* is limited in scope; it does not pretend to investigate the genesis of the totalitarian state, nor the laws of its economy, nor the prospect for its survival; it simply evokes the "tone" of life in a totalitarian society. And since it is not a realistic novel, it can treat Oceania as an *extreme instance*, one that might never actually exist but which illuminates the nature of societies that do exist.

Orwell's profoundest insight is that in a totalitarian world man's life is shorn of dynamic possibilities. The end of life is completely predictable in its beginning, the beginning merely a manipulated preparation for the end. There is no opening for surprise, for that spontaneous animation which is the token of and justification for freedom. Oceanic society may evolve through certain stages of economic development, but the life of its members is static, a given and measured quantity that can neither rise to tragedy nor tumble to comedy. Human personality, as we have come to grasp for it in a class society and hope for it in a classless society, is obliterated; man becomes a function of a process he is never allowed to understand or control. The fetichism of the state replaces the fetichism of commodities.

There have, of course, been unfree societies in the past, yet in most of them it was possible to find an oasis of freedom, if only because none had the resources to enforce total consent. But totalitarianism, which represents a decisive break from the Western tradition, aims to permit no such luxuries; if offers a total "solution" to the problems of the twentieth century, that is, a total distortion of what might be a solution. To be sure, no totalitarian state has been able to reach this degree of "perfection," which Orwell, like a physicist who in his experiment assumes the absence of friction, has assumed for Oceania. But the knowledge that friction can never actually be absent does not make the experiment any the less valuable.

To the degree that the totalitarian state approaches its "ideal" condition, it destroys the margin for unforeseen behavior; as a character in Dostoevsky's *The Possessed* remarks, "only the necessary is necessary." Nor is there a social crevice in which the recalcitrant or independent mind can seek shelter. The totalitarian state assumes that—given modern technology, complete political control, the means of terror and a rationalized contempt for moral tradition—anything is possible. Anything can be done with men, anything with their minds, with history and with words. Reality is no longer something to be acknowledged or experienced or even transformed; it is fabricated according to the need and will of the state, sometimes in anticipation of the future, sometimes as a retrospective improvement upon the past.

This four-paragraph section of the book centers upon a main idea presented in an opening topic statement; the writer commits himself to explain how *1984* "renders the essential quality of totalitarianism." The remaining sentences in the first paragraph explain this main idea by eliminating what the novel does not say, in order later to concentrate on "the essential quality" of totalitarianism. Each of the succeeding paragraphs points back to the topic statement. The second paragraph describes Orwell's "profoundest insight" into the "essential quality" of totalitarianism, that it removes "dynamic possibilities" from life. The third paragraph contrasts totalitarianism in *1984* with "unfree societies in the past," emphasizing the completeness of controls in the world of the novel. Then the final paragraph discusses one implication of the "perfected" totalitarianism, that it leaves no "margin for unforeseen behavior."

The obvious procedure for unifying a segment of a composition, as the examples above indicate, is to control the segment through a clearly expressed main idea and to focus all subdivisions of the section on this main idea. Usually, prose that lacks unity fails for one of the following reasons: (1) it lacks a clear statement of a main idea; (2) the opening statement misdirects the reader because it makes a commitment that the writing does not — perhaps cannot — meet; (3) subdivisions are not so selected or phrased that they clarify their relation to the main idea. Compare, for example, the following versions of the beginning of a student theme.

ORIGINAL

I like Walt Kelly's comic strip, *Pogo.* One of my favorite characters is Albert the Alligator; good old lazy Albert is somewhat of a big, conceited show-off. And of course everybody loves Pogo. As for Deacon Muskrat and the Buzzard, they are anything but lovable, though they are not so short-tempered as Albert, who though he is loyal to his friends and even sentimental on occasion will sometimes throw a towering tantrum. His friend, Churchy La Femme. . . .

[*At the beginning this composition threatens to become confused because it lacks any unifying main idea.*]

REVISION

Walt Kelly's comic strip, *Pogo,* gains part of its charm from the fact that each of the swamp creatures becomes a satire on some recognizable type of human being. Albert the Alligator is an irresponsible but genial ne'er-do-well, a lazy, rather cowardly show-off, short-tempered enough to throw a towering tantrum, but loyal to his friends and even, on occasion, sentimental. Deacon Muskrat, on the other hand. . . .

[*With the unifying idea that each of Kelly's creatures can be equated with a human type, the writer can give order to his composition.*]

The lack of unity in the original appears from the beginning; the writer's revelation of his personal interest in *Pogo* is not a promising unifying idea. The revision, based on the assertion that each of

Walt Kelly's characters can be equated with a human type, has a main idea on which the development can focus.

The following opening paragraph flounders because the first sentence sounds like a statement of the main idea but does not control what follows it.

ORIGINAL

[1] Freedom of speech has always been a tradition in America, supposedly guaranteed by the Constitution. [2] Tapping of private telephones is certainly a violation of privacy and freedom of speech. [3] Government agents posing as students and reporting what they hear in classrooms threaten both faculty and students. [4] This is bad for education, and students are understandably disturbed by it. [5] Students can see the same kinds of dangers in attempts to pressure newspaper or television or radio reporters to influence their opinions and attitudes. [6] Censorship of bookstore or library materials is also a threat to freedom of speech. [7] Threats to free speech can come from various quarters, from officials trying to retain political power or from groups wanting to maintain their economic status.

REVISION

Because successful education requires unrestricted communication, many serious students are worried about what seem to them threats to freedom of speech. They are disturbed when news reporters are pressured by their advertisers or by government officials to avoid criticizing foreign policy or army expenditures or government support of a particular industry. They are disturbed by stories of official wiretapping. They feel threatened by government agents posing as students and reporting what goes on in classrooms or student conversations. When an instructor or student is disciplined for expressing an unpopular opinion or when a book is banned from the library or from a course, students fear that the quality of their education is in danger.

The first sentence of the original commits the writer to discuss freedom of speech as a Constitutionally guaranteed tradition in America. The details selected, however, indicate that the writer is really concerned with signs that freedom of speech is threatened. As a result, the paragraph does not focus on the idea of the first sentence or on any other main idea. The writer might have moved in a second sentence to introduce a topic that at least some of his details would support—for example:

At present, however, there are signs that this tradition is being threatened by both political and economic power.

The writer could have developed his paragraph by supporting this sentence, which incorporates part of sentence 7 of the original, with the examples he has used. The revision uses an idea in sentence 4 of the original to frame a new opening statement which can be supported by the details the writer has collected.

Commitment and the Main Idea

In other words, a good topic statement works for the writer because it appropriately directs his commitment. When a writer frames a topic statement, he commits or obligates himself to develop his paper in certain ways. As he narrows his topic, he is thinking of what he may say about it. When he writes his comment in a sentence, he focuses his attention still more precisely. The student who narrows his topic to "Campus Politics as Education" (see chapter 1) will have reasons for his selection — his attitude toward the subject and his purpose in writing. He might now adopt a controversial point of view and phrase his main idea as:

> Campus politics provides the opportunities for practical education that are lacking in formal courses in political science.

Such a statement commits and limits the writer in a number of ways. He will need to list specific educational opportunities provided by campus politics; furthermore he must show that courses in political science cannot provide these opportunities. Another student might phrase his idea as:

> Campus politics, because it deals with artificial situations and insignificant problems, has no place in an educational institution.

This student has committed himself quite differently, to show artificiality and insignificance in campus political activity and still further to maintain the rather awkward logical assumption that anything artificial or insignificant has no place in an educational institution. A third student might decide to take no controversial stand, to describe and not to argue:

> Campus politics is sometimes educational and sometimes a waste of time, but it is almost always exciting for the participating student.

At first glance, this student may seem to have committed himself less because his statement is broader; actually he has given himself a considerable task: to illustrate both the educational and the wasteful aspects of campus politics and then to show that campus

33

politics is always exciting. All of these statements, because they commit the writer so extensively, suggest papers of some length. For the kind of paper usually required in college classes, the student would need to limit his main idea, to restrict his commitment, still further. The first student, for example, might think of specific opportunities for education in campus politics, using a process of dividing and selecting like that outlined above for limiting a topic. His statement might become one of the following, more specific and more workable:

> Campus politics teaches students the psychological principles of political campaigning.
>
> Campus politics is a practical way of teaching a student public speaking.
>
> Campus politics teaches the methods of organizing a large group of people and directing their efforts toward a single goal.
>
> Campus politics gives students practice in operating the machinery of government.
>
> Campus politics tests the student's integrity because it often requires him to choose between his selfish interests and the general good.

As he writes, the student may, of course, change his mind or collect new evidence that will result in a modification of his main idea; but until he can tie himself down to some tentative view, he has not thought enough.

Among the most common sorts of propositions that provide usable commitments are the following.

1. *Generalization.* Most propositions involve generalization: that is, they result from observing facts and discovering something worth recording that is common to all of them. The student writing on campus politics, for example, might check the files of the student paper for five years and produce a generalization, a proposition, like the following:

> During the past five years every campaign for student body president has turned about trivialities rather than issues of educational policy.

The generalization identifies a characteristic that the student considers common to all the campaigns he has examined. Used as a theme or thesis sentence, the proposition would commit the writer to provide illustrations and examples of the trivialities. More serious and more extensive study did in fact produce the following generalization, which serves as a thesis statement:

First of all, it is certain that we of Western society have never, in our five thousand years of recorded history, kept peace for long within an area save by bringing that area within the authority of a single government.

CRANE BRINTON, *From Many One*

2. *Definition, classification, description.* A proposition may characterize a topic and thus commit the writer to explain it in more detail. As a thesis statement, such a proposition usually is specific enough to stimulate further comment. A definition like "A dictionary is a book" is so broad that it tends to end discussion, but consider the following:

A good dictionary lists a selection of the words of a language, providing information about their origin, spelling, pronunciation, meaning, and uses.

The fuller definition refines the proposition and gives the writer some basis for continuing, suggesting that subsequent sentences illustrate each of the dictionary's functions. Other propositions, although they take the form of definitions or classifications, may express opinions that require support:

Campus politics is one of our most successful methods of miseducation.

Such a thesis sentence would commit the writer to illustration and perhaps to argument. Descriptive propositions may require lists of the kinds of details on which the generalization is based:

The room was a garden of wax fruit and plastic flowers.

A description based on this sentence would mention specific things: the bowl of pink and lavender grapes on the table, the shiny calla lilies on the piano, the planting area with its imitation tropical greenery.

Propositions that describe may also include implied judgment or opinion:

Ten minutes of his conversation was enough to convince the girls that they should have stayed at home.

Such a thesis sentence would require the writer to describe this conversation more fully.

3. *Relational propositions.* Propositions may develop from a writer's speculations about how things or events are related—how one thing may be a part of another or the cause or effect of an-

other. Such propositions often open discussions that list reasons, cite evidence, develop an argument. For example:

> Campus politics persists mainly as an outlet for the energies of a few students who need to build their egos and are incapable of doing it in athletics or scholarship.

Such a proposition, involving a fairly complicated causal relationship, may require complex development. Consider:

> *Our Town* is popular as a school play mainly because it can be staged easily.

The proposition obligates the writer to supply some support for both ideas—that the play is easily staged and is popular—and to argue that the easy staging leads to the popularity.

4. *Practical propositions.* Propositions may be called practical when they advocate action, indicate something that should exist or should happen.

> Campus politics should be reformed by strict university regulations and faculty control.

Actually, propositions of this sort introduce brief essays less frequently than might be imagined, probably because they require argument. Writers are often more successful with propositions that introduce factual support.

PHRASING TOPIC STATEMENTS

2b

As we have seen, clear writing gains unity by focusing on main ideas, which are usually given formal expression in topical statements. Such statements may control the whole composition or any segment of it—a group of paragraphs, a paragraph, or a group of sentences within a paragraph. The phrasing of topic statements, however, can be most readily studied in topic sentences of paragraphs. Well-organized paragraphs need to meet the same requirements for unity as a longer composition. Their topic sentences need to be phrased precisely and specifically. And in learning to draft topic sentences for paragraphs we learn also to draft topic statements for any other units of composition.

A topic sentence rests on definition in the etymological sense of that word, thereby setting up boundaries. A good topic sentence blocks out enough space for the paragraph and sets limits to it. It

2b   **TS**

*Provide a topic sentence or rephrase the existing topical
statement, making it better suited to control a segment of
the composition, or to provide a transition.*

ORIGINAL

REVISION

I shall always remember an experience I had last summer; it was
the most exciting thing that has
ever happened to me.

[*This has the earmarks of a poor topic
sentence. The writer probably does not
intend to demonstrate that he will remember this incident while forgetting others,
or to make a comprehensive study of his
exciting moments.*]

Last summer, while I was trying
out my new skin-diving equipment,
I blacked out and nearly drowned.

[*This sentence, although it may have
no great virtues as a topic sentence, says
something, and what it says is to the
point. It is briefer than the original,
does not mislead the reader, and introduces the subject with some exactness.*]

. . . My mother's graduation present
was tied up in two neatly ironed
strips of gingham, which I recognized as her apron strings.

I got the job I had applied for,
and I also received a letter saying I
had been admitted to the university.

[*The lack of transition leaves the
reader wondering where the account is
going.*]

. . . My mother's graduation present
was tied up in two neatly ironed
strips of gingham, which I recognized as her apron strings.

These apron strings soon became
a symbol for the new life that, I
discovered, I was now beginning to
lead.

[*Not all topic sentences require repetition of words, but most of them require
some transitional material.*]

is general enough to provide scope for the idea in the paragraph,
but it restricts the subject in order to exclude other materials. Consider a paragraph from Gilbert Highet's *The Classical Tradition:*

Nineteenth-century writers admired this culture for two chief
reasons: because it was beautiful, and because it was not Christian.
They saw their own civilization as squalid and greedy; they praised
the Greeks and Romans as noble and spiritual. They felt contemporary Christianity to be mean, ugly, and repressive; they admired
the cults of antiquity as free, strong, and graceful. Looking at the
soot-laden sky, pierced by factory chimneys and neo-Gothic steeples,
they exclaimed

Great God! I'd rather be
A Pagan suckled in a creed outworn.

Highet wishes to say that nineteenth-century writers admired the Greek and Roman culture for two reasons, "it was beautiful" and "it was not Christian," and his topic sentence restricts the discussion to just these subjects, although he carries them parallel through the paragraph. He might have written:

> In this connection it is interesting to note that earlier periods exerted a certain charm over many of the more sensitive spirits of the nineteenth century and that among the reasons for this charm were the differences between theirs and an earlier day. They saw in their own civilization. . . .

As a topic sentence this could have been worse. It would have permitted the writer to say almost anything he pleased; but it is clearly a worse topic sentence than Highet's, partly because it is less exact, less precise. It tells the reader too little of what he should know; it does not restrict the paragraph to just those materials that are to be its content.

Similarly, Highet might have begun his paragraph in this manner:

> Nineteenth-century writers resented living under a soot-laden sky. They resented the growing ugliness of an industrial society. They disliked the factory chimneys that thrust up everywhere, and not only the factories but the neo-Gothic spires, which suggested that the Christianity of the day, like the industry, was ugly. They saw in their own civilization. . . .

Again, he did not, and the reason is obvious. He would have been starting with material so specific that it provides no proper introduction to the whole.

Topic Sentences and Transition

A topic sentence can appear anywhere in the paragraph. It may appear at the end as a summary; it may appear as a sort of hinge in the middle, looking both forward and backward within the paragraph. Most frequently, however, it appears at the beginning, and hence it usually includes some transitional matter, relating the paragraph to material elsewhere, especially in the immediately preceding segment of the composition. One of the most common types of topic sentence opens with a reference to what has preceded, a repetition of it, or even a kind of summary, and then goes on to introduce a new topic. Notice, for example, how the

38

following sentence from an essay of W. H. Hudson links what has preceded and what is to follow: "Although the potato was very much to me in those early years, it grew to be more when I heard its history." The opening subordinate clause summarizes generally what has preceded, a narrative comment on the author's interest in the potato; the second clause introduces a new topic, the history of the potato, which is the subject of the paragraph the sentence introduces. The following sentence, from a *Time* report on the telephone business, does the same kind of thing less directly but succinctly: "Not all calls end so happily." The paragraph that preceded had reported pleasant experiences with the telephone; the sentence itself introduces a paragraph listing less fortunate incidents. Often, as in the following, the first sentence of a paragraph is almost entirely transitional material: "The return of fatalism in our modern world leads us to another general question." The preceding material discussed the return of fatalism; the sentence presents the transition directly, and a second topic sentence proposes the question to be discussed.

Not all writing is as simple as the Hudson essay or a *Time* account, but topical statements can be made to show relationships within relatively complex material. Peter Shrag, in an article entitled "The Decline of the WASP," endeavors to analyze subtle shifts in American social mentality. Early in the essay he points out that persons born before World War II shared an unquestioning attitude toward America, "wanting only to be accepted according to the terms that history and tradition had already established." The next paragraph begins as follows:

> What held that world together was not just a belief in some standardized version of textbook Americanism, a catalogue of accepted values, but a particular class of people and institutions that we identified with our vision of the country.

The phrase "that world" provides the transition from the previous segment of the essay; the remainder of the sentence indicates rather precisely what had held American society together, what it was and what it was not. The next sentence refines this topic statement more precisely; as Shrag expresses it, "The people were white and Protestant; the institutions were English; American culture was WASP." He concludes, "The American mind was the WASP mind."

The next two paragraphs continue in a similar pattern; the topic sentences announce new aspects of the general topic and relate them to previous paragraphs. The first of these begins as follows:

> We grew up with them; they surrounded us; they were the heroes of the history we studied and of the fantasy life we sought in those Monday-through-Friday radio serials.

Here the transition is even stronger; the topic sentence links the paragraph to *they*, who were the WASPs, and establishes *we*, who were other than WASPs, but who accepted and even furthered the WASP mind. As Shrag says, "Hollywood's Jews sold the American dream strictly in WASP terms." The first sentence of the next paragraph begins as follows:

> They—the WASPs—never thought of themselves as anything but Americans, nor did it occur to others to label them as anything special until, about twenty-five years ago, their influence began to decline and they started to lose their cultural initiative and pre-eminence.

One might notice that the transition here is relatively subtle and complex. It continues the reference to *they* and the distinction between the persons so referred to and the ethnic groups referred to as *we*, but it mentions, also, the contents of the two preceding paragraphs, that "they . . . never thought of themselves as anything but Americans" (the first paragraph), "nor did it occur to others to label them as anything special" (the second paragraph). In addition the whole third paragraph is transitional in that it is preparing for the "decline of the WASP."

Uses of Topic Statements

A good topic statement can do at least four sorts of things; an author, especially in his rewriting, may do well to check his topic statements for adequacy. The following should always be considered and should usually be present.

1. *Transition.* For every segment of writing the reader should know how it relates to other writing, either other parts of the same composition or other compositions. The most usual transitions of this sort are brief references, relying upon words or phrases, to previous segments of the composition. Occasionally, a transition is so clearly implied that it need not be expressed; a series of segments may be so obviously part of a larger segment that each one need not be linked in a formal way, but such instances are rare and the young writer may well remind himself, "Better too much transition than too little."

2. *Structure.* The reader usually needs to know how a composition is put together, how he can expect it to develop. At a

minimum, he should understand before he finishes a composition how it has been structured. Usually, the writer need not go so far as to open a passage by saying, "I believe that the women's liberation movement warrants our support for three reasons," but some indication of structure can be a useful part of a topic statement.

3. *Topic.* At a minimum, a topic statement should announce a topic, usually the more precisely the better.

4. *Commitment.* The topic statement should commit the writer to what he wants to say, ideally, to no more and no less. Of course, the developing of the topical material will inevitably become a refinement of it, but careful drafting of a topic statement can do much to clarify the writing as well as the reading process.

FOR STUDY AND WRITING

A Criticize the following topics and statements of main ideas; which are suitable for student themes? Consider what commitments are implied in the statements of ideas.

1. TOPIC: Orientation
   MAIN IDEA: This theme will show various problems of the freshman at a large university and how his courses are different from his high school work and something should be done to remedy the situation.

2. TOPIC: Sweaters in the College Wardrobe
   MAIN IDEA: Uses of sweaters in a girl's wardrobe. Many kinds. Sizes, colors, styles, etc. What will go with what? How many should a girl have? Styles. Goods from which made.

3. TOPIC: Improving Bus Service
   MAIN IDEA: Bus service in my city could be made better, and even profitable, if the bus company would change some of the routes to fit shifts in population, adjust schedules to popular need, and teach drivers some common courtesy.

4. TOPIC: Learning American History from Stamps
   MAIN IDEA: Collecting American stamps is a painless but profitable way to learn the facts of American history.

5. TOPIC: Making Your Own Drapes
   MAIN IDEA: Making drapes for your room requires consideration of texture and color in choosing material, selection of a suitable and practical style, patience, and a sense of humor.

6. TOPIC: Woodchucks as Game Animals
   MAIN IDEA: Hunting woodchucks provides good sport; woodchucks are plentiful and never out of season, and properly dressed the flesh is excellent food.

7. TOPIC: Sutpen's Mansion
   MAIN IDEA: An hour wandering through the ruins of the old mansion makes one feel a sense of loss for a way of life that has disappeared from the South.

8. TOPIC: Ballet
   MAIN IDEA: I would expect to give a brief sketch of the invention, history, and development of ballet, say something about the recent popularity of ballet in this country, the leading ballet companies, especially the New York City Ballet, and the amateur and semiprofessional groups that are growing up everywhere, very much like the little theater movement of the last generation, the ballet in movies and TV, and give some of my own opinions of ballet as an art, based on my lessons in ballet.

9. TOPIC: Becky Thatcher's Home
   MAIN IDEA: When we visited Hannibal, Missouri, we went to see it.

B Each of the following sentences appears early in an essay or book and may be taken as an expression of the main idea of some part of the composition. Describe what each sentence commits the writer to do.

1. Probably the most powerful effect of literature on us is a moral effect, and this effect, rightly appreciated, is what gives literature its unique value.

2. One of the most precise clues to what is actually going on psychologically in a culture is its use of language.

3. The question of form in language presents itself under two aspects.

4. As an undergraduate Kittredge had acquired a taste for clubs and societies, and the taste proved lasting.

5. The English drama arose out of two compulsions: the natural instinct to imitate and the evangelical desire to teach.

6. *Winnie-the-Pooh* is, as practically everyone knows, one of the greatest books ever written, but it is also one of the most controversial.

C Consider the following as topic sentences:

1. Mrs. Jones was even stingier than her daughter.

2. Mrs. Jones was the stingiest woman I ever knew.

3. Mrs. Jones's name was a synonym for *stingy* in our town, and everybody had some anecdote to tell about her.

Each of these sentences might serve as a topic sentence, but each makes a different sort of commitment to what is to follow. The first implies that the daughter's stinginess has been discussed in a previous paragraph. The second seems to imply that Mrs. Jones is to be compared with all other stingy women the writer has known; probably he has no such intention, and the reader would probably assume that these words mean no more than "Mrs. Jones was very stingy,"

42

but the writer would do well to say what he means. The last sentence could suitably introduce a paragraph of tales told about Mrs. Jones. Now examine the following groups of possible topic sentences and distinguish the implications of each.

1. **a)** Janet is the most tiresome salesgirl I ever dealt with in my whole life.

   b) I do not like Janet as a salesgirl.

   c) Obviously, Janet is a poor salesgirl.

   d) Janet is a poor salesgirl because she wants to do all the talking.

   e) Janet is a poor salesgirl because she has never learned to let the customer do a little healthy griping.

   f) Janet is the worst salesgirl in the store.

   g) Janet would be a better salesgirl if she would cultivate a little interest in her customers.

   h) Janet would be a better salesgirl if she were a kind and sympathetic person who could take a natural interest in her customer's wishes.

   i) Janet might be a better salesgirl if she would read a book on selling.

   j) Janet would not be such a bad salesgirl if she would remember what she was told in her course in salesmanship.

2. **a)** The American attitude toward Chinese affairs is wholly wrong.

   b) The American attitude toward Chinese affiars seems to me wrong.

   c) The American attitude toward Chinese affairs seems to me unrealistic.

   d) The American attitude toward Chinese affairs seems to me shrewd but dangerous.

   e) Ping-Pong may be more effective than diplomacy in solving the Chinese problem.

   f) Washington does not understand the Chinese problem.

   g) If Washington understands the Chinese problem, our recent moves do not reveal the fact.

   h) Washington may or may not understand Chinese problems, but we are endeavoring to give the impression of knowledge, not to say clairvoyance.

   i) Washington cannot be expected to reveal its Chinese policy until we have studied the reactions of London and Moscow.

3. **a)** All that I can now remember learning in high school I gained from playing basketball.

   b) Until I started playing basketball, I had no interest in high school.

   c) Chemistry is now my major interest, but I got started in chemistry only through my high school basketball coach.

   d) For me, basketball was a bridge between bumming around town and studying chemistry.

   e) If I ever become a chemical engineer, one reason is to be sought in a tricky backhand shot I have, which brought me to the coach's attention.

   f) I think basketball should be a required course for every student.

g) Basketball is an American invention, and the more people live in cities where there is no room for baseball diamonds, the more basketball becomes our national sport, and that was my experience, that it changed my life.

h) The lessons learned on the basketball court are the factors needed for success in the classroom and in the world of today.

i) For all-around fun and character building, give me basketball.

j) Basketball, so called because the first games were played with a peach basket with the bottom knocked out, provided a turning point in my life.

D The following paragraph—minus its topic sentence—is taken from a letter from an officer in the Second Iowa Regiment describing what he saw and heard of the Battle of Shiloh, April 6, 1862. Construct topic and closing sentences that, taken together, will give the paragraph unity.

> "What was the plan of the battle, General?" asked Gen. Buell of Acting Brig. Gen. Tuttle. "By God, sir, I don't know!" he replied. Gen. Sweeney on our right said he gave all his orders on his own hook, and so of many others. The army was scattered over about twenty miles. The greenest regiments were on the outposts, and not a shovel full of dirt thrown up to protect them until they could be reinforced from the interior of the camp. As a natural consequence, they were panic stricken and retreated in, reporting their regiments "all cut to pieces." Col. Peabody's brigade, on the left, had none but green regiments, viz.: the 12th Michigan, 16th Wisconsin, and the 23d and 25th Missouri. They lost both their batteries, which soon were turned upon us. Sherman's regiments on the right and Prentiss in the centre had few troops that had ever seen a fight.

E The following is part of a paragraph concerning David Crockett, a picturesque frontier figure who got himself elected to Congress, partly by his outrageously tall tales.

> . . . He [Crockett] was quite willing to have it known that he had waded the Mississippi and whipped his weight in wildcats and leaped over the Ohio, that he salted his bear-steaks with hail and peppered them with buckshot and broiled them with a flash of lightning, after riding on it. He had hugged a bear out of breath and caught and tamed an alligator and set him up beside his cabin and used him as a bench, and his little boy brought bear-cubs home in his pocket. He even wrote the story of his life, in which a friend helped him to "classify the matter." He liked the kind of real life that made a book "jump out of the press like a new dollar fresh from a mint-hopper," he said; and this *Narrative,* with its fresh images and homespun style, at once became, and remained, a frontier classic.
>
> VAN WYCK BROOKS, *The World of Washington Irving*

Obviously, Brooks has set limits to this piece of writing; it is about Crockett, and furthermore it is about a certain aspect of Crockett. Discuss each of the following as a theme sentence that will make clear the commitments that Brooks has accepted for this passage.

1. Crockett had his own means of attracting attention.
2. Crockett had a language of his own, a mixture of fantasy, poetry, and backwoods wit.
3. Crockett had quite a career, and even got himself elected to Congress.
4. Crockett, son of a tavern keeper, was hunter, trapper, scout, and itinerant farmer.
5. Crockett never tired of recounting his truly remarkable exploits.

F Let us assume that you have only limited admiration for some of the lectures you have attended and have decided to write a theme about what is wrong with the way professors conduct classes. Then you decide to be somewhat less blunt about it, and while noticing that various professors lecture quite differently, have a little fun suggesting that some of them are not too good. You produce the following paragraph.

A student expects to find certain qualities in a good classroom lecture. At a minimum, it should be well organized and directed to a known purpose. My instructor in anthropology has almost a set pattern for his lectures, but you always know where he is going and why. His first sentence may be something like this: "Last day, I found occasion to mention the words *nation, language,* and *race.* Of these, the first two are roughly definable, but the word *race* cannot be defined with anything like scientific accuracy." He will then develop his criticism of the concept of race, breaking down his discussion under various headings, and letting you know when he goes from one to another. This sort of treatment can be dull, but at least the student comes out of the class with an orderly set of notes that he can understand when he goes back over them for review. My art instructor, on the other hand, although he may get you excited about a painting, sometimes leaves you wondering what the class was about. He may start by showing a picture, repeat something he said last week, get to talking about the brushwork in the picture, without ever explaining what he means by brushwork, and then go off on a story of how Holbein designed his own brushes. The result is that when you try to review for an examination you do not know where to begin.

Now if you will look back at the topic sentence you should notice that although it might serve for some paragraphs, it is not a good topic sentence for this paragraph. Unless you now wish to change your mind about what you want to say, you should rewrite the topic sentence. The beginning of the sentence, "A student expects to find" leads to nothing and had better be cut. Of the "certain qualities," a vague expression even if the reader knows which use of *certain* is intended, only one, organization and direction, enters into the paragraph. As it stands, the paragraph seems to be mainly concerned with producing usable class notes, an idea not incorporated in the topic statement. Try writing a better topic sentence.

G Go back to the journal you have been keeping, with a view to selecting a subject that can be developed into a theme of 500–1,000 words.

Do you see any larger implications in some of them, now that you have mulled them over? Or take one and examine it more closely. For example, let us assume you have made an entry about a good lecture you heard, or an interesting book you have been reading. Now try to write out a dozen different statements about the lecture or book, about its contents, its impact upon people, its limitations, the ways in which you find it inadequate, or whatever. Then select one of these statements, accept it as a commitment, and plan the theme, writing first a theme sentence, then a topic sentence for each paragraph. Then write the theme. When you have done so, reconsider the theme sentence, then each topic sentence, and rewrite each of them in at least two ways. You will want to consider whether these topical statements are broad enough or too broad, and whether the structure and wording of the sentences can be improved. When you hand in your theme, hand in also the two other versions, and explain why you preferred the one you finally use.

DEVELOPMENT: COMMITMENT AND RESPONSE

CHAPTER 3

*Controlled writing is developed through a response
to a commitment.*

Topic statements, as we have seen, provide the focal points for writing; an entire composition or any segment of it gains unity by focusing on a main idea. But every statement, especially every topic statement, makes a commitment; it promises or implies that some kind of response will follow. Prose develops by providing responses to commitments.

A series of unfulfilled commitments does little to move a discussion forward because the sentences only project the writer's opinion; the assertions have no support. Consider the following:

> The abortion laws in this state need radical revision. The present laws are discriminatory, favoring people with money. The religious arguments against abortion are unrealistic. Overpopulation is already a major hazard to our civilization, and the problems are getting steadily worse. Most of our present ecological problems have developed because there are too many people on this planet. In fact, every family should be restricted to two children.

The second sentence does respond to the commitment of the first, suggesting one reason to support the idea that the laws need revision. But the train of thought stops with the second sentence, which commits the writer to explain how the laws favor people with money. Instead, the writer introduces another topic, religious arguments, and again drops it without a response and proceeds to introduce overpopulation. In fact, every sentence in the paragraph would serve as a topic statement for at least a paragraph.

47

The writer who has difficulty producing a 500-word paper because "he has said everything he knows" in the first paragraph often produces judgments like the above. His writing stalls because he has begun by recording every opinion or conclusion he can muster. He has not really started his writing. He should provide facts to support judgments, to clarify the general with the specific, to meet the commitment of each sentence with a response.

GUIDE TO REVISION

3a   Fact

*Revise, limiting the unit of composition to no more than
one judgment and supplying facts to support it.*

ORIGINAL

College education is much too expensive in America, and it is getting worse every day. Many deserving students either have to postpone college indefinitely or to work so much of the time that they neglect their studies. If democracy is to survive, the government must provide some method for enabling more capable students to get college educations. Scholarship awards are unfair because they put a premium on memory and mental ability and not on character and need. If our country is to survive, something must be done about this problem.

[*It is no wonder that this paper stopped short of the required number of words; except for the second sentence, the paragraph is made up of undeveloped judgments, so broad that they discourage development. The writer should begin by abandoning the unnecessary judgments.*]

REVISION

The cost of a college education in the United States has more than doubled in the last fifteen years. It is no longer easy for a young man to save enough from his paper route and a job mowing lawns on Saturdays to see him through four years at a university. In most colleges and universities tuition and fees have more than doubled, and getting along without a car is harder than it used to be. The textbook that cost $5.00 a few years ago is likely to cost from $10.00 to $20.00 now. Inflated food prices have affected college cafeterias, and even the soft drink or cup of coffee that used to provide recreation for a nickel is now fifteen or twenty cents. . . .

[*The revision narrows the scope of the paragraph; instead of broad judgments, it uses a general factual statement that can be illustrated. It leaves the writer with a chance to develop his topic.*]

Fact

Compare the following sets of statements:

JUDGMENT: Martha is a bad girl.
FACT: Martha took two pieces of candy without asking.

JUDGMENT: Snidhart is a murderer.
FACT: Two witnesses saw Snidhart shoot twice at the cashier who died in the hospital this morning.

JUDGMENT: Smith's dog kills sheep.
FACT: I saw Smith's dog kill a sheep.

JUDGMENT: College football is on the way out.
FACT: In many major universities, football costs are increasing more rapidly than gate receipts.

The judgments are opinions, decisions, pronouncements. They characterize or classify; they express approval or disapproval; they make a general statement. Their truth or falsity cannot finally be demonstrated. The facts report what has happened or exists; they result from observation or measurement or calculation; they can be tested or verified.

Most statements, however, cannot be distinguished so sharply as these examples. A comment like "I believe that Martha is a bad girl" can be called fact—presumably the writer knows what he believes—but it obviously includes a judgment. Or a primarily factual statement like "We saw the murderer Snidhart shoot the cashier" includes a judgment in the label *murderer*. Furthermore, judgments are not always so nearly final as those above. Many are plausible opinions that provoke thought or lead to factual development:

A little learning is a dangerous thing.
Athletics is a valuable part of an educational program.

Many statements are somewhere between, seemingly factual but not clearly verifiable. They may introduce substantiating evidence or illustrative fact.

The trouble with youth is that those who have it are too young to enjoy it.
College football has ceased to have any relation to education.

Obviously, not all statements can be clearly classified, but fact and judgment can usually be distinguished as products of different kinds of thinking, and judgments and facts have different uses in writing.

49

Judgments are deceptively easy to come by. We hear them all about us; and often, especially if we think uncritically, we accept them because other people do. When we need to put words on paper, judgments and opinions often occur to us first, but they impair writing unless they introduce factual material. Facts are harder to collect than judgments, but judgments are useless without them.

Furthermore, accepted at face value, judgments impede the writer because they tend to bring his thinking to a dead end. In serious writing, judgments as nearly final as those cited above leave the reader only two choices: agreement or denial. Confronted by "John is a fool" a reader can only agree or say, "He is not." The judgment opens no further discussion. It begins by settling the matter. Such a judgment, in other words, is so sweeping that it cannot be substantiated, even by evidence that John behaved foolishly. The writer can only reassert his opinion, and repetition does not convince. The successful writer recognizes the limited usefulness of judgments, preferring statements he can develop with evidence.

General and Specific

Judgments are usually more general than facts, although *general* and *specific* are relative terms. That is, things or expressions are not absolutely or finally general or specific, but only more general or more specific than something else. *Automobile* is more general than *passenger car* but more specific than *automotive vehicle*, and *passenger car* is more general than *dune buggy*. The general expression is broader, more inclusive; it tends to refer to a whole class, a type, or a group. As a statement becomes more specific it approaches pointing to a particular, to a single object. *Man* is more specific than *living being; American citizen* is more specific than *man; John Jones* is more specific than *American citizen*. Compare the following examples:

College activities are bad.

Extracurricular activities in college are harmful to the student.

Extracurricular activities in college prevent good academic work.

Adrian failed Chemistry 101 because he spent too much time in dramatics.

Each statement is more specific than the one preceding it.   **50**

Development can be looked on as a process of responding to commitments. Whenever we use a word or clause or sentence, we commit ourselves; we limit or restrict in some ways what can follow. The choice we make of a sentence subject, for instance, does much to dictate what the remainder of the sentence will be like. And every sentence we write determines in part what the next sentence is to be — or what the next several sentences will be. Each sentence commits the writer to proceed with some development or to shift to another sequence of ideas. Consider the following first sentence of an article with five alternate possibilities for a second sentence.

I used to love to get into the thick of crowds.

1. Moving along in a crush of pulsing humanity was one of my greatest pleasures.
2. More recently, however, I find myself mistrustful and frightened in even a small group of strangers, with my hand automatically hovering near my billfold.
3. It was these interests and enthusiasms that started me in the life of the circus.
4. I felt enlarged, recharged, much as I did when climbing on a mountainside.
5. I loved the subway rush hour, the crush at ticket windows, the squeeze of New Year's Eve on Forty-second Street, or the night street market in Boston.

Each of the alternatives might follow the first sentence, and the five represent the main ways of responding in one sentence to the commitment of a preceding one. They represent the possibilities from which a writer may select in moving prose forward, in developing an idea.

1. *Repetition.*　The first alternative sentence is a possible response, but it provides little development. It does little more than repeat, adding perhaps a bit more information to the idea of crowds. In general, a sentence that merely repeats a preceding one does nothing to advance discourse, to develop an idea, although sometimes it may provide emphasis. Here the first alternative does not seem a profitable way to continue the discussion.

2. *Diversion.*　The second alternative would turn the writing in a new direction, as the *however* signals. The sentence moves the discussion from the writer's love of crowds in the past to a new topic, his fear of crowds in the present. This type of response is useful

whenever the writer wants to move from one topic to another; it does not provide development for the sentence it follows but establishes a new topic to be developed.

3. *Generalization.* The third alternative is possible here, but it assumes that the sentence before it is not an opening sentence but one of a series of sentences listing early interests of the writer. A generalization of this sort is a possible response; but it does not develop; it summarizes development that has preceded it. It may work as a topical statement coming after the material that develops it.

4. *Specification.* The fourth and fifth alternative sentences exemplify the most common type of response to any commitment. They move the thought ahead, developing it by making the preceding sentence, or part of it, more specific. Sentence 4 develops the first part of the opening sentence, making more specific the idea behind "I used to love." Sentence 5 provides specific examples to develop the other part of the opening sentence, to show more precisely what the writer means by "the thick of crowds." Sentence 5 follows the opening sentence in the article from which it is taken.

Prose moves as a sequence of commitments and responses, but it develops mainly as it moves toward the specific. The kind of response that develops an idea is usually a specification.

SPECIFIC DEVELOPMENT

3b

This kind of sentence-to-sentence movement, pushing toward the specific, characterizes the direction of expository writing. Generalization has its uses, since the idea that ranges widely may express the purpose or point of a piece of writing, but understanding sharpens as the writer explains his general observations in specific terms the reader can grasp. Modern prose, even in a unit as small as the single sentence, develops in large part through specification. The following sequence of sentences illustrates a typical movement.

[1] Change in meaning is frequently due to ethical, or moral, considerations. [2] A word may, as it were, go downhill, or it may rise in the world; there is no way of predicting what its career may be. [3] *Politician* has had a downhill development in American English; in British English it is still not entirely without honor.

THOMAS PYLES, *The Origin and Development of the English Language*

The three sentences open a paragraph by moving successively toward greater specificity. Sentence 2 moves to a level of greater specificity than 1 by pointing out a precise way in which a word may change for ethical or moral reasons—by going up or down hill. Then 3 moves to another stage with a particular illustration of meaning change in the word *politician*. The paragraph continues at the same level of specification, using other words as examples of the kind of change described in 2.

The following opening of a paragraph begins in the same way:

[1] Like most of the American Indians, except those of the Southwest pueblos, the tribes of the Northwest Coast were Dionysian. [2] In their religious ceremonies the final thing they strove for was ecstasy. [3] The chief dancer, at least at the high point of his per-

GUIDE TO REVISION

3b   **Spec**

Revise to make development more specific, adding details or making diction more precise (see Chapter 20).

ORIGINAL

Obviously, the theater was everything that a university theater should be. It had all the qualities that one wants to find in a campus playhouse. In size and equipment it was almost perfect. It is no wonder that drama was so popular on the campus and that plays were so well attended. We should attempt to get something like it for our university. And the responsibility for action rests in part with the students themselves.

[Like most examples of inadequate development, this passage from a student theme is general rather than specific; it repeats judgments; it includes in one short paragraph material that could be developed into a long theme. The writer gets into trouble at the beginning by failing to illustrate. The writer may be willing to make his obvious statement on the basis of his knowledge, but the reader does not have enough information to accept it.]

REVISION

The theater was everything that a university theater should be. It was small and intimate, holding only about two hundred and fifty, and you could hear and see from every seat. The seats were comfortable but not new, and an occasional rip in the leather gave the place an atmosphere of permanence; it did not have the kind of polish that makes you expect to smell fresh paint when you walk in. There was no revolving stage or other complex machinery, but the stage was large and there was plenty of room to get around backstage. There was enough equipment to make possible all kinds of experiments—good and bad—but there was not enough to keep the stage crew from using ingenuity.

[The first sentence of the original can be developed into a paragraph. If the other general statements of the original are to remain, they need similar illustration.]

formance, should lose normal control of himself and be rapt into another state of existence. [4] He should froth at the mouth, tremble violently and abnormally, do deeds which would be terrible in a normal state.

RUTH BENEDICT, *Patterns of Culture*

The paragraph begins with a general statement. The second sentence explains the first, and the term *Dionysian,* with a statement a little more specific. The third illustrates the second and the meaning of *ecstasy.* The fourth becomes more specific still in illustrating the third. As it becomes more specific, the writing becomes more vivid.

Responses as Development

The process of composing is not simple, but at some stage it emerges as the very practical matter of putting one word after another, one sentence after another. Words and sentences must be produced in some kind of sequence that leads the thought of the reader. Each word or sentence relates in some way to what has preceded and points to what is to follow. The writer constantly makes rhetorical choices, selecting, often almost automatically, among possibilities. These choices produce and control development. Development in any piece of writing depends on the step-by-step choices a writer makes among the four types of responses to commitments.

A writer does not, of course, examine every alternative for every sentence and conduct a debate with himself before he makes a choice. But speculation about some of the kinds of considerations behind the development of a segment of prose may illustrate something of the complex composing process. Consider the following selection from a discussion of the demolition derby, a variation on automobile racing, in *The Kandy-Kolored Tangerine-Flake Streamline Baby.* Tom Wolfe describes the events of a derby, but he also has an "idea for writing," an interpretation of the significance of the derby. The passage, with the sequence of responses described in marginal notes, develops part of that interpretation, opening with a proposition that asserts the importance of the automobile in our society.

[1] As hand to hand combat has gradually disappeared from our civilization, even in wartime, and competition has become more and more sophisticated and abstract,

(1) The sentence responds to the preceding description as a generalization and also commits the writer to develop the contention that the automobile is a symbol of aggression. Without explana-

54

Americans have turned to the automobile to satisfy their love of direct aggression. [2] The mild-mannered man who turns into a bear behind the wheel of a car—i.e., who finds in the power of the automobile a vehicle for the release of his inhibitions—is part of American folklore. [3] Among teen-agers the automobile has become the symbol, and in part the physical means, of triumph over family and community restrictions. [4] Seventy-five per cent of all car thefts in the United States are by teen-agers out for "joy rides."

[5] The symbolic meaning of the automobile tones down but by no means vanishes in adulthood. [6] Police traffic investigators have long been convinced that far more accidents are purposeful crashes by belligerent drivers than they could ever prove. [7] One of the heroes of the era was the Middle Eastern diplomat who rammed a magazine writer's car from behind in the Kalorama embassy district of Washington two years ago. [8] When the American bellowed out the window at him, he backed up and smashed his car again. [9] When the fellow leaped out of his car to pick a fight, he backed up and smashed his car a third time, then drove off. [10] He was recalled home for having "gone native."

[11] The unabashed, undisguised, quite purposeful sense of destruction of the demolition derby is its unique contribution. [12] The aggression, the battering, the ruination are there to be enjoyed. [13] The crowd at a demolition derby seldom gasps and often laughs. [14] It enjoys the same full-throated participation as Romans at the Colosseum. [15] After each trial or

tion this judgment would lack conviction; the following paragraphs all respond to this opening commitment. (2–3) Sentence 2 responds by moving toward the specific with an example—the mild man who becomes an aggressive driver, and 3 provides another, the teen-ager for whom a car means a triumph over restrictions. (4) Sentence 4 responds to 3, with one item of specific evidence for the teen-ager's respect for cars.

(5) The second paragraph begins with a sentence that responds to 1 as a specification parallel with 2 and 3, but also responds to 3, carrying on the reference to teen-agers by having them grow up. (6) Sentence 6 offers a specification of 5, one symptom of adult aggressiveness in automobiles. (7–10) The final three sentences narrate an incident that provides a response to 6, with sentence 10 emphasizing the application of the incident by suggesting that the diplomat had acquired American aggressiveness.

(11) The opening of the third paragraph is again primarily a specifying response to sentence 1, as 1 has been developed through two paragraphs. Sentence 11 classifies the demolition derby as a manifestation of aggressiveness expressed through the automobile, which is associated with a "purposeful sense of destruction." (12–14) The second sentence of the paragraph, 12, picks one aspect of the derby for con-

heat at a demolition derby, two drivers go into the finals. [16] One is the driver whose car was still going at the end. [17] The other is the driver the crowd selects from among the 24 vanquished on the basis of his courage, showmanship or simply the awesomeness of his crashes. [18] The numbers of the cars are read over loudspeakers, and the crowd chooses one with its cheers. [19] By the same token, the crowd may force a driver out of competition if he appears cowardly or merely cunning. [20] This is the sort of driver who drifts around the edge of the battle avoiding crashes with the hope that the other cars will eliminate one another. [21] The umpire waves a yellow flag at him and he must crash into someone within 30 seconds or run the risk of being booed off the field in dishonor and disgrace.

[22] The frank relish of the crowd is nothing, however, compared to the kick the contestants get out of the game. . . .

sideration, the enjoyment, and commits the writer to develop this. Sentence 13 responds, referring to the crowd with a more specific observation, specified still further by the allusion to the Romans in 14. (15–19) Sentence 15 begins a series of sentences that narrate the events of the derby as a way of specifying how the crowd participates. Sentence 17 applies the information of 15 and 16, pointing out that the crowd selects the second driver for the finals. Sentence 17 specifies the "participation" mentioned in 14, and then 18 and 19 specify the way the crowd participates in selection. (20–21) Then two sentences provide more specific information about the kind of driver introduced in 20.

(22) The new paragraph, with a transition from the description of the crowd in the third paragraph, introduces a new specification of sentence 1, the enjoyment of the contestants, which also becomes the commitment for the new paragraph.

Comments after the fact, like those accompanying the passage from Wolfe, may seem both artificial and needlessly complex. Wolfe probably did not consciously ponder alternatives for every sentence or mechanically contrive the patterns of specification. The comments are only one kind of analysis of what the writer finally produced; and though they may seem complex, they are actually grossly simpler than the thinking behind the passage, thinking that may have extended over a long period of time before the actual writing and that used all the facilities of an active mind. We know little about the composing process, but we know it is not simple.

From the writer's point of view, however, thinking in terms of progressive specification can have practical advantages. The writer working to develop an idea, groping for his next sentence, can profitably direct his thinking toward responding to an earlier commitment, usually that in the preceding sentence, with some kind of specification. Consider, for example, the student working on a paper on "The Status of Women at State University" (see chapter 6). The student has considered the topic for some time, has perhaps discussed it informally with friends, and has settled on the general thesis that "women on the campus do not have rights and privileges equal to those of men." In the course of writing he discusses what he considers discriminatory rules and then decides to move to another topic that has occurred to him earlier, the university's support of activities for women.

He provides a transitional sentence to open a new paragraph:

> [1] Although some of these regulations may be justified on the ground that they reflect general attitudes of society, especially of parents, no such rationalization can explain why the university should favor men in supporting extracurricular activities.

The sentence suggests more than one direction for further development. The writer might clarify the assertion that this discrimination cannot be justified, or he might support the contention that the university does discriminate. Because of the general purpose of the paper, he decides to accumulate relevant examples — swimming pool hours, provisions for meeting rooms, rooms for social activities, gymnasium facilities. These seem to fall into two groups, those relating to social life and those relating to athletics, and the student decides on a second sentence to introduce one of these groups:

> [2] For example, no logical explanation justifies the university's apparent unfair solicitude for the social life of the male.

The student might, of course, reject any sentence like this, moving directly to citing specific examples. But the sentence provides a transition from the opening sentence by carrying on the idea of explanation, and by taking an intermediate step toward specification it helps the reader group the more specific examples that can follow:

> [3] There is a men's lounge in the Union Building, but no women's lounge. [4] Of the organizations officially recognized by the university eight are exclusively for men, two for women. [5] Four of these organizations have permanent offices in the Union; neither of the women's organizations has been assigned any space. [6] The two new dormitories built last year, with large living rooms, study rooms, and even kitchen facilities, have both been assigned to men; women remain in the old dormitories with inadequate space for social activities.

Sentences 3–5 are simple factual statements that illustrate sentence 2 without further development, but the student recognizes that sentence 6 could provoke opposing arguments. He decides on further development to forestall these:

[7] The new dormitories, of course, were needed to relieve overcrowding in the old men's dorms, but at least one of the new buildings might have been assigned to women, with men taking over one of the old women's dorms to get necessary space.

The writer can now turn to his second group of examples with another specification of sentence 1, paralleling sentence 2:

[8] Discrimination is even more obvious in support for athletic activities.

The student can then move again to specific examples to support sentence 8, as he has supported sentence 2, so that the entire paragraph might develop as follows, with levels of specification indicated by indentation.

[1] Although some of these regulations may be justified on the ground that they reflect general attitudes of society, especially of parents, no such rationalization can explain why the university should favor men in supporting extracurricular activities.
　　[2] For example, no logical explanation justifies the university's apparent unfair solicitude for the social life of the male.
　　　　[3] There is a men's lounge in the Union Building, but no women's lounge.
　　　　[4] Of the organizations officially recognized by the university eight are exclusively for men, two for women.
　　　　[5] Four of these organizations have permanent offices in the Union; neither of the women's organizations has been assigned any space.
　　　　[6] The two new dormitories built last year, with large living rooms, study rooms, and even kitchen facilities, have both been assigned to men; women remain in the old dormitories with inadequate space for social activities.
　　　　　　[7] The new dormitories, of course, were needed to relieve overcrowding in the old men's dorms, but at least one of the new buildings might have been assigned to women, with men taking over one of the old women's dormitories to get necessary space.
　　[8] Discrimination is even more obvious in support for athletic activities.
　　[9] Although the university has ample facilities for extensive athletic activities, intercollegiate competition has first call on all of them, and this is exclusively for men.

58

[10] Women are allowed to use the swimming pool one night a week—unless the swimming team needs it for practice or a meet.
[11] Women almost never have access to the fieldhouse or the gymnasium.
[12] There is an extensive program of intramural athletics for men, but women presumably get enough exercise walking to classes.

The paragraph is not a masterpiece, but it does illustrate one way the student can develop his writing, moving from sentence to sentence by responding to previous commitments with some kind of specification.

Types of Development

Every commitment requires its individual development, but the human mind tends to think according to discernible patterns, and these patterns are reflected in the types of development writers frequently employ. Classical rhetoricians, in fact, created an extensive system to aid in the discovery or "invention" of arguments suitable for different subjects or occasions, developing a list of "topics"—"places" where arguments might be found—in definition, for example, or in relationships like cause and effect, or in appeals to authority. Although modern writers do not often work from a formal system as elaborate as that of classical rhetoric, they do appeal to the tendencies of the human mind on which the topics were based. Accordingly, development commonly records thought processes like those discussed in chapters 9–11 or those behind the following types of development. These types, of course, are only samples of some of the kinds of information or reasoning a writer may exploit.

1. *Citing particulars, instances, examples, illustrations.* Probably the easiest way to clarify a general statement is to provide instances. For example, assume that a paragraph opens with the following sentence: "The houses in our block represent the worst characteristics of modern tract-house architecture." The sentence commits the writer to say more on at least two general topics—the houses in the block and his ideas about architecture. The obvious course is to cite particulars, examples of houses in the block or examples of characteristics of architecture illustrated by the houses. A second sentence might read: "The new house on the corner has a picture window with a view of the neighbor's clothesline and garbage cans, shutters that were never intended to work but are nailed to the siding, and a heating system that keeps the living

59

room at 85 degrees and provides no heat for the bathrooms." Or the writer might pick a different set of particulars, listing the architectural characteristics he objects to rather than describing individual houses. He might use as his second sentence: "Viewed from the street the houses are identical, except that the doors of the two-car garages are painted in different bright colors."

The following selection develops with examples, introduced by a structural topic sentence.

> The foregoing are particularly striking examples, but hundreds of others could be cited. We find generalization in such everyday words as *picture*, once restricted, as the etymology would suggest (compare: the Picts, "painted ones"), to a *painted* representation of something seen, but now applicable to photography, crayon drawing, and so forth; *butcher*, who once slew one animal only, the goat (French *bouc*); the verb *sail*, which has been transferred to steam navigation, just as *drive* has been transferred to self-propelled vehicles . . . .
>
> STUART ROBERTSON and FREDERIC G. CASSIDY,
> *The Development of Modern English*

The paragraph continues with examples, as the topic sentence promises it will. The writer cannot, of course, collect all possible examples or instances, but he has enough to illustrate what he means by his generalization. Similarly, the following paragraph begins with a topic sentence that introduces more detailed questions that flow from it.

> From the moment that one doesn't take composing for granted in our country, a dozen questions come to mind. What is the composer's life in America? Does it differ so very much from that of the European or even the Latin American composer of today? Or from the life of United States composers in other periods? Are our objectives and purposes the same as they have always been?
>
> AARON COPLAND, *Music and Imagination*

The writer does not complete the dozen he has promised, but he does develop by listing particulars. The following paragraph opens with a sentence that less obviously dictates structure but introduces two topics—the evening and the crowds—each developed by citing specific characteristics of the scene.

> It was early evening of a day in the late fall and the Winesburg County Fair had brought crowds of country people into town. The day had been clear and the night came on warm and pleasant. On the Trunion Pike, where the road after it left town stretched away between berry fields now covered with dry brown leaves, the dust from passing wagons arose in clouds. Children, curled into little

60

balls, slept on the straw scattered on wagon beds. Their hair was full
of dust and their fingers black and sticky. The dust rolled away over
the fields and the departing sun set it ablaze with colors.

SHERWOOD ANDERSON, Winesburg, Ohio

As in the following, the topic sentence may offer a proposition
that can be illustrated with specific instances.

> But, indeed, the dictum that truth always triumphs over persecu-
> tion is one of those pleasant falsehoods which men repeat after one
> another till they pass into commonplaces, but which all experience
> refutes. History teems with instances of truth put down by persecu-
> tions. If not suppressed forever, it may be thrown back for cen-
> turies. To speak only of religious opinions: the Reformation broke
> out at least twenty times before Luther, and was put down. Arnold
> of Brescia was put down. Fra Dolcino was put down. Savonarola was
> put down. The Lollards were put down. The Hussites were put
> down.

JOHN STUART MILL, On Liberty

The passage uses two sentences to expand the topic sentence and
to make it more specific, then shifts to consider one kind of opinion — religious — and cites specific instances.

2. *Incident, extended illustration.* Instead of offering a series of
instances, a writer may make his point by telling a story or describing a single illustration in some detail. Ruth Benedict, supporting
the proposition that happiness depends upon social customs, begins her book *Patterns of Culture* by recounting her conversations
with a chief of the Digger Indians of California. Alan Bullock, in
the following paragraph, uses one event in the life of Adolf Hitler
to illustrate a general observation about his tactics.

> Surprise was a favourite gambit of Hitler's, in politics, diplomacy,
> and war: he gauged the psychological effect of sudden, unexpected
> hammer-blows in paralysing opposition. An illustration of his ap-
> preciation of the value of surprise and quick decision, even when on
> the defensive, is the second presidential campaign of 1932. It had
> taken Goebbels weeks to persuade Hitler to stand for the Presi-
> dency at all. The defeat in the first ballot brought Goebbels to de-
> spair; but Hitler, now that he had committed himself, with great
> presence of mind dictated the announcement that he would stand a
> second time and got it on to the streets almost before the country
> had learned of his defeat. In war the psychological effect of the
> *Blitzkrieg* was just as important in Hitler's eyes as the strategic: it
> gave the impression that the German military machine was more
> than life-size, that it possessed some virtue of invincibility against
> which ordinary men could not defend themselves.

ALAN BULLOCK, Hitler: A Study in Tyranny

61

The first sentence generalizes about Hitler's reliance on surprise; the second introduces an illustration; the next three describe what happened in 1932; the final sentence generalizes again, relating the incident of 1932 to the general proposition of the first sentence.

3. *Cause and effect.* People clarify their thinking by speculating about causes and results, and the writer can capitalize on this tendency in his search for ideas to use for development. The following topic-comment unit develops by providing reasons to support an opening thesis.

> The Yellow or Silver Pine is more frequently overturned than any other tree on the Sierra, because its leaves and branches form the largest mass in proportion to its height, while in many places it is planted sparsely, leaving long, open lanes, through which storms may enter with full force. Furthermore, because it is distributed along the lower portion of the range, which was the first to be left bare on the breaking up of the ice-sheet at the close of the glacial winter, the soil it is growing upon has been longer exposed to post-glacial weathering, and consequently is in a more crumbling, decayed condition than the fresher soils farther up the range, and therefore offers a less secure anchorage for the roots.
>
> JOHN MUIR, *The Passes of the Sierra*

The development presents a series of sentences justifying the opening assertion that the Yellow Pine is the most frequently overturned tree.

4. *Analogy.* In analogy, a special kind of illustration, the writer draws a parallel, explaining the unknown by something familiar. The device is common; to explain the rotation of the earth to a child, we might use a rubber ball or a top. Victor Hugo describes the Battle of Waterloo as a giant letter *A*. Thomas Henry Huxley in a famous analogy says that life is like a game of chess. The following paragraph uses a literary analogy to begin its discussion of man's failure to resist mass pressures that can drive him back toward savagery.

> Of all the sad experiences of these last twelve years this is perhaps the most dreadful one. It may be compared to the experience of Odysseus on the island of Circe. But it is even worse. Circe had transformed the friends and companions of Odysseus into various animal shapes. But here are men, men of education and intelligence, honest and upright men who suddenly give up the highest human privilege. They have ceased to be free and personal agents. Performing the same prescribed rites they begin to feel, to think, and to speak in the same way. . . .
>
> ERNST CASSIRER, *The Myth of the State*

5. *Comparison and contrast.* The paragraph of analogy above demonstrates also another technique of development, in which the writer cites similarities and differences. A proposition like "Boston is not a small New York" would require noting differences between the cities. The following paragraph uses the method in a rather complex pattern, citing contrasting incidents.

> But there is another side to the War and one that it would be wrong to ignore or minimize—the side of glory. There was glory enough for each side. The North has its legends (true legends) as well as the South. There is the desperate and fruitless courage of Fredericksburg; there is the rush by Missionary Ridge; there are the heroic stories of units like the 20th Maine at Gettysburg; there is Sheridan riding on to the field at Cedar Creek and turning the tide of battle like Desaix at Marengo. There is most impressive of all, the disciplined and despairing advance at Cold Harbor. Here is glory. But whether the South has more glory than the North or not (I think it has), it needs it more and, as is right, cherishes it more. It cherishes the fame of the most Plutarchian (and greatest) American soldier, "Marse Robert." It cherishes or should cherish, with Pickett's attack, the memory of Hood's men advancing to their doom at Franklin. And for the individual heroic actions, their name is legion. It should remember with pride, not that there were so few under arms to surrender with Lee or Johnston, but that there were still so many.
>
> D. W. BROGAN, *A Fresh Appraisal of the Civil War*

The first three sentences develop the topic, establishing parallels and contrasts between legends of the North and South; then the paragraph breaks into two divisions providing particulars. The following selection, which introduces an article on basketball, provides details through a series of contrasts.

> Basketball is the city game. Its battlegrounds are strips of asphalt between tattered wire fences or crumbling buildings; its rhythms grow from the uneven thump of a ball against hard surfaces. It demands no open spaces or lush backyards or elaborate equipment. It doesn't even require specified numbers of players; a one-on-one confrontation in a playground can be as memorable as a full-scale organized game. Basketball is the game for young athletes without cars or allowances—the game in which the drama and action are intensified by its confined spaces and chaotic surroundings.
>
> Every American sport directs itself in a general way toward certain segments of American life. Baseball is basically a slow, pastoral experience, offering a tableau of athletes against a green background, providing moments of action amid longer periods allowed for contemplation of the spectacle. In its relaxed, unhurried way, it is exactly what it claims to be—the national "pastime" rather than

an intense, sustained game crammed with action. Born in a rural age, its appeal still lies largely in its offer of an untroubled island where, for a few hours, a pitcher tugging at his pants leg can seem to be the most important thing in a fan's life.

Football's attraction is more contemporary. Its violence is in tune with the times, and its well-mapped strategic war games invite fans to become generals, plotting and second-guessing along with their warriors on the fields. With its action compressed in a fairly small area and its formations and patterns relatively easy to interpret, football is the ideal television spectacle. Other sports have similar, if smaller, primary audiences. Golf and tennis belong first to country-club members, horse racing to an enduring breed of gamblers, auto racing to Middle Americans who thrive on its violent roaring machines and death-defying risks. But basketball belongs to the cities—and New York, from its asphalt playgrounds to the huge modern arena that houses the professional basketball champions of the world, is the most active, dedicated basketball city of all.

PETE AXTHELM, The City Game

6. *Restatement and amplification.* Almost all the examples above are variations on the use of particulars to support a topic or a proposition. Most paragraphs do develop in such patterns, illustrating the general with the more specific. Sometimes, however, a paragraph—especially an introductory paragraph or a short summary paragraph—may need mainly to restate or to amplify an idea, sometimes revealing varying implications of the topic. Consider the following:

Another obvious practical point is that the goal of education, in a cognitive world as eclectic, as ignorant, as accidental, as disorganized as ours inevitably will be, needs very much to be rethought. We need, certainly in higher education, to be sure that some genuine experience of discovery and rediscovery is a part of the life of everyone who is educated; we need to be sure that some genuine appreciation of the gulf which separates knowledge and ignorance is also a part of it. I say this because only people who have been through these experiences are intellectually prepared to live in a world in which they are surrounded by knowledge of which they will largely remain ignorant, prepared not to take the vulgar and superficial account of knowledge for the reality.

J. ROBERT OPPENHEIMER, ACLS Annual Lecture

Even in this kind of paragraph the movement is primarily toward specification; the second sentence restates the proposition of the first somewhat more specifically, and the third sentence produces a reason to support the proposition.

FOR STUDY AND WRITING

A Which of the following statements are mainly fact and which mainly judgment? Answers may vary; in sentence 3, for example, your conclusion may be altered by the degree of objectivity you attribute to words such as *perceptive, interested,* and *favorable.* Some statements may be considered more or less factual, depending upon the circumstances. If an entomologist says, "That is a golden-eyed fly," he may be identifying a tabanid of the genus Chrysopa, but if a five-year-old child makes the same remark he may be implying much less fact.

1. Water freezes at 32 degrees Fahrenheit.
2. The early bird catches the worm.
3. Joseph Wood Krutch, who died in 1970, known for his drama reviews in *The Nation* and his perceptive essays collected in such volumes as *The Modern Temper* (1929), became interested in desert ecology long before environmental studies had attracted favorable national attention.
4. The road was a ribbon of moonlight across the purple moor.
5. Patriotism is the last refuge of a scoundrel.
6. If a man in someone else's house calls another a perjurer or accosts him insultingly with scandalous words, he shall pay 1*s.* to the householder, 6*s.* to the man whom he insulted, and 12*s.* to the king.

   Anglo-Saxon Law, A.D. 685–86
7. In the seventeenth century, although three hundred crimes in English law were punishable by death, the Massachusetts Body of Liberties listed only ten, and in some of the other states there were fewer.
8. Being in a ship is being in a jail—with the chance of being drowned.
9. We cannot continue forever to solve Asia's problems for her.
10. Parallel lines will never meet, no matter how far extended.

B Rearrange the roughly synonymous expressions in each of the following groups in order of their specificity, with the most general first and the most specific last. The answer to 1 is *c, d, a, b.*

1. **a)** dark outfit
   b) Mary's black jersey ensemble
   c) wearing apparel
   d) garment contrived for the purpose of covering the female figure
2. **a)** drum
   b) musical instrument
   c) percussion instrument
   d) band instrument
3. **a)** It was a lovely scene.
   b) The western sky was deep blue-green with feathered gold spots where the sun broke through.

65

    c) The sky was bright-colored and lovely.

    d) The greenish western sky was mottled with gold spots.

4. a) The three major composers of the postromantic revolution are like the three brothers in the fairy tale who set off in different directions, follow divergent paths, and after sundry adventures arrive at much the same destination.

    b) The three major composers of the postromantic revolution used different methods and different procedures to achieve their ends but finally achieved new types of music.

    c) The three major composers of the postromantic period sought to move away from what they considered the sterility of nineteenth-century music—Schoenberg through mathematics, Bartók through ethnography, Stravinsky through history.

    d) The changes that characterize the postromantic revolution in music came about through varying influences on composition.

5. a) The sculpture sat in the Museum of Modern Art garden impressive for its unusual materials and its effective symbolism, combining mass and void in a complex symphony of light and shadow.

    b) Reuben Nakian's sculpture *The Rape of Lucrece,* in the Museum of Modern Art garden, is two interacting abstract figures constructed of variously shaped, movable plates of sheet metal mounted on a framework of black pipe.

    c) Nakian's sculpture in the Museum of Modern Art garden is a complex construction of metal sheets mounted in different planes, on which light and shadow play.

    d) The sculpture in the garden was exciting and moving because of the sculptor's unusual approach to his subject and his skillful handling of materials.

C Following are a number of sentences from paragraphs about language, each of them followed by four alternative succeeding sentences. Indicate which of the alternatives makes an adequate response to the commitment of each sentence, which would not move the development ahead. One alternative in each group appeared in the original paragraph, but frequently more than one of the alternatives would be a suitable second sentence.

    1. Of course there are many ways of making sound.
                       L. M. MYERS, *The Roots of Modern English*

      a) Most of these, however, are not suitable to the production of language.

      b) Crickets rub their legs together and ruffed grouse drum on hollow logs, but neither method seems to permit much variety.

      c) Variations in pitch depend on the frequency of vibrations of the sound waves.

      d) Sounds are the basis of human speech; communication is possible because different sounds are arbitrarily given different symbolic significances.

2. Loan words not only alter their meaning in the course of the borrowing process, but they are equally liable to change after they have become a naturalized part of the English language.

ALBERT H. MARCKWARDT, *American English*

a) A loan word is a word borrowed from another language.

b) Examples include even words adopted in the seventeenth century from American Indian languages.

c) Borrowing accounts for much of the rapid expansion of the vocabulary of the English language, and especially for the growth of American English.

d) *Powwow,* one of the very early American Indian adoptions, originally bore its etymological meaning of priest or medicine man.

3. There is practically no limit to the number of social affinities revealed in differences of language.

DWIGHT BOLINGER, *Aspects of Language*

a) Many of these social distinctions, however, produce only insignificant language differences.

b) The bases of social class distinctions in America differ, of course, from those in many other countries.

c) To age, sex, occupation, and occasion, it would be necessary to add religion, politics, lodge affiliation, preference as to sports or amusements, and any other circumstances under which people meet and speak.

d) Language differences are of many kinds, but among the most interesting are those that distinguish geographical dialects.

4. The era of discovery and exploration brought new knowledge about the languages of the world.

JOHN B. CARROLL, *The Study of Language*

a) Travelers and missionaries wrote grammars and dictionaries of languages they found in Africa, America, and other parts of the world.

b) There are certainly more than two thousand different languages in existence throughout the world today.

c) Much of this knowledge was inaccurate, based on hasty descriptions and colored by prejudices and misconceptions, but it stimulated the kinds of speculation that led to modern linguistics.

d) Using this language, however, required ingenuity and imagination.

D The following groups of sentences are from published paragraphs but are not necessarily in their original order. Arrange them according to increasing specificity; that is, so that the most specific is last. Then decide whether this order seems the most logical one for the sentences within their paragraph.

1. a) All our energies ought to be going into the attempt to get world attention for this objective, so that a framework will be created within which sources of income will not depend on voluntary offerings or payments, any more than individual citizens may decide when, how, and if their taxes are to be paid.

b) The United Nations is not a country club for privileged members who have access to the facilities so long as they keep up their dues.

c) The United Nations is, or should be, a world constitutional body with complete jurisdiction in those matters concerning the common safety of the world's peoples.

NORMAN COUSINS

2. a) However, the Chinese are a proud people.

b) They are not partial to foreigners, and they are thoroughly confident of the superiority of their age-old culture.

c) They have not yet recovered from the wounds and indignities which the Western world unjustly and arrogantly inflicted upon them during the last century.

JAMES S. DUNCAN

3. a) *Huckleberry Finn* deals directly with the virtue and depravity of man's heart.

b) *Tom Sawyer* has the truth of honesty — what it says about things and feelings is never false and always both adequate and beautiful.

c) It is more intense truth, fiercer and more complex.

d) The truth of *Huckleberry Finn* is of a different kind from that of *Tom Sawyer*.

LIONEL TRILLING

E Study the following student theme and determine which statements are primarily judgment and which primarily fact. Then select two judgments, rewrite them as generalizations limited enough to permit illustration, and make a list of facts you might use in a paragraph illustrating each of your generalizations.

A good campus newspaper can be a great asset to any college or university. However, it must be truly a campus paper, and it should be very outstanding. Many campus papers are more concerned about national or international news than about affairs right on the campus. They are all ill-advised. It is much more desirable for a campus paper to concentrate its efforts on local matters and to leave major news stories to larger papers, which have the advantages of a huge staff and expensive news services.

Local news is just as important as the events that make the headlines in the large dailies. Students are often more interested in the campus prom queen election than in the election of a representative to Congress. Interest in local affairs is highly desirable. Everyone should be interested in what goes on in his immediate surroundings.

A paper that is primarily concerned with campus events also provides better training for budding journalists. This country, and every country in the world today, has need for good journalists. Journalism has much to do with the formation of public opinion, and in a democracy public opinion is very important. It is therefore of the greatest significance for a country like ours that papers should train the best type of journalist.

A local paper is also more interesting because it does not pretend to be something more important than it is. Any pretension is always unpleasant. We can, however, really be interested in a campus paper that tells us the things we want to hear about.

For these reasons I believe that a campus newspaper should be concentrated on reporting campus news.

F Rewrite each of the following in specific terms, inventing specific details to develop the general statements:

> EXAMPLE: Later the two women were sitting outside looking as usual at the scenery.
>
> After lunch Milly and her mother were sitting as usual on the balcony beyond the salon, admiring for the five-hundredth time the stocks, the roses, the small, bright grass beneath the palm, and the oranges against a wavy line of blue.
>
> KATHERINE MANSFIELD, *The Dove's Nest*

1. The shelves were packed with books of a great many kinds and varieties.
2. When we rose in the morning, we could see all over the streets the signs of the storm of the night.
3. Mary was always doing the kind of thing that gave her the reputation of being a girl you could not trust.
4. The kitchen was well equipped with all the modern conveniences.
5. The white tablecloth was almost invisible because it was so thoroughly covered with so many good things to eat.
6. At the university David had fewer academic than social triumphs.
7. The children came to the Halloween party in the many kinds of costumes customary to such celebrations of an old holiday.
8. The desk was piled in high confusion with numerous evidences of Wendy's varied interests.
9. When Susan sat down to study, she always found her thoughts wandering to unrelated subjects.
10. Before he started in college, Phil had not realized that he would constantly be needing money for a variety of incidental and miscellaneous expenses.

G List fifteen specific details you might use in describing any three of the list below. Make the details concrete; prefer "the soiled brown chair with protruding springs" to "the furniture in the room."

1. A college room
2. A favorite restaurant
3. A teacher I know
4. A classroom
5. The lakefront
6. A campus politician

List specific details you might use to illustrate each of the following statements:

1. A university provides wide opportunities for wasting time.
2. Drugstores have become more than places that sell drugs.

3. The modern automobile has developed with concern for increased safety and decreased pollution.

4. Those who attend musical concerts are guilty of a variety of discourtesies.

5. Comic books are not designed exclusively for children.

Describe a specific instance that might be used to illustrate any five of the following statements:

1. People who endeavor to improve the environment sometimes ruin it.

2. Incidents of childhood may have profound effects on human beings.

3. Not all beautiful places in America have been discovered by tourists.

4. Athletes are not necessarily poor students.

5. Proverbs are not always applicable.

6. Pets can be nuisances.

7. Emergency measures sometimes become permanent parts of a social system.

8. Economy does not always pay.

9. Newspaper columnists are not always right in their prophecies.

10. Some people may profit from a war.

H If you wish to demonstrate that a computer has limitations and can do only what it has been programmed to handle, you might point out that computers can be instructed to count the number of times a word occurs in a given passage, because ability to count has been built into the machine, but that as yet no means has been devised so that a computer can define a word. That is, you might give an example. You might also promote understanding by using an analogy, saying that a typewriter designed to write English can be used to write Chinese or the International Phonetic Alphabet only if human beings design and construct suitable keys and insert them into the typewriter. For each of the following statements, supply (a) a possible example and (b) a possible analogy.

1. As private airplanes become more popular, prices are likely to drop.

2. A rocket attains its great speed through the propulsive powers of discharging gas.

3. The central portion of the United States is a great, shallow bowl.

4. An end run can be a deceptive play.

5. A personnel manager should have training as well as experience.

6. Animals can be taught more with kindness than with whipping.

7. Race prejudice should be discouraged in the public schools.

8. This year's automobiles are designed more to sell cars than to promote safety.

I Write down a sentence at random. When you have done this, look back at Exercise B and notice how statements that are mainly general can be made more specific. Then rewrite your sentence to make it more specific. Next write down every detail you can think of that could be pertinent for this statement, even minute or highly exact details. For example, let us assume that you have seen the title of an article in a magazine, "Why Students Want Their Constitutional Rights Now." This gives you an idea, and you write down the sentence, "Students should be allowed their constitutional rights." Checking B, above, you remind yourself that one way to be specific is to divide something into its parts and find examples. What are constitutional rights that are sometimes refused to students? You think of the right to assemble, to protest peacefully, to dress and appear as one pleases, so long as he is not offensive. You decide that this last will be broad enough, and you try to think of every instance you know of in which your former teachers have tried to control the dress and the hair length of the students, and just what happened in each confrontation—one student, trying an assignment like this one, goaded his principal into saying, "but the constitution of this school supersedes the constitution of the United States." When you have collected a good body of details, select from them, draw a new general statement as a thesis sentence, and write a paper.

J Set yourself a project in which you try to record as many details as possible and as accurately as you can. Determine beforehand that you will observe at least one speech in a conversation or a discussion that you witness. You might plan to record a question asked by a student in class and the instructor's reply. Record exactly what each says; note the tone of voice and anything else about the ways the sentences are spoken. Record how the person looked, how he stood, what he did with his hands, everything that you can see or hear. Then write a report as precise and as detailed as you can make it.

MATERIALS
FOR DEVELOPMENT

CHAPTER 4

Good writing requires development; ideas must be elaborated,
illustrated, refined, supported with detail.

Writing is a growth, a becoming. A composition does not spring
from the head of its creator in full armor, like Athena from the
brain of Zeus. It grows — with false starts, new ideas, and revisions,
changing directions sometimes to accommodate fresh insights. As
it grows the writer needs details, examples, and evidence — materials for adequate development.

ADEQUATE DEVELOPMENT   4a

Usually the purpose of writing is to make a
reader understand as the writer understands — to help him see
from a particular point of view, to guide him along a line of reasoning, to show him relationships among particular facts or events.
The reader needs to be shown. The writer must do more than
assert an opinion or express a generalization that he believes. A
student might, for example, decide to write a paper to show that
"Many American teachers have not been trained for the jobs they
are required to do." His generalization may shock some readers
into interest, but other readers will neither understand nor change
their views unless this idea is supported with adequate development — examples of teachers who have been put into jobs for which
they were not prepared, information about practices in schools

in assigning teachers, or statistics on teacher training. Such information might not establish the generalization, but it would clarify it.

Providing adequate development may not be easy, but materials for development are always available, in general from two sources—from within the writer and from outside sources. Everyone has within him a reservoir of information from which memory can draw. By thinking about the information stored in his mind—relating one fact to another, putting facts into groups, evaluating ideas—the writer can produce reasons, arguments, examples, and illustrations as materials for development. In addition, the writer has available the accumulated knowledge of the world, accessible in books, films, and paintings or in events that can be investigated.

GUIDE TO REVISION

4a   **Dev**

Revise, supplying material for adequate development.

ORIGINAL

The old Union Building at Winnemac University must be replaced. We must have a modern building that will be worthy of an institution like Winnemac. The present building is a disgrace and a shame, far from providing any beneficial college atmosphere. Both inside and out the building is inadequate. It does not, even in the most elementary way, fulfill the needs of student body and faculty. The building stands out on the campus like a sore thumb.

[*The writer of this paper also had trouble finishing, probably because he found a limit to the number of times he could say the same thing in different words. The paper fails because no idea is developed; it is a series of judgments —or repetitions of one judgment.*]

REVISION

The old Union Building at Winnemac University is not meeting the needs of the student body. Its cafeteria offers only seventy-five seats to a student body of eight thousand residents. Its dance floor is so small that a hundred couples crowd it; as a result, Union dances are becoming more and more unpopular. The bookstore is so crowded that it cannot keep texts in stock. Furthermore, many important activities are entirely neglected. No rooms are available for meetings of student or faculty groups. There is no space for accommodation of guests of the University. There is no theater, no auditorium, no office space for publications or other activities.

[*The addition of some facts makes the judgments more plausible.*]

We have already observed something of the sources within the writer in our consideration of the uses of a journal. We have noted that a writer may record what he sees, hears, or otherwise experiences, as these events happen or so soon thereafter that he can record the immediacy of an event. This is what a newspaper reporter often does; he attends a football game or a political meeting knowing why he is there, to see and to hear the most important happenings and to record them. He is likely to notice more than do others, partly because he is a professional observer, but partly also because he works at the job of observing. Many journal entries are of this sort, immediate or almost immediate responses, events as they filter through someone's awareness.

Other materials that come through the activities of the writer appear more remotely in time. Everyone old enough to write has been alive many years, and from the moment of his birth—or even before—the world has been pouring information into him, through his eyes and ears, through his senses of smell, taste, and touch, and perhaps through other sorts of perception of which we know very little. Even when he is unconscious, being asleep or otherwise unaware, information has poured in on him. Most of all this he has lost, but much will have been retained, buried deep perhaps and not very well ordered, but more subject to recall than a beginning writer may at first assume. Professional writers, notably creative writers, make much use of such resources, so much that the observable difference between some great writers and mediocre writers is that the genius has a more abundant reservoir of information. He can recall more.

Notice the following from Thomas Wolfe's *The House of the Far and Lost*. Wolfe tells us that once when he was living in England he had a room where he could look out over some college playing fields, where the students were practicing rugby, and one afternoon, while he was passing one of these fields, the ball bounded into the road, and Wolfe went to pick it up. He continues as follows:

One of the players came over to the edge of the field and stood there waiting with his hands upon his hips while I got the ball: he was panting hard, his face was flushed, and his blond hair tousled, but when I threw the ball to him, he said "Thanks very much!" crisply and courteously—getting the same sound into the word "*very*" that they got in "*Amer*ican," a sound that always repelled me a little because it seemed to have some scornful aloofness and patronage in it.

For a moment I watched him as he trotted briskly away on to the field again: the players stood there waiting, panting, casual, their hands upon their hips; he passed the ball into the scrimmage, the pattern swayed, rocked, scrambled, and broke sharply out in open play again, and everything looked incredibly strange, near, and familiar.

I felt that I had always known it, that it had always been mine, and that it was as familiar to me as everything I had seen or known in my childhood. Even the texture of the earth looked familiar, and felt moist and firm and springy when I stepped on it, and the stormy howling of the wind in that avenue of great trees at night was wild and desolate and demented as it had been when I was eight years old and could lie in my bed at night and hear the great oaks howling on the hill above my father's house.

We might notice that the scene is being developed with three sorts of material, which as creative bits come from within Wolfe as he writes, however they came to be a part of him. First, there are the results of recent observation, now recalled. We can observe that Wolfe has observed acutely and has recorded his observations revealingly; not only does he see the pattern of scrimmage, in which the bodies "swayed, rocked, scrambled, and broke sharply out in open play again," but also he notices the tone of speech, and he senses the feel of the springy earth. In one sense all this is strange to him; he had never played rugby as a boy, and he somewhat resents the young Briton's manner of speaking, which he suspects of being patronizing to an American. But if the whole is "incredibly strange," it is also "near and familiar."

This idea sets him thinking and transports him to his childhood. Now the reader gets a different sequence of details, sharply apprehended and reported, but all dredged up from Wolfe's memory of his life twenty years or so before. Thus the development follows a pattern something like this: immediate observation $------\rightarrow$ awareness of the observation $------\rightarrow$ thinking about this awareness $------\rightarrow$ recalling earlier experience $------\rightarrow$ more thinking, combining both sets of details and inferences from them.

Two entries in Thoreau's *Journals* provide an even clearer example of how the various sorts of material from within the writer provide development during the course of prewriting, writing, and rewriting. His entry for April 19, 1854, includes the following:

> A man came to me yesterday to offer me as a naturalist a two-headed calf . . . but I felt nothing but disgust . . . . I am not interested in mere phenomena, though it were the explosion of a planet, only as it may have lain in the experience of a human being.

Thoreau was disturbed that the man presenting him with the calf could not distinguish between a phenomenon that Thoreau thought insignificant and one that revealed meaning. He thought enough about the event to generalize that phenomena are interesting only as part of human experience. But he did not develop the idea, did not explain it fully enough to show a reader its implications. The experience and the idea apparently continued to concern him. He thought more, refined and elaborated his concept, and a few weeks later, May 6, 1854, made the following entry in his *Journals.*

> There is no such thing as pure *objective* observation. Your observation, to be interesting, *i.e.* to be significant, must be *subjective.* The sum of what the writer of whatever class has to report is simply some human experience, whether he be poet or philosopher or man of science. The man of most science is the man most alive, whose life is the greatest event. Senses that take cognizance of outward things merely are of no avail. It matters not where or how far you travel, — the farther commonly the worse, — but how much alive you are. If it is possible to conceive of an event outside to humanity, it is not of the slightest significance, though it were the explosion of a planet. Every important worker will report what life there is in him.

The repetition of the phrase "though it were the explosion of a planet" indicates that in May Thoreau was still thinking about his earlier reaction to the two-headed calf.

Meanwhile, like Wolfe recalling the rugby players, Thoreau has thought more, but whereas Wolfe mainly dredged up older detail to support a new idea, Thoreau mainly matures his ideas, using both recent and older recalled detail. The processes are similar, although the results are somewhat different. Thoreau is now able to draft a succinct topic sentence, one that provides him with a clear commitment: "There is no such thing as pure observation." He can respond to this commitment, using two ideas that he had already been toying with: (1) that to be significant observation must be subjective, and (2) not travel but the intensity of one's life determines what he can do. These ideas can be supported both with the detail from the immediate observation of the two-headed calf and from other evidence that Thoreau had been accumulating. Thus, although the results of writing and rewriting are rather different in Wolfe and in Thoreau, the processes are similar; each man starts from an immediate stimulus and the detail it provides. This detail is supplemented by recall from within the writer, and the writer thinks about both the ideas and the evidence, going from detail to ideas to more detail and refined ideas, until the whole emerges as a finished piece of writing.

Thus the old injunction "Look in thy heart and write" has its pertinence, but there are also other places to look, notably in the library and the laboratory, into materials already assembled by other people. A student projecting a paper on some

GUIDE TO REVISION

4b   **Sources**

Consider using library or other outside sources to obtain material for more adequate development.

ORIGINAL

More than one American statesman has revealed aptitude in fields quite unrelated to politics and diplomacy. It is possible to find men in our history who were capable of all sorts of tasks, ranging from manual labor to technical science. Many men were not only skillful in political affairs but really achieved a great deal in such occupations as printing, medicine, science, agriculture, finance. They were always trying to reach out beyond new horizons. Among the men with broad interests in addition to their interests in affairs of state were Washington, Jefferson, Franklin, and others. Many such men were always doing things not directly connected with national or foreign affairs.

[*The paper starts well, but it remains general and not very revealing because it lacks concrete development. If the writer would consult an appropriate book, or even a good article, on any of the statements he mentions, he could improve the paragraph.*]

REVISION

More than one American statesman has revealed aptitude in fields quite unrelated to politics and diplomacy. There was Jefferson, for example. An astute politican, he was also an important political philosopher, developing in his writing his theories that government should rest in the hands of the producing class. His interest in science was practical as well as theoretical; he is credited with a mathematical formula that still governs the shape of plowshares, with the invention of the swivel chair, and with the design of a leather buggy top. He contributed to the University of Virginia not only his knowledge as an educator but also the plans for the campus, one of the most beautifully arranged in America. He studied language and was one of the first Americans to learn Anglo-Saxon. His was the kind of inquisitive mind that found interest and new ideas in many subjects.

topic connected with military training might draw from his own experience for material. He might recall incidents from a high school ROTC course, from military service, or from conversations with friends. He might have thought about the subject enough to have worked out reasons or arguments that he could use to develop an opinion about whether military training should be part of a college curriculum, or whether it should be compulsory, or whether it should admit women. For any extended discussion, however, he is likely to find that he needs more material and more carefully screened evidence than he can recall offhand.

He may set out to create this material. Particularly if he wishes his paper to concern his own campus, he may elect to investigate the local military program, and the reactions of students to it. He may interview military officers and tape their responses, take a poll, or call a mass meeting and summarize the discussions. He may consult with alumni of the campus to amass information as to what graduates have or have not done with whatever they got from military drill. Such efforts would constitute research of a sort; the student might not be in a position to set up sufficiently rigid controls so that his investigation could be called research in any very exact sense, but he is endeavoring to promote new understanding by making use of hitherto unrecorded truth. This question of research and the writing that grows from it will be considered in more detail in chapter 24.

Locating Library Materials: The Card Catalog

For most writing that does not grow out of the author's experience, a good library provides the best source, and the key to it is the catalog. A general library must be calculated to compass all knowledge; a great library will contain millions of volumes. Endeavoring to bring order into such a mass is essentially cataloging all that man has ever recorded about himself and the universe — no easy task. Inevitably, no catalog can be entirely satisfactory, and any catalog that approaches adequacy will be complex, but if it is too complex it will become unusable to all but experts. Dozens of librarians have attempted to devise adequate means of cataloging, but two systems have been so obviously superior that most American libraries now use one or the other, or a combination of them, the Dewey Decimal System and the Library of Congress system.

Melvil Dewey was a remarkable man. During his eighty active years he founded two library schools, a library journal, and various library organizations, directed several libraries, and in the process of putting the Amherst College Library in order, devised the

Dewey Decimal System. It is marvelously simple and functional. Relying on the ten Arabic symbols of the decimal system, Dewey divided all the world's knowledge into ten areas, divided each of these into ten, and divided each of these again into ten. That is, a book like Eric Partridge's *The World of Words* would be numbered 410, with *4* the symbol for language, *1* for English, and *0* for a general book. Any cataloger knowing the Dewey system would give it the same number, and any informed user would know this number and could go to any library using the system and find Partridge's book there with other general books on the English language. The second and third lines of the book's call number would distinguish it further: a capital letter, the initial of the author's last name, would start the second line, followed by a number identifying the book more particularly, and a letter in lower case for the main word in the title of the book; thus for Partridge's book the second line would be P259w. The third line could be the date of the publication, so that the whole would become 410/P259w/ 1944. A number so derived would serve for most books, and if necessary a decimal point could be added at the right and more numbers added for more subdivisions. Special collections could be handled with letters like *B*, for biography, *R* for Reference, *F* or *X* for fiction. The system was so successful that it became standard, and now, a century later, many American libraries still use it.

From the first, however, great libraries found it inadequate. It had too few categories and was too rigid. Areas of knowledge may not fall readily into ten groups, and each of these may not divide logically into ten. For example, Dewey had assigned *8* to literature; thus a general book on world literature became *800,* on American literature *810,* and English literature *820.* European literatures took up most of the remaining numbers. That worked for local libraries in the nineteenth century, but now the literatures of all the Latin American countries must huddle under Spanish, and what is one to do about burgeoning Africa and the vast reaches of Asia, with no more numbers available? Likewise, Dewey had allowed no numbers for space travel, for the sea floor, for race relations, for ecology, for two world wars, for all sorts of areas that have arisen since 1874. Dewey's system, excellent for general libraries of moderate size, proved too limited in his own day for the great libraries and has since become progressively less adequate. Accordingly, many libraries developed their own systems.

The most successful was the Library of Congress. Dewey had decided logically what a system should be; the Library of Congress librarians approached the problem more inductively, devising categories from the books themselves. They assorted the books and recognized groupings that would bring like books together; the original job continued for more than three years, and the library still maintains a staff to enlarge and to revise the system as new interests arise and new sorts of books appear. Thus the system never gets out of date, and it allows for more expansion than does the Dewey system. It starts with a letter, and can use two letters; that is, *H* is for social sciences, but *HD* is for land agriculture and *HQ* for the family. Where Dewey has ten main categories based on the arabic numerals the Library of Congress system starts with a possible twenty-six letters, which can readily become hundreds when a second letter is added. These letters are followed by numbers, and the banks of these letters and figures can be extended indefinitely; usually two are enough, but some books now use five, and more are possible. The result is that most of the bigger libraries in the United States today, especially the college and university libraries, have switched to the Library of Congress system — known as the LC system — or are doing so. Many use both systems until they can afford to recatalog and to reshelve the older books.

The LC system cannot be readily described. The Dewey system is so simple that an experienced user of libraries can guess a great deal about a book by its call number; the LC system is too complicated to permit any but an expert to do that, but the loss is a small one. The LC system is more likely to bring similar books together than is the Dewey, and it greatly facilitates the cataloging and shelving of volumes, thus helping both the library and the user. In it, *A* is used for general works, and *Z* for bibliography; *B* through *P* are assigned to the humanities and the social sciences, *Q* through *V* to the physical sciences; at this writing, *I, O, X*, and *Y* have not been used. The second letter does not have a uniform use, as some numbers do in the Dewey system; that is, *KD* will be a subdivision of law as *PD* will be a subdivision of literature, but *D* will not represent the same subdivision of each, since the subdivisions of law do not parallel those of literature, and the LC system is arranged to assort books, not to maintain consistency in subdivisions.

By whatever system the call number is determined, it is copied onto the spine of the book and into the library catalog. The number will lead the user to the proper shelf, if the library operates on an open-shelf plan, or provide a number to be copied out and handed to a library attendant. Most American libraries use a card file system with cards filed alphabetically; for each volume or set of volumes in the library there will be a card for the author, for each author if there are several, and for an editor if there is one. There will be cards also for the title and for the main subjects treated in the work. A typical author card is shown opposite.

80

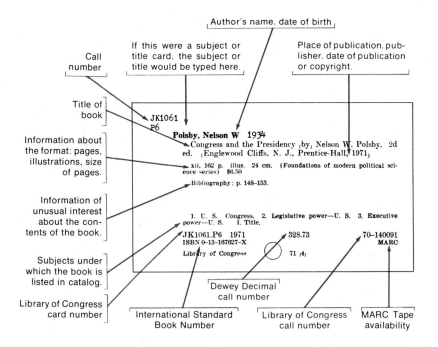

Author's name, date of birth

If this were a subject or title card, the subject or title would be typed here.

Place of publication, publisher, date of publication or copyright.

Call number

Title of book

Information about the format: pages, illustrations, size of pages.

Information of unusual interest about the contents of the book.

Subjects under which the book is listed in catalog.

Library of Congress card number

JK1061
P6

Polsby, Nelson W 1934
Congress and the Presidency ⌈by⌉ Nelson W. Polsby. 2d ed. ⌈Englewood Cliffs, N. J., Prentice-Hall, 1971⌉

xii, 162 p. illus. 24 cm. (Foundations of modern political science series) $6.50

Bibliography: p. 148-153.

1. U. S. Congress. 2. Legislative power—U. S. 3. Executive power—U. S. I. Title.

JK1061.P6 1971
ISBN 0-13-167627-X

Library of Congress

328.73

71 ⌈4⌉

70-140091
MARC

Dewey Decimal call number

International Standard Book Number

Library of Congress call number

MARC Tape availability

Printed Catalogs and Bibliographies

Books not available in the local library can be obtained from other libraries, borrowed by interlibrary loan, or, if they are in print, purchased. For these purposes, printed catalogs of the great libraries and printed bibliographies are indispensable. At this writing the most useful, since it is recent, extensive, and all in one series, is *Author-Title Catalog: Library, University of California* (Boston, 1963), 115 vols. The catalog of the Library of Congress is available in some libraries on cards and has also been printed with supplements that bring the whole up to more than two hundred volumes. For the greatest of the British libraries, the British Museum *General Catalogue of Printed Books* (London, 1966; Supplement, 1968), 263 vols., prints the catalog to 1955; it is excellent for older books, for British and Continental books, and for rare books. Useful for recent books are *Subject Guide to Books in Print* and *The Publishers' Trade List Annual*, which is conveniently indexed as *Books in Print* and cumulated in five-year volumes as *U. S. Catalog of Books in Print*. Other bibliographies can be found through *Bibliographic Index: A Cumulative Bibliography of Bibliographies, 1938–* (New York, 1939–   ). Some libraries have a union card catalog made up of cards for books in many libraries. Bibliographies for many subjects can be located conveniently through Constance M. Winchell's *Guide to Reference Books*, 8th ed. (Chicago, 1966).

The student should also be alert for bibliographies and bibliographic footnotes in books. These are often the best sources because they are prepared by experts in particular subjects. A good beginning bibliography can usually be found in an authoritative encyclopedia.

Periodical and Newspaper Indexes

With rare exceptions, magazine articles are not included in card catalogs of libraries or in general bibliographies, and they must be located through special indexes. Magazine articles may be extremely important, more important than the writer who knows only popular magazines is likely to expect. There are scholarly, technical, scientific, and professional journals in all subjects of any consequence. They print highly technical material, some of which is never reprinted in book form, and they report the latest findings before this material can possibly be incorporated in books. Thus, information may appear first in periodicals, and some material is available only in periodicals.

Many periodical indexes are "cumulated"; that is, they are constantly re-edited and republished in accordance with a system that keeps them up to date. For instance, *The Readers' Guide to Periodical Literature,* which indexes relatively popular magazines, appears every month. In February of any year, the library will receive a number that indexes the January issues of magazines and in March a number that indexes the February issues. In April, however, a cumulative number will arrive, in which all the issues of January, February, and March have been re-edited into one list. Thereafter one-month numbers will continue, but the July issue will cumulate the articles for six months. The following January a number will cumulate the entire preceding year. Similarly, there will be two-year, three-year, and five-year cumulations, by which time the book has become so large that the cumulation begins all over again. In this way, the index can be kept constantly up to date, while the user need not thumb through the numbers for each month. Not all indexes are cumulated so frequently as is *The Readers' Guide,* but the principle is the same. The investigator should be sure, however, that he uses all the copies of the index that cover the time in which he is interested, and that the periodicals he needs are indexed in the periodical index he is using; there will be a list somewhere, usually in the front of any volume. Most periodical indexes use a highly skeletonized style; the user should consult the list of abbreviations.

The following are the most useful indexes to periodical material published in English:

Readers' Guide to Periodical Literature, 1900– . The most useful general index in English, although it includes fewer serious or specialized periodicals than the *International Index.* It succeeds *Poole's Index to Periodical Literature,* 1802–1907, still useful for older periodicals.

International Index to Periodicals, 1907– . Unusually useful for investigative papers, since it includes leading American and foreign periodicals in the sciences and humanities. It does not index highly specialized or technical journals.

Indexes to special subjects. Almost every field of study and every subdivision of a large field of study has a specialized periodical index. Many of these are published in an issue of a periodical; for example, the most widely used current bibliography of the study of language and literature is that published in an annual number of *PMLA* (*Publications of the Modern Language Association*), and bibliographies of periods are likely to appear in journals of more restricted interest. This set is now being expanded to become the *MLA International Bibliography,* 1970– . Specialized indexes, not all of which are cumulated, include the following:

Agricultural Index, 1916– . Includes pamphlets.

Annual Bibliography of the Modern Humanities Research Association, 1924– .

Art Index, 1929– .

Book Review Digest, 1905– . Indexes reviews, with excerpts; not cumulated.

Dramatic Index, 1909– .

Education Index, 1929– . Includes both professional and academic journals.

Engineering Index, 1906– . Indexes, also, subjects related to engineering.

Essay and General Literature Index, 1900– . Invaluable for locating essays by subject, fiction by theme, and the like.

Industrial Arts Index, 1913– . Indexes a large number of trade, technical, and industrial periodicals, many of them obscure. Includes pamphlets.

New York Times Index, 1913– . Cumulation available, but not in all libraries.

Public Affairs Information Service, 1915– .

The Times Index, 1907– . Indexes the London *Times.* Detailed and cumulated. Excellent for British and foreign news. From 1914–1957 the index was called *Official Index of the Times.*

Wall Street Journal Index, 1957– . Valuable for financial and industrial news.

For additional indexes, see Constance M. Winchell, *Guide to Reference Books*, 8th ed. (Chicago, 1966).

Bulletins and Pamphlets

Bulletins and pamphlets vary, both in the manner of their publication and in their value; accordingly, libraries handle them variously. Some bulletins come out more or less regularly and in series. For example, the Bureau of American Ethnology publishes what are called *Bulletins*, which may run to hundreds of pages of original research not elsewhere available. On the other hand, a pamphlet issued to describe the beauties of a lake resort may be almost worthless. Accordingly, such questions arise as when is a pamphlet a pamphlet and when is it a book or a periodical, which so-called pamphlets are worth cataloging, which are worth keeping but not worth cataloging, and which should be thrown away? No simple statement can be made about pamphlets. Some are treated as though they are books; they are cataloged in the regular way and appear in the card catalog. Practice varies, especially with the purposes of the library. In a university library having an active anthropology department, the Bureau of American Ethnology *Reports* and *Bulletins* are likely to be cataloged. In a public library they are likely not to be. If they are not cataloged as individual volumes, they are likely to be cataloged as a series with authors and titles on a central card under the name of the series. As indicated above, some pamphlets are listed in periodical indexes, even though they are not periodicals. Government bulletins — and they include quantities of valuable material — appear in the *United States Document Catalogue*. Many libraries collect documents by subject, especially on local topics.

Reference Books

Some books are so useful for ready reference that most libraries keep them on special reference shelves or at a reference desk. The most important works in all fields, including reference works, can be located through Winchell's *Guide to Reference Books*, cited above. Some reference works are so useful that everyone should know them without reference to Winchell.

Dictionaries. For the foremost dictionaries of English, see chapter 20.

Encyclopedias and specialized dictionaries. Encyclopedias and specialized dictionaries are good to start with but not to finish with. They should be used mainly to acquire a reliable introduction, for brief bibliographies, and to verify routine details. They should not be used as crutches to avoid serious investigation. Useful general encyclopedias include the following:

Encyclopaedia Britannica, 14th ed., 1929, 24 vols. This work is in continuous revision, so that important articles may be quite recent; some articles are signed. Scholarly articles in the eleventh edition are still valuable, as are some in the thirteenth. For many purposes this is the best general encyclopedia in English, although far from authoritative.

The Encyclopedia Americana, rev. ed., 1945, 30 vols. In many ways similar to the *Britannica;* less detailed on most subjects.

New International Encyclopedia, 2nd ed., 1914–1916, rev. 1922–1930, 25 vols. Older and briefer than the two previous items and with fewer signed articles, but useful.

Encyclopedias are available in most European languages, some of them excellent. In addition, some encyclopedias, although limited by area or a sectarian approach, are yet sufficiently inclusive that they serve for general reference work. They include the following:

Catholic Encyclopedia, 1907–1922, 17 vols.

Encyclopedia of the Social Sciences, 1949–1950, 13 vols.

Hastings' *Encyclopedia of Religion and Ethics*, 1908–1927, 12 vols. and index.

New Schaff-Herzog Encyclopedia of Religious Knowledge, 1940–1950, 13 vols.

Encyclopedias and handbooks of more specialized subjects can save time and trouble.

Bartlett's *Familiar Quotations*, 14th ed., 1968.

Grove's Dictionary of Music and Musicians, 5th ed., 1954, 9 vols.

Handbook of Chemistry and Physics, 1914– .

Harper's Dictionary of Classical Literature and Antiquities, 1897.

Mencken's *A New Dictionary of Quotations*, 1942.

New Oxford History of Music, 1957.

The Mythology of All Races, 1916–1932, 13 vols.

The Oxford Companion to American Literature, 4th ed., 1965.

The Oxford Companion to English Literature, 4th ed., 1967.

Collections of biographical accounts in English include the following:

Dictionary of American Biography (called *DAB*), 1928–1936, 20 vols. and index. Supplements, 1944, 1958. *American* refers to the United States.

Dictionary of National Biography (called *DNB*), 1882–1949, 22 vols. Accounts of dead British notables.

Briefer accounts are included in the following:

International Who's Who, 1935– .

Who's Who, 1849– . Biographical accounts of living British subjects and some others of great prominence.

Who's Who in America, 1899– . Biographical accounts of living citizens of the United States. For names not in the general volume, see *Who's Who in New England*, 1915– ; *in the East*, 1943– ; *in the Midwest*, 1949– ; *in the West*, 1949– .

Who Was Who, 1897– . Useful for those not included in *DAB;* supplements roughly by decades.

Similar works are available in the native language for most populous countries. More specialized dictionaries of biography include the following:

American Men of Science, 11th ed., 1965.
The Century Dictionary and Cyclopedia, 1911, 12 vols.
Current Biography, 1940– .
Directory of American Scholars, 4th ed., 1964, 4 vols.
Twentieth Century Authors, 1942– .
Webster's Biographical Dictionary, 1943.

Almanacs and yearbooks. Some publications bring within ready compass statistics and miscellaneous information about a variety of subjects of general, and especially of current interest. Most of them are revised annually, with statistics brought down to date for the previous year or the most recent compilation. They include the following:

Facts on File, 1940– . A weekly digest under headings like *Sport, World Affairs.*

The New York Times Encyclopedic Almanac, 1967– , perhaps now the best of several annuals published by newspapers. *The World Almanac,* long the favorite, is still good, as is that published by the *Chicago Daily News.*

Statesman's Yearbook, 1864– . Standard; strong international bent, with emphasis on political and commercial subjects.

Statistical Abstract of the United States, 1878– . The most extensive body of general statistical information readily available in English.

Encyclopedias publishing annual supplements, surveys for the year, include *Encyclopedia Americana, Encyclopaedia Britannica,* and *New International Encyclopedia.*

Taking and Preserving Notes

No writer can hope to remember accurately everything he can locate in a library, and he cannot have every book he may need at hand for immediate reference. He therefore needs to develop a

86

system for selecting and recording and organizing the material he needs so that he can use it after a book has been returned to the library or a newspaper has been thrown away. Sometimes he may wish to copy a document entire, and with the development of mechanical copying devices by such companies as Xerox this is often practical. Usually, however, he will want to select from his reading the material pertinent to his subject and to record it in notes.

The wrong way to take notes is to write them down consecutively in a notebook. They soon become a jumble. They follow the order of the book from which the information was taken — usually not the order the investigator will require. They are unidentified. They cannot be classified, particularly if the investigator writes on both sides of a sheet of note paper. As a result, the investigator knows only that he "has that somewhere" and has to spend half his time hunting for notes he cannot find. Most research workers find that cards or uniform slips provide the most practical means of taking and preserving notes; they permit the most flexible system, and in the end are the most economical. The procedure takes a little time to learn, and using it makes the recording of material a little slower, but in the end it more than pays for itself. The investigator should begin by providing himself with cards or slips; usually three-by-five bibliography cards prove to be too small. Four-by-six cards will serve many purposes, but some writers prefer half-sheets of paper; if slips are used, the paper should be heavy enough to be handled easily, and slips should be cut uniformly so that they can be filed. Basic rules for taking notes are:

1. *Adopt a system and follow it.* The writer must doggedly resist the temptation just "to jot this one down in my notebook" or "to remember this until I get some note cards."

2. *Copy notes directly onto cards.* Putting notes into a notebook and then copying them onto cards wastes time and encourages error.

3. *Identify the source of the information on the card.* Any note must be precisely identified. If the writer is working with a bibliography, he can abbreviate the reference on the note card to the author's last name, a short title of the book or article, and a page reference. Notice that if a quotation runs over to a second page, the location of the page break should be indicated.

4. *Indicate with quotation marks on the note cards any passages taken verbatim from the source.* Knowing when to take material verbatim and when to summarize is difficult. In general the writer may want word-for-word accounts for the following: material that has been very well phrased; material extremely important for the discussion; and controversial material, especially if the writer ex-

pects to examine the statement and comment on it adversely. Any direct quotation—even a two- or three-word phrase—must be enclosed in quotation marks on the card to avoid apparent plagiarism later. If the quotation is not marked on the card, the writer forgets that the passage was written by somebody else and writes it into his paper as his own work.

5. *Write only one piece of information on a card.* If a card contains only a single piece of information, it can be classified by subject with cards containing similar information, no matter from what source it comes. Thus the investigator has all his material on one aspect of his subject filed together.

6. *Indicate with key words the nature or use of the material taken.* When the card is complete, it should be filed according to subject. For this purpose, the investigator should adopt a number of words under which material can be filed; usually these words are headings of his outline.

7. *Avoid taking unnecessary notes.* Some material important for a general understanding of the subject will soon become so familiar that the writer will not need to collect further notes on it. A writer does well to read generally on a subject before starting to take notes and to skim through a book before collecting material from it.

8. *If in doubt, take the note.* Taking just the right material, just enough material and no more, is hardly possible. The investigator will save time by taking too much rather than too little. Copying a few extra words takes a few minutes, but trying to get a book after it has been returned to the library and someone else has borrowed it may take hours.

9. *Take concrete, specific, exact material.* Occasionally generalities are useful, but, on the whole, the more specific the notes, the better. Facts, figures, dates, statistics, verbatim quotations, or factual digests are useful. Most beginners collect too much general material, not enough concrete, objective material.

10. *On the whole, avoid long quotations.* When long quotations are necessary, a facsimile reproduction may save time and errors.

11. *Be accurate and neat.* Type or write legibly; take especial pains with titles, figures, the spelling of names, or with any material in which blunders cannot be caught by context.

12. *Double check every note card.* A wrong page number or an omitted title can cost hours of time and frustration in locating a quotation, and if the final paper contains misquotations, misspellings, or mispunctuation in copied material, the reader cannot be expected to trust much else in the paper.

The following card contains material on the importance of clothing and supplies in the Revolutionary War. Clothing and supplies, of course, are subjects of all the cards and need not be entered on any of them. One important subtopic of the subject, however, is the importance of uniforms. Thus *uniforms* becomes the first key word to identify the note. *American* subdivides the cards concerning uniforms, and *from France* further identifies this note.

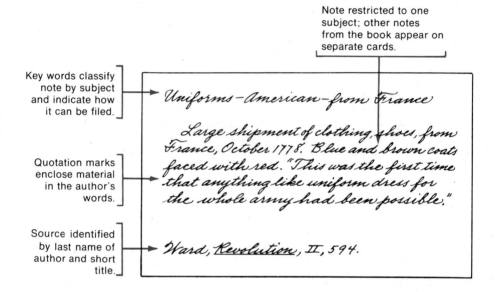

Note restricted to one subject; other notes from the book appear on separate cards.

Key words classify note by subject and indicate how it can be filed.

Quotation marks enclose material in the author's words.

Source identified by last name of author and short title.

Uniforms — American — from France

Large shipment of clothing, shoes, from France, October 1778. Blue and brown coats faced with red. "This was the first time that anything like uniform dress for the whole army had been possible."

Ward, *Revolution*, II, 594.

Selecting Material for Notes: Summary, Paraphrase

Note-taking requires deciding what to record and how to phrase the note—whether to copy a passage verbatim, to write a fairly full paraphrase of it, to reduce it to a brief summary, or to pass it by as not likely to be pertinent to the investigation. The clearer the writer is about his subject and the purposes of his investigation, the easier this procedure becomes, but some waste motion will be inevitable.

Consider alternatives available to a writer looking at the following passage from Mark Twain's *Roughing It* as he collects notes for a paper intended to discuss the peculiar qualities of Twain's humor.

He [Hyde] said it was pretty well known that for some years he had been farming (or ranching, as the more customary term is) in Washoe District, and making a successful thing of it, and furthermore it was known that his ranch was situated just in the edge of the valley, and that Tom Morgan owned a ranch immediately above it on the mountainside. And now the trouble was, that one of those hated and dreaded landslides had come and slid Morgan's ranch, fences, cabins, cattle, barns, and everything down on top of *his* ranch and exactly covered up every single vestige of his property, to a depth of about thirty-eight feet. Morgan was in possession and refused to vacate the premises—said he was occupying his own cabin and not interfering with anybody else's—and said the cabin was standing on the same dirt and same ranch it had always stood on, and he would like to see anybody make him vacate.

"And when I reminded him," said Hyde, weeping, "that it was on top of my ranch and that he was trespassing, he had the infernal meanness to ask me why I didn't stay on my ranch and hold possession when I see him a-comin'! Why didn't I *stay* on it, the blathering lunatic—by George, when I heard that racket and looked up that hill it was just like the whole world was a-rippin' and a-tearin' down that mountainside—splinters and cordwood, thunder and lightning, hail and snow, odds and ends of haystacks, and awful clouds of dust! Trees going end over end in the air, rocks as big as a house jumping 'bout a thousand feet high and busting into ten million pieces, cattle turned inside out and a-coming head on with their tails hanging out between their teeth!—and in the midst of all that wrack and destruction sot that cussed Morgan on his gatepost a-wondering why I didn't *stay and hold possession!* Laws bless me, I just took one glimpse, General, and lit out'n the country in three jumps exactly."

MARK TWAIN, *Roughing It*

If the writer is quite sure that he will want to do no more than refer to the passage generally, perhaps mentioning it as one example of exaggeration in Twain's humor, a brief summary may be all he needs to record. A good summary, however, requires some care. The writer needs to read the entire passage, thinking about it to extract its essence, and he needs to think about how it applies to his purposes. In reading the Twain passage, for example, he needs to consider particularly what it tells him about Twain's humor. He might make a summary note like the following:

> T. makes a rancher called Hyde give very funny account of how another ranch landed on top of his. Good picture of way landslide came down mountain, using exaggeration and wild details.

A note like this would serve as a reminder, but it would not provide much material for development. A longer paraphrase like the following would be more useful:

> T. makes rancher named Hyde tell how in a landslide "Morgan's ranch, fences, cabins, cattle, barns, and everything" slid down and "exactly covered up every single vestige of his property, to a depth

of about thirty-eight feet." Morgan refused to vacate, saying cabin "was standing on the same dirt and the same ranch it had always stood on," and asked Hyde why he had left when he "see him a-comin'." What Hyde had seen was "just like the whole world was a-rippin' and a-tearin' down that mountainside," bringing with it "odds and ends of haystacks . . . trees going end over end in the air, rocks as big as a house jumping 'bout a thousand feet high and busting into ten million pieces, cattle turned inside out and a-coming head on with their tails hanging out between their teeth!" In the face of this, Hyde "lit out'n the country in three jumps exactly."

The longer note preserves some of the flavor of Twain's humor by including direct quotations — carefully distinguished by quotation marks. It records picturesque details of the story and would give the writer something specific with which he could illustrate generalizations about Twain's humor.

Fact and Opinion in Notes

No matter what kind of notes he takes, the writer must understand and record the basis on which each piece of material can be evaluated. That is, he must know whether information is a confession of faith or belief, an opinion fabricated from thin air, a judgment based on expert observation, or a factual report that can be tested objectively. Compare the following comments about a heavy rainstorm:

> I believe that last night's storm was divine punishment to the farmers of this county for their sins.

> Crop damage from last night's storm, according to insurance company estimates, will run to more than $2,000,000.

> According to weather bureau reports, the storm last night brought 2.2 inches of rainfall in ten hours.

The first is obviously belief or opinion; no means of verification is available. The others, with the qualifications specified, are factual; they could be checked. As already indicated (see 3a), fact cannot be strictly separated from judgment or opinion; the last two comments above are approximations and involve the judgments of the insurance company and the weather bureau. The objective writer, however, especially concerned with "facts," must be aware of the type of information with which he is dealing.

For an example, consider a passage in a book by a modern American critic-historian; he is discussing Thomas Jefferson.

Scarcely leaving his native province, he had become a great humanist there and one of the most cultivated men the world could boast of,—and all this thanks to the kind of advantages that he shared with thousands of other young men and that any Virginian of means might have had as well. . . . He had developed early the eager curiosity that marked him as an architect, an inventor and a linguist, for he was also more or less familiar with the languages of forty Indian tribes.

VAN WYCK BROOKS, The World of Washington Irving

Let us assume that an investigator, using this passage, has taken the following note:

Jefferson had become one of the most cultivated men in the world; his eager curiosity developed early, and helped make him an architect, an inventor, and a linguist.

Assertions recorded in this note are not equally factual; consider the three following: (1) "Jefferson was one of the most cultivated men the world could boast of," (2) his "eager curiosity" developed early, and (3) he was an inventor. The last should be subject to documentation, and in fact Brooks does document it in a footnote, where he notes that Jefferson invented "a plough, a sundial, an adjustable bookcase, a portable reading and writing desk, a phaeton, a swivel-chair, a lock-dock for laying up vessels, a chaise longue, a leather buggy-top, a folding ladder, a hexagonal lantern, a two-way dumb waiter, and a sheltered weather vane," along with a device to open and shut double doors. Since documentary evidence could be produced for all of these inventions, presumably, we may say relatively factually that Jefferson was an inventor.

The other statements are not equally subject to verification. All normal children are curious, but how does Brooks know that Jefferson's curiosity was developed, not inborn, how early it was, or whether it was unusual enough to be called "eager curiosity"? Probably he does not, but he certainly could have found—and doubtless he did—that Jefferson, as a young boy, gave much more evidence of curiosity than do most youngsters. Brooks could not have been so sure about the state of Jefferson's curiosity as he was about Jefferson's standing as an inventor, but roughly speaking the statement can probably be called factual.

What about Brooks's assertion that Jefferson was "one of the most cultivated men the world could boast of"? How can one determine degrees of cultivation factually? Is it likely that Brooks had studied intimately the lives of all men in the eighteenth century, the state of learning of individual Tibetan monks, for example? Obviously, this is an opinion, although an opinion based upon sufficient evidence that it is plausible.

All this subtle variation in fact and opinion would probably be inferred by anyone reading the book because Brooks obviously endeavored to write factually. He reports that Jefferson as a boy "pored over Virgil stretched out under an oak tree," and we are confident that these details came out of a document. He usually qualifies when he makes generalizations, saying that some of Jefferson's courtesy "he may possibly have owed to the example of Franklin," and as evidence he cites Jefferson's praise of Franklin's manners. This judicious weighing of fact and opinion has disappeared, however, from the investigator's injudicious note, which jumbles all statements together as though they were equally factual. He might better have written something like the following:

> Brooks considers Jefferson "one of the most cultivated men" of his day and attributes his abilities as architect, inventor, and linguist in part to an "eager curiosity," which had developed early.

By clearly attributing the opinions to Brooks and making use of direct quotations, the writer produces a more useful note.

Plagiarism and Intellectual Maturity

At least one matter that has entered into the previous discussions in various ways calls for more detailed treatment; plagiarism. It is the academic and literary equivalent of burglary, taking another person's property and treating it as though it were one's own. Some plagiarism involves unadulterated dishonesty; the student, being overworked, lazy, or incompetent, copies printed material or another student's work and submits it as his own, knowing quite well what he is doing, but hoping he will not be caught. He is a petty criminal, and he deserves the contempt that society reserves for petty criminals as well as the treatment that the law endeavors to provide for them. But this book does not purport to be a treatment of morals or ethics, and most student plagiarism, particularly in papers resting upon library investigation, stems not so much from dishonesty as from intellectual immaturity. Since intellectual maturity is surely one of the goals of higher education, it warrants careful attention.

That many students grow up intellectual copycats is not to be wondered at; they have been taught no better. With young children this is inevitable; small children have to be told, and they may learn most readily by repeating what they are told. They have to assume that everything they are told is true, and they early learn that, relatively speaking, it is likely to be. But of course a time

93

comes when they ought to outgrow this childishness. Sometimes they are not much encouraged to do so; they go on through the secondary schools praised if they can produce a "correct" answer, even though the answer is something they have parroted out of a book or a lecture without knowing what it means and without being expected to know. They continue to take matter out of text-books and to record it in lecture notes, and again, they may be encouraged to regurgitate this jumble uncritically in examinations. Many examinations are calculated to encourage original thinking, but under the pressure of an examination, routine correctness may be preferred to judgment, and even an intelligent student may go on for years without discovering that higher education is training the mind, not stuffing the mind with relatively reliable statements that can be reproduced on call. Thus, the student may be slow to recognize that at last he is being treated as an adult and that he is expected to act as, and to assume the responsibilities of, an adult.

Thus, intellectual honesty and intellectual maturity go to-gether. Most students want to be intellectually honest, but they may not know how; they may not have trained their minds to dis-tinguish what they believe they know from what they are accepting because they assume that a writer knows. Or they may not have become much aware that they should not steal another man's phrasing and treat it as their own. They may never have learned to paraphrase intelligently and carefully; they may not even have learned to be careful to distinguish their own material from other people's material, and thus they become unwitting criminals, but criminals all the same. Perhaps an example may be instructive.

> The life of all great mystics consists of the same steps. We must accept their experiences as described by them. Only those who them-selves have led the life of prayer are capable of understanding its peculiarities. The search for God is, indeed, an entirely personal undertaking. By the exercise of the normal activities of his conscious-ness, man may endeavor to reach an invisible reality both immanent in and transcending the material world. Thus, he throws himself into the most audacious adventure that one can dare. He may be looked upon as a hero, or a lunatic. But nobody should ask whether mystical experience is true or false, whether it is auto-suggestion, hallucination, or a journey of the soul beyond the dimensions of our world and its union with a higher reality. One must be content with having an operational concept of such an experience. Mysticism is splendidly generous. It brings to man the fulfillment of his highest desires. Inner strength, spiritual light, divine love, ineffable peace. Religious intuition is as real as esthetic inspiration. Through the contemplation of super-human beauty, mystics and poets may reach the ultimate truth.
>
> ALEXIS CARREL, *Man the Unknown*

94

The following is one student's paraphrase of the passage:

> All the great mystics go through the same steps, and we have to accept their experiences. For people who have lived a life of prayer the search for God is personal, and they get outside the world around us. Mysticism is the greatest adventure that one can dare, and although a mystic may be called a hero or a lunatic, he is concerned with a higher reality. Mystics are splendidly generous people, and religious intuition is as real as esthetic inspiration.

This is a weak paraphrase, mainly because it does such scant justice to Carrel, but secondarily because it could scarcely be used without some plagiarism. The student has not understood the passage, but he has recognized that it contains intelligent comment. Accordingly, he has gone through it, picking up familiar words and stringing them together so that they make a sort of sense, although certainly not the sense that Carrel intended. When he changed "mysticism is splendidly generous" to "mystics are splendidly generous people" he was misunderstanding the use of *generous* and hence the whole sentence. He ignored whole passages, probably because they made no sense to him, but he incorporated verbatim the sentence "Religious intuition is as real as esthetic inspiration," probably in a sort of desperation, and because the comparison appealed to him; but by using it as the closing idea he distorts the meaning of the whole. Furthermore, when he comes to write his paper he would probably be attracted by these words and write them into his paper without indication that they constitute a direct quotation. Now notice another purported paraphrase:

> Only those who have themselves led the life of prayer, that is, the mystics, are capable of understanding its peculiarities, because the search for God must inevitably be a personal undertaking. A man who endeavors to reach an invisible reality both immanent in and transcending the material world throws himself into the most audacious adventure that one can dare. Nor should anyone ask whether mystical experience results from auto-suggestion, hallucination, or a journey of the soul beyond worldly dimensions in its unions with higher reality. Mysticism, being splendidly generous, brings its fulfillment in inner strength, spiritual light, divine love, and ineffable peace, and mystics may share with poets the ultimate truth.

In one sense this is much better; the student has gained some grasp of what Carrel is saying, and if he has stolen unabashedly, he has at least had the taste to steal Carrel's best passages and not to corrupt them much. But, obviously, if he treats this paraphrase as his own notes and makes any use of it, plagiarism of a good many sorts is inevitable.

An adequate paraphrase of a paragraph like this may well be beyond the student's ability, but any student should be able to take better notes than these paraphrases represent if he will consider the following injunctions:

1. Endeavor to understand a passage as a whole before attempting to paraphrase any of it.
2. State in your own words anything you summarize, and note carefully that your wording is not colored by the original.
3. When you can provide no adequate summary of your own, or when the wording of the original is so good that you wish to preserve it, scrupulously surround it with quotation marks.

The following paraphrase may not be adequate, but it could be used without plagiarism.

The activities of mystics, although they may strike more worldly people as strange, or even as insane, have their justification in that mystics, like poets, "may reach the ultimate truth." We must assume that mystics are describing their experiences to us honestly, and that only those who have experienced a mystical life can understand it. The mystic "throws himself into the most audacious adventure that one can dare"; mysticism is "splendidly generous," and the mystic's end is to "reach an invisible reality both immanent in and transcending the material world," and thus to cultivate "inner strength, spiritual light, divine love, and ineffable peace."

FOR STUDY AND WRITING

A The Duke of Wellington, examining the roll of officers sent him for a campaign, is said to have remarked, "I only hope that when the enemy reads the list of their names, he trembles as I do." Presumably the warlike duke thought he had been sent a staff of incompetents. If so, the reason may be the working of "The Peter Principle." This theory, devised by Laurence J. Peter, comprises several theses, of which the following may be the most important: (1) everything almost always goes wrong, since (2) the work of the world is delegated to people incompetent to handle it, because (3) everybody rises to the level of his incompetence and stays there. The second accounts for the first and the third for the second.

For example, a young chemistry professor delighted everybody. He loved to lecture, and he had a ready wit and a knack for making difficult problems seem easy. Students packed his classes, and the administration, wanting to encourage a good man, made him chairman of the department with an advance in salary. Unfortunately, although he talked engagingly, he hated paper work and

96

was only bored by administrative details. He talked so much to his colleagues that they shunned him and would not attend staff meetings; students could not get registered because he interviewed them interminably; his laboratory assistants quit because he forgot to requisition their wages; the laboratory itself was a shambles because he did not bother to order equipment. In short, the department became a mess because a good professor proved to be a bad administrator; he had risen to the level of his incompetence, and there he remained—because his superior, also, had risen to the level of his incompetence and was incapable of replacing the chairman and sending him to the level of his competence, in the classroom.

Does the Peter Principle work at other levels? Do you know a good housemother who became an incompetent dean of women? A good chairman of the membership committee who was a bad president? A skillful dropkicker who wrecked the team when he became captain? A convincing car salesman who failed as a garage owner? A skillful political organizer who became a clumsy governor? Re-examine some of your acquaintances—or even some of your own past experiences—and use the material to develop a theme on the Peter Principle.

B Recently, an editor of a dictionary, trying to suggest that language always changes, said that there are now more than a quarter of a million words in English that Shakespeare would not have known. Is this an exaggeration? Try to find out. Here would be one possible way. Use the best dictionary you can get readily—your desk dictionary should serve, but a larger dictionary like the *New International,* either the second or third edition, would be better. By counting a few sample pages, estimate how many entries it has. Modern English has at least a half million words, so that if your dictionary has about a hundred thousand words, you will have to multiply your results by five. Then take a few sample pages and ask yourself which of the words Shakespeare could have known. For example, on a pair of pages you might notice the following: *mumps, Munchausen, municipalism, murid,* and *muscadine. Mumps* he may well have known; children no doubt had them. *Munchausen* he would not have known; Baron Munchausen was not born yet. *Municipalism* he probably could have known, because cities are old and this word derives from Latin, but maybe, because cities were not much studied in Shakespeare's time, this rare word had not developed. *Murid* he probably would not have known; Latin names for plants were much later than Shakespeare's time. *Muscadine* he would not have known; it is an American grape, and American flora were practically unknown to Renaissance Englishmen. Try to assort the words on the pages you select into three groups: (1) words Shakespeare could probably have known; (2) words Shakespeare could not have known, and (3) words about which you are uncertain.

Does the editor's guess look like a good one? Of course he probably had sources of information with which you are not familiar;

he could, for instance, by using the *Oxford English Dictionary,* know that *municipalism* was not used until long after Shakespeare's time. Without such helps, you may find that your third category is so big that you cannot make a good guess. But make due allowances, and come as close as you can. Write a statement of your results.

C Let us assume you have written the following:

> The car hit a patch of ice, and I suddenly had that "gone" feeling, that the brakes and the steering wheel had no effect on the car. Then I heard a crash. I realized that the car had tipped over on its side. I felt as though I was floating, far off somewhere. Then, suddenly, I began to hurt, in several places at once.

If you had experienced this yourself, you could probably now take any one of these sentences and use it as a topic sentence for a whole theme, at least for a paragraph. Now look at something you have written that embodies your own experience; an entry in your journal should serve. Pick from it a sentence or two, or even a phrase or so. Turn this bit of your own writing into a carefully drawn topic sentence or theme sentence, and write a paper from this commitment.

D Read carefully the following selection from Bergen Evans's *Natural History of Nonsense* (New York: Knopf, 1953), pp. 258–59:

> In the *New York Evening Mail* for December 28, 1917, Mr. H. L. Mencken diverted himself by greeting what he called "A Neglected Anniversary." On that day seventy-five years before, he averred, one Adam Thompson, an adventurous cotton broker in Cincinnati, had created quite a splash by lowering his naked form into the first bathtub installed in America. His act had precipitated a storm of protest. Bathing was universally condemned as an affectation and a menace to health and morals. Medical societies expressed their disapprobation, state legislatures imposed prohibitive taxes to prevent the custom from spreading, and the city of Boston—then as now zealous to protect its citizens from harmful contacts—passed a special ordinance forbidding it. There was strong public resentment when President Fillmore had a tub installed in the White House, but ultimately his example carried the day and bathing came to be tolerated if not practiced by our grandfathers.
>
> This story in its author's words, "of spoofing all compact," was "a tissue of heavy absurdities, all of them deliberate and most of them obvious," but it was seized upon with avidity by all sorts of people and related as one of the most sacred facts of our history. Quacks used it as evidence of the [end of p. 258] stupidity of doctors. Doctors used it as proof of medical progress. Bathtub manufacturers used it as proof of their foresight, and assorted reformers used it as proof of the public's lack of it. Editors used it as proof of their own knowledge. It appeared as a contribution to public welfare in thick government bulletins. The standard reference works incorporated it. It was solemnly repeated by master thinkers, including the president of the American Geographical Society

and the Commissioner of Health for the City of New York. Dr. Hans Zinsser communicated it to his readers as one of the esoteric facts of medical annals, and Alexander Woollcott shared it with the radio public as one of those quaint bits of lore with which his whimsical mind was so richly stored.[1]

By 1926 Mencken, "having undergone a spiritual rebirth and put off sin," felt that the joke had gone far enough. He confessed publicly that his story had been a hoax and pointed out what he felt should have warned the critical reader against accepting it as a fact. His confession was printed in thirty newspapers "with a combined circulation, according to their sworn claim, of more than 250,000,000," and the gullibility of the public (which had consisted largely in believing these same papers) received many an editorial rebuke.

[1] H. L. Mencken: "Hymn to the Truth," *Prejudices. Sixth Series* (New York: Alfred A. Knopf, Inc.; 1927), pp. 194–201. See also Vilhjalmur Stefansson: *Adventures in Error* (New York: Robert M. McBride & Company; 1936), Chapter 8; and Curtis D. MacDougall: *Hoaxes* (New York: The Macmillan Company; 1941), pp. 302–09.

Prepare note cards, with key words suggesting the content, and with indications of the source, for the following:

1. A note card for a paper to be entitled "Mencken, Master Spoofer," in which you reduce the first paragraph to about half, but retain the most interesting passages in direct quotation. Make clear that you are quoting Evans' summary of Mencken.

2. A note card for the same paper, in which you recount Mencken's confession and quote both Mencken and Evans.

3. A note card for a paper to be called "Learned Gossip," in which you try to show how rapidly learned errors may spread. This note might in effect be a paraphrase of the second paragraph.

4. A note card to yourself for the same paper in which you record the information so that you can look up treatments of the bathtub hoax by Stefansson and MacDougall.

5. A note card for a paper on "Bergen Evans: Modern Mencken."

E Study carefully the following paragraph.

Strictly speaking, we know in advance that it is impossible to set up a limited number of types that would do full justice to the peculiarities of the thousands of languages and dialects spoken on the surface of the earth. Like all human institutions, speech is too variable and too elusive to be quite safely ticketed. Even if we operate with a minutely subdivided scale of types we may be quite certain that many of our languages will need trimming before they fit. To get them into the scheme at all it will be necessary to overestimate the significance of this or that feature or to ignore, for the time being, certain contradictions in their mechanism. Does the difficulty of classification prove the uselessness of the task? I do not think so. It would be too easy to relieve ourselves of the burden of constructive thinking and to take the standpoint that each language has its unique history, therefore its unique structure. Such a standpoint expresses only a half truth. Just as similar social, economic, and religious institutions have grown up in different parts of the world from distinct historical antecedents, so also languages, traveling along different roads, have tended to converge toward similar forms. Moreover, the historical study of language has proven to us beyond all doubt that a language changes not only gradually but consistently, that it moves unconsciously from one type toward another, and that analogous trends are observable in remote quarters of the globe. From this it follows that broadly similar morphologies must have been reached by unrelated languages, independently and frequently. In assuming the existence of comparable types, therefore, we are not gain-saying the individuality of all historical processes; we are merely affirming that back of the face of history are powerful drifts that move language, like other social products, to balanced patterns, in other words, to types. As linguists we shall be content to realize that there are these types and that certain processes in the life of language tend to modify them. Why similar types should be formed, just what is the nature of the forces that make and dissolve them—these questions are more easily asked than answered. Perhaps the psychologists of the future will be able to give us the ultimate reasons for the formation of linguistic types.

EDWARD SAPIR, *Language*

Criticize the following attempts to paraphrase this passage.

1. Trying to put the thousands of languages and dialects spoken on the surface of the earth into a limited number of types makes it necessary to ignore certain contradictions in their mechanisms, and hence classification becomes a useless task. In assuming the existence of comparable types, therefore, we are gainsaying the individuality of all historical process. Perhaps the psychologists of the future will be able ultimately to put the languages of the world into types.

2. Although Sapir recognizes that speech, like all human institutions, is too elusive to be ticketed, he believes that endeavoring to type sorts of speech develops constructive thinking. He points out that historical study of language has proven that a language changes not only gradually but consistently, and that accordingly, we must assume that similarities in language in different parts of the globe represent powerful drifts that move language, like other products, to balanced patterns, in other words, to types.

Now try to write a more adequate paraphrase of not more than a hundred words.

F Below are eighteen titles of reference works and twenty questions that have answers in the books. For each question indicate which reference book would be likely to supply the answer.

    a) *World Almanac*

    b) *Statesman's Yearbook*

    c) *Encyclopaedia Britannica*

    d) *Dictionary of National Biography*

e) *Dictionary of American Biography*

f) *Catholic Encyclopedia*

g) *Statistical Abstract*

h) *Facts on File*

i) Hastings' *Encyclopedia of Religion and Ethics*

j) *Harper's Dictionary of Classical Literature and Antiquities*

k) Winchell, *Guide to Reference Books*

l) *American Men of Science*

m) Bartlett's *Familiar Quotations*

n) *Who's Who in America*

o) *The Times Index*

p) *New York Times Index*

q) *The Cambridge History of English Literature*

r) *Grove's Dictionary of Music and Musicians*

1. Where and when was R. Buckminster Fuller born?

2. What is the title of a standard bibliography of works concerning the poet John Donne?

3. What is the area in square miles of the Republic of Ghana?

4. Where is the original of the Magna Carta?

5. What public offices were held by Horace Walpole (1678–1757)?

6. What beliefs are associated with the god Krishna?

7. Who discovered electric welding?

8. Who won the championship of the National Professional Football League in 1959?

9. What is the story told of the Virgin of Guadalupe?

10. Is it true that James Watt became interested in steam engines while watching his mother's kettle?

11. Who attended the funeral of Sir Winston Churchill in 1965 in London?

12. Who wrote, "A pen is a pistol let off at the ear"?

13. Who were the earliest composers of fugues?

14. What Greek plays deal with stories of the family of Atreus?

15. What was the significance of Thomas Warton's *Observations on the "Faery Queene" of Spenser*?

16. What college or university did the head of your department of chemistry attend as an undergraduate?

17. What is known about the actors who performed in the Greek comedies of Aristophanes?

18. Is there a prepared bibliography on diamond cutting?

19. Who were the Nobel Prize winners of 1969?

20. At what university did Thorstein Veblen teach?

G By using conventional reference aids, answer the following questions and specify where you found each answer.

1. What was the maiden name of the mother of James Maitland, eighth Earl of Lauderdale (1759–1830)?

2. How tall was the winner of the Miss America contest in 1964?

3. What is the origin of the word *pamphlet*?

4. In Jewish religion, what is the length of the knife to be used in Shehitah, the ritual slaughtering of animals?

5. Where and when was Dickens' *Great Expectations* first published?

6. What are two theories about the origin of the word *Dixie*?

7. What is the native name of the Friendly Islands?

8. What is the most recent article published on extracting salt from sea water?

9. Is there a concordance to the poems of W. B. Yeats?

10. Who are two of the people who accompanied Thomas Edison on a camping trip in August, 1918?

11. What is the leading feature of the form of religion whose adherents are elkesaites?

12. Of what type is the government of Liberia?

13. What is the origin of the quotation, "Where ignorance is bliss, 'tis folly to be wise"?

14. How many barrels of crude petroleum were produced in North Dakota in 1969?

15. When was the word *gig* current to refer to a rowing boat used for racing?

16. Who is holding the hero captive at the beginning of Dryden's play *Don Sebastian*?

17. In Greek mythology is there any difference between Pallas and Athena?

18. Of what New York periodicals was Noah Webster once editor?

19. What was the maiden name of the wife of one of the senators of your state?

20. Who are the authors of a bibliography of the writings of Washington Irving published in 1936?

ORGANIZATION: ANALYSIS AND CLASSIFICATION

CHAPTER 5

The organization of a composition develops from analysis of subjects and classification of materials.

Composition is, in essence, a process of imposing order, of organization. All writers have the same words at their disposal. The problem is to put them into patterns—sentences, paragraphs, chapters, books. "To write," said Jean Cocteau, "is to disarrange the dictionary." Furthermore, in expository prose, at least, the writer does not invent material or make up facts; rather, he finds them and puts them in order and thus expresses his personal view of their relationships. He converts his raw material into a creation of his own by organizing details to suit his particular purposes. The new insights he reveals by his selection and arrangement give the composition its individuality or originality or significance. Hundreds of good books can be written about the Elizabethan theater or the French Revolution because the material can be ordered in almost infinite ways to suit the purposes and main ideas of different writers.

Usually the clues for an organizational plan are implicit in the very beginning stages of composition, in the prewriting that produces an "idea" for a paper; organizing is part of getting an idea. Two processes, analysis and classification, are most useful in the prewriting, in restricting the topic (see chapter 1) and suggesting materials for development. They also provide basic processes to give a composition its final organization, because they can bring order out of chaos. Indeed, they work even in so ordinary an activity as cleaning a room after a Saturday night party. The student can analyze the mess, breaking it into its elements or parts;

he discovers clothes, books and papers, food, dirty dishes, trash. Then he considers each of these parts of the confusion as if it labeled a class, and classifies the items under one or another head — clothes in a pile for the closet, dishes in another pile for the kitchen, trash in the wastebasket, and so on.

These two processes — actually, different ways of looking at the same process — constantly work together. By analysis, wholes are divided into parts — directions into north, east, south, and west; colors into primary and secondary, and then primary colors into red, yellow, and blue. By classification we can attain the same result by a reverse process, by bringing like things together. Given a number of colors we can assort them on the basis of one of their characteristics into primary and secondary. These two approaches supplement each other, and both are fundamental for handling ideas.

Scientific and Literary Analysis

Roughly speaking, analysis is of two sorts: scientific or formal, and literary or informal. The first, scientific analysis, attempts to be complete and exact. A biologist making an analysis of animals, for instance, would endeavor to include every sort that exists: he would establish the families, the subfamilies, the genera, and the species, and continue his subdivisions until every known sort of animal is accounted for. For example, the Canadian lynx, which clearly belongs in the cat family or Felidae, is placed within the genus *Lynx* and becomes *Lynx canadensis* to distinguish it from *Lynx rufus*, the bay lynx. If a new sort of lynx were now to be discovered, a Canadian lynx but different from previous known lynxes of the species, a new category within *Lynx canadensis* would be required to differentiate it from the first. This sort of analysis is useful in bringing permanent order into a complex subject, but it is necessarily exacting and time consuming for both the analyst and those who utilize his work.

Literary or informal analysis, being less exacting, is usually used for practical and relatively immediate ends. The same ornithologist who spends his lifetime endeavoring to correct and to complete the classification of Pacific Ocean birds may open a lecture as follows: "Birds that frequent the Hawaiian Islands represent several aquatic species in such families and subfamilies as the Sternidae, the Pelecanidae, the Sulidae, but I am concerned this morning with only *Pterodroma phaeopygia sandwichensis*, the Hawaiian race of the dark-rumped petrel." He is using literary anal-

104

ysis. He feels no obligation to enumerate all the main categories of Pacific birds or to pursue any category to its final subdivision. He has said enough to indicate that there are a number of sorts of birds and to center attention upon the subject of his discussion. A lecturer in history may say, "Land fighting in the War Between the States divides roughly into campaigns in the East and those in the West. The western campaigns were important, but by the very nature of southern population distribution they could never be decisive." He has been systematic so far as he has gone, but he will certainly feel no obligation to analyze either campaign to the last skirmish—he would have few students left if he did—and he has provided, in his word *roughly,* for the fact that he has ignored minor actions like raids into the North and Indian action in the Far West. Furthermore, some subjects are not amenable to scientific analysis. A lecturer on recent American literature, for instance, might mention the southern school of novelists, the midwestern regionalists, the proletarian novelists, the psychological novelists, the novelists concerned with race problems, the novel of philosophical bawdry and black humor. This rough, informal analysis would be adequate for his purposes, but it is not, because of the nature of the material, a scientific analysis. What would the lecturer do, for instance, about a satirical novel written by a southern writer and concerned with psychological problems of a black steel worker? Literary or informal analysis is not so detailed or so systematic as scientific analysis, but it is much more common and, for most purposes, more useful. In this book we shall be concerned with some common types of literary or informal analysis.

ANALYSIS AND WRITING **5a**

Almost any topic can be approached analytically. The following paragraphs suggest how analysis can be applied to a few common sorts of writing problems.

1. *Division in time.* The history of English literature is traditionally approached in chronological stages—the heroic age, the Middle Ages, the early Renaissance, and so on. An account of a fire might consider the discovery, the alarm, the arrival of the fire trucks, the fire fighting, and then the scene after the fire is controlled. Almost any narrative, report of an event, or historical account can be divided by analysis into periods of time.

2. *Parts of a system, institution, mechanism, or area.* A writer analyzing the government of the United States might begin by considering three branches: legislative, executive, and judiciary.

5a   An

Strengthen organization through better use of analysis.

ORIGINAL

When my brother and I set out to remodel an old car into a dune buggy we had no notion we were becoming two of the polluters of the environment we had complained about. Of course all cars pollute the environment, and probably always will, somewhat. But there are differences, too. A four-wheeled vehicle of the military scout type, for example, can do more damage than the conventional hardtop that must stay pretty close to the paved roads. To make a dune buggy you need a strong chassis and a good motor, along with some skills, especially how to handle an acetylene torch. . . .

[*The composition is confused, partly because the author has no clearly defined main idea.*]

REVISION

All fuel-driven vehicles pollute the environment, and within limits no doubt they always will, but one group of them is especially damaging to all that conservationists try to protect. I refer to those vehicles that permit the inexperienced vacationer to penetrate sparsely inhabited regions where ecosystems have not previously been much disturbed. Among these are the four-wheel-drive scout-type cars, motorcycles, and the dune buggy. My own experience with the last of these, a dune buggy that my brother and I put together, has convinced me that. . . .

[*The original might have been revised in any of several ways, but one is to clarify the organization by analysis.*]

Prior to the Communist occupation there were more than four million Christians of all denominations in China. Matthew Ricci, S.J., who arrived in the sixteenth century was one of them. . . .

[*The writer has used analysis, although not in an orderly manner, and he has not made the basis of his analysis clear.*]

Christianity has been introduced into China three times, but the missionary ventures of the seventh and thirteenth centuries proved abortive. Not until Matthew Ricci, S.J., arrived in 1582 to replant the faith of the West did Christianity play a leading part in Chinese life. . . .

[*The chronological analysis is now clear to the reader.*]

In sections treating each of these branches he could analyze further, perhaps dividing the discussion of the executive branch into chapters on the president, the cabinet, the presidential advisers, and the executive bureaus. One writer discusses the weather by considering each of the "seven American airs." Another, discussing pollution, might consider effects upon the earth, the air, fresh water, and the sea. Analysis can break anything complex into its parts.

3. *Parts of an argument.* A student preparing an appeal for more lenient dormitory regulations might describe practical problems presented by existing rules, make comparisons with rules in other schools, and discuss possible effects of the proposed changes. Analysis of a logical discussion can produce divisions to make the case orderly.

4. *Parts of a process.* Description of a simple process like building a campfire might proceed in chronological steps — selecting and preparing a site, gathering fuel, building the fire. Jacques Barzun in a more complicated discussion of how a teacher conducts a class analyzes the problem into methods: "The three basic ways are the lecture, the discussion group, and the tutorial hour."

5. *Aspects of a character.* A writer planning a sketch of a character from fiction or from life might use analysis to isolate such subjects as personal appearance, attitudes and prejudices, activities and accomplishments, and family background.

6. *Characteristics of a literary work.* Criticizing a story, a writer might consider its theme, its imagery, its characterization, and its diction. Or he might examine the story through its parts — its introduction, its early development, its climax, its denouement.

Analysis, in other words, need not be scientifically thorough to be useful, especially in the prewriting stages of gathering material and planning and in keeping ideas in order.

CLASSIFICATION

5b

Classification relies on similarities and differences. For example, considering all living things on earth, we could observe that some are similar in that they have four feet. We could group them as quadrupeds. But within this class, brought together because of a particular similarity, we would also find differences, and distinguish cows, horses, sheep, pigs, and lions. Furthermore, each of these subclasses could again be subdivided — cows into Guernseys, Jerseys, Holsteins, Herefords, Aberdeen Angus, and so on.

The same items can be grouped in a number of ways by using different points of similarity as the basis of classification. Consider the following items: fire truck, bluebird, violet, yellow convertible, goldfinch, poinsettia, sunflower, blue bicycle, cardinal. They can obviously be classified by kind, as listed on page 108.

5b Class

Reclassify, using only one basis of classification at a time.

ORIGINAL

During the period 1932–1936, the government of the United States created a large number of temporary bureaus and agencies. In this paper I shall be concerned with the question of why some of the supposedly temporary agencies were accepted permanently. I shall consider four groups of agencies: agricultural agencies, financial agencies, agencies established after 1936, and agencies that exist today. . . .

[*Classes have been established on different bases. The first two depend on matter the agencies dealt with; the third is based on time of establishment of the agency, and the fourth on permanence of the agency. The material needs to be reclassified on a consistent basis — probably a basis indicated by the central purpose of the paper.*]

REVISION

During the period 1932–1936, the government of the United States created a large number of temporary bureaus and agencies. In this paper I shall be concerned primarily with the question of why some agencies were accepted permanently whereas others were soon abandoned. I shall consider the agencies in four groups: those abandoned after a short trial, those replaced by other agencies, those abandoned because their purpose was accomplished, and those still in existence.

[*The classification of the final sentence is changed to one that depends on a single principle — the permanence of the agencies This basis for classification is suggested by the statement of the purpose.*]

Vehicles	Birds	Flowers
fire truck	bluebird	violet
yellow convertible	goldfinch	poinsettia
blue bicycle	cardinal	sunflower

But a painter might classify them by color:

Red	Blue	Yellow
fire truck	blue bicycle	yellow convertible
cardinal	bluebird	goldfinch
poinsettia	violet	sunflower

The students in a classroom can be classified by the registrar as freshmen, sophomores, juniors, and seniors; by a minister as Baptists, Roman Catholics, Episcopalians, Methodists; by the instructor as A students, B students, C students; by the football coach as potential spectators, potential halfbacks, potential linemen; by a boy in the back row as men and possible "dates." The important consideration is that *material can be classified on only one basis at one time.* The women in a class can be classified by the color of their hair as blondes, brunettes, and redheads. The redheads can be reclassified on the basis of their grades, and the B-student redheads can be classified into Pan Hellenics, members of local sororities, and independents. They cannot be classified on any two of these bases at one time, since some students would belong to both classes and some to neither.

The interests of the classifier determine the basis for the classification. There is an old story of a college dean who had no trouble dealing with a parrot that had become a nuisance in a dormitory, even though its presence did not violate any existing rule. "I suggest," he told the owner of the offending bird, "that you dispose of your parrot before I am forced to classify it as a dog or a television set."

Analysis and Classification for Organization

In organizing a composition, analysis and classification work together, as the following discussion of the wide appeal of the English language illustrates.

The English language is spoken or read by the largest number of people in the world, for historical, political and economic reasons; but it may also be true that it owes something of its wide appeal to qualities and characteristics inherent in itself. What are these characteristic features which outstand in making the English language what it is, which give it its individuality and make it of this world-wide significance? Some of the more obvious of these are the following. First and most important is its extraordinary receptive and adaptable heterogeneousness —the varied ease and readiness with which it has taken to itself material from almost everywhere in the world and has made the new elements of language its own. English, which when the Anglo-Saxons

The writer begins by using analysis to prescribe the limits of his discussion. He analyzes the broad topic, reasons for the appeal of English, into four divisions—historical, political, economic, and inherent. Then he indicates that he will discuss only the last reason.

He then analyzes again, breaking the reasons inherent in the language into five "characteristic features." He qualifies even this analysis, not pretending that it is exhaustive, but calling these five the "most obvious."

He then discusses each of these features in turn, marking his organization very obvious with first, second, *and so on.*

From the opposite point of view, it can be said that the writer is classifying these five features under the heading "reasons." And under each of these five features he is classifying illustrative details.

first conquered England in the fifth and sixth centuries was almost a 'pure' or unmixed language — which could make new words for new ideas from its own compounded elements and had hardly any foreign words — has become the most 'mixed' of languages, having received throughout its history all kinds of foreign elements with ease and assimilated them all to its own character. Though its copiousness of vocabulary is outstanding, it is its amazing variety and heterogeneousness which is even more striking: and this general receptiveness of new elements has contributed to making it a suitable and attractive vehicle in so many parts of the world.

Under the first, the "heterogeneousness" of English, he points out that English has become a "mixed" language, that it has assimilated elements from other languages, and that this variety makes it suitable throughout the world.

A second outstanding characteristic of English is its simplicity of inflexion — the ease with which it indicates the relationship of words in a sentence with only the minimum of change in their shapes or variation of endings. There are languages such as Chinese, that have surpassed English in the reduction of the language in the matter of inflexions to what looks like just a series of fixed monosyllabic roots: but among European languages, taken as a whole, English has gone as far as any in reducing the inflexions it once had to a minimum. A natural consequence of this simplifying of inflexion by reduction, however, is that since the relationship of words to each other is no longer made clear by their endings, this must be done in other ways.

To illustrate the second feature, "simplicity of inflexion," he points out that English has reduced inflection as much as any European language and that it therefore shows relationships in other ways. "Other ways" provides a transition to the third feature.

A third quality of English, therefore, is its relatively fixed word-order. An inflected language like Latin or Russian can afford to be fairly free in the arrangement of its words, since the inflexions shew

Under the third quality, "fixed word-order," the writer classifies his details about order, including a contrast with Latin or Russian.

clearly the proper relationship in the sentence, and ambiguity is unlikely. But in a language which does not change the forms of its words according to their relationship in the sentence-significance, the order of the words is likely to be relatively fixed; and a fixed word-order in relation to meaning in the sentence takes the place of the freedom made possible by the system of inflexions.

Another consequence, fourthly, of the loss or reduction to the minimum of the inflexions which English once had, is the growth of the use of periphrases or roundabout ways of saying things, and of the use of prepositions to take the place of the lost inflexions. The English simplified verb uses periphrases and compound tenses made with auxiliary verbs to replace the more elaborate system of tenses that once existed (though tenses had already become fairly simple before the Anglo-Saxons came to England). Similarly, English, which once had nearly as many case-endings as Latin, has come to use prepositions instead of these, as can easily be seen if one translates any piece of Latin into English.

A fifth quality of English — though this, like the loss of inflexions and its consequences is shared with some other languages — is the development of new varieties of intonation to express shades of meaning which were formerly indicated by varying the shapes of words. This is perhaps somewhat comparable (though only in a small way) to the vast use of intonation in Chinese as a method of expressing meaning in sentences which would otherwise seem like series of unvarying monosyllabic roots. Consider, for instance, the wonderful variety of shades of meaning we

The fourth quality is linked to the second and third as "another consequence" and is divided into two sub-qualities, the use of "roundabout ways of saying things" and of "prepositions to take the place of lost inflexions." The writer then cites an example to illustrate each: expanded forms of the verb to illustrate the first and prepositions instead of case endings to illustrate the second.

Under the fifth quality, "intonation," he classifies two illustrations: a comparison with Chinese and our ways of saying do.

111

may put into the use of the word 'do', merely by varying the intonation—that is the pitch and intensity, the tone of the voice.

Not all the above qualities are in themselves necessarily good, nor have they all contributed to the general success of English. But it seems probable that of them all it is the adaptable receptiveness and the simplicity of inflexion that have done most in this regard. On the other hand, the very copiousness and heterogeneousness of English leads to vagueness or lack of clarity. Its resources are too vast for all but the well educated to use to full advantage; and such phenomena as 'pidgin English', 'journalese', jargon, woolliness of expression and slatternly speech and writing, are everywhere likely to be met with. It may fairly be said that English is among the easiest languages to speak badly, but the most difficult to use well.

C. L. WRENN, *The English Language*

In the final paragraph the writer summarizes with a comment on the advantages and disadvantages of these qualities, classifying here his comments on the effects of the five features.

The writer uses analysis to determine the main divisions of his discourse and classifies his information appropriately in each division. Often, of course, prose does not indicate its use of analysis and classification so obviously or formally as this, but the following passage shows the same approach used to organize a humorous and ironic proposal for what the writer calls a "handy-dandy college system for honest paranoids."

No fair-minded cretin can deny that our colleges—so lovingly nourished, so costly to maintain, so irreplaceable in the knowledge they augment and dispense—are in one hell of a mess. If the stupid Establishment would only *listen* to our idealistic children, to the sincere college students who only want to *communicate* their superior wisdom in meaningful monologues, then the answer to all our college problems would become as clear as the nose on my face, which few observers fail to notice.

We must unmask the broad *social* causes that underlie campus unrest. Once we understand that, or them, the cure is a cinch.
I. Causes
Millions of decent young Americans annually complete what we

112

call "high" school. (This usually occurs between the age of 16.) These innocent youngsters are cursed with materialistic *parents who do not understand them.* The insensitive parents fall into three inhuman groups.

A. Parents who insist that their children go to college because they are naïve sentimentalists and want to give their offspring the best education possible.

Going to a college is, of course, not the same as getting an education; but parents in Group A are ecstatic if their progeny simply use up four years on a campus—even though Junior hates to read, Missy is incapable of understanding why water runs downhill instead of up, and both will get a B.A. under the illusion that the Generalissimo of Nationalist China is Shanghai Jack.

B. Parents who force their kids to go to college only because they (the parents) don't want them (the kids) hanging around the house. Nothing so destroys American parents' peace of mind as having nubile boys and girls in physical proximity when they (the parents) don't want them (the children) around, especially while they (the parents) want to get loaded enough to ask each other how in the world they (the parents) had ever been crazy enough to decide to have them (the children).

C. Mothers and fathers who nag, nag, nag their sons and daughters into surrendering to a college official only because of social ambitions that are based on the outmoded American dream of providing your offspring with every chance to better themselves. There is a widespread illusion in parental circles (even parents who are "square" move in circles) that the quickest way to better yourself, when you are between 16, is to spend the next four years in a college dorm—playing house, or conducting imaginative experiments in biology with bad boys and girls from good families.

But these foolish parents fail to recognize how many of our young people want to spend four years *not* with boys and girls, but with boy-girls, or girl-boys, or boys/girls—who are the most picturesque of all in dress, posture and dangling particles.

LEO ROSTEN. "Handy-Dandy Plan to Save Our Colleges"

The essay continues with the second of the two divisions into which the writer has analyzed the topic, "Cure." Then as his cure Rosten describes six types of universities he proposes to institute, labeling each class: "1. Useless Universities, 2. Playmate Universities, 3. Institutes of Technology," and so on. Even though the analysis is not serious—nobody is likely to accept his three classes of parents as a total representation of "the broad *social* causes that underlie campus unrest"—analysis and classification are the basis for the organization. In fact, with his numbers and letters the writer is perhaps partly parodying formal organizational schemes.

In any composition, analysis and classification can be used to provide order. Topics and subtopics can be analyzed into parts,   **113** and materials can be classified under appropriate headings. For example, a historian trying to find out why Lee's army lost at Gettysburg considers Longstreet's failure to move as he was ordered, Stuart's failure to arrive until the battle was essentially over, the questionable tactic of Lee in ordering Pickett to charge, and a number of other factors; he then decides to consider the question of the unexpected effectiveness of the Union artillery. He has now narrowed his subject by analysis, but he is not done. He has still to ask himself why the Union batteries wrought such havoc. Another analysis suggests that the key reason was that Brigadier General Henry J. Hunt had managed to trick the Confederate command into believing he was out of ammunition, although he was not. How did he manage to do this? Of all the artillery actions, of all the evidence from spies and skirmishers, which will be significant and which will not be significant for this question? Now the job becomes one of classification; evidence must be sorted, rejected if it is not pertinent, and grouped with other like evidence if it is pertinent. This process may become complicated, with new analysis of minor questions, new categories into which evidence must be classified, and with the historian moving as his evidence and his interpretation of this evidence lead him. Through it all he will be using analysis and classification, sometimes one, sometimes the other, and often both.

Coordination and Subordination

In writing, the results of analysis and classification are indicated by two structural devices, coordination and subordination. In addition to creating sentences or parts of sentences (see chapters 15 and 16), they reveal organization in large units of composition (see chapters 6 and 7), and promote the construction of paragraphs (see chapter 8). They depend on nothing inherent in ideas or things themselves, but they clarify the kinds of relationships we want to give them. *Ham and eggs*, to take an oversimple example, may be coordinated in sentences—"He ate ham and scrambled eggs." Here the two are put into a coordinate pattern; that is, they are presented in such a way that the reader finds them bearing the same—an equal—relationship to the rest of the sentence. Nothing in the nature of the two foods requires this sort of comment, however, and the sentence with equal logic might be "He ate eggs scrambled with ham," in which *ham* is subordinate to *eggs*, or "He ate ham garnished with scrambled eggs," in which *eggs* is subordinate. In the second and third sentences, ham and eggs are not

114

shown to be coordinate; they are not listed as two items of equal rank, independent of each other, as they are in the first sentence. One is subordinate to the other, not because one is less important, but because the writer wants to talk about them differently—about eggs as they are prepared in a particular way involving ham, or about ham as it is served along with eggs. The sentence with co-ordination is like "He ate ham and cabbage"; the sentence with subordination is like "He ate poached eggs on whole wheat toast." The writer has signaled the coordination by using *and* to connect the two items; he has signaled the subordination by putting one item into the pattern and position for modifiers (see chapter 16).

On a larger scale, the same two structural devices show read-ers of the two selections above how the writers have analyzed and classified. The diagram (page 116) of the first sentences of the selec-tion from Wrenn above uses indentation to suggest roughly the broad patterns—that is, coordinated items have the same indenta-tion and are marked by the same superscript number; subordi-nated items are indented farther, and the colored lines suggest the idea in one sentence to which another element is subordinate. A simple diagram like this can barely suggest the intricate play of coordination and subordination in a carefully built piece of writing. The diagram indicates broadly that the opening sentence, with two coordinate elements, establishes a topic, to which all the remaining material is subordinate. The second and third sentences may be considered coordinate with each other but subordinate to the first sentence, introducing an enumeration of the "qualities and char-acteristics" named as topics in the first sentence. The third sentence moves to a third level of subordination, mentioning the first of the five "characteristic features" described in the selection. These five are made coordinate in the selection—the final item of the diagram is marked at level 3. Wrenn indicates the coordination in several ways—by introducing each "feature" in a topic statement, by mak-ing these topic statements similar in form, by labeling each as one of the features, and by marking them from first to fifth. But these five features are all subordinate to the main contention of the selection, that English has its wide appeal partly because of quali-ties inherent in itself, and the selection itself is subordinate to the general purpose of Wrenn's book, to describe the nature of the English language. Furthermore, each of the five features is sup-ported by material subordinate to it—material marked at level 4 in the diagram—and the sentences have coordinated and subordi-nated elements within themselves, beyond the obvious ones indi-cated on the diagram. In the first sentence, the phrase "for his-torical, political, and economic reasons" is subordinate to the basic predication that "English . . . is spoken or read by the largest num-

[1] The English language is spoken or read by the largest number of people in the world, for historical, political and economic reasons;

[1]but it may also be true that it owes something of its wide appeal to qualities and characteristics inherent in itself

[2]What are these characteristic features which outstand in making the English language what it is, which give it its individuality and make it of this world-wide significance?

[2]Some of the more obvious of these are the following.

[3]First and most important is its extraordinary receptive and adaptable heterogeneousness,—the varied ease and readiness with which it has taken to itself material from almost everywhere in the world and has made the new elements of language its own.

[4]English, which when the Anglo-Saxons first conquered England in the fifth and sixth centuries was almost a 'pure' or unmixed language—which could make new words for new ideas from its own compounded elements and had hardly any foreign words—has become the most 'mixed' of languages, having received throughout its history all kinds of foreign elements with ease and assimilated them all to its own character.

[4]Though its copiousness of vocabulary is outstanding, it is its amazing variety and heterogeneousness which is even more striking;

[4]and this general receptiveness of new elements has contributed to making it a suitable and attractive vehicle in so many parts of the world.

[3]A second outstanding characteristic of English is. . .

ber of people," but the words *historical, political,* and *economic* are coordinate with one another. That is, these two structural devices work at the same time among major units of a composition and within the sentences of which these units are composed.

In the Rosten selection the letters *A, B,* and *C* signal that the three types of parents are coordinate. Each of these is subordinate, however, to the broader notion of causes of social unrest in colleges. The idea of causes is coordinate with cures, but both of these are subordinate to the idea of explaining the "mess" in colleges.

Writing, in other words, is a complex of coordination and subordination, which reflects analysis and classification and reveals how the writer wants to relate his ideas. Items are coordinate with other items of the same class, but they are subordinate to items of which they are a part, on which they depend, or of which they are illustrations.

FOR STUDY AND WRITING

A Select any five of the following general topics and list subdivisions — parts, elements, stages, etc. — revealed by analysis. For example, for the first you would probably make your initial analysis on the basis of the position of the players; that is, you would divide the men into linemen and backfield. Then you might make a second classification and analyze on the basis of type of play, noticing that the ends and tackles are likely to become involved in offensive play, whereas the center and guards have the primary responsibility for holding the center of the line. You could then distinguish further between the function of ends and tackles, and the like. For the backfield you might want to distinguish the offensive backs from the defensive backs, and among the defensive backs distinguish linebackers from safety men. Or you might want to distinguish the work of defensive backs against a line play, a pass, or a kick.

1. A football team
2. A newspaper
3. A storm
4. Building a tree house
5. A university
6. Snobbishness
7. Registration day
8. A gasoline engine
9. Learning to swim
10. A garden

B Consider the following subjects; obviously they are much too broad for brief papers. Limit these subjects by analysis, and then write a theme sentence for each in which you announce the subject of the proposed essay and give sufficient indication of the basis on which the analysis was made. Review of chapter 1 may help. For number 1 you might produce a sentence like the following: "Viewed from the vantage point of 1970, Asia presented three areas of greatest tension; in the southwest because of the conflict between Israel and the Arab countries, in the southeast because of China and other Communist states that threatened lands from India to the Malaysian Peninsula, and in the central east because of the rivalry between China and Russia."

1. Political tension in Asia
2. The teacher surplus
3. A recent political campaign
4. Modern music
5. Automation and the labor problem
6. Juvenile delinquency
7. The farmer in the modern world
8. Picking the right college
9. Summer vacations
10. The economic problems of the emerging African nations

C Make two separate classifications for the items in each of the following groups, classifying each time on a different basis and being sure to classify on only one basis at a time:

1. canned peas, frozen pears, canned peaches, a can of wax, a dozen clothespins, 10 pounds of potatoes, a dozen oranges, frozen peaches, a can of kitchen cleanser
2. baseball, tennis, swimming, basketball, diving, skiing
3. advanced economics, freshman chemistry, beginning history, physics seminar, beginning German, first-year Italian, freshman biology, senior French

D Indicate one item in each of the following classifications that is inconsistent because it has not been classified on the same basis as the other items:

1. Pictures: *into* oil, landscape, watercolor, pastel, tempera
2. Books: *into* novels, collections of poems, collections of short stories, leather-bound books, collections of plays, histories, textbooks
3. Dresses: *into* evening dresses, afternoon dresses, sports dresses, cotton dresses, dinner dresses
4. Criminals: *into* burglars, murderers, incorrigibles, arsonists, embezzlers
5. Stylistic qualities of a poem: *into* alliteration, rhyme, meter, consistency, stanzaic pattern
6. Causes for water pollution: *into* industrial waste, pesticides, untreated garbage, inadequate government regulations, refuse from boats

E The following paragraph is confused for a number of reasons, but it can be put in order if it is revised after clear analysis of the problem. What light do our presidents throw on the question of humor as an asset in politics? Analyze the problem, classify the evidence on the basis of your analysis, and rewrite the paragraph with a central idea and clear evidence of organization.

Neither Richard Nixon nor John F. Kennedy was devoid of a sense of humor, but neither was notable for it; Kennedy's victory seems to provide little evidence one way or the other. Calvin Coolidge did have a sense of humor, a salty Vermont wit. Very few people liked it much. George Washington was a great general and a great president. He had dignity, but apparently not much sense of humor. William Howard Taft is said to have been a very genial man in private, but he was also a very heavy man, and thus in public life he was more frequently the butt of humor than the creator of it. Most of our presidents, if they do not illustrate the assertion "The people expect their statesmen to be solemn asses," give us little reason to suppose that a sense of humor is a political asset. Woodrow Wilson had a sense of humor, which he used in his scholarly writing and in the privacy of his home. John Adams and John Quincy Adams were men of subtle mind, but they seem not to have enjoyed laughing. Adlai Stevenson, who convulsed his audiences when he was campaigning against Dwight D. Eisenhower, was defeated twice, whether because of his humor or in spite of it. Of the early presidents, only Thomas Jefferson seems to have enjoyed a joke, a very quiet joke well screened from public view. Theodore Roosevelt was perhaps not subtle enough to have much humor; as Professor T. V. Smith has said, "He exclaimed 'bully' from the larynx more often than he laughed from the belly." Franklin Roosevelt used his humor sparingly and for calculated effects. When Peter Cartwright, a frontier evangelist, was campaigning against Lincoln for Congress, he accused Lincoln of not knowing where he wanted to go because he would stand neither with those who were certain they would go to heaven nor with those who expected to go to hell. "I aim, of course, to go to Congress," Lincoln drawled. More recently, both Lyndon B. Johnson and Barry Goldwater could crack jokes, but Goldwater's wit did not save him and Johnson's homely humor probably brought him few votes. It did not save him from having to decline a second term. Presidents like Zachary Taylor and Andrew Jackson were blunt, almost humorless men, but they were triumphant vote getters and popular presidents. Even Madison and Monroe were notably solemn. Abraham Lincoln, whose sense of humor became legend, offers the only notable exception to the general rule that our presidents have not been characterized by their sense of humor. Some presidents seem to have had some sense of humor, but hesitated to use it in politics, or in any connection suggestive of state affairs. Harding probably lacked the liveliness of mind either to engender or to appreciate much humor. When Nixon did run successfully he became famous for his oft-repeated "Now let me make this perfectly clear," not for any subtlety or wit.

F Turn back to the diagram above of the first sentences of the selection from Wrenn's book. Continue the diagram, working through the subsequent paragraphs, identifying subordination and coordination as evidenced in the larger units within the selection. Obviously, the remaining "characteristic features" are subordinate to the thesis statement in the first paragraph and are coordinate with one another, but within the four paragraphs that develop these "features" subordination and coordination are everywhere. What will you do about the final paragraph? Could it be called either clearly coordinate or subordinate, and if so, related to what?

PATTERNS OF
ORGANIZATION:
THE OUTLINE

CHAPTER 6

*Organization, planned in the outline, reveals the relationships among
ideas, the essentials of the composition.*

The ancient world had a pleasant if erroneous idea that divine
order regulated the entire universe. Planets, stars, angels, men,
animals, or stones all fit set places, and each of these had order
within it. The pattern for order was established and clear, and it
fit man or beast or the heavens. The great world, for example, the
macrocosm—*macro-* meaning great and *cosmus* a universe—com-
prised the earth and heavens with all the stars and planets. Man,
the microcosm, was a little universe, supposed by early thinkers to
be like the physical universe in nature and organization, with some
necessary variations for size. Arteries and veins, they observed,
were like the rivers of the greater world; the seven openings in
man's head—two eyes, two ears, two nostrils, and a mouth—corresponded to the seven planets. While this order was preserved,
all went well. When it was violated in any part, chaos prevailed.

As a scientific explanation, this elaborate analogy has long
been abandoned; there are differences between blood and river
water. As a description of expository composition, the old system
is still at least interesting, both for its insistence on the importance
of order and its enthusiasm for correspondences in patterns.

APPROPRIATE ORGANIZATION

6a

There is, of course, no single plan of organiza-
tion; the Almighty was not so systematic about composition as the
ancients thought he was about the universe. But the old analogy be-

tween the small and great worlds can be applied to composition in another way, to a correspondence in general patterns of order between small and larger units of composition. For example, one can think of the paragraph as a kind of "microcomposition," reflecting in miniature the same sorts of order that govern longer pieces of writing. The same general principles for ordering ideas apply to sentences, to paragraphs, and to larger units.

All writing units fall into patterns of order, corresponding to conventional ways in which human beings think. Certain of these patterns are obviously appropriate to certain kinds of subjects and purposes. The writer telling a story is likely to find chronological order most convenient; the writer advancing an argument may need a logical pattern. A single composition may, of course, include units organized on different bases. Often, for instance, within an overall logical pattern, a writer may illustrate a point with a story presented in chronological order.

Usually, however, one kind of general scheme for a composition most readily keeps ideas in order. For example, a student writ-

GUIDE TO REVISION

6a   **Org**

Revise, providing an organizational scheme that is clearer and more appropriate to the purpose of the paper.

ORIGINAL

The first sort of pollution to the environment to attract wide attention was municipal garbage, but not much was done about it. From New York City garbage barges were hauled farther out to sea before they were dumped, but not much farther. The second kind of pollution to attract much public notice was air pollution, particularly as it was apparent in city smog. London and Los Angeles. . . .

[*Chronology provides an adequate basis for organizing some exposition — for example, an orderly survey — but it may not focus attention on the main idea the writer wants to present.*]

REVISION

Although less immediately lethal than either lead poisoning from exhaust gas or mercury poisoning from factory wastes, crude oil spilled in the sea may in the end do the most to render the earth uninhabitable for man. Lead poisoning is rather readily subject to control; it need not be put into gasoline, which is explosive without it. As for mercury wastes. . . .

[*Since the author of the original intended to center attention on the long-range dangers of oil spillage, an ascending order would probably work better than chronology.*]

ing a paper on *Hamlet* might select as a statement of his main idea:

> Fortinbras, although a minor character in the play, is important because he serves as a foil for the main character and also represents stability in the chaotic world of the play.

The resulting paper might well have two logical divisions — Fortinbras as a foil for Hamlet and Fortinbras as a representative of stability. The writer would analyze each of these subtopics and classify and arrange evidence from the play under them. If he were to fall into the easier chronological pattern of simply recording in order Fortinbras's actions in the play, he would have more trouble showing how the evidence supported the main proposition.

The following are common patterns a writer may use in organizing his paper to show relationships among ideas.

Chronological Organization

In the following sentences, order shows a chronological relationship.

> A yellow convertible flashed by the billboard and screamed around the curve. A traffic policeman wheeled his motorcycle from its hiding place and roared into the highway.

Because one sentence precedes the other, the reader assumes that the event it describes precedes the other event. Reversing the order of the sentences would reverse the order of events and save a fine for the driver of the convertible.

Any record of happenings can almost always be planned around related times — often by the simple procedure of putting first things first. The following description of Mary Stuart's preparation for execution is organized in this way.

> She laid her crucifix on her chair. The chief executioner took it as a perquisite, but was ordered instantly to lay it down. The lawn veil was lifted carefully off, not to disturb the hair, and was hung upon the rail. The black robe was next removed. Below it was a petticoat of crimson velvet. The black jacket followed, and under the jacket was a bodice of crimson satin. One of her ladies handed her a pair of crimson sleeves, with which she hastily covered her arms; and thus she stood on the black scaffold with the black figures all around her, blood-red from head to foot.
>
> JAMES ANTHONY FROUDE, *History of England*

A description of a process — how to do something or how something is made or how it works — is one obvious application of chronological order. A recipe for making beef Wellington, directions for the construction of a rabbit hutch, or the tracing of a proposed statute through a bicameral legislature can be arranged as a step-by-step account. In a long discussion the writer usually divides the sequence of operations or events into stages, describing each in adequate detail and sometimes commenting on its significance. The following, part of a much longer account of how earth and sea were formed, is an adaptation of the process method.

> The new earth, freshly torn from its parent sun, was a ball of whirling gases, intensely hot, rushing through the black spaces of the universe on a path and at a speed controlled by immense forces. Gradually the ball of flaming gases cooled. The gases began to liquefy, and Earth became a molten mass. The materials of this mass eventually became sorted out in a definite pattern: the heaviest in the center, the less heavy surrounding them, and the least heavy forming the outer rim. This is the pattern which persists today — a central sphere of molten iron, very nearly as hot as it was 2 billion years ago, an intermediate sphere of semi-plastic basalt, and a hard outer shell, relatively quite thin and composed of solid basalt and granite.
>
> RACHEL CARSON, *The Sea Around Us*

Spatial Organization

Order can show relationship in space as well as in time. To help the reader picture relative positions, the writer reflects spatial arrangement by the arrangement of his sentences. Describing a scene, he can arrange details as they meet the eye.

> The ship turned sharply and steamed slowly in. It was a great landlocked harbour big enough to hold a fleet of battleships; and all around it rose, high and steep, the green hills. Near the entrance, getting such breeze as blew from the sea, stood the governor's house in a garden. The Stars and Stripes dangled languidly from a flag staff.
>
> SOMERSET MAUGHAM, "Rain"

Even though the writer's purpose may be to set a scene and center attention on a particular object, the method may be by spatial arrangement, as in the following, where relationship words are notably those of space — *on, among, removed, near, above, under,* and *where.*

> On the shelving bank of the river, among the slimy stones of a causeway — not the special causeway of the Six Jolly Fellowships,

which had a landing place of its own, but another, a little removed, and very near to the old windmill which was the denounced man's dwelling-place—were a few boats; some, moored and already beginning to float; others, hauled up above the reach of the tide. Under one of these latter Eugene's companion disappeared. And when Eugene had observed its position with reference to the other boats, and had made sure that he could not miss it, he turned his eyes upon the building, where, as he had been told, the lonely girl with the dark hair sat by the fire.

CHARLES DICKENS, Our Mutual Friend

Ascending or Descending Order

Material may be arranged, more or less formally, in an ascending or descending order. Although a newspaper reporter does not say so, he usually goes from the events or results that he considers the most newsworthy to those he considers least newsworthy, since he knows that many readers do not bother to read all of a news account. On the contrary, a teacher may start with the easiest part of a discussion and proceed to the more difficult. A writer or speaker endeavoring to gain an effect is likely to use the order of climax, from the least interesting to the most interesting, from the least damaging to the most damaging, or whatever. Or he may select one detail that will attract attention, and thereafter use the order of climax.

Usually the writer does not draw undue attention to his ordering of material in an ascending or descending order. He does not say, "The least important is . . . ," "The next least important is . . . ," but he has, himself, worked out the order with considerable care, and the reader is likely to be aware of this order. For example, J. N. Hook and E. G. Mathews, in *Modern American Grammar and Usage*, list what they call the seven groups of the users of American English as follows: linguistic paupers, unschooled linguistic colorists, the semischooled self-satisfied, linguistic aspirants, linguistic purists, linguistic self-adjusters, and schooled linguistic colorists. They never say that they are going from the least desirable to the most desirable, but their discussion makes this order obvious. Of the "linguistic paupers" they say, "Limited in ideas, in vocabulary, and in knowledge of linguistic devices, the members of this group tend to express themselves repetitiously, unimaginatively, often incoherently." The "unschooled linguistic colorists" are clearly more promising, for "Members of the second group . . . pay no more attention to 'correctness' than do the linguistic paupers, but their language is much more interesting because their observation and imagination are brighter, their vocabu-

lary is somewhat larger, and their use of grammatical constructions
is somewhat more varied." This sequence becomes clearer when
we get to the seventh level, to the schooled linguistic colorists,
of whom the authors say, "Take and give him an education that
does not dull his sensibilities, his play instinct, his love of experiment, his vitality. He will then be a member of Group 7. He will
write with gusto. . . ."

The ascending or descending order, although it has been
carefully worked out by the writer, may be apparent only in his
treatment of his material, not by any formal statement he makes.
Notice the following, the opening paragraph of a study the author
entitles "Southern Imperialism."

By the year 1824 a change was becoming evident in the South
that was to affect profoundly the course of southern thought in
regard to her peculiar institution. The passing of the long Virginia
hegemony was a sign that southern opinion was undergoing a
revolutionary overturn, and that leadership henceforth would rest
with men of a different philosophy. The humanitarian spirit that
marked the thought of the preceding generation was dying out, to
be replaced by a frank recognition of local economic interests.
Expectation that slavery was on the way to natural extinction was
yielding to the conviction that the system was too profitable to the
South to permit its extinction, and this in turn bred an imperious
desire to spread it westward to the Pacific. With this significant shift
from apology to imperialism, it became clear to ardent pro-slavery
men that lukewarm Virginians of the old tradition were not the
spokesmen to entrust with the fortunes of the South, and leadership
passed to the South Carolina school. In that momentous shift much
was implied. It was more than a shift from Jefferson to Calhoun,
from humanitarian idealism to economic realism. It marked the
complete ascendancy of a small minority of gentleman planters over
the inarticulate mass of southern yeomanry, and the assertion of the
aristocratic ideal as the goal of southern society. It denied the
principle of democracy as that principle was understood in the
North and West, and it rejected the new humanitarian spirit of
western civilization. It abandoned the Jeffersonian equalitarianism
that was so deeply rooted in the southern mind from Kentucky to
Georgia; it cast aside the agrarianism of John Taylor and the older
Virginians; and it set up in place of these congenial conceptions the
alien ideal of a Greek democracy. More momentous still, it threw
down the gauntlet to the ideals of the middle class, then in the first
flush of a triumphant career, and in the armed clash that eventually resulted, it was destroyed by that class.

VERNON LOUIS PARRINGTON, *Main Currents in American Thought*

One might notice that Parrington never says he is moving
from matters of lesser import to the fundamental issues, but his

treatment makes this organization clear. He mentions various minor matters, that the hegemony of Virginia was "undergoing a revolutionary overturn," that the "humanitarian spirit" was dying. Toward the middle of the paragraph he says that a "significant shift" occurred, so that the apologists for slavery gave way to "the South Carolina school." Then he includes a subtopic sentence, "In that momentous shift, much was implied." The remainder of the paragraph develops this idea, which is clearly identified as the most important by this climactic treatment and by the more extended attention given to it.

Logical Organization

In much expository writing, the chronological and spatial patterns common in narrative and descriptive writing are inadequate. The writer must reveal complicated relationships between the elements of his main idea, relationships that can be loosely described as "logical"—such as cause and effect, conclusion and reasons, comparison or contrast, or the steps in a chain of reasoning. Sometimes organization is logical in relatively strict senses. Commander X receives unexpected reinforcements just at the time the river freezes over between him and his enemy, and his scouts report that the opposing forces have been decimated by a plague. Commander X decides to attack. The organization of a description of this decision is clearly that of cause to effect. Conversely, consider the situation of a householder who discovers water leaking into his living room. The leak is an effect; what is the cause? He checks the flashing of the chimney, the calking around essential nails, the flue, and the concrete cap on the chimney. All seem to be in order. Then he remembers that although the chimney is built of porous blocks it has never been waterproofed. He concludes that the chimney needs waterproofing. The order here is clearly that of effect back to cause.

Most writing is essentially logical, if only loosely so. Consider the following, in which Thomas Jefferson is writing to a young student friend of his, urging him to examine objectively the claims of truth made by different religions.

For example, in the book of Joshua, we are told, the sun stood still several hours. Were we to read that fact in Livy or Tacitus, we should class it with their showers of blood, speaking of statues, beasts, etc. But is it said, that the writer of that book was inspired. Examine, therefore, candidly, what evidence there is of his having been inspired. The pretension is entitled to inquiry, because millions believe it. On the other hand, you are astronomer enough to know how contrary it is to the law of nature that a body revolving on its axis, as the earth does, should have stopped, should not, by that sudden stoppage, have prostrated animals, trees, buildings, and should after a certain time have resumed its revolutions, and that without a second general prostration. Is this arrest of the earth's motion, or the evidence which affirms it, most within the law of probabilities?

THOMAS JEFFERSON, Letter to Peter Carr

Jefferson is presenting a problem logically, and he orders his material with respect to logic, stating a proposition, breaking it into parts, presenting evidence, moving toward a conclusion.

The following paragraph is essentially logical, but less strictly so because the logical requirements are less rigid. The authors have said that language grows, and in this paragraph they are providing an example; their presentation, however, differs from Jefferson's in that they are presenting evidence, not balancing one set of evidence against another set.

> The history of *torpedo* offers a good illustration. It was originally the name of a fish of the ray family (*torpedinidae*), capable of emitting electric discharges. The name is derived from Latin *Torpere*, "to be numb or stiff." There existed in English names for this fish, as for instance, *cramp-fish, cramp-ray,* and *numb-fish,* which, however, were early superseded by the Latin term. The fish's curious electric power provided an atmosphere of mystery to a people who knew nothing of electricity. Naturally they regarded it as venomous and thought of it with horror. The *Oxford Dictionary* illustrates the use of the word in the sixteenth century with the quotation (1589), "like the fish Torpedo, which being towchd sends her venime alongst line and angle rod, till it cease on the finger, and so mar a fisher for euer." The traditionally dangerous nature of the fish made it early a source of metaphor. Christopher Marlowe applied it to a dangerous human being:
>
> > Fair queen, forbear to angle for the fish
> > Which, being caught, strikes him that takes it dead;
> > I mean that vile torpedo, Gaveston,
> > That now I hope floats on the Irish seas.
>
> Another metaphorical use is illustrated by Dr. Johnson's remark, "Tom Birch is as brisk as a bee in conversation; but no sooner does he take a pen in his hand, than it becomes a torpedo to him, and benumbs all his faculties."
>
> ROBERT M. ESTRICH and HANS SPERBER, Three Keys to Language

The organization of the material is to a degree chronological, but mainly logical, telling how the word came from Latin, how it acquired new implications by superstition, and then how it developed metaphorical uses.

Using an Outline

Outlining is a useful skill, both as an aid to reading and as a tool for organizing writing. For the reader an outline may provide a method of seeing more sharply the main plan of a piece of difficult prose, or of extracting main points in notes for future reference. Some technical reports, in fact, require an accompanying outline — sometimes the only part of the report that is read. For the writer an outline is a useful guide, a preliminary plan for organization, and also a useful way for testing the organization of a composition in revision.

Student writers often resist the suggestion that they should write from an outline. An outline, they insist, is too limiting; it "stifles inspiration." Usually such students either have the wrong notion of what an outline should be or have found that outlining requires clear thinking and do not want to think. Actually, an outline provides the easiest method of doing preliminary thinking and of keeping ideas in order as the writing progresses. The following versions of a theme suggest the advantages of working with an outline.

ORIGINAL

A word not only indicates an object but can also suggest an emotional meaning. The essence of poetry depends upon words that arouse the emotions of the reader. An experiment may be conducted to prove how much words mean in poetry. Replace the emotionally filled words with neutral ones, and all the poetic value will be knocked out of the poem by the change. Politicians are apt at changing the public's opinion merely by the use of words. *"Bolshevik," "Fascist," "reactionary," "revolutionary"* are examples of emotional words used by politicians. Emotional words find their place in poetry but are out of

REVISION

A word not only "means"; it conveys emotion. If we refer to a dog as a *mongrel,* we objectively define his pedigree, but we also reveal an attitude toward the dog.

The emotional meanings of words are useful, especially if the writer's purpose is to sway opinion. Poetry, for example, depends on words that arouse the emotions of the reader, as anyone may demonstrate if he will replace the emotion-filled words of a poem with neutral ones; all the poetic value will be knocked out of the poem by the change.

Emotional words have their place in poetry, but they are misplace in modern science where exact thinking is required. The scientist wants only the facts. He does not want to be swayed by words, only facts. This type of straight scientific thinking results in new discoveries. Science has worked hard ridding their books and discussions of emotional words; politics should do the same. The use of emotional words makes it hard for us to think straight in national and social problems. If clear unemotional words were used by people in the government, it would benefit our civilization. People would then be able to form their opinions by facts, not words.

Emotion-filled words are used not only by politicians but also by critics. By the use of words a critic can sway the public opinion against a writer, simply because he does not like the work.

We need to be careful not to form opinions on emotionally filled words.

[*The student theme printed above contains inaccuracies. Worse, it lacks any clear plan. An attempt to outline the theme reveals its weakness, for a meaningful outline proves to be almost impossible. An attempt might look like this:*

INTRODUCTION: Words have emotional as well as denotative meaning.

   I. Importance of emotional words to poetry
  II. Use of emotional words by politicians
 III. Avoidance of emotional words by scientists
 IV. Danger of emotional words in politics
  V. Use of emotional words by critics

leading when we are concerned with facts rather than attitudes. The scientist, for example, wants facts; he does not want to be swayed by words. He has worked to rid his books and discussion of emotional words, and by straight scientific thinking has made important discoveries. Politicians have not done the same. They are apt at changing the public's opinion merely by the use of such emotional words as *Bolshevik, Fascist, reactionary,* or *revolutionary.* They prevent straight thinking about national and social problems. If people in the government would use clear, unemotional words, we could form opinions on facts, not words, and society would benefit.

Emotional words can present a danger as well as an advantage, and we need to be careful not to form opinions on them.

[*The theme is still undeveloped, in spite of the addition of an illustration or two. But it does come nearer than the original to showing how ideas are related. The revision involved first of all a new outline:*

MAIN IDEA: Emotion-filled words are a handicap to scientific thinking.

INTRODUCTION: Words not only "mean"; they convey emotions.

  I. Usefulness of emotional words
    A. Usefulness in swaying opinions
    B. Usefulness in poetry
 II. Dangers of emotional words
    A. Use in science
    B. Use in politics

CONCLUSION: We should avoid emotion-filled words to form opinions.

The new outline classifies topics under two main headings and organizes the

CONCLUSION: We need to be careful in using emotion-filled words.

Topic II *is out of order. The outline reveals the lack of classification of material and the failure to subordinate minor to major topics.*]

paper around a central idea. It changes the illogical order revealed by the original outline. The writing follows the outline, corrects the obvious errors in accuracy, revises many of the sentences, and leaves out the undeveloped and nonessential example of the critic.]

Classification, Coordination, and Subordination

The basic processes for successful outlining have already been discussed, since the outline plans the classification of materials and indicates coordination and subordination (see chapter 5) while it develops from a main idea (see chapter 2). A statement of this idea, in a clear, complete sentence, is the first step in preparing an outline. For example, a writer has decided that he wants to say something about equal rights for students and has narrowed his topic to "Rights of Women at State University." Tentatively he decides that he wants to show that "At State University women do not have rights and privileges equal to those of the men." He begins his outline with this statement. He then jots down at random ideas that he thinks he might use, producing a list like the following:

1. Rules requiring women to live in dormitories
2. Rules regulating hours women must come in at night
3. The paragraph in the University Catalog concerning equal rights for all students
4. Women in student-body offices
5. Men's lounge in Union Building, but no women's lounge
6. As many women on campus as men
7. Women not willing to assert their rights
8. Rules requiring women to eat in dining hall
9. Swimming pool privileges
10. Rules on leaving campus
11. Intercollegiate athletics
12. College women just as responsible as college men
13. Attitudes of parents
14. The time Anne Wilkins was expelled but the boy who was equally guilty was not
15. Married women students
16. Women not interested in student government

17. Gymnasium and athletic facilities
18. Modern women taking equal responsibilities in the world
19. Military service of women

The list is a beginning, a record of random thoughts about a subject; it is not a record of organized thinking. To organize his material, the writer needs to analyze his subject and classify his details.

He may do so in a more or less systematic way. He may ask himself: What are the principal aspects of the life of women on the campus, and which of these do I wish to consider? That is, he may start by analyzing his subject and stating a main idea that can be used as the basis of classification. Or, he can start by examining his jottings to see whether he can observe any general groups and by classifying material under general headings. He can check his findings later by asking himself whether the headings he gets do or do not constitute an adequate analysis. As a matter of practice, of course, most writers use analysis and classification pretty much unconsciously as twin means of restricting a subject, ordering it, and developing it.

The student may now appropriately look over his jottings. If he is to write on discrimination against women at State University, some material is obviously inappropriate and can be thrown out, items 4 and 13, for instance. On the other hand, items 1 and 2 begin a list of discriminatory rules. Items 5 and 9 suggest a class of inequalities in university facilities. Items 3 and 6 might suggest reasons for equality. Item 7 might suggest a class that would require new material, reasons for inequalities. If the topic is restricted to unmarried women, item 15 would be eliminated. The list, then, could be rearranged and expanded by classification somewhat as follows:

Rules that discriminate against women
1. Rules requiring women to live in dormitories
2. Rules regulating hours women must come in at night
8. Rules requiring women to eat in dining hall
10. Rules on leaving campus
14. Expulsion of Anne Wilkins (might fit here as example of use of rules) Rules for sororities stricter than those for fraternities [*The writer thinks of a new point as he is making the classification.*]

Inequalities in university facilities
5. Men's lounge in Union Building
9. Swimming pool privileges
11. Intercollegiate athletics

17. Gymnasium and athletic facilities

Reasons why there should be equality

3. The statement of the University Catalog

6. As many women on campus as men

12. College women just as responsible as college men

18. Modern women taking equal responsibilities in the world

19. Military service of women

Causes for inequalities

7. Women not willing to assert their rights

16. Women not interested in student government
Tradition in colleges and world
Prevalence of men in administration and on faculties
Old prejudices against educating women
[*The writer adds new items.*]

Such classification is the beginning of an outline but the writer must still give the outline form by considering the classes in terms of the main idea and in terms of the proposed length of his paper. Strictly speaking, only the first two of the classes listed above apply to the proposed subject. Reasons for equality and causes of inequalities could be incorporated, but they would expand the paper beyond manageable length. The writer therefore limits his main headings to:

I. Rules that discriminate against women

II. Inequalities in university facilities

He then subordinates details to these main headings, thinks of further details to support his ideas, and chooses an order for his topics.

The degrees of subordination are conventionally indicated in an outline by indenting and by labeling subdivisions alternately with numbers and letters. A conventional form is shown below.

I. _____
    A. _____
        1. _____
        2. _____
    B. _____
II. _____
    A. _____
    B. _____
        1. _____
            a. _____

   (1) _____
   (2) _____
  b. _____
 2. _____
  a. _____
  b. _____
C. _____

THE COMPLETE OUTLINE   **6b**

    For a single paragraph or a short theme, a writer can keep his plan in mind without a written record, and an experienced writer knows basic patterns so well that he can compose still larger units without a written outline. A skilled carpenter can put together a considerable structure without a blueprint. But a contractor is not likely to start construction on a house without a set of carefully worked-out plans. A writer working seriously on an extensive piece of writing will not proceed without an outline.

    The outline is a means to an end, not an end in itself. Since it is practical, it should have the most useful form the writer can devise. For a paragraph or two or for an answer to an essay question on an examination, a few scribbled headings may be sufficient. For

GUIDE TO REVISION

6b   **Out**

Revise the outline so that each item is specific, coordinate items are in parallel form, and subdivisions are logical.

Getting a Deer

MAIN IDEA: How to get a deer

 I. Planning the hunt
  A. Reasons
  B. There are several methods
 II. Finding the deer
  A. Methods
  B. Incidents
   1. Tell about tracking one
 III. The kill
  A. Incidents
  B. Results

[*The outline shows almost no planning beyond suggesting a chronological arrangement in three stages. The statement of the main idea only repeats the topic. Items are so general that they provide no help in arranging material. Items I.B and II.B1 are not in parallel form, and if II.B1 is the only "incident" it is not a subdivision. One suspects that the writer has not thought much about what the "methods" and "incidents" are.*]

a longer composition a more careful outline is practical, but it should never be static. The writer should not hesitate to add to his outline any kind of note that may help him later. Often as he works he has useful ideas for a transition, a striking introduction, an incident or illustration, an apt phrase. He can add them to his outline so he will not forget to use them in appropriate places.

In general, the complete outline includes a statement of the main idea, a note on the introduction and conclusion, and a summary of the main topics to be discussed in the body of the paper, with relationships between them indicated by numbers and indentations. The outline should indicate how the paper is to be proportioned, so that the introduction, for example, does not include so much material that there is no room to develop main ideas. Items should be as specific as possible and should be parallel in form. Subdivisions should be elements of the topic they divide. Single subdivisions are illogical; it is impossible to divide something into one part. The following outline might be developed from the materials collected above for a paper on "Rights of Women in State University."

MAIN IDEA: At State University, women do not have rights and privileges equal to those of men.

INTRODUCTION: Use the statement in the University Catalog that all students have equal rights and privileges and point out that the paper will show the statement to be false.

[*A detail that the writer recalled when first thinking about the topic seems to provide a possible introduction. The writer gives himself a reminder.*]

I. Rules that discriminate against women
   A. Dormitory rules (begin paragraph with story of expulsion of Anne Wilkins)

   [*Again the writer sees a place to use a detail and makes a note.*]

      1. Rules requiring women to live in dormitories

      [*The writer sees need for classification more detailed than in preliminary organization.*]

      2. Rules on hours
      3. Registration and signout system
      4. Rules forbidding leaving dormitory and campus
   B. Sorority rules — regulations stricter than those for fraternities

   [*The expansion of point B is not illogically made a single subdivision.*]

   C. Rules requiring women to eat in dining hall
      1. Expense of dining hall
      2. Quality of food

134

II. Inequalities in university facilities. (Possible transition pointing out that above rules can be justified on ground that they are for students' "own good" but that other inequalities cannot.)

    [A lengthy note for future use records an idea that occurs to the writer as he makes the outline.]

  A. Social facilities

    [Coordination of topics is indicated by parallel form.]

    1. Lack of meeting places for women's organizations
    2. Lack of a room comparable to the men's lounge in the Union Building

  B. Athletic facilities

    1. Lack of women's sports comparable to men's intercollegiate athletic program
    2. Lack of equal swimming-pool privileges
    3. Restriction on women's use of gymnasium

CONCLUSION: Use idea that there are as many women on the campus as men, that they will have equal responsibilities in later life, and that they should have equal rights and privileges in college.

    [A possible conclusion is suggested by another of the groups of details rejected in preparing the body of the outline.]

The outline is a working guide. It should be used but should not be followed slavishly. Obviously a writer cannot visualize a paper perfectly. He will change his mind as he works out paragraphs and sentences, and he will think of new material. He should use his outline as a preliminary sketch, as a record of his prewriting, constantly subject to revision and expansion as the writing proceeds.

The Sentence Outline

Many writers prefer a sentence outline, which differs from the sample outline above only in that it employs sentences rather than topics. The outline above, put in the form of a sentence outline, would start as something like the following:

MAIN IDEA—At State University, women do not have rights and privileges equal to those of men.

INTRODUCTION—The University Catalog includes the statement that all students have equal rights, but this statement is not true, either in light of the regulations or the interpretation of regulations.

I. University rules discriminate against women.
   A. Dormitory rules discriminate against women, as is apparent in the case of Anne Wilkins.
      1. Rules require that all freshmen women live in dormitories, sorority houses, or private dwellings approved by the dean.

A respect for form and parallelism in an outline requires either that all headings in the outline be sentences or that none of them be, and certainly any outline used for itself should use one form or the other consistently. An outline, however, is usually practical; when the paper is written the outline has become useless, and many a competent writer pays little attention to whether his headings are parallel or not. The extra thinking required to make items parallel certainly does no harm, and most writers find it useful, even for a strictly utilitarian outline.

The following is an example of a sentence outline.

TOPIC: Satire in Washington Irving's *Knickerbocker's History of New York.*

[*The outline starts well; clearly, the author has thought his subject through. He has a main idea and he has phrased it with some care.*]

MAIN IDEA: The character of the satire in Irving's *History* changed as the work progressed and as the author matured, from genial persiflage and parody in the earlier chapters, to salty high comedy toward the middle, and to trenchant, even bitter satire after the death of Irving's fiancée.

INTRODUCTION: Writing is inevitably associated with the writer; Irving's *History* seems to provide a good example, reflecting the changing emotions of a brilliant but disturbed young man.

[*After the introductory material an outline should reveal levels of subordination and coordination. That is,* I *should be parallel with* II *and* III, *which should approximate the whole of the main idea. In this outline they will, if* III *reads something like the following:*

III. The latter chapters, written after the shock that followed his fiancée's death, are feverish, bitter, and a little sad.]

[*Similarly,* A *and* B *should approximate* I.]

I. The early chapters reflect Irving as an impudent young litterateur in a provincial city.
   A. In the early years of the nineteenth century, Irving was one of a group who wrote gay, witty articles.

136

1. The pieces were intended to poke good-natured fun at the stodgy burghers and to flaunt a zeal for the arts.
    a. The pieces were published as the *Salmagundi Papers.*
        (1) A salmagundi is a sort of stew.

    [*Obviously* a *and* (1) *are illogical; nothing can be subdivided into fewer than two. If there is no* b, *that is, if there was no second group of published papers,* a *can be incorporated within* 1. *Certainly* (1) *can be incorporated, if it is not so trivial as to be omitted.*]

2. Irving and his bachelor friends had gay parties in which they planned the next "paper" and laughed hilariously at the effect it would have.
    a. They delighted in listening to the lively speculation as to who the authors were.
    b. The authors, members of socially prominent families, knew all the important gossip, but wrote under pseudonyms.
    c. Irving and such friends as James K. Pauling thought these satirical pieces great good fun.

    [*Clearly, something is wrong here;* 1 *and* 2 *do not add up to* A. *Furthermore,* a, b, *and* c *do not add up to* 2. *Examination of the entries will reveal that the difficulty arises from the handling of what is now* 2. *If what is now* 2 *is made subordinate as* c, *and what is now* c *is made coordinate with* 1 *as* 2, *the whole will become relatively logical.*]

B. The earlier chapters of the *History* read like an extended *Salmagundi* paper.
    1. There is a tendency to try to be funny by using learned words to say nothing and to parody local history writers.
    2. The content is similar; here we find the same twitting of important people, especially venerated Dutchmen.
    3. Style.
        a. Irving seems to be trying to show off and to be funny—even when he is funny.
        b. Irving is a great American writer.

    [*Again, something is wrong.* A *and* B *do add up roughly to* I, *but* 1, 2, *and* 3 *do not add up to* B. *The trouble is that* B *should apparently have two parts, one for content, one for style. The present* 1 *is not parallel with the present* 2 *and* 3, *which should become* 1 *and* 2. *Then the present* 1 *will find its appropriate place along with the present* a *under* 3. *The present* b *probably has no business in the outline, at least not here. Number* 3 *should be rewritten; it is not a sentence and hence not parallel with the other sentences.*]

II. The body of the work reflects Irving as an unwilling law student, who took out some of his hatred of law by satirizing the foibles of officialdom.

[*The last two thirds of the outline are omitted. To round it out,* II *should be developed and* III *should read something like heading proposed above.*]

Utilizing the Outline To Check Logic

Obviously, an outline provides an orderly guide to writing, but it can have other uses as well. We have already noticed that it encourages thinking prior to writing; it also encourages continuity in thinking and in collecting material. Weeks, months, or even years may elapse during the preparation of an extensive piece of writing, but if the author has prepared a good outline with which to refresh his memory he can always return to his original plan. More immediately, the writer can use his outline to check the adequacy and logic of his planning or to guide him in revision of his first draft. Checking the finished draft against the outline or sketching a new outline of the draft can help the writer test for adequate planning, proportion, and logical relationships among items.

FOR STUDY AND WRITING

A Indicate which of the types of organization described in this chapter — or what combinations of organizational plans — you think would work best for each of the following compositions; be able to explain your choice.

1. A pamphlet explaining to incoming students what they should do during orientation week and registration.

2. A description of the library building intended to help new students find their way in it.

3. An essay for a campus magazine advocating the inclusion of students in the membership of all faculty committees dealing with the hiring, tenure, and salaries of faculty members.

4. A critical paper for a class in literature discussing Vachel Lindsay's poem "The Congo" and advancing the thesis that various kinds of sound effects are important to the total effect of the poem.

5. A report on discrimination in housing in your city presenting the results of two surveys, one a questionnaire to real estate companies asking for statements of their policies, the other a house-to-house canvass by black students attempting to rent.

6. A report for a physics course on a laboratory experiment on the speed of falling bodies.

7. A report to a club on a national convention to which you have been the club's delegate.

8. A letter to the editor of the campus newspaper protesting an editorial in a previous issue on the grounds that the editorial contained a number of factual errors.

B Below are preliminary notes for a theme called "Education for Women Today." They are not complete and are not necessarily pertinent or sufficiently specific. Using the list as a start, select a main idea for a possible theme and then construct an outline for it, using the notes that are pertinent. You will probably need to eliminate some notes, revise others, and add new ones to fit your main purpose.

1. Women in industry
2. Practical or cultural education
3. Education for successful marriage
4. Dormitory regulations for women
5. Women's physical education
6. Extracurricular activities for women
7. Discrimination between the sexes
8. Beauty shop apprenticeship
9. Teacher-training courses
10. Liberal arts training
11. Special course for social workers
12. Nurses' training
13. Laboratory technology for women
14. Preparation for life
15. Home economics
16. Courses in preparation for marriage
17. General culture
18. Business courses
19. The importance of English composition for the secretary
20. Number of women in college last year
21. Adult education
22. Schools of music and dance
23. Business colleges
24. The old-fashioned finishing school

C Comment on the weaknesses of the following outlines.

Outline 1

TOPIC: Satire in Movie Cartoons

MAIN IDEA: Satire in today's movie cartoons

I. Introduction
   A. Increasing tendency toward satire in cartoons
II. Caricatures of human beings
   A. Caricatures of types
      1. The man who loses his temper
         a. Donald Duck
      2. The pedant
         a. Examples
      3. Sentimental lovers
         a. Examples
   B. Actors may appear in cartoons
III. Satire on situations in life
   A. Domestic life
   B. National affairs
IV. Conclusion
   A. General quality of satire
   B. Conforms to attitudes already present in most people

Outline 2

TOPIC: Success in the American University

MAIN IDEA: To write about success at the university

I. Introduction
   A. The purpose of a university
      1. Details of the purpose
      2. Further details
   B. The organization of a university
      1. Schools and colleges
      2. The campus
      3. The administration
      4. Registrar's office, comptroller, etc.
      5. Fraternities and sororities
   C. Types of students in a university
      1. Men
      2. Women
      3. Foreign students
      4. Black students
      5. Independents
      6. Alumni organizations
II. Methods of attaining success in a university
   A. Attaining social success
      1. Fraternities and sororities
      2. Minority groups
      3. Ethnic groups
      4. Dances
      5. Games and athletic events
      6. Snack bars, soda fountains, etc.
         1. Make new friends, get dates, etc.
      7. The library
      8. Contacts that will be valuable in later life
      9. Religious life
   B. Athletic successes
      1. Major sports

140

2. Minor sports
3. Passing your courses
   1. Choosing courses you can pass
      a. Advice about choosing courses
III. Conclusion
   A. Success in college and social activity

D Below are numbered sentences that might be arranged into a short essay describing the group of sea animals that includes squids and octopuses. Make an outline arranging the sentences in the order they might have in a theme. Do not copy the statements; refer to them by number.

1. Among the animal's most interesting characteristics is its system of jet propulsion.

2. With this jet engine the cephalopod attains extraordinary speed.

3. They are octopuses, cuttlefish, and squids, and they are remarkable organisms in a variety of ways.

4. Among the thousands of creatures that inhabit the oceans of the world none is more interesting than those known as *Cephalopoda* or "head-footed ones."

5. The cephalopod can protect itself not only with its speed and remarkable strength for its size; it also has two physical properties with which it can become almost invisible.

6. Some of the tiny, slim varieties streak through the water as fast as flies move through the air.

7. They can leap from the water and dart by so fast that the eye cannot follow them.

8. Cephalopods may not live up to all the fantastic yarns about them told by ancient mariners, but they are certainly among the most interesting of the animals of the sea.

9. First, it developed the technique of the smoke screen long before modern navies.

10. The cephalopod is encased in a long, slim cloak, with a muscular collar that rings its neck and a funnel that sticks up in front.

11. Larger varieties, it is estimated, move over the surface of the ocean faster than the fastest speedboat.

12. The cephalopods have little ink sacs that manufacture and store ink, and they can squirt sepia cloud screens to shield them from their enemies.

13. It can then close the collar and squeeze its body suddenly and violently.

14. Swimming on its belly, the octopus or squid can pump water into its body cavity through the space between this collar and its neck.

15. They also can hide themselves because of their chameleon-like ability to change colors.

16. The water shoots out the funnel, propelling the animal backward.

17. The propulsion system of the squid or octopus is no more remarkable than its special devices for defense.

18. They can turn purple when annoyed, or on white sand they can pale to near invisibility.

E Use the following as a main idea: "The story of the letter *A* reflects the history of the alphabet." Construct a suitable outline by classifying, coordinating, and subordinating. Reject any material not pertinent, and note any main divisions that need to be further divided or developed and any details that have no general heading. Remember that Greek and Roman times are often referred to as *classical,* that the Egyptians, Babylonians, and Semites were preclassical peoples, and that the periods between the classical age and the Renaissance are often lumped together and called the Middle Ages, for which the adjective is *medieval.*

Changes in Latin

Sounds of the various letters

Early known forms of *A*

Introduction—Story of how I learned letter *A*

Changes during the Middle Ages leading to modern upper-case *A*

Lost Greek forms of *A*

Greek reversal of the letter

Development of North Semite *A* into Phoenician *A*

The North Semites and the earliest known form of *A*

Modern upper-case *A* from the medieval book hand

Difference between *a* and *an*

Contributions of medieval Irish scribes to modern upper-case *A*

Changes in Greek

Interesting details about *U* and *V*

Medieval and more recent forms of the letter

Influence of Greek "boustrophedon" writing on *A*

Symbol for Egyptian sacred bull as possible ancestor of *A*

Contributions of medieval French scribes to modern upper-case *A*

Hypothetical origins of *A*

Modern upper-case *A* from medieval court hand

Developments in classical times

Babylonian aleph as possible ancestor of *A*

Preclassical history of *A*

COHERENCE: CONTINUITY, INTRODUCTIONS, CONCLUSIONS

CHAPTER 7

Devices for guiding the reader give writing coherence and clarify organization.

No matter how skillfully the writer has ordered his materials, he needs also to direct the reader from one idea to the next, to help him see the plan of the composition. The writer must blaze the trail, pointing the direction at the beginning, providing signs along the way, and marking the end of the route. Consider the following comments about the American opossum, which might serve as a list of details for the development of a paragraph.

The opossum has survived in definitely hostile surroundings for seventy million years.

The opossum is small; it can easily find hiding places.

The opossum can always find a little food, while big animals starve.

The individual opossum is not very delicate; it can stand severe punishment.

It "plays 'possum" when it gets into trouble.

It can go without food for a long time.

Many different things are food to an opossum.

Traits of the opossum have a high survival value.

The opossum is a survivor from the Age of Reptiles.

The details have been abstracted from a paragraph and are listed in the order in which they originally appeared, but merely running the items together would not produce a clear paragraph. The material would have a kind of unity, because the details all refer to the same topic, but the reader would lack guidance in seeing relationships, in following the writer's plan. Compare the original:

> The reasons our opossum has survived in definitely hostile surroundings for 70 million years are evident. One is his small size: small animals always find hiding places, they always find a little food, where the big ones starve. Another of its assets was its astounding fecundity: if local catastrophes left only a few survivors, it did not take long to re-establish a thriving population. Also the individual opossum is not exactly delicate: it can stand severe punishment— during which it "plays 'possum" and then scampers away—and it can go without food for a considerable time. Finally, a great many different things are "food" to an opossum. Each of these traits has a high survival value, and their combination has presented the United States with a survivor from the Age of Reptiles.
>
> WILLY LEY, *The Lungfish and the Unicorn*

The paragraph differs from the list largely because it has coherence. The writer of the paragraph has framed his sentences to provide smooth transitions from one idea to the next. The opening sentence provides an introduction, indicating the significance of the details that follow, that they are reasons. The final sentence provides a conclusion, summarizing the significance of the details. On a small scale the paragraph demonstrates the main ways in which a writer can gain coherence.

CONTINUITY

7a

As indicated in chapter 3 writing can be thought of as a flow or sequence, with every unit making a commitment for what is to follow while responding to what has preceded. The writer can use a variety of structural devices to smooth this flow. For one thing, almost every sentence in clear prose is linked with the sentences around it by direct or implied references. Pronouns in one sentence may refer to words in the sentence before. The idea of one sentence may be briefly rephrased in another. Repeated references to the central idea of the paragraph may serve to bind sentences together. These central ideas echoing through the composition—along with transitional expressions—make the parts of the writing cohere and draw the reader effortlessly along the trail of the writer's thoughts. The following passage indicates how parts of clear writing are linked together.

7a

Con

Revise, using such devices as repetition, transitional words, and parallel order to make sentences "track."

ORIGINAL

Modern scholars now agree that the ancestor of the Romance languages is not now much taught in our schools. It was Vulgar Latin, which is usually taught today only in graduate schools. The kind of language that was written by Virgil and Cicero is the kind that is usually taught both in high school and in college, but it is not the kind from which French or any other language of that sort has come. In English we have words from the language of the Romans, and some of those words did come from the language written by famous Romans. However, what are called Romance languages did not. The working men were the ones who determined the language in the various countries that had been conquered by Caesar and other classical generals. Church Latin is still spoken but is not much taught. Vulgar Latin is made up of words spoken by the common people, or *vulgus.*

[*This paragraph is confused, partly because of faulty order, but partly also because sentences are not linked by synonyms and repeated words. Three ideas run parallel in the paragraph: the kinds of Latin, the descent of the Romance language, the teaching of Latin in the schools. These ideas should be distinct but should also be tied together.*]

REVISION

The modern Romance languages descended from Latin, but not from the Latin usually taught in the schools. There are several Latins, notably Classical Latin, Church Latin, and Vulgar Latin. Of these three divisions of the Latin language, Classical Latin is taught almost exclusively. Church Latin is still spoken but is seldom taught to undergraduates. Vulgar Latin is taught only in a few graduate schools. Yet Vulgar Latin is the ancestor of all modern Romance languages—Italian, French, Spanish, Portuguese, and Romanic. Classical Latin has accounted for words borrowed by these languages, as it accounted for words borrowed by English, but all scholars now agree that the Romance languages did not come from the classical speech of Virgil and Cicero. French and Italian and Spanish came from the Latin speakers who were working in France and Italy and Spain, the soldiers, the merchants, the laboring men, that is, the *vulgus* whose speech is known as Vulgar Latin.

[*The three ideas are carried through the paragraph by repetition of such words as* Latin, *and the generous use of such synonyms and partial synonyms as "Vulgar Latin" and "the classical speech of Virgil and Cicero."*]

A driver doesn't have to look at his road map once he starts on a highway, as long as he doesn't come to any intersections. He doesn't have to worry about which way to go if he has no choice about it. But when he comes to a crossroads, with signs pointing in various directions — then he can't just let the road decide where he is to go; he has to make up his mind. He has to stop and think.

MONROE C. BEARDSLEY, *Thinking Straight*

The passage carries through a single subject, *driver,* designated by the pronoun *he* after the first mention. Sentences cohere, also, by the repetition of patterns like *doesn't have to* and *has to, intersections* and *crossroads;* the connective *but* holds the two main parts of the paragraph together, marking the contrast between them.

Another passage relies on different echoes of meaning:

In time of peace in the modern world, if one is thoughtful and careful, it is rather more difficult to be killed or maimed in the outland places of the globe than it is in the streets of our great cities, but the atavistic urge toward danger persists and its satisfaction is called adventure. However, your adventurer feels no gratification in crossing Market Street in San Francisco against the traffic. Instead, he will go to a good deal of trouble and expense to get himself killed in the South Seas. (In reputedly rough water, he will go in a canoe; he will expose his tolerant and uninoculated blood to strange viruses.) This is adventure. It is possible that his ancestor, wearying of the humdrum attacks of the saber-tooth, longed for the good old days of pterodactyl and triceratops.

JOHN STEINBECK and EDWARD F. RICKETTS, *Sea of Cortez*

A pronoun subject, standing for *adventurer,* carries through, but references to adventure and danger also hold the paragraph together. *However* and *instead* mark shifts in the thought.

As the examples above indicate, repetition of a subject from sentence to sentence is one of the most obvious ways to promote **146**

continuity. A repeated subject, often expressed through synonyms or pronouns, helps to keep attention focused. Compare the
following versions of the start of a student theme:

ORIGINAL

I can remember when tires were
quite different from what they are
today. Twenty to thirty thousand
miles is not now considered unusual tire mileage, provided tires
are kept at proper inflation and
are not run at excessive speeds.
Also, anybody can change a tire
with ease now. The modern tire
is a marvel and a joy. A good tire,
when it is new, will turn most nails
and almost any old tire ought to
zip through broken glass from milk
bottles without a scratch. You can
buy tires in nonskid, high-speed,
and antisnow types. Some tires
come reinforced with steel plates
or fiberglass belts.

REVISION

To anyone who knew touring in
the old days, the modern automobile tire is a marvel and a joy. It will
run, with proper care, twenty thousand to thirty thousand miles. It
will zip through smashed milk bottles without a scratch. When new,
it will turn most tacks and nails.
At reasonable speeds and with
proper pressure, it is almost blow-
out-proof, especially when reinforced with steel plates or fiberglass
belts. It is available in nonskid,
high-speed, and snow types. Best
of all, it can be changed in a few
minutes.

The ancestor of the modern tire,
however, was quite different. . . .

The original is needlessly confusing because the subject shifts from
sentence to sentence. The revision improves continuity and coherence because the subject of discussion, modern tires, has become
the grammatical subject of the sentences.

Synonyms and pronouns are especially useful for coherence.
They provide a means of continuing key ideas without the dis-
tractions of excessive repetition of the same word. *It* as a substitute
for "the modern automobile tire" in the example promotes clarity
and economy. Even repetition is likely to be less annoying than
attempts to avoid it with contrived substitutions, but notice the use
of synonyms for *mayor* in the revision of the following.

ORIGINAL

More and more black mayors
are taking over our cities, and as
yet we do not know what effect
these black mayors may have on
government. These mayors, who
get their power through the growing ghettos, are bound to influence
politics generally, because mayors
become powerful figures by virtue

REVISION

More and more black mayors,
raised to eminence by voters in the
ghettos, are taking over our cities,
but as yet we cannot assess their
influence on government. The
power that resides in City Hall,
however, strengthened by the size
of municipal budgets and the fact
that a municipal leader may become

147

of the money a mayor controls and through the possibility that a mayor may become a governor or a national figure. a state or national leader, is bound to influence politics generally.

Some of the uses of *mayor* can simply be omitted, and some can be replaced by pronouns. Furthermore, the shifts to substitutions like "the power that resides in City Hall" and "municipal leader" work here because they have connotations more precise for the context.

Continuity and Word Order

The links between sentences, the structural indicators of the commitment-response patterns of ideas, can be reinforced through word order.

Repetitions of sentence patterns emphasize parallels or contrasts in ideas and help the reader move smoothly from sentence to sentence, from paragraph to paragraph. In both paragraphs above, the sentence subjects link one sentence to the next, mainly because each sentence repeats the order of the preceding one. The following two sentences are linked, even though the subjects differ, because the subjects appear in the same relative place in each:

> An old man stood in front of the monkey cage excitedly throwing peanuts at a score of begging arms. A small boy only a few feet away sat with his face buried in a comic book.

The repetition of word order sharpens the contrast between the two main actions. On the other hand, variations from usual word order may provide bridges, carrying special emphasis from one sentence to another:

> In front of the monkey cage stood an old man, excitedly throwing peanuts at a score of begging arms. A few feet away sat a small boy, his face buried in a comic book.

The shift in order throws emphasis on the location, heightens the contrast in the actions by stressing the nearness of the two persons, and helps link the sentences through the repetition of the reversed pattern. There is some loss of continuity when the word order pattern is not repeated, as in the following:

> In front of the monkey cage stood an old man, excitedly throwing peanuts at a score of begging arms. A small boy only a few feet away sat with his face buried in a comic book.

148

Consider the following sentence: "This volunteer they rejected." Standing alone, it seems unnecessarily backward, but when it is put into its context, the reasons for the irregular order are clear: "One volunteer refused to undergo the rigorous arctic training course. This volunteer they rejected." Similarly, "The ashes Daniel spread over the floor" at first seems an unjustifiable inversion. In its context, however, the inversion proves valid: "The servant brought a gleaming torch and a sack of ashes. He set the torch in a bracket on the wall. The ashes Daniel spread over the floor."

Sometimes coherence and continuity may justify quite unusual word order or variations on usual sentence patterns (see chapter 18). More frequently, however, continuity is enforced by the repetition of standard sentence patterns beginning with a subject and verb, as in the following passage (with italics marking subjects and verbs in main patterns).

> In Connecticut the *chickadees came* to see me when I did not go to see them. In Arizona the desert *birds do* the same, though the attraction—which was certainly not me in either case—is water rather than food. A curved-billed *thrasher,* his threatening beak half-open like the mouth of a panting dog, *approaches* defiantly, scattering the smaller birds as he comes. A cactus *wren,* the largest and boldest of the wren tribe, impudently *invades* my porch and even *jumps* to a window sill to peer at me through the glass. And as I know from experience, *he will invade* even the house if I leave a door open and *will carry* away for his nest any material available. Only the large white-winged *dove does* not *seem* to notice that this is an unusually warm day. *He will fly* away to Mexico at the first hint that summer is over and now, when the temperature in the sun must be at least 120 degrees, *he seems to be saying,* "But we don't call this hot in Campeche."
>
> JOSEPH WOOD KRUTCH, *The Voice of the Desert*

The reader moves easily from sentence to sentence, because the sentence pattern continues.

The following versions of a paragraph from a theme illustrate the use of repeated constructions to provide continuity.

ORIGINAL

Most co-eds at State University did not come here to get married, though the president did make a joke something like that. We didn't come to get dates, either, at least not mainly, though the Dean kind of hinted that. And I suppose the

REVISION

Whatever the administration may imply, the co-eds at State University have not come here mainly to get married. Whatever the Dean of Women may say, they have not come mainly to get dates. And whatever the faculty may think, they

| profs think we are just being nice to them to get good grades without working. | have not come mainly to get good grades by flashing their smiles at professors. |

The effect of the parallel sentences in the revision may be more dramatic than most writing requires, but the revision does guide the reader more clearly than the original.

Continuity Through Transitional Words

Relationships can be clarified further by transitional words, words that identify the relationship between the parts of a paragraph and thus improve continuity. The following are some of the more useful transitional words:

> To mark an addition: *and, furthermore, next, moreover, in addition, again, also, likewise, similarly, finally, second*
>
> To introduce or to emphasize a contrast or alternative: *but, or, nor, still, however, nevertheless, on the contrary, on the other hand, conversely*
>
> To mark a conclusion: *therefore, thus, then, in conclusion, consequently, as a result, in other words, accordingly*
>
> To introduce an illustration or example: *thus, for example, for instance, that is, namely*

Others indicate shifts of time or introduce clauses; almost all connectives can provide transitions. Overuse of transitional expressions makes stiff prose; careful use of them helps make clear prose.

TRANSITIONS

7b

Coherence requires continuity to carry a topic through its development, but it also requires easy movement from one topic to another, smooth transitions. Most frequently topic sentences (see chapter 2) provide such transitions, leading the reader from one topic-comment unit to another, introducing a new topic while linking what is to come with what has preceded. Consider, for example, the following three topic sentences, taken at random from a discussion of the formation of a national government in America:

> This solution was achieved under the Articles of Confederation, a formal agreement which had loosely unified the colonies since 1781. . . .

Thus a new colonial policy based upon the principle of equality was inaugurated. . . .

Unfortunately, however, in the solution of other problems the Articles of Confederation proved disappointing.

In the first of the topic sentences, "This solution" refers directly to what has preceded; then the sentence goes on to introduce the Articles of Confederation as the topic of its paragraph. The second sentence refers with the word *thus*, but it provides continuity also because it summarizes the entire preceding paragraph, putting the material into new terms that emphasize the new aspect of the topic to be considered, the use of equality as a basis of the policy. The third provides a transition in two ways, by echoing the word *solution* from the first sentence and by referring to previous material with "other problems."

GUIDE TO REVISION

7b   **Trans**

Revise to provide adequate transition, through either a topic sentence or a transitional paragraph.

ORIGINAL

. . . *Derring-do* is an example of a meaning that has developed from misunderstanding, the original being something like "He was one of few daring do it."

Edward Sapir, in his book, *Language,* makes use of the English word *foot, feet* to illustrate linguistic change, what he calls drift.

[*This transition is clumsy; concluding and topic sentences would smooth it out, but since this is a turning point in the discussion, a transitional paragraph like that in the revision is useful. The writer is discussing two books on language. In the section with which the passage above opens, he has said that the first of the books is concerned with stories about odd words. He is now ready to turn to a more penetrating book by Sapir.*]

REVISION

. . . *Derring-do* is an example of a meaning that has developed from misunderstanding, the original being something like "He was one of few daring do it."

Thus, the first of the two books under discussion is mainly concerned with telling engaging stories about the origin or growth of odd words. The second, Edward Sapir's *Language,* is quite different; Sapir studies words—common words more than odd ones—to try to understand the nature and working of language.

Take, for example, his illustrations for his theory of linguistic change of the sort he calls drift. He starts with the common English words *foot* and *feet,* and by tracing these to such early forms as *foti* in Gothic. . . .

Frequently, in order to clarify a transition, a writer uses two sentences, making his transition in the first sentence of the paragraph and stating his topic in the second. For example, DeWitt H. Parker moves to a new section of an essay on aesthetics as follows:

> In our discussion thus far, we have been assuming the possibility of aesthetic theory. But what shall we say in answer to the mystic who tells us that beauty is indefinable?

The first sentence summarizes what has preceded. The second introduces the topic of the paragraph, the possibilities of defining beauty.

Transitional Paragraphs

For brief papers, well-written topic sentences can supply all the transitional material necessary. Longer compositions may be broken into large divisions containing several paragraphs with transitions important enough to require brief transitional paragraphs. Thomas Henry Huxley, in an essay on the method of scientific investigation, moves from a series of examples of how we behave "scientifically" in everyday life to a more serious discussion of causal relationships, relying on the following relatively formal paragraph:

> So much, then, by way of proof that the method of establishing laws in science is exactly the same as that pursued in common life. Let us now turn to another matter (though really it is but another phase of the same question), and that is, the method by which, from the relations of certain phenomena, we prove that some stand in the position of causes toward the others.
>
> THOMAS HENRY HUXLEY, "Darwiniana"

The paragraph has the qualities of a good topic sentence used transitionally, although it is developed more fully. Its first sentence summarizes what has preceded; the second tells us precisely and directly what is to follow.

Transitions and Organization

As one of their major contributions to coherence transitional devices reveal the main outline of a composition. The selections in chapter 5 illustrate the use of fairly obvious signposts—*first, second, third,* etc. The following passages from a longer essay by

152

Sir Arthur Keith show how topic sentences and transitional paragraphs may provide a map for a composition's organization.

In all the medical schools of London a notice is posted over the door leading to the dissecting room forbidding strangers to enter. I propose, however, to push the door open and ask the reader to accompany me within. . . . We propose to watch them [the students] at work. Each student is at his allotted part, and if we observe them in turn we shall, in an hour or less, obtain an idea of the main tissues and structures which enter into the composition of the human body.

[These passages appear in the opening paragraph, which serves as an introduction showing the reader the overall purpose of the essay and the writer's plan for achieving it—by observing the students as they dissect. The paragraph commits the writer to describe the "main tissues and structures" of the human body.]

By good fortune a dissection is in progress in front of the wrist, which displays, amongst other structures the radial artery. . . .

[The second paragraph locates the reader near the first student.]

Lying side by side with the sinews of the wrist there is another cord. . . . It is the median nerve. . . .

[The third paragraph opens with a sentence linking the preceding topic, "sinews of the wrist," with a new one, "the median nerve."]

We propose to observe the dissector as he traces the radial artery to the heart. . . .

Before leaving the dissection we have been surveying it will be well to see one of those marvelously contrived structures known as a joint. . . .

[The reader is led to another stage in this dissection and is also warned of a change to come.]

We have surveyed the anatomy at the wrist in some detail and with a very distinct purpose. . . .

[A summary or transitional paragraph marks the end of this episode; the reader is led to a turn in the trail.]

We now propose to transfer our attention for a short time to two students who are uncovering the parts in front of the neck between the chin and breastbone or sternum. . . .

[The writer indicates a major shift to a new dissection.]

Our time with the students in the dissection room has almost expired; there remains only a moment to glance at a dissection which is exposing the important organs which are enclosed within the thorax and abdomen. . . .

[The writer marks another turn and also prepares the reader for the end of the trail.]

Our cursory visit to the dissecting room has not been in vain if the reader has realized how complex the structure of the human body really is, and how necessary it is that those who have to cure its disorders should try to understand the intricacy of its mechanism. . . .

"Man: A History of the Human Body"

[Transitional materials have kept the reader informed of the author's subsidiary commitments as these have developed. The conclusion reminds the reader of the purpose of the discussion, of the writer's overriding commitment.]

The essay includes even more guides to its general pattern than have been excerpted here, but these samples, most of them opening sentences of paragraphs, illustrate the importance of such aids. These passages outline the complete essay:

MAIN IDEA: A visit to the dissecting room reveals the complexity of the human body and the importance of studying it.

  I. The anatomy at the wrist: the first dissection
      A. The radial artery
      B. The median nerve
      C. Tracing the radial artery to the heart
      D. The joint
  II. The parts in front of the neck
  III. Organs within the thorax and abdomen

The reader can follow clearly and easily because the writer has revealed his outline step by step.

INTRODUCTIONS

7c

"The beginning," Plato wrote long ago, "is the most important part of the work." It is important because it fixes the reader's attention, sets the tone of the work, and suggests what it is to be about. It may also, of course, in a longer work, provide any necessary background information about the subject or the circumstances of the writing or the validity of the material. It need not be long; in fact, papers suffer more frequently from top-heavy, rambling introductions than from brevity in the beginning. But whatever else it does, the introduction must introduce.

An introduction usually presents the main idea of the paper, either in a direct statement or by implication; it makes the commitment that the remainder of the paper is to fulfill. It identifies the subject and leads gracefully into the body of the discussion. There is no recipe for introductions; various approaches may serve, and the writer may change his introduction half a dozen times before he finishes the final draft. He may prepare a very formal introduction he knows he will discard, go on to complete the writing, and then return to work out a more interesting beginning, or he may hit upon an idea for an introduction when he is first considering his subject. The following are some characteristics of good introductions.

GUIDE TO REVISION

7c   **Intro**

Revise the introduction so that it presents the subject, is connected to the main idea, is independent, is in proportion, and is not merely an apology.

ORIGINAL

REVISION

Proper Feeding of Cattle

Proper Feeding of Cattle

[*The main idea of the paper is that scientific feeding of cattle has improved the entire beef industry.*]

I have always been interested in cattle, and I have noticed the growing importance of the cattle industry in all parts of the country. Not only has the quality of American beef improved in recent years, but the raising of beef cattle has spread throughout the nation.

The first requirement of proper feeding for beef cattle is. . . .

The American beef industry has shown important developments in recent years. Not only has cattle raising been introduced in areas formerly thought unsuitable; at the same time the quality of beef has improved. The progress is due primarily to the introduction of scientific feeding.

The first requirement of. . . .

[*The revision omits superfluous, confusing material and tells what the paper is about; it introduces.*]

College Humor

College Humor

[*The main idea of this paper is that practical joking in college has remained about the same for many years.*]

Last week four mechanical engineering students dismantled a Model-T Ford, carried the parts quietly up the back stairs of the dormitory one night, and reassembled the car in the third-floor hall. It was an interesting example of college humor, of the practical variety, as it exists in colleges today.

[*The incident attracts the reader's attention, but the second sentence does not relate it to the main idea of the paper.*]

Last week four mechanical engineering students dismantled a Model-T Ford, carried the parts quietly up the back stairs of the dormitory one night, and reassembled the car in the third-floor hall. Undergraduates admired, janitors were puzzled, and the incident made the national news reports, but it was only a repetition of a pattern that has characterized practical jokes in college for many years.

[*The new transitional sentence interprets the introduction in terms of the main idea of the paper.*]

---

1. *An introduction should introduce.* The introduction should present both the topic and the writer to the reader. The writer may wish to hold back a bald statement of his topic, while preparing his reader for it, but the reader should be able to sense that a piece of writing is moving in an orderly way, and that he will know the topic by the time he needs it. Even a blunt statement, however, is better than a vague or puzzling introduction. Inevitably, the opening of a composition introduces the writer; the author may not wish to attract attention to himself, but the reader, consciously or unconsciously, starts making estimates of the writer. An author does well to consider how he wishes to appear before the reader, and draft his introduction accordingly.

The Porn Capital of America

Everything's up to date in San Francisco these days, which means, according to some, that they've gone about as far as they can go. Too far for Dianne Feinstein, the attractive brunette who happens to be president of the city's Board of Supervisors. Mrs. Feinstein and a party of concerned citizens recently made an educational tour of the town's booming pornographic establishments, or porn shops, as they're more familiarly known to thousands of contented patrons. What they found appalled them. "Appalling is a modest term," wrote one, columnist Merla Z. Goerner . . .

WILLIAM MURRAY

[*The author announces his subject at once: he will write about the fact that pornography has recently become common and blatantly frank in San Francisco and that important people disapprove. Less formally, he introduces himself; he does not say that he is a published novelist, but his whole manner lets the reader know that he is an accomplished writer. He is a conversant person; he recalls the song from* Oklahoma! *about everything being up to date in Kansas City. He has a sense of humor; notice the reference to "contented patrons." He expects to be objective; he tells what people did and quotes what they say.*]

2. *The introduction should be independent of the title.* The title may be changed or may be dropped from a paper submitted for publication. Especially, a pronoun or adjective like *this* or *these* referring to the title should not open a paper. Compare:

ORIGINAL

Freedom of Speech

This subject is basic to the survival of democracy in America.

[*The reference to the title betrays the writer into imprecise diction.* Freedom, *not the* subject, *is basic.*]

REVISION

Freedom of Speech

Freedom of speech is basic to the survival of democracy in America.

[*Repetition of the title makes the introduction independent, and also more accurate.*]

156

3. *Exemplary material should be related to the composition.* If the writer begins with an anecdote or example, he should connect it clearly with the main idea of the paper. No matter how amusing a story may be, it is useless as an introduction if its relevance to the topic is not made clear.

Once, many years ago, 9 West 102nd Street certainly housed a respectable family, probably with a maid to open the door. Even now, it looks rather shabbily respectable from the outside. Inside, it is probably the closest thing to hell to be found in New York City, where there are a lot of hellish places.

For 9 West 102nd Street is known throughout the East as a place where a desperate man can get a sure heroin fix.

STEWART ALSOP

[*The first brief paragraph provides a startling example, based on contrast. The next paragraph begins with an explanation and an application of the example to the article as a whole. The conclusion, that something must be done about the drug problem, and soon, is only foreshadowed.*]

4. *The introduction should be in proportion.* Introductions should be as brief as may be practical. Most student themes are short enough that they require only a brief introduction. The writer who rambles through 200 words to introduce a 500-word paper is obviously slighting his main point. Compare:

ORIGINAL

Decorating a Living Room

As a hobby, I draw house plans, one of which I hope to have blueprinted and built in the near future. I have been working on various plans for many years, and I find the hobby fascinating. It is instructive as well as pleasant, and I have learned many things from my experiments. My first plans were amateurish and impractical. The plans I draw now are more detailed and more concerned with functional requirements. I have been especially interested in plans for decorating living rooms because actually the living room sets the theme for the rest of the house.

REVISION

Decorating a Living Room

Decorating the living room is the most important step in decorating a house, since the living room sets the theme for all the other rooms. . . .

[*The introduction was obviously too long for a paper of 300 words. The solution, as usual, is to omit material not relevant to the main purpose of the paper. The omission makes the paper more direct as well as better proportioned. The student might appropriately write, on another occasion, a paper detailing his experiences as an amateur architect, but the material is not appropriate here.*]

5. *An introduction should not apologize.* Although qualifying the goals of a composition may be appropriate in an introduction,

the apologetic introduction seldom succeeds. If the apologetic writer means what he says, he should have kept his pen in his pocket. If he does not mean it and is being falsely modest, the reader sees the deception. Compare:

ORIGINAL

Illegal Gambling

I have no firsthand knowledge of illegal gambling, and perhaps I should not write about it. But I do have some opinions. . . .

[*One suspects that the writer's first impulse was right; he should have changed his topic.*]

REVISION

Illegal Gambling

Illegal gambling is dangerous to our society mainly because of the other crimes that accompany it.

[*The writer has thought of the "opinion," which is what he planned to discuss, and he has used it to start the paper.*]

Types of Introductions

The following paragraphs illustrate some common ways of getting a paper started.

1. *Statement of proposition.* Often a direct statement of the proposition to be defended provides a good introduction.

The Growing Power of Admen

America's advertising industry is moving into a commanding role in our society. Its executives are becoming masters of our economic destiny, the engineers behind some of our most successful political campaigns. . . .
         VANCE PACKARD

[*Here Packard begins with his general thesis, continues with general illustrations, and goes on to more specific evidence.*]

2. *Presentation of factual background.* An opening offering factual statements to provide some justification or background or reason for the proposition of the composition is one of the most common and most successful.

What Every Writer Must Learn

The teaching of writing has become practically a profession by now. There is hardly a college in the land that does not offer at least one course in "creative writing" (whatever that is) by some "teacher of writing" (whoever he is). There are, moreover, at least fifty annual

[*The introduction continues, after this opening, to assert that writing requires inventiveness and then to consider six ways in which the writer's talents for creation may be realized.*]

158

writers' conferences now functioning among us with something like fifty degrees of competence. And there seems to be no way of counting the number of literary counselors, good and bad, who are prepared to promise that they can teach a writer what he needs to know.

JOHN CIARDI

3. *Questions to isolate a problem.* Opening a paper with a series of questions to lead to the main topic can be effective, but this device must be used with caution, for in unskilled hands it can seem over-oratorical and affected.

Force and Freedom

Can there be a moral basis for freedom in a world of force? This is one of the ugly questions that disturb many intelligent people at this moment. Can we reconcile the doctrine of military force—the idea of killing men in war—with a moral purpose? As a matter of history, freedom has often emerged from the successful use of force; yet we abominate war as intensely as we love freedom. How are we to resolve this paradox?

JAMES BRYANT CONANT

[*A series of questions leads to the basic problem of the paper: the relationship between force and freedom. The first question is the main one the writer will try to answer.*]

4. *Analysis.* The introduction may divide the subject into its parts and indicate which parts will have emphasis (see chapter 6).

Prospects in the Arts and Sciences

The words "prospects in the arts and sciences" mean two quite different things to me. One is prophecy: What will the scientists discover and the painters paint, what new forms will alter music, what parts of experience will newly yield to objective description? The other meaning is that of a view: What do we see when we look at the world today and compare it with the past? I am not a prophet; and I cannot very well

[*The introduction is an excellent model of the careful analytic opening. It divides the topic into two parts, "prophecy" and "view," announces that it will consider only the second of these, and tells the reader why.*]

159

speak to the first subject, though in many ways I should like to. I shall try to speak to the second, because there are some features of this view which seem to me so remarkable, so new and so arresting, that it may be worth turning our eyes to them; it may even help us create and shape the future better, though we cannot foretell it.

J. ROBERT OPPENHEIMER

5. *Statement of view the writer is to oppose.* The writer may begin by describing a popular opinion he thinks erroneous; he may comment on earlier writings with which he expects to disagree; he may mention a person with whom he differs. With this device the writer can gain the interest that always attaches to an argument and at the same time define his own stand by its opposite.

Has the Education Industry Lost Its Nerve?

The leaders of many so-called education companies, especially those formed through marriages of electronics and publishing, seem to be losing confidence in the premise that technology can change education. Having eagerly embraced that enticing proposition a few years ago, and having since discovered that it is more difficult to consummate than they expected, some now appear ready to abandon it.

ROBERT W. LOCKE

[*The introduction, relying on a figurative comparison with matrimony, suggests that the educational conglomerates have become disillusioned. This statement prepares for (1) a survey of the disillusionment and (2) development of the idea that times have now changed sufficiently so that a cautious development of new devices and techniques could be both useful and profitable.*]

6. *Justification or explanation of paper.* The writer may have been an eyewitness to an important event; he may have done exhaustive research; he may have conducted controlled experiments. Many research papers begin with a presentation that allows the reader to judge the validity of the material presented.

Thomas Couture

My first meeting with Couture, who became one of my best and dearest friends, was odd and characteristic. It was in 1834; I was not yet one and twenty, and had just arrived from the United States, well

[*The introduction has the easy grace of familiar narration, but it also lets the reader know that the writer is speaking on the basis of long and intimate acquaintance with his subject.*]

160

provided for in the way of courage and determination, with a stock of youthful illusions, and very little besides.

GEORGE P. A. HEALY

7. *A relevant incident, a striking illustration, an anecdote.* An account of something that has happened can catch the reader's interest and also lead into the main topic of a composition.

A Pig from Jersey

Among those who passed through the general clinic of Lenox Hill Hospital, at Seventy-sixth Street and Park Avenue, on Monday morning, April 6, 1942, was a forty-year-old Yorkville dishwasher who I will call Herman Sauer. His complaint, like his occupation, was an undistinguished one. He had a stomach ache.

BERTON ROUECHE

[*The incident, which the writer develops in detail, not only introduces the discussion of a disease, trichinosis, but serves as a unifying thread running through the entire essay. Notice the details that make it convincing.*]

The Blood Jet Is Poetry

On a dank day in February, 1963, a pretty young mother of two children was found in a London flat with her head in the oven and the gas jets wide open.

[*The opening perhaps sensationalizes a* Time *review of a book of poems by Sylvia Plath, but it sets the tone of the article, which is mainly biographical.*]

8. *A quotation.* A quotation may serve as a starting point because it illustrates the main idea to be presented.

The Uses of Flexibility

Thackeray wrote, "The wicked are wicked, no doubt, and they go astray and they fall, and they come by their deserts; but who can tell the mischief which the very virtuous do?"

J. WILLIAM FULBRIGHT

[*Fulbright goes on to discuss the dangers of inflexible and intolerant attitudes growing from the purest of motives.*]

CONCLUSIONS

7d

Like introductions, conclusions vary widely, from long summaries to brief suggestions, from formal deductions to illustrative incidents. Even a short paper, however, will profit

7d   # Conc

*Revise the conclusion so that it
rounds out the composition logically.*

ORIGINAL

REVISION

[*The paper attempts to show that football is a business in this student's university.*]

All too frequently scholastic standards have been subordinated to
football. I know of one instance in
which an important player was
allowed to take a final examination
over twice, for no reason except
that it took him that long to pass it.
All of us have heard of exceptions
to entrance requirements made for
athletes.

[*The final sentences concern only
one aspect of the theme; they do not
return the reader to the main idea.*]

I may be condemned for lack of
school spirit or for idealism or for
something worse, but I cannot help
hoping that someday football in
State University may become a
sport instead of a business.

[*The addition of a concluding paragraph that returns to the central topic
rounds out the composition. It suggests
that the writer has concluded, not just
stopped. The conclusion here presents
the point of view the writer has explained by the evidence already submitted.*]

[*The body of the paper presents reasons to justify the heavy expenditures
on modern college football.*]

On Saturday afternoon in the
crowded stadium twenty-two young
men are fighting for the kinds of
ideals that have made this country
great. May the best team win!

[*The conclusion is a string of stock
statements that happen to fit football,
but it has no intimate relationship with
the point of the paper.*]

Football may have become big
business, but it is a business worth
preserving because its aims are the
aims of education.

[*When the writer starts thinking
about what he has said—not just
vaguely putting together sentences that
happen to get associated in his mind
with the subject of football—he finds
that he can make a general statement
that sums up his main argument and
effectively concludes his theme.*]

from evidence that the discussion is finished, that the writer has
completed what he had to say—not stopped because he heard a
bell or came to the end of a page. Usually this concluding comment
recalls what the composition has done, reinforces its theme or
argument; sometimes it adds final suggestions or advice that the
writer wants to emphasize.

In a short paper, a single sentence may provide an adequate conclusion. An extended conclusion, like an overlong introduction, may destroy the proportion of a composition. The conclusion should show succinctly that the writer has completed his job, but it should not begin a new essay or make assertions not justified in the body of the paper. The following paragraphs exemplify some possible types of conclusions.

1. *Restatement of main idea.* Modern exposition tends to conclude with a restatement of the main idea of the composition — usually not a formal summary but a fresh presentation of the idea.

The Illusion of the Two Cultures

Today we hold a stone, the heavy stone of power. We must perceive beyond it, however, by the aid of the artistic imagination, those humane insights and understandings which alone can lighten our burden and enable us to shape ourselves, rather than the stone, into the forms which great art has anticipated.

LOREN EISELEY

[*A scientist uses a prehistoric, shaped stone as a unifying device for his essay and turns his conclusion about it, emphasizing his point that the artistic and the practical can work together.*]

2. *A supplementary comment.* A writer may reinforce his argument by adding a new but related observation, which serves to emphasize what the essay has said.

Walt Whitman: He Had His Nerve

Let me finish by mentioning another quality of Whitman's — a quality, delightful to me, that I have said nothing of. If some day a tourist notices, among the ruins of New York City, a copy of *Leaves of Grass*, and stops and picks it up and reads some lines in it, she will be able to say to herself: "how very American! If he and his country had not existed, it would have been possible to imagine them."

RANDALL JARRELL

[*The essay has discussed a variety of aspects of Whitman's poetry. The final comment, although technically presenting a new quality, actually epitomizes the attitude of the essay.*]

3. *Statement of importance, plea for change.* Many kinds of conclusions suggest the importance of what has been presented (for example, 1 above). They may also make a plea for a change of attitude or for specific action.

The Smell of Death

Thus the meaning of 9 West 102nd Street is this: *any* measure, no matter how radical, which holds out *any* promise of controlling the heroin malignancy must be taken, and soon. It must become an over-riding first priority of American policy—and especially foreign policy—to control the production and distribution of this city-killing drug.

STEWART ALSOP

[This is the close of the editorial by Alsop of which the introduction is quoted above. Alsop deftly recalls the introduction and draws his conclusions.]

The Technique of the Modern Political Myths

We should carefully study the origin, the structure, the methods, and the technique of the political myths. We should see the adversary face to face in order to know how to combat him.

ERNST CASSIRER

[After describing the nature and importance of political myths, the writer concludes by suggesting what we should do—which is what his essay does.]

Moonlight and Poison Ivy

Better marriage relations in this country await an extensive revaluation of our attitude towards life and living. If our values are shabby and our attitudes adolescent, how can American marriage, made in our image, be anything but a monumental failure?

DAVID COHN

[An essay on the weaknesses of our attitudes toward marriage ends by suggesting that we change and by pointing out the necessity for change.]

The conclusion, then, is designed chiefly to make sure that the reader leaves the essay with its main point clearly in mind. It helps the reader recall the pattern of ideas the essay has followed; and it may make a final effort to show him the special significance of the whole.

FOR STUDY AND WRITING

A Of the following sentences, assume that *a* is the concluding sentence of one paragraph and that *b* is the topic sentence of the next paragraph. Consider the following pair:

a) Thus a thundershower saved us from losing the first baseball game of the season, and gave us another week to tighten our team play.

b) A week later our pitchers were in better condition.

This is not a good transition. The opening of the second sentence, *a week later,* does something by setting the time; but the end of the preceding paragraph had seemed to promise some account of the practice during the week to develop team work, and sentence *b* does not fulfill the promise. Something like the following would be better:

c) The next Monday afternoon the coach started a series of drills intended to show us how to work together.

Now consider the following sequences of sentences. Which provide good transitions? Which are inadequate, and why?

1. **a)** Drug addiction on campuses is quite different from the same problem as it appears in secondary schools.

   b) First, let us consider the rash of drug addiction in junior and senior high schools.

2. **a)** Everybody had left by midnight, and we went to bed.

   b) I put the coffee on and started to mix batter for pancakes.

3. **a)** The poll to assess student sentiment showed overwhelming enthusiasm for the proposed Student Union Association.

   b) They decided I should be chairman of the membership drive committee.

4. **a)** Here with a view of the mountains on three sides and the tiny creek near the center of the area was a perfect site for the new school.

   b) The site was nearly fifty miles from a sizable town. Supplies and help would be a problem. Building costs would be high.

5. **a)** Literary merit is, then, a possible attribute, not essential but also not wholly casual, of any nonfictional writing.

   b) But isn't this also true of what goes more strictly by the name of literature itself: . . .

6. **a)** Interpreting local news, therefore, is perhaps the most important single function of the college newspaper.

   b) National affairs should be of interest to college students and college journalists.

7. **a)** Thus for a century or two, the natives of Southeast Asia have associated extortion, brutality, and bad manners with white men.

   b) They are making white men pay—all white men, from whatever country they come and whatever their previous connection with Asia—for the mistakes and crimes of a few.

B The following opening sentences of paragraphs from essays on language provide various sorts of transitional material. Study each one and try to determine what has preceded the sentence and what is to follow. Some reveal more than others.

1. This new concept of the phoneme has revolutionized modern grammatical study.

2. In addition to the great stock of Latin words that have entered our language through the French, or under its influence, we have a huge mass of words and phrases taken directly from the Latin without change.

3. At no point is the intelligent traveller inconvenienced by these hitherto unfamiliar, but easily assimilable, expressions. The more difficult task is to understand the living and ever-changing idioms of American slang.

4. From yet another Romance language, Italian, English has acquired a good many words, including much of our musical terminology.

5. A third premise arising from the two just discussed is that the difference between the way educated people talk and the way they write is a dialectal difference.

C Below are beginning paragraphs, with the sentences that follow them, taken from papers discussing action-oriented courses as against the more conventional courses directed toward academic or professional ends. Comment specifically on the appropriateness of each as an introduction.

1. In this theme I shall consider action-oriented courses. Action-oriented courses have both advantages and disadvantages.

2. Not being a member of the faculty, or the administration, or the student committee that has been investigating the relevance of the new or the old courses, I do not have much information about this subject, but I will write about it as well as I can.
   I am sure, however, that drastic changes are needed.

3. When my older brother came to the university, the word *relevance* was not much used in regard to courses, but he soon found out what irrelevance can be. He took a course in English in which he learned how to spell and punctuate and to parse sentences, but he had already won a spelling contest and he had been parsing ever since the sixth grade. He failed a course in trigonometry, but what he needed, if he was to take over his father's business, was some accounting. If the courses he registered for in Spanish, history, and art appreciation meant anything in his life, he did not know what it was.
   When I arrived things had changed a little, but not much.

4. Like a good many of my friends, I came to the university because I could not get a good job, and I did not know what else to do. I am having a good time, and that is all right, but a good time isn't everything.
   That gets me to my subject, because I have been thinking about the courses I have been taking.

5. Two years as a hippie taught me very little, but I did learn one thing: a serious student can get an education and the kind of courses he takes make a difference.
   From my point of view, courses offered in most universities and colleges are of two sorts: those that center upon a body of material and those that attempt to do what we used to call "turning a cat on."

6. This subject is important for all college students, because in this day and age almost everybody has to be able to make a living, and all of us have to learn how to live in a modern world.

I am going to break my subject down into four main parts.

D Below are concluding paragraphs taken from papers having the same general subject as those in C, above, the role of action-oriented courses in collegiate curricula. Comment on the appropriateness of each as a conclusion.

1. [*The paper argues that students should be allowed to elect courses like anatomy and surveying if they expect to have use for them, but that all required courses should stimulate students, not provide organized information.*]

The courses I am taking are dull, dull, dull! I cut class and I don't read the assignments. After all, why should I?

2. [*The paper contrasts a course given in an ethnic-studies program on the role of emancipated slaves in the War Between the States and a course given in the Department of History on the same struggle.*]

I learned more about mankind and the nature of civilization from my history professor, but I learned more about what history means in men's lives from the ethnic studies course.

3. [*The paper describes a beginning course in French and tells how much time the student is spending learning to conjugate French verbs, and trying to remember which nouns are masculine and which feminine.*]

I suppose some people would like this course — I guess some actually do — and I guess some other sections of the course may be better. I do not know about that, but I do not see any reason why students should waste their time studying courses that are no good to them.

4. [*The paper describes several courses the writer took in an ethnic-studies program; he found them repetitious, vague, and lacking in content.*]

As a result of my experience with ethnic studies, I have concluded that I want two things out of college, to learn how to think and to learn facts to think with. I need no course to "turn me on"; until I can turn myself on I have no business in college.

5. [*The paper surveys five courses the student is registered for and endeavors to examine each of them to see what its relevance may be for her.*]

The fifth course I am taking is called "Introduction to Home Economics." It meets three times a week, but one class is a kind of laboratory and lasts from one to four p.m. The instructor is quite jolly, and I like her a lot.

6. [*The paper surveys the offerings of the university, describes sample courses, and endeavors to assess the reactions of students to the different sorts of courses.*]

So far as I can observe, younger students tend to like courses centered in themselves and their interests; older students want facts, principles, techniques, and no nonsense.

E Describe methods used in the following paragraphs to gain continuity, and point out specific examples of each method. Then select at least one of the paragraphs and analyze in detail the commitment each sentence makes to what is to follow and the way in which each sentence responds to this commitment.

[1] The story of Galahad and the Grail quest may well have been included by Malory as a metaphor of the transcendence of the epic's war and adultery, hate and lust. It serves that function in any theoretical analysis of the book. But in the act of reading and appreciation it does not. It separates itself out as a different story. However carefully Malory strives to connect the main story of Launcelot, Arthur, and Gawain with their failure in the Grail quest, and however symbolical the relation of Launcelot and his bastard son, Galahad, may be, the two plots are really incongruous. The story of the Grail stands best alone. In spite of tedious detail and naïve style, the medieval French Grail romances transmit more of the mystery that has attracted generations of cranky interpreters and spinners of learned fantasy as well as the whole tribe of occultists to the Grail legends. However, Malory's version is all most modern readers are likely to read and it is sufficiently awe-inspiring. In *Le Morte d'Arthur* the major actors in the drama of King Arthur's court will find their transcendence, not in supernatural vision, but in the common human illumination that comes with the acceptance of tragedy.

KENNETH REXROTH, *Le Morte d'Arthur*

[2] The doctrine of energy has to do with the notion of quantitative permanence underlying change. The doctrine of evolution has to do with the emergence of novel organisms as the outcome of chance. The theory of energy lies in the province of physics. The theory of evolution lies mainly in the province of biology, although it had previously been touched upon by Kant and Laplace in connection with the formation of suns and planets.

A. N. WHITEHEAD, *Science and the Modern World*

[3] I have already given you a summary account of the manner in which young misses are educated in this country. They are all sent early to school; where they are taught to spell, and read, and write. From parochial schools, many of them are transferred to boarding-schools and academies. Here they learn to understand arithmetic, which indeed is usually taught them in parochial schools, and study English grammar, geography, history to some extent, criticism, and composition. In a few instances they are taught moral science, and in some ascend to higher branches of mathematics, the Latin and French languages. To these are added embroidery, drawing, and music.

TIMOTHY DWIGHT, *Travels in New England and New York*

[4] I am therefore led to my final assumption, that the admission of a principle of relativity and uncertainty should not be simply depressing. It does not destroy all possibility of knowledge and judgment. Rather, it is the outcome of comprehensive knowledge, and the means to further knowledge of man's history. It enables a higher objectivity, a fuller understanding of present and past. It enables wiser choices among the possibilities open to us—among goods that are no less real because they are relative, and that are more relevant than arbitrary absolutes. Above all, this principle encourages a positive faith in

168

positive values: of liberality, of breadth of spirit, hospitality to new ideas, willingness to adventure, humility in admitting one's own fallibility and the limitations of the human mind — of the tolerance that is indispensable for the pursuit of truth, for social harmony, and for simple humanity. If these are not the highest values, none are more essential to the hopes of world order and peace.

HERBERT J. MULLER, *The Uses of the Past*

F Following are sentences taken from published paragraphs. Frame a sentence that might follow each, one that seems to you a possible response to the commitment made by the sentence quoted. Your instructor can tell you what sentence actually did follow in the original paragraph.

1. The American, probably more than any other man, is prone to be apologetic about the trade he follows.

2. The vanishing father is perhaps the central fact of the changing American family structure.

3. Not only were the potatoes of that land as large as any in the world, but they were probably the best in the world to eat.

4. We humans have had very little experience in any environment save one in which we can travel in any path at any speed we wish.

5. The human animal has survived by virtue of his ability to perceive, decide, and react.

6. Teen-agers could hardly live without the telephone — and many parents can hardly live with it.

7. It does not take a linguist to know that language changes.

8. Football is a game which simply does not lend itself to intelligent spectatordom.

9. In one large city, the principals of the junior high schools and the superintendent are now holding firm against interscholastic games.

10. Almost no feature of the interior design of our current car provides safeguards against injury in the event of collision.

G Rewrite the following paragraphs from student themes, attempting to improve the continuity from sentence to sentence:

[1] The mythology and folkways of a primitive people are the basis of their society. Wise men and priests explain the mysteries of the universe. Folkways are learned by the young by imitation and under the pressure of authority. Traditions of a different society are sometimes imposed on a primitive group, and then the old folkways are submerged and covered by superficial acquired habits. The dress and language of the new society are adopted. You have to probe beneath the surface to find the old beliefs persisting.

[2] What to wear was a very important problem to me. Blue was the color which my mother considered most flattering to me, but I liked red. I was only in the seventh grade. It was very hard for me to find a formal that fit me. Dress designers apparently did not take sufficient account of the special problems of seventh-graders. Many dresses,

both blue and red, were presented. I did not seem to have curves in the right places. When I did find a suitable dress, the alterations turned out to be more complicated than making the dress could have been.

H Select a paragraph from a theme you have written. Using the paragraphs in 7a as models, draw lines tracing the continuity from key word to key word. Then revise the paragraph, attempting to improve its continuity, and draw lines on the revision to test whether more ideas carry from sentence to sentence.

PARAGRAPH
PATTERNS

CHAPTER 8

Writing develops in topic-comment units, in paragraphs that may be organized in a variety of patterns of coordination and subordination.

Writing can be thought of as interlocking passages—the whole made up of units, each of which contains other units, which—and so on. None of these units can be sharply defined or limited; even relatively established bits like the sentence or the word vary so much that exact definition is difficult. But units can be recognized; they and their patterns can be usefully described. One such topic-comment unit is the paragraph. It participates in the general principles of ordering materials, discussed in chapters 5–7, but while contributing to the larger patterns of development it has also its own organization.

Topic-Comment Units

Any unit of writing, even a brief sentence, can be described as a topic plus a comment; "Dogs bark" is a comment about the topic "Dogs". The next largest topic-comment unit is typically a sentence plus whatever additional development may be necessary to respond to its commitment. When a sentence turns back to an earlier commitment or shifts to a new topic, it usually starts a new topic-comment unit. Following are two such units.

[1] At the moment, as for many years past, the chances to see silent comedy are rare. [2] There is a smattering of it on television—too often treated as something quaintly archaic, to be laughed at, not with. [3] Some two hundred comedies—long and short—can be

rented for home projection. [4] And a lucky minority has access to the comedies in the collection of New York's Museum of Modern Art, which is still incomplete but which is probably the best in the world.

[5] In the near future, however, something of this lost art will return to regular theaters. [6] A thick straw in the wind is the big business now being done by a series of revivals of W. C. Fields's memorable movies, a kind of comedy more akin to the old silent variety than anything which is being made today. [7] Mack Sennett now is preparing a sort of potpourri variety show called *Down Memory Lane* made up out of his old movies, featuring people like Fields and Bing Crosby when they were movie beginners, but including also interludes from the silents. [8] Harold Lloyd has re-released *Movie Crazy,* a talkie, and plans to revive four of his best silent comedies (*Grandma's Boy, Safety Last, Speedy,* and *The Freshman*). [9] Buster Keaton hopes to make at feature length, with a minimum of dialogue, two of the funniest short comedies ever made, one about a porous homemade boat and one about a prefabricated house.

JAMES AGEE, *Agee on Film*

Sentence 1 presents a topic, that there are now only rare chances to see silent comedy; sentences 2, 3, and 4 list three of these opportunities. Sentence 5 also introduces a topic, that silent comedy will return, signaling the shift to a new topic with *however;* sentences 6–9 provide four examples of coming events. The two units are combined in their essay as a single paragraph. They might have appeared as separate paragraphs; the paragraph just preceding this one in the essay is a single topic-comment unit, with two sentences developing a topic, that the trouble with screen comedy today is "that it takes place on a screen which talks."

Obviously no single formula for construction can govern the paragraph. As indicated in chapter 7 paragraphs are sometimes set off as units because they have special purposes — as transitions, introductions, or conclusions. Paragraphing of newspaper stories and dialogue is conventional. Narrative writing may be almost innocent of structure in its paragraphs, divided into segments of chronology rather than logic. Paragraphs may vary in length from a single sentence to several hundred words. Perhaps all that can be said of paragraphs in general is that they include one or more topic-comment units that a writer has chosen to mark with indentation as segments in the discourse. The indentation signals a new topic, a shift in direction, or perhaps just a pause in a continuing movement.

The student working on writing skills, however, can profitably look at some common patterns for expository paragraphs, thinking of them as small compositions, combinations of topic-comment units.

The easiest type of paragraph to put together, and probably the most useful, is a single unit composed of elements already discussed. Typically it includes (1) some topical

GUIDE TO REVISION

8a   ¶

Use standard paragraph patterns to replace choppy paragraphs, to develop isolated statements, or to order paragraphs lacking organization.

ORIGINAL

[1] In the suburbs and on the highways of many large American cities, young men are killing themselves by the thousands.

[2] Many of the accidents could be avoided if a little common sense were used. When a boy gets behind the steering wheel of a car, the first thing he thinks of is how fast he can go.

[3] Speed is the reason for so many deaths. The teen-ager does not seem to realize that his car is dangerous if it is not used sensibly.

[4] There is another reason for a large number of teen-age automobile accidents.

[5] This is the playing of games with cars. These senseless games kill hundreds of teen-agers every year.

[6] The most popular game is "Chicken." Two or more cars. . . .

[*The body of the theme concerns the game mentioned in paragraph 6, but the preceding matter is broken into what appear as five paragraphs. This introduction is not well planned or closely knit, but such plan as it has is obscured by the meaningless indentations.*]

REVISION

On the highways in and around many large American cities, young men are killing themselves by the thousands in automobile accidents that could be avoided by the use of a little common sense. First, young drivers must learn to be sensible about speed. When a boy gets behind a steering wheel, the first thing he thinks of is how fast he can go. He does not seem to realize that his car is dangerous if it is not used sensibly. Second, young drivers must learn some sense about the senseless games played with cars, which kill hundreds of teen-agers each year.

The most popular game is "Chicken." Two or more cars. . . .

[*Five paragraphs have been combined into one, but the revision has involved more than removing the indentations. For example, the first two sentences have become a single sentence, with its elements subordinated. The three sentences of paragraphs 4 and 5 have become a single sentence. Sentences have been reworked to provide continuity, and the remark of the original about common sense has been exploited to provide unity.*]

material introducing the subject (see chapter 2), (2) development with materials such as details, illustrations, examples, reasons, comparisons (see chapter 3), and (3) sometimes a conclusion. Of these, the topical material is usually brief; it may consist only of a topic sentence, often the first sentence in the paragraph, which sometimes is supported by restatement or amplifying comments at various points throughout the paragraph. The development is likely to comprise the bulk of an expository or argumentative paragraph. In very informal or unsophisticated prose it may comprise only a sentence or two presenting relatively few details in support of the topic sentence, but most closely reasoned or adequately developed paragraphs are likely to include a hundred or perhaps several hundred words of development. The conclusion, if one is required, is almost always brief, and often is merely implied in the topical material opening the next paragraph.

The following paragraph illustrates the pattern at its simplest.

> His folks talked like other folks in the neighborhood. They called themselves "pore" people. A man learned in books was "eddicated." What was certain was "sartin." The syllables came through the nose; "joints" were "j'ints"; fruit "spiled" instead of spoiling; in corn-planting time they "drapped" the seeds. They went on errands and "brung" things back. Their dogs "follered" the coons. Flannel was "flannen," a bandanna a "banddanner," a chimney a "chimbly," a shadow a "shadder," and mosquitoes plain "skeeters." They "gethered" crops. A creek was a "crick," a cover a "kiver."
>
> CARL SANDBURG, *Abraham Lincoln: The Prairie Years*

The paragraph begins by summarizing the main idea. The remainder of the paragraph lists particular instances to illustrate and support the opening statement. No conclusion is needed. The following has the same general pattern.

> I am no better than a procrastinating cuss, and since being married I do less than ever before. Here is another winter gone and I am again nursing nasturtiums and feeding mosquitoes. I am going on to thirty-eight years old, the yawning gulf of middle-age. Another, the fifth, year of professordom is expiring this week. I am balder, duller, more pedantic, and more lazy than ever. I have lost my love of travel. My fits of wrath and rebellion against the weaknesses and shortcomings of mankind are less violent than they were, though grumbling has become my favorite occupation. I have ceased to grow rapidly either in public esteem or in mental development. One year resembles another, and if it weren't for occasional disturbing dreams of decay, disaster, or collapse, I should consider myself as having attained as much of Nirwana as a man of my race and temperament can expect to do.

174

¶

The paragraph is from a letter by Henry Adams, one of America's most cogent writers. For other purposes and more subtle ideas, Adams often wrote more complicated paragraphs. Here he needs only to announce a subject, develop it with a series of details having no expressed order, and finish with a more general illustration of the topic to serve as conclusion.

The same pattern will work for more formal material, as the following paragraph developed from a topic sentence used in chapter 1 illustrates.

> Sometimes the Scandinavians gave a fresh lease of life to obsolescent or obsolete native words. The preposition *till*, for instance, is found only once or twice in OE. texts belonging to the pre-Scandinavian period, but after that time it begins to be exceedingly common in the North, from whence it spreads southward; it was used as in Danish with regard to both time and space, and it is still so used in Scotch. Similarly *dale* (OE. *doel*) "appears to have been reinforced from Norse (*dal*), for it is in the North that the word is a living geographical name" (NED.), and *barn*, Scotch *bairn* (OE. *bearn*) would probably have disappeared in the North, as it did in the South, if it had not been strengthened by the Scandinavian word. The verb *blend*, too, seems to owe its vitality (as well as its vowel) to Old Norse, for *blandan* was very rare in Old English.
>
> OTTO JESPERSEN, *Growth and Structure of the English Language*

The author follows his opening topic sentence with others presenting four words as examples of his opening generalization.

In some paragraphs the two or three parts are not sharply distinct, and the organization of the development may be rather loose. In brief paragraphs, particularly those that are quasi-narrative, little organization may be needed. The details may be in chronological order, for example, and the author may be endeavoring to record no more than the details and their order. Notice the following consecutive paragraphs.

> Henry Adams's first venture into published scholarly writing was an essay entitled "Captain John Smith," appearing in the January, 1867, issue of the *North American Review*, then edited by Charles Eliot Norton. As candidly admitted in *The Education*, the young man was eager "to make a position for himself," and such an article seemed calculated for an effect, since it struck at the Pocahontas legend, particularly precious to self-conscious exemplars of Virginian chivalry. Adams had done some research on Smith as early as 1861, after hints obtained in conversation from John Gorham Palfrey, author of *A History of New England*, but he owed most to Charles Deane, whose edition of Wingfield's *Discourse of Virginia*

contained notes casting doubt on Captain John Smith's veracity. Adams finished a draft of his study in 1862 but laid it aside until 1866, when at Palfrey's urging he revised and sent it to the *North American.*

In essence the article virtually establishes that the famous story of Smith's rescue by Pocahontas is not history but hoax, invented by Smith in his later years, presumably to call attention to himself so that he might mend his tattered fortunes. At least it is highly suspicious that Smith's first account of the incident was that in his *General Historie of Virginia,* published in 1624, seven years after the death of the Indian maiden who was said to have laid her head upon his when the clubs of her father's warriors were about to fall. In his *True Relation* (1608) and subsequent writings, published before 1624, Smith had not mentioned the episode.

ROBERT A. HUME, *Runaway Star*

Here Hume is attempting nothing very complicated; in the first paragraph he is recounting the details of the publication of an article, and in the second he is summarizing the import of the article. He is laying the groundwork for more serious writing to come; the material is not difficult, and much of it is narrative with chronology making the order clear. He needs no elaborate organization; as a matter of fact the organization of the two paragraphs is similar, although as usual this basic similarity does not seem repetitious because it is obscured by minor differences. In each paragraph the topic is announced at once, in the first part of the first sentence, but the topical material is brief enough so that the author can use part of the sentence to add details. Thereafter more details are presented in a few sentences and the details are kept in order by chronology, in the first paragraph through the chronology of the writing, revising, and printing of the article, in the second paragraph through the chronology of Smith's published works. The first paragraph has a sort of conclusion; it starts with the implication that the paragraph is to concern the publication of an article, and the last sentence sees the study published. The second paragraph has nothing much that can be called conclusion; the topic sentence had made the subject quite precise, that the Pocahontas legend was "not history but hoax." Hume then presents the evidence, and presumably assumes that in so brief a paragraph he need not remind his reader of the subject, particularly since this is all background as far as Hume's book is concerned, and whether Smith was or was not a genial liar makes little difference in his discussion.

Elsewhere, Hume feels he must make points more precisely. Consider the following:

A man's birth is indispensable to his physical existence but is intellectually unimportant, belonging on the same level with his conception about nine months earlier, or with his taking successive breaths and imbibing maternal milk. It is difficult, therefore, to identify the author of *The Education of Henry Adams* with a certain helpless, presumably intractable male brat that appeared on February 18, 1838, in Boston, Massachusetts, to be promptly designated the fourth child and third son of Charles Francis Adams, who was the son of John Quincy Adams, who was the son of John Adams. That complicated entity Henry Brooks Adams—diffident, contemptuous; energetic, indolent; rebellious, tradition-conscious; eye-twinkling, dour—did not indubitably emerge for a number of years, just how many it is hard to say.

The structure is still relatively simple. Again, the topical element is in the first part of the first sentence—birth is physically indispensable but not intellectually important. The remainder of the first sentence and the second sentence provide development of this idea, that for a time Adams was more brat than brain. The final sentence pins down the conclusion rather sharply, that Adams as an entity did not emerge for some time. The one-two-three sequence noted above is here sharper, but not much more complicated.

Combining Topic-Comment Units

The standard paragraph with a single topic-comment unit is simple to handle, but a variation on it that combines two or more units is equally useful. The following paragraph, also from Hume's book on Henry Adams, combines two units, both of them commenting on the opening topic sentence.

[1] He [Adams] knew, surely, what any competent scientist is aware of: that no one method or set of experiments can be regarded as final. [2] The scientist works not in terms of certain, ultimate cause (though in the name of human dignity he holds this forever before him as an ideal), but in terms of probability. [3] Probability arises from the findings in one experiment. [4] If the findings in a second experiment are at least roughly equivalent, the probability becomes stronger. [5] It becomes still stronger with similar findings in a third experiment, and so on. [6] If findings in continual and repeated experiments all point to the same end, the scientist gains confidence in his original hypothesis and eventually may cease to regard it as a mere hypothesis but as something so strongly impreg-

nated with probability that it can be adopted for convenience as a workable fact. [7] But the scientist, if he be worthy of his name, will never quite lose sight of the lurking latency of error. [8] He will be sufficiently a philosopher to feel the force of David Hume's contention that causation is never established in a manner answerable to logic. [9] To invoke the humdrum instance, although the sun has punctually risen on a hundred thousand successive days, it may not rise tomorrow.

The main idea of this paragraph, that Adams understood that probability can become a workable "fact" but never an absolute fact, breaks naturally into two parts: the first exploring the nature of probability and the second defining the scientist's responsibility to the possibility of error. The pattern might be analyzed somewhat as follows:

TOPIC: (1) Adams knew as a scientist that no set of experiments can be final.

SUBTOPIC 1: (2) Scientist works in terms of probability. (*In this second sentence, the writer selects one aspect of the topic for detailed explanation.*)

DEVELOPMENT: (3–5) How probability becomes stronger with additional experiments.

CONCLUSION: (6) When probability becomes strong enough, in practice it can be considered workable fact. (*This first unit, 2–6, illustrates a logical progression in thought as the writer adds to the topic of probability introduced in 2, so that he can come to the conclusion in 6, which looks back to 1, the original topic sentence of the paragraph.*)

SUBTOPIC 2: (7) Scientist must beware of lurking latency of error. (*After the conclusion of 6, the writer must look at the other side of the coin: 7 partly repeats 1, the original topic.*)

DEVELOPMENT: (8) Justifying 7 by citing a general contention of David Hume and (9) providing a familiar instance.

Obviously, patterns of this sort can vary widely, but the most common and most useful system for building paragraphs relies on topic-comment units. The single-unit pattern may be adequate, but often the topic of a paragraph lends itself to subdivision and is followed by two or three units in which subtopics are supported by details. Furthermore, the units themselves may vary; sometimes, for example, the supporting details precede a summary topic statement, and in longer compositions further variations may develop in paragraphs that are themselves subdivisions of larger topics or main ideas.

178

Coordination and Subordination in Paragraphs

Coordination and subordination reveal relationships in all units of composition, among the parts of the total composition (see chapter 5) or within a single sentence (see chapter 15). In the paragraph the writer can use coordination and subordination to produce a wide variety of structural patterns to match the multiplicity of complex relationships. In the examples above, the patterns of coordination and subordination are generally simple, in the paragraphs by Sandburg and Adams, for example, primarily coordinate sequences. Each begins with a topic sentence leading to a series of sentences coordinate with one another but all subordinate to the opening sentence. The sentences can be said to have only two levels of subordination—that of the topic sentences and that of the subordinate illustrative sentences.

More complex patterns, however, can be constructed—and described—in terms of different levels of subordination. Consider the following paragraph, which has been arranged so that indentation and superscript numbers mark levels of subordination. Sentences with the same left margin and the same small numbers are coordinate; indentation indicates subordination.

[1] [1] The intellectual life of the nineteenth century was more complex than that of any previous age.

 [2] [2] This was due to several causes.

  [3] [3] First: The area concerned was larger than ever before; American and Russia made important contributions, and Europe became more aware than formerly of Indian philosophies, both ancient and modern.

  [3] [4] Second: Science, which had been a chief source of novelty since the seventeenth century, made new conquests, especially in geology, biology, and organic chemistry.

  [3] [5] Third: Machine production profoundly altered the social structure, and gave men a new conception of their powers in relation to the physical environment.

  [3] [6] Fourth: A profound revolt, both philosophical and political, against traditional systems in thought, in politics, and in economics, gave rise to attacks upon many beliefs and institutions that had hitherto been regarded as unassailable.

   [4] [7] This revolt had two very different forms, one romantic, the other rationalistic.

    [5] [8] (I am using these words in a liberal sense.)

    [5] [9] The romantic revolt passes from Byron, Schopenhauer, and Nietzsche to Mussolini and Hitler; the rationalistic revolt begins with the French philosophers of the Revolution, passes on, somewhat softened, to the philosophical radicals in England, then acquires a deeper form in Marx and issues in Soviet Russia.

BERTRAND RUSSELL, *A History of Western Philosophy*

179

The patterns stand out partly because the writer has used obvious, almost superformal, signals to help the reader. Sentences 3–6, for instance, are shown to be coordinate not only by their parallel form but by the introductory words that label them as items in a list of coordinate clauses. Similarly, the repetition of *revolt* from sentence 6 to open 7 helps the reader see that 7 will expand 6 and be subordinate to it, that it will not be coordinate and offer a fifth cause. The same device relates 9 to 7.

Here, as usual, the levels of subordination in structure correspond to levels of specificity in meaning (see chapter 3). That is, each step in subordination is likely to accompany a step toward specification. In the paragraph above, for example, sentences 3–6, at the third level of subordination, all specify "causes" of sentence 2 at the second level. Sentence 9 at the fifth level is a specification of the meaning of sentence 7 at the fourth.

The following paragraph, which may be described with four levels of subordinarion, follows a somewhat different pattern.

[1] [1] Something of the same kind is true of animal species.

[2] [2] The more specialized an animal species is, the more genetic possibility has become somatic actuality.

[3] [3] A species with selective adaptation to an environment *and with genetic or geographic isolation from closely related species* (which is one of the basic criteria of what constitutes separate species) is poorer in genes than the total mother-stock.

[3] [4] That is, any one species of animal is poorer in total variety than is a whole group of related species.

[4] [5] For example, there is a greater variety of genes in the sum total of South African antelopes (springbok, steenbok, hartebeest, duiker, eland, nylghau, gnu, etc.) than there is in any one of the species alone.

[4] [6] But a springbok's adaptations are not a bit of good to the gnu, or the gnu's to the springbok, so long as they are genetically isolated from one another as separate species.

[2] [7] As a result, the non-inter-breeding of these species makes the great total variety of antelope genes mutually unavailable in the separate species.

WESTON LA BARRE, *The Human Animal*

The opening sentence refers to the previous paragraph and announces a new subject. Sentence 2 might be called a subtopic sentence. Sentences 3 and 4 specify the idea in sentence 2, and sentences 5 and 6 provide specific examples of the statements in 3 and 4. Sentence 7 concludes.

Sometimes, however, indication of levels of subordination does not totally reveal complexities of the pattern of a paragraph. Consider the following:

¹[1] It is sometimes said to be characteristic of our time that we undo the spiritual structures of our ancestors; whatever they sacralized we desacralized.

²[2] They retreated from the evident unholiness of the world into images which stored up the strength of those moments when it seemed holy or terrible in a different way.

²[3] They built in order to make space sacred, and in their rites they abolished the terrors of time, as spring kills winter and St. George the dragon.

²[4] They made books which were compact of all the world and of all its history, syllabically inspired and, like nature itself, signed with the secret meanings of a god.

²[5] We build to serve human functions, and not to make models of a divine world; cathedrals that were living bibles, churches proportioned as the music of the spheres.

²[6] We live, more than any of our ancestors, in a time become linear and patternless.

²[7] Our books inform or divert in a purely human sense.

³[8] Where a book continues to be venerable, we attribute its power to different causes: we demythologize, find reasons in nature for its being as it is; we see it as figuring not the whole world of knowledge but dead men's knowledge of the world.

³[9] It sinks into history, becomes the victim of our perspectival trick, falls under the rule of time.

¹[10] So we desacralize the world.

FRANK KERMODE, *The Patience of Shakespeare*

The paragraph is perhaps more difficult than those above because it remains relatively abstract, occupied with ideas. Moreover it is more complexly organized than the levels of subordination reveal. Sentences 2–7 appear on the same level of subordination, but the diagram does not reveal that 2–4 comprise one topic-comment unit and 5–7 another, each unit subordinate to a different part of the topic sentence. The topic sentence breaks into two parts: (1) "the structures of our ancestors" or what "they sacralized" and (2) what "we desacralized." Sentences 2–4 illustrate the first part of the topic, sentences 5–7 the second part.

Revealing the Plan of the Paragraph

A paragraph, like a longer composition (see chapter 7), should give the reader enough guidance that he can see how ideas are related. Usually the topic sentence provides the first guideposts, especially when a paragraph falls into parts, as many expository paragraphs do. A paragraph may begin with such obvious structural markers as in "These results can be accounted for in any of three ways." The writer will then treat the three ways one after the other and will indicate when the first stops and the second begins; he may even label them, *first, second, third*. He may feel no occasion to be so pedestrian; but if he is a careful, orderly writer he will still keep his three parts separate and will let his reader know when he passes from one to the other, as the author does in the following description of a neighboring genial maniac whom he had known as a child.

> One of Mrs. Sedley's inner convictions was that she was the nymph of the spring in the valley which provided our drinking water. This conviction usually smote her in the evening shortly after sundown. Once she had been smitten, Mrs. Sedley got into a white nightgown, let down her stringy gray hair, and walked to the spring. She then washed her feet in the water and sang original little songs as she dabbled about the rim of the pool. If anyone came near her, she called a cheery greeting and said: "I am the nymph of this spring. Won't you be a nymph too?" No one ever accepted her invitation, but that didn't trouble Mrs. Sedley. She stuck a few flowers in her hair, sang another song, and went on being the nymph of the spring until someone from her house missed her and sent a servant down to lead her home. There were rumors afloat that if the servant didn't get to the spring soon enough, Mrs. Sedley was smitten by a conviction that a nymph wore no clothes, but my sister and I, though we watched her a number of evenings, never saw anything to confirm this.
>
> JOHN J. ESPEY, *Minor Heresies*

The paragraph runs so smoothly that it can be read with no more than a vague awareness of its organization, but it is developed in three parts as carefully controlled as though Espey had marked them *first, second, third*. The first sentence is clearly the topic sentence, after which the first portion begins with "This conviction," the second with "If anyone came near," and the third with "There were rumors afloat."

If the paragraph dealt with difficult material, such easygoing indications of plan would probably be insufficient; the writer might well feel that he needed what would amount to three minor paragraphs within his paragraph, each with its own clear topic sentence, perhaps each with its own conclusion. The organization should be adapted to the material, but all careful writing should have plan, and within the paragraph it should contain sufficient evidence of this plan, the subject matter and the reader being what and who they are.

Compare the following two versions of a paragraph as evidence of the importance of a clearly revealed paragraph plan.

ORIGINAL

Gail McDermott is likely to win the election as president of the Associated Students. He is both a quarterback and an actor, and he has support from organizations all over the campus. Meanwhile, some candidates for offices are running unopposed or are opposed by candidates who have little support. The widest interest in the election is being drawn by the races for the three vacant seats in the Student Senate. Many campaigners believe that the election of so many as one candidate for the Senate supported by the Associated Resident Halls Party, known as the Barbs, will assure the decline or abolishment of football at State University. The reasons for this belief are complicated and will later require some analysis. Meanwhile, Nancy Jenkins and Dorothy Cochran are leading a lively field of candidates for the presidency of AWS. That race is attracting no attention off the campus, and very little on the campus, though the question of who is to be elected to the Student Senate has become a statewide issue. The other contests, except for the race for the Student Senate, are sideshows. None of the freshman candidates, for instance, is well known or widely supported. But the Senate race has raised questions of such interest and has stimulated so much electioneering that billboard space is getting scarce on the campus, with placards plastered all the way from the president's gate to the back door of the Aggie Greenhouse.

REVISION

Interest in the State University student elections this year centers in the race for the three vacant seats in the Student Senate. The other contests are likely to be sideshows. Gail McDermott, known as both an actor and a quarterback, has support from so many organizations that his election as president of the Associated Students is practically conceded. Some of the class officers are running unopposed, and other races are attracting little attention. None of the freshman candidates, for instance, is well known or widely supported. For the presidency of AWS, Nancy Jenkins and Dorothy Cochran are leading a lively field of candidates, but the race is attracting no attention off the campus and relatively little on the campus. The election of three members to the Senate, on the other hand, has become a question of interest throughout the state and has led to so much electioneering that placards are plastered all the way from the president's gate to the back door of the Aggie Greenhouse. The issue, of course, is the future of football at State University, and many campaigners believe that the election of so many as one candidate from the Associated Resident Halls Party, known as the Barbs, will assure the decline or the abolishment of football at State University. The reasons for this belief are complicated and will require some analysis.

183

The original not only lacks signals to reveal its plan; it lacks a plan. The revision reorganizes the material and provides indications of the paragraph pattern. A topic sentence announces the purpose. The second sentence introduces a subtopic, the campaigns of minor interest, and a series of illustrations support this subtopic. Then a second subtopic is introduced by "The election of three members of the Senate, on the other hand," and the sentences discussing this topic lead to a conclusion and a transition to the next paragraph. Devices for continuity (see chapter 7) help make the organization clear.

CONVENTIONAL INDENTATION, DIALOGUE

8b

The paragraphing procedures described above serve for most ordinary prose composition, but for a few purposes indentation is used conventionally, to mark stages in the discourse

GUIDE TO REVISION

8b **¶Di**

Revise dialogue using indication to make the words of each speaker a separate paragraph.

ORIGINAL

"Good evening. It's a cold night," said Holmes. The salesman nodded, and shot a questioning glance at my companion. "Sold out of geese, I see," continued Holmes, pointing at the bare slabs of marble. "Let you have 500 tomorrow morning." "That's no good."

REVISION

"Good evening. It's a cold night," said Holmes.

The salesman nodded, and shot a questioning glance at my companion.

"Sold out of geese, I see," continued Holmes, pointing at the bare slabs of marble.

"Let you have 500 tomorrow morning."

"That's no good."

but not necessarily to set off structural units. Newspaper stories, for example, are conventionally divided every eight to ten lines, partly to break up the narrow columns of type and partly because newswriting style proceeds in a series of short units for quick scanning. The practice of setting off almost every sentence by indentation has been adopted by some modern writers who use a journalistic style. The most common other conventional use of paragraphing is to present dialogue. To help the reader identify speakers, writers of dialogue begin a new paragraph whenever the speaker changes.

FOR STUDY AND WRITING

A Analyze the following paragraphs. A full analysis would attempt to answer such questions as: What is the main idea of the paragraph? Is there a topic sentence; what is it and to what does it commit the writer? What is the plan of the paragraph; which parts are coordinate and which subordinate? How does the writer reveal the plan of the paragraph to the reader? Does the paragraph have adequate development? What are the relations between general and specific material in the paragraph? Does the paragraph cohere? What devices are used to give the paragraph continuity? Can you think of ways in which the sentences could be improved by better organization or continuity? Sentences are numbered for reference.

1. [1] Their sufferings, they told him, were too great to be endured. [2] All the men had received one, most of them two or three wounds. [3] More than fifty had perished, in one way or another, since leaving Vera Cruz. [4] There was no beast of burden but led a life preferable to theirs. [5] For when the night came, the former could rest from his labors; but they, fighting or watching, had no rest, day or night.

   WILLIAM H. PRESCOTT, *Conquest of Mexico*

2. [1] Then it is said of the American woman that, in order to satisfy her ambition, she urges men to killing extremes of competition. [2] Undoubtedly, there are greedy women in America, just as there are lazy men. [3] But they are the exception, not the rule. [4] The economic rat race, as men like to call it, far from being a female creation, terrifies the American woman, who by and large would make almost any sacrifice to reduce the work pressure on her husband and keep him healthy. [5] But the American man is certain he is loved for his money, not for himself—he brings this idea into marriage, and nothing his wife can do will disabuse him of it. [6] It is he, far more than his wife, who is the victim of the materialism he deplores in her. [7] The American man, unlike the American woman, doesn't have to be conspicuously shallow, he has only to be average in his society, to measure his personal worth by the kind of house he lives in, the car he drives, the show his family makes in the community.

   DIANA TRILLING, *Look Magazine*

3. [1] In any event, it might be useful for the newspapers themselves to undertake a scientific survey of the effects on public opinion of headlines and news angling. [2] It might be useful, too, to look into specific cases in which members of Congress or Government officials have spoken or acted on the basis of spot headline news rather than the full story. [3] One such instance comes to mind. [4] Two weeks ago the

185

State Department issued a new statement of policy on its book and library program overseas. [5] That statement was carefully worded and attempted to state the basic principles governing the acquisition and retention of books. [6] It tried to deal with the complexities of the library program. [7] Yet one sentence from the statement was featured in the news lead of one of the wire services to make it appear that the State Department had gone "soft on Red writers." [8] A number of headlines emphasized this erroneous, out-of-context reference. [9] Within minutes Congressmen were publicly denouncing the statement, though admittedly they had not read it in full. [10] Public investigations were ordered and the library program was again in jeopardy.

NORMAN COUSINS, *Saturday Review*

4. [1] The development of language is the history of the gradual accumulation and elaboration of verbal symbols. [2] By means of this phenomenon, man's whole behavior-pattern has undergone an immense change from the simple biological scheme, and his mentality has expanded to such a degree that it is no longer comparable to the minds of animals. [3] Instead of a direct transmitter of coded signals, we have a system that has sometimes been likened to a telephone-exchange, wherein messages may be relayed, stored up if a line is busy, answered by proxy, perhaps sent over a line that did not exist when they were first given, *noted down and kept* if the desired number gives no answer. [4] Words are the plugs in this super-switchboard; they connect impressions and let them function together; sometimes they cause lines to become crossed in funny or disastrous ways.

SUSANNE K. LANGER, *Philosophy in a New Key*

5. [1] Among medieval and modern philosophers, anxious to establish the religious significance of God, an unfortunate habit has prevailed of paying to Him metaphysical compliments. [2] He has been conceived as the foundation of the metaphysical situation with its ultimate activity. [3] If this conception be adhered to, there can be no alternative except to discern in Him the origin of all evil as well as of all good. [4] He is then the supreme author of the play, and to Him must therefore be ascribed its shortcomings as well as its success. [5] If He be conceived as the supreme ground for limitation, it stands in His very nature to divide the Good from the Evil, and to establish Reason "within her domination supreme."

A. N. WHITEHEAD, *Science and the Modern World*

6. [1] As for our brand of humor, the tall tale of the nineteenth century, being the expression of a young, healthy, hell-raising frontier people, gave something new and exhilarating to the humor of the world. [2] Our contributions in the twentieth century—the gag, the wisecrack, the comeback, the nifty, the clincher—are nowhere so good. [3] As long as it was expertly used—indeed, scrupulously stylized—in old vaudeville routine; as long, too, as it represented a second stage of the American humor, a kind of retort on the tall tale's boastfulness, the American gag had its real virtues. [4] But we have turned the gag into a mechanical, ubiquitous, incessant national tool so brassy as to be vulgar, so unchanging as to be dull. [5] As for the comeback, though fond of it, we have never been very good at it; in terms of cussing and repartee alike, our truck drivers are mere duffers by com-

parison with even the average cockney. [6] After all, the essence of a good comeback is a certain delayed sting, a certain perfection of surface politeness. [7] Two Frenchmen who had been brilliant and bitterly hostile rivals at school went on to become a famous general and a distinguished cardinal. [8] The cardinal, seeing the general, after many years, on a railway platform, approached him haughtily and said, "Mr. Stationmaster, when does the next train leave for Bordeaux?" [9] The general paused, smiled, and said, "At half past two, madame." [10] By comparison, how very American at bottom is the most famous of modern comebacks; how lacking in all subtlety and in any final wit is Whistler's "You will, Oscar, you will."

LOUIS KRONENBERGER, *Company Manners*

7. [1] There are, however, one or two minor points in Rabelais that may be worth notice. [2] I might, you know, analyze it as I attempted to analyze *Don Quixote.* [3] There is in *Gargantua and Pantagruel* that same complexity of thought and construction: you may note, first of all, the great essence which is common to these masterpieces as to all literature—ectasy, expressed in the one case under the similitude of knight-erranty, in the other by the symbol of the vine. [4] Then, in Rabelais you have another symbolism of ecstasy—the shape of *gauloiseries,* of gross, exuberant gaiety, expressing itself by outrageous tales, outrageous words, by a very cataract of obscenity, if you please, if only you will notice how the obscenity of Rabelais transcends the obscenity of common life; how grossness is poured out in a sort of mad torrent, in a frenzy, a very passion of the unspeakable. [5] Then, thirdly, there is the impression one collects from the book: a transfigured picture of that wonderful age; there is the note of the vast, interminable argument of the schools, and for a respond, the clear, enchanted voice of Plato; there is the vision, there is the mystery of the vast, farlifted Gothic quire; and those fair, ornate, and smiling *chateaux* rise smiling from the rich banks of the Loire and the Vienne. [6] The old tales told in the farmhouse kitchens in the Chinonais, the exultation of the new learning, of lost beauty recovered, the joy of the vintage, the old legends, the ancient turns of speech, the new style and manner of speaking: so too the old world answers the new. [7] Then one has the satire of clergy and lawyers—the criticism of life—analogous, as I said, with much that is in Cervantes, and so from divers elements you see how a literary masterpiece is made into a whole.

ARTHUR MACHEN, *Hieroglyphics: A Note Upon Ecstasy in Literature*

B Analyze the following paragraphs and prepare diagrams for them, using as models the diagrams in the section above entitled "Coordination and Subordination in Paragraphs."

1. [1] There were two ancient Greek philosophers, long before even Socrates haunted the streets of Athens, who had diametrically opposed views about reality. [2] There was Parmenides, who argued that all change is illusory, transitory, imperfect, unreal. [3] And later there was Heraclitus, who saw reality as a flowing river, apparently the same but never the same, to whom all was constant flux and change, and who dismissed the permanent as unreal, as evidence of human imperfection, as a distortion of reality.

EMMANUEL G. MESTHENE, *Learning to Live with Science*

2. [1] I do not mean to suggest that this portrait of America, composed by fifty years of history and two world wars, was wholly flattering. [2] No nation is universally admired until time has left it 3,000 years behind, and even then there will be Alcibiades in the stern of the ship and Socrates' murderers. [3] We had our critics—as many critics, indeed, as we had contemporaries. [4] We were too rich. [5] We talked in a rather childish way about brinkmanship, like two boys daring each other to walk out on a railroad trestle. [6] Our principal exports —tourists and Coca-Cola—were not everywhere well received. [7] Nevertheless, the essential figure was still the figure Wilson had presented—Wilson and that innocent doughboy of the First World War. [8] We still talked in the vocabulary of the vast ideal and backed it up with enormous gifts of goods and money. [9] And above all, though we had more power than any nation in the history of the world had ever had, we still refrained from the use of power except as a deterrent.

ARCHIBALD MACLEISH, *What Is "Realism" Doing to American History?*

3. [1] I have been emphasizing the importance of study and investigation as ends in themselves and insisting that the *raison d'être* of the universities is to further those ends for their own sakes and not as means to anything else. [2] But I am not advocating that academic work should be treated as a closed mystery, or that every undergraduate should be regarded as carrying a professorial chair in his knapsack. [3] To say that study is an attitude of mind and way of life with criteria and interests peculiar to itself is not to deny that someone who has been trained in that way of life may for that very reason be the more successful in quite different walks of life. [4] To bring this out it is necessary to distinguish between the concept of the "life of an individual" and that of the "life of an institution." [5] To speak of the life of an institution is, I have suggested, to speak of a specific tradition, a definite way of doing things, involving interests, methods, and criteria peculiar to itself. [6] But it would be a mistake to regard the life of an individual person in this circumscribed way. [7] Just as a society contains many different ways of life, so does an individual participate in many different ways of life. [8] And the ways in which the various kinds of activity in which a person participates influence each other (and therefore him) in the course of life may be compared to the ways in which different forms of activity may influence each other within a whole society. [9] Only if academic institutions maintain the integrity of their own specific ways of working will academic training continue to be of value to someone who proposes to devote most of his life to the service of some other institution.

PETER WINCH, *Universities and the State*

C A rather ignorant and illogical woman visited the Comstock Lode during the mining boom and wrote a description of the mines. It reads in part as follows:

In many of the mines the miners cannot strike the pick more than three blows before they have to go to the cooling station and stay double the time they are at work.

The cooling stations are where they have a free circulation of air. These stations are on every level. They have large tanks or reservoirs to hold the water that is pumped from one level to another. These vats are often full of boiling water. In many of the mines the water is so hot that if a person slips into one of these tanks, he is generally scalded to death before he can be rescued.

If he is rescued alive, it is only to linger a few days, suffering the most intense agony, till death relieves him of his sufferings. He is often so completely cooked in the scalding vats that the flesh drops from the bones while taking him out. His suffering and agony are terrible to witness.

The heat of the mines is very great. In some mines it is almost unendurable. In such mines it is almost impossible to work, while in others they can work without such excessive heat.

Miners are brought to the surface almost daily from overheat.

There is scarcely a day in the year that there is not from one to two funerals among the miners; and I have known of there being five in one day.

There are a great many different causes of death. Sometimes death is caused by the caving in of rock, or by falling into the scalding tanks, or by a misstep, by falling hundreds of feet down the shafts or inclines.

MRS. M. M. MATHEWS, *Ten Years in Nevada, or Life on the Pacific Coast*

This writing is not without promise. It contains concrete observation and some significant generalization, but the whole is jotted down in a scatterbrained way. Try to make a good paragraph of this material, expressing a central idea in a topic sentence, developing the paragraph in accordance with some orderly plan, and omitting extraneous matter.

D Below are paragraphs from student themes that are faulty because they lack plan, fail to turn about a topic sentence, include irrelevant material, or lack continuity. Criticize each paragraph; then supply a plausible topic sentence for each, and rewrite it into a coherent unit.

1. There are many dictionaries on the market, and some of these are reprints of older dictionaries. Some are good and some are bad. Some of these reprints reproduce books that were badly prepared when they were new, and some of them are reprints of books that were once good, but are now out of date. Many of them carry the name *Webster* on the title page. In fact, more than 140 dictionaries have that name on the cover, and the word *Webster* has been declared by the Supreme Court as part of public domain. Thus anyone can now use the word if he wants to, although anyone who uses it must be able to show that he follows principles laid down by Noah Webster. This, however, is not hard, and thus the word *Webster* does not tell much about what is inside a dictionary.
2. Although it is far from the largest museum in New York, the Cloisters is one of the most interesting for its size in the city, well arranged and well managed. It provides ready and revealing insight into the Middle Ages. Here, within a few miles of the greatest industrial concentration in the world, is a little bit of the Middle Ages. Parts of five French cloisters, with their ancient stonework from corbels to statues, have been taken down stone by stone and re-erected here.
3. In his story *"The Devil and Daniel Webster,"* Stephen Vincent Benét uses the Devil, or Mr. Scratch, to stand for evil. There is entirely too much evil in this world of ours. Mainly the story teaches a very important rule, that evil can win over almost anything but not over goodness.

This appears at the end of the story. Daniel Webster has been losing almost all the time in the trial, because he is not dealing with a fair judge or a fair opponent. In the beginning of the trial a legal battle is fought between Mr. Scratch and Daniel Webster, with Webster trying to argue fine legal points with the Devil. Finally Daniel Webster realized that he could not fight his opponents with their own weapons. You cannot win fighting evil with evil. The tactics of Daniel Webster changed, and a long speech about the good things in the world was the next order of business. "The simple things that everybody's known and felt" were what he talked about. The rule has been taught to society in many ways, but this method of teaching it through fiction is one of the most effective. Evil cannot conquer goodness is the rule that is the main theme of the story.

4. For one thing, cotton had to be picked by hand in the eighteenth century. The pickers had to spend long hours working with the cotton if they were to get anywhere. Cotton is an example of how the Industrial Revolution developed in the eighteenth century. From the fields the cotton went to the home. Here seeds were removed from the cotton by hand. This job required a considerable amount of time and patience. Then the cotton was spun into thread and woven into cloth. Men finally became tired of slow and tedious manual labor, and they began to seek new methods of producing cotton textiles. It was about the middle of the century when a number of inventions appeared that tended to shift the cotton industry from the home to the factory. Hundreds of workers could be replaced by the new machinery. Factories were built in order to house this machinery.

5. She has native aptitude as a literary critic, or at least as a critic of current magazines. Unless restrained, she literally devours *The Atlantic,* concentrating on the front and back covers, if she can stuff them into her mouth. My young brother attributes this preference for *The Atlantic* to the whisky advertisements on the back page, but I am convinced she genuinely has taste for a good thing, something solid enough so that she can get her teeth into it. This theory of mine gains support from her other tastes. She prefers the woodpulp of the *New York Times* to that of the local paper, and I confess that I prefer the *Times,* also, to read as well as to swat flies. She will have none of the sleazy magazine digests. She throws them on the floor with a squawk of disgust. My sister's magazine for teen-agers and Mother's home-building magazine intrigue her for short periods — she likes to chew the square binding at the back, for there is a certain four-square practicality in Barbara — but not for long. I gather she finds them jargonic and repetitious, lacking in the sort of body required by a young woman with three teeth. *The New Yorker* she toys with, but never consumes. I suspect that it is too brittle for her taste, caviar to the nursery. Mother, I am happy to report, encourages Barbara in her literary leanings; Mother approves of *The Atlantic,* partly because the covers are so tough that Barbara can seldom chew anything loose. Think what might happen to her taste and her stomach if she were some day to swallow a chunk of a true confession magazine.

DEFINITION

CHAPTER 9

Definition can both organize and develop writing.

Samuel Johnson, who spent years producing definitions for his great dictionary, was aware of the dangers.

> It is one of the maxims of civil law that all definitions are hazardous. . . . I see a cow. I define her: *Animal quadrupes ruminans cornutum.* But a goat ruminates and a cow may have no horns. *Cow* is plainer.

Cow may be plainer than "a ruminating animal having horns and four legs," but when Johnson turned to the use of language, where he found "perplexity to be disentangled, and confusion to be regulated," he relied on definition. Others have used definition for purposes less academic than lexicography. Joseph Wambaugh in *The New Centurions* puts the following passage into the mouth of a sergeant talking to a class of police cadets:

> Okay you guys. . . . We're supposed to be talking about searches incident to a lawful arrest. How about this one: Two officers observe a cab double-parked in front of a hotel. The fare, a man, gets out of the front seat. A woman comes out of the hotel and gets in the rear seat. Another man not with the woman walks up and gets in the back seat with the woman. Two policemen observe the action and decide to investigate. They approach and order the occupants out of the cab. They observe the man remove his hand from the juncture of the seat and the back cushion. The officers remove the rear cushion and find three marijuana cigarettes. The man was convicted. Was the decision affirmed or denied by the appellate court? Anyone want to make a guess?

No doubt neither the sergeant nor his students thought of this speech as definition. To be good policemen, the students needed to know what they could and could not do as officers of the law, and therefore they needed a working definition of both *arrest* and *search*. In discussing the case the cadets found they had to consider the limits of action — *definition* comes from Latin *de finitio*, concerning boundaries. Time was involved: if the search, to be legal, had to take place in conjunction with an arrest, and the charge was the possession of marijuana, could the arrest be conceived as having started before the discovery of the marijuana, and if not, how was the search legal? Could the fact that a man moved his hand from the juncture of the seat and the back cushion be interpreted as a "furtive gesture," suggesting a concealed weapon? If so, an overt act preceded the search. Similarly, space became involved; could the cab be considered "in control" of the man who had hired it? Suppose the man, ordered out of the cab, had just walked away; would his leaving affect "control," in view of a court decision that a man arrested ninety-five feet from his home could not be used as justification for a search, since he was too far away to control the house? The discussion continues for the remainder of the chapter, and not all of it can be considered definition, but the need for definition controls the organization and provides part of the development.

DEFINITION AS ORGANIZATION AND DEVELOPMENT

9a

Definition can dominate a piece of writing. W. H. Auden organized a discussion of detective stories by various sorts of definition:

> The vulgar definition, "a Whodunit," is correct. The basic formula is this: a murder occurs; many are suspected; all but one suspect, who is the murderer, are eliminated; the murderer is arrested or dies.
>
> This definition excludes:
>
> (1) studies of murderers whose guilt is known, e.g., *Malice Aforethought*. There are borderline cases in which the murderer is known and there are no false suspects, but the proof is lacking, e.g., many of the stories of Freeman Wills Crofts. Most of these are permissible.
>
> (2) thrillers, spy stories, stories of master crooks, etc., when the identification of the criminal is subordinate to the defeat of his criminal designs.

The interest in the thriller is the ethical and eristic conflict between good and evil, between Us and Them. The interest in the study of a murderer is the observation, by the innocent many, of the sufferings of the guilty one. The interest in the detective story is the dialectic of innocence and guilt.

As in the Aristotelian description of tragedy, there is Concealment. . . .

The Guilty Vicarage

Similarly, definition may provide the development, as in the following paragraph.

GUIDE TO REVISION

9a **Def**

Strengthen organization and development by better use of definition.

ORIGINAL

In the true sense of the word, a conservative is the person who really keeps our society from disaster. He is the man we should honor as the preserver of our traditions, not vilify as a foe to progress. . . .

[*The opening sentence appears to define, but does not. The remainder of the paper suffers because the reader does not understand a key term in the writer's special sense.*]

Jamaica Bay Wildfire Refuge is near the Kennedy· International Airport. It has suffered from the jet fuel and the oil slushed out from the airport. It has also suffered from two Nassau County sewage plants. They dump more than a quarter million gallons of partially treated sewage every day. Some of these solids collect on the bottom of the bay to the detriment of clams and other shellfish.

[*The paragraph can be read, but it lacks a sense of order and direction.*]

REVISION

If we consider a conservative as the person who is reluctant to change until he is convinced that the new is better than the old, we can see that the conservative keeps our society from disaster. He is. . . .

[*A definition, distinguishing the term* conservative *as a type of person, clarifies the remainder of the discussion. The reader may not agree, but he at least understands.*]

Part of the bay floor of the Jamaica Bay Wildlife Refuge has become fouled with what one marine biologist called "black mayonnaise." It is composed in part of sludge from the jet fuel and waste oils flushed out from nearby Kennedy International Airport and in part of incompletely treated sewage.

[*The paragraph is now centered upon the definition of the picturesque phrase, "black mayonnaise," which provides at once organization and picturesque detail.*]

It is this association of culture with every aspect of daily life, from the design of his razor to the shape of the bottle that holds his sleeping pills, that distinguishes the highbrow from the middlebrow or the lowbrow. Spiritually and intellectually the highbrow inhabits a precinct well up the slopes of Parnassus, and his view of the cultural scene is from above. His vision pinpoints certain lakes and quarries upon which his special affections are concentrated—a perturbed lake called Rilke or a deserted quarry called Kierkegaard—but he believes that he sees them, as he sees the functional design of his razor, always in relation to the broader cultural scene. There is a certain air of omniscience about the highbrow, though that air is in many cases the thin variety encountered on the tops of high mountains from which the view is extensive but the details are lost.

RUSSELL LYNES, *Highbrow, Lowbrow, Middlebrow*

More frequently, however, definition is used with other intellectual processes in writing, with analysis and classification (see chapter 5) for instance, with induction or deduction (see chapters 10 and 11).

Writings relying upon definition can vary greatly in extent. The following is only a footnote in Isaac Taylor's *Words and Places.*

Grenades have no connection with the famous siege of Granada, but are so called from their resemblance to the granate or pomegranate. The tallest and strongest men in the regiment, who were chosen to throw them, were called *Grenadiers.*

In other books definition almost dominates, in both its senses, that of setting up boundaries and that of determining the character of what lies within these boundaries. For example, A. L. Kroeber, a professor of anthropology, wrote a long book entitled *Configurations of Cultural Growth;* he used analysis to break movements into their parts and narrative to trace their growth, but definition permeates his study. First he must distinguish the patterns of culture, a concern of anthropology, from the history of culture. To make these distinctions he must define history and distinguish it from anthropology; he must also distinguish anthropology from philosophy, from sociology, from the philosophy of history—more definitions. He must define what he calls configurations, and define the character of the parts of various configurations. The word *definition* seldom occurs in his book, but the need to define was constantly with him as he wrote. Many a disputant has discovered that once he has defined his terms, the argument is over, and many a writer, facing the need to understand or to explain, has found that once he has defined his subject, he sees the directions his discussion should take.

194

"What's that?" "It's a faucet."

This is the simplest sort of definition, pointing. Small children expect it and use it constantly, but pointing is difficult in writing. Not very different is the simple equation of synonyms: a faucet is a tap or valve. This sort of definition is useful in word choice (see chapter 20), but it is too simple to have much value as either development or organization.

If we complicate this definition slightly, however, it becomes quite different so far as its use in writing is concerned. It might read: "A faucet is a device with a hand-operated valve for regulating the flow of a liquid from a pipe, barrel, etc." The statement has now become a definition of the type made famous by Aristotle and long recognized as the standard definition. It is made up of two parts: (1) a generic term, denoting a class, in this example *device* and (2) qualification to place the defined object within the class, in this instance description, "with a hand-operated valve," and purpose, "for regulating the flow." In theory, this method of definition will work for anything; everything can be classified, as we have seen in chapter 5, and with enough qualifying details any object could be distinguished from all other objects in the same class. Obviously, this method can be used for both development and organization of writing.

Both modern semanticists and modern rhetoricians, however, point out that the method has its limitations. If we relate definition to experience this method may not define anything at all. We might say, "A swoosher is a three-winged bird operating by jet propulsion." This assertion fills the requirements of an Aristotelian definition, having both a generic class and restricting details that would surely exclude all other known members of the class, but in any real sense the predication is no definition at all, because there are no swooshers, no three-winged birds, and although some sea animals move by jet propulsion, birds apparently do not.

Even if we restrict definitions of this sort to words that refer to something known to exist, the Aristotelian definition still has limitations. No word has exact meaning, and hence a definition made up of a combination of words can be at best only a combination of inexactitudes. In the definition above, who is prepared to define *device* exactly? And would a faucet cease to be a faucet if an armless man operated it with his foot? Such a query is only a quibble in a definition like this one, designed only to be helpful and directed toward a relatively simple object, but consider a definition of religion in the same dictionary (*Webster's New World Dictionary*, 2nd ed.): "a belief in a divine or superhuman power or powers to be obeyed and worshipped as the creator(s) and ruler(s) of the universe."

Such a statement would require pages, chapters, whole books if it were to attain anything approaching exactness. The fault is not in the definition; it is a good definition. The fault, if there is one, appears through the inevitable inexactitude of language. If the Zoroastrians believed that their god had not created the world, that he was only in the process of creating it, and that he did not rule it because he was fighting for it against the powers of evil, is Zoroastrianism therefore no religion? What is worship? Is saying prayers worship, but doing good deeds not worship, and what deeds are good? That is, in most areas and for most subjects, a statement or a series of statements of the Aristotelian sort are so far from providing a precise definition that modern semanticists prefer a term like "propositional function"—that is, such a proposition has definitional use, although in any strict sense it does not define.

The rhetorician, likewise, finds the Aristotelian definition inadequate, but for rather different reasons. That the Aristotelian statement is not logically exact does not bother him much; it does provide details for development and means of organizing details. It may not, however, provide the most useful definition. Isolating an object in a class—saying that a faucet is a device or that religion is a belief—may serve few practical purposes; notably, it may not much serve the needs of a writer. A mystic's account of his religious experience may tell us more about religion than could any Aristotelian proposition. The following may be a good definition of a stria: "any of the several parallel lines or abrasions on a surface," but the glacial scratches on a rock are not likely to have much meaning until we know about glaciers, how they have inexorably plowed their way, leaving stria upon rocks where they ground smaller rocks across them. Thus semanticists may prefer what is called operational definition, telling how something works and why, finding a description based upon nature and function more meaningful than definition by Aristotelian propositions. The rhetorician is inclined to agree with him, while adding that operational definition has other advantages in writing. It is likely to be more vivid, more flexible, more adaptable to an audience, and the like.

As a matter of working fact, most definitions result from the application of both procedures. The definition of a faucet, above, mainly follows Aristotelian lines, but it makes use, also, of an operational approach in the explanation of purpose, "for regulating the flow of a liquid." A sharper example of the Aristotelian method is provided by the classic definition of man as "a featherless biped."

It places man in the category of creatures having two feet, no more and no fewer, and excludes birds with the qualification "feather-less." This restriction begs such questions as whether kangaroos have two or four feet, what is a bat, whether emus are covered with feathers or a hairlike substance, and whether imaginary creatures like Mephistopheles, the anthropophagi, and Albert the Alligator can be classed as bipeds—not to mention plucked poultry. But from the rhetorician's point of view the limitation of the definition is not so much its imprecision as its inadequacy. It tells more about what a man is not than what he is. He is not a quadruped or a reptile, and he has no feathers, but of all the qualities that make man what we call human there is little hint. An operational definition of man would inevitably be much longer, but it would also be more revealing.

Types of Definition

The following are some of the sorts of definition selected for their usefulness in writing:

1. *Logical or formal definition.* This has been described above; it defines by identifying within a class—a triangle is a plane figure with three sides. It is much used in science, where it has the virtue of brevity and, within limits, of precision. With it natural phenomena can be classified with great exactitude, but as is suggested above it is usually not pictorial nor does it necessarily lead to much understanding. It is useful in organizing and developing a piece of writing mainly when used with other sorts of definition. The following is the zoological definition of man in the *Century* dictionary: "a featherless plantigrade biped mammal of the genus *Homo*."

2. *Definition by description.* Some terms can be at least partly described by enumerating or picturing physical qualities such as size, shape, color, weight, height, length, degree, and the like. The following is part of the description of man in *Webster's New International Dictionary,* 2nd ed.:

> Man is the highest type of animal existing or known to have existed, but differs from other animals more in his extraordinary mental development than in anatomical structure. . . . The main structural characters distinguishing man are: his completely erect posture and gait, from which follow the modification of the feet for walking instead of prehension (the hallux or great toe being nonopposable) and the greater development of certain muscles (as the gluteus maximus or those of the calf) which hold the body erect; the shortness of the arms and the size and perfect opposability of the thumb;

the scarcity of hair on most parts of the body; the distinctness of the chin; the comparative uniform size and even arrangement of the teeth; and most of all the enormous development of the brain, especially of the cerebrum, and the smooth rounded skull and high facial angle.

3. *Definition by example.* Examples clarify and may help to define, especially when there are not many examples of whatever is to be defined. A definition of an epic as "a poem like *The Iliad, Beowulf,* and *The Song of Roland*" could conceivably be extended to include all the poems to be classified as epics. A definition like "Nouns are words like *horse, typewriter, disease,* and *happiness*" lacks scientific validity, unless it lists all the thousands of words of the class, but it may be one of the best ways of giving a student some notion of what a noun is. Franz Boas in *The Mind of Primitive Man* finds he must define the working of man's mind. He concludes that certain ideas are inevitable in man, but that they appear in different guise in various societies. This rather complex idea he establishes with several sets of illustrations, of which the following presents the first set.

> Instances of such lack of comparability can easily be given. When we speak of life after death as one of the ideas which develop in human society as a psychological necessity, we are dealing with a most complex group of data. One people believes that the soul continues to exist in the form that the person had at the time of death, without any possibility of change; another one that the soul will be reborn at a later time as a child of the same family; a third one that the souls will enter the bodies of animals; and still others that the shadows continue our human pursuits, waiting to be led back to our world in a distant future. The emotional and rationalistic elements which enter into these various concepts are entirely distinct; and we perceive that the various forms of the idea of a future life have come into existence by psychological processes that are not at all comparable. In one case the similarities between children and their deceased relatives, in other cases the memory of the deceased as he lived during the last days of his life, in still other cases the longing for the beloved child or parent, and again the fear of death — may all have contributed to the development of the idea of life after death, the one here, the other there.

4. *Definition by significant detail.* All description presumes selection of detail, as in the description under number 2 above, but highly revealing definition may be provided by concentration upon one or relatively few significant details, as in the following:

> Man is but a reed, the most feeble thing in nature, but he is a thinking reed. The entire universe need not arm itself to crush him.

A vapor, a drop of water suffices to kill him. But if the universe were to crush him man would still be more noble than that which killed him, because he knows that he dies, and the advantage which the universe has over him: the universe knows nothing of this.

BLAISE PASCAL, *Thoughts*

Man, with all his noble qualities, with sympathy which feels for the most debased, with benevolence which extends not only to other men but to the humblest living creature, with his god-like intellect which has penetrated into the movements and constitution of the solar system — with all these exalted powers — man still bears in his bodily frame the indelible stamp of his lowly origin.

CHARLES DARWIN, *The Descent of Man*

5. *Definition by content.* Objects, and even the more difficult concepts, may be defined in part by noticing what they are made of. The following is presumably anonymous:

A man weighing 150 pounds approximately contains 3,500 cubic feet of gas, oxygen, hydrogen and nitrogen in his constitution, which at 70 cents per 1,000 cubic feet would be worth $2.45 for illuminating purposes. He also contains the necessary fats to make a 15-pound candle, and thus, with his 3,500 cubic feet of gases, he possesses great illuminating possibilities. His system contains 22 pounds and 10 ounces of carbon, or enough to make 780 dozen, or 9,360 lead pencils. There are about 50 grains of iron in his blood and the rest of the body would supply enough to make one spike large enough to hold his weight. A healthy man contains 54 ounces of phosphorus. This deadly poison would make 800,000 matches or enough poison to kill 150 persons.

6. *Definition by comparison.* Analogies and figures of speech may serve as the basis of extended definitions, and they are especially useful when combined with other approaches. They are usually not appropriate in restrictive definition, but they may promote clarity, charm, and insight.

[Man is] a map of misery. JOHN TAYLOR

Man is a rope stretching from the animal to the superman — a rope over an abyss. F. W. NIETZSCHE

Man is a god in ruins. R. W. EMERSON

The world is a pot and man is a spoon in it. Old Proverb

This is the state of man: today he puts forth
The tender leaves of hope; tomorrow blossoms,

And bears his blushing honors thick upon him;
The third day comes a frost, a killing frost,
And, when he thinks, good easy man, full surely
His greatness is a-ripening, nips his root
And then he falls, as I do.

WILLIAM SHAKESPEARE and JOHN FLETCHER

7. *Definition by interpretation.* A description can be combined with an interpretation; the result is not likely to be objective, but by combining information with an attitude toward the information it may gain effects denied to strictly objective writing. In the following, figurative devices are combined with interpretation:

What a piece of work is a man! how noble in reason! how infinite in faculty! in form and moving how express and admirable! in action how like an angel! in apprehension how like a god! the beauty of the world! the paragon of animals! And yet, to me, what is this quintessence of dust? man delights not me: no, nor woman neither.

WILLIAM SHAKESPEARE, *Hamlet*

8. *Defining by contrast.* Within limits the writer can tell what something is by demonstrating what it is not. The following is part of an epitaph for a dog, criticizing man by describing his characteristics as contrasts to the virtues of the animal.

O man! thou feeble tenant of an hour
Debased by slavery, or corrupt by power,
Who knows thee well must quit thee with disgust,
Degraded mass of animated dust!
Thy love is lust, thy friendship all a cheat,
Thy smiles hypocrisy, thy words deceit!
By nature vile, ennobled but by name,
Each kindred brute might bid thee blush for shame.

LORD BYRON, "Inscription on the Monument of a Newfoundland Dog"

Man is neither an angel nor a brute, and the very attempt to raise him to the level of the former sinks him to that of the latter.

BLAISE PASCAL, *Thoughts*

9. *Definition by origin.* Objects, and even principles and beliefs, can be profitably described by noting their origin and growth, or the process can be reversed, deducing an origin by an eventual development. Often the two work together, as in the following:

Since fossil evidence for man's ancestry is fragmentary and unsatisfactory, we can only try to deduce the form from which he evolved by studying what he is. Most of the living primates are tree-dwellers, and there can be little doubt that our own ancestors were so at one time. The structure of the human arm and shoulder bears mute witness to a long-lost habit of swinging from branch to branch. So do the flexible human hand and the five toes of the human foot, once a grasping organ. Even the adaptation of our bodies to a vertical posture probably goes back to the days when our ancestors hung by their arms much more than they stood on their legs. It seems almost certain that, somewhere in our line of ancestry, there was an arboreal form not very different from some of the existing Old World monkeys. He did not swing by his tail, since only the New World monkeys developed that refinement, but we may be sure that he was educated in the higher branches.

RALPH LINTON, The Study of Man

In practice, of course, various methods of definition tend to merge into one another, very much as definition as a mental process tends to combine with other processes like induction and deduction.

FOR STUDY AND WRITING

A Examine the following statements and comment upon the adequacy of each as definition. For which can you identify the "route" or method described above?

1. A skeleton is a man with the outside taken off and the inside taken out.

2. Slang is language that tears off its coat, spits on its hands, and gets the job done.

3. Slang is to language what an automatic elevator is to a stairway; it may get you there, and you may be able to go without thinking, but it gives neither your legs nor your mind any exercise.

4. Mental agility is not necessarily jumping at conclusions.

5. Rhetoric is speech designed to persuade.

6. Persuasion involves choice, will; it is directed to a man only insofar as he is *free*.

KENNETH BURKE

7. A narcotic is a drug that in moderate doses allays sensibility, relieves pain, and produces profound sleep, but in poisonous doses produces stupor, coma, or convulsions.

8. A chocolate éclair is like a cream puff stretched oblong and frosted or glazed with chocolate.

9. An *F* can be defined as the lower end of a grade scale that has *A* at the top.

10. A hammer is what you use to drive nails or to break rocks or to beat smooth the dented fender of a car.

11. An example of a palindrome is "Able was I ere I saw Elba."

12. In other words, education is the instruction of the intellect in the laws of Nature, under which name I include not merely things and their forces, but men and their ways; and the fashioning of the affections and of the will into an earnest and loving desire to move in harmony with those laws.

THOMAS HENRY HUXLEY

13. Moreover, man is the sole possessor of language. It is true that a certain degree of power of communication, sufficient for the infinitely restricted needs of their intercourse, is exhibited also by some of the lower animals. Thus, the dog's bark and howl signify by their difference, and each by its various style and tone, very different things; the domestic fowl has a song of quiet enjoyment of life, a clutter of excitement and alarm, a cluck of maternal anticipation or care, a cry of warning — and so on. But these are not only greatly inferior in their degree to human language; they are also so radically diverse in kind from it, that the same name cannot justly be applied to both.

WILLIAM DWIGHT WHITNEY, *The Life and Growth of Language*

14. Aircraft carriers are the backbone of a Naval task force. They are slower than planes, but, of course, faster than fixed land installations.

U.S. Navy pamphlet

15. A square is anybody who has been around but became so flat he missed the point.

B Consider the adequacy as definitions of the statements below. Describe any fault you find in them.

1. Experience is the name everyone gives to his mistakes.

2. A good book is the precious lifeblood of a master spirit embalmed and treasured upon purpose to a life beyond life.

3. A genealogist is one who traces your family back as far as your money will go.

4. *Toves* are something like badgers — they're something like lizards — and they're something like corkscrews.

5. A straight line is the shortest distance between two points.

6. Network: anything reticulated or decussated at equal intervals, with interstices between the intersections.

7. Liberty is the right to do anything that does not interfere with the liberty of others.

8. History is the lengthened shadow of one man.

9. History is philosophy teaching by examples.

10. A highbrow is a man who has found something more interesting than women.

11. A tie rack is a rack for holding ties.

12. A fallacious argument is an argument used by somebody else to prove a conclusion you do not agree with.

C Define each of the following terms, using three different methods for each.

1. the now generation	3. turn on	5. student power
2. relevance	4. confrontation	6. longhair

202

D The following are definitions of the novel or an aspect of the novel. Examine them, noting sorts of definitions used in each; as is usual in written definitions, the author has in most instances used more than one approach. Be prepared to identify the different methods in definition and to comment on the apparent strength of each.

1. Novel. An extended, fictional, prose narrative which portrays characters in a plot. The novel may stress adventure for its own sake or character development or a partisan position on some issue or a blend of these and other emphases. The plot of the novel is more extended than that of the short story, having usually many more episodes. In modern fiction it is possible to find novels that treat at length one or a few episodes in psychological depth and with a modified concept of time that plays down sequence and stresses relationship. Especially in our day, the distinction between a novel and a novella becomes difficult.
   ALFRED L. GUERIN, et al., *A Handbook of Critical Approaches to Literature*

2. One generalization about the form offers itself immediately: the short novel seems to invite each author to sum up his most basic beliefs. Short stories more often take the form of tentative sketches, ruthlessly foreshortened episodes, "crucial instances," "epiphanies," "little disturbances of man," monologues of lonely voices, anecdotes of ordinary citizens in Winesburg or Dublin. Novels, on the other hand, encourage development and ramification of their subjects, a larger rendering of society or history or biography, and great particularity of character and event. Balanced between these, the short novel seeks the utmost depth and complexity by means of radical simplifications. It often becomes a philosophical fable, often resorts to blunt summary statements and an extreme symbolism.
   DEAN S. FLOWER, *8 Short Novels*

3. It is a large mirror of life, and has a far greater range than any other form of literature. Fiction can be approached and enjoyed in so many different ways that it is almost as bewildering as life itself. I will enumerate some of these ways. We may regard fiction as a narrative pure and simple, or as a picture of manners, or as an exhibition of character, or as the vehicle of a certain philosophy of life. Again, we may approach a novel with none of these things in our minds, but with an intense desire to be more fully acquainted with the personality of the novelist himself, whose every little turn of phrase has a fascination for us. And though we may declare that not all these interests are on the same level, we have no right to say that they do not exist and have nothing to do with fiction. There are critics who tell us that we go to a novel for this or that, whereas in truth they are only telling us what their own interests happen to be.
   J. B. PRIESTLEY, *The English Novel*

4. The house of fiction has in short not one window, but a million—a number of possible windows not to be reckoned, rather; every one of which has been pierced, or is still pierceable, in its vast front, by the need of the individual vision and by the pressure of the individual will. These apertures, of dissimilar shape and size, hang so, all together, over the human scene that we might have expected of them a greater sameness of report than we find. They are but windows at the best,

mere holes in a dead wall, disconnected, perched aloft; they are not hinged doors opening straight upon life.

HENRY JAMES, Preface to *The Portrait of a Lady*

5. We considered a Novel to be a rendering of an Affair. We used to say, I will admit, that a Subject must be seized by the throat until the last drop of dramatic possibility was squeezed out of it. I suppose we had to concede that much to the Cult of the Strong Situation. Nevertheless, a Novel was the rendering of an Affair: of one embroilment, one set of embarrassments, one human coil, one psychological progression. From this the Novel got its Unity.

FORD MADOX FORD, *The Lordly Treasure House*

6. The novel, then, is a perpetual quest for reality, the field of its research being always the social world, the material of its analysis being always manners as the indication of the direction of man's soul. When we understand this we can understand the pride of profession that moved D. H. Lawrence to say, "Being a novelist, I consider myself superior to the saint, the scientist, the philosopher and the poet. The novel is the one bright book of life."

LIONEL TRILLING, *Manners, Morals and the Novel*

7. Fiction, to borrow a figure from chemical science, is life distilled.

CLAYTON HAMILTON, *Materials and Methods of Fiction*

8. Enough has been said, in summarizing the development of the novel, to show that it is a growth from various roots, that it has flourished with different results in different soils, that with time it has given forth new shoots, taken on new colors, and served different purposes. In fact, since its earliest beginning, it has at no time been static. It is as though having struggled for hundreds of years to get itself born into the light of day, it were not content with its development and had persisted in further changes. But the truth of the matter is, the novel is so vigorous a literary form, so capable a vehicle of thought and art, that different writers have adapted it to their differing purposes.

WILLIAM FLINT THRALL and ADDISON HIBBARD, *A Handbook to Literature*

9. They're all little Jesuses in their own eyes, and their "purpose" is to prove it. Oh Lord!—*Lord Jim! Sylvestre Bonnard! If Winter Comes! Main Street! Ulysses! Pan!* They are all pathetic or sympathetic or antipathetic little Jesuses *accomplis* or *manqués*. And there is a heroine who is always "pure," usually, nowadays, on the muck-heap! Like the Green Hatted Woman. She is all the time at the feet of Jesus, though her behaviour there may be misleading. Heaven knows what the Saviour really makes of it: whether she's a Green Hat or a Constant Nymph (eighteen months of constancy, and her heart failed), or any of the rest of 'em. They are all, heroes and heroines, novelists and she-novelists, little Jesuses or Jesusesses. They may be wallowing in the mire: but then didn't Jesus harrow Hell! *A la bonne heure!*

Oh, they are all novelists with an idea of themselves! Which is a "purpose," with a vengeance! For what a weary, false, sickening idea it is nowadays! The novel gives them away. They can't fool the novel.

... Secondly, the novel contains no didactive absolute.... The man in the novel must be "quick" [that is, acutely alive]. And this means one thing, among a host of unknown meaning: it means he must have a quick relatedness to all the other things in the novel:

snow, bed-bugs, sunshine, the phallus, trains, silk-hats, cats, sorrow, people, food, diphtheria, fuchsias, stars, ideas, God, tooth-paste, lightning, and toilet-paper. He must be in quick relation to all these things. What he says and does must be relative to them all.

D. H. LAWRENCE, *The Novel*

E Making use of any of the material in D above, write a 300-word definition of *definition*. When you have completed it analyze your own definition as you analyzed those in D. Then rewrite your theme using somewhat different approaches—and if possible, more appropriate ones—and hand in both your versions with an explanation of why you made the changes.

F Try to write three one-sentence definitions of a novel. For example, you might write one which distinguishes a novel from a short story, one that distinguishes a novel from a textbook, or one that distinguishes a novel from a history. Or you might think of the difference between a novel written by John Barth or Joseph Heller or Peter De Vries as contrasted with a novel by Walter Scott, and try to define the novel as a particular novelist apparently conceives it. If you cannot devise three different one-sentence definitions of novels, adopt some from the definitions of D above; the first excerpt from the *Handbook* and the selection from Priestley each starts with a one-sentence definition of a novel. Write down your three definitions.

Next, accept these three definitions as the thesis sentences for three possible extended discussions of the novel. How would the discussion based upon the three different thesis sentences differ from one another? Describe these differences in a brief paper.

G Go back to your journal and reread an entry that interests you. Notice an idea in the journal, write a one-sentence definition of the idea, accept this as a thesis sentence, and write a paper in which you develop this thesis by definition. By way of example, let us assume that you have made an entry as follows:

Dull lecture in poly sci today. The prof got off on one of the subjects he's hipped on, that Eisenhower when he was president misunderstood what is meant by offshore oil, and how his well-intentioned support of the wrong people led to the corruption of Texas politics, the pollu- of Gulf shores, and the creation of dozens of tax loopholes. I wish he'd stick to his subject, which is the history of political parties, not graft in Texas. There's graft everywhere, but he's anti-Texas.

There are dozens of concepts here that might be thought about, and even investigated. What is dullness in a lecture, and what makes it dull? What is being "anti-Texas"? Between these two ideas, the sentences are thick with concepts that might be considered; the author could pick one, try to define it, and develop a paper delineating his own concept of an idea that he uses frequently.

Try this on your own journal, defining a term you use and accepting this statement as a thesis sentence to be developed by definition.

EVIDENCE:
INDUCTIVE REASONING

CHAPTER 10

Generalizations are developed by induction and supported by evidence.

A state commission on equality in housing recently received a number of complaints from one city that landlords were consistently refusing to accept black tenants. The commission interviewed representative landlords and officers of the city's real estate association, who assured the commissioners that no discrimination existed. Complaints continued, however, and the commission was puzzled. Finally one member of the commission took a list of the apartments, real estate offices, and rental agencies in the city and started telephoning, pretending he had just arrived in the city and needed a place to live. Whenever he discovered a vacancy he immediately sent a member of the black student group cooperating with him to rent the available house or apartment. Although the telephone calls revealed a large number of vacancies, only two of them still seemed to exist when the students arrived, and those two carried impossibly high rents. The survey convinced the commission; it was "logical"; it was based on evidence. The commissioner's process was inductive. He proceeded from specific instances to a general conclusion and collected data in order to form a generalization.

The process is fundamentally related to writing, and to several matters discussed earlier in this book that concern applications of inductive reasoning—the main idea (chapter 2), which is usually a generalization based on induction; development (chapters 3 and 4), which frequently includes evidence; and even organization of the whole composition or of a paragraph (chapters 6–8), which may depend on ordering materials logically.

To generalize is to point out a common element in a number of different phenomena. A generalization can concern as few as two instances. If there are only two girls enrolled in a class, we can pick a common element and generalize, "Both the girls in my class have red hair." We may be able to find more than one common element in the same group of instances, although identifying generalizations becomes more difficult as the number of instances increases. With the two girls we can generalize that they both wear green pants or make good grades. Or we could phrase the generalization differently, "All the girls in my class are married," and it becomes misleading.

Generalizations about only two instances are not likely to be worth making, unless the common element is especially striking; usually generalization is useful in thinking and writing because it is economical. It allows us to make observations about a large number of instances without commenting separately on each one. It allows us to select a common element with which we may be able to affect many instances—the causes of a disease, for example. It also allows us to put items in groups or classes (see chapter 6).

We use induction every day, to reach conclusions, to determine causation, to make decisions. We must work with varying kinds of evidence; as a result our conclusions vary in reliability and in usefulness. For example, a man goes out in the yard on a cool morning in spring wondering whether a frost the night before has killed the cherries. He examines a dozen blossoms in different parts of his tree and finds black spots in the center of each where the fruit should be forming. A neighbor's tree shows similar black spots. He believes that he has found enough specific instances to warrant the generalization that there has been a killing frost. He has noticed a number of unharmed blossoms on a small tree partially protected by an overhanging porch roof, but he rejects these because they are not typical examples. The generalization is reliable because it is induced from a sufficient number of typical relevant instances.

Other generalizations develop in much the same way, but less directly. We can generalize that if we flip a light switch the light will turn on, even though we are aware that current is sometimes off and bulbs burn out. The generalization rests on evidence of a pattern of occurrences; although it is a prediction, a statement of probability, it is practically useful. With less assurance, but on the same basis, we can generalize that if we pull a cat's tail we shall provoke some kind of noise.

Similarly we can generalize from statistical probability. If statistics record 607 traffic deaths during the Fourth of July holiday last year and reveal that holiday traffic deaths have tended to increase annually, we can predict with some assurance that there will be more than 607 traffic deaths over the holiday this year. But statistical evidence is likely to be reliable only within limits, which may be unpredictable. Safety campaigns, blustery weather that discourages outings, or new safety devices may introduce unexpected trends.

Analogy provides another type of evidence for inductive generalization. We may conclude, for example, that the chukkar partridge will flourish in western American semideserts because it lives in parts of India that have similar climate. The generalization may be useful if the two areas are sufficiently similar. That is, analogy is reliable as evidence if the instances compared are similar in all important respects and if any differences between them can be explained. Most often, it serves best to illustrate or to clarify (see chapter 3), not as evidence.

Causation, Hypotheses

Arguments involving causation also employ induction. Usually they lead to hypotheses that are useful but require further testing. For example, a girl comes into her dormitory room late at night and finds her roommate's clothes spread about. She sees an empty flower box on the dresser. She finds a new bottle of perfume open. She remembers that this is the night of a formal dance. She discovers that her roommate's new gown is missing from the closet. She forms a hypothesis to explain the facts she has observed: that her roommate received a last-minute invitation and has gone to the dance. A hypothesis is usable if it provides a better explanation for all known facts than does any alternative; but it can be only a tentative explanation, requiring verification from the observation of more data.

Induction in Writing

Induction affects writing in two ways: in its conception and its expression. A student walking about the campus notices a "no-parking" sign blocking his vision of the fountain in front of the library. Mildly annoyed, he keeps an eye out for similar intrusions and finds another traffic sign partly covering two azalea bushes. He is now alerted, and he observes more signs, garbage cans beside the entrances to two buildings, and a large, unpainted storage bin, with hoses hanging out of it, beside the university greenhouse.

He makes a tentative generalization that the appearance of the campus is being spoiled by the carelessness of the buildings and grounds department. He decides to write a letter to the campus newspaper. By induction, he has moved from observing a number of instances to a generalization that will serve as his main idea for writing. He reverses the process, using the specific instances as evidence to support and to illustrate his generalization. He probably needs to look for additional evidence in order to develop his paper adequately. Furthermore, part of his generalization is a hypothesis, that the building and grounds department is responsible for the signs and cans. He needs to verify the causal relationship he has assumed.

Similarly, Ruth Benedict, in *Patterns of Culture*, observes wide diversity in social habits and attitudes. Induction provides the statement, but she does not leave the statement as an unsubstantiated judgment. She examines in various cultures the customs concerning adulthood, warfare, and marriage. The facts gathered both support and refine her main idea, providing substance for her writing. The structure of her entire discussion might be described as a pyramid, a pyramid that is solid and convincing because its foundation is factual. Specific details support each general statement, and the analysis could be carried down to even smaller units of composition, supported by even more specific details. The lower left block of the pyramid below, for example, is the paragraph that follows it.

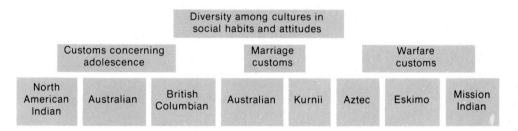

Adulthood in central North America means warfare. Honour in it is the great goal of all men. The constantly recurring theme of the youth's coming-of-age, as also of preparation for the warpath at any age, is a magic ritual for success in war. They torture not one another, but themselves; they cut strips of skin from their arms and legs, they strike off their fingers, they drag heavy weights pinned to their chests or leg muscles. Their reward is enhanced prowess in deeds of warfare.

The paragraph also resembles a pyramid, with details supporting statements that support another more general statement.

```
            ┌─────────────────────────┐
            │    Adolescence rites     │
            │  in preparation for war  │
            └─────────────────────────┘
      ┌──────────────────┐   ┌──────────────────┐
      │   Magic ritual for│   │     Torture      │
      │   success in war  │   │                  │
      └──────────────────┘   └──────────────────┘
┌──────────────────┐ ┌──────────────────┐ ┌──────────────────────┐
│  Cutting skin from│ │ Striking off fingers│ │ Dragging heavy weights│
│   arms and legs   │ │                  │ │   pinned to flesh     │
└──────────────────┘ └──────────────────┘ └──────────────────────┘
```

In the scheme of the whole chapter, however, as shown above, the apex of this pyramid becomes another statement that the writer uses to document further conclusions.

HASTY GENERALIZATION   10a

Since the writer uses induction both to produce and to support generalizations, the phrasing of generalizations can be crucial for any composition. We have already noticed difficulties that develop when a writer commits himself to more than he can fulfill (see chapter 2). Usually his impractical commitment results from hasty generalization, jumping to conclusions, asserting more than the facts warrant.

GUIDE TO REVISION

10a   Gen

Revise the generalization so that proof is possible or so that it does not commit the writer to proof.

ORIGINAL

Purebred dogs are essentially stupid. When I was a child, I had a fine pedigreed Dalmatian. I tried for months to teach him to shake hands. I succeeded only in encouraging him to jump up and wipe his front feet on anyone who came in sight. An expensive spaniel that succeded him was no better. I tried to teach him to bring in the newspaper; he learned only to chew the paper to bits.

REVISION

I never expect to own another purebred dog; my experiences have prejudiced me thoroughly in favor of curs. When I was a child. . . .

[*The too sweeping pronouncement about purebred dogs in the original is unjustified and unnecessary. With an opening like that in the revision, the writer can use his details as illustrations, avoid the problem of proof, and write a convincing paragraph.*]

A reporter spends an afternoon on the campus and interviews half a dozen professors, whom he knew when he was an undergraduate. His story in the morning paper begins, "Professors oppose student membership on faculty committees." Obviously his sweeping conclusion is not justified. Or someone relies on one or two persons he has known — or perhaps only on hearsay — and generalizes, "Poets and artists cannot be successful politicians." Such broad generalizations have the obvious disadvantage of being untrue, but they are also impractical for the writer. They commit him to the impossible. He cannot produce evidence to support them, because the evidence does not exist. Furthermore, the sweeping generalization is usually unnecessary even for a striking effect. Making the two generalizations cited above accurate would not weaken them: "At least six professors oppose student membership on faculty committees" and "There are no poets or artists among the present members of the state legislature."

Especially difficult to manage are the kinds of broad generalizations that come from general impressions. They may embody a judgment and be highly abstract: "College is nothing but anxieties" or "The new fashions are all designed to make women look awful." Generalizations less sweeping, less dependent on opinion, can be more convincingly supported: "Many college students are disturbed by the pressures of grading," "Some of the new fashions require a slim figure." There is at least a chance of supporting the less abstract generalizations with evidence.

ADEQUATE AND RELIABLE EVIDENCE **10b**

Even when a generalization is based on induction it needs to be developed in writing, to be supported with reliable evidence. To be reliable, evidence must be adequate, relevant, typical, and accurate. If the man examining his cherry trees had looked at only one blossom, he might have seen one damaged by the neighbor boy's baseball; his evidence would have been inadequate. If he had considered only the size or color of the blossoms, or even whether the petals had dropped off, his evidence would have been irrelevant to his conclusion. If he had looked at only the tree protected from frost, he would not have seen typical instances. If the man had taken his information from the testimony of a nearsighted neighbor, who had mistaken a dead bee for a frozen blossom, his evidence would have been inaccurate. To be useful to the writer in developing his ideas, evidence should be able to withstand tests of its authority.

10b   Ev

Revise, supplying additional evidence, substituting facts
for hearsay, or replacing irrelevant comments.

ORIGINAL

Some of the most important discoveries of modern times have been the result of accidents. For instance, according to the story, the great strike at Goldfield, which uncovered more than three billion dollars in gold and silver, resulted from the random kick of a bad-tempered jackass. Old Jim, while he was prospecting the area, had made camp, and was boiling his nightly coffee. The coffee pot tipped over, and splashed some boiling water on the jackass, which kicked at the pot, missed, but hit a ledge of rock instead. Old Jim stood staring, and with good reason. The sharp little hoof of the jackass had knocked loose a chunk of high-grade gold ore.

[The writer admits that his story, improbable on the face of it, has no reliable authority; yet he proceeds to use it as evidence.]

"The Windhover" is obviously not a good poem. I read it twice and was unable to make any sense at all of it. Many of the words were unclear to me, and some of them are run together in unusual ways. I do not see any reason for this kind of writing. . . .

[The comments following the opening sentence are not relevant to the topic introduced. They are pertinent only to some kind of confession by the writer about his difficulties in reading; they tell nothing of the quality or excellence of the poem.]

REVISION

In spite of the great advance in science, individual curiosity and even pure luck still play a part in important discoveries. As a matter of course the so-called miracle drugs have in the main resulted from careful planning, deliberate search, and vast technical knowledge. But even here, chance observations have helped make pharmaceutical history and save lives. Consider, for instance, penicillin. . . .

[To substantiate his serious generalization about important discoveries, the writer needs a more reliable instance than the kind of folk legend that can be given no more authority than "according to the story." If he knows the interesting story of the development of penicillin, he can proceed to write a convincing paper, with authoritative support for his generalization.]

The diction of Hopkins in "The Windhover" causes much of the poem's complexity. His description of the falcon's wing as *wimpling*, for example, combines effects of meaning, sound, and a slightly archaic flavor. Or the compounded *dapple-dawn-drawn*. . . .

[The writer should try to collect evidence relevant to the topic, not merely to his own feelings, or he should revise his topic sentence so that it becomes more specific and more susceptible to proof with relevant evidence.]

1. *Is the evidence adequate?* A generalization that all cows are black and white, made by a city boy after his first visit to a farm specializing in Holstein-Frisian cattle, is not reliable; it is based on too few instances. A vistor's "firsthand account" of the attitude of the Chinese toward the United States, based on a two-day guided tour of Peking, is not trustworthy; his evidence is inadequate.

Human beings readily jump to conclusions without adequate evidence. A mother, quite innocently, indulges in what is known as wishful thinking to select only a small part of the evidence and to conclude that her child has been grossly wronged by a teacher. Reporters from newspapers of rival political parties, perhaps not innocently, make different generalizations by selecting only part of the facts in their report of a mass meeting.

2. *Is the evidence relevant?* A writer who uses statistics about football gate receipts as evidence that football builds character is not convincing; his evidence is not relevant to his generalization. It might be pertinent to some other proposition — that football helps finance college athletic programs, for instance. Testimony of a large number of students that examinations should be abolished is not evidence for the proposition that examinations are not fair tests of knowledge.

Various kinds of emotional appeals are usually irrelevant as evidence. Name-calling is one variety. Slipping in a clever — but irrelevant — comment or slogan is another. Advertising relies heavily on information that pretends dramatically to relevance and significance but often is quite beside the point. The number of ingredients in a headache tablet is not necessarily relevant to the efficacy of the medication. Neither the absence nor presence of suds guarantees that a soap cleanses well. Charming girls in bathing suits are not relevant evidence for the virtues of cigars, beer, or automobiles. Juries are cautioned to avoid such irrelevancies as the diction of the defense attorney or the dress worn by the defendant.

3. *Is the evidence typical?* A poll of its subscribers conducted by a business magazine is not likely to provide reliable evidence on the attitudes of Americans toward taxing corporations. The instances considered would not be typical. The kind of student paper that begins "Cats can never be trusted. I once had a cat that . . ." is probably unconvincing both because the instance cited is not typical and because the evidence is inadequate. Consider the following beginning:

> Required physical education courses tend to improve study habits and to raise grade point averages for college students. A poll of physical education majors at State College reveals that more than 90 per cent testified that they studied better and made better grades while they were taking the required physical education courses.

Obviously the group surveyed does not supply typical evidence.

4. *Is statistical evidence complete and pertinent?* Statistics can be useful evidence, but incomplete or unanalyzed statistics can lead to false conclusions. A campus newspaper once reported, quite accurately, that during the year 50 per cent of the women in one college of the university had married their instructors. Outraged conclusions had to be withdrawn when it was revealed that the college was the college of engineering and the total number of women students for the year was two. Consider the following:

> Statistics show that everyone in the office is making enough money to live comfortably. The average salary, computed on certified figures for last year, was a little more than $9,800 per year per employee.

At first glance the statistics may seem to apply to the generalization. But it is possible that only two salaries, those of executives at $35,000 each, are as high as the average and that some are very low.

5. *Is the evidence up to date?* National statistics from ten years ago do not provide a reliable basis for determining present salary scales. The Battle of Gettysburg does not necessarily provide evidence for current military strategy.

6. *Is the evidence unprejudiced?* A biography commissioned by a political party for its major candidate is suspect as evidence. A probable partner in crime is not a reliable character witness for an alleged criminal.

7. *Does the evidence come from a reliable witness?* If a nine-year-old reports that his neighbor is a political spy, his evidence must be discounted because of his limited knowledge and experience. A baseball fan in the right-field bleachers probably has less reliable information than the umpire about the last pitch.

8. *Is the evidence more than an illustrative analogy?* Analogy is a useful device for development and even definition (see chapters 3 and 9), but it is usually not valid as evidence, at least not as proof. A writer trying to explain the breeds of horses to city children might wish to say that just as racing automobiles have light wheels and chassis, and trucks have very heavy running gear, racing horses are relatively light and draft horses very heavy. This is an analogy. But a horse is not a machine, and an automobile is not an organism, even though the two have common use and some common qualities. The writer cannot prove anything about a horse by evidence from an automobile, but he may be able to promote understanding of the structure of the horse by noting similarities. Consider the following use of analogy:

> The modern corporate businessman, in his use of ingenuity, is like the Indians of western Canada. Needing light during their foggy winters, they discovered a new use for the candlefish, which had long been a staple of their diets. This fish is so fat when it swims inland to spawn in the spring that the Indian has only to stick a rush into the fish's back and light it. The fish will then burn like a candle. It is evident, therefore, that modern business owes its success to the ability of Americans to take advantage of their natural resources.

The comparison of the ingenuity of the businessman with that of the Indian is an interesting analogy, but it does not justify the conclusion of the final sentence.

9. *Does the evidence show cause or only coincidence?* When possibly related events occur near each other in time, both the careless and the unscrupulous are tempted to jump to the conclusion that the first caused the second. Mere sequence in time does not provide evidence of causation, even though superstitions, false political claims, and false accusations are often based on such a sequence. Establishing a causal relation requires direct evidence that one event led to the other. The fact that a bomb was tested just before a storm broke does not prove that the explosion caused the storm.

A person dealing with causes may be tempted to generalize quickly or to admit as evidence material that is not properly evidence at all. He plays with a toad on Monday and discovers a wart on his finger on Friday. He finds a horseshoe at ten o'clock, throws it over his left shoulder at 10:02, and finds a $10 bill at noon. If he concludes that playing with the toad caused his wart or that finding the horseshoe was responsible for his good luck, he is making the error known as the *post hoc ergo propter hoc* fallacy, "after this therefore because of this." The following passage illustrates the fallacy as it often appears in writing.

> Governor Jones was elected two years ago. Since that time constant examples of corruption and subversion in government have been unearthed. It is time we got rid of the man responsible for this kind of corrupt government.

Although there is no evidence of causation, the coincidence is cited as evidence of cause.

FOR STUDY AND WRITING

A The passages given below contain generalizations that are illustrated or supported by evidence. Comment on the reliability of each generalization, indicating whether it is merely illustrated or is supported by evidence; point out especially instances of inadequate or unreliable evidence, of misused analogies, or of faulty causation. Examine each passage in light of the requirements listed in 10b.

1. Except for the encouragement that television broadcasters give to student radicals there would be little or no trouble on our campuses. Every time there is any trouble on the campus, a television cameraman will be right there, filming the bloodiest scenes he can find, and I have heard that some of these same scenes are set up by the television newsmen themselves.

2. The Japanese people are completely in accord with American democratic principles. This is the conclusion of Mr. J who has just returned after spending a week in Tokyo visiting his son who has been in Japan for some time as the American representative of a large corporation. Mr. J reports that in spite of his handicap in not knowing the Japanese language he was able to collect many favorable opinions about this country in his conversations.

3. "People of discrimination smoke Foggs," says beautiful debutante Debbie Dune, "because scientific tests have proved that they contain more fresh goodness."

4. The enclosed manuscript contains about 22,000 words. In order to arrive at this figure I counted the words on ten typical pages, computed from this total the average number of words per page, and multiplied this average by the number of pages.

5. If the Jews are legally or morally entitled to Israel, then Italy is entitled to claim Britain as a colony of the ancient Roman Empire.

6. Some people think there is nothing in spiritualism, but they have never seen any of the proofs. I was convinced last year when a friend of mine told me what he had actually seen. He had been to a meeting where a woman went into a trance, and then pretty soon people all over the room started trying to talk with spirits out of the other world. It couldn't have been faked, because the spirits knew the people they were talking to and could remember things that happened a long time ago. And a couple of the spirits even materialized and floated around the room. They didn't look much like real people, of course, because they were spirits, but you could see them so plainly there was no doubt about them.

7. The learned man will say, for instance, "The natives of Mumbo-jumbo Land believe that the dead man can eat and will require food upon his journey to the other world. This is attested by the fact that they place food in the grave, and that any family not complying with this rite is the object of the anger of the priests and the tribe." To anyone acquainted with humanity this way of talking is topsy-turvy. It is like saying, "The English in the twentieth century believed that a dead man could smell. This is attested by the fact that they always covered his grave with lilies, violets, or other flowers."

G. K. CHESTERTON, *Heretics*

8. Clearly Mr. B cannot be guilty of using his business offices to disguise the headquarters of a worldwide syndicate distributing illegal drugs. Two of his business partners testify without reservation to his honesty and good character.

9. The Roman Empire collapsed when Rome became too prosperous.

We should be sure to avoid too much prosperity for the United States.

10. During the past month living costs in America have risen .4 per cent. This figure is based on statistics compiled by governmental bureaus through sampling prices of selected commodities and on rents in important areas throughout the United States. It does not take any account of changes in federal or state taxes.

11. Sir, a woman's preaching is like a dog's walking on his hinder legs. It is not done well, but you are surprised to find it done at all.
JAMES BOSWELL, *Life of Samuel Johnson*

12. There is no doubt that the students at State University want football to be continued. The campus newspaper in a recent issue invited letters showing why the present sports program should be continued, and more than two hundred students replied. Every letter favored retention of football.

B Select any three of the following generalizations and list various sorts of evidence that might be used in support of each.

1. Campus reform can be expected only as a direct result of student protest.

2. Extracurricular activities in college require a great deal of the student's time.

3. Fraternities and sororities are valuable parts of college life.

4. Fraternities and sororities foster snobbishness.

5. Television advertising is often misleading.

6. Lobbies may discourage honest legislation.

7. Convenience does not dictate fashions.

8. Comic books encourage juvenile delinquency.

9. The mass media handicap education.

C What evidence would be required to establish the following assertions?

1. The Green Bay Packers will win the next football championship.

2. The big utilities can be expected to take every advantage of scientific discoveries in their attempts to protect the environment.

3. Dance has a great future on television.

4. The Mississippi and the Missouri drain the world's largest river basin.

5. International treaties can be relied upon.

6. Lemmings march by hordes to drown themselves in the sea.

7. The airplane was invented, not by the Wright Brothers, but by Samuel P. Langley.

8. There are 5,280 feet in a mile.

9. Taxes are high because of corruption in government.

10. Using filters on cigarettes will prevent lung cancer.

D Each of the following generalizations is followed by four statements, some of which might be relevant as supporting evidence for it, some of which are not. Comment on the suitability of each of the proposed supporting statements as relevant evidence.

1. Nobody knows who should be blamed for campus unrest, authoritarian administration, faculty that supports antiquated academic programs, the so-called street people, or liberal but possibly misguided students seeking to build a better world.

   a) The conduct of the Chicago police during the Democratic convention brought widespread criticism.

   b) Confrontations like those at Berkeley, San Francisco State, and Columbia announced to a shocked American public that a new day had arrived in campus relations.

   c) American educational disturbances were paralleled abroad in Japan, France, Italy, and Latin America, where campus revolts were mainly part of local left-wing political programs.

   d) Less sophisticated campuses like those at Kent State and a number of southern colleges seemed to reflect a notable change from the Berkeley-Columbia pattern.

2. In the half century preceding World War I, the United States came of age.

   a) In fifty years it was transformed from a rural republic to an urban state.

   b) Woodrow Wilson, who brought the Democrats into power at the end of the period, after three Republican administrations, was a native of Virginia.

   c) Great factories, steel mills, and railroad systems developed throughout the land.

   d) The Civil War, according to one writer, "cut a great white gash through the land."

3. The first quarter of the twentieth century in America brought a flood of important inventions.

   a) The principle of the dynamo was developed as early as 1831 and held great interest for Henry Adams.

   b) The first successful motor-driven airplane was invented in 1903 by the Wright brothers.

   c) Nearly a million patents were issued in the United States between 1900 and 1925.

   d) The X-ray tube was invented in the United States in 1916.

4. After the first rush of gold mining in the West, cattle raising developed as a major industry in many states.

   a) Between 1866 and 1888 some six million cattle were driven from Texas to winter on the high plains of Colorado, Montana, and Wyoming.

   b) In the late 1860's and 1870's cattle raising spread from Texas throughout much of the western territory, and herds moved annually on the "long drive" to shipping points in Kansas.

   c) Now the ranch hand with a Jeep and a truck-trailer rig has largely supplanted the cowboy with his horse and his cattle drives.

   d) The cowboy was one of the most picturesque figures of American life in the nineteenth century.

E The following table is adapted from statistics prepared by the United States Office of Education. Study it with a view to drawing generalizations.

COLLEGE DEGREES CONFERRED BY AREA OF STUDY: 1967/68

Area of study	BACHELOR'S AND FIRST PROFESSIONAL			MASTER'S			DOCTOR'S		
	Total	Men	Women	Total	Men	Women	Total	Men	Women
All areas	666,710	390,507	276,203	176,749	113,519	63,230	23,089	20,183	2,906
Agriculture	6,722	6,476	246	1,482	1,408	74	561	549	12
Architecture	3,160	3,020	140	536	509	27	6	6	—
City Planning	102	102	—	485	444	41	9	9	—
Biological Sciences	31,826	22,986	8,840	5,506	3,959	1,547	2,784	2,345	439
Business and Commerce	79,528	72,575	6,953	17,848	17,239	609	445	431	14
Computer Science and Systems Analysis	459	404	55	548	518	30	36	36	—
Education	134,905	32,492	102,413	63,503	30,798	32,705	4,079	3,249	830
Engineering	37,368	37,159	209	15,182	15,083	99	2,932	2,920	12
English and Journalism	52,340	18,288	34,052	8,646	3,972	4,674	1,009	744	265
Fine and Applied Arts	25,521	10,390	15,131	6,563	3,704	2,859	528	428	100
Foreign Languages and Literature	19,254	5,253	14,001	4,849	2,068	2,781	707	503	204
Forestry	1,586	1,569	17	315	312	3	87	87	—
Geography	2,623	2,050	573	549	461	88	96	94	2
Health Professions	31,175	16,782	14,393	3,677	1,852	1,825	243	212	31
Home Economics	7,350	198	7,152	966	51	915	71	20	51
Law	16,931	16,254	677	724	696	28	36	34	2
Library Science	814	79	735	5,165	1,051	4,114	22	15	7
Mathematical Subjects	23,513	14,782	8,731	5,527	4,199	1,328	947	895	52
Military Science	2,029	2,028	1	—	—	—	—	—	—
Philosophy	5,751	4,716	1,035	654	545	109	278	251	27
Physical Sciences	19,380	16,739	2,641	5,499	4,869	630	3,593	3,405	188
Psychology	23,819	13,792	10,027	3,479	2,321	1,158	1,268	982	286
Religion	8,541	6,959	1,582	2,724	2,134	590	401	382	19
Social Sciences	120,668	76,757	43,911	20,336	13,952	6,384	2,821	2,477	344
Trade and industrial Training	3,173	3,151	22	65	65	—	1	1	—

You might, for example, notice that library science is one of the few subjects in which more students earn graduate degrees than undergraduate degrees, that women are much less likely to take a doctoral degree in computer science than in biology. Now phrase the five most interesting generalizations you can on the basis of this table.

F The table on page 220 is adapted from statistics collected by the United States Department of Labor concerning the education of the United States labor force over eighteen years of age in recent years. Study the table, being alert to interesting generalizations.

Again, make the five most interesting generalizations you can. You might, for example, note that the nonwhite members of the labor force who were college-educated increased much more during the period 1962–1969 than in the corresponding period 1952–1959. Of course this is not the whole story; no doubt the campuses attended by the whites were generally better than those attended by the non-whites, but even the raw statistics are revealing.

EDUCATIONAL ATTAINMENT OF UNITED STATES LABOR FORCE

Percent Distribution

Date and color	ELEMENTARY		HIGH SCHOOL		COLLEGE		Median school years completed
	Less than 5 years	5 to 8 years	1 to 3 years	4 years	1 to 3 years	4 years or more	
White							
October 1952	5.2	29.3	18.7	28.3	8.8	8.5	11.4
March 1957	4.3	25.8	19.0	30.8	9.0	9.7	12.1
March 1959	3.7	23.6	19.4	32.0	9.7	10.2	12.1
March 1962	3.3	21.4	18.8	33.5	11.3	11.8	12.2
March 1964	2.7	19.8	18.5	36.0	11.1	11.9	12.2
March 1965	2.7	18.9	18.4	36.8	11.0	12.2	12.3
March 1966	2.3	17.8	18.3	37.7	11.2	12.5	12.3
March 1967	2.2	16.9	18.1	37.7	12.3	12.8	12.3
March 1968	1.9	16.1	17.4	38.6	12.8	13.2	12.4
March 1969	2.0	15.1	16.9	39.7	13.0	13.4	12.4
Nonwhite							
October 1952	26.7	38.7	15.9	10.8	3.7	2.6	7.6
March 1957	21.2	34.9	19.3	14.8	3.9	3.4	8.4
March 1959	17.9	34.3	20.6	15.8	4.5	3.9	8.7
March 1962	15.4	29.8	23.2	21.0	5.7	4.8	9.6
March 1964	11.6	29.2	24.7	22.2	6.6	5.7	10.1
March 1965	11.8	25.7	24.9	24.4	6.1	7.0	10.5
March 1966	11.1	26.7	24.3	24.8	7.1	5.8	10.5
March 1967	10.4	25.5	23.6	27.5	7.2	5.8	10.8
March 1968	9.5	23.5	24.3	28.3	7.7	6.7	11.1
March 1969	8.6	22.6	24.7	28.4	9.0	6.7	11.3

G Look again at the tables of statistics in E and F above. Select one of the generalizations you made—or another that you can now make, which you prefer—and use it as the basis of a brief composition. You can, of course, add to these statistics; obviously, for the second table you might need to notice that a "year" of education is not a reliable unit, since some schools are obviously much better than others. Similarly, in the table in E, there might be many reasons why no women in 1967–1968 took doctoral degrees in either military science or trade and industrial training, but the statistics can be used as an important part of a piece of inductive writing.

LOGIC: DEDUCTIVE REASONING

CHAPTER 11

Orderly writing should embody the principles of logic.

"To begin with," said the Cat, "a dog's not mad. You grant that?"

"I suppose so," said Alice.

"Well, then," the Cat went on, "you see a dog growls when it's angry, and wags its tail when it's pleased. Now I growl when I'm pleased, and wag my tail when I'm angry. Therefore, I'm mad."

The logic of the Cheshire Cat, revealed in the extract above, would fool few people outside Wonderland. The absurdity more than the validity of his argument suggests his madness; but consider this paragraph.

Nobody would accuse American industry of communistic tendencies. American business traditionally supports the Republican party and the interests of investors. On the other hand, labor traditionally supports the Democratic party and seeks the welfare of the worker rather than the prosperity of the investor. Naturally, therefore, labor tends toward communism.

The passage is not obviously silly. Some persons reading it might agree with the final controversial statement, but they could not have formed their opinion on the basis of the argument presented. The information does no more to establish that labor tends toward communism than the argument above does to prove that the Cheshire Cat is mad. The illogicality in both examples involves the same sort of faulty deduction.

Most thinking almost always combines at least two processes. For example, the man described in chapter 10 recognizing a frost by observing the blossoms of cherry trees could not have reached his conclusion by induction alone. He could observe that some blossoms had black spots in the center, but he could interpret this change in color only with the aid of another process. He had to call inductively on his experience or his knowledge to give him a generalization: blossoms that have black spots in the center may have been frozen. Then he could apply this generalization to a specific instance—that the blossoms on his tree had black spots— and reach the hypothesis that these blossoms had been frozen. Testing this hypothesis by his knowledge of recent weather and his further investigation, he could generalize that there had been a killing frost. The process by which he interpreted the meaning of the black spots on the cherry blossoms is called deduction, that is, the carrying of understanding further by the application of generalizations to specific cases in order to learn more about these cases.

Thinking, in other words, progresses by chain reaction, in which induction and deduction constantly work together. By induction we examine specific instances until we are justified in making a generalization. Then we can apply this generalization to specific instances and understand the instances more fully. Even though we do not consciously follow steps in formal logic, we use logical procedures to reach dozens of everyday conclusions. By induction we learn that the dormitory dining hall always serves macaroni and cheese for lunch on Mondays. Since today is Monday, we can deductively apply the general principle to the specific instance, conclude that macaroni and cheese will be on the menu in the dining hall, and decide whether to go there for lunch.

A lawyer building a case to prove that Elbridge Dangerfield is guilty of murder uses inductive reasoning. He observes that a victim was shot through the heart; Dangerfield was found in the victim's room just after the shooting with a smoking revolver in his hand; the bullet taken from the victim's body was fired from the gun Dangerfield was holding; the victim had been blackmailing Dangerfield; thus the lawyer reaches the generalization that Dangerfield is probably guilty of murder. He has reasoned inductively, but an insurance agent sitting in the courtroom as the jury announces its verdict uses deduction to conclude that Elbridge Dangerfield is a bad insurance risk.

Fully understood, deduction is a complicated process, but viewed simply it consists in putting two and two together. It applies generalizations—the results of induction, or general principles, or laws, or even definitions—to specific cases. The reasoning of the insurance agent making a professional estimate of Elbridge Dangerfield might be formalized as follows, in a series of patterns known as syllogisms.

MAJOR PREMISE: Any man judged guilty of murder has an excellent chance of hanging.

MINOR PREMISE: Elbridge Dangerfield has been judged guilty of murder.

CONCLUSION: Elbridge Dangerfield has an excellent chance of hanging.

MAJOR PREMISE: Any man who has an excellent chance of hanging is a bad insurance risk.

MINOR PREMISE: Elbridge Dangerfield has an excellent chance of hanging.

CONCLUSION: Elbridge Dangerfield is a bad insurance risk.

The insurance man has seen the relationship between generalizations he knows about and has been able to reach a valid conclusion.

Deduction operates by putting together ideas or statements with a common term, called in logic "the middle term." In the first group of statements above, the element common to each premise is "has been judged guilty of murder"; in the second group each premise contains "has an excellent chance of hanging." Oversimplified, then, deduction is sometimes like an algebraic formula: if *a* equals *b* and *b* equals *c*, then *a* equals *c*. Two terms *a* and *c* can be related on the basis of the common term *b*. If John is the same age as Bill and Bill is the same age as George, then John is the same age as George. If we know that Sir Philip Sidney was killed in the Battle of Zutphen and we know that the Battle of Zutphen occurred in 1586, then we know the date of Sidney's death.

We can look at deduction in another way by thinking of it as a process of relating groups or classes. The statement "Daisy, as she is a cow, is a ruminant" involves three elements, or terms, which might be represented by three circles varying in size according to the relative sizes of the classes they name.

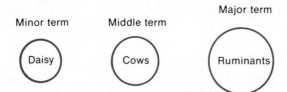

Minor term   Middle term   Major term

The minor term indicates the small class, the major term the large class, and the middle term the class somewhere between the other two in size. When the statement about the terms is put into its logical steps, it reads:

MAJOR PREMISE: All cows are ruminants.

MINOR PREMISE: Daisy is a cow.

CONCLUSION: Daisy is a ruminant.

The statements say something about how the terms are related or, if we think of the terms as circles, about which term includes the others. By the authority of the major premise, the middle circle can go into the larger one; but the minor premise puts the small circle into the middle one. Necessarily, therefore, the small circle must also be included in the large one.

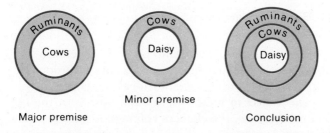

Major premise   Minor premise   Conclusion

Clearly Daisy belongs among the class of ruminants; the conclusion is *valid* because it follows logically from the premises stated. It is *true* if the premises are true.

VALID DEDUCTIONS: THE MIDDLE TERM

11a

      Reasoning turns about a middle term; if conclusions are to be valid, the middle term must be clear and stable. It must have the same meaning each time it appears. *Cow*, the middle term of the syllogism above, here refers to a recognizable object not readily confused with anything else. A century or so

224

ago, however, the word could refer to another sort of object, which one traveler defined as follows: "A cow is a kind of floating raft peculiar to the Western rivers of America, being composed of immense pine trees tied together, and upon which a log cabin is erected." Obviously, this object was not a ruminant, and if one confuses the two kinds of cows the result is nonsense. With the

GUIDE TO REVISION

11a **Ded**

Revise to make a deductive sequence valid, with the middle term stable and distributed at least once.

ORIGINAL

The things that have real educational value should obviously be the core of a college curriculum. Nobody who has ever tried to get a job will deny that typing is valuable. Certainly, then, all students should be required to take typing.

[*The terms, especially the middle term* value, *shift and slide:*
    Courses of value should be required.
    Typing has value.
    Typing should be required.
    The term* value, *as it is used in the passage, changes from a vague general idea to a more specific practical idea.*]

Great poetry becomes richer on successive reading. This must be a great poem, since it has revealed so much more to me on each reading.

[*The argument implied is:*
    Great poetry improves on successive readings.
    This poem improves on successive readings.
    This is a great poem.
    The statement does not exclude the possibility that bad poems also improve on successive readings and that this is a bad poem.*]

REVISION

I think that typing, because of its practical value, should be a required course in the college curriculum.

[*Making the conclusion both true and valid is probably impossible. Revised so that the middle term is tied down, the statement is logical:*
    All courses with practical value should be required.
    Typing has practical value.
    Typing should be required.
    But the major premise — and thus the truth of the conclusion — is now in doubt. Few college curricula could find room for every practical subject.*]

Only great poetry improves on successive reading. This must be a great poem because it has revealed more to me on each reading.

[*The addition of* only *distributes the middle term in the major premise and makes the conclusion valid. There is, of course, a question about the truth of the major premise and therefore of the conclusion. The writer needs to rethink his main idea.*]

navigating cow, as against the ruminating one, a syllogism might read as follows:

MAJOR PREMISE: A cow has a log cabin on her.

MINOR PREMISE: My Daisy is a cow.

CONCLUSION: My Daisy has a log cabin on her.

Distinguishing the two kinds of cows is not difficult, and even raft-men, who were never notable for their conscious use of syllogisms, would have been unlikely to start a piece of deduction using *cow* as the designation of raft and to finish the same deduction using *cow* to mean a ruminating animal. Not all uses of words are so readily distinguished, however; consider the following:

MAJOR PREMISE: All acts that threaten the American way of life are treasonable.

MINOR PREMISE: The new bill on civil rights threatens the American way of life.

CONCLUSION: The new bill on civil rights is treasonable.

The common element, "threatens the American way of life," is vague to begin with; the writer probably has never defined it for himself, and thus, part of his trouble may be inadequate definition. As he uses the term its meaning changes from one sentence to the next. When Mark Twain said, "It is easy to give up smoking. I have done it thousands of times," he was shifting the meaning of "to give up." The effect is humorous but not logical.

The middle term must also be "distributed" at least once in any valid logical statement. A term that is distributed includes or excludes all members of the class it denotes; "all cows" or "no cows" is a distributed term. That is, in "All cows are ruminants," *cows* is distributed, made by *all* to embrace an entire class. Similarly, in the following syllogism "no cows" is distributed: "No cows read books; this female student is reading a book; this female student is not a cow." The following syllogism is not valid because the middle term is not distributed: "Cows have horns; this animal has horns; this horned toad is a cow." The middle term is not distributed; the syllogism does not say either that all cows have horns or that all animals that have horns are cows. In any logical pattern, one premise must say something about all members of a class or no members of a class.

To be valid, then, a syllogism must contain a firm middle term distributed at least once. To be true, a syllogism must be valid and contain premises that are true. The following is valid, though not necessarily true.

226

MAJOR PREMISE: All communists read Karl Marx.

MINOR PREMISE: Mr. Jones is a communist.

CONCLUSION: Mr. Jones reads Karl Marx.

The middle term, *communists*, is distributed in the first statement. Or "reads Karl Marx" could be distributed once and used as the middle term.

MAJOR PREMISE: Anyone who reads Karl Marx is a communist.

MINOR PREMISE: Mr. Jones reads Karl Marx.

CONCLUSION: Mr. Jones is a communist.

"Reads Karl Marx," the middle term, is distributed in the major premise. The conclusion is valid, though untrue; but it would not be valid if the middle term were undistributed.

MAJOR PREMISE: All communists read Karl Marx.

MINOR PREMISE: Mr. Jones reads Karl Marx.

CONCLUSION: Mr. Jones is a communist.

One term, "all communists," is distributed, but it is not the middle term. The middle term, "read(s) Karl Marx," is not distributed, and the conclusion is not valid. Although arguments like the above are often accepted—especially when there are emotional reasons for liking the conclusion—they are no more valid than the following:

MAJOR PREMISE: All chickens have feathers.

MINOR PREMISE: This canary has feathers.

CONCLUSION: This canary is a chicken.

LOGIC IN DEVELOPMENT **11b**

If every statement in writing had to be analyzed into logical patterns like those above, writing would be both wordy and dull. Deductive patterns, however, are basic to writing, even though they are not labeled premises and conclusions. The following sentences, for example, develop mainly by deductive reasoning.

As enemy territory becomes more thoroughly protected by fighter planes during daylight hours, it becomes increasingly difficult to take the desired reconnaissance photographs each day. Therefore, the trend is toward more night photography, when darkness lends to planes increased safety from antiaircraft fire and aerial pursuit.

GEORGE RUSSELL HARRISON, *Atoms in Action*

11b   # Log

*Make development logical by supplying necessary steps in
the reasoning, revising circular arguments, or
avoiding untenable assumptions.*

ORIGINAL

REVISION

When clarinets are not playing, a
band sounds dull, because the notes
of the clarinet are so high and shrill.
[*The sentence makes no sense as it
stands, although the reader can guess
that the writer had some logical notion
in mind. The reader cannot see how
highness and shrillness prevent the band
from being dull.*]

The high, shrill tones of the clarinets are needed in a band to give it
life and color. Therefore, when the
clarinets are not playing, a band
sounds dull.
[*With all the steps of the argument
stated, the conclusion is valid, although
many readers might reject the premise,
and hence the conclusion.*]

There is a kind of basic sense or
voice within everyone that tells him
to be careful and to resist when a
possible act is wrong. Cheating is
that kind of act. Cheating is wrong,
because our consciences tell us so.
[*The statement, purporting to be an
argument, merely turns in a circle.*]

Cheating is one of the acts that
our consciences tell us are wrong.
[*There was no material for a logical
conclusion in the original, but with a
general statement that says what he
wishes to say, the writer can try to substantiate his main idea with facts or
arguments.*]

A liberal arts course is a waste of
time because it trains students for
no profession.
[*The assumption that any course that
does not train for a profession is a waste
of time may be more doubtful than the
writer realized.*]

1. A liberal arts course trains students for no profession.
2. A liberal arts course is a waste
of time.
[*The writer should select one of the
two statements combined in the original,
or perhaps drop the whole idea.*]

Fraternities are obviously valuable parts of college life. Consider
how long they have existed.
[*Is the implied reason one the writer
would try to maintain? Gangs of hood-
lums also have a long history.*]

1. Fraternities contribute to college life.
2. Fraternities have been a valuable part of college life for many
years.

The logic behind the development of the passage might be put as
follows:

MAJOR PREMISE:	Pictures cannot be safely taken over areas protected by fighter planes.
MINOR PREMISE:	In daylight, areas are protected by fighter planes.
CONCLUSION:	Pictures cannot be safely taken in daylight.

MAJOR PREMISE:	The trend is toward photography in periods of increased safety.
MINOR PREMISE:	Darkness is a period of increased safety.
CONCLUSION:	The trend is toward photography in darkness.

The reasoning could be described in other ways and broken down more completely, but clearly the paragraph develops as a series of syllogisms.

When deduction is the basis for development of an idea, such telescoping is imperative if the writing is not to be unendurably ponderous; and deduction is so natural to the human mind that deductive procedures permit great economy. But if an argument loses its clarity or validity, it loses its value as development. The writer need not record all the steps of his deduction, but he needs to provide enough information that the reader can follow. In particular, as the following comments indicate, he must not omit essential steps in his reasoning, argue in a circle, or base an argument on an untenable assumption.

1. *Including steps in the argument.* A logical conclusion is not likely to convince a reader unless it is supported by at least the essential parts of the deduction behind it. An argument may be clear in a writer's mind, but it will be obscure to his reader if he fails to record the main steps of his progress from one idea to another. Compare, for example, the following statements:

ORIGINAL

Apparently the *Titanic* had been built very well, for the crew did not know the lifeboat assignments.
[*The ignorance of the crew about lifeboat assignments is not conceivably a reason for believing that the ship had been well built.*]

REVISION

Everyone on the ship considered the *Titanic* so well built that she was unsinkable. Members of the crew were so confident of the ship's safety that they had not even learned their lifeboat assignments.

The original skips so many steps of the deductive process that its thinking seems confused. As the revision shows, however, a logical connection can be established between the ignorance of the crew and the soundness of the ship.

2. *Arguing in a circle.* One of the more subtly destructive sorts of omission leads to what is called arguing in a circle. In this sort of fallacy the discussion starts with a generalization, perhaps with a definition, but includes no further steps of a logical deduction. This omission is obscured, however, because the discussion returns to the original generalization; and if the reader accepts the original premise as true, he may feel that the whole discussion is logical. Consider the following:

ORIGINAL

The Bellelli Family by Degas is a remarkable psychological group portrait. The portrait shows the master's sense of composition and color, but its enduring charm grows from its revelation of family relationships. The psychology of the family makes it truly a group painting, not just a depiction of a collection of people on one canvas.

[*The passage starts with the idea, "psychological group portrait," but instead of developing this idea the writer merely repeats it in slightly different ways.*]

REVISION

The Bellelli Family by Degas is a remarkable psychological group portrait. With relaxed poses and naturalistic lighting the artist has centered attention upon the two children, who in turn center upon the mother. The image of the father breaks patterns of both composition and color, and the artist seems to be saying that this father, like so many others, has his interests elsewhere.

[*The reasoning is no longer circular; the paragraph develops logically from the topical idea.*]

3. *Assumptions as major premises.* As indicated above, when deduction is used for development, it seldom follows the form of the complete syllogism. More frequently it has the pattern of a variation on the syllogism, sometimes called the enthymeme, a logical sequence in which at least one essential, usually the major premise, is omitted, presumably because it can be assumed. Notice the following: "Students should oppose violence on the campus, because seeking and disseminating truth are essential to education." If this statement were analyzed logically, it would involve a whole series of syllogisms, including several that would include such major premises as these: that violence impedes or prevents the finding and dissemination of truth, that a student's overriding concern should be getting an education, and that disseminating truth is essential to education. Many students, although obviously not all, would accept most of these generalizations as true, but as they are implied in the sentence above they are assumptions.

Assumptions lie behind almost everything we do or say. We plan tomorrow and next week on the assumption that the sun will continue to rise, that there will be a tomorrow, that the earth will not burst into a shower of meteorites. These are tolerably safe as-

230

sumptions. Students go to class on the assumption that the instructor will be there. This assumption is somewhat less certain and is more or less reliable depending upon a number of conditions, including the instructor's health. Formerly, everybody assumed that if a line looked straight it was, for all practical purposes, straight. Then Einstein demonstrated that all lines curve. Now we have two assumptions. Philosophically we assume that all lines curve. Meanwhile, carpenters work on the assumption that a plumb bob or a square will provide a straight line.

Often assumptions in writing are as reliable and acceptable as that of the carpenter. An editorial writer states, "Police records prove that the old pool hall on Jones Street is encouraging juvenile delinquency; it should be closed." He is assuming, as a major premise, that anything that encourages juvenile delinquency is bad. Probably most readers will accept his assumption and therefore his argument. A writer states, "The sight-seeing tour into the mountains should begin at five so that it can be completed before dark." His assumption that sight-seeing is better in daylight than darkness will probably not meet serious opposition.

Suppose, however, that a student writes a theme recommending geology as a liberal arts subject because it promotes an understanding of the world in which we live. He is making many assumptions, among them that knowing about the physical world is so good that it is helpful to everybody. A reader says, "Yes, but geology casts doubt on the truth of Genesis, and anyone who does not believe every word of the Bible will be damned. Saving our souls is the only purpose in life, and thus geology does more harm than good." The reader has not accepted the assumption. For him the discussion proposed by the theme is not adequate, and if discussion with him is to continue, the earlier assumption—that knowledge of the physical world is absolutely good—must itself become the subject for discussion. Another student comments, "The man had been on relief for three years; he was obviously lazy." His assumption, the major premise of his argument, that only lazy men are on relief, is questionable, and therefore his argument is questionable.

Clearly, the writer needs to be aware of the assumptions on which he is basing his statements. He needs to change his argument if the assumed major premise is untenable. Or sometimes he needs to state his assumption so that the reader can judge its acceptability. By 1946, a writer on military tactics could assume, perhaps without comment, that the blitzkrieg would be part of any subsequent war; but if he was to assume, also, that atomic weapons would determine strategy, he had to say so in order to make the basis of his discussion clear. By 1970, the writer could assume silently that subsequent weapons would be atomic; but if he assumed that an aggressor nation would attack from a space platform, he would need to state his assumption. Sometimes a writer may even adopt an unreal assumption for the sake of discussion. A writer on child psychology, for instance, might begin an article with "Let us assume that you are only three months old."

A writer can readily trick himself into relying on an untenable major premise, since as an assumption it is unexpressed. Consider the following: "Although there have been a few highly publicized instances of serious injury, football is not really harmful to students and should be retained as part of every university program." The statement appears in valid form, and some readers might accept it without question. When, however, the basic assumption of the statement appears as the major premise in a syllogism, it is absurd:

MAJOR PREMISE: Anything not harmful should be on a university program.

MINOR PREMISE: Football is not harmful.

CONCLUSION: Football should be part of every university program.

The syllogism is valid, but it is not true because it is based on an untenable major premise; even the writer probably would not maintain that anything harmless—eating a cream puff, for instance—belongs on all university programs. Consider another statement of the same type: "He found himself actually enjoying the plays of Shakespeare." The statement does not explicitly state a logical proposition, but behind it is the assumption that Shakespeare's plays are dull.

FOR STUDY AND WRITING

A Indicate which of the sets of premises and conclusions given below are valid and which are true. Give reasons for your decisions. The first is valid, since it follows the logical form of the syllogism, but it is not true because the major premise is false.

1. MAJOR PREMISE: All athletes eat Crumples for breakfast.
   MINOR PREMISE: Jerry is an athlete.
   CONCLUSION: Jerry eats Crumples for breakfast.

2. MAJOR PREMISE: Any golfer who makes a hole in one is lucky.
   MINOR PREMISE: Francis made a hole in one.
   CONCLUSION: Francis was lucky.

3. MAJOR PREMISE: Men of distinction drink Old Overshoe.
   MINOR PREMISE: I drink Old Overshoe.
   CONCLUSION: I am a man of distinction.

4. MAJOR PREMISE: All cats have nine lives.
   MINOR PREMISE: Tabby is a cat.
   CONCLUSION: Tabby has nine lives.

5. MAJOR PREMISE: All good citizens vote.
   MINOR PREMISE: Al Capone voted.
   CONCLUSION: Al Capone was a good citizen.

6. MAJOR PREMISE: Money is the root of all evil.
   MINOR PREMISE: Time is money.
   CONCLUSION: Time is the root of all evil.

7. MAJOR PREMISE: No tigers have wings.
   MINOR PREMISE: This creature has wings.
   CONCLUSION: This creature is not a tiger.

8. MAJOR PREMISE: Sixty men require one-sixtieth the time required by one man.
   MINOR PREMISE: One man can remove an automobile tire in sixty seconds.
   CONCLUSION: Sixty men can remove the same tire in one second.

9. MAJOR PREMISE: No cat has eight tails.
   MINOR PREMISE: One cat has one more tail than no cat.
   CONCLUSION: One cat has nine tails.

10. MAJOR PREMISE: Man is the only creature capable of reason.
    MINOR PREMISE: Mary is not a man.
    CONCLUSION: Therefore Mary is incapable of reason.

B Discuss the logical truth and validity of the reasoning in the following passages:

1. We should rely exclusively on the opinions of young people, because everybody over thirty is untrustworthy.

2. Students, like all young people with active minds, are easily susceptible to any idea like communism, which seems to be advanced and at first glance may hold out hope for the impractical idealist. It is easy to see why our colleges should be shot through with communism.

3. People who are poor lack ambition; if they did not lack ambition they would not be poor.

4. The editorial in the last student newspaper says that only a student can understand the need for a better intramural program on the campus. Well, I am a student, and I certainly think that the program we now have is all anyone could ask for. The editorial writer should be more logical about what he says.

5. The money was taken between eleven o'clock and noon from the desk in this room. Nobody has left the room since eleven o'clock. One of the persons who have been present in the room must have taken the money. John was in the room. Obviously, he took the money.

6. All governments, for reasons of security, must deceive the public from time to time. This bulletin issued by the government therefore must be false.

7. Houses with shallow foundations should be avoided at all costs; but since this house has an unusually deep, reinforced foundation, you can have no reason for rejecting it.

8. It was plain as a pikestaff. Anyone traveling on the African mailboat would be three days late. Mr. Sims was three days late. Therefore he must be on the mailboat from Africa.

9. Of course, art is dying. The capacity of one man among ten million to create, whether in art or thought, whether in science or invention, is the hallmark of men's inequality, so that democracies, which aim at equality, have neither reward nor honor to offer to genius.

10. "There's more evidence to come yet, please your Majesty," said the White Rabbit, jumping up in a great hurry; "this paper has just been picked up."

"What's in it? said the Queen.

"I haven't opened it yet," said the White Rabbit, "but it seems to be a letter, written by the prisoner to—to somebody." . . . He unfolded the paper as he spoke, and added, "It isn't a letter after all: it's a set of verses."

"Are they in the prisoner's handwriting?" asked another of the jurymen.

"No, they're not," said the White Rabbit, "and that's the queerest thing about it." (The jury all looked puzzled.)

"He must have imitated somebody else's hand," said the King. (The jury all brightened up again.)

"Please, your Majesty," said the Knave, "I didn't write it, and they can't prove I did: there's no name signed at the end."

"If you didn't sign it," said the King, "that only makes the matter worse. You *must* have meant some mischief, or else you'd have signed your name like an honest man. . . ."

"That *proves* his guilt," said the Queen.

LEWIS CARROLL, *Alice in Wonderland*

C Each of the statements below assumes a major premise that is not stated. Supply the assumption behind each statement.

1. Many television serials are bad for children as they deal with wild and improbable adventures.

2. She must be intelligent if she is on the honor roll.

3. All high school students should have courses in driver education; careful driving is something they should know about.

4. The people next door go to church regularly; they will want to make a contribution to the Red Cross.

5. It is ridiculous to suppose that we can ever get rid of anything that has existed in our society as long as nationalism has.

6. He cannot be expected to be in sympathy with American ideas of democracy; he was born in Europe.

7. It should be a good dress; it cost more than any dress in the store.

8. You could tell she was a gossip because she criticized some of the most important clubwomen in town.

9. General B is certain to make a good university president; look how successful he was during the war.

10. Socialists really support the American system of government, for they believe in government by the people.

D In this selection from *Macbeth,* Lady Macbeth is berating her husband because, having proposed murdering the king, he now prefers not to do so. Upon what general assumptions (major premises) is Lady Macbeth relying, even though she does not express all of them, but assumes their truth?

> *Lady M.*   Was the hope drunk
> Wherein you dress'd yourself? and hath it slept since?
> And wakes it now, to look so green and pale
> At what it did so freely? From this time
> Such I account thy love. Art thou afeard
> To be the same in thine own act and valour
> As thou art in desire? Wouldst thou have that
> Which thou esteem'st the ornament of life,
> And live a coward in thine own esteem,
> Letting "I dare not" wait upon "I would,"
> Like the poor cat i' the adage?
>
> *Macb.*   Prithee, peace:
> I dare do all that may become a man;
> Who dares do more is none.
>
> *Lady M.*   What beast was't, then,
> That made you break this enterprise to me?
> When you durst do it, then you were a man;
> And, to be more than what you were, you would
> Be so much more the man.

E Examine the cartoon below and the caption that accompanies it. What are the assumptions of the writer? Do they differ from the assumptions of the cartoonist? Are any of them untenable? Write a 500-word analysis of some of the assumptions behind the cartoon and the caption, indicating why some of them may be untenable.

The Wall of Perfections; Tear It Down. Admire and respect the men and art works composing it, but don't let anybody make you think they are immortal or perfection. There's no surer way to destroy man than to confront him with a wall and make him think he can't go beyond it. It's death by inanition and despair.

SENTENCE RHETORIC: BASIC PATTERNS

CHAPTER 12

The basic sentence is a brief comment about a topic.

Ben Jonson, who was a great worker with sentences, lived as a bricklayer before he became one of England's great poets and playwrights. About sentences he concluded:

> The congruent and harmonious fitting of parts in a sentence hath almost the fastning and force of knitting and connexion: As in stones well squar'd, which will rise strong a great way without mortar.

Of course mortar does no harm; what we might call "sentence mortar" has its uses, as have the mortars used to cement paragraphs and longer compositions, but Jonson had a point. Mainly, good sentences result from appropriate units of language well fitted together.

All languages are composed of units of various sizes, most frequently of three sorts: small units of meaning (conventionally in English they are called words), extended compositions (discussed in chapters 1–11), and intermediate combinations of words or other semantic units. In English these intermediate groups are called sentences; they are the subject of chapters 12–17. On the whole they can be studied in two ways: the way they are made and the way they work, a study called *grammar;* or the way they may be appropriately used to suit the needs of speaker or writer, a study called *rhetoric.*

Since this book concerns problems of writing, it discusses grammar only as grammar illuminates rhetoric. Rhetoric involves

236

choice; it examines probable effects of different sorts of expressions in order to help a writer select from the many patterns available. Because grammar describes what is available (particularly in the sentence), we need to understand it if we are to make wise rhetorical choices.

Furthermore, understanding the working of a grammar is usually quite easy, once we have the key to it. Languages — all languages, not only English — are extremely complicated, and understanding the grammar in all its details requires long and exacting study, but the basic principles are likely to be few and relatively easy to grasp. Fortunately, for those of us who are trying to learn to write, usually only the basic principles are fundamental for rhetoric. We shall need to understand the basis of English grammar, and know it well, but we can ignore most abstruse and technical problems.

Kinds of Grammar

Grammar can be approached in many ways; one is to notice that most languages include two sorts of things, units of language and ways of using these units. The units may be of several kinds, perhaps most frequently units of sound or meaning or both. In English, for example, we usually think of words as units of meaning, but a word has also a characteristic sound or a form in writing that distinguishes it from other words. Nobody confuses *pig* with *extrapolate*, on whatever basis we distinguish them. English can be broken, also, into units smaller than words. For example, the *s*-sound in *cups* could be thought of as a sound and at the same time as a unit of use or meaning, indicating plural number. Since distinctive sounds are often identified by putting a symbol between slant lines, we could rewrite the word *cups* as sound by writing it /cup/ + /s/. In modern terminology, such units are called *morphemes;* they may comprise what are popularly known as words, like /cup/, but they can also include units smaller than words, units like /s/, which can be parts of words. Thus, whatever the units in a language, or however we conceive them, all languages have some kind of units, the sort of thing that most of us think of as vocabulary in English.

Indicating Grammatical Relationships

Linguistic units can be changed or left unchanged. If we change them we can change them variously; for example, starting with the word *capital* we can add something to it and make it *cap-*

italize. In conventional terminology we have made a noun or a modifier into a verb, but however we describe this change, the fact is that *capital* and *capitalize* work differently in a sentence and they do so because we have added something to one of them. We can also change a word internally; *write, wrote,* and *written* work differently, and we know they should work differently because of differences within the words. This procedure, revealing grammar by changes in form, is called *inflection* or *synthesis.* It is very common in the languages of the world; it was characteristic of the ancient ancestor of English, Indo-European, and it survived extensively in Classic Latin and Greek, and in Old English. In recent centuries, however, it has been going out of fashion in many languages, especially in Modern English, so that it survives only scatteringly in distinctions like the following: "The player*s* play," but "The player play*s.*"

Similarly, if linguistic units remain unchanged we can do various things with them. For example, we can change the order of the words; in the sentence "Man the pump" and "Pump the man" we know how the words *man* and *pump* work because of the words that come before and after them. We can also reveal grammar by using some words to show relationships; for example, in "hundreds of students" the construction can work only because the word *of,* which here has little semantic use, shows how *students* and *hundreds* work together. The system of revealing grammar by the order of words or by the use of words showing relationships is called *analysis, isolation,* or *distribution.* It is characteristic of Modern English. In fact, the grammar of modern American speech can be roughly defined as the grammar of a language that has been moving from synthesis toward analysis, and this fact has implications for modern rhetoric and for modern sentence structure.

Grammatical Statements

Thus far we have been using *grammar* to mean the way a language works, but this word, like most words, can also be used in other ways. It can be used in the sense of "grammar book," as a description of the way the language works. For clarity, we might call a grammar book a grammatical statement; that is, a statement that attempts to describe the way the language works. Of course, ideally, the grammatical statement should describe the grammar of the language exactly, but in fact it never does. In the first place, grammatical statements are made by human beings, and all human statements are more or less wrong, more or less inaccurate and

238

inadequate. Furthermore, language is always changing, so that even if a grammarian could devise a perfect statement about a language, by the time the statement had been worked out and published it would be inaccurate. More important is the fact that, if by *grammar* we mean a grammatical statement, there is no such thing as *the* grammar, the one and only grammar, of English or of any other language.

This assertion may need explaining. As we have seen above, languages can work in various ways, can make use of various grammatical principles, and can use various devices to reveal these principles. Scholars have never found any language that used one grammatical device and only one. Accordingly, the grammatical statement will vary depending upon which of the grammatical devices in a language we accept as the most important. For example, in the sentence "Some plays play to large audiences," we all know that *plays* is a noun and the subject of the sentence, and that *play* is a verb, involved in the predication. But how do we know? Do we know this because *plays* has an *s* in the printed form and a /z/ in the spoken form, and that these are characteristics of nouns, or do we know it because *plays* comes before *play*, and the standard English sentence pattern is subject-verb-complement? In practice, both principles may be working (perhaps not equally for all users of the language), but in preparing a grammatical statement a grammarian is likely to have to prefer one principle to the other. The result is that two grammarians can produce two somewhat different grammatical statements, depending upon which principles each assumes to be primary and which secondary. Furthermore, both may be what we should call "correct" or "true," since each provides a recognizable description of the language, and both may be useful. One approach may most tellingly reveal the philosophy of the language, another may be handy in teaching ghetto speakers, and still another may be useful for oral speech.

The older grammatical statement, still taught in many schools, started with the assumption that English would be best described by identifying the parts of speech. This approach was based upon Latin grammars, and led to parsing; in Latin it worked fairly well, because Latin made much use of inflection, and thus the parts of speech could be identified by their endings. Few English words, however, now have endings, and modern grammarians tend to become unhappy when they try to apply Latin grammar to English. They find that a grammatical statement based upon the parts of speech is often inaccurate, generally inadequate, and subtly confusing. In short, it does not tell us enough.

On the other hand, this approach cannot be entirely invalid. Modern grammarians believe that in all languages certain locutions have what they call "privilege of occurrence." That is, some linguistic units can occur in certain ways but not in certain other ways. Take the word *the*. Practically speaking, it cannot occur as subject; we do not say "The is the brightest boy in class." Neither can *the* be a verb; we do not say "He can the the problem." *The* is not privileged to occur as subject or verb. Whenever the word *the* occurs we know it is the first word of a sequence that must end with a word like *man*, as in the following: "the man"; "the public-spirited man"; "the slovenly, slack-jawed, moronic, sack-of-potatoes sort of man." Once the word *the* appears, we know that a word like *man* must come eventually, and that only certain sorts of words can intervene between them. That is, in the sense that all words have some sorts of privilege of occurrence, parts of speech must be a very real part of English grammar if not the whole of it.

Modern grammarians, therefore, have attempted to describe parts of speech or classes of words more precisely than did traditional grammarians. They have observed, for example, the inadequacy of a definition like "A verb is a word that expresses action, being, or condition"; applied literally it suggests that *collision, game,* and *violently* might all be verbs since they express action. They have substituted two kinds of descriptive criteria: form and function. For example, a noun may be distinguished by its form as a word that can have an *s* or *es* plural or a possessive form with *'s* or *s'*. Some nouns can also be distinguished by derivational endings like the *–tion* or *–ness* or *–dom* in *prevention, happiness,* and *kingdom.* A verb can be distinguished as a word that changes its form to mark the difference between present and past tenses. Functional or positional definitions can supplement these. A noun can be described as a word that can be put into the blank in a test frame like "The _____ seemed ready." Or an adjective can fit into a frame like "the _____ house." Such definitions do not solve all problems, and they become more complicated as they become more inclusive, but they are revealing, and used with caution and with due attention to exceptions, they do not tell fibs about the language.

Consideration of the function of parts of speech or words of different classes can lead to another approach to grammar. That is, grammarians recognized that not only was a noun a noun, but that it acted as *subject* of a sentence; it might be the "subject" in the sense that it was the subject under discussion. A verb was a verb as a part of speech, but it acted as *verb* in predication. It might be incomplete itself, and if so, the words that followed it, whatever their parts of speech, functioned as what could be called *complements.* The verb along with whatever accompanied it, often including a complement, constituted a predication about the subject, and thus could be called a *predicate.* Accordingly, from the point of view

240

of function, a sentence was seen to consist of a subject and a predication about it, or a predicate, and the whole followed the subject–verb–complement pattern. Perhaps we should notice here that any one of these parts can be zero, can be missing; a sentence might have no expressed subject ("Get out!"), no verb ("John, a hero?"), or no complement ("I wonder"), or it might even lack two or more of the usual parts ("Fire! What?"). Usually, however, in connected discourse, most sentences contain all three parts, and thus *subject–verb–complement* becomes a revealing description of a sentence.

The So-Called New Grammar

These are some of the answers a grammarian will get if he assumes that English will be best described by starting with the parts of speech or with the functioning of words, but he can start with other assumptions. He can, for example, notice that all languages employ sound; in fact, all languages existed as speech long before anybody wrote or read, and languages seem still to change on an oral basis. Grammar must be basically oral, and hence it must have structure; one sound has to come after another because nobody can utter two sounds simultaneously. We are not violins, capable of double-stopping; we have only one set of vocal cords. Thus, the grammarian may plausibly break a language into its sounds and observe their structure. This is essentially what we were doing earlier, when we broke *cups* into /cup/ + /s/—although, to be more exact, we should have used phonemic symbols and produced /kəp/ and /s/. Each of these symbols represents what is called a *phoneme*, a working unit of sound, and each working group of sounds is called a *morpheme*, a unit of language. The structuralist starts with a segment of language, usually a sentence. He cuts this into its *immediate constituents*, that is, into the two parts of which it is made, and then cuts each of those into its two most important parts, and so on until only phonemes are left.

This kind of analysis has been very successful. It has been used to analyze primitive, unwritten languages, to teach strange languages to the armed forces, and to teach English and other tongues as a second language, especially to primitive or uneducated people. It is being used in some schools to teach composition to Americans. It can provide a revealing description of a language, because it can record the stress, pitch, and pauses within a sentence that reflect the grammar orally. It is sometimes called *structural analysis, phonemic analysis,* or *structural linguistics*. It is too complicated to treat in any detail here, but we might notice that when a structuralist makes his first immediate constituent cut (called an

IC cut), he divides the sentence into the two conventional parts, the subject and the predicate. The next cut in the predicate severs the verb from the complement.

Thus language can be thought of as a string of things to be cut apart; equally, it may be thought of as units to be put together in a string. In writing, *loves* and *solve* are composed of the same units, but the order is different. In spelling, the order is usually rigid; in grammar it may not be so rigid but still regular enough to provide what can be called a *string grammar*, of which a particular sort is *slot and filler* grammar. Let us assume that a sentence can be thought of as a series of variously shaped slots, as follows:

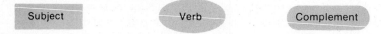

Fillers of certain shapes could be used to fill these slots; let us assume we have the following:

Obviously, blocks like these could be inserted in the slots above to make various sentences:

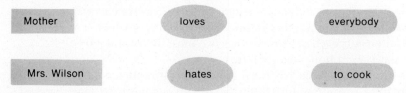

To expand such a system of slots into anything like a grammatical statement would require more shapes, but more could be provided, like the following:

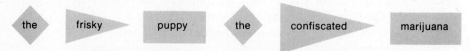

One of the most interesting grammatical statements, called *tagmemics*, is at least partly slot-and-filler. It relies upon the tagmeme, which can be defined roughly as any unit of language, but the concept of the tagmeme is complex. Both the slot and the filler, for example, can be tagmemes, and tagmemes involve concepts like those described in physics as *particle*, *wave*, and *field*. That is, a sentence can be thought of as particles—in conventional terminology as words—but it must be thought of at the same time as wave, the action of the words, and field, the interaction of words. And of course all other levels of language, from phonemes to bodies of composition like paragraphs can be tagmemes, and can be thought of from the various tagmemic points of view. This approach to language has apparently been used with success by experts working with unwritten languages, but perhaps understandably it has not yet been applied to English in any form simplified enough that it has become popular in the schools.

At least in practice, the grammatical statements we have considered thus far start mainly with language in existence, with a written sentence or with a recorded oral sentence. But of course grammar exists as speech coming to be, as sentences being written and as words being spoken and building into sentences. What is the grammar that allows language to come into existence? In an attempt to answer this question, some scholars are producing what are called *generative grammars*, embodying a set of relatively simple rules that will account for the generation of all sentences.

One such grammatical statement starts with the following rule:

$$S \longrightarrow NP + VP$$

In this formula, S stands for *sentence*, for any sentence. The symbol $\longrightarrow$ stands for "write as." NP stands for *noun phrase* and VP for *verb phrase*. Thus the formula means, "A sentence is written as a noun phrase plus a verb phrase." A noun phrase is defined roughly as any word or combination of words that users of the language would recognize as a subject. Thus NP could be "students," "all the students," "any group of students that you happen to be thinking of," or anything else that could be a subject along with whatever can accompany the subject. Similarly, VP is a verb phrase, a verb plus one or more complements, and anything that may go along with the verb and the complements. With this start the generative grammarian can write more specialized rules; one of the first will inevitably look something like the following:

$$VP \longrightarrow V + \begin{cases} NP \\ mod \\ zero \end{cases}$$

Anyone who knows the conventional grammatical statement about sentences may be able to read this as "A verb phrase can be written as a verb plus a noun phrase, a modifier, or nothing." The first alternative includes predicates containing direct objects ("Fran watched television"), predicates containing predicate adjectives ("Fran looked bored"), and predicates having no complement ("Fran sulked").

This approach has been rendered graphic through what are called branching tree diagrams. It is now being widely taught, even in elementary schools, but it can be used, also, for deeply philosophical purposes. Many grammarians distinguish between *surface grammar* and what is variously called *deep grammar, meta-linguistics,* and *universal grammar,* with differences in the terms too abstruse to be pursued here. Surface grammar is the way a particular language can be seen to work—English sentences rely upon the working together of the subject, verb, and complement, whereas in some American Indian languages the subject and the verb are parts of one expression, and in others verbal ideas are extensively drawn into nouns and modifiers.

Thus languages as we know them through surface grammar all differ from one another. Any language will differ in time from what it was before, and from speaker to speaker. But there must be something universal about language, also. Why do all people have names for things, but so far as we know no other creatures do? Dogs distinguish among people, but we doubt that they have names for us, and if they do, they have not built these names into a system that is passed on from bitch to whelp. Language seems to be the means as well as the mark of being human, and as language is universal in man, so within limits must grammar be universal.

Deep Grammar as Mind in Action

One group of modern grammarians, the sort of generative grammarians that are called *transformationalists,* have been unusually active in seeing deep grammar as evidence of the working of the human mind. They observe that very many languages use some variation upon the subject–verb–complement pattern, and they postulate that the mode of expression embodied in the formula S $\longrightarrow$ NP + VP represents the basic and characteristic working of the human mind. Such a sentence represents deep structure, and all other possible grammatical structures are believed to be *transforms* of it. That is, "Does John love Mary?" is a transform of "John loves Mary," and "Sandra's green skirt" is a

244

transform of something like "Sandra wears a skirt; the skirt is green." Not all grammarians—not to mention all psychologists or philosophers—believe in transforms, or that the mental process diagrammed in S $\longrightarrow$ NP + VP is the inevitable basic thought, but the work of the transformationalists has done much to suggest the importance for grammar in understanding communication, for the nature of the human mind, and even of whatever makes human beings human.

Obviously, some other grammarians, the tagmemists for instance, could take advantage of generative approaches, and even of transforms, but at least one group, while they probe deep grammar, deny the use or validity of the idea of the transform. These scholars believe that language should be examined as strata, and they are constructing a *stratificational grammar,* growing from the presumably universal concepts of contrast that can be expressed as direction (*up* and *down*), association (*and* or *or*), and systemization (*ordered* or *unordered*). They believe that these tendencies in language are not restricted to the grammar of the sentence but that they explain all working of language, from the phoneme through an extended composition. As yet stratification exists mainly in monographs and scholarly journals; it may someday be of great use to writers, but even its supporters would agree that at present it is too complex and uncertain to be applied.

Grammar and Writing

Thus far, these are the main approaches to English grammar. If we were to pursue any of them very far, we should become involved in many complexities, and in contradicitions between the approaches, but viewed in their elements, we may observe that the various sorts of grammatical statements produce remarkably similar results. Whether we start by naming parts of speech, by identifying the functions of words, by inserting fillers into slots, by splitting sentences according to their structures, or by generating sentences in accordance with formulas, we get much the same answers. The core of English grammar, and probably of English sentence structure, is to be sought in the way in which the subject, the verb, and the complement work together. Of course the whole job of writing must be more complicated than this makes it sound; thought and life are complex and language is a subtle and variable instrument, but we shall do well to make the use of language as simple and orderly as we can. Apparently the subject-verb-complement pattern should be a good place to start, for the pattern must be central, yet it must have variations, and these variations must be important. What a writer does or does not do with this pattern must have much to do with what makes good writing good and bad writing bad.

The working of this basic pattern—henceforth called the SVC pattern—should repay further scrutiny. Observe it in the following passage, where subjects, verbs, and complements have been italicized.

> [1] *Government* in America *has* always *regarded* the *operation* of industry as a purely private function. [2] To return to an earlier example, even the *newest-biggest* of all governmental agencies, born in the early days of the Atomic age and the Fair Deal—the AEC— *operates* its vast, complex, "monopolistic," and largely secret *domain* through private industrial contractors. [3] But *business has* yet *to show* a comparably broad and tolerant *understanding* of the legitimate domain of government. [4] In fact, some *sections* of the business community *could not do better than follow*, in this regard, Dr. Johnson's *advice*, and *clear* their *minds* of cant and prejudiced misinformation, not to say the downright nonsense about "governmental dictator-ship," and, of course, "creeping Socialism" that all too often, as a species of businessman's groupthink, takes the place of responsible consideration of the proper functions of government in free society.
> ADLAI STEVENSON, *My Faith in Democratic Capitalism*

The paragraph can be thought of as extended comments on two topics, government and business. Within the paragraph each of the four sentences introduces a topic and then adds a comment. The italicized words establish a framework for each sentence.

Subject	Verb	Complement
[1] Government	has regarded	operation
[2] newest-biggest	operates	domain
[3] business	has to show	understanding
[4] sections	could not do better than follow	advice
	clear	minds

In English even the most complicated sentences can be pro-duced by established grammatical procedures from a relatively small number of SVC patterns, such as the following:

Subject	Verb
Fish	swim.
Blue	fades.

Subject	Verb	Object Complements
Maxine	broke	her engagement.
Jack	threw	Evelyn the orchid.
The children	consider	her stupid.
The voters	made	him an ex-president.

Subject	Linking Verb	Subject Complement or Modifier
The moon	was	a ship.
The pumpkin	became	a coach.
Life	is	real.
The coat	felt	warm.
Nobody	was	there.

Most adult writers find few uses for sentences as simple as "Fish swim," but one adult writer did produce "Most fish of which we have any record, either contemporary or geologic, swim with the digestive organs downward." The precise grammatical rules by which "Fish swim" can generate a longer sentence are the materials of modern grammars; in general the processes involved are the following:

1. *Collocation.* Groups of words as well as single words can function as any of the main parts of the SVC pattern; the complement, especially, is frequently a word group.

Jack hated *washing the car.*

Jerry learned *how to retouch the photographs.*

The new boss promised *that nobody would be fired.*

Where you hide the bottle is not my concern.

The meeting *should be starting* now.

In the first three sentences the italicized word group serves as a complement, in the fourth as a subject, in the last as a verb.

2. *Combination or coordination.* Words or groups of words can be combined or coordinated to serve as any of the main parts of the pattern.

Music and *poetry* can open *hearts* but no *purses.*

The children *ran out the door* and *jumped on their bicycles.*

They knew *what they wanted* and *what they could get.*

In the first example *music* and *poetry* are joined by *and* as the subject and *hearts* and *purses* are joined as compound object complements. In the second, two predicates, verb-complement combinations, are joined by *and*. In the third, two word groups are joined as object complements. Furthermore, complete patterns can be joined to develop complicated sentences.

> Tam O'Shanter sang a sonnet, but his wife made him change his tune.

Almost infinite combinations of patterns and parts of patterns are possible.

3. *Subordination.* Any part of the sentence pattern can be modified by a word or group of words subordinated to it.

> When it is exposed to strong sunlight, blue often fades to a dull gray.

The basic pattern is "blue fades"; the beginning word group modifies the whole pattern and *often* and *to a dull gray* modify the verb *fades*.

For the last two of these processes, coordination and subordination, see chapters 15 and 16; following are further illustrations of the composition of each of the main part of the sentence pattern.

The Subject

We recognize a subject in English mainly from its position, at the beginning of the SVC sequence, except in a few inverted patterns (see chapter 14). The order is so nearly standard in English that we identify it even without anything that can be called words, as in "The quigquig obled a biscum." We know at once, because it is preceded by the determiner *The*, that *quigquig* is a symbol like *girl* or *wind* and not a word like *off*. From its position and the absence of any signs that identify it as not the subject we assume that it is, that it obled the biscum.

Most frequently subjects are what modern grammarians call *noun phrases*, composed of a pronoun or a noun and its modifiers. "Salesgirls," or "the salesgirl," or "the new salesgirl with the motheaten wig" may be a noun phrase working as a subject. Pronouns may make good subjects, since they indicate specific persons or things and by referring to an antecedent provide continuity with what has preceded; for forms of pronouns suitable for subjects, see the Glossary (chapter 27). Various verbal constructions may serve as subjects. They include clauses, which themselves include subjects and verbs, and are usually distinguished by an introductory word like *that, how, what, whether, whoever.*

What you decide to do is your own business.

That he pocketed the commission himself seemed obvious.

A verbal (see Glossary) or a verbal and its object may be used as a subject.

Watching television was his only recreation.

To solve that problem will take more than a slide rule.

The Verb

The second main part of the SVC, the verb, is the focal point of the comment about the topic; its nature and function provide the distinctions among the types of sentence patterns listed above. That is, the following three types of verbs are characteristic of the three general SVC types of clauses.

1. *Intransitive.* An intransitive verb has no complement. It does not *transfer* or *transmit* meaning; along with modifiers it can complete the comment on the topic.

The tide *turned.*

She *sang.*

In spite of her incipient laryngitis, the drafty old barn in which she was asked to perform, and the handicap of a foreign audience, she *sang* very well, reaching high C with scarcely a suggestion of a squeak.

2. *Transitive.* The transitive verb takes at least one object complement.

The car *turned* the corner.

Johnny *gave* his mother a green apple.

Johnny *ate* an apple.

3. *Linking.* A linking verb, usually some form of *to be*, carries little meaning but links a subject with a subject complement.

The milk *turned* sour.

Life *is* real, life *is* earnest.

The man *was* a traitor.

In each example, the verb is primarily a function word; *turned* joins *milk* and a complement that modifies it, *sour; was* joins *man* and *traitor*, a subject complement that restates the subject in other terms.

Notice that *turned* appears in all three groups, with some change of meaning in its different functions. Most verbs can function as either transitive or intransitive, and some may also function as linking verbs (*seem, appear, look, get, become, feel, taste, smell, sound.*) Notice also that *turned* can function in sentences like the following:

> The car *turned over.*
> The cook *turned off* the gas.

The verbs in these sentences may be called *separable suffix verbs* or *merged verbs.* Verbs of this type have been developing rapidly in the English language, apparently as combinations of verbs with various sorts of words that are not verbal. Compare the following:

> Frankie looked over the transom.
> Frankie looked over the contract.

In the first, *looked* can be thought of as the verb with "over the transom" telling where Frankie looked. In the second, this kind of interpretation obviously will not work; the contract is not a barrier over which Frankie cast her glance. *Look over* has become a verb, and a single synonym like *examined* might be substituted for it. Consider other sentences:

> The globe turned on its axis.
> The cook turned on the stove.
> Agnes called up the dumb waiter.
> The airplane blew up.

In the first, the verb is *turned,* modified by "on its axis." But in the second, the verb must be *turned on,* unless the family can expect broiled cook for dinner. In the third, we do not know whether the verb is *called* or *called up* unless we know the intended meaning. If Agnes put her head into the dumb waiter shaft and said "Yoo-hoo," the verb is *called,* and "up the dumb waiter" prescribes direction. If Agnes went to a telephone and tried to speak with a waiter who was either unable to talk or not very bright, then the verb is *called up.* In the final sentence a new verb has been created in which both parts have lost original meanings. *Up* certainly does not have its usual meaning; the plane, or what was left of it, came down. And *blew* in the combination does not mean the same thing as *blew* without the suffix. The two words have become a new word meaning exploded.

New verb combinations reflect a significant historical change in the English verb, part of the shift in the nature of the language. As we have noted before, English comes from an ancient language known as Indo-European, which was heavily inflected. Different forms of the verb indicated different uses. We retain remnants of these forms, as in "I write, I wrote, I have written." English, however, has been losing its inflected forms and stringing words together to increase the varieties of meaning possible in verbs. Compare the following:

Janet   is going   to Europe.
Janet   is going   to marry Walter.

Divided this way, to indicate that the verb is *is going*, the second sentence apparently means that Janet is walking or riding and at the end of her journey will have arrived wherever the wedding is to take place. In most contexts this meaning would not be intended; in Modern English, sense dictates that the words be divided as:

Janet   is going to marry   Walter.

The verb seems to be *is going to marry*, a future of the verb *to marry*. In recent centuries such forms have increased in number and complexity, so that we now find word groups, like those in the following, that serve as verbs.

We *look forward to being able to consider* your plan.
They *should be trying to maneuver* the lunar module.
The dean *expects to get around to offering* them some advice.

These combinations have become very numerous, with different combinations making distinctions in time or *tense*. Forms like *eat, am eating, am to eat* indicate present or future time, depending on context ("I am eating now." "I am eating a light lunch tomorrow.") Forms like *ate, was eating, had eaten, have been eating* indicate various stages of past time. These same forms and others may indicate much more. They may indicate the speaker's concepts of the sentence, the *mood* (see Glossary). "He ate the cake" is indicative; "If he were to eat the cake" is conditional; "He could have eaten the cake" is subjunctive; "Eat that cake" is imperative. Verbs may also indicate the *aspect* from which the action is viewed. "I eat in the cafeteria" implies customary action; "I keep eating too much" suggests that an action repeats itself; "I am about to start dieting" implies that an action is to begin.

Complements are not always easy to define or to distinguish from complex verbs, but in general they are of two sorts, the *object complement* and the *subject complement*.

The *object complement* completes the verb by introducing the name of something that is not the subject and that receives the predication of the verb.

Tam O'Shanter saw a *witch*.

He admired her short *skirt*.

The devil was going to roast *him*.

His wife was nursing her *wrath* to keep it warm.

These object complements are highly varied, and a complete analysis of them is not easy. For instance, in the sentences "Mary made a cake" and "The cake made Jimmie sick," the cake, clearly, did not make Jimmie in the same sense that Mary made the cake. Fortunately, however, the student need not be able to distinguish all the different sorts of objects complements in order to understand fundamental English sentence structure, or to write vigorous sentences.

The *subject complement* completes predication but also elaborates or modifies the idea expressed in the subject. It may give another name for the subject, mention a class that includes the subject, or include the subject in a group and sharpen our understanding of it.

Tam O'Shanter was a *Scotsman*.

He was an old *soak*.

The student may know this type of complement as a *predicate noun* or *predicate nominative*, since it is the name of something and it appears in the predicate. The subject complement may also give a characteristic or quality of the subject.

Tam seemed *thirsty*.

He was *drunk* every Saturday night.

The student may know this type of complement under such names as *predicate adjective*, *predicate attribute*, or *attribute complement*.

The distinction between these two kinds of complements has practical importance in usage because pronouns used as subjective complements traditionally take the subjective or nominative forms.

Often in conversation and sometimes in writing, some parts of the basic sentence are not expressed; they are understood from the context. They are incomplete in form, but they can stand independently in their contexts and are punctuated as sentences. Among the most common are exclamations, like "Oh, wonderful!" or "Incredible!" or "Good morning," and replies to questions, like "No," "Yes," or "Of course." Also used in both speaking and writing is the command, in which no subject is expressed: "Go wash the dishes" or "Let sleeping dogs lie." Our feeling for usual word order is so firm, moreover, that other types of incomplete sentences can make complete statements in context. "How old are you?" might be answered by the complete sentence "I am twenty years old," but the incomplete sentence "Twenty" is more likely. "Years old" can be omitted because we habitually state ages in years (we could specify two decades), and "I am" can be omitted because it is so obvious a part of the regular word order that the question implies it. The following passage from Dickens' *Pickwick Papers* concludes with a properly independent incomplete sentence.

> But bless our editorial heart, what a long chapter we have been betrayed into. We had quite forgotten all such petty restrictions as chapters, we solemnly declare. So here goes, to give the goblin a fair start in a new one. A clear stage, and no favour for the goblins, ladies and gentlemen, if you please.

A paragraph from Thomas Wolfe's *Of Time and the River* illustrates a modern writer's use of the incomplete sentence, punctuated like a complete sentence and making a statement.

> The coming on of the great earth, the new lands, the enchanted city, the approach, so smoky, blind and stifled, to the ancient web, the old grimed thrilling barricades of Boston. The streets and buildings that slid past that day with such a haunting strange familiarity, the mighty engine steaming to its halt, and the great trainshed dense with smoke and acrid with its smell and full of the slow pantings of a dozen engines, now passive as great cats, the mighty station with the ceaseless throngings of its illimitable life, and all of the murmurous, remote and mighty sounds of time forever held there in the station, together with a tart and nasal voice, a hand'sbreadth off that said: "There's hahdly time, but try it if you want."

Such sentences are incomplete as grammatical units because they

12a   # Frag

*Revise for clarity or the consistency of prose patterns
by completing the SVC sequence.*

ORIGINAL

A communistic government attempts to distribute the products of industry equally. It often restricts individual liberty, however. The system requiring careful control of the means of production.

[*The final group of words contains no verb.* Requiring *could work as part of a combination of verbs,* is requiring *or* had been requiring, *but alone it is not a verb. Here it seems only a modifier of* system, *a verbal. The fault can be corrected, as the revisions show, by making the fragment dependent (1); changing the part of a verb to a verb (2); making the fragment a modifying phrase (3).*]

He failed the course in physics. Either because of laziness or because of stupidity.

[*The final group of words fills no basic sentence pattern. The writer probably only mispunctuated, having meant something like (1). He could revise also by adding a verb (2) or by making the subordination clearer (3), which is often preferable.*]

Looking out toward the horizon she saw only the old cabin in which Mary had been born. A single cottonwood that had escaped the drought. The apparently boundless expanse of sunburned prairie.

[*The last two groups are actually additional objects of* saw; *they name and do not tell anything about what they name: They are not complete. They can be placed in usual order as complements (1), or they can be made sentences by adding verbs (2).*]

REVISION

(1) A communistic government attempts to distribute the products of industry equally, but since the system requires careful control of the means of production, it often restricts individual liberty.

[*Often this method of revision is best, since it clarifies relationships of ideas although it may require, as does this sentence, that the author rethink his statement and subordinate some of it.*]

(2) The system requires careful control of the means of production.

(3) It often restricts individual liberty, however, requiring careful control of the means of production.

(1) He failed the course in physics, either because of laziness or because of stupidity.

(2) He failed the course in physics. Either laziness or stupidity was his trouble.

(3) Because of either laziness or stupidity, he failed the course in physics.

(1) Looking out toward the horizon, she saw only the old cabin in which Mary had been born, a single cottonwood that had escaped the drought, and the apparently boundless expanse of sunburned prairie.

(2) Looking out toward the horizon, she saw the old cabin in which Mary had been born. A single cottonwood that had escaped the drought stood near it. The apparently boundless expanse of sunburned prairie spread into the distance.

omit one of the essential elements, subject or verb, but they may
be successful, because basic word order has become standard in
English. We anticipate missing elements, and in successful incomplete sentences we automatically supply them. The writer establishes a pattern in his style that helps the reader perceive unexpressed thoughts. The incomplete sentences in the Wolfe paragraph
above are subjects; the reader can understand what the writer
means to say about these subjects—that they are observed or were
part of his experience.

Most writers, however, use the incomplete sentence sparingly,
except in reports of conversation. It is a special device, to be used
for special effects. In the hands of anyone but an expert, it may
cause trouble because basic patterns have not been established, and
missing ideas cannot be supplied. The fragment in the following
suggests only that the writer has been careless.

> The actor had to strap his ankle to his thigh. In this manner giving
> the impression that he had only one leg.

Combining not only avoids punctuating as a sentence the second
sequence of words, which lacks a verb, but also relates ideas more
precisely.

> The actor had to strap his ankle to his thigh in order to give the
> impression that he had only one leg.

The following also suggests mainly carelessness, perhaps mispunctuation.

> In the morning Thoreau was released from jail. Although he still
> refused to pay the tax.

The second group, labeled by *Although* as a modifier rather than
an independent pattern, could easily be combined with the first
sentence.

> Although he still refused to pay the tax, Thoreau was released from
> jail in the morning.

FOR STUDY AND WRITING

A Sentences developed from the different patterns described above
have different uses. The following paragraphs have been rewritten—
often distorted—by changing sentences from one pattern to another,

so that patterns with linking verbs predominate. Rewrite each paragraph, changing sentences to subject-verb or subject-verb-object patterns whenever you think you can make the writing more direct. Your instructor can supply the original paragraphs for comparison.

1. [1] My father was as unmechanical a man as ever lived, and the gasoline engine was a complete mystery to him. [2] Sometimes as far as he went was to lift the hood and stare at the engine, or maybe it was to reach in and wiggle a wire to see whether it would wiggle. [3] But mostly his procedure was to confine himself to kicking the tires. [4] It was never clear to me, and I doubt that it was clear to him, what he expected to learn from this, but he was very serious and professional about it. [5] His attitude was that of thumping a patient's chest. [6] It is a wonder to me that he never placed a stethoscope to the casing or stuck a fever thermometer down the valve stem.

2. [1] The fact that courses are the means by which information is made available to students is one reason for there being textbooks. [2] Knowing where you are going in a class is easier for both student and teacher if there is a textbook available to them. [3] That is, to make the point briefly we could say that a textbook helps to show where the course is going and that it provides a kind of record of how the teacher and the class are getting on. [4] A lot of people are going to have their feelings hurt by this statement, especially those teachers that are liberal and progressive, who are the same ones who deplore there being any kind of prescription in teaching, and who may also have various reasons for not wanting textbooks, perhaps partly because of the name, textbook, because the word *text* has echoes of scripture and authority.

3. [1] The great migratory wave in American life is from country to city. [2] What happens to tens of thousands of children is that they are swept up in this wave and transplanted from a rural variety of poverty to the more oppressive urban ghetto. [3] Something from which they suffer is what social scientists call "cultural shock." [4] Little conception of what happens in cities or even what they look like is the rule for such children. [5] Trips to and around the city, routine for more privileged children, are the instruments whereby it is possible to help equalize the impoverished child's knowledge of modern realities.

4. [1] One of the important features of Boston today is a fairly stimulating atmosphere for the banker, the broker, for doctors and lawyers. [2] "Open-end" investments are prosperous, a major product at the dock is still fish, the wool market is still good, and employment is available for workers in the shoe factories in the nearby towns. [3] For the engineer, the physicist, the industrial designer, for all the highly trained specialists of the electronic age, Boston and its area are of seemingly unlimited promise. [4] Sleek, well-designed factories and research centers popping up everywhere are characteristic of the area; in the Sunday papers are pleas from the companies for more chemists, more engineers, and humble expressions of the executive benefits of salary and pension and advancement the companies are prepared to offer.

5. [1] Internationally, in the Fifties, intellectuals in Europe and America were the counter force to a dull, blatant Communist cultural offensive in a long weary effort. [2] They were what might be called successful, in a kind of Korean success. [3] Whether it was the boring quality of

the enemy, the boring quantity of the support received at home—or the boring quality of home itself, which in those years, was after all being defended—this conflict was one that can scarcely be said to have produced much in the way of intellectual monuments. [4] Those who engaged in this battle of the books and journals became possessors of what knowledge about the matter was available years before. [5] There were no new positions, only long heavings at the mired axles of cultural lag. [6] It was a stalemate, painful to some, boring to others, to some few, death; very like the Korean War. [7] Hungary in 1956 was a proof that there was no real point to it, but it went on.

B The passage below contains a number of fragments used as sentences. Revise the passage, using methods outlined above, to make the fragments complete sentences or to combine the fragments with other sentences.

[1] Catherine II, called Catherine the Great, came to the throne of Russia in 1762. [2] Her reign being the most notable of those that followed the long rule of Peter the Great. [3] Although she was not a Russian by birth, Catherine remained on the Russian throne for thirty-four years. [4] Since she was a German princess whose marriage to Peter III had been arranged by Frederick the Great. [5] Peter III being half-insane when he took the throne.

[6] Catherine, a despot who wished to be regarded as an "enlightened" despot like Frederick II of Prussia, more concerned with maintaining prestige than spreading culture through her country. [7] She continued some of the work of Peter the Great, ruling the country firmly and strengthening the central authority by administrative reorganization. [8] Divisions of the government under appointed governors and vice-governors, all responsible to the tsarina. [9] A church dependent for its property and power on the desires of the central authority. [10] By maintaining a strong foreign policy and striking her rivals when they were weak, she established the international position of the Russian empire. [11] A war against the Ottoman Empire, 1768–1774, was highly successful. [12] Which led to navigation rights for Russian ships and added considerably to Russian territory. [13] Poland, weakened by internal strife, and easily preyed upon by surrounding empires. [14] By 1795 Poland had virtually ceased to exist as an independent state. [15] Her territory partitioned among Austria, Prussia, and Russia. [16] With Catherine getting the lion's share.

[17] Catherine's internal policies did bring about a number of reforms. [18] The establishment, for example, of schools and academies. [19] Reform, however, being carefully regulated. [20] In order to prevent genuine enlightenment of the masses that might weaken the position of the aristocracy.

C Analyze the sentences in a theme you have written recently, underlining subject, verbs, and complements in the main patterns of each. Which of the main patterns appear most frequently? Try changing any of the sentences you can to another pattern, and decide whether the original or the revision is better.

PREDICATION

CHAPTER 13

Subject, verb, and complement must interact logically.

Predication is the relationship expressed when subject, verb, and complement interact. Selection of the subject, verb, and complement, therefore, directs the course of the sentence—determines its structure, controls its plausibility. This sequence usually begins with the subject. English grammar being what it is, the first word in a sentence that can be a subject automatically becomes one, whether the writer chooses it for that purpose or not, unless he does something to keep it from being a subject. Consider, for example, a student attempting to tell why he came to college. If the first word that comes to his mind is *reason* and he writes it down as a start, he restricts what is to follow. He cannot very easily use a verb like *growls* or *objects* or *admires*. He is almost committed to *is* or a verb like it. One student, starting in this way, muddled on to the following:

> The reason why I came to college is because, there being a law you have to have a degree for a license in the field of embalming in this state, which is my goal in life.

This production, of course, is not a sentence at all. A good sentence might have been written even with *reason* as the subject, but the writer's troubles began when he chose to begin with the relatively abstract word.

He might have chosen another abstraction: "My desire to meet the state requirements for an embalming license. . . ." He would have had a somewhat larger group of verbs to select from—

258

cause or *make* or *influence,* as well as *is*—but he would still have been likely to write an indirect and perhaps wordy sentence. In conversation, if the student had been asked why he came to college, he probably would have stayed out of trouble. He might have said something like "I want to be a mortician" or "I need a degree so I can get a mortician's license." He would have chosen the actor as the subject and produced a straightforward, clear sentence.

CHOOSING SENTENCE SUBJECTS

13a

Usually, a writer chooses the subject as the first important word in a prospective sentence, and the subject, once it is chosen, does much to chart the predication. The verb must work with the subject, and the complement must follow from the verb.

GUIDE TO REVISION

13a   **Subj**

Select a new subject and revise the sentence, preferably with a verb other than to be.

ORIGINAL

The important thing is that shifting your weight is necessary on a turn if the centrifugal force is to be accommodated for.

[*The abstract subject and the unnecessary frame lead to a clumsy construction.*]

The reason for Gary's wanting to major in molecular physics was because of his interest in a graduate degree in rocket engineering.

REVISION

You must shift your weight to accommodate for the centrifugal force developed in the turn.

[*With a pronoun as the subject the sentence becomes simpler and clearer.*]

Gary wanted to major in molecular physics as preparation for a graduate degree in rocket engineering.

Thus, when a writer chooses a subject, he limits his choice of subsequent words and structures, and unless he chooses a subject that can be developed with an appropriate verb, he is likely to be led into a clumsy, rambling sentence.

The principle applies most readily to descriptions of events or acts. If a pencil drops off the table and a speaker wishes to comment, he is likely to say "The pencil dropped" or "The pencil fell on the floor." He picks the actor for the subject and uses the verb to specify what the actor did. Writers of fiction draft most of their sentences so that someone or something does, says, or is something. Writers of factual, expository prose may have to use abstractions, but the following passage illustrates how even a scholarly subject may be discussed mainly in sentences with the actor as subject.

> Two sages of a later day actually preached that the independent growth of American English was not only immoral but a sheer illusion. They were Richard Grant White, for long the most widely read writer upon language questions, and Thomas R. Lounsbury, for thirty-five years professor of English language and literature in the Sheffield Scientific School at Yale. White's "Words and Their Uses" (1872) and his "Everyday English" (1880) were mines of erudition. Lounsbury effectively attacked the follies of the grammarians; his two books "The Standard of Usage in English" and "The Standard of Pronunciation in English," not to mention his excellent "History of the English Language" and his numerous magazine articles, showed a sound knowledge of the early history of the language, and an admirable spirit of free inquiry. But when these laborious scholars turned from English proper to American English, they tried to deny its existence altogether, and to support that denial brought a critical method that was anything but scientific.
>
> H. L. MENCKEN and RAVEN I. MC DAVID, JR., *The American Language*

A less skillful writer might have been tempted to start sentences differently, to begin the first one, for example, with "A major contribution to the study of. . ." or "The attitude of two sages of a later day. . . ." The resulting sentences would have been less direct and less clear.

Expository writing sometimes requires relatively abstract subjects followed by a form of *to be*—to fit a context, for introductory matter, or in topic sentences, for example. The following sentences, for good reason, all have subjects that take the verb *to be:*

> Our lives are the creation of memory and the accompanying power to extend ourselves outward into ideas.
>
> At the other pole, the spread of attitudes is wider.
>
> This polarization is sheer loss to us all.

These are good sentences. The student writer, however, can do nothing more important to improve his writing than try whenever possible to pick a subject that will allow him to use a vigorous verb rather than *to be*. Compare the following:

260

> The origin of the classic prose that Mark Twain developed was his knowledge of the actual speech of America.
>
> Out of his knowledge of the actual speech of America Mark Twain forged a classic prose.

The second sentence is obviously stronger and more direct than the first, which is a bad remolding of the original. Compare another distortion with its original:

> The demand for creation in science is a high level of imaginative insight and intuitive perception.
>
> Creation in science demands a high level of imaginative insight and intuitive perception.

Again, the second sentence, the original with the subject-verb-object pattern, seems stronger. Although the writing may attempt only to inform the reader of the existence of facts and ideas, sentences turning about an actor and an action usually say more and say it more briefly.

Even within the subject-verb-object sentences a specific subject usually works better than a more general one. Abstract nouns (*heroism, nutrition, importance, reason*) tend to require more general, less active verbs than concrete nouns (*quarterback, candle, creek*). In many confused sentences the trouble starts with the selection of abstract subjects that betray the writer into indiscriminate use of verbs like *mean, provide, result, prove.* Because transitional sentences and topic sentences may need to deal in abstractions, they are particularly susceptible to weakening through imprecise subjects.

Since the sentence begins to take written shape when a possible subject is put on paper, the following practical suggestions can save the student from verbal quagmires.

1. *Prefer actors as subjects.* On the whole, make the subject the actor if there is one; in other words, use as the grammatical subject the actual subject, what the sentence is mainly about.

2. *Avoid abstract subjects.* Whenever possible, prefer concrete, specific subjects to abstract or general ones. Especially treacherous are abstract words that usually must be followed by *is* or *was*—words like *reason, aspect, explanation, conclusion, situation,* and *attitude.* Often, of course, a context demands a sentence beginning with such a subject, but more often a better sentence emerges when the writer avoids abstract subjects.

3. *Consider the verb.* Choose the subject in light of the verb that is to follow it, for the subject alone cannot make the sentence, but usually a concrete, precise subject will permit the choosing of an appropriate verb.

4. *Rewrite for clarity.* If a sentence causes trouble, try finding a new subject and starting over. Often you can ask yourself, "What am I trying to say?" and make the simplest answer you can. The subject in your answer often makes the best subject for the sentence you are trying to write.

Choosing Verbs

Even with a good subject, an inadequate verb may weaken a sentence, since after the subject the verb mainly determines whether the most appropriate sentence pattern will develop. Consider "Johnny is a dropout." The writer begins with the actor as subject, but *is* does little more than fill the sentence pattern and link *Johnny* and *dropout.* If the writer has no more to say than to establish this connection, the sentence is adequate; but usually a writer has more to say. He could go on with the same pattern: "Johnny is a dropout. He was the owner of a convertible. It was new. But he was in a wreck with it." This sounds wordy and immature largely because verbs carry none of the meaning. Compare "Johnny, a dropout, wrecked his new convertible." With an expressive verb, *wrecked,* for the main predication, *is* and *was* can be dropped and *dropout* and *new* can be subordinated (see chapter 16).

Furthermore, sensitive choice of verbs permits subtle distinctions. In the example above, the devastation to Johnny's car could be altered by changing *wrecked* to *scratched, dented, crumpled, smashed,* or *demolished.* Such precision through verb choice characterizes poetry and much narrative writing, but verbs can specify also in the sort of exposition that students need to write. For example, students quoting material often overuse the verb *state,* when they might gain at once variety and exactness by judicious use of dozens of synonyms like *write, declare, assert, imply, infer, admit, insist, concede, suggest, explain, postulate, amplify, propose, conclude, reveal, doubt, argue, point out, wonder if, question whether, add, continue.*

LOGICAL PREDICATION

13b

The following sentences embody the basic patterns described in chapter 12; they look like basic sentences:

The prejudice ambushed inconsequentials.

The lampshade promised Albert.

The person meant the failure.

Wilbur seemed the artichoke.

The words in each position have privilege of occurrence where they are used; that is, the "sentences" differ from "Wilbur artichokes seem," which makes no sense because *artichoke* does not have privilege of occurrence as a verb nor *seem* as a complement.

GUIDE TO REVISION

13b　　　　　　　　　　　　　　　　**Pred**

Revise so that main parts of sentence patterns—subjects, verbs, and complements—are compatible in meaning.

ORIGINAL

REVISION

My mother being unable to resist installment buying meant the difference between a comfortable existence and constant fear of poverty.

[*Mother makes no sense as a subject for* meant. *The subject probably intended is buried as a modifier.*]

My mother's inability to resist installment buying meant the difference between a comfortable existence and constant fear of poverty.

[*Not* mother, *but "mother's weakness" was probably intended as the subject.*]

The lack of a proper diet and work as heavy as lumbering demanded a man with a strong body.

[*The second part of the compound subject fits logically with the verb, but the first does not.*]

Work as heavy as lumbering, carried on without a proper diet, demanded a man with a strong body.

[*The main subject is selected and the inappropriate idea becomes a modifier.*]

They should not have allowed such tragedies to exist in their community.

[Tragedies *do not* exist.]

(1) They should not have allowed conditions in their community that further such tragedies.

(2) They should not have allowed such tragedies to occur in their community.

Perhaps there are omissions that should have been included.

[*Even though the verb* should have been included *is in a subordinate clause, it must make sense with* omissions, *represented by* that.]

He managed during his life to defy all the traditional qualities of an outstanding politician.

["*To defy qualities" makes no sense.*]

(1) Perhaps there are omissions that should have been remedied.

(2) Perhaps material has been omitted that should have been included.

[*The second revision is clearer.*]

He managed during his life to defy all the traditions associated with success in politics.

They also differ from grammatical sentences that err factually, like "Rabbits eat elephants." Nevertheless, these groups of words obviously do not work as basic sentences. Modern grammarians would call them ungrammatical, because the words chosen to be subject, verb, and complement in each example do not represent meanings that can conceivably work together. The predication, the interaction of the main sentence parts, is here not logical.

Nobody is likely to write a sentence like any of the absurdities above: "The person meant the failure," for example. The following sentence, however, was taken from a student paper:

> Any person ill on the day of that first performance would have meant the failure of the entire summer theater.

Embedded in the longer sentence, the basic pattern does not parade its lack of sense so obviously. The reader can guess at what the writer intended to say, even though the sentence appears confused and obscure, but essentially the longer sentence is as illogical as the pattern on which it is based. The writer has not produced a meaningful predication, has not combined a compatible subject, verb, and object. He probably meant:

> The illness of any member of the cast on the day of that first performance would have led to the failure of the entire summer theater.

The sentence remains awkward, however, and in most contexts the following would be better:

> If any member of the cast had been ill on the day of that first performance, the entire summer theater would probably have failed.

A better subject allows the use of a more vigorous verb and permits a more vigorous sentence.

Consider a similar sentence:

> The basis for the continuing unrest, which was partly misunderstanding and partly understanding too well what our motives were, held little hope among our representatives for success in negotiating new treaties.

The words seem at first glance to communicate; they sound like a sentence. But they communicate only confusion because the basic pattern is confused: "The basis held little hope." The subject, verb, and complement do not make sense together, even though the length of the sentence momentarily obscures the confusion. With a new subject and verb the sentence comes nearer sense:

264

> Our representatives had little hope of negotiating new treaties because of the continuing unrest, based partly on misunderstanding our motives and partly on understanding them too well.

Clear communication requires a basic sentence pattern that makes a plausible predication.

Subjects, Verbs, and Predication

A plausible predication requires first of all a subject and verb that make sense together, and obviously not all combinations work. The possible subjects for *sparkle* are numerous, but they are also limited; *gold, eyes,* and *hair* would work, and metaphorically even *wit* and *conversation,* but *clamor, participation, sneeze,* and *appetite* are not likely. In a broad way certain classes of nouns point toward different kinds of verbs. For example, animate nouns (*boy, dog, captain*) can be followed by verbs that will not work with inanimate nouns (*book, opinion, cup*). A clear sentence must derive from a plausible basic pattern; when the writer loses sight of his main predication he may produce sentences like the following:

> If present trends continue, by next year the applicants who want to be considered for the benefits of free advanced education will have doubled.
>
> Many people may find homes there and expand into towns.

Isolating the basic patterns from which the two sentences derive, "applicants double" and "people expand," reveals the absurdity — with applicants splitting like amoebas and people becoming balloons.

Two sorts of structure warrant special notice. In one, predication becomes confusing because the writer picks a verb that would logically follow a word used as a modifier but does not follow the word in the subject slot. Consider the following sentence:

> The setting of this picturesque little town was filled with a colorful history.

The sentence is confused in more ways than one, but central is the incompatibility of the subject and predicate; the town, mentioned as part of a modifier, can be "filled with a colorful history," but the setting, used as the subject, cannot be. Whatever the writer intended to say, apparently he did not wish to talk about the setting at all, but about the town. The sentence could be revised as follows:

This picturesque little town has a colorful history.

In another kind of structure, *it* appears as a dummy subject, perhaps in a futile attempt to disguise illogical predication. Consider the following sentence:

With a knowledge of the history of words it will enable a student to read with keener understanding.

Insertion of the vague *it* makes the basic predication unclear—"it would enable." The writer could have solved his problem by using either of two available logical subjects, "knowledge" or "student." Possible revisions include:

Knowledge of the history of words will enable a student to read with keener understanding.

With a knowledge of the history of words, a student can read with keener understanding.

Object Complements and Predication

Like subjects and verbs, verbs and objects must make sense together. Consider the following sentence:

Economists are still piecing together the overall situation.

The metaphor implied by the verb *piecing together* aggravates the disorder here so that *situation* cannot logically follow it as an object; one cannot piece together a situation. If the metaphor is to be retained the sentence might read:

Economists are still piecing together the overall picture.

Or the trite metaphor could be abandoned:

Economists do not yet understand what happened.

In the following sentence, a passive structure disguises a similar inconsistency between a verb and its complement:

They let the discussion continue until after midnight in order that a consensus might be garnered.

Extraction of the basic pattern behind the final clause, "they garnered a consensus," exposes the awkwardness. Impossible complements can also be produced by modifying clauses, as in the following:

He tried to borrow money from everybody in the room that he was acquainted.

As the sentence stands, the final clause derives from "he was acquainted everybody"; presumably the writer intended "with whom he was acquainted" or "he was acquainted with."

LOGICAL EQUATION WITH TO BE   **13c**

The verb *to be*—which appears most frequently as *am, is, was, were* or in combinations like *will be* and *has been*—presents special problems in predication, partly because of the variety of ways in which it may link the subject and verb. It may carry some meaning, as in "To be or not to be" and "Whatever is, is right," where it can mean to exist. It may imply definition or classification ("Music is an art"), supply a name ("This is John"), connect a subject with a modifier ("The apple is ripe"), or act as part of another verb ("The picture is being made now"). In all these the "meaning" of the verb is relatively insignificant; the verb mainly joins or links other meanings. Used in this way, to link a subject and a complement, the verb *to be* almost always implies some kind of identity. Compare the following:

The coat is in the closet.	My sister is a trained nurse.
Happiness is where you find it.	Alcoholism is the root of his trouble.
Happiness is oblivion.	Beauty is truth.
Two and two is four.	Life is a dream.

In the first two examples the verbs are modified by "in the closet" and "where you find it"; they retain much of the meaning of *exist* and do not link the subject with a complement. In the other sentences, however, the verb forms of *to be* resemble the equals sign in mathematics; the sentences are a kind of equation. Whatever comes before the verb is conceived to be equal, from at least one point of view, with what comes after it.

Sentences developed from patterns with *to be* need not, of course, be mathematical equations; life is not literally a dream. But a sentence in the form of an equation must link ideas that can plausibly be identified with each other. Abstractions in either the subject or complement position are especially treacherous:

Ranching is an idea that has always attracted me.

Ranching is not an "idea"; the implausible equation spoils the sentence. The equation could easily be improved:

267

13c

Eq

Revise to avoid an implausible equation of subject with subject complement. Usually the best solution is to change the basic sentence pattern, shifting from to be *to a different verb.*

ORIGINAL

The only knowledge I have had about horses is living on a farm and raising them.

[Knowledge *is not* living.]

REVISION

The only knowledge I have of horses comes from living on a farm and raising them.

[*Changing the verb makes the sentence logical.*]

Perhaps the most important action regarding the teacher's technique of adjusting behavior problems in the classroom is her attitude toward the problem child.

[*An* action *is not an* attitude, *and the sentence is further complicated by other inexact constructions. Various revisions are possible.*]

(1) Perhaps the most important decisions for the teacher facing problems of classroom behavior grow out of her attitude toward the problem child.

(2) The teacher who wishes to solve her problems of classroom behavior should be careful of the attitude she adopts toward the problem child.

The trouble was the many difficulties that complicated the sending of the invitations.

[Trouble *is singular and* difficulties *plural. As a result the meaning is not precise.*]

(1) The trouble was that many difficulties complicated the sending of the invitations.

(2) The trouble grew out of complications in sending the invitations.

The only uniform I have been issued was in camp last August.

[*The sentence is unclear because* was *links no complement with* uniform. *Either supply a complement (1) or change the verb (2).*]

(1) The only uniform I have been issued is the one I received in camp last August.

(2) I have been issued only one uniform, which I received in camp last August.

A syllogism is where you use a major and minor premise to get a logical answer.

[*A syllogism is not a place.*]

In a syllogism, you use a major and minor premise to obtain a logical answer.

> Ranching is a profession that has always attracted me.

A better revision eliminates the equation, shifting to a different sentence pattern:

> Ranching has always attracted me.

Even a difference in number between the subject and the complement may make an equation sound illogical:

> The problem for the students was the instructor's many personal anecdotes, which distracted them.

The sentence is awkward mainly because the singular subject, *problem*, is linked with the plural complement, *anecdotes*. Changing the pattern solves the problem:

> The instructor's personal anecdotes distracted the students.

Modifiers as Complements

The list of basic sentence patterns set forth in chapter 12 includes three types with the linking verb *to be*.

> Subject–*to be*–subject complement — Integrity is a virtue.
> Subject–*to be*–modifier of subject — Violets are blue.
> Subject–*to be*–place adverb — Jerry is outside.

That is, the only kind of sentence with *to be* that does not in some sense equate a subject and complement is the third type, in which a modifier after *to be* designates place or area: "Love is where you find it," "The moon was over his left shoulder." Other kinds of adverbial modifiers — like *quickly, prominently, with gay abandon, whenever he was ready*, will not work in the third position in this pattern. If such modifiers are used after *is*, they often produce ambiguity, because the reader tends to relate them to the subject, not the predication. Consider the following:

> The method of holding a club that some golfers find produces the longest drives is with the hands locked together.

The sentence derives from "method is with the hands locked"; the adverb of manner, "with the hands locked," will work neither as a subject complement nor as an adverb of place. The pattern is not characteristic of the language. As usual, choosing a different subject, the actor, begins the best revision:

> Some golfers find that they can make longer drives if they grip the club with locked hands.

Similar pattern faults can be seen in the following:

ORIGINAL	REVISION
The process of cutting hay in the early days was by means of the scythe, which was manipulated by hand.	(1) In the early days hay was cut by hand with a scythe. (2) Pioneers mowed with a scythe.
The way in which Mary wore her clothes was with an air of sophistication.	Mary wore her clothes with an air of sophistication.

Both original sentences develop from equations that do not fit basic patterns: "The process was by means of the scythe" and "The way was with an air." The revisions change the basic patterns, with new subjects.

"Is because," "Is when"

In conversation and some informal writing a few constructions usually used as adverb modifiers are treated as if they were subject complements. *Because, when, where,* in particular, traditionally introduce modifying clauses, but in sentences like the following they introduce noun clauses used as complements:

> Radicalism is when you jump to conclusions.
>
> The study of mathematics is where I get my lowest grades.
>
> The reason Johnson wrote *Rasselas* was because he needed money for his mother's funeral.

None of these presents much danger of serious misunderstanding, but the equations are hardly precise. Whatever radicalism may be, it is not time, and study is not place. Furthermore, *that*, not *because*, is the standard introduction for a noun clause. Sentences of this sort are almost always wordier and less precise than more direct constructions:

> Radicalism usually involves jumping to conclusions.

270

I get my lowest grades in mathematics.

Johnson wrote *Rasselas* because he needed money for his mother's funeral.

Such constructions can have uses, as in the witticism, "Summer is when parents pack up their troubles and send them off to camp," but in general, clauses relying on *is when, is where, is why,* and *is because* are best revised.

Equations in Frame Sentences

In most of the sentences we have considered, the main predication, the SVC, has carried the important part of the meaning of the sentence. Consider, however, the following:

The most important thing to remember is that nobody has ever reached the peak without oxygen tanks.

The first matter to consider is how far we can go without letting the administration express its attitude.

I think that somebody must have picked the lock and taken the examinations.

Each of these sentences has a standard basic pattern, subject-verb-complement, with the complement slot filled by a clause. But the three subjects, *thing, matter,* and *I,* are not what the sentences mainly concern, and the verbs *is* and *think* do not embody significant assertions. In each sentence the complement makes the important comment; the basic pattern works only as a kind of "frame" to present the idea in the complement.

Such sentences are useful, especially in introductions and transitions. Often context requires them, to carry on a subject or to provide special emphasis, as in the following, which use a possible object to construct a frame:

Algebra was the only course John studied last year.

This quarrel with his son was now his only regret.

Both of these, however, are indirect and carry the hazards of the *to be* sentence, with its need for a logical equation. Often the more direct sentence, with the actor as subject, can improve the writing:

John studied only algebra last year.

Now he regretted only this quarrel with his son.

English sentences are clear only if they develop consistently from one of the relatively few patterns described in chapter 12. That is, no matter how complicated they may become,

GUIDE TO REVISION

13d   **Shift**

Revise to avoid shifted structures, either shifts within the basic pattern of a sentence or illogical shifts in pattern from one sentence or clause to another.

ORIGINAL

Any passage that pleased him he tried to write something in the same style.

[*What promises to be the subject, passage, never becomes one.*]

I looked out over the pines toward the tiny lake a thousand feet below us. You could hardly see the cabin where we had spent the night.

After the textbook had been mastered, he had no trouble with chemistry.

[*The impersonal passive construction shifts awkwardly to the active with the subject* he.]

REVISION

(1) Any passage that pleased him was likely to become the model for a composition in the same style.

(2) He would imitate any passage that pleased him.

I looked out over the pines toward the tiny lake a thousand feet below us. I could hardly see the cabin where we had spent the night.

After he had mastered the textbook, he had no trouble with chemistry.

[*Both structures are now active.*]

---

sentences must continue with the sort of structure established at the beginning. The writer who begins with one pattern in mind, then forgets and shifts to another, inevitably produces something other than sense. Consider the following:

For information concerning almost any event that is too minor to be found in periodical articles may be located through *The New York Times Index.*

The writer apparently started his sentence assuming that he would supply a subject, perhaps *you* or *one;* but by the time he had finished his long modifier, he had lost any sense of a pattern. The "sentence" never acquired a subject. He might have followed the structure he began, supplying a subject:

> For information concerning almost any event too minor to be found in periodical articles, the research worker can use *The New York Times Index.*

Probably, however, the writer got into trouble originally because he started in a way that did not allow him to select the most workable subject for his sentence. With a new subject, the sentence works better:

> *The New York Times Index* includes information about almost any event too minor to be reported in periodicals.

The same sort of forgetfulness can weaken continuity (see 7a) and sometimes produce confusion by shifting patterns unnecessarily from one clause to the next. Consider the following sentence:

> We packed the baskets of food and the seven children into the old car, and a very pleasant afternoon at the lake was enjoyed by everyone.

The sentence shifts from a regular subject-verb-complement pattern in the first clause to a passive variation of it in the second clause. Maintaining the first pattern produces a more direct sentence:

> We packed the baskets of food and the seven children into the old car and enjoyed a pleasant afternoon at the lake.

Consider another sequence in which the writer needlessly shifts subjects from sentence to sentence and in effect changes his point of view (see 21b):

> You may find summer school more intensive than regular sessions. If you choose your courses carefully, however, a person may find that he learns more in the concentrated program.

The point of view would remain consistent if either *you* or *a person* and *he* were kept as subjects throughout the passage.

A Revise each of the following sentences by choosing a new subject and following it with a verb other than a form of *to be.* For example, the revision of the first sentence might read: "He hoped to win the election by promising everybody everything they might ever want."

1. By promising everybody everything they might ever want was the system by which it was his hope that he would be victorious in the election.

2. The result he hoped to achieve was frightening the girls by holding the skull on a stick outside their window.

3. The reason for the confusion of the people with the new regulations was the ambiguous way in which they were written.

4. The influence that he had over his wife was only in regard to her political attitudes.

5. The way in which he taught his daughter to swim was by throwing her into the middle of the lake without her water wings.

6. Realizing that society had more important goals than producing wealth was the guiding force in his decision to start a cooperative community.

7. Because he was stalking her calf was why Bryan was chased by the moose.

8. Some self-confidence is an extremely important item for any young person to have.

9. The information that we needed to discredit the first witness was from an old man who had seen the accident occur.

10. The method by which the fence was built by the new gardener was by the use of plum saplings planted and twisted so that they would grow together.

B The sentences below contain equations with the verb *to be.* Identify subjects and complements. Then revise each sentence, changing subject or complement to make them work more logically together or using a more expressive verb than *to be.*

1. College spirit is an experience long remembered after school is over.

2. In the play, the weavers' situation, which in broad terms is a people born into a society where they must struggle to develop in all ways, is a basic problem of humanity.

3. Journalism is not a romantic life as some books play it up to be, and as some people believe; it is a hard job for anyone to undertake.

4. It can clearly be seen from the story that the desire to return Cassio to her husband's favor was because she honestly felt that it was best for him.

5. The source of my material is from two books.

6. A tragedy is when all the main characters die at the end.

7. The plans of a log cabin should be very compact and not too roomy.

8. The value of this book, in my opinion, was in the fact that it showed more than one cause of juvenile delinquency.

9. The story is where a group of men find themselves the sole survivors of a civilization destroyed by war.

10. The nature of the adult illiterate has been one who has not had a chance to go to school and has never learned to read and to write.

11. The subject of *The Washerwoman's Day* is about the situation in which a girl finds herself.

12. One other example of Shakespeare's humor being portrayed in his characters was Bottom.

13. The primary purpose of colleges was intended to be an institution of higher learning.

14. The most outstanding of their rivalries were over a woman.

15. A follower and a leader are both qualities he must possess to enable him to achieve his goals.

C The sentences below contain faulty predication; that is, the basic sentence in each is illogical. Point out the main SVC in each sentence, analyze relationships, and revise each sentence so that the subject, verb, and complement work together.

1. As soon as they are corrected these disadvantages will improve the club a great deal.

2. The sidewalk, being old and broken in many places, made our progress slow.

3. He did not recognize how difficult were the many facets he must play in his role as director.

4. In two years in the club she managed to break every situation required by the rules.

5. My mother objected to everybody whom I associated.

6. The reason for our delay in prompt processing of this application is caused by staff shortages.

7. A parrot can be stroked on the chest, but anywhere else usually costs the admirer a sore finger.

8. Her mental attitude is disturbed and may not return for several hours.

9. For a person to not obey the duke's wishes would mean the person's death.

10. The friends that you make often result from your manners.

11. This method took as long as three days to plant three hundred acres.

12. For a rifle team to become a success, many points must be accomplished.

13. The amount of money lost by both the strikers and the employers took a matter of years in order to regain them.

14. The main idea of Donne's "Song" seems to be about a man who has been jilted by his mistress.

15. After intensive courses in hairdressing at the new college, everyone on our staff is trained to accentuate your beauty needs.

D Try writing sentences in which you use each of the pairs of subjects below with each of the verbs following it. Some of the subjects may not work with some of the verbs; for these be able to discuss why you could not write a grammatical sentence.

Possible Subjects	*Possible Verbs*
1. Andrew, intention	was, implicated, smiled
2. sharks, conclusions	conspired, jumped, indicated
3. water, book	presented, fell, promised
4. tendency, painter	splashed, developed, forced
5. nutrition, horse	saved, prevented, occupied
6. play, actor	frightened, awoke, broke
7. Breaking the appointment, Jeremy	was, called, contributed
8. What I want to know, happiness	is, requires, smashed

E Rewrite the following passage improving the predication. As the paragraph stands, several sentences rely upon SVC patterns in which the various parts cannot work together.

Everyone knows that one of the worst places where the ecosystems are being disrupted is where the great whales are being systematically exterminated. Ocean-going refineries are the aspect of the fishing industry that some whalers are exterminating these wonderful mammals. Especially, whalers from Japan and Russia, even though those countries are supposed to be in civilized circumstances, with all the advantages that are modern educational systems. All this is what has been known for quite some time, but now a new discovery is the artistic abilities of some whales. The reason we know this is because a new record has just come out, *The Songs of the Humpback Whale* having been just issued is a revelation of what some sea life is capable. The artistic capabilities of the whales of this species is the variations they produce on musical sequences. They sing in what one reviewer of the record stated, perhaps because of the resonating bones in the whale's head, the music being electronic in character and it becomes almost stereo. One can only hope that the wide acceptance being accorded this record will be the occasion for renewed determination to put a stop to the environment that is our national and international heritage.

VARIATIONS
IN PATTERNS:
EXPLETIVE, PASSIVE

CHAPTER 14

Basic sentence patterns can be varied for special purposes.

Most of the sentences in contemporary prose expand and combine the basic patterns described in chapter 12, following the subject-verb-complement order. Language and thought are complicated, however, and particular uses may call for other structures that can be thought of as variations on the basic patterns. For example, "The children are happy" readily changes to "Are the children happy?" for the purpose of asking a question. "Horses eat grass" can be changed to a question, "Do horses eat grass?" Variations like these present no significant rhetorical problems, but two more complicated patterns need attention because undiscriminating use of them may mar writing.

POSTPONED SUBJECT, EXPLETIVES

14a

The following sentence combines patterns that vary from the SVC.

It is simply impossible to exhaust the variety of significant change in linguistic growth: there is no conceivable direction in which a transfer may not be made; there is no assignable distance to which a word may not wander from its primitive meaning.

WILLIAM DWIGHT WHITNEY, *Language and the Study of Language*

14a   Expl

Revise to remove expletives and to restore the subject-verb order.

ORIGINAL

It was after a long argument that we decided to push on. It was soon agreed among us, however, that we had made a mistake. Within an hour all our patrols were pinned down by sniper and mortar fire. It was obvious that we should have stayed at the base camp.

[*The needlessly inverted sentences slow and obscure the passage.*]

His escape set England again on fire. There were Llewelyn wasting the border, the Cinque Ports holding the sea, the garrison of Kenilworth pushing their raids as far as Oxford.

[*Postponement of the subject weakens the second sentence and blocks the continuity of ideas from one sentence to the next.*]

REVISION

After a long argument we decided to push on. Soon, however, we agreed that we had made a mistake. Within an hour all our patrols were pinned down with sniper and mortar fire. Obviously, we should have stayed at the base camp.

[*Normal order strengthens and shortens the passage. For variety some writers might prefer to leave the last sentence:* It was obvious that we should have stayed at the base camp.]

His escape set England again on fire. Llewelyn wasted the border; the Cinque Ports held the sea; the garrison of Kenilworth pushed their raids as far as Oxford.

[*With normal order restored, the reader can see that the second sentence develops the general idea of the first.*]

In each of these three patterns *it* or *there* serves as an expletive. That is, in each clause *it* or *there* fills the subject slot, although it is not a noun and carries no meaning, serving mainly as a function word to fill the sentence pattern. The ideas being talked about, the usual material for the subject, appear in the complement position after *is*.

This sentence is unusual in the book from which it is taken, in which Whitney relies mainly on subject-verb-complement sentences. Here, however, he has good reasons for the variations. Sentences of this sort, with the expletive used in the subject slot, can be derived from basic patterns, most frequently from the subject-*to be*-adverb pattern. That is, a sentence like "There was a mouse in the soup" could be derived from "A mouse was in the soup." Whitney's opening clause could be derived from a different pattern: "To exhaust the variety is impossible." For each of these variations, Whitney could have employed a subject-verb sentence, but his choices can be explained by considering the following main uses of the expletive sentence.

1. *To provide a simple predication.* The expletive provides a simple means of saying that something exists, as in "There are two reasons for doubting his word" and "There will be time for one more question." These ideas could be expressed in other ways, as in "We could find two reasons . . ." and "Two reasons are apparent . . .," but for most purposes such devices would offer no improvement. For Whitney's second and third sentence, "No direction is . . ." and "No distance is . . ." would have been awkward. Whitney could have contrived a subject to replace the expletive and produced a sentence like "Nobody can conceive any direction in which a transfer may not be made." The result is clumsy; for simple purposes like identification, expletives may provide the smoothest, most economical structure. Expletive sentences of this sort frequently appear as topic sentences: "There were three good reasons for preferring the safer course."

2. *To permit a parallel structure.* Expletives permit the writer to assemble parallel details, especially materials too complicated to serve well in the subject, which usually should be followed by a verb without much intervening matter. Consider the following:

> But there was a class of residents which appears to be perennial in that University, composed out of the younger masters; a class of men who, defective alike in age, in wisdom, or in knowledge, were distinguished by a species of theoretic High Church fanaticism; who, until they received their natural correction from advancing age, required from time to time to be protected against their own extravagance by some form of external pressure.
>
> JAMES ANTHONY FROUDE, *History of England*

If the subject, *class*, were to appear in its usual position at the beginning of the sentence it would be separated from the verb by more than fifty words of elaborate modification; and when the verb finally appeared it would be only *was* or perhaps some such wordy device as *was in existence*. The expletive construction allows the subject to come after the verb but near it; *there was* in effect introduces the subject and then allows it to carry the major emphasis of the sentence.

3. *To promote continuity.* The expletive variation can provide continuity from clause to clause or give special emphasis. Whitney probably preferred the expletive structures mainly because SVC

patterns would have been labored, but his repetition of the patterns aids continuity. The following example illustrates more obviously.

> There is no such thing in America as an independent press, unless it is in the country towns. You know it and I know it. There is not one of you who dare to write his honest opinions, and if you did you know beforehand they would never appear in print.
>
> JOHN SWINTON, "Five-Minute Talk"

The final sentence could easily have been phrased in the SVC pattern: "Not one of you dares. . . ." By making the sentence parallel with the first sentence, however, the writer expedites the flow of thought.

Except for these purposes, the expletive pattern is usually less effective than a direct sentence. The construction is by its nature roundabout; often it is wordy, and it obscures the parts of the sentence that are potentially strongest, the subject and the main verb. Consider, for example, "It is a fact that it is hard to get people to see that there is a lot of sport in snowshoeing." The sentence limps along mainly because so many subjects are needlessly postponed. Compare "Although few people know it, snowshoeing can be a good sport."

The feel of the basic pattern persists strongly enough in these variations so that the noun after the verb is traditionally thought of as the subject. Since *to be* has different forms to agree with its subject, this identification of the subject can become practically important: "There *is* one house on the hill," but "There *are* two houses on the hill" (see 17g).

THE PASSIVE   14b

Usually the agent or actor should be mentioned first in a sentence, so that we know who or what we are talking about. Sometimes, however, the agent or actor is less important than the action or the result; sometimes the actor is unknown or should not be mentioned; and sometimes continuity requires that some word other than the name of the actor appear first. The passive construction provides for such variations. Compare:

> The rebels fired the first shot.
> The first shot was fired by the rebels.

In the first, the more direct sentence, the actor, *rebels,* is the subject, with *shot* as object. The second reverses the pattern, and *shot* becomes the subject in the passive sentence. Either pattern would work, of course, depending on the context and the emphasis desired. Compare the following, however:

> In June somebody completed the new road.
>
> The new road was completed in June.

The second, passive, sentence omits the subject *somebody,* and for most purposes this passive sentence would be preferable to the active. The useless subject *somebody* can be omitted.

GUIDE TO REVISION

14b   **Pass**

Strengthen by replacing unwarranted passives with subject-verb-complement structures.

ORIGINAL

    That there were many difficulties whereby women were unable to use the new union lounge was the attitude that was stated by the first speaker. It was her contention that women were resented in the lounge by the men students and that this resentment was clearly made known by the men in their actions. A different point of view was introduced by the second speaker, by whom it was stated that the reason for the inability of the women to make full use of the lounge was caused by the attitude of the women themselves. The views expressed by this speaker were the objects of sharp criticism from the other members of the panel.

    The trouble was caused by John's insistence that he begin.

    [*Nothing here warrants departing from normal order, since the actor-action elements are present and important.*]

REVISION

    The first speaker insisted that women were unable to use the new union lounge because men students resented having women there and made their resentment clearly known. The second speaker introduced a new point of view, that women were unable to make full use of the lounge because of their own attitude. The other members of the panel sharply criticized the views of this speaker.

    [*The original has many weaknesses, but basic to most of its difficulties is overuse of unwarranted passive sentences. The revision still needs development, but it improves the passage, mainly by recasting sentences in the actor-action pattern.*]

    (1) John's insistence that he begin caused the trouble.

    (2) John caused the trouble by insisting that he begin.

Passive constructions are frequently misused and overused. Inversion through use of the passive construction throws stress on the receiver of the action, draws attention away from the actor-action patterns, and may produce roundabout sentences like the following:

> The lake where the meetings of our gang are held is reached by an old road that was found by me when I was hidden out there by the kidnappers.

Two of the passives in the sentence may be justified, but revising at least two of them strengthens the sentence:

> The lake where our gang holds its meetings can be reached by an old road that I found when I was hidden out there by the kidnappers.

Whenever an actor is named, it usually works best in the subject slot. Like the expletive sentence, however, the passive sentence has important uses.

1. *When the subject for an SVC sentence is not known.* A historian writes, "The world of St. Paul was steeped in guilt and wretchedness." He does not know who steeped it; the agent, even if it could be determined, would be much too complicated for expression in a single sentence. Or consider "Nations that have lost their moral self-respect are easily conquered." This generalization does not depend at all on who conquers these nations; no one actor could be specified.

2. *When there are reasons for not naming the actor.* Suppose, for example, we wish to mention the publication of a book in 1623, but we have no reason to name the publisher. We want the publishing to be the main action, but if we use the subject-verb-object pattern, we are faced with something like "A person or persons whom we do not wish to mention just now published the book in 1623." In this sentence, the receiver of the action, *book*, is more important than the missing actor. We therefore solve the problem by putting *book* into the subject position and using a passive form of the verb: "The book was published in 1623." For a statement as simple as this, however, a separate sentence is usually inappropriate; the writer might better reduce the idea embodied in this sentence to a modifier and go on to another idea: "The book, *published in 1623*, has provided the basis for all subsequent editions of Shakespeare's works." There may even be legal reasons for not specifying an actor. A newspaper reporter might be telling the truth if he were to write, "John A. Scrogum murdered Joseph Meek at 7:45 this morning in the Hot Spot Lunch." This state-

ment is libelous; the reporter and the newspaper that publishes the sentence can be sued for accusing a man of murder who has not been legally convicted. Accordingly, the reporter would probably write something like "Joseph Meek was shot and killed at 7:45 this morning in the Hot Spot Lunch." The actor has now been removed, and the statement is legally publishable.

3. *For stylistic reasons, especially for the following purposes:*

a) To provide continuity by maintaining the same subject in a sequence of sentences.

> The new student body president gained immediate support when he proposed a campaign to clean up the campus. He was severely criticized, however, by the student senate committee when he suggested that the campaign should be financed with student body funds.

Using *he* as the subject of the second sentence continues the subject from the first sentence. Using *student senate*, the actor, as the subject would break the continuity. The same motives may justify the passive pattern in a dependent clause:

> The Progressive Mills Company, although it was considered by the investigating committee to be the chief polluter of the river, escaped regulation because it provided the town's only substantial payroll.

b) To give special prominence to the receiver of the action.

> An investigation was authorized by the legislature an hour after the protest march began.

c) To avoid inserting extensive material between a subject and verb. Compare:

> The hearing was opened by the chairman of the committee, who was known for his ruthlessness in smirching the reputation of innocent witnesses and for his cleverness in beclouding the issue by his own witticisms and innuendoes.
>
> The chairman of the committee, who was known for his ruthlessness in smirching the reputations of innocent witnesses and for his cleverness in beclouding the issue by his own witticisms and innuendoes, opened the hearing.

The first version has the advantage of keeping subject and verb together.

Except in these special situations, the passive usually weakens English prose. Consider the following passage, in which most of the verbs are passive:

Zoroaster's spirit was rapidly caught by the Persians. A voice that was recognized by them as speaking truth was responded to eagerly by a people uncorrupted by luxury. They have been called the Puritans of the Old World. Never, it is said, was idolatry hated by any people as it was by them, and for the simple reason that lies were hated by them.

Compare this passage with the original:

The Persians caught rapidly Zoroaster's spirit. Uncorrupted by luxury, they responded eagerly to a voice which they recognized as speaking truth to them. They have been called the Puritans of the Old World. Never any people, it is said, hated idolatry as they hated it, and for the simple reason that they hated lies.

JAMES ANTHONY FROUDE, "Calvinism"

Froude's version keeps the actor-action pattern everywhere but in the third sentence and the parenthetical "it is said" of the fourth — in which the subjects of the action are unknown. Obviously, his paragraph is more economical and more expressive.

FOR STUDY AND WRITING

A Revise each of the following sentences by removing the expletive and recasting the sentence in normal order with a subject followed by a verb.

1. It is obvious that there should be more courses in fine arts taken by the average student.
2. There were more than a dozen cats waiting for the children to feed the birds.
3. There was no reason why Wayne had to doubt his mother's word.
4. There was a tall white stallion standing all alone at the edge of the cliff.
5. It is in his book *The Diary of a Writer* that Dostoevsky describes how a mother hen defended her chickens from a brutal and sadistic boy.
6. If there is the desire to help, there are always lots of ways for a father to be saved money by the student.
7. It was when I was waiting in a registration line and I was talking with a graduate student that the realization came to me of how complicated a university is.
8. That was the time when there was an opportunity for me to buy my first colony of bees.
9. There were two chaperons in attendance at the dance, but still the uninvited guests soon outnumbered the invited ones.

10. It was because so many students had forgotten to register for the examination that there were new rules passed by the academic council.

B Revise each of the sentences below by converting it to usual word order and using active verbs.

1. The corsage was worn by Wilma on her left shoulder.

2. The election was arranged by a group of dishonest party hacks so that the success of the reform movement was prevented.

3. A very rigid censorship was imposed by the commanding officer on war news.

4. By using a spectroscope it is possible for many metals to be identified by a laboratory technician.

5. After working for fifteen minutes, the ground was finally cleared and leveled by the men enough for the sleeping bags.

6. Provisional governments were set up by the military forces as soon as an area had been conquered.

7. Citizens of the United States were guaranteed freedom of speech by the First Amendment to the Constitution.

8. If the petition is signed by enough people, it will be considered by the assembly.

9. Drifting down the river out of control, a series of dangerous rapids was approached by the boat.

10. Although still eager to write a great epic, many prose pamphlets had to be turned out by Milton.

11. The ball was thrown accurately by the first baseman, but it was missed by the catcher, and the runner was waved home by the third-base coach.

12. The introduction of the speaker was made by the past president of the club.

13. Undeterred by the stories in the papers, a trip around the lake after midnight was contemplated by Jane and her roommate.

14. At the end of the passage our progress was arrested by a pile of huge boulders.

15. Tickets were bought by Mr. Sims from a scalper for twice their value.

16. A small shop was opened on Fifth Avenue by two of my classmates where clothes could be designed by them to suit both the figure and the purse of the average girl working in an office.

C The following paragraph has been altered from the original, largely by including more passive and more expletive sentences. Revise it, changing any sentence patterns that seem to you inappropriate. Your instructor can supply the paragraph as Rachel Carson originally wrote it.

[1] Of all the elements present in the sea, probably men's dreams have been stirred by none more than gold. [2] There is gold there—in all the waters covering the greater part of the earth's surface—enough in total

quantity so that every person in the world could be made a millionaire by it. [3] But how is it possible that the sea can be made to yield it? [4] The most determined attempt to wrest a substantial quantity of gold from ocean waters — and also the most complete study of the gold in sea water — was made by the German chemist Fritz Haber after the First World War. [5] There was the idea conceived by Haber of extracting enough gold from the sea so that the German war debt could be paid, and there was from his dream the result that there was the German South Atlantic Expedition of the *Meteor*. [6] The *Meteor* was equipped with a laboratory and filtration plant, and between the years 1924 and 1928 the Atlantic was crossed and recrossed by the vessel, with the water being sampled. [7] But the quantity found was less than had been expected, and there was far greater cost of extraction than there was value of the gold recovered.

D Mark every sentence in one of your themes in which you vary from usual word order. Then revise these sentences to the actor-action pattern and judge whether or not the change improves the theme.

E Select a brief incident in the current news — or accept your instructor's selection. Recount it as a narrative, using your own words. Then make some comment upon the incident, explaining how it is beneficial or harmful, suggesting how such incidents can be prevented or encouraged in the future, or evaluating the importance of the incident.

When you have done so, classify your sentences for structure. You will probably find that in your narrative you have used mainly sentences and clauses having SVC patterns. You may find that in your second piece, an exposition based upon a narrative, either you have used more structure employing expletives and passives or you have been tempted to do so. Can you find good reason for using these expletives and passives? Change those you cannot defend and notice the effect.

COORDINATION
AND
PARALLELISM

CHAPTER 15

For most purposes the basic sentence pattern requires elaboration;
coordination, revealed in parallel structure, provides means
to develop complicated ideas.

"I see the kitty" is a sentence, but few writers who have progressed beyond nursery school find much use for it. As indicated in chapter 12, such sentences can be expanded in three ways, one of which is coordination. With coordination, the writer can relate and order ideas — parts within sentences, sentences in paragraphs, or paragraphs in longer compositions. In sentences coordination may be as simple as "John and Mary" or "ham and eggs," a structure that any child can handle. In fact, childish talk is likely to be a combination of the basic and the coordinational sentence patterns — "I took my fish pole, and I took Rover, and I took my Daddy, and I went fishing." That is, *coordination* is bringing like things together, combining them; the term *parallelism* is often used to describe the patterns that reveal coordination. These patterns are not all as simple and easy to manage as "ham and eggs." The newspaperman who wrote the following sentence had trouble indicating coordination accurately:

Among the items in the collection are the only known document bearing the signatures of Queen Elizabeth and Sir Walter Raleigh and a cigar-store Indian.

The reporter's copy may have included a comma after the name Raleigh, but even so the sentence seems to attribute more skill to the Indian than the writer probably intended.

Among the grammatical groups that can be coordinated within the sentence are varieties of the basic sentence pattern itself. Consider the following:

> The sun had set. A cool breeze was blowing across the lake. The tiny cabin was still too warm to be comfortable.

Here are three sentences, each of which can be considered independent, one concerning the sun, one the breeze, and one the cabin. More revealingly, the three can be considered as parts of one idea, that in spite of certain cooling agents the cabin was still too hot. Obviously, the three sentences had better become one, somewhat as follows:

> Although the sun had set and a cool breeze was blowing across the lake, the tiny cabin was still too warm to be comfortable.

The subject-verb patterns of the three short sentences are preserved here, but the patterns work together to make a single sentence. That is, clauses of like nature can be coordinated; consider the following:

> Marriage and hanging go by destiny. Matches are made in heaven.
>
> Marriage and hanging go by destiny; matches are made in heaven.
>
> Marriage and hanging go by destiny, but matches are made in heaven.

In the first version, the two ideas stand as independent sentences, although they are obviously to be taken together. In the second version the ideas are still independent — neither relies on the other — but their interrelation is emphasized by their being joined into one sentence with a semicolon between them. What were formerly sentences have become independent clauses. The author of the sentence understandably preferred the idea in this form. The third version also contains two clauses that could serve as independent sentences, with the contrast between them emphasized by the signal word *but*. For the punctuation of such sentences see 25b, 25c.

Not all clauses can be coordinated because they are not all of like nature; that is, they have different uses and follow different clause patterns. Conventionally, clauses are divided into two sorts, *independent* and *dependent* or *subordinate*. Grammatically, the distinction is not always sharp in English; but of course clauses can coordinate only with other clauses like themselves, independent with independent, dependent with dependent. For purposes of sentence structure the distinction is sharp enough, since we recognize like patterns. Observe the following:

If you have any ideas about how
we can improve our product

or

you know any ways of improving
our service,

I advise you to
keep quiet about
them.

Two dependent clauses connected by *or* are coordinate, and their working together is made clear by their parallel form and position.

Coordinating Lesser Sentence Elements

Often ideas that might be expressed in a sentence or a clause may be reduced to a phrase or a word coordinated with another phrase or word. Consider the following:

In the Indian Parliament a member may call his colleague a simian.

In the Indian Parliament a member may not call his colleague a baboon.

Obviously, the sentences are alike except for one part of the complement. The whole can be said with one sentence having a coordinate complement:

In the Indian Parliament a member may call his colleague a simian, but not a baboon.

Buffon was using a similar sort of coordination, although he coordinated more parallel complements, when he wrote:

The human race excepted, the elephant is the most respected of animals. . . . We allow him the judgment of the beaver, the dexterity of the monkey, the sentiment of the dog, and the advantages of strength, size, and longevity.

Using a sentence for each of the elephant's virtues would expand the statement to a paragraph. In these sentences, only the complements are coordinated, but most elements of a sentence can be used coordinately, and most sentences of any complexity have more than one sort of coordination. For instance, H. L. Mencken re-

corded his disapproval of zoos as follows, without, of course, itali-
cizing his coordinate elements:

> The sort of man who likes to spend his time watching *a cage of mon-
> keys chase one another,* or *a lion gnaw its tail,* or *a lizard catch flies,* is
> precisely the sort of man whose mental weakness should be *combated*
> at the public expense, not *fostered.*

COORDINATION AND PARALLEL STRUCTURE 15a

Coordination can be more or less elaborate.
When a zookeeper remarked that "We need good, strong cages to
protect the animals from the public," he was using coordination
very simply to join the words *good* and *strong.* The same device can
knit together extremely complicated structures; for instance, in the
sixteenth century, balanced and contrasted constructions became a
fad, and when John Lyly wrote the following he was gaining a
number of effects and also having fun with language:

> This young gallant, of more wit than wealth, and yet of more wealth
> than wisdom, seeing himself inferior to none in pleasant conceits,
> thought himself superior to all in honest conditions, insomuch that
> he deemed himself so apt to all things that he gave himself almost to
> nothing but practicing of those things commonly which are incident
> to these sharp wits, fine phrases, smooth quipping, merry taunting,
> using jesting without mean, and abusing mirth without measure.
>
> *Euphues*

The style is exaggerated, but the passage illustrates how intricately
words, phrases, and clauses can be balanced against one another
in writing.

Whether coordination is simple or complicated, parallel
structure will help to clarify it. The following are practical devices.

1. *Give coordinate elements the same grammatical form.* In the
phrase "good, strong cages," the similarity of the words *good* and
strong, both modifiers of *cage,* indicates that they are coordinate.
The more complicated pattern of the Mencken quotation uses
similar grammatical parallelism:

. . . watching { a cage of monkeys chase one another
a lion gnaw its tail
a lizard catch flies

15a   **Paral**

Revise to make coordinate elements parallel in structure.

ORIGINAL

Today a secretary has to be attractive in appearance and a high intelligence.
[Attractive *is here a modifier,* intelligence *a noun. Revise by making both modifiers or both nouns.*]

Buffalo Bill could ride like the wind and who shot a bottle cap thrown into the air.

I told him that he should have an agreement about his situation at home, he needed a room to himself with a good light, and specified hours when he could have freedom to study.
[*Failure to repeat the signal word* that *leaves the sentence confused. The reader starts to read* he needed *without understanding that he has begun the second of three things* I told him.]

On the first day we visited the Metropolitan Museum, the Planetarium, and rode the ferry to Staten Island.
[*Museum, Planetarium, and* rode *are not parallel in meaning, and should not appear in parallel form.*

Penicillin was found to cure most diseases more quickly, effectively, and less dangerously than did the sulfa drugs.
[*The series is not a series as it stands. The sentence can be revised either to avoid the illogical series or to make it logical.*]

REVISION

(1) Today a secretary must be attractive and intelligent.
(2) Today a secretary must have an attractive appearance and high intelligence.

Buffalo Bill could ride like the wind and shoot a bottle cap thrown into the air.

I told him that he should have an agreement about his situation at home, that he needed a room to himself with a good light, and that he should be allotted specified hours when he could have freedom to study.
[*The three clauses that follow* I told him *are now marked off by the repeated signal word* that.]

On the first day we visited the Metropolitan Museum and the Planetarium and rode the ferry to Staten Island.
[*Insertion of* and *in place of the first comma breaks up the illogical series and makes the parallels clear.*]

(1) Penicillin was found to cure most diseases more quickly and effectively and less dangerously than did the sulfa drugs.
(2) Penicillin was found to cure most diseases more quickly, more effectively, and less dangerously than did the sulfa drugs.

The parallel structure of the three clauses emphasizes that they are coordinate. Consider the following sentence, however:

Mary enrolled for painting, harmony, music appreciation, and to study art history.

Four items are coordinated in a series, but the last is not parallel in form. Revision reinforces the coordination:

Mary enrolled for painting, harmony, music appreciation, and art history.

2. *Use function words to signal coordination.* In the passage from *Euphues* quoted above Lyly might have written "of more wit than wealth, and yet more wealth than wisdom." The phrases would have been understandable, but the reader might hesitate before recognizing which words *and* coordinates. As Lyly wrote the sentence, repeating the word *of,* even momentary misunderstanding is scarcely possible. The following student sentence is clear because it repeats *in.*

Bacon's "idols" dwell in the minds of men, but their temples are in London, in Moscow, and in Washington.

Compare the following sentence in which the parallelism is broken by inconsistent use of *the.*

The only enemies of the sloth are the eagles, jaguars, and the large boas.

Either inserting *the* before the second element or dropping it before the final element would restore the rhythm of the sentence and keep the coordinate items parallel:

The only enemies of the sloth are the eagles, jaguars, and large boas.

3. *Use word order to support coordination.* Signal words especially need to be placed carefully. Compare:

You are either *late* or *early.*
Either *you are late* or *I am early.*
You are either *late* or *I am early.*

The first two sentences are clear because the signal words *either* and *or* appear just before the two expressions to be coordinated.

292

The third is not clear because *either* is out of position. The following howler from a student paper illustrates a similar danger.

> To be polite he first poured some of the wine into his glass so that he would get the cork and not the lady.

The intention of the writer is clear enough; in speech he could have made himself understood by emphasis. In writing he would need to put the parts of his compound subject together.

> To be polite he first poured some of the wine into his glass so that he, and not the lady, would get the cork.

4. *Use coordinating structures only for items that can be logically coordinated.* Sometimes apparent inconsistencies in parallelism misrepresent coordination. Notice the following sentence: "The play was lively, witty, and the audience responsive though not very many of them." A diagram reveals at once that the coordinated elements are not parallel:

$$
\text{The play was} \begin{cases} \text{(1) lively} \\ \text{(2) witty} \\ \text{(3) the audience} \end{cases} \begin{cases} \text{(1) responsive} \\ \text{(2) not very many of them} \end{cases}
$$

Audience is not parallel with *lively* and *witty,* nor are the coordinated modifiers of *audience* parallel. The sentence seems to be coordinating elements that cannot logically be made parallel. The writer probably intended a pattern like the following:

$$
\text{(1) The play was} \begin{cases} \text{(1) lively} \\ \text{and} \\ \text{(2) witty} \end{cases}
$$

and

$$
\text{(2) the audience was} \begin{cases} \text{(1) responsive} \\ \text{though} \\ \text{(2) small} \end{cases}
$$

Or consider "New Orleans is exciting, surprising, and which I should like to visit again." *Exciting* and *surprising* are parallel in form and can be readily coordinated, but the final clause cannot easily be made parallel with them. The solution is to coordinate the two complements and also to coordinate the two clauses: "New Orleans is exciting and surprising, and I should like to visit it again."

Coordination, as examples above indicate, may promote economy, since parallel patterns are so well established that entire structures need not be repeated:

He knew the rules and (*he knew the*) regulations.

GUIDE TO REVISION

15b **Inc**

Revise, supplying words to clarify an incomplete parallel structure.

ORIGINAL	REVISION
The water cask was nearly empty by noon and drained for evening rations.	(1) The water cask was nearly empty by noon and was drained for evening rations.
[Drained *must be preceded by* was (*understood*), *but the* was *after* cask *is a complete verb; it cannot be understood as part of the verb* was drained.]	(2) The water cask was nearly empty by noon; we drained it for evening rations.
Many of the soldiers saw only what hundreds of tourists always had and always will be seeing.	Many of the soldiers saw only what hundreds of tourists always had seen and always will be seeing.
D'Artagnan was interested and skillful at fencing.	(1) D'Artagnan was interested in and skillful at fencing.
[*No connective follows* interested; at, *which does not make sense, is the only word available.*]	(2) D'Artagnan was interested in fencing and skillful at it.

Coordination makes expression of the italicized repetition unnecessary. The stability of English word order allows similar shortcuts in other patterns. Parts of verbs, for example, need not be repeated in a parallel passage:

In a few minutes the stakes had been driven and the canvas (*had been*) spread on the ground.

The children started to work just as their parents had (*started to work*).

Even when the idea is not expressed in the form later required, it need not always be repeated:

> They did all they could (*do*).
>
> He ran as fast as he could (*run*).

Similarly, connectives need not always be repeated in parallel constructions:

> They fought on land and (*on*) sea.
>
> He had not learned how to read or (*how*) to write.

Usually, however, such economies work only when the ideas to be carried over establish a form that will fit the second part of the parallel pattern. Consider, for example, the following sentence in which the reader is asked to supply part of the verb in one of two coordinated elements:

> The liquor was confiscated and the barrels dumped into the sea.

The reader must supply a verb to precede *dumped;* the pattern of coordination suggests repetition of *was,* but *was* will not work after the plural *barrels.* Both verb forms need to be supplied to make the parallel clear.

> The liquor was confiscated and the barrels were dumped in the sea.

Or consider the following, in which a preposition is intended to carry over from one coordinate element to another.

> He was helpful and considerate of his friends.

If *friends* is intended to attach to *helpful* as well as to *considerate,* a second preposition is needed; *of* does not work after *helpful.*

> He was helpful to his friends and considerate of them.

PATTERNS OF COMPARISON **15c**

Parallel patterns may express comparison, usually with function words like *than* or *as.* The word order for these constructions is so well established that parallel elements need not be completely repeated; the following sentences illustrate standard economy.

15c $\qquad\qquad\qquad$ # Comp

Revise to make items compared parallel in form and comparable in meaning.

ORIGINAL

During the war the value of black troops was found to be on a par with white service forces.
[*The sentence compares* value *and* forces, *which are not logically comparable. The writer probably intended to compare the value of one force with the value of the other, or to compare the two forces.*]

The foreman insisted that his job was harder than a laborer.
[*Job* and laborer *are not comparable.*]

Cyrano is more popular than any of Rostand's plays.
[Cyrano *cannot be more popular than itself, and "any of Rostand's plays" includes* Cyrano.]

I knew her better than Mary.
[*With parts of the comparison omitted, two meanings are possible.*]

The people had been as kind if not kinder than my own family.
[Than *cannot serve both comparisons. Revision* (2) *is accurate, though stiff;* (1) *lacks logical connectives, but follows a familiar pattern.*]

The heroine was so charming.
[*The writer probably did not intend a comparison but added the intensifier under the impression that it made his statement more convincing.*]

REVISION

(1) During the war black troops were found to be on a par with white service forces.
(2) During the war black troops were as valuable as white forces.
[Troops *and* forces *can be logically compared. The idea of value can be retained by making it the basis for comparison.*]

(1) The foreman insisted that his job was harder than a laborer's.
(2) The foreman insisted that his job was harder than that of a laborer.

Cyrano is more popular than any other of Rostand's plays.
[Cyrano *can logically be compared with the* other *plays of Rostand.*]

(1) I knew her better than Mary did.
(2) I knew her better than I knew Mary.

(1) The people had been as kind as my own family, if not kinder.
(2) The people had been as kind as, if not kinder than, my own family.

(1) The heroine was charming.
(2) The heroine was so charming that I paid no attention to the other characters.
[*If the writer has a comparison in mind, he should complete it.*]

It was easier to take a cab *than it was easy to take* a bus.

It was easier to take a cab *than to take* a bus.

It was easier to take a cab *than* a bus.

The shorter final version has obvious advantages. Furthermore, these patterns are so well established that they permit ideas to carry over even though they would have to be understood the second time in a different form:

> Plants grow more rapidly in California than (*plants grow*) in New York.
>
> Plants grow more rapidly in California than they do (*grow*) in New York.
>
> She was treated more politely than he (*was treated*).
>
> The joke was as old as the hills (*were old*).

The sentences are clear and also economical. Like other patterns of coordination, however, these constructions serve only when the elements to be compared are parallel in form.

> *My cousin* was older than *any other freshman.*
>
> It is easier *for a camel to go through the eye of a needle* than *for a rich man to enter into the kingdom of God.*

In each example the items are in parallel form.

They are also comparable in meaning, but consider "His teeth were sharper than a tiger." *Teeth* and *tiger* are parallel in form, but obviously they do not represent the ideas to be compared. The sentence was presumably intended to compare teeth with teeth: "His teeth were sharper than a tiger's (*teeth*)." Such comparisons may be absurd — "His ears were longer than a jack rabbit" — but sometimes the illogicality of a comparison is not so apparent and a sentence may seem only vaguely confused. Consider:

> The battle against eating pumpkin seeds in school continues, as gum chewing does in most American schools.

The words coordinated are *battle* and *gum chewing,* but their ideas are not logically comparable. The writer may have intended to compare two battles:

> The battle against eating pumpkin seeds in school continues, as does the fight against gum chewing in most American schools.

Or he may have intended to compare the two activities:

> Eating pumpkin seeds in school continues, as gum chewing does in most American schools.

One idiomatic pattern in English involves a special problem. Sentences like the following are common colloquially: "That night the team was as good if not better *than* any other team in the league." But the connective *than* cannot be logically understood after *good*, where *as* is required. Standard English, therefore, requires some kind of completion of comparisons of this sort.

In another troublesome colloquial pattern, expressions like *so beautiful, most wonderful, biggest, finest, prettiest* appear as vague indications of enthusiasm: "It was *such* a lovely party," "He was the *nicest* man." Logically such expressions begin a comparison, and in formal English the writer should finish the comparison or substitute a modifier not implying comparison.

FOR STUDY AND WRITING

A Combine the materials of each of the following groups of sentences into a single sentence using parallel structure.

1. Seated on the steps were a tan spaniel and brindle boxer. Angela, the Manx cat, was also there.

2. A good nurse possesses a willingness to do more than her required tasks. She is also constantly alert to guess her patient's wishes.

3. The brown pup seemed to possess intelligence. None of the other dogs in the litter seemed so intelligent.

4. In this corrupt system we see the cruelty of the totalitarian kind of government. There we also see the craft of this type of government. And we see there its ambition.

5. Upon the chair hung a neatly folded suit. There was also a crumpled red tie there. A crushed gardenia was on the same chair.

6. Every person in the tournament knew bridge thoroughly. Each one was intelligent in his playing. A firm determination to win was in every player.

7. A nationalistic rather than a sectionalistic attitude developed in the West. This was partly because the West needed a national government to protect it from the Indians. It also looked toward the national government to provide aid in the development of transportation facilities. Furthermore, foreign affairs could be handled by a strong national government.

8. Without the mariner's compass, Columbus could not have discovered America. Neither could Vasco da Gama's trip to find a sea route to India have occurred. Magellan's sailing around the world would not have taken place without it, either.

298

9. Jean spent an hour with the tea committee. After it she knew that she had never before known how intricate planning a tea could be. She did not believe that the event was worth the trouble it took. She would never be on another tea committee, she was sure.

10. A course of study in music may prepare a student for concert performances. It may also provide preparation for a career in teaching. And many students gain preparation for occasional recreational activity through their entire lives.

B Recast each of the following sentences so that items intended to be coordinate are parallel in form and meaning, or remove unwarranted parallel structures.

1. Escalators should not be used by barefooted persons, pets, or for transporting strollers or wheelchairs.

2. He is a person of great integrity, vision, and has the rare ability to stimulate the best efforts of his associates.

3. He stated in his complaint that the defendant owned a large dog that walked the floor most of the night, held noisy midnight parties, and played a radio so that sleep was impossible until 1:30 in the morning.

4. The typical hero wears light clothes as opposed to the "bad man" dressed in black.

5. I still remember the smell of burning candles, incense, and Greek chanting.

6. The professional players were more skillful, accurate, but less enthusiastic than their amateur opponents.

7. The dean told Alice that she should find a better place to study, she needed to spend less time at the movies, and ought to attend class more frequently.

8. She seemed pretty, clever, perceptive, and the courtesy required of an airline hostess.

9. To survive without a guide in the north woods one has to be well trained as a woodsman as well as excellent physical condition.

10. She told her mother she wanted either a wedding in a church with flower girls, organ music, long trains, or a quick elopement to a justice of the peace.

11. I much prefer listening to concerts on the radio rather than to sit in the heat and discomfort of our auditorium.

12. His career, unlike most people who played a musical instrument, ended when he left school.

13. His job consisted mostly of planning and constructing roads, bridges, and various forms of surveying.

14. From the air the stream looked languid, twisted, and flowed on its course like some giant caterpillar en route to its cocoon.

15. He accused the senator of being a fool and too stupid to know the real issues.

C Revise the following sentences to assure clarity in comparisons and other parallel structures.

1. When I looked into the cell I disliked Dandy Jack as much as the police officer.
2. He learned respect and obedience to the new officers.
3. People say that reading a book a week increases your vocabulary and your manner of speaking.
4. The girls found the cabin so beautiful, and Aubrey was such a handsome man.
5. There were great scientific advances, but precious little chance to use them until government regulations had been removed.
6. She looked as old or older than Methuselah.
7. After an hour of this conversation, I decided that I disliked Mary's cousin as much as Mary.
8. In *Othello* the structure is somewhat different from the other tragedies.
9. She liked Picasso better than any painter.
10. Because cars are so well built, the driver drives much faster than he can safely handle the car.
11. The lecturer compared his life with a medieval peasant.
12. His arms dangled down longer than a baboon.
13. Wordsworth's *Prelude* was written, not like Rousseau wrote his *Confessions,* to reveal himself, but for the happiness and moral betterment of men.
14. His career was more brilliant than any musician who had graduated in his class.
15. Geology, unlike most professional men, seems to have entered into a period of shrinkage in job opportunities.

D Improve the following paragraph by making more and better use of coordination.

The census of 1970 provided some surprises. Some were in education. There were also some in the way students vote. Then there were some divorce problems, too. There were some in society, the circumstances of the relations of the numbers of young adults and those younger than young adults. As for education, statistics revealed that America has no "dropout" generation. There was increase in school attendance among young adults especially. There was some, also, among teen-agers. It was less so. Among the fourteen- to seventeen-year-olds, nine tenths were in school in 1960. By the time it was 1969, this percentage had increased so that it was 94. Among eighteen- and nineteen-year-olds, fewer than 40 per cent were enrolled in 1960 compared with nearly 50 per cent in 1969. Meanwhile, education boomed among young adults. Above the average, blacks were those who were getting more education. For the period 1940–1970, the percentage of college degrees among all twenty-five- to thirty-year-olds rose from 6 to 16 per cent, percentages rising from a low of 1.6 for the blacks in 1940. And in 1970 it became a percentage of 10. That is, for the entire population the percentage of college graduates among young adults nearly tripled. It got to be more than that, in percentages, among the blacks, up six times and more. As for student political interests, although 1969 was a year of dissent and revolt against the Establishment, the resentment that the students had did not get expressed in the voting aspects of college life. When the elections came along in 1968 the eighteen- to twenty-year-olds turned out in numbers figured at about 33 per cent. On the other hand, of the 1969 voters, same ages, the people voting were only 26 out of 100. Meanwhile, divorced persons increased, the women increasing in numbers more than men increased. During the 1960's divorced women increased from 42 to 60 per 1,000 of the population, whereas the divorced men increased only 28 to 35. Such statistics suggest that divorced women are finding it harder and harder to remarry. As for youth and middle age, the statistics generally suggest that the twenty-eight- to thirty-five-year-olds will increase in numbers at the expense of those whose ages are between fifteen and twenty-five years. That is, in the 1970's the accent is likely to shift from youth to being somewhat older persons.

SUBORDINATION: MODIFICATION

CHAPTER 16

Sentences develop through addition, primarily by the addition of sub-ordinated materials, usually modifiers.

A child, with a few strokes of a crayon, can draw something identifiable as a man, but his creation is not a finished likeness. A portrait painter does more. He makes his outline more accurately, adds details to distinguish his subject, and heightens some effects by subduing others. Similarly, a child can communicate with a simple sentence like "Willie eats bananas," but an adult user of the language would probably need a statement that would distinguish Willie from a monkey and specify more accurately Willie's behavior. He might retain the basic sentence, but he would add to it, providing subordinate details that would modify the central pattern. He might say something like

> Sometimes, when he is tired of his regular baby food, Willie eats very ripe bananas crushed to a paste and mixed with a little milk.

The sentence has been developed by modification, one of the three main ways of expanding basic patterns (see chapter 12).

We have already observed how subordination of some material affects communication generally, in extended discourse (see chapter 3). In sentences, subordinated materials work as modifiers —limiting, restricting, specifying—sometimes modifying subject, verb, or complement, sometimes an entire predication, sometimes another modifier. Structures for subordination or modification, like those for coordination, allow a writer to combine for economy but, more important, to clarify relationships.

302

Subordination permits a writer to direct the reader's attention; it helps the reader to focus on some ideas and to view others as related to them. Writing that lacks subordination sounds immature because it restricts itself to the relatively simple

GUIDE TO REVISION

16a	Sub

Use subordination to improve an immature style, characterized by strings of short sentences or clauses joined by and *or* so, *by clumsy repetitions, or by excessive use of* this *and* that *as subjects.*

ORIGINAL

Louise was tired of listening to the concert and it was dark enough that her grandmother could not see her and so she slipped out into the lobby.
[*The relationships between the three clauses are not accurately marked by linking them with* and *and* so.]

When Lord Byron was at Cambridge, he published *Hours of Idleness.* This was in 1807. The volume was Byron's first book of poems.

[*Repetition of a subject or* this *as a subject may signal a need for subordination.*]

Andrea stepped confidently into the hall. Joe pulled the rug from under her, when she fell down.
[*A minor detail assumes major importance so awkwardly that the subordination seems illogical or upsidedown.*]

REVISION

Since Louise was tired of listening to the concert, she slipped past her grandmother in the dark into the lobby.
[*With ideas subordinated to a main subject-verb framework*—she slipped—*the sentence is clearer and more economical.*]

In 1807, when Lord Byron was at Cambridge, he published his first book of poems, *Hours of Idleness.*
[*The combination says everything in the original more clearly and more economically.*]

(1) Andrea stepped confidently into the hall. When Joe pulled the rug from under her, she fell down.
(2) Andrea stepped confidently into the hall. Joe pulled the rug from under her, and she fell down.
[*Reversed subordination (1) or coordination (2) seems more likely.*]

relationships of the basic sentence pattern—subject, verb, and complement. The following passage makes little use of subordination.

> We are offered a penny for our thoughts. We consider what we have been thinking. Many things have been in our minds. From these many things we can select a few. The things we select do not compromise us too nakedly.

Even though the sentences are short and direct, the passage is not easy to understand; the reader gets no help relating ideas, in seeing which are to be considered parts of others. In the original the author used subordination to combine ideas:

> When we are offered a penny for our thoughts we always find that we have recently had so many things in mind that we can easily make a selection which will not compromise us too nakedly.
>
> JAMES HARVEY ROBINSON, *Mind in the Making*

The sentence is more complicated than the series of short sentences, but it is clearer.

The need for adequate subordination becomes even greater when unrelated short sentences are strung together in a more extended passage. Compare the following two versions of a student theme on a Hemingway short story:

ORIGINAL

Margot Macomber must have been a very beautiful woman. She had everything except wealth. When she married Francis Macomber she acquired this wealth. Although she was married to Francis, she was very untrue to him.

One day they went on a hunting expedition to Africa. They took a white man as a guide. His name was Wilson. Of course, Margot had to have his attention, and she did. Francis felt very sorry for himself. He knew that she would never leave him because of his wealth. He would never divorce her because of her beauty.

One day Francis and Wilson went out hunting lions. They came upon one and wounded it. It ran into the

REVISION

Margot Macomber was a very beautiful woman who had everything except wealth. When she married Francis Macomber, she acquired that. Although she married Francis, she was untrue to him, and during a hunting expedition to Africa, she sought the attention of their white guide, Wilson. Although Francis felt very sorry for himself, he knew that his wealth would keep Margot from leaving him and that her beauty would keep him from divorcing her.

One day while Francis and Wilson were out hunting, they wounded a lion and let it get away to hide in the brush. They moved into the brush after him, although getting him out was dangerous. Suddenly

304

brush and hid. Getting the lion out would be a very dangerous job. Wilson and Francis began moving into the brush looking for the lion. All of a sudden, the lion jumped out of the brush. Macomber became frightened. He turned and ran. Wilson stood his ground and shot the lion, killing it. Francis knew that he would be the laughingstock of the party.

Some time later, they went on a buffalo hunt. They came upon a herd of buffalo. A buffalo was wounded and ran into the brush. Previous incidents seemed to be repeating themselves. Francis saw a chance to redeem himself. He began going through the brush. All this time, his wife had been watching him from a distance. All of a sudden, the buffalo jumped up and charged Francis. Francis held his ground and aimed at the animal's nose. In the meantime, Margot saw the animal charge too. She brought a heavy rifle to her shoulder. Then there was the sound of two shots. Francis and the buffalo both toppled to the ground dead. When she saw that Francis was dead, she became hysterical. She began to realize that Francis was really the man she loved.

the lion jumped out. Macomber, frightened, turned and ran. Wilson stood his ground and killed the lion. Francis knew he would be the laughingstock of the party.

Some time later they went after buffalo, found a herd, and wounded one, losing him in the brush. As the earlier situation re-occurred, Francis saw a chance to redeem himself and began to go into the brush. Suddenly the buffalo jumped up and charged Francis. He held his ground and aimed at the buffalo's nose. Margot, who had been watching from a distance, saw the charge, too, and raised a heavy rifle to her shoulder. Two shots sounded. Francis and the buffalo both toppled to the ground dead. When Margot saw that Francis was dead, she became hysterical, realizing that Francis was really the man she loved.

Neither version is very successful; what purports to be a character sketch of Margot Macomber turns out to be merely a plot summary revealing some curious misinterpretations of the story. But the revision illustrates that much can be done to improve the childish style of the original by subordinating some parts to others.

Subordination and Economy

As examples above illustrate, subordination sharpens prose, makes it more economical, avoiding repetition and removing unnecessary words. The following provides a simple example:

> Dramatics develops assurance. This is very valuable.
>
> Dramatics develops valuable assurance.

A sentence opening with a *this* that refers to the whole preceding idea is almost always a candidate for subordination. And in general both economy and clarity are best served when subordination reduces an item to the briefest form in which it makes sense. Consider the following:

> Calling a spouse vile names is grounds for divorce, *and this is true if the names are put into language composed only of signs.*
>
> Calling a spouse vile names *that are couched in the language of signs* is grounds for divorce.
>
> Calling a spouse vile names *by using the language of signs* is grounds for divorce.
>
> Calling a spouse vile names *in sign language* is grounds for divorce.

Notice what has happened to the idea of using signs for marital epithets. In the first sentence, this idea requires all the words after the function word *and;* that is, it is an independent clause and a rather complicated one. In the second sentence the idea has been reduced to the italicized dependent clause. In the third sentence this idea has been subordinated still further to the italicized group of words introduced by *by,* and in the last sentence the idea has become "in sign language." The groups of words that express this idea in the last three sentences can all be thought of as modifiers; they all show subordination, but the subordination is progressive. Naturally, the Spokane court that made this ruling preferred the last sentence, in which the modifiers show the greatest evidence of subordination.

Selecting Items for Subordination

Deciding what to subordinate in what patterns is one of the most complicated and difficult tasks of writing. Compare the following, all of them descriptions of the same phenomena:

The girl in the green sweater	The green sweater on the girl
The girl wearing a green sweater	The girl's green sweater
The girl who wears a green sweater	The green sweater the girl is wearing

The two items being considered, the girl and the green sweater, appear in all the expressions, with the physical relationship maintained; the sweater remains on the girl. In those on the left the sweater is grammatically subordinate to the girl; in the others the

306

girl is subordinate to the sweater. That is, either the girl or the sweater can be selected as the object to be talked about and the other can be subordinated to it. The writer makes his choice not because either item is necessarily more important than the other, but because for his immediate writing purposes he wants to relate the items grammatically in a certain way. He wishes to say something about the girl and uses the sweater to distinguish her, to point out which girl he means, even to suggest what kind of girl she is. Or he wishes to say something about the sweater using the girl to specify which sweater. In other words, the writer's purposes determine which items he subordinates. In the following the subordination differs; so does the meaning:

> The green sweater is ugly.   The green on the sweater is ugly.

Contexts, then, and the author's desire for particular emphases and meanings determine what should be subordinated; for certain purposes almost any idea can be placed in a subordinate position.

Some sorts of details, however, are more likely to profit from subordination than are some others.

> That night in a drafty hall at Red Lion Square, having escaped from an importunate hostess who wanted me to meet her niece, I heard a little, graying old man, England's leading living novelist, Thomas Hardy, read Greek poetry with an understanding and love that bespoke a lifelong devotion to the classics.

One might notice the sorts of material that are here subordinated; they include the following: time ("that night"), place ("in a drafty hall at Red Lion Square"), incidental information ("having escaped . . ."), details of description ("little, graying old"), identification or apposition ("England's leading living novelist, Thomas Hardy"). Such details are usually best subordinated; they provide attendant circumstances, offer explanations, fill in minor bits, and keep the relationships of the main predication clear in light of other predications. Of course, a very minor notion may provide the sentence's grammatical framework (see chapter 12):

> Not until long after my vacation was over and I had returned to my studies at Oxford did I realize that the quiet little gray man whom I would occasionally overhear as he trudged the hedgerowed lanes muttering Greek poetry was England's leading novelist, Thomas Hardy.

The main pattern of the sentence is "I did realize" plus a long subordinate clause used as the complement and carrying most of the meaning of the sentence.

Choosing the appropriate details to subordinate requires taste and long practice, but all good writers have learned to do it.

FORMS OF MODIFIERS: ADJECTIVE AND ADVERB   16b

Modifiers can be single words or groups of words; they can be joined as compounds; they can be modified by other modifiers, or as word groups they can contain other modifiers. Modifiers can also be classified on the basis of what they modify, as modifiers of nouns, of verbs and other modifiers, and of sentences or clauses.

GUIDE TO REVISION

16b   **Adj, Adv**

Revise using the form of adjective or adverb that the context requires.

ORIGINAL	REVISION
Jack can sure sing. [*Sure has developed a special meaning in this colloquial use.*]	Jack can surely sing. Jack can sing very well. [*More formal expressions do not translate the original exactly.*]
When I called, they came quick.	When I called, they came quickly.
The dog smelled badly. [*Adjectives rather than adverbs are required after linking verbs. Unless the writer intends a reflection against the dog's ability as a bloodhound, he needs the adjective.*]	The dog smelled bad. [*Since is could be substituted for the verb without making nonsense, smelled acts as a linking verb.*]
She looked well in her new dress. [*This suggests that she either is skillful at looking or has recovered her health.*]	She looked good in her new dress. [*Good modifies she and produces the meaning probably intended.*]

Noun modifiers, traditionally called adjectives, appear as complements in one basic sentence pattern ("Sugar is sweet," "The proposal looks good"), but modifiers that function in other ways can be derived from these and other patterns.   **308**

Pattern	*Modifier and Noun*
The plan seems dangerous.	The *dangerous* plan
The boat looks leaky.	The *leaky* boat
The university is Cornell.	*Cornell* University
The boy grows.	The *growing* boy
The boat is a house.	The *house* boat
The coat is for the house.	The *house* coat
The builder builds houses.	The *house* builder
The man works in the house.	The *house* man

As the last four sentences indicate, modifiers may have different meanings. Out of context "the orange crate" is ambiguous, depending on whether it implies that the crate is painted orange or that the crate is for oranges.

Adverbs modify verbs or other modifiers, and single-word adverbs are characteristically distinguished by an *–ly* ending.

> They attacked the food *eagerly*.
>
> The children swam *before breakfast*.

Eagerly modifies *attacked*, and *before breakfast* modifies *swam*. But modified terms are not always single words, nor can they always be positively identified. A sentence like "He did not come because he was a member of the club," for example, may be ambiguous, depending on whether the *because*-clause modifies *come* or the entire predication "He did not come." If it modifies only *come*, he presumably attended the meeting; if it modifies the entire predication, he stayed away.

Frequently modifiers are intended to modify not a single word but an entire actor-action pattern; these are best considered as sentence modifiers.

> *Before lunch*, he read two novels.   He read, *before lunch*, two novels.
> He, *before lunch*, read two novels.   He read two novels *before lunch*.

Since it modifies the entire action of the sentence, "before lunch" can occur in various positions, although it is least awkward at the beginning or end.

Although a few words can function as any type of modifier (*better*, *early*), most single-word modifiers are restricted to use as either adjective or adverb. (For further distinctions see *Adjective* and *Adverb* in the Glossary, chapter 27.) Some adjective forms are common in adverb positions in nonstandard English:

Nonstandard	*Standard*
She played her piece real good.	She played her piece very well.
None of the work was done satisfactory.	None of the work was done satisfactorily.

Usage variations are especially common when modifiers follow a copula or linking verb. After such a verb a single-word modifier refers to the subject, a noun, and should be an adjective. Difficulties develop because some verbs can be either transitive or linking. *Tastes,* for example, can be a transitive verb ("He tastes wine") or a linking verb ("The wine tastes good"). *Good,* in the second sentence, is an adjective modifying *wine.* To say "The wine tastes well" would be nonsense. We cannot speak of the skill of wine in tasting. We could say "He tastes well" or "He tastes the wine well," a compliment for a professional wine-taster. To say "He tastes good" implies cannibalism. As a kind of rough test, the writer can sometimes substitute a form of *to be* for the verb. If it can be substituted without creating nonsense, the original verb is a linking verb and should be followed by a subject complement, not an adverb. Compare the following:

He looked timidly standing all alone before the judge.	He looked timid standing all alone before the judge.

The adverb form *timidly* is probably not intended; compare "He looked timidly about the room." *Timid*, the adjective form, modifies *he; was* might plausibly be substituted for *looked* in the revised version.

DEGREE OF MODIFICATION: COMPARATIVE AND SUPERLATIVE 16c

Form changes in modifiers indicate three different degrees of modification; positive, comparative, and superlative (see *Comparison of Modifiers* in the Glossary). Handling modifiers in these forms produces usage problems. For example, using both *more* or *most* and an ending to indicate comparative or superlative is now considered nonstandard, although it was once a device for emphasis—Tennyson called Paris "more lovelier than all the world beside."

Another problem develops because some modifiers have meanings not logically subject to comparison (*opposite, final, dead* in the sense of "deceased," *waterproof, entirely, previous, diametric,* for example). Strictly speaking, *fatal* cannot be thought of in degrees; a wound is fatal or not fatal. Colloquially, however, the function words indicating comparison (*more* and *most*) are often used to mean *more nearly* or *very*, and they are sometimes used with such words even in standard writing ("more dead than alive," "more perfect union"). Furthermore, many of these words are losing their traditional meanings and assuming meanings that are comparable. *Unique*, for example, once meant "only" as in *his unique son*, but it has broadened in its meaning to "unparalleled," or more broadly still "remarkable" or "unusual." Formal usage, however, often resists these new meanings and avoids comparison of modifiers like *complete* or *perfect*, and many writers avoid loose uses of words like *unique*, especially the comparative and superlative, along with compounds like "rather unique," even in informal use.

Formal practice also restricts use of superlative forms to comparisons among not fewer than three, although informal usage has never supported the distinction:

GUIDE TO REVISION

16c   # Degree

Revise to provide the degree of modification appropriate to the variety of English you are using.

ORIGINAL

REVISION

Stanley's singing was more better than his dancing.

Stanley's singing was better than his dancing.

Her sincerity is the most unique characteristic of her singing.
[Unique *originally meant "single" or "sole," but it has come colloquially to be a vague blanket term meaning "extraordinary." Some writers find this use loose and misleading, especially in comparative and superlative forms.*]

(1) Sincerity is the distinguishing characteristic of her singing.
(2) Her sincerity is the most unusual characteristic of her singing.

He was the most outstanding scholar in the school.
[*Although* outstanding *has developed a meaning like "excellent" or "distinguished," it often seems redundant when compared.*]

He was the outstanding scholar in the school.
[*Without* most, *the modifier is more economical and more forceful.*]

The Rush Memorial represents Gutzon Borglum's most artistic achievement.
[*A judgment of this sort can be no more than an opinion and is likely to impress the reader as an unreliable one.*]

(1) Some critics consider the Rush Memorial Gutzon Borglum's most artistic work.
(2) The Rush Memorial is impressive in its mass and grand in its conception.

Between the flatboat and the life raft, I should say that the raft offers *the better* (not *the best*) chance of shooting the rapids.

Extravagant superlatives trap a writer into making statements he cannot substantiate and ultimately make his writing weaker and less convincing than more soberly qualified prose. Careless use of superlatives may lead to incomplete constructions (see chapter 15).

ORIGINAL

The Byington Parkway is the most modern highway in all the world.

REVISION

The Byington Parkway embodies many recent developments in highway construction.

POSITION OF MODIFIERS

16d

Adjective modifiers occupy relatively fixed positions, with single-word adjectives immediately preceding and phrases and clauses immediately following the nouns they modify:

The *old* man *in the boat* grinned happily.
I was the *first student* witness *the board interviewed.*

There are a few variations. For example, appositive modifiers, which repeat in different words the expressions they modify, follow what they modify:

The plainclothesmen, detectives, took charge of the investigation.

Adjectives, usually more than one, may gain prominence in a position immediately after the noun they modify.

The convertible, *red and shiny,* looked like a fire engine.

In this shifted position, modifiers are usually set off by commas, which mark the change from usual order. Sometimes, also, variations in order change meaning or emphasis. Compare:

Our hearts were *gay.*
They found the *deserted* village.

Gay were our hearts.
They found the village *deserted.*

Adverbs do not usually have fixed positions in sentence order. Phrasal and single-word modifiers of verbs, for instance, may ap-

16d   **Mod**

Revise so that modifiers appear in positions where their meaning is clear, where they do not cause ambiguity or "squint," or distort emphasis.

ORIGINAL

He gave the book to his father that was bound in leather.

[*The final clause should modify the* book, *but it does not appear in the usual fixed position immediately after what it modifies. Moreover, the word* father *intervenes, and thus the man rather than the book seems to have the leather binding. The word order can be changed (1, 2), or the sentence revised (3, 4). Usually misplaced modifiers are symptoms of wordiness; the cure is cutting and revising.*]

REVISION

(1) He gave the book that was bound in leather to his father.
(2) He gave his father the book bound in leather.
(3) He gave the leather-bound book to his father.
(4) He gave his father the leather-bound book.
[*Obviously the last two revisions are preferable to the longer versions above.*]

To understand the importance of the magazines, we investigated their sources of popularity.

[*The sense of the sentence suggests that* their *was probably intended to modify* popularity.]

To understand the importance of the magazines, we investigated the sources of their popularity.

[*The single adjective is placed in its fixed position before the word it modifies.*]

The youngest girl only thought of new clothes.

[*The context might make the sentence clear, but a reader could be temporarily misled to take* only *as a modifier of* thought — *suggesting that the girl only* thought *of clothes, did not, for instance, buy any.*]

The youngest girl thought only of new clothes.

[*In some colloquial idioms* only *appears before the verb even though it modifies the complement: "He only paid me a quarter." Here the sentence is clearer with the modifier in its usual position.*]

He fired three shots at the lion with a smile of triumph on his face.

[*Often a sentence modifier may appear at either the beginning or the end, but at the end it may fall into a fixed position.*]

With a smile of triumph on his face, he fired three shots at the lion.

[*In this sentence the reader has no trouble locating the smile.*]

She told me as soon as the dance was over she would marry me.

[*With the modifier so placed the sentence is ambiguous.*]

(1) As soon as the dance was over, she told me she would marry me.
(2) She told me she would marry me as soon as the dance was over.

pear in any of several positions, sometimes without much shift in meaning or emphasis. They occur most frequently immediately after the verb ("He drove *slowly* down the street"). They may appear within complex verbs ("She was *always* losing her gloves"). Or they may precede the verb ("I *soon* recovered"). Some modifiers, especially those that indicate direction, regularly appear after the verb but either before or after an object ("Take *back* what you said," but "Take that *back*"). Sometimes one position is obligatory, or almost so ("Set the clock *ahead*," not "Set *ahead* the clock").

A few limiting modifiers (like *only, nearly, very, just, almost, merely, ever, hardly, scarcely, quite*) are expected to modify whatever expressions immediately follow them, especially if they accompany other modifiers:

> They supplied *too* little *too* late.
>
> Very *quickly* we were *thoroughly* disgusted.

Compare the following:

> *Only* Williams could hope to win the hundred dollars.
>
> Williams could *only* hope to win the hundred dollars.
>
> Williams could hope to win *only* the hundred dollars.

Movable Modifiers in Fixed Positions

Since the same words or groups of words can be used as either fixed or movable modifiers, the reader must depend on word order to see how they apply and what they mean. He interprets according to his expectations of word-order patterns. From the sentence "The man *in the boat* was a tyrant" the reader understands automatically that "in the boat" in a fixed position, is a modifier specifically locating the man. If the phrase is moved, the reader interprets it as a movable modifier that applies to the entire sentence, and he understands the sentence differently. "*In the boat,* the man was a tyrant." The first sentence makes clear that the man was a tyrant, presumably all the time. The second preserves a little respect for him, limiting his tyranny to his time in the boat. So long as the sentence modifier is kept out of a fixed position, it may be moved, with changes in emphasis but no alteration of essential meaning. Observe the changes in meaning as the modifier moves in the following:

> *Walking in the park* the man found a mushroom.
>
> The man *walking in the park* found a mushroom.
>
> The man found a mushroom *walking in the park*.

314

In the first sentence, "walking in the park" modifies the action of the entire sentence. In the second, however, the phrase identifies the man. In the third, it has moved into the position of a fixed modifier of *mushroom* and causes either awkwardness or absurdity.

Negative sentences are especially troublesome if a modifier intended to apply generally is placed where it can apply to a specific word. Compare:

> Nobody was ever punished *because the camp was run so carelessly.*
>
> *Because the camp was run so carelessly,* nobody was ever punished.

With the clause at the end, the sentence is ambiguous; it can mean either what the second version says or that the managers of the camp were never punished for their careless administration.

Movable modifiers may be misplaced so that they apply with equal ease in more than one way. They "squint," seeming to look in two or more directions at once. The difficulty arises when an adverbial modifier follows a word that it would normally modify but also precedes another word that it can modify. Consider, for example, "The person who lies frequently gets caught." *Frequently* can be taken to modify either what precedes it or what follows it. If the modifier is intended to modify the whole sentence, it should precede it. If it is intended to modify *lies,* the sentence should probably be recast: "Anybody who lies frequently is likely to be caught."

Position of Conjunctive Adverbs

Modifying words that serve also as connectives (*however, therefore, moreover, consequently,* sometimes called *conjunctive adverbs*) appear at the beginning of a clause when they modify its entire action; placed within a clause they throw stress on the words they follow. Preceding clauses or sentences usually indicate which sentence parts need emphasis and therefore indicate where conjunctive modifiers should be placed.

> John was afraid to look at me; *however* he was eager to look at Alice.
>
> John was afraid to look at me; he was eager, *however,* to look at Alice.

The position of *however* in the second sentence stresses *eager* and accents the contrast between *eager* and *afraid.* Compare the following:

ORIGINAL

He ate baseball, slept baseball, and dreamed baseball; and when he thought he thought baseball. Therefore, a mere football game could hardly make him blink an eye.

[*Therefore has stress at the beginning of the sentence, which it probably does not deserve; thus it fails to emphasize a significant contrast.*]

REVISION

He ate baseball, slept baseball, and dreamed baseball; and when he thought he thought baseball. A mere football game, therefore, could hardly make him blink an eye.

[*Placed as it is here,* therefore *emphasizes* football game *and the contrast between football and baseball that is crucial for the sentence.*]

"DANGLING" MODIFIERS 16e

Sentence modifiers that do not themselves contain subjects, especially verbal modifiers, tend to be related to the subject or to the nearest noun. Compare:

Eating lunch on the lawn, the children were amused by the speeding cars.

Eating lunch on the lawn, the speeding cars amused the children.

The first is clear, but the second is ludicrous because the subject, *cars,* cannot logically supply the sense of a subject for the verbal, *eating.* Similarly, the modifier that opens the following sentence dangles:

Sitting on the bridge, the huge steeple looked like part of a toy village.

The subject, *steeple,* seems to govern *sitting,* but the huge steeple could scarcely be sitting on the bridge. The sentence can be revised by using as a subject whatever was sitting on the bridge ("Sitting on the bridge, *we* could see . . ."). The sentence can be revised, also, by providing the modifier with a subject of its own ("As *we* sat on the bridge, the huge steeple . . ."), or by changing the modifier in some other way so that it does not rely on anything in the main clause ("From our position on the bridge, the huge steeple . . .").

Since introductory modifiers readily refer to the subject, confusion may result if the subject is postponed in favor of an

316

16e   **DM**

*Reword a "dangling" modifier or revise the main
sentence so that modification is clear.*

ORIGINAL

Having rotted in the damp cellar, my brother was unable to sell any of the potatoes.

[*The modifier applies automatically to the main action as it is expressed, to the subject-verb of the sentence. The result is the absurdly unsanitary state of the decomposing brother. The modifier should apply to an SVC pattern* with potatoes *as subject, but* potatoes *is not in the subject position.*]

Convinced that people of the state are not well informed about the university, pamphlets were printed describing the space-age educational program.

[*The sentence is not obviously absurd, but it is unclear because the reader needs to know who was convinced, and* pamphlets *does not tell him accurately.*]

The fields had been burned by the soldiers, thus causing suffering in the valley.

[*The sentence seems to say that the fields caused the suffering; the intention obviously was to say that "the burning of the fields," not expressed in the sentence, caused it.* Soldiers *cannot complete the meaning of* causing *because it is put into a dependent position in the passive sentence.*]

He hit a home run in the eighth inning, resulting in the winning of the game.

[*The modifier has nothing to modify, but the confusion arises from obscuring "He won the game" in the modifier.*]

REVISION

(1) Having rotted in the damp cellar, my brother's potatoes were unfit for sale.

[*Word order is changed so that the subject referred to by the modifier becomes the subject of the sentence.*]

(2) Since the potatoes had rotted in the damp cellar, my brother was unable to sell any of them.

[*The modifier is changed to a clause, which can include its subject,* potatoes.]

(1) Convinced that people of the state were not well informed about the university, the committee published pamphlets describing the space-age educational program.

(2) Since the committee was convinced that people of the state were not well informed about the university, it published. . . .

(1) Because the soldiers had burned the fields, there was suffering in the valley.

[*The dangling expression, since it is really the most important idea of the sentence, is made the main clause.*]

(2) By burning the fields, the soldiers caused suffering in the valley.

(3) The inhabitants of the valley suffered because the soldiers had burned the fields.

(1) His home run in the eighth inning won the game.

(2) By hitting a home run in the eighth inning, he won the game.

(3) He won the game with a home run in the eighth inning.

expletive or if the sentence is passive (see 14b). Notice the following:

Finding something important, there are complete details to be recorded by the secretary.

When finding something important, complete details were recorded by the secretary.

The modifiers make sense only if the reader can tell who was doing the finding. Usually the name of the actor used as the subject of the sentence, in the position just after the modifier, supplies such information. In sentences like the above, in which the actor is not the subject, the modifiers dangle. Compare:

When the staff found something important, the secretary recorded complete details.

When they found something important, the staff dictated complete details to the secretary.

These revisions name the actor in the normal position in the actor-action pattern. In English the feeling for this pattern is sufficiently strong so that it will work even though the subject is only implied, as in a command:

To avoid a cold, wear a piece of red flannel around your neck.

If normal order is not followed, the modifier dangles:

To avoid a cold, a piece of red flannel may be worn around the neck.

The initial modifying phrase is so common in the pattern of the English sentence that an introductory modifier without its own subject may still seem relatively clear in itself and be useful because it is economical.

Talking with students, the same questions arise time after time.

Since *talking* is so nearly complete in its meaning—like *fishing* or *swimming*—that it relies but little on the subject, *question*, the sentence is reasonably clear. Or consider:

When lunching at the Union, conversation must be sacrificed for speed.

The conversation is not lunching, of course, but the sentence is not confusing, and the use of an impersonal *one* or *a person* would not improve it.

318

Normally modifiers should not be allowed to split constructions by separating closely related sentence elements, particularly if the separating element is long or complicated, although sometimes separation is unavoidable or is desirable for special effects. Subject and verb, parts of the verb, verb and complement, parts of a verbal, or elements of a series should be separated only with caution.

GUIDE TO REVISION

16f

Split

Revise to strengthen a split construction.

ORIGINAL

REVISION

He expected that they would in the shortest possible time agree to our terms.

[The long modifier obscures the pattern by separating words that logically belong together.]

He expected that they would agree to our terms in the shortest possible time.

[The modifier should be placed where it does not interrupt the main sentence movement.]

I promised to quickly remove my incomplete, and to never again for any cause whatever get another.

[Revision of the first split infinitive is advisable and revision of the second is imperative.]

I promised to remove my incomplete quickly and never again to get another for any cause whatever.

[Revision both tightens the sentence structure and promotes ready comprehension.]

We may, if the weather clears, go to Birmingham.

Separation of parts of the verb *may go* might be desirable to put special emphasis on *may,* but usually the modifier, "if the weather clears," would appear at the beginning of the sentence. Or consider the following in which subject and verb are separated by long modifiers:

The *driver,* confused by the snow icing on his windshield wiper and the tires skidding on the ice and his wife yanking at his elbow, *yelled.*

The unnecessary division of the basic pattern obscures meaning.

Notable partly because it has become popularly celebrated as a usage "error," the split infinitive is a similar construction. Usually a modifier does not work best between *to* and the remainder of an infinitive, where it may produce false emphasis.

He promised to *firmly* hold our position.

The meaning is clear, and *firmly* would "squint" before *to*, but the sentence gains strength if *firmly* is moved.

He promised to hold our position *firmly*.

On the other hand, a split infinitive sometimes seems almost a necessity. Herman Melville in *The Confidence Man* preferred to split an infinitive for the sake of clarity in modification.

The sick man seemed to have *just* made an impatiently querulous answer.

Placed either before *to* or after *made* the modifier *just* would change meaning, carrying something of the sense of *only*. Usually, however, the split infinitive should be regarded as a deviation from normal word order, warranted only by special circumstances. The temptation to split an infinitive is a reliable signal that word order or sentence pattern should be changed.

FOR STUDY AND WRITING

A Combine each of the following groups of sentences into a single sentence.

1. Patton was an American general. He was a tank commander. He participated in the Normandy landing.

2. There were two Scarlattis. They were both composers. Alessandro Scarlatti was the father. He wrote 115 operas. Domenico Scarlatti was his son. He composed 545 sonatas. Each sonata was in one movement. He was a harpsichord virtuoso. Both Scarlattis were prolific composers.

3. My mother had ideas of her own. My mother believed that all members of the Students for a Democratic Society were communists. It was another of her beliefs that all Young Republicans were members of the Ku Klux Klan.

4. Many flowers come out in the spring. They include violets, anemones, bloodroot, and trilliums. This is in the Middle West. These flowers appear about May. They cover the ground in woods and parks.

5. I am not a very good swimmer. This is because I have always been afraid of the water. I have spent many hours on the beach, however.

320

6. In *Jane Eyre* Charlotte Brontë describes abuses of education. These were in a real school. Miss Brontë had once attended the school, and it was at Cowan Bridge.

7. The oboe is a difficult instrument. This is because it has a double reed. This is hard to blow.

8. First all the girls in the camp had to take exercises. Then all the girls had breakfast and had to clean up the bunks. Then all the girls of the camp reported for swimming. I liked swimming better than any other activity.

9. In 1864 Atlanta was one of the most important cities of the South. This was so for the reason that the Confederacy had developed it as an important railroad center. It was also developed as a manufacturing center. This was done in the belief that it was far from the center of military activity. It would therefore be safe.

10. I grew up in a small town. It was in the South. I have not visited this town for many years. To be exact, I have not been there for eight years. It is still, however, the place I think of as home.

B Revise any sentences among the following that you think might be improved by subordinating different elements. Be able to explain the effect of any changes you make.

1. I was still very young, although I thought it was getting to be time for me to make up my mind about whether I wanted to be a teacher or a librarian or an airline stewardess.

2. Although we had been warned against hiking over the rocky slope in the dark, we started before daylight. The sun peeped over the horizon just as I fell and sprained my ankle.

3. After three months of haunting casting offices and leaving her phone number with TV producers, Jane decided to go back to St. Louis. The telephone rang when she was almost too disgusted with Los Angeles to answer it.

4. Irvin was seven years old, although he had never seen grass growing. He had never been outside the area about four blocks square that surrounded the ghetto apartment house.

5. The man who was peeping in the window and who was immediately noticed by me was on the outside.

C The sentences below probably do not say what their writer intended. Revise them, paying particular attention to modification.

1. The nurse brought in Robert, Jr., to see his father in his bassinet.

2. No one is allowed to dump anything along this road except a city official.

3. He is asking the reader to adopt his point of view as well as the lady to whom the poem is addressed.

4. "The Secret Life of Walter Mitty" by James Thurber is the typical story of a daydreamer.

5. He knew that the boat had been sunk because he had seen the battle.

6. The old man was not arrested because he had befriended the natives.

7. Joan decided that she would not marry him at the last possible moment.

8. They should not move the old road so that the trees will shade travelers.

D Revise the following sentences so that modification is clear and logical.

1. When hardly more than a baby, a gang of older boys threw me into the creek and told me to sink or swim.

2. Knowing that the whole future of the club was at stake, the investigation found us reluctant to say a word.

3. At the age of nine my father's interest in languages was already developing.

4. Every promise had been broken by the new governor, causing widespread dissatisfaction.

5. On approaching the village the gold spire was the only evidence of civilization that we could see.

6. Although only pretending to shoot, the gun suddenly went off with a loud roar.

7. Having had no sleep for two nights, the dirty haystack actually seemed inviting.

8. Trying to climb in the dormitory window at night, the Dean of Women caught her and recommended her suspension.

E Revise the following sentences by reducing italicized expressions to shorter modifiers, by making clauses into phrases or phrases into shorter phrases, or complex constructions into single words:

1. She specializes in answers *that are in the negative.*

2. He avoided tall girls *because of the fact that he was only five feet two in height.*

3. He did not believe *in the factor of hereditary influences.*

4. Hybrids are formed by crossing two species *that are pure before they are crossed.*

5. *Smoking when a person is in bed* is prohibited.

6. The will, *which can never be conquered,* sustains the rebel.

7. *When breakfast had been finished,* the boys got out their fishing tackle.

8. She was *the kind of girl who is a blonde type.*

F Combine the sentences below with the *introductory modifier* suggested for each, leaving the modifiers as they are but revising the sentences so that the combinations are clear and logical. Notice that the sentences as they now stand have passive verbs. Most of the sentences join logically with the modifiers if the verb is made active.

1. Having turned off the light. Ominous shadows were seen by Marie lurking in every corner.

2. After walking for an hour. The camp was finally seen by our leader.

3. Unable to get materials. A new product was put on the market by my father's company.

4. Playing the last ten minutes with a broken finger. The game was finally won by Jack with a free throw.

5. While flying a kite in a storm. Information about electricity was discovered by Benjamin Franklin.

6. While raking the yard. Her left knee was twisted.

7. To prove that there were no hard feelings. A dinner was given for us by the winning team.

8. Working without rest for two afternoons. The oil pollution was finally cleaned up by volunteer students.

G Below are groups of slightly varied sentences. Comment on distinctions in emphasis or meaning you can discern among the versions in each group.

1. **a)** Hope springs eternal in the flunking breast.
   b) Hope springs eternally in the flunking breast.
   c) Eternal hope springs in the eternally flunking breast.

2. **a)** With the field glasses the girl found the dog.
   b) The girl with the field glasses found the dog.
   c) The girl found the dog with the field glasses.

3. **a)** Suddenly the clown jumped up and slapped the acrobat.
   b) The clown suddenly jumped up and slapped the acrobat.
   c) The clown jumped up and suddenly slapped the acrobat.

4. **a)** The past, at least, is secure.
   b) The past is secure, at least.
   c) At least the past is secure.

5. **a)** The duke still lives that Henry shall depose.
   b) The duke still lives that shall depose Henry.
   c) The duke that Henry shall depose still lives.

6. **a)** The law smiles in your face while it picks your pocket.
   b) While it picks your pocket, the law smiles in your face.
   c) While the law smiles in your face, it picks your pocket.

7. **a)** In the long run, we are sure to lose.
   b) We are sure to lose in the long run.
   c) We are, in the long run, sure to lose.

8. **a)** This was a better way of making a living.
   b) This was a way of making a better living.
   c) This was a way of making a living better.

9. **a)** Just before noon we decided that the program was too long.
   b) We decided that the program was too long just before noon.
   c) We decided that the program just before noon was too long.

10. **a)** Although he hated everyone there, John stayed at the party.

b) John stayed at the party, although he hated everyone there.

c) John stayed—although he hated everyone there—at the party.

H Use the facts given below for a brief composition. Subordinate as many of the details as the material warrants.

Alice Marriott wrote an article.

The article is called "Beowulf in South Dakota."

Alice Marriott is an ethnologist.

Alice Marriott studies American Indian tales.

The New Yorker published the article.

The New Yorker is a sophisticated magazine.

The author was collecting stories from an old Indian.

The Indian lived in South Dakota.

One day the old Indian was bored and restless.

The Indian looked as though he did not want to tell more stories.

The Indian asked a question.

The Indian wanted to know why the white people wanted his stories.

The Indian wanted to know if the white people had no stories of their own.

The author said she wanted to compare the stories of the Indians with the stories of the white people.

The old Indian became interested.

He acted pleased.

The Indian said that the author's idea was a good idea.

The Indian said he wanted the author to tell him one of the white people's stories.

The author retold the story of *Beowulf*.

The author used Indian terms and Indian concepts.

The author made Beowulf a great war chief.

Beowulf gathered the young men of the tribe around him.

Beowulf and the young men went on a war party.

Beowulf and the young men attacked the Witch of the Water and her son.

The Witch of the Water lived under a great stone in a rushing, dangerous river.

A great fight took place under the water.

There was blood welling up through the water.

The water was as red as the sun rising.

Beowulf killed the Witch of the Water and her son.

The Indian liked the story.

The author had to tell it over and over.

The Indian told it to his friends and the friends talked about it.

The Indians talked about Beowulf.

The Indians sounded like a seminar in literature.

The Indian did not tell any more stories that day.

The author had to go home and wait until the Indians recovered from *Beowulf.*

The old man told the author many stories.

The storytelling continued for weeks.

Another ethnologist was trying to get the old Indian to tell him stories.

Ethnologists have methods of working and standardized ethical practices.

An ethnologist who tries to use another ethnologist's information is unethical.

Two ethnologists are likely to confuse an informant.

A confused informant gives unsatisfactory evidence to both scientists.

The old Indian said he liked the author.

The author was the friend of the old Indian.

The Indian offered not to tell the other ethnologist Indian stories.

The author went back to her university.

The author heard that the other ethnologist wanted to question the old Indian.

Two or three years passed.

The author was reading a learned journal.

The author found an article signed by the other ethnologist.

The article was called "Occurrence of a Beowulf-like Myth among North American Indians."

The author wondered whether or not she should tell what she knew.

SENTENCE COHERENCE: FUNCTION WORDS, REFERENCE, AGREEMENT

CHAPTER 17

Word order, function words, and referential devices give English sentences coherence.

We have observed that paragraphs must be tied together and to one another (see chapter 7), and that coherence among larger units relies upon sentences. Sentences, also, must cohere within themselves, and the immediately preceding chapters of this book, discussing basic sentences, their variations, and their developments through coordination and subordination, have treated devices that incidentally promote coherence. In addition, English utilizes special means to knit sentences together, some of which can be most readily observed in their historical growth.

Growth of Structural Coherence

We have seen that English has developed from an archaic ancestor, Indo-European, and that in doing so it has moved from a language relying heavily upon inflection to one relying upon analysis or distribution. Notice the differences among three versions of a passage from Boethius's *Consolation of Philosophy:*

Latin of Boethius

Tandem,	"Vincimur,"	arbiter	Umbrarum	miserans
At length	*"We are overcome,"*	*the judge*	*of Hades,*	*pitying,*

ait;	"Donamus	comitem	viro,	emptam
said;	*"Let us give*	*a consort*	*to the man,*	*bought*

carmine	conjugem."
with song	*a wife."*

326

Old English of King Alfred

Tha	cleopode	se	hellwara	cyning,	ond	cwaeth
Then	*spoke*	*the*	*of Hell*	*king*	*and*	*said:*

"Wuton	agifan	thæm esne	his	wif,	for thæm
"We ought	*to give back*	*to the husband*	*his*	*wife,*	*because*

he	hi	hæfth	gearnad	mid	his	hearpunga.
he	*her*	*has*	*earned*	*with*	*his*	*harping.*

Middle English of Chaucer

At the laste the lord and juge of soules was moevid to misericordes, and cryede: "We been overcomen," quod he; "yeve we to Orpheus his wif to beren him compaignye; he hath wel y-bought hire by his faire song and his ditee."

The first passage, in Latin, illustrates a synthetic grammar, in which signs of meaning and signals of grammar are combined; *vincimur* not only indicates its meaning but includes inflections to show that *we* is its subject and that it is passive in voice. The English passages show the language developing an analytic grammar, which tends to use one word to signal a grammatical relationship and another word to convey meaning. As the grammar becomes more analytic, more words are needed—twelve for the Latin, twenty-two for the Old English, and forty-two for Middle English. Translation into Modern English would require a few more words: "we been overcomen" would be "we have been overcome," and "yeve we" would be "let us give." The additional words—like *at*, *to*, or *by*—work mainly as signals of grammar.

Function Words and Content Words

As in the passages above, Modern English attaches increasing importance to what may be called function words or relationship words. Because these words are intimately connected with language change and because many of them have multiple functions, using them can produce problems. But because they are increasingly important in specifying grammatical relationships, the writer needs to give them particular attention.

Partly because English is still in process of becoming a language with an analytic grammar, words cannot be sharply classified as either content words or function words, and such classification is not necessary. Distinction between the two kinds of uses, however, can be revealing. Compare the following groups of sentences:

I *have* two apples.   I *have* eaten two apples.

Up is the right direction.	He blew *up* the balloon.
The balloon blew *up*.	The wind blew the balloon *up* the road.

In the first sentence, *have* is clearly a content word, a sign of meaning; but in the second it is a function word, a sign of the tense of the verb. In the second group, *up* appears in a variety of uses: first as a content word naming a direction, second as a part of a verb *blow up* which works as a sign of meaning, third as a part of the same verb representing a different meaning in its transitive use, and fourth as both a function word joining *road* to the sentence and a content word indicating direction. Since most function words formerly had other uses and since they did not lose entirely their old uses when they began to fill new functions, they have now developed remarkable variety and adaptability. In the following sentence, nearly half the words, those in italics, act as function words.

> *Although the* room contained many women *who would have* died unhesitatingly *for their* children, *when a* mouse appeared, courageous mothers *who had been* sitting *on* chairs found themselves standing *on the* tops *of* piano benches *or* clinging *to* strange men *for* protection.

Although relates the words before the first comma to the rest of the sentence, but it also suggests that the clause it introduces presents a seeming contrast to the main assertion. *The* warns us that we are concerned with a specific room. *Who* relates the following words to the rest of the sentence, especially to *women*, and implies that the idea involved in *women* will serve as the subject of a dependent clause. *Would have* has little meaning but specifies the form of the verb. *For* is best thought of as part of the verb, but it shows the relationship of *children* to the remainder of the sentence. To see how subtly function words blend into content words, try to find a definition that will fit both this *for* and the *for* toward the end of the sentence. *Their* carries meaning as a pronoun, but it also refers to an antecedent, *women*, and points to the word after it, *children*. *When* warns us that a dependent clause is coming and that the action in the clause determines the time of an event expressed elsewhere in the sentence. *A* introduces one particular mouse, but with the understanding that this mouse might as well have been any mouse. *On, of,* and *to,* like *for,* may be parts of verbs, but they also show how words like *chairs, tops,* and *piano benches* are related to other parts of the sentence. *Or* has a meaning, indicating a location in space, but what is the meaning of *of*? *Or* joins *standing* and *clinging,* suggesting that there is an alternative between the ideas expressed in the two words. And so on.

Function words may give the sentence additional coherence by specifying grammatical ideas beyond those conveyed by word

328

order. For example, we can often know that we are dealing with a question only because certain words signal questions. Compare "He spoke" and "Who spoke?" We recognize the second as a question only because *who* serves partly as a function word. Also compare "Jack *has* told a lie" and "Jack *was* told a lie." Only the fact that *has* and *was* signal different relationships distinguishes the active sentence pattern from the passive variation of it. "He had no basis for his charges" and "*Although* he had no basis for his charges . . ." differ only by a function word. The first is a sentence; the addition of a function word makes the second not a sentence but a possible modifying clause.

Since function words or relationship words have recently shifted within the language and are still shifting, they cannot be sharply classified. As this book is being written, for example, *like* and *as* are shifting in usage. Function words are sometimes grouped as *determiners, auxiliaries, relatives, intensifiers, conjunctions,* and *prepositions,* with subdivisions among these, but distinctions are not always sharp. Two of these groups, however, conjunctions and prepositions, are especially important to sentence coherence.

COORDINATING CONJUNCTIONS **17a**

Theoretically, a *coordinating conjunction* joins like or parallel expressions, linking either complete sentence patterns or parts of patterns.

> Although it was Sunday *and* although I knew I ought to get up for church, I turned over to take another nap.
>
> I cannot stand that yapping dog; it goes *or* I go.
>
> I jumped into the car without trouble, *but* Mary slammed the door on her fingers.

Although only a few words function as coordinating conjunctions (see *Conjunctions* in the Glossary, chapter 27), they can be used to show how ideas are related. *And* normally signals the addition of a parallel idea; *but* emphasizes a contrast; *or* offers a choice.

Coordinating conjunctions sometimes introduce a sentence, when a writer puts coordinate ideas into separate sentences to avoid a long or involved construction:

> The wolf is today what he was when he was hunted by Nimrod. But, while men are born with many of the characteristics of wolves, man is a wolf domesticated, who both transmits the arts by which he has been partially tamed and improves upon them.
>
> R. H. TAWNEY, *Religion and the Rise of Capitalism*

17a   # Conj C

Use coordinating conjunctions to reflect accurately the relationship between the sentence elements they join.

ORIGINAL

The sea was like glass, and that was the last calm day we had at the beach.
[*Probably, a contrast is intended.*]

You can play all sorts of games, and if you want to, you can spend the afternoon under a tree reading a book.
[*A choice seems intended.*]

At first I thought I would decorate the table with flowers. But I found that the roses had gone to seed.
[*Opening the second sentence,* but *is unduly emphatic.*]

REVISION

The sea was like glass, but that was the last calm day we had at the beach.

You can play all sorts of games, or if you want to you can spend the afternoon under a tree reading a book.

At first I thought I would decorate the table with flowers, but I found that the roses had gone to seed.
[*Within a compound sentence,* but *is appropriately inconspicuous.*]

Although the sentences might have been combined, the separation sharpens the contrast between ideas, because *but,* the sign of the contrast, is in the position of emphasis at the beginning of the sentence. This device is easily overworked. It is useful when the writer needs the special emphasis given the coordinating conjunction in initial position, when combining would produce an unwieldy sentence, when a more formal connective like *in addition* or *however* would seem ponderous, or when a sentence beginning with *but* is to be contrasted to more than one preceding sentence.

Correlative conjunctions also join coordinate elements but work in pairs, with their position distinguishing which items are coordinate (see *Conjunction* in the Glossary, chapter 27).

CONJUNCTIVE ADVERBS   # 17b

Conjunctive adverbs, like coordinating conjunctions, connect parallel clauses but at the same time modify within a clause (for a list see *Conjunctive Adverb* in the Glossary). Observe the following:

330

I wanted one of the then fashionable slit skirts; however, I got Jinny's old plaid.

She was in no mood to take advice. I was angry, however, and I told her what I thought of her leaving the party.

GUIDE TO REVISION

17b	# Conj Adv

Avoid overuse of conjunctive adverbs.

ORIGINAL

   Clubs for girls can serve useful functions. However, they should not take up all of a girl's time. Then, they merely prevent a girl's achieving social maturity. Nevertheless, there is a time in a girl's life when a club can be helpful and even exciting.

REVISION

   If clubs take up all a girl's time, they can only prevent her achieving social maturity. At some time in a girl's life, however, a club can be helpful, even exciting.
[*The original suffers mainly from repetition and a failure to relate ideas, but the overuse of conjunctive adverbs aggravates the confusion.*]

In both examples *however* functions partly as a sentence modifier, modifying the subject-verb pattern in which it appears; but it also links two clauses in the first example and two sentences in the second. Conjunctive adverbs readily acquire false emphasis (see 18b) when they appear too frequently at the beginning or end of a sentence.

SUBORDINATING CONJUNCTIONS   **17c**

    Subordinating conjunctions are used mainly to convert sentence patterns into clauses that can function as parts of other patterns. Thus words like *when, although, because, since, as, so that,* or *whereas* at the beginning of a clause mark the clause as a modifier, usually of the whole predication that follows or precedes it. Words like *that, how, what,* or *whoever* signal that clauses they introduce can function as nouns. Relative pronouns, *who, whom, whose,* and *that,* also function as subordinating conjunctions, introducing modifying clauses. Since subordinating conjunctions indicate the use of a clause and specify how it is related in meaning to its sentence, they should be chosen to reveal both functions. Compare, for example:

Although she was his wife, she stayed at a hotel.

Because she was his wife, she stayed at a hotel.

Before she was his wife, she stayed at a hotel.

Until she was his wife, she stayed at a hotel.

After she was his wife, she stayed at a hotel.

While she was his wife, she stayed at a hotel.

Whenever she was his wife, she stayed at a hotel.

GUIDE TO REVISION

17c   # Conj S

Choose subordinating conjunctions to define relationships precisely. Some expressions used as subordinating conjunctions are nonstandard (but what *for* but that, so as *or* so *for* so that, as *or* as how *for* that).

ORIGINAL

REVISION

While Father did not approve of alcoholic beverages, he always had some in the house for guests.

[While *is loosely used as an equivalent of* although *or* because. *Strictly used it means that one event takes place at the same time as another.*]

Although Father did not approve of alcoholic beverages, he always had some in the house for guests.

[*The subordinate clause mentions a concession, and the concessive conjunction,* although, *has accordingly replaced* while.]

Karen finished addressing the envelopes, while Georgianna could not get the ditto stencils typed in time.

[*Apparently a contrast is intended.*]

Karen finished addressing the envelopes, but Georgianna could not get the ditto stencils typed in time.

[*With* but *replacing* while *the meaning is immediately clear.*]

Since my mother was a little girl, she was not allowed to sit at the table.

[Since *often refers to time, but it is also used in the sense of* because.]

Because she was only a little girl, my mother was not allowed to sit at the table.

I washed my face so as I would be allowed to go in for dinner.

I washed my face so that I would be allowed to go in for dinner.

I arrived on time so I could leave early.

I arrived on time so that I could leave early.

Because they indicate different kinds of relationships between the ideas in the clauses, the various conjunctions give the sentences different meanings. Some subordinating conjunctions may be used in contexts where coordinating conjunctions would be more suitable. Doubtless with the laudable purpose of avoiding excessive use of *and* or *but*, careless writers may use *while* as a coordinating conjunction, as in the following:

> Arnold helped our scoring by winning the shot put, while he placed only a poor third in his favorite event, the javelin.

Read with the usually accepted meaning of *while*, indicating that one event takes place at the same time as another, this sentence is ridiculous, but *while* is growing so rapidly as a coordinating conjunction that many readers would readily accept it.

PREPOSITIONS

17d

Unlike conjunctions, prepositions function only within the basic sentence, joining a noun or noun substitute to some part of a sentence. The preposition and the noun following

GUIDE TO REVISION

17d   **Prep**

Choose prepositions that are appropriate and idiomatic in standard English.

ORIGINAL	REVISION
He went in the house and stopped at the mirror.	He went into the house and stopped before the mirror.
I had never heard about him or of his famous rescue.	I had never heard of him or about his famous rescue.
I found the keys in back of the water pitcher.	I found the keys behind the water pitcher.
He spoke in regards to the paving of the alleys. [*When the construction is appropriate, the word is* regard, *not* regards.]	(1) He spoke about paving the alleys. (2) He discussed paving the alleys.

it constitute a *prepositional phrase,* which can function as almost any sentence element, usually as a modifier. Choosing prepositions accurately is not always easy because convention, often arbitrary, may dictate which prepositions determine which meanings. For example, British English requires the idiom "He lives in Oxford Street;" whereas American English requires "He lives on Oxford Street." *Street* in England retains some of its medieval meaning and designates both the thoroughfare and the areas alongside it. Most users of the language cannot be expected to know such historical backgrounds for differences and accordingly must rely on their sense of idiom when they distinguish among speaking *to, with, for, of,* or *about* the devil. They must sense that they agree *with* a friend, *to* a proposal, *on* terms, and *about* somebody's character. For further discussion, see *Preposition* in the Glossary.

PRONOUN REFERENCE 17e

Ideas carry from sentence to sentence and paragraph to paragraph partly as they are repeated or echoed, either in the same words or in synonyms or substitute words (see 7a). This device, which contributes to coherence within the sentence as well as between sentences, may be called reference, signifying the relationship between one expression and another that restates its idea or refers to it. The word referred to, especially by a pronoun, is called the antecedent (see Glossary).

Reference works in a variety of ways, as the following sentences illustrate (antecedents are in italics):

My *sister* said she had found the *book* that was missing from the shelves. (*She* refers to *sister* and *that* to *book.*)

He believes that *everyone who attends the dean's teas receives special favors,* but this is not true. (*This* refers to the idea of the entire clause.)

In his criticism of student government, the *speaker* alleged that students were naturally irresponsible. (*His* refers ahead to its antecedent, *speaker.*)

Although these sentences vary, they are clear primarily, not only because customary word-order patterns are followed, but also because pronoun forms and meanings point a word toward its antecedent.

17e   Ref

Revise to clarify reference of pronouns, supplying needed antecedents, substituting nouns for pronouns that refer vaguely, or recasting the sentence.

ORIGINAL

Some critics have accused Chaucer of Frenchifying English, which has been disproved.
[Which *has no certain antecedent.*]

Charles lacked refinements, which annoyed her.
[Which *seems to refer to* refinements.]

The next morning he decided to fly to Phoenix, and this was where he made his fatal mistake.
[*With the vague reference of* this, *several meanings are possible.*]

If they are taken into the army, it means they will not graduate.
[It *lacks an antecedent. Even the loose idea that the reader might supply for* it, *their induction into the army, does not make a good subject for the main clause.*]

In Hemingway's book *For Whom the Bell Tolls,* he tells about an American teacher in the Spanish Civil War.
[He *must refer to a person, but* Hemingway's *is not a person. It helps identify* book.]

In the paper it says the weather will change.
[*Colloquially* it *and* they *sometimes refer loosely to "people" or "society."*]

REVISION

Some critics have accused Chaucer of Frenchifying English, but the accusation has been disproved.
[*No antecedent is necessary.*]

Charles's lack of refinements annoyed her.
[*Revision to remove the indefinite reference clarifies.*]

(1) The next morning he made his fatal mistake in deciding to fly to Phoenix.
(2) The next morning he decided to fly to Phoenix where he was to make his fatal mistake.

If they are taken into the army, they will not graduate.
[*In the original vague reference is a symptom of roundabout writing. The vague pronoun usurps the position of the real subject of the sentence,* they.]

In his book *For Whom the Bell Tolls,* Hemingway tells about an American teacher in the Spanish Civil War.
[*With the pronoun in the dependent position and* Hemingway *as the subject, the reference of* his *is clear.*]

The paper says the weather will change.
[*In standard written prose* it *and* they *are seldom appropriate as indefinite pronouns.*]

Often we must rely on word order to establish reference relationships, and the patterns of reference in English sentences can vary enough to make vague and inaccurate references a hazard for the writer. In general the following principles apply:

1. *Subject as antecedent.*   The subject, as the most important noun or pronoun in a clause, and especially the subject of a main clause, tends to become an antecedent of a personal pronoun. Consider:

> Shakespeare was two months younger than Marlowe; a record of *his* baptism April 26, 1564, has been preserved.

Even though *his* could apply sensibly to either *Shakespeare* or *Marlowe,* and even though *Marlowe* is nearer *his* in the sentence, the reader knows that *Shakespeare,* the subject, is the antecedent of *his.*

2. *Complement as antecedent.*   If the subject is obviously impossible as the antecedent of a personal pronoun, a complement tends to be the next choice.

> She took the rooster out of the sack and put a rock in *its* place.

Its cannot refer to the subject, but it does refer to *rooster.* Notice that while the meaning helps clarify reference, the order is essential here. We could change the chicken's fate by transposing *rock* and *rooster.*

3. *Subordinate word as antecedent.*   The less important the position of the word in a sentence, the greater is the difficulty of making the word an antecedent. Modifiers and other words in subordinate uses, however, may work as antecedents of pronouns in parallel structures.

> I visited the library and spent an hour looking through the book. I found nothing in *it.*

It refers to *book;* pronoun and antecedent have parallel uses and positions.

4. *Immediately preceding noun as antecedent.*   A noun expression immediately before a relative pronoun tends to be its antecedent. Notice what happens when a relative pronoun is used in one of the sentences above.

> Shakespeare was two months younger than Marlowe, a record of *whose* baptism in February, 1564, has been preserved.

The relative pronoun *whose* refers to *Marlowe,* and the date has to be changed to keep the sentence accurate.

Deviations from these patterns usually cause awkward sentences. Consider the following:

> I should like to find out how authors were affected during the Depression and how it changed *their* styles of writing.

Even though *their* is widely separated from its antecedent *authors,* it refers clearly to the word in the subject position. *Depression,* however, in a prepositional phrase, is not immediately recognized as the antecedent of *it.* If the sentence is revised to put antecedents and pronouns in parallel positions, the reference becomes clear:

> I should like to find out how the Depression affected authors, and how *it* changed their styles of writing.

Pronoun Forms and Reference

Pronouns are related to their antecedents not only by word-order patterns but in some instances by form. That is, the writer can make reference clear both by word order and by selecting pronoun forms that agree in person, number, and gender with their antecedents. Often choice of proper forms, along with attention to meaning, establishes reference, as in the following example:

> John showed *his* sister *his* copy of the book that *she* had written.

Since *she* is feminine in form it must refer to sister; the authorship is clear.

Notice, however, the difference if John had met his brother.

> John showed *his* brother *his* copy of the book that *he* had written.

Because of meaning and order we could probably guess whose copy is involved, but we cannot guess who wrote the book. Since no form distinctions are present, reference is unclear.

Indefinite Pronoun Reference

Pronouns, especially *this, that, it,* and *which,* may refer to a general idea rather than a specific antecedent:

> I had thrown a loaf of bread at the Marquis, which hit him on the cheek, and *that* made me feel good.
>
> ROBERT GRAVES, "Avocado Pears"

No particular noun can be labeled the antecedent of *that*, but the meaning is clear, with *that* referring to the entire action described in the first part of the sentence. This use of the pronoun, however, is subject to considerable abuse. Too often the construction disguises careless thinking; the pronoun is used to stand for an idea that the writer assumes the reader understands, but that he has not made clear to the reader and may not have made clear to himself. The indefinite use of pronouns may also be a symptom of inadequate subordination (see 16a). Consider the following:

> Beret was constantly reminded of Norway and home and this made her nostalgic, which helped cause her insanity.

The meaning of *which* is implied in what precedes it, but indefinite reference muddies the sentence. The broad reference of *this* is clear, but revision can improve the sentence by subordinating the material in the first clause and avoiding the indefinite references:

> Constantly reminded of Norway and home, Beret developed nostalgia, which helped cause her insanity.

Sentences may begin with a dependent clause followed by a pronoun referring to a noun in the clause:

> If this article makes a few people take democracy seriously, it will have served its purpose.

It has a clear antecedent in *article*, with both antecedent and pronoun in the subject position. The construction has perhaps led to the colloquial popularity of a similar pattern in which the pronoun lacks even a vague antecedent.

> If there were some way to get all people to use the same dialect, it would be much simpler.

The general idea of the opening clause makes no sense as a subject for the main clause. Logical predication (see chapter 13) will require a subject.

> If there were some way to get all people to use the same dialect, communication would be much simpler.

Although pronouns exemplify reference most obviously, sentence coherence may depend on the accurate refer-

GUIDE TO REVISION

17f   **W Ref**

Revise to make words that refer to other expressions reflect the meanings of their antecedents accurately.

ORIGINAL

The field of interior decorating holds vast opportunities for the people who want to apply themselves to the task.
[*A* field *is not a* task, *and the faulty reference helps make the sentence ambiguous.*]

He started out as a senior economist, very difficult for a person without much experience.
[*The writer probably did not mean to say that the economist was difficult, but that his work was.*]

Bowling Green, the name of my home town, is in the southern part of Kentucky.
[Bowling Green *can be either a name or a town, but the town, not the name, is in Kentucky.*]

We saw a little adobe house and rode over. The man and his wife greeted us pleasantly.
[The *suggests a man who has been mentioned before.*]

If he has any time for fooling around after class he will do so.
[*He cannot* do *fooling around.*]

REVISION

(1) Interior decorating holds vast opportunities for people who want to apply themselves.
(2) People who become interior decorators have vast opportunities.
[*Here, as often, confusion can best be cured by deletion.*]

He started out as a senior economist, doing work very difficult for a person without much experience.
[Work *provides a plausible idea for* difficult *to modify.*]

Bowling Green, my home town, is in the southern part of Kentucky.

We saw a little adobe house and rode over. A man and his wife greeted us pleasantly.
[A *indicates that the man is being introduced; the false reference disappears.*]

If he has any time to fool around after class, he will.
[*With the form changed, no substitute is necessary.*]

ence of other words (antecedents in the following are in italics):

> I *place* more faith in her judgment than you do. (*Do* repeats the idea of *place* and can be said to refer to it.)

> People in America believe *that everyone should share the good and the bad*, but this principle does not apply here. (*This principle* refers to the clause *that everyone should share the good and the bad; principle* is a plausible name for the idea of the clause.)

> He annoyed many people by his *smugness and intolerance*, attitudes developed from his early training. (*Attitudes* adequately restates its antecedent, *smugness and intolerance*.)

The accuracy of the reference depends partly on word order but primarily on meaning, the accuracy with which a word can embody the meaning of the expression to which it refers. Consider the last two of the sentences above in the form in which they originally appeared in student papers:

> Our country's democracy believes in everyone's sharing the good and the bad, and in this case the assumption would not hold true.

> He annoyed many people by being smug and intolerant, attitudes developed from his early training.

The first sentence is unclear in its predication, but the word *assumption* causes further trouble because there is no previous idea for it to refer to—no assumption has been expressed. In the second sentence, *attitudes* presents the same problem. It cannot logically repeat the meaning of *smug and intolerant*, which are modifiers and do not name attitudes or anything else.

Difficulties with word reference can take several forms. Sometimes forgetfulness or a careless shift in thinking seems the only explanation.

> Of all the regulations for women, I hated most being in by nine o'clock.

Being in is not a regulation; the general term does not logically include the specific one. The easiest revision avoids the reference problem:

> I hated most the regulation requiring women to be in by nine o'clock.

340

Confusion may arise because a modifier cannot refer logically to the word it seems to modify.

> Finally she was appointed head dietician, vacated only the day before by a sudden resignation.

Probably the position, not the dietician, was vacated. A revision might supply an expression for *vacated* to refer to:

> Finally she was appointed head dietician, filling a position vacated only the day before through a sudden resignation.

Some words used as modifiers are much like pronouns in their reference to antecedents — words like *the, such, there, here, other, another, this, that, these, those.*

> He offered to rewrite the examination, but *this* solution did not satisfy his instructor.
>
> After Wilfred had read the poem, the instructor announced that he would not allow *such* doggerel in his class.

This and *such* help identify *solution* and *doggerel* as words that restate and refer to other ideas in the sentence. In the following, however, the words do not refer clearly:

> He meant no harm by his pranks, but *this* result did not always come of his mischief. *Such* result came from one prank.

This and *such* only expose more sharply the inaccurate reference of the words they modify. The sentence was probably intended to mean something like the following:

> Although he intended no offense, his mischief was not always harmless, and one prank ended unhappily.

In the following sentence *there* has no antecedent, except perhaps in the writer's mind:

> I feel that harbor dredging will be a very interesting subject. Since I have lived *there* for fifteen years, I am well acquainted with it.

The writer needs to reveal where he has lived:

> I feel that harbor dredging will be a very interesting subject, and I am well acquainted with it, since for fifteen years I have lived where I could observe an extensive dredging project.

Do frequently acts as a substitute to avoid repetition of a verb:

Joan never wears her hair the way her sister *does.*

In effect, *does* stands for the entire predicate, but it refers to *wears* as an antecedent. The following sentence provides no logical antecedent for the form of *do:*

He expresses the revolt against bondage and the desire to be free. His argument centers around the possibility *to do so.*

Expresses is the only possible antecedent for *to do so,* but reference to it makes no sense. Compare the following:

He speaks of revolting against bondage and being free. His argument assumes the possibility of *doing so.*

The revision at least provides clear reference, with the antecedent, *revolting,* and the substitute, *doing so,* parallel in position and form.

AGREEMENT OR CONCORD   **17g**

Although word order and function words establish sentence coherence, a few surviving inflections or form changes reinforce it. Older forms of English used inflections extensively to specify relationships between words, even requiring a modifier to change its form to agree with the form of a noun. Most inflections have disappeared from English; those that remain apply to only a few grammatical relationships, and clarity seldom requires the inflectional signals of agreement. No one would miss the meaning of "The man walk [rather than *walks*] to work," even though the sentence sounds like pidgin English. Since agreement is not often essential for communication, it is not always observed in nonstandard English and in many constructions agreement is only partially observed in spoken English. Agreement is, however, characteristic of standard English, and writers need to know common practices.

The inflections in English involved in agreement are four.

1. *Pronoun forms.* Forms of personal pronouns that distinguish person (*I, you, it*), number (*I, we*), and gender (*him, her, it*).

2. *Noun endings.* The ending on nouns, or sometimes the form change, that distinguishes the plural number.

3. *Third person present singular* –s. The –s ending on the third person present singular of verbs that distinguishes person and number.

342

17g   Agr

*Revise to make verbs agree with their subjects in person
and number or to make pronouns agree with their
antecedents in person, number, and gender.*

ORIGINAL

When everybody has given their opinion, the committee can decide.
    [*Everybody has a singular meaning here and is used with a singular verb. The pronoun referring to it should be singular.*]

A horde of little Mexicans and one lone donkey was trooping down the road.
    Donkey *is singular, but the subject,* horde *and* donkey, *is plural.*

Either French dressing or mayonnaise go well with tomatoes.
    [*The subject is singular,* dressing *or* mayonnaise, *not both.*]

There is two good reasons for protesting the decision.
    [*There, although in the subject position, does not govern the number of the verb.*]

My father was one of the many businessmen who was ruined by inflation.
    [*The subject of* was ruined *is* who, *which almost certainly is intended to refer to* businessmen *and thus is plural.*]

Orrie, with his little sister, were squatting in the middle of the puppy pen.
    [Orrie *is a singular subject, modified by* with his little sister.]

REVISION

When everybody has given his opinion, the committee can decide.
    [*The singular* his *has replaced the plural* their.]

A horde of little Mexicans and one lone donkey were trooping down the road.
    [Were *agrees with* horde *and* donkey.]

Either French dressing or mayonnaise goes well with tomatoes.
    [*The singular* goes *has replaced the plural* go.]

There are two good reasons for protesting the decision.
    [*Even though it follows the verb, the plural subject requires a plural verb form.*]

My father was one of the many businessmen who were ruined by inflation.
    [*The plural form* were *replaces the singular* was; *only in an unusual context would* one *be the antecedent of* who.]

Orrie, with his little sister, was squatting in the middle of the puppy pen.
    [*The singular* was *has replaced the plural* were.]

4. *Forms of* to be.   Form changes of the verb *to be* that distinguish number and person (*am, is, are*).

These forms affect mainly two relationships in English, between a pronoun and its antecedent and between a subject and verb. In general, two principles apply.

1. *A pronoun agrees with its antecedent in gender, number, and person.*   That is, if a pronoun refers to a feminine, singular antecedent (*woman* or *Evangeline*), a feminine, singular pronoun (*she* or *her*) is used.

2. *A subject and its verb agree in number and person.*   That is, if a subject is third person and singular (*goat* or *salesmanship*), the inflected form of the verb (*is, does, works*) is used.

Since inflections in English are simple and relatively few and since rules for agreement are clear, difficulties usually occur only when the number of the subject or antecedent is in doubt or when the structure of the sentence obscures the pattern for agreement. The following passages are concerned with some of these special circumstances.

Number of Subject or Antecedent

In English, meaning usually determines the number of a subject or antecedent, as in "Two *hours* of his last twelve *were gone*" and "Two *hours is* a long time." In the first sentence *hours* is plural, according to the sense of the sentence, but in the second sentence, in spite of its plural form, *two hours* specifies a single unit of time and is therefore in agreement with a singular verb. Usually form and meaning are the same, and often when a subject plural in form is used in a singular sense it is imprecise. Consider "Late *hours was* the cause of his illness." The sense of the subject is singular, but revision would make the meaning more exact: "*Keeping* late hours *caused* his illness."

Indefinite pronouns like *everybody, anybody, everyone, each, somebody* are traditionally considered singular, as specifying one of a group. They have been used so often, however, with a plural sense—to mean "all people," for example—that colloquially they have long been used as plurals. Even in formal writing, *none* is used as either singular or plural, depending on the sense intended; in the phrase "none but the brave," *none* must be plural, but *none* is clearly singular in the denouncement by a psalmist, "There is none that doeth good; no, not one." Words like *everybody* are occasionally considered plural when they clearly have a plural sense. Generally, however, in serious writing such pronouns are considered singular; pronouns referring to them are singular in form and verbs of

344

which they are subjects are also singular. Confusion becomes acute if the verb and pronoun do not interpret the subject in the same way—that is, if an indefinite pronoun is followed by a singular verb and then referred to by a plural pronoun.

> *Anybody knows* it is to *his* [not *their*] advantage to have a college degree.

When the verb does not designate that an indefinite pronoun is singular, a pronoun referring to it, at least informally, is often plural.

In written American English, a collective noun is treated as singular unless the meaning clearly shows that the parts in the collection, not the collection as a whole, are being considered. Colloquially, however, plural verbs and pronouns are common even when the sense of the noun is not clearly plural ("The staff *were* willing to work late"). Certainly, in writing, the verb and any pronouns referring to the subject should agree:

> The company considers John one of *its* [not *their*] best men.

The singular verb here marks the subject as singular, but consider:

> The committee *differ* [not *differs*], some supporting the motion, some opposing it, and some calling it irrelevant.

Here the various members of the committee, not the committee as a unit, serve as subject.

A compound subject usually is plural, even though its parts are singular. *Corn and lettuce* combine into a subject as clearly plural as a plural form like *vegetables*. The meaning of the subject, however, usually determines its number, and occasionally compound subjects join to form a noun expression whose sense is singular. Compare:

> *Ham and eggs are* among his most profitable products.
> *Ham and eggs is* a good dish.

The compound is plural in the first sentence, but in the second it names a single item for a menu.

Either, neither, or, nor, usually separate alternatives and do not combine elements as compounds. Colloquially, alternative subjects are often considered plural ("Neither of them were afraid"), but in writing, at least formal writing, alternative subjects govern verbs individually. If both alternates are singular, a singular verb or pronoun follows; if both are plural, verb and pronoun are plural.

Virtue or honesty *is* [not *are*] its own reward.

Neither Columbus nor Henry Hudson achieved *his* [not *their*] ambitions.

If one is singular and the other plural, usage varies. Some writers follow a rule that the verb or pronoun should agree with the item nearest it:

Either the boys or their father is going to help.

Either the dog or the chickens were doomed.

But most writers would avoid either sentence, especially the singular construction.

A clause or phrase used as a subject is considered singular and is followed by a singular verb.

What you are looking for is in the closet.

To know birth and death is to know life.

Agreement with Obscured Subjects or Antecedents

In some constructions subjects or antecedents may be hard to identify. For example, subject-verb-complement order is so well established in English that speakers may have trouble recognizing a subject that follows the verb and fail to make the verb agree with it. Colloquially, an introductory *there* or *it* may be taken for a singular subject and followed by a singular verb, even when the real subject is plural. In standard writing, however, the verb takes the number of its subject, even though the subject may follow it.

There *were* [not *was*] only a few seats left.

Behind the tree *were* [not *was*] two squirrels.

A similar problem arises when the subject and complement of a linking verb differ in number; is the subject the word following or the word preceding the verb? Usually the basic word-order pattern prevails, and the verb agrees with the word preceding it:

Oranges were his main product.

His main product was oranges.

When a subject is modified, a writer may carelessly mistake the modifier for a part of a compound subject or may make the verb agree with the modifier rather than the subject. Colloquially,

346

a subject modified by a prepositional phrase is sometimes used as a compound. ("The captain with most of his crew were standing on deck"), but in standard written English the verb agrees with the subject.

> Jim, as well as his brothers, *plans* [not *plan*] to enter the university.

Even when subject and verb are widely separated they should agree.

> The employer of all sorts of people, highly trained scientists, igno-rant laborers, callow youths, and love-sick stenographers, *has* [not *have*] wide understanding of human nature.

Employer is the subject, even though it is almost forgotten by the time the verb appears.

Within a clause the verb agrees with its subject, but when the subject is a relative pronoun it takes its number from its antecedent. In a few types of sentences, therefore, the number of the verb form chosen may reflect different meanings in different contexts. Com-pare:

> The court is concerned mainly with the group of delinquent children responsible for the vandalism. John is one of those children who *seems* unaffected by punishment.
>
> The courts have to deal with many different types of children. John is one of those children who *seem* unaffected by punishment.

Usually no distinction in meaning is involved, and logic requires a plural verb.

> She is one of those people who always *complain* [not *complains*] about the weather.

Who takes its number from its antecedent *people*, which is clearly plural, although colloquially users of the language ignore logic and employ a singular verb in such sentences.

Consistency in Impersonal Pronouns

Modern English has no graceful device for impersonal con-structions. Expressions like "we find," "they say," and "you go" are common but ambiguous. The indefinite *one* is less ambiguous, but it can become awkward, especially when the possessive *one's* is re-quired or when the impersonal subject is continued. For all but the most formal writing *one* can be combined with *he* and *his*. The writer should not, however, shift to pronouns designating another person (see 13d).

> When one is abroad, *he* [not *you*] will almost always find somebody who can speak *his* [not *your*] language.
>
> I think everybody should be careful of *his* [not *one's*] grammar.

Agreement of Nouns that Refer

When one noun refers to another, it agrees with the antecedent in number. In the following sentence *an equal* refers to *women*.

> Women are treated as an equal when they work in the fields.

Several women can scarcely be treated as one equal, and the sentence needs to be revised so that the noun agrees with its antecedent.

> Women are treated as equals when they work in the fields.
>
> A woman is treated as an equal when she works in the fields.

In the following *dresses* is plural to agree with *robes*.

> The men wear long robes that somewhat resemble *dresses* [not *a dress*].

FOR STUDY AND WRITING

A In the following sentences select for each blank the appropriate present tense form of the verb in parentheses:

1. A sales lot full of old cars, some with battered fenders and bashed grills, some badly needing paint, and some with broken glass and missing chrome, _____ (*resemble*) a portable junk yard.

2. In the United States, everyone who _____ (*want*) an education can have it.

3. Neither Darwin nor his critics today _____ (*understand*) the full implication of the theory of evolution.

4. Clarence is one of those men who never _____ (*do*) tomorrow what can be put off until next week.

5. Clark, with all his little brothers and sisters, _____ (*be*) trying to squeeze through the closing subway door.

6. Each of them, in spite of the most stubborn resistance to education, _____ (*find*) that he cannot entirely escape learning something.

7. If either of you _____ (*like*) the sweater, you can have it.

8. If either Helen or Judy _____ (*like*) the sweater, I will give it up.

9. He was one of those lucky soldiers who _____ (*seem*) always to be where there is no battle.

10. There _____ (*be*), after all is said and done and your life has mostly run away, only two rewards that make life worth living.

B In the following sentences choose a pronoun to agree in number with the collective noun that is its antecedent:

1. The fraternity bowling team has just won (its, their) first victory.

2. If one is in a national park (you, he, they) can find drinking water if (you, he, they) will ask a ranger.

3. The herd of wild burros follows (its, their) path up the canyon.

4. The gang held (its, their) regular meeting Wednesday after school.

5. The Chamber of Commerce cast (its, their) ballots for various candidates for beauty queen.

6. The team took (its, their) positions about the field.

7. The Security Council will endeavor to reach (its, their) decision today.

8. The convention of nurses kept busy brushing (its, their) respective teeth.

C Revise the following sentences so that all pronouns or other reference words refer clearly to logical antecedents:

1. In the pterodactyl the hind legs were poorly developed, and thus we do not see any of them walking or crawling around on land.

2. If anything wrong has been done, I hope they put them in jail.

3. Television requires little mental activity, and in my opinion this is what we need.

4. When Admetis discovered that the veiled woman was his wife, it certainly had a significant effect on his thoughts.

5. Some of Cortez's horses were so outstanding in battle that it caused the Indians to consider them gods.

6. In the time of Shakespeare there existed much anti-Jewish prejudice and their religion set them apart from the rest of the people.

7. The chest had been her mother's, and she remembered the sorrow she had felt when she left for America.

8. The only used trailers we found for sale had been lived in by families with children that had been all scratched up.

9. Later several experimenters added more keys to the clarinet to give it range, and this is why its popularity increased.

10. Glassmaking flourished in very early times; it was made and used by the Egyptians before 1400 B.C.

11. In the first chapter of Miss Langer's book she talks about symbols.

349

12. Macbeth fears that Banquo knows that he has killed Duncan, the king, and this necessitated his death.

D If the italicized function word in each of the sentences below is faulty, choose a better form, or revise the sentence.

1. *While* I don't usually eat green onions, I sometimes do.

2. The reason I do not approve of federal aid for education is *because* we must protect our liberties.

3. He told me to move into the light *so as* he could watch the expression on my face.

4. I wrote a letter *in regards to* the advertisements for hair tonic.

5. Wilma liked to swim in the warm pool, *while* Joan preferred the invigorating water of the ocean.

6. *Being as* I have never learned to play bridge, I do not enjoy Mrs. Blackwell's parties.

7. *While* I do not like to complain about my guests, I do object to anybody who comes in with his shoes dripping mud.

8. I had expected to love Venice, *and* when I got there I could not stand the smell of the canals.

9. Mother always said that childhood is *when* you have the best time.

10. We spent our vacation in the Great Smokies, *and* we knew it would be cool there.

E Revise the following sentences, correcting any examples of illogical word reference.

1. His long punts and accurate passes, qualities that made him feared by all opponents, helped us to win the championship.

2. Many students spend all their time in extracurricular activities, and I am glad I am not in that category.

3. He was always boasting about his conquests in love, and I have never admired this characteristic.

4. The girls decided to restrict membership in the club to members of the white race, an attitude that seemed to me undemocratic.

5. Of all the people in our neighborhood, the sadness of one case affected me most.

6. The field of chemistry is exciting for anyone who undertakes this great adventure into science.

7. All the men were looked on as a brother in the camp.

8. An important part of a student's life, especially a man, is activity in student government.

9. College, the word dreamed about by so many high school students, was not what I had expected it to be.

10. The other secretaries all conspired to give me the most unpleasant jobs, aspects I had not anticipated.

11. Although there are many faults in the unicameral system of legislation, there are not enough to make it an unprofitable change.

12. Some feel that they do not have the ability to study, and others feel that they have better things to do. The latter include marriage, traveling, or work.

F Combine each of the pairs of clauses below into five different sentences, varying meanings or shades of meaning by varying conjunctions or conjunctive adverbs. You may change the order of the clauses and make necessary changes in forms of the words.

1. Mary asked me to go skating   I developed a headache
2. I slid down the drain pipe   I heard somebody scream upstairs
3. I have fast reaction time   I like sports
4. I have to ride the subway to school   I study the advertising on the car cards
5. The boat heeled over   He worked at the sails

G Notice carefully the occurrences of *this* in the paragraph below, and revise so as to remove any vague reference.

Acetylene is usually only mildly poisonous and it is commonly available; this makes it a handy way of getting rid of vermin. It has other properties aside from being poisonous and convenient, and this is not always remembered. A Swedish garage owner recently provided an example of this. While he was driving to work, he became aware that a rat was chewing the cushion of the rear seat of his car, and hearing this, he stopped to kill the rat. This did not help much, because the rat scrambled under the back of the seat, which could not be removed although the seat could have been. Knowing this, the garage owner drove to his place of business, determined to poison or to smoke out the rat. This was sensible, and the garage owner got out his acetylene welding kit with a good fresh tank of gas, thinking this would kill the rat or get him out. It got him out. Shortly after the car was filled with gas, the garage owner saw his roof flying seventy-five feet into the air, this presumably being due to a short circuit in the automobile that had ignited the acetylene. Along with the roof went much of the owner's automobile, and parts of five others. This was not the only damage the owner saw around him. Six men had to be hospitalized because this was so unexpected that people stood still in the street staring while pieces of garage fell on them. The rat has not been seen since. Neither has the cushion. In spite of this, the garage owner is not taking out a patent on his rat exterminator.

EMPHASIS
IN WRITING

CHAPTER 18

*The skillful blending of rhetorical devices can give
writing appropriate emphasis.*

Exploding bombs are notably emphatic, but they do little of the
work of the world and produce little of lasting beauty. Good writing seldom requires bombs. Forceful prose gains its power not
from unlimited fireworks but from steady use of standard patterns
with variations to produce special effects when they are appropriate. Excessive or unwarranted variation has the effect of no variation at all. Some stylistic devices, however—variations in sentence
length, structure, and rhythm—can strengthen writing.

Sentence Length and Variety

The most obvious difference among sentences is that some
are longer or shorter than others. Similarly the most obvious
difference between modern American prose and the prose of two
centuries ago is that the modern tends to run to shorter sentences,
although the apparent difference is deceptive because habits of
punctuation have changed so that writers now often use periods
where their predecessors used colons or semicolons. Even in contemporary prose, however, sentences vary in length as one can
observe by comparing the following two paragraphs from Ernest
Hemingway's *A Moveable Feast* that concern the American writer
F. Scott Fitzgerald and his wife Zelda at a time when she was near a
nervous breakdown. Hemingway and Fitzgerald, unaware of

Zelda's illness, assumed she was just behaving badly and drinking too much.

> Zelda had a very bad hangover. They had been up on Montmarte the night before and had quarreled because Scott did not want to get drunk. He had decided, he told me, to work hard and not to drink and Zelda was treating him as though he were a kill-joy or a spoilsport. Those were the two words she used to him and there was recrimination and Zelda would say, "I did not. I did no such thing. It's not true, Scott." Later she would seem to recall something and would laugh happily.

The sentences tend to be short, and even the longer sentences are mainly built up from brief patterns strung together. The writing is choppy, but intentionally so. The most staccato passage is that quoted from Zelda, and the style of the whole is appropriate as a reflection of the character of the conversation behind the scene; the style itself contributes something to the meaning of the passage.

That Hemingway did not always write this way is clear from his preceding paragraph:

> Scott Fitzgerald invited us to have lunch with his wife Zelda and his little daughter at the furnished flat they had rented at 14 rue Tilsitt. I cannot remember much about the flat except that it was gloomy and airless and that there was nothing in it that seemed to belong to them except Scott's first books bound in light blue leather with the titles in gold. Scott also showed us a large ledger with all of the stories he had published listed in it year after year with the prices he had received for them and also the amounts received for any motion picture sales, and the sales and royalties of his books. They were all noted as carefully as the log of a ship and Scott showed them to both of us with impersonal pride as though he were the curator of a museum. Scott was nervous and hospitable and he showed us his accounts of his earnings as though they had been the view. There was no view.

The sentences are longer, more subtle in structure and more crowded in detail than those of the other paragraph. The only notably short sentence is the final one, and it is short for a purpose. It provides a kind of epigrammatic close, giving the paragraph a sudden, dramatic, ironic turn at the end, establishing the attitude of the entire paragraph, the disapproval of Fitzgerald's display of shallow pride. Concentrating the final blow in four words accents the shock.

Differences in sentence length obviously affect style, but the differences do not occur because writers have consciously set out to write either long or short sentences or because they have consciously mixed the lengths to gain some kind of variety. Sentence length depends on the material to be presented, the audience addressed, and the purposes of the writer. Sometimes sharp changes in sentence length can produce special effects; short sentences can nail an idea down, accent a climax, provide a transition, or concentrate attention.

Since sentence length normally depends on what is said to whom and why, and since these needs vary, adequate sentence variety usually follows naturally. The notion that variety is inevitably a virtue, that student writers should consciously set out to regulate sentence length or to avoid repeating a subject or a structure, does more to muddy writing (see chapter 7) than to develop a style. The expository writer, particularly, seldom needs the kinds of special effects Hemingway employs in narrative fiction; exposition is likely to go along without monotony but with no dramatic attempts to provide variety. Consider the following, for example, the conclusion of an introductory section in a book on literary scholarship:

> Despite these formidable barriers—the necessity for discovering authentic records in the first place, and then peeling off the successive layers of embroidery with which later generations have adorned them—the scholar persists in trying to find out the truth. From the time that Chaucer, according to a contemporary legal document, was accused "de rapto meo" by a lady with the enchanting name of Cecily de Chaumpaigne, literary biography has been thickly sprinkled with ladies whose relationships with men of letters require exegesis. "Cherchez la femme" is a motto of the literary detective as much as it is of the fictional criminologist; and scholars would not be human if they did not betray a certain zest in running down the often delectable details. But they must draw a careful line between the episode which, however sensational it may have been, lacks real relevance to the literary productions of an author, and that which can be an important clue to his personality or a profound influence on his later life and his work. In the following pages we shall see an example of each type.
>
> RICHARD D. ALTICK, *The Scholar Adventurers*

The sentences, except the last, are of middle length, not notably different in structure. The last sentence, making a transition, is appropriately short. But like most modern expository prose the passage has adequate variety, which develops naturally from the variety in the material.

354

Most modern prose is intended primarily for silent reading, but sound patterns echo even in silent reading and a sense of underlying intonation or rhythm is part of total comprehension. A device like alliteration, for example, the repetition of initial sounds ("flight of fancy"), may bind a phrase together but may also become obtrusive with overuse. An unexpected rhyme may call attention to itself ("He couldn't brook the book's attitude") and hinder understanding. Some writers even avoid combinations of sounds that are hard to pronounce. Certainly the rhythm of prose, the pattern of accents in the sentences, is part of stylistic effect. Notice, for instance, the following from a seventeenth-century prose writer.

> How all the kinds of Creatures, not only in their own bulks, but with a competency of food and sustenance, might be preserved in one Ark, and within the extent of three hundred Cubits, to a reason that rightly examines it, will appear very feasible. There is another secret, not contained in the Scripture, which is more hard to comprehend, and put the honest Father to the refuge of a Miracle; and that is, not only how the distinct pieces of the World, and divided Islands, should be first planted by men, but inhabited by Tigers, Panthers, and Bears.
>
> THOMAS BROWNE, *Religio Medici*

The passage, in the rhythmic style common in its time, has almost the regularity of verse. Modern prose tends to be less mannered, less regular, but tends also to cultivate subtlety and variety of rhythm. The skillful writer has developed an ear for prose as for poetry. John F. Kennedy, addressing the Canadian Parliament, probably did not analyze the rhythms in the following very carefully, but he certainly knew what he was doing:

> Geography has made us neighbors. History has made us friends. Economics has made us partners. And necessity has made us allies. Those whom nature hath so joined together, let no man put asunder.

Obviously, there are two sorts of rhythm here. The first four sentences are short, blunt, and parallel. Ordinarily so skillful a writer as Kennedy would never use four childishly simple sentences one after the other, but here he had a purpose. He wanted those four salient facts to strike his hearers like blows, and probably he wanted the rhythm to become just a bit monotonous before he changed it. When he did change the rhythm the effect is dramatic, and partly because the new rhythm is a parody of a marriage ceremony, as

355

though he were the officiating priest solemnizing the sacrament joining two great nations.

The next day Kennedy said essentially the same thing again, but he said it in a different way and with different rhythms.

> In the effort to build a continent of economic growth and solidarity, in an effort to build a hemisphere of freedom and hope, in an effort to build an Atlantic community of strength and unity of purpose, and in an effort to build a world of lasting peace and justice, Canada and the United States must be found, and I am certain will be found, standing where they have always stood, together.

In a sense this sentence is like the earlier passage; the four parallel clauses beginning with *in* suggest the four staccato sentences, but here, instead of establishing something, the rhythm seems to suggest that the speaker is building up to something. He is; the final word, *together*, climaxes and clinches the whole.

EMPHASIS THROUGH STRUCTURE 18a

A basic sentence, composed of a subject, verb, and sometimes complement, serves most of the utilitarian needs of language—to greet friends, to get food, to ask directions. Adult communication concerned with complex problems, however, relies on longer sentences composed of various parts. Inevitably the parts must be organized, must develop in accordance with some pattern. Two patterns are natural: (1) The SVC pattern can be completed at once, with various modifying and coordinated elements following it; or (2) some elements of the basic pattern can be withheld while modifying elements build up until the final word closes at once the SVC and the sentence. Compare the following:

> Tolerance, good temper, and sympathy are no longer enough in a world which is rent by religious and racial persecution, in a world where ignorance rules, and science, who ought to have ruled, plays the subservient pimp.

> In a world which is rent by religious and racial persecution, in a world where ignorance rules, and science, who ought to have ruled, plays the subservient pimp, tolerance, good temper, and sympathy are no longer enough.

The first version, with subordinate material appended to an initial SVC, exemplifies what may be called a *cumulative sentence;* E. M. Forster wrote the sentence this way. The second version, changed so that modifiers appear first and the SVC is postponed for a final climax, exemplifies the *periodic sentence.*

Patterns, of course, can be combined, and not all sentences follow models like these; but the sentences illustrate two general kinds of emphasis characteristic of complex English sentences. For a language like English, relying heavily on word order, the cumulative sentence may provide the natural emphasis — making a statement and then appending qualifications. The cumulative sentence seems to have grown naturally in English; the author of *Beowulf* used it extensively, as did Chaucer and other early writers. The periodic sentence, however, also has a long tradition in English, fostered by the school rhetoric founded on Classic Latin and Greek. Both types of sentence — the cumulative sentence, apparently native, and the periodic sentence, assiduously cultivated — have uses in modern writing.

GUIDE TO REVISION

18a   **Em**

Revise for appropriate emphasis, making use of periodic or cumulative structures, or both.

ORIGINAL

    Karen, because she was so changeable and was sometimes openhearted and friendly but sometimes selfish and calculating, was a source of continuing bafflement to me, although she did have a way that I found completely charming, in spite of being uncertain of herself.

    Man is continuing to pollute the surface of the earth, and so suicide is a very real possibility, and there is also the possibility that he will devour the resources of the earth, especially since there are too many of him now, and populations are getting bigger and bigger.

    [*The sentence is jumbled, lacking emphasis because it lacks pattern.*]

REVISION

    Karen baffled me, sometimes openhearted and friendly, sometimes selfish and calculating, always uncertain of herself, and yet occasionally exhibiting a warmth that I found completely disarming.

    [*With a clear opening statement followed by cumulating details, the sentence falls into a pattern.*]

    If man cannot curb his appetite to overpopulate the globe, if he cannot cease to decimate the earth's natural resources, if he cannot learn to live without polluting the world around him, he will shortly commit race suicide.

    [*With the sentence cast into periodic mold the qualifying clauses are brought together and the sentence builds to a climax.*]

Classical rhetoric mainly described oral prose as exemplified in ornate speeches for formal occasions or persuasive speeches addressed to judges or political audiences. Since Latin and Greek seldom used word order or position for grammar, classical orators could place words anywhere they pleased for emphasis, and accordingly orators devised what were called "colors of rhetoric," cultivating figurative language and elaborate displays of word patterns. These patterns, including balance, contrast, climax, and the tricolon, fitted readily into the periodic sentence. English and American orators have imitated such sentences; notice the following from Lincoln's Gettysburg Address: "But, in a larger sense, we cannot dedicate—we cannot consecrate—we cannot hallow this ground." With a tricolon, three parallel elements—"cannot dedicate, cannot consecrate, cannot hallow"—the sentence builds a climax from human dedication to divine hallowing, closing sense and structure at once. The next sentence is balanced as well as essentially periodic, as the following suggests:

$$\text{The world will} \left\{ \begin{array}{c} \text{little note} \\ \text{(nor)} \\ \text{long remember} \end{array} \right\} \text{what we say here}$$
$$\text{(but)}$$
$$\text{it can never forget} \qquad\qquad \text{what they did here.}$$

The oration comes to a crashing conclusion with a period that builds through a tricolon and a tricolon within a tricolon:

that we here highly resolve
   that these dead shall not have died in vain
   that this nation, under God, shall have a new birth of freedom
      (and)

$$\text{that government} \left\{ \begin{array}{c} \text{of the people} \\ \text{by the people} \\ \text{for the people} \end{array} \right\} \text{shall not perish from the earth.}$$

The longer sentence quoted from Kennedy makes similar use of balance, developing to a climax as a periodic sentence.

Most modern writers do not compose orations, particularly not orations modeled upon the classics, but notice the following from Macaulay's review of Boswell's biography of Samuel Johnson:

Johnson grown old, Johnson in the fullness of his fame and in the enjoyment of a competent fortune, is better known to us than any other man in history. Everything about him, his coat, his wig, his figure, his face, his scrofula, his St. Vitus's dance, his rolling walk,

358

his blinking eye, the outward signs which clearly marked his appro-
bation of his dinner, his insatiable appetite for fish sauce and veal
pie with plums, his inextinguishable thirst for tea, his trick of touching the posts as he walked, his mysterious practice of treasuring up
scraps of orange peel, his morning slumbers, his midnight disputa-
tions, his contortions, his mutterings, his gruntings, his puffings,
his vigorous, acute, and ready eloquence, his sarcastic wit, his
vehemence, his insolence, his fits of tempestuous rage, his queer in-
mates, old Mr. Levitt and blind Mrs. Williams, the cat Hodge and the
negro Frank, all are as familiar to us as the objects by which we have
been surrounded from childhood.

Macaulay was admired for sentences like these, and they do assort
numerous details into a neat order, but most modern prose is more
relaxed. Restrained use of parallelism continues, however, and
good modern writers find use for the periodic structure, as in the
following description of the birth of an Americanism:

> When head, wings, and claws were added by Gilbert Stuart, the
> celebrated painter, the result was by a stroke of genius called a *gerry-*
> *mander*.
>
> THOMAS PYLES, *Words and Ways of American English*

The Cumulative Sentence

Nevertheless, periodic sentences, even sentences as inconspicuous as this one, do not do the work of most modern paragraphs, however useful they may be for variety and for special
effects. For whatever reasons — and the reasons are probably rooted
in the nature of the English language and in the needs of modern
society — good American writing relies heavily on cumulative sentences.

Such structures appear readily in fiction; consider the following:

> He took all his pain and what was left of his strength and his long
> gone pride and he put it against the fish's agony and the fish came
> over onto his side and swam gently on his side, his bill almost touch-
> ing the planking of the skiff and started to pass the boat, long, deep,
> wide, silver and barred with purple and interminable in the water.
>
> ERNEST HEMINGWAY, *The Old Man and the Sea*

This sentence carries with it a great weight of detail, but it does so
with ease and with no sense of strain. Instead of building to a climax the sentence moves like waves, instinct with life, and with
crests and valleys. Sentences like these, because they can move in

varied rhythms, team well together. Notice the following paragraph from later in the same book:

> The two sharks closed together and as he saw the one nearest him open his jaws and sink them into the silver side of the fish, he raised the club high and brought it down heavy and slamming onto the top of the shark's broad head. He felt the rubbery solidity as the club came down. But he felt the rigidity of bone too and he struck the shark once more hard across the point of the nose as he slid down from the fish.

These sentences could, of course, be cast into periodic form, but a succession of formally wrought periods would ill consort with the story of an old man catching a fish. Hemingway's sentences not only carry the detail better, and move more easily from the sharks to the club, to the man, and back again to the sharks, but they suggest better the time and the place, the temper of a tale more concerned with suggesting than with persuading.

Similar structures serve, also, for modern nonfictional prose. The following describes a teen-age delinquent on trial for having participated in the gang murder of a helpless old man:

> It was not hard to see evil in Jack Koslow, the oldest defendent. So manifest was his sickness of soul that he could have posed as one of the tormenting demons that populate Hieronymus Bosch's vision of hell. His skin had been described as "sallow," but that gave no hint of its dead green-whiteness, in eerie and surprising conjunction with thick hair that was dark red and wholly without shine, receding from his forehead in a high crest. His features were delicately ugly; a long thin curved nose with a sharply articulated ridge; a thin, down-turned, and usually derisive mouth, lips colorless, the upper extending slightly above the lower; weak but bony chin; a white, undeveloped neck. His eyes were strangest of all. They were dark brown and seemed pupilless, and their look was hooded as if by a transparent extra lid. When Koslow walked in and out each day manacled to his guard, you could see how tall and thin he was, and how his narrow head hung forward from his body like a condor's.
>
> MARYA MANNES, *But Will It Sell?*

The fourth sentence, the one beginning "His features were delicately ugly," may profitably be compared with the sentence quoted above from Macaulay describing Samuel Johnson, which begins, "Everything about him, his coat, his wig, his figure, his face, his scrofula," and closes, "are as familiar to us as the objects by which we have been surrounded from childhood." Of course this conclusion is not true; nobody since Boswell has known Johnson that well, but even if we concede Macaulay his innocent hyperbole, the fact remains that his periodic conclusion was concocted for the structure of his sentence, and the whole long list of Johnsonian qualities impresses us as brought together for effect. Macaulay sounds as though he were composing in his study, which doubtless he was; Miss Mannes sounds as though she were sitting in the courtroom, acutely examining Koslow feature by feature, detail by revealing detail. We believe her, as we do not believe Macaulay, partly because we sense that we see these horrible scraps of evidence as she saw them. Yet she achieves a climax at least as devastating as Macaulay's; the sentence closes with the mention of Koslow's "white, undeveloped neck," and we realize that this young scavenger upon the body of society has never worked, and that the aimlessness of his life has something to do with his congenital evil. These effects of Miss Mannes are deliberate; the "white, undeveloped neck" foreshadows the conclusion of the paragraph, when we learn that Koslow's "narrow head hung forward from his body like a condor's." Such climaxes are the more effective because they are not flaunted as they would be in periodic sentences, but are slightly veiled beneath the shifting patterns of cumulative structures.

Emphasis by Subordination

Periodic and cumulative sentences, as examples above indicate, differ in the location of subordinated material. The periodic sentence keeps subordinated material toward the opening of the sentence; the cumulative sentence tends to append subordinate material. The writer's decisions about what to subordinate, therefore, can regulate emphasis both by influencing structure and by influencing meanings. Subordination (see chapter 16) offers the writer a useful means for combining the following relatively simple ideas:

> I was twelve years old.
> I got my first long pants.
> I took the girl next door to the movies.

Most obviously, perhaps, the first idea might be subordinated to the others as an indication of the time, with the last two ideas sharing equally the stress of the sentence:

> When I was twelve years old, I got my first long pants and took the girl next door to the movies.

A change in the subordinating word would vary both meaning and emphasis.

> Although I was only twelve years old, I got my first long pants and took the girl next door to the movies.

Centering attention on the second idea could produce a sentence like the following:

> Since I was now twelve years old and about to take the girl next door to the movies, I was allowed to buy my first long pants.

Or both the first two ideas might be subordinate:

> When I was twelve years old and in my first long pants, I took the girl next door to the movies.

The trip to the movies becomes the event that the writer wants primarily to talk about, and the acquisition of the pants drops out.

Subordination should vary with the sentences that precede and follow. The last version above, for example, might be appropriate in a paragraph narrating a story about the friendship of a boy and girl. The context might suggest even wider variations in the pattern of subordination. Consider:

> When I had my first long pants and had taken the girl next door to the movies, I was twelve years old.

This unusual emphasis might be logical if the preceding sentence had read:

> The actual date of my twelfth birthday meant nothing to me.

A different preceding sentence might suggest the wisdom of a parallel pattern of subordination following it.

> At the age of eleven, I tore my knickers trying to catch a toad with which I hoped to frighten the girls at the Sunday School picnic. At twelve, I wore my first long pants to take the girl next door to the movies.

The second sentence fits the pattern of the first, draws the contrast between the events, and enforces the continuity (see chapter 7).

EMPHASIS BY INVERSION 18b

Any variation from a usual pattern may work as a device for special emphasis. As indicated below, a modifier moved into an unusual position may attract attention. Compare:

He turned *slowly* toward the open door.

Slowly he turned toward the open door.

Slowly gains emphasis in the second example. The effects of such variations, however, are usually dramatic and are warranted only by special contexts. Rhetorical questions, for example—"Why did these atrocities occur?"—or words like *well* or *now* or *no* inserted specifically for emphasis are likely to have a false ring in ordinary prose, to suggest that the writer is pushing too obviously for an effect.

One of the most common variations for emphasis is inversion. A word is drawn out of its normal place in the sentence; and since Modern English makes much use of normal order, the change,

GUIDE TO REVISION

18b   **F Em**

Revise to avoid false emphasis, restoring normal order or deleting words attempting unwarranted emphasis. (See also 16a.)

ORIGINAL

I was only a child, inexperienced and trusting. Little did I know what was in store for me.

[*The second sentence is trite, but the staleness is obvious because the inversion is unwarranted. The unusual word order makes the sentence overdramatic.*]

There are five reasons for joining a sorority in college. What are those reasons? The first is. . . .

[*The question dramatizes a prosaic statement, which should be clear without repetition in inverted order.*]

This nation must return to the ideals that inspired its founding. Yes, we must re-examine our goals.

[*The insertion of words like yes, indeed, well, now can overemphasize insignificant parts of the sentence.*]

REVISION

I was only an inexperienced and trusting child, unaware of what was in store for me.

[*Restoration of usual word order removes most of the affectation from the sentences, although the reader is still suspicious of the significance attached to the facts.*]

There are five reasons for joining a sorority in college, of which the first is. . . .

[*Omission of the rhetorical question makes the emphasis more appropriate to the meaning. For Rhetorical Question see Glossary, chapter 27.*]

This nation must return to the ideals that inspired its founding. We must re-examine our goals.

[*Even with the yes omitted, the sentence is oratorical enough in its tone.*]

even when slight, is forceful. The following lines from Alexander Pope's "Elegy to the Memory of an Unfortunate Lady" are an extreme example:

> By foreign hands thy dying eyes were clos'd,
> By foreign hands thy decent limbs compos'd,
> By foreign hands thy humble grave adorn'd,
> By strangers honour'd, and by strangers mourn'd!

Usual order was changed in each clause in a curious way so that each involves a kind of double inversion. The usual pattern would be:

Subject	Verb	Complement
Foreign hands	closed	thy dying eyes.

The poet followed two procedures for varying word order. He reversed subject and object, making the verb passive: "Thy dying eyes were closed by foreign hands." Then he went a step further and moved the modifier, which would have been the subject of the action in a conventional sentence, into the position of emphasis at the beginning. The result is stress on the initiator of the action, "foreign hands"— even more stress than normal word order would provide. Repetitions of this pattern throughout the clauses multiply the stress. The first three clauses build on the importance of "by foreign hands" so that the meaning of "by strangers" is sharp and clear. The result is that the reader remembers most vividly, even in the presence of death itself, the circumstance that only strangers were present at the death.

Emphasis so strong as this would not be appropriate in most prose, but unusual order may enforce continuity (see chapter 7) or provide special emphasis, as in the following passage from a monologue in Virginia Woolf's novel *The Waves:*

> "I have signed my name," said Louis, "already twenty times. I, and again I, and again I. Clear, firm, unequivocal, there it stands, my name. Clear-cut and unequivocal am I too. Yet a vast inheritance of experience is packed in me. I have lived thousands of years. I am like a worm that has eaten its way through the wood of a very old oak beam."

FOR STUDY AND WRITING

A Revise each of the sentences below, moving the italicized modifier to the different possible positions. Then explain any changes in meaning or emphasis effected by the shifts in word order.

1. We found the girl *breaking into the back room.*
2. The hill is not really pretty *because of the big rocks on it.*
3. The girl *with the broken arm* grabbed the new doll.
4. The children promised to *faithfully* chew every bite.
5. *In complete confusion* the speaker finally found his audience.
6. *Happily* the old man watched the children singing.
7. He ordered them *at once* to dump the nerve gas into the sea.
8. I decided I would get up *when my roommate threw a glass of water on me.*
9. The room looked filthier than any stable I had ever seen *by daylight.*
10. She *nearly* threw away all her diamonds.

B Rewrite the following selection from a student theme, improving its style in any way you can and paying particular attention to opportunities for clarifying relations between ideas by subordination:

> On the night of the flood four of us drove across the river away from home to see what damage had been done. We drove around on the other side for about an hour and a half. We finally decided to start home. We came back to the bridge. There was about three feet of water over the road. We had to get across for classes the next day, so we had to find some way to cross to the other side. After considerable debate we decided to drive across. We had gone about a fourth of the way and the ignition got wet. The car stalled in about two feet of water. The water started pouring in under the doors. The heat of the engine dried the ignition, and the car started again. We went about half way and stalled again. This time we were in about three feet of water. The water poured in. We talked about pushing the car across. The three boys got out and pushed. I steered. The water was deep, and so they could not push the car. They got back in. I thought maybe the water would get deeper. It was very exciting. The water was swift. Finally a large truck came in behind us. He pushed us across. We still could not start the car, and so we had to leave it. The water was still rising. We came back the next day. The car was still there and the water had not come to it again. We tried to start it. It would not start. We pushed the car for three or four blocks. It did not fire at all. We pushed it to a garage, and the mechanic said the carburetor was full of mud. The river water was very muddy in the flood. We left the car at the garage to be cleaned.

C Revise for emphasis and clarify the faulty sentences in the following student theme; often sentences can appropriately be combined.

> [1] When our Constitution was written, the thing foremost in the people's mind was to have freedom of speech. [2] People were tired of listening to the government tell them what to say and what not to say. [3] They had come over here to escape from a society where there were always government agents, and the people could be persecuted by them. [4] Town meetings were broken up unless the speakers were told by a government official exactly what to say.
>
> [5] After the Constitution took effect, freedom of speech began to be used by the people in its true meaning. [6] Opinions could be voiced by

anyone on any subject. [7] No longer did a person have to be afraid of landing in jail or getting deported from the United States. [8] Often there were soapbox speakers, and they stood on boxes in the streets or in the city squares and gave speeches. [9] Sometimes public officials were attacked by these speeches. [10] These speeches were finished without punishment by the speakers.

[11] It seems that nowadays nothing can be said by a citizen, or he will be in danger of being thrown in jail by the government. [12] If a person talks against our government or any high official in it, he may be labeled a communist. [13] I wish a different system could be found by the government to enforce its laws. [14] Yes, what people say should not be used as evidence against them. [15] If it were not, there would be for us more of the kind of freedom of speech we used to have.

D The following paragraph is the next one after Marya Mannes's description of Jack Koslow quoted above, and the *his* in the first sentence refers to Koslow. Rewrite the paragraph in three ways: (1) using only short sentences, (2) using only long or relatively long periodic sentences, incorporating balance if you can, and (3) using only long, cumulative sentences. You need not rewrite sentences that fit the type you are using in any given paragraph; that is, the final sentence as Mannes wrote it is periodic and need not be changed in version (2) unless you want to. When you have written three versions of the paragraph, compare them with Mannes's original for their effects as pieces of writing, and embody your results in a written paragraph.

> Melvin Mittman, seventeen, was physically his antithesis. His body was barrel-thick and strong, and his shoulders wide, his head square, his features blunt. He had an upturned, broad-based nose, small, thick-lashed eyes under glasses, dense hair growing low on his brow, and a strong round chin. Throughout the trial until the verdict, when he wept and buried his face in his hands, he was expressionless. You would not have picked him out of a group, as you would Koslow, as having something "wrong" with him; he seemed just stolid and enclosed. Yet where Koslow's hands were white and thin and smooth as a girl's, lacing and interlacing during the trial and drumming little dances, Mittman's hands, abnormally short and thick, with hair on the fingers, made one inevitably imagine them pounding flesh.

E As the sense for sentence patterns has become stronger in English, writing has become more economical. The following, from chapter 2 of Exodus in the King James Bible, recounts the birth and some incidents in the early life of Moses. To follow the action, one should recall that by order of Pharaoh all male Hebrew children were to be killed. The writing represents good English prose of about three hundred fifty years ago. Retell the story as best you can in modern English. Then compare the versions, noticing where you have been able to be briefer and terser than the original by omitting parts of constructions that the authors of the King James Bible thought essential.

1 And there went a man of the house of Levi, and took to wife a daughter of Levi.

2 And the woman conceived, and bare a son: and when she saw him that he was a goodly child, she hid him three months.

3 And when she could not longer hide him, she took for him an ark of bulrushes, and daubed it with slime and with pitch, and put the child therein; and she laid it in the flags by the river's brink.

4 And his sister stood afar off, to wit what would be done to him.   .

5 And the daughter of Pharaoh came down to wash herself at the river; and her maidens walked along by the river's side; and when she saw the ark among the flags, she sent her maid to fetch it.

6 And when she had opened it, she saw the child: and, behold, the babe wept. And she had compassion on him, and said, This is one of the Hebrews' children.

7 Then said his sister to Pharaoh's daughter, Shall I go and call to thee a nurse of the Hebrew women, that she may nurse the child for thee?

8 And Pharaoh's daughter said to her, Go. And the maid went and called the child's mother.

9 And Pharaoh's daughter said unto her, Take this child away, and nurse it for me, and I will give thee thy wages. And the woman took the child, and nursed it.

10 And the child grew, and she brought him unto Pharaoh's daughter, and he became her son. And she called his name Moses: and she said, Because I drew him out of the water.

11 And it came to pass in those days, when Moses was grown, that he went out unto his brethren, and looked on their burdens: and he spied an Egyptian smiting an Hebrew, one of his brethren.

12 And he looked this way and that way, and when he saw that there was no man, he slew the Egyptian, and hid him in the sand.

13 And when he went out the second day, behold, two men of the Hebrews strove together: and he said to him that did the wrong, Wherefore smitest thou thy fellow?

14 And he said, Who made thee a prince and a judge over us? intendest thou to kill me, as thou killedst the Egyptian? And Moses feared, and said, Surely this thing is known.

15 Now when Pharaoh heard this thing, he sought to slay Moses. But Moses fled from the face of Pharaoh, and dwelt in the land of Midian: and he sat down by a well.

16 Now the priest of Midian had seven daughters: and they came and drew water, and filled the troughs to water their father's flock.

17 And the shepherds came and drove them away: but Moses stood up and helped them, and watered their flock.

18 And when they came to Reuel their father, he said, How is it that ye are come so soon to day?

19 And they said, An Egyptian delivered us out of the hand of the shepherds, and also drew water enough for us, and watered the flock.

20 And he said unto his daughters, And where is he? why is it that ye have left the man? call him, that he may eat bread.

21 And Moses was content to dwell with the man: and he gave Moses Zipporah his daughter.

22 And she bare him a son, and he called his name Gersham: for he said, I have been a stranger in a strange land.

LANGUAGE
AND
VOCABULARY BUILDING

CHAPTER 19

An enriched and extended vocabulary can develop
from knowledge about language.

The Anglo-Saxons had a revealing word for a vocabulary. They called it a "word-hoard," a treasury of words that each man owned and on which he could draw whenever he wanted to speak. Our ancestors seem to have understood that if a man is to be intellectually rich he needs a great store of words; the more words he acquires the richer he becomes. The analogy has its limitations, however; for a word is not so simple or so readily employed as the gold objects that were wealth to the Anglo-Saxons.

One major complication is that almost everyone has at least four basic vocabularies. He uses a relatively small number of words that we may call the *speaking vocabulary*, composed of words that come readily to the speaker's tongue. A dull person may use only a few hundred words in this way; even a moderately articulate speaker uses only a few thousand. Every literate person has a second vocabulary, a *writing vocabulary*, which includes the words in the speaking vocabulary, plus other words that he can call up. A good writer may employ a vocabulary of ten thousand, twenty-five thousand, perhaps fifty thousand words. Another person may suffer from a writing vocabulary little larger than his speaking vocabulary. Every literate person has also a *reading vocabulary*, including words he would not speak in conversation or use when he writes but would know when he sees them written. For most people the reading vocabulary is much larger than either the speaking or writing vocabulary—fifty thousand, seventy-five thousand, a hundred thousand words, perhaps more. The fourth vocabulary, the largest of all, we may refer to as the *acquaintance vocabulary*. It includes the other three, but it includes, also, words that the owner has seen or heard before, although he can do little more with them than guess their meaning in context. Vocabularies of this sort can be very large.

The description of these four vocabularies suggests one obvious way for a writer to expand his working vocabulary. Since speaking and writing vocabularies are relatively small and reading and acquaintance vocabularies relatively large, he has only to move words from his reading and acquaintance vocabularies into his speaking and writing vocabularies.

Building a Vocabulary

Much building of word-hoards is unconscious. We all have a wealth of vocabulary because we have, in effect, inherited it, and it has continued to grow without our conscious help. Babies start learning vocabulary shortly after birth, and they acquire the language to which they were born, quite literally as a birthright. They start, unconsciously, with a hearing vocabulary, including terms that are moved into a speaking vocabulary, and eventually into reading and writing vocabularies. The shapes of words, especially, are learned in these ways, but uses are learned unconsciously, also. Native children learn sequences like "the ice-cream cone"; they never need be told that "cone cream ice the" is wrong. Such acquisition is probably the best language learning; certainly it is the fastest and easiest.

Few human beings, however, could ever become fluent in a language if they commanded only unconsciously learned linguistic data, which are limited in quantity and to a degree in character. Thus the more language anyone needs, the more he must learn consciously. A person of any consequence in a modern society needs much more language than is ever likely to seep into him, and once a speaker must rely on language learned consciously, principles, understandings of language as a phenomenon, and linguistic devices become important. In fact, in a broad way, the more a speaker needs language the more he must expect to learn it deliberately.

This chapter should help deliberate attempts to expand a vocabulary. In particular it concerns where words come from — how they are formed, how they move from one language to another, how they shift, and how an understanding of these changes can promote language learning. Following are practical suggestions for using the information in the chapter, both to add new words to a vocabulary and to make fuller use of words already there.

1. *Learn words by groups.* Many English words can be related to words in other languages through a common root in an ancestor language. Starting with a native word and adding loan words, you can work with the group as a family and may learn a dozen words more easily than you could learn one word otherwise.

2. *Work with prefixes and suffixes.* By learning the significance of some of the basic affixes in the language, you can increase your recognition vocabulary almost at once. Since affixes are used widely in word formation, each one you learn has the potential of adding many new words.

3. *When you learn a word, learn enough about it to make it your own.* The history of a word is not only interesting in itself; it also is an excellent aid to memory and a clue to how the word may be used.

4. *Learn words you will use.* You may be able to amaze your friends if you know the meaning of *ento-ectad* — it means from inside out — but words completely strange are hard to learn and quick to forget. Learn more about words you have encountered and are likely to encounter again, or need in your own writing and speaking. Move words from your acquaintance vocabulary to your working vocabularies, from your reading vocabulary to your writing and speaking vocabularies.

5. *Once you learn a word, use it.* Do something deliberately to keep your new words; find work for them. Introduce them into conversation, or into your next theme.

Similarities Among Languages

Until recently — say, less than two centuries ago — man knew relatively little about the growth of language on the earth. Most languages were not well recorded. For those that were at least skimpily analyzed, no patterns of relationships had been observed, only patchy bits of evidence for which interpretations were mainly conjectural. Scholars knew that the Anglo-Saxons had borrowed the Latin word for a harbor, *portus*, and made it *port*. The French had the same word, although pronounced differently, but the French had not borrowed the word, since French was Latin, or a Latin-like language that developed while Romans dominated what is now France. Scholars knew also that modern languages have changed; Modern English came from Middle English and Middle English came from Old English. Old English had been brought to the island of Britain from northern Europe, where there remained languages that somewhat resembled it, Dutch, German, Danish, and the like. Evidence from other parts of the world was no better, and the whole did not seem to add up to any comprehensive understanding of anything so complex as language.

By the late eighteenth century more linguistic evidence had been assembled. The new knowledge led to new insights, and the insights prompted more knowledge. New relationships became apparent, so that almost suddenly all scholars conversant with the progress of learning were aware that a breakthrough had come in language, reducing the worldwide confusion into something like order. The following table, prepared by the American philologist William Dwight Whitney, suggests the emerging patterns:

English	Lithuanian	Celtic	Latin	Greek	Persian	Sanskrit
three	tri	tri	tres	treis	thri	tri
seven	septyni	secht	septem	hepta	hapta	sapta
me	manen	me	me	me	me	me
mother	moter	mathair	mater	meter	matar	matar
brother	brolis	brathair	frater	phrater		bhratar
night	naktis		noctis	nuktos		nakta

The similarities are remarkable. Look, for example, at the words for *mother*. There is some difference in the vowels, but not more than can be observed in almost any language; there is more variety in the way Americans say *aunt* than there is in the main vowel in words for *mother* scattered halfway around the world. All the examples begin with the same nasal representing the sound /m/, and they all end with some sort of /r/ — sounds may be distinguished from letters by putting them between slant lines. The medial consonant varies between sounds spelled *t* and *th;* these are both made in the same place in the mouth, differing as the flow of air is stopped in *mater* or not quite stopped in *mother.* This consistency is much too great to be accidental, particularly since hundreds of other words show like resemblances in the same languages.

These similarities cannot be accounted for by borrowing from one language to another. English could borrow a word like *port* from Latin because the Romans occupied the island of Britain, stayed for hundreds of years, and built ports. Only the kind of installation the Romans built was called a port; natural harbors were designated by *haven,* or by other words not borrowed from Latin. But Englishmen could not have borrowed a word for *mother* from Sanskrit, or vice versa, because by the time this word was common in Old English no speaker of Sanskrit, so far as we know, had ever visited the island of Britain nor had any speaker of Old English gone to India. Certainly there was no exchange sufficient to account for extensive borrowing.

Language by Descent

Obviously, language must have evolved, much as did the earth and its inhabitants. Words for concepts indicated by *mother* and *three* must be similar because they had a common ancestor. Crustaceans have no backbones and something approaching a shell because an ancestor had these characteristics, and for similar reasons dogs and wolves are four-footed carnivores covered with skin and more or less hair. English, Celtic, Latin, Greek, Persian, and Sanskrit have a word written *me,* with similar pronunciations and uses, whereas Chinese, Arabic, and Sioux do not have a sound so used. English is related to similar languages like Sanskrit and Latin, but not, unless very remotely, to dissimilar bodies of speech such as Chinese and Sioux.

Once this suggestion was made, dependable study of language became possible as never before. The evidence built up so fast, and it fitted into patterns so readily, that for more than a century, nobody with more than a smattering of knowledge about language could doubt the essential truth of the new insights. Long-dead ancestors of extant languages could be reconstructed; the growth and filiation of languages could be described, and the principles by which language grows could be outlined. Characteristics of different lines of descent could be traced and fitted into patterns; scholars could account for both the similarities and the differences between English and Sanskrit, and they could trace the history of linguistic bits, pronunciations, meanings, grammatical devices, even patterns of stress. What is true of English and its relatives is true in a broad way of all other languages; they have descended from earlier languages, are or have been parts of language families, and can be understood in the light of their relatives and their ancestors.

The basic understandings were worked out using a body of speech that includes English, most of the languages of Europe, and some others. Triangulating from languages still living, and from dead languages like Sanskrit, Gothic, and Latin, scholars reconstructed an ancient parent language that has been conveniently called Indo-European, or more technically, Proto-Indo-European, and its speakers are known as Indo-Europeans.

372

What do we know of these Indo-Europeans? Directly, very little; even the name, Indo-European, has been made up for them. History is no help; we have little history from before 5000 B.C., and none at all from then barbaric central Europe. Archaeology does not help much; presumably the Indo-Europeans built no buildings that would endure. Their tools, if we have them, cannot be identified as theirs. Written records do not help; presumably the Indo-Europeans could not write; at least no scrap of writing has survived from them. But we can reconstruct their language, at least approximately, and from language much can be inferred. We know, for example, that they had words for bears, wolves, and pine trees; they had no words for alligators, rhinoceroses, and palm trees. Accordingly, we assume they lived in a cool climate. They had horses; they rode them, and drank their milk, but did not use them as draft animals. They knew a number of grains, which they cultivated, and they had domesticated various animals, but they still hunted and fished. We assume they were no longer barbaric nomads but had as yet developed only simple agriculture. They spoke a highly inflected language, with some sixteen case distinctions for nouns in more than a dozen classes, and many conjugations of verbs; even adjectives were declined in three ways. Their language had some affinity with that of the Hittites, although what is not yet clear.

During the millennia before Christ the Indo-Europeans underwent a population explosion and spread in almost all directions, although especially west, south, and southeast. Possibly their acquisition of the horse gave them a fighting advantage over their neighbors. Whatever the cause, they initiated one of the most significant population movements of all time. Working east and southeast from their ancestral home — probably in what is now east central Europe or southwestern Russia — they broke into the subcontinent of India, perhaps about 1500 B.C., where they established the Indo-European language that we call Sanskrit, ancestor of modern Indic. Another branch, speaking what we call Iranian, has given us modern Persian. Indo-Europeans appeared north of the Himalayan Mountains, also, in what is now the Gobi Desert, speaking at least two dialects of a language called Tocharian, which may be an offshoot of Indo-Iranian or may represent an unrelated surge to the east. Armenian and a number of minor languages fit in here somewhere. Indo-Europeans whom we call Hellenes worked into southern Russia and eventually down into the Balkan peninsula; by this time places like Crete, the Nile valley, and the Tigris-Euphrates valley were highly civilized. The Hellenes became civilized, too, in time; we know them as the Greeks. Meanwhile, peoples speaking a branch of Indo-European we call Italic worked past the Alps and down into the Italian peninsula; they gave us Latin, and by descent, the Romance languages. People we call Celts, near-relatives of the Italic group if we may judge from the similarities of the languages, spread west through northern Europe, and even took over the offshore islands, now England and Ireland. Another group, speaking what we call Proto-Germanic or Teutonic, followed them, and overran them almost everywhere; other Germanic peoples spread north into the Scandinavian peninsula. Those who migrated less, who spoke what we call Balto-Salvic, account for modern languages like Russian, Bulgarian, and Lithuanian, which has preserved the old Indo-European inflection system to a remarkable degree.

Thus the branches of the Indo-European family account for most of the languages of Europe, some of the more important in Asia, and all the tongues likely to survive in Australia and in North and South America. Extensive charts appear in most good dictionaries; for our purposes the concise chart opposite will suffice. It should not be taken literally. The figure of speech of the family, by which we describe linguistic relationships, works well enough if we remind ourselves that it is a figure of speech, not an accurate statement. A parent language does not give birth to a daughter language, as a mother bears a child, at a certain time and place. Rather, dialects of a language drift apart, usually because the speakers have drifted apart, and since language is always changing, it changes differently in the two groups. These two groups of speakers will have differing experiences, which will be reflected in language change, and the groups will coalesce in varying degrees with other linguistic communities. For a time the two ways of speaking can be thought of as two dialects of the same language, but eventually they change so much that the speakers of one group cannot understand the speakers of the other, and we must recognize two languages, which of course will already have developed dialects.

Linguistic evolution differs from biological evolution in at least one other way, in that acquired characteristics of a language are inherited. If a father knows calculus and his wife bookkeeping, the children will not be born commanding these bodies of knowledge; if they want them, they must learn them themselves. In language, however, the descendants will inherit most of the acquisitions of a parent language. For example, as we have seen, *port* was borrowed into Old English from Latin; that is, it was not an inherited part of Old English but a bit of speech that we can call an acquisition, even though a word is rather different from what a

374

SIMPLIFIED CHART OF THE INDO-EUROPEAN LANGUAGE FAMILY

The chart emphasizes Western languages, especially those leading to English.

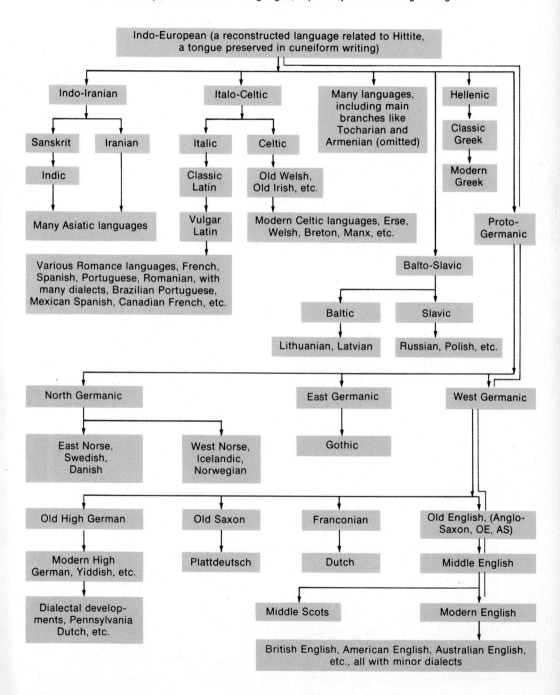

biologist means by the term *acquired characteristic*. Once it is part of English, however, it will be treated like any other English word. We have developed *carports*, *airports*, and *spaceports*, and if we should now colonize our moon, and Moon-Americans become so detached from Earth-Americans as to develop their own language, *port* and words like *portal* and *portable* would appear as readily in Moon-English as would the words that descended within the language.

Evolution: Changes in Words

Indo-European languages have changed so much that they are now mutually unintelligible. In part, modern tongues work as they do because they have grown by different patterns, patterns of sound, grammar, word form, and the like. Compare the following:

for	für	por	peri	*per–
father	Vater	pater	patēr	*peter
foot	Fuss	ped(estal)	(tri)pod	*ped–

You will recognize the first column as English, and those who have studied German will know that the second column is composed of the corresponding words in that language. The third column consists of related words in Latin, and the fourth of related words in either Greek or Sanskrit. The fifth column gives the Indo-European word or root from which the other four words, and many more like them, have come — the asterisks indicate that the forms have been reconstructed, not recorded. Presumably the Indo-Europeans could not write; if they could, none of their writing has survived, and all that we know of the language comes from reconstruction.

Two generalizations can be made at once. If the Indo-European base, whether root or word, began with *p* as here spelled, that is, with /p/ in sound, this sound was roughly preserved in Latin and in some other languages. In English and German, however, this /p/ changed to /f/, spelled *f* in English, although sometimes *v* in German, as in *Vater*. Now we might notice that this variation in sound is not so great as it would seem if we think only of spelling. The letters *p* and *f* are separate, and used quite differently, but the sounds /p/ and /f/ are very close together. The initial consonant of the root *per–* is a bilabial voiceless stop; that is, it is made by stopping the unvoiced air completely with both lips. The initial consonant in English and German, /f/, is a bilabial or labio-dental voiceless fricative; that is, it is the fricative corresponding to /p/, or in simpler words, it is like /p/ except that the air is not entirely stopped. Thus the difference between English *for* and Latin *por* is that the Latin word, as well as the Indo-European root, **per-*, starts with the breath completely stopped, whereas the English word starts with the breath not quite stopped.

Other differences become simpler when we look upon them as sound, not as spelling. Take the next row, in the table above, *father, Vater, pater, pater,* and **peter.* The medial consonant is identical, except that in English it is spelled *th*, representing a sound that can be written /ð/. But this is only the voiced fricative that corresponds to the voiceless stop /t/. That is, the breath is not entirely stopped in English and is voiced. Similarly, in the third line, the difference between the final consonant in English *foot* and the Indo-European root **ped–* is that /t/ is the voiceless sound corresponding to voiced /d/. One of the most common confusions is that involved in the last line of Whitney's table above, where English *night* is equated with Latin *noctis*, both descending from the root **nekwt.* Here the problem stems from what are called palatals, sounds made along the roof of the mouth. They are notably unstable; many of them have disappeared from English, leaving behind spellings like *gh* in *night*, but one may expect to find palatals in many languages, spelled in many ways, such as *h* in Old English, *x* or *ts* in Latin, *ks* in Greek, or *g, j, c, ch,* in Modern English.

Thus throughout the Indo-European language family, differences that seem highly divergent if one considers only the spelling can be seen to resemble one another when the variations are viewed as sound. These differences can mostly be explained if one studies sound, whether as phonetics or phonemics, but the student who is not conversant with linguistics can still make use of Indo-European bases to learn vocabulary. He has only to recognize that differences can be explained, that they are probably in reality not so great as they appear, and that he can learn from similarities while not letting differences in spelling stop him.

The Great English Vowel Shift

Another type of change, which occurred much later in the history of English, helps explain why words may look quite different from each other and still be closely related. We have already observed that broad changes may move through language in movements technically called *drift.* In English an unusually important drift, known as the Great English Vowel Shift, began in the Middle Ages, operated for several centuries in the dialects that are the ancestors of both British and American standard English, and may still be working in some dialects.

By this drift, most of the English vowels commonly called *long* or *tense* moved forward or upward in the mouth, or both, or became diphthongs. The corresponding short or slack vowels did not change much. That is, our word *he* used to be pronounced like the modern word *hay*, but the vowel in *get* has not much changed. Our word *like* used to be pronounced like the modern word *leek*, but the vowel in *hill* has remained. Our word *loaf* used to be pronounced so that it would rhyme with our word *cough*, *tooth* used to be pronounced so that it would rhyme with our word *oath*, and *town* was pronounced so that it would rhyme with our word *boon*.

As a result, letters in English words may be identical with letters in another body of speech, but the same letter represents different sounds in the two languages. In English the letter *e* when tense is likely to represent the sound of the vowel as in *heat*, *cheek*, and *meek*. The same letter in any other related language is more likely to represent the sound of the vowel in *hay*, that is /e/. Thus English *feet* is related to Latin *pes*, but *pes* is pronounced about like our *pace*. English *feline* is spelled like the corresponding French word, which is pronounced more nearly like *fay-lean*—if there were such a word—in English. The same drift can account for doublets being borrowed into English; our word *pike* presumably came from Latin *picus*, but early enough to get into Old English, and hence to be changed with the Vowel Shift; but the same word was borrowed again, after the Middle Ages, and hence remained almost unchanged, our word *peak*, as in our place-name *Pike's Peak* where the two have curiously come back together, and a third time as our word *pique*.

Cognates and Vocabulary

These changes have implications for vocabulary development. They help us relate words in groups so that the meaning of one word explains another, and they help us clarify meanings by using cognates—words in different languages that derive from the same root. Suppose, for example, that a student has encountered the phrase strange to him, "the cynosure of all eyes." A dictionary informs him that *cynosure* means "anybody or anything that is the center of attention or interest." This information would probably permit him to interpret the passage, but unless he has genius for this sort of thing, he will probably soon forget the word and be as badly off the next time he encounters it. Now suppose he tries the etymology. He will find that the Indo-European root was something like *kwon-*, giving *hound* in English and *canine* in Latin,

378

meaning "dog"—the K-9 corps is of course a pun. (He need not let the difference between the spellings *h* and *kw* bother him; the sound is one of those unstable palatals.) *Cynosure* meant literally a dog's tail, since the Greeks called the constellation we know as the Little Bear the Dog, and the North or Pole Star appears in its tail. For a time it was the center of much attention, the *cynosure* of all astronomers. Meanwhile, the student may have been amused to discover that a *cynic* is one who snarls in a doglike manner. Once the student has acquired such information and can relate the Greek words to *hound*, he is not likely to forget either *cynosure* or *cynic*.

Assume that a student wants to indicate that the present development of an individual can be understood from the past development of a class or species; he is trying to recall a phrase from a science course, "Phylogeny repeats ontogeny." Or is it "Ontogeny reflects phylogeny"? He has looked it up before and forgotten it. If he looks it up again he will probably forget it again, but etymologies might help. He will find that *ontogeny* comes from the Indo-European root *esti-* or *es-*, our word *is*, appearing through borrowing in all sorts of words like *essence, interest*, and *present*. The –geny part derives from *gen-*, seen in our word *kind* (especially in the sense of "nature" or "sort"), and embodied in dozens of words he knows like *genus, genius*, and *genuine*. This root appears also in *phylogeny*, but the first part of the word comes from the root *bheu*, which became our word *been* and the Greek word *phule*, meaning "tribe." The principle is "Ontogeny recapitulates phylogeny," because it means that the individual as he *is* repeats the species development that has *been*. The vowel of *is* equates with the vowel of *ontogeny*, the *b* of *been* with the *ph* of *phylogeny*.

Borrowing and Vocabulary

Speakers of English have been great borrowers of language, some kinds of language. They had no need to borrow a grammar; they had one, descended from Indo-European and adapted to their changing wants. They had no need to borrow sounds; those, too, came from Indo-European, with some drifting. As to words, they had no need to borrow those of human existence, like *live* and *die;* for the obvious parts of the universe, like *sun, moon, earth;* for family living, like *mother, brother, child;* for a simple home, like *house, roof, bed;* for the names associated with primitive means of making a living, like *hunt, fish, plow, corn*. They did not need to borrow such linguistic tools; their ancestors had been using them for thousands of years. But one of the facts of English and American history is that most of the ideas, techniques, tools, and materials associated with complex modern living—from abscissa to zucchini squash—have been borrowed, and this cultural borrowing set up a corresponding stream of linguistic borrowing that changed the complexion of English terminology.

The cultural flow began early and has continued ever since. It moved west from one of the cradles of civilization at the eastern end of the Mediterranean, clothed in Greek words. In the Italian peninsula it took on Latin dress, and with the spread of the Roman Empire terms were carried north. Germanic tribesmen, including the Angles and the Saxons, picked up a few names for Roman cooking utensils, our word *street* for Roman roads, and for Roman coinage, several terms including *mint* and *pound*. After the Angles and Saxons were established in their island home, they were swept over by one cultural wave after another, each bringing more words, most of them Greek or Latin, directly or through French. Christianity brought words, chivalry brought them, schools brought them, government and the courts brought them—the government was heavily French after the Norman conquest—learning and the arts brought them, so that philosophical terminology is heavily Latin and musical words heavily Italian. This borrowing has gone on for some two thousand years, and it continues; recently we have acquired *hors d'oevres* and *chic* from French, *rodeo* and *hoosegow* from Spanish via Mexico, *cruller* and *Santa Claus* from German by way of Pennsylvania Dutch, *cosmonaut* and *commissar* from Russian, although these last words were themselves borrowed into Russian. Many of these terms were cognates of English words, since most European speech descends from Indo-European, but English has of course borrowed from other languages also, *tea* and *typhoon* from Chinese, *magazine* and *coffee* from Arabic, *pajamas* and *shampoo* from Hindustani, *sauna* from Finnish, *kimono* from Japanese and hundreds more.

Most of these words have been borrowed naturally. That is, we or our ancestors acquired the idea or the goods or the method, or something, and the word came with it. We borrowed the word *ski* with the skis, and nobody planned it that way. But some borrowing has been deliberate. When the Swede Carolus Linnaeus tried to classify all plants, he adopted Latin terminology with which to describe a plant, providing what has become known as its "Latin name." The common tiger lily is *lillium tigrinum*. He set a fashion; botanists and zoologists continued to import Latin loan words, and when physics developed, physicists turned to the other great reservoir of little-used words, Greek, so that we now have *telephone* and *telegraph*. In our day, scientists and technologists generally mine the classical tongues in devising new terms for new inventions, for *antibiotics, hallucinogens, microclimatology*, and the like.

In origin, most of our words have descended from Indo-European or they have come to English as loan words from another language. As words are used, however, they are mainly what the users of English have done to them, and consequently words come to reflect human minds, human society, and the ways speakers of a language use their vocal equipment. Our word *theater* comes from Greek, but a Greek theater was not a building; most Americans would not recognize the word if presented in Greek spelling, θεᾱτριστής, or comprehend it if he heard a Greek pronounce it. Even a word like *stet*, which is spelled as it was in Latin, and means what it meant in Latin, in the sense that it can be defined in both languages as "let it stand," is employed as it never could have been in Roman times. It is now mainly used by an author, editor, or proofreader instructing somebody like a typesetter to print the passage without change. The Romans could have had no such use for the word because they had no printing.

Thus words as they are used reflect human societies and human minds, and these facts, too, help users of the language to learn words in groups. Minds work by generalizing from a particular, and words result from such generalization. Our word *car* developed from the Roman two-wheeled war chariot, perhaps from the running horses that drew it; it was generalized into any vehicle that traveled on wheels. Now it has become specialized in America — but not in England — to mean an automobile, not only a self-moving four-wheeled instrument of transport, but a particular kind of automotive vehicle, one that cannot be called a truck or a tractor, for example. Similarly, minds work by mental leaps, by contriving figures of speech and jokes; our word *cranium* comes from a Latin word for horn. Presumably the idea was that somebody's head was as empty as a cow's horn. Man needs names, and names in turn become words; *quisling* comes from the Norwegian collaborator Vidkun Quisling, and *tawdry* presumably reflects the quality of cheap mementos used to celebrate a pious lady, Saint Audrey. Some words seem to reflect the imitation of a sound — *cuckoo, bang, hiss, fizz, murmur.* Some result from blends, words run together; *smoke* and *fog* become *smog, motor* and *hotel* become *motel.* Fun can play a part, also; a woman expecting a baby can be said to *infanticipate*, and "a store selling psychedelic posters" has been called a *psychedelicatessen.* Among the most rapidly growing bodies of speech in present-day English are the acronyms; a recent dictionary of such terms includes more than forty-five thousand like ZIP code for Zone Improvement Plan. Obviously, many names are now determined by the acronym, not the acronym by the name; the suggestion of speed in *zip* must have influenced the selection of a name for the plan, and it can be no accident that Students Tired of Pollution produces the acronym STOP.

One of the commonest means of reflecting human and social needs in vocabulary is compounding. When something new appears, one of the easiest ways to describe it is to put together two familiar ideas, perhaps with a figure of speech; the Anglo-Saxons, confronted with the white flowers that spangle English countryside combined *dæges*, "day's," with *eage*, "eye," to make *dægeseage*, the eye of the day, our word *daisy*. This device has become a characteristic of American English; pioneers encountered new phenomena, somewhat like the Old World fauna and flora. They used the familiar word; a bear or a duck can usually be recognized, but creatures in the New World were different from those in the Old, and hence they were called *black bears, cinnamon bears, grizzly bears, canvasback ducks, buffle-headed ducks*, thousands of new compounds.

The characteristic of a compound is that in combination the words acquire a meaning different from that of any of its parts and also different from the words written separately. A blackbird is different from a black bird, a hothouse is different from a hot house. The meanings of individual parts of a compound may be sufficiently subdued that we can speak of a green blackboard or round icecubes without being aware of any contradiction.

Compounding flourishes in contemporary English, especially to label new phenomena—*spaceship, moonshot, jetway*. And compounds tend to become faddish, to extend rapidly by similarities. Perhaps by analogy with *drive-in*, we have *sit-in, camp-in, sing-in, love-in*, and *be-in*, which may be as far as one can go. By analogy with *horsepower* or *waterpower*, we have *black power, Indian power, gay power*, and with the increasing concern for ecology, *green power*.

Rather similar to compounding in the building of words is affixation. Some linguistic units having meaning, and known use can be attached to other units but cannot be used alone. In the newer terminology they are called *bound morphemes*, in the older terminology *affixes—prefixes, suffixes*, and *infixes*—bits like *un-, retro-*, and *-ible*. Sometimes they are combined with one another, as in *inventiveness*, in which none of the units can be used in this sense alone, but more frequently they are combined with words, as in *unstable, retroactive, irresistible*. Some of these affixes can be confusing. Consider *in-;* it can mean not, as in *inactive, inescapable*, and *inappropriate*, but it can also mean something like *into*, as in *inroad, include*, and *induce*. That is, *in-* can mean not, or almost its opposite. The explanation is that these linguistic bits, like our words, mostly go back to Indo-European, and that the affixes have changed in some ways coming to us through Old English, and in other ways as they descended into the languages from which English has borrowed.

Let us look again at the *in-* prefixes. Indo-European had a root **en-*, which gives us the prepositions *in* and *into*, and the prefix *in-* in words like *indoors*. It also descended into Latin, where it appears in a few words we have borrowed, like *invade*, and in prefixes like *inter-*, *intro-*, and *intra-*. Indo-European had quite a different root, **ne-*, meaning not. It is involved in our words *not* and *naught*, probably in our word *nay*, and certainly in our prefix *un-*, meaning not, as in *unable, unusual, unkind*. This is the root that provided the common Latin prefix, the *in-* that means not, and in parallel forms becomes *im-* in *immaterial*, *ir-* in *irrelevant*, *il-* in *illogical*, and the like.

These prefixes are not illogical at all, although changes in form make them seem so. The Indo-European root **en-* provides *in-* in both English and Latin, meaning "into" in both languages, although few words with this meaning have been borrowed into English from Latin. The contrasting Indo-European root, **ne-*, meaning not, became both *un-* in English and *in-* in Latin (along with variant forms *ir-, il-, im-*,) again meaning not in both languages, but so many of these words were borrowed into English that, to the casual observer, "not" seems to be the only meaning of Latin *in-*. This Latin *in-* appears mainly in words having other classical syllables, like *intellect* and *irreligious*, but recently we have tended to prefer the native prefix and have produced *unorthodox* and *unsophisticated*. In fact, this pattern is so strong that we can predict confidently that when we need the terms we shall coin *unorbited* and *unfissioned*, not *inorbited* and *infissioned*.

A look at the origin of an affix may help clarify its meaning and make it easier to remember. As indicated above, English *for* comes from the Indo-European root **per-*, which survived in Latin without much change of its initial sound from /p/ to /f/. In other words, the same root that became the English prefix *for-* produced in Latin a number of prefixes beginning with /p/, including *per-*, *por-*, *par-*, *pro-*, *pur-*, and *peri-*. English has borrowed thousands of cognates that included one of these prefixes when it was borrowed and has also imported the prefixes, which can be applied widely (*pro-American, pro-student*). Recognizing the relationship among these cognates does much to clarify meanings, especially for words with a prefix akin to *for* in the sense of *forward*—*perfect*, "to carry through to a finish," *permeate*, "to go through"—as well as for words in which the prefix has a different sense of *for*, as *profess*, "to stand for publicly," *program*, "something written beforehand."

Many affixes from the classical languages have no parallel terms in English, but they may have cognates in English that are not used as affixes. Thus the Indo-European root may help the writer to remember what the borrowed affixes mean and have more feeling for them. Greek *mega-*, seen in words like *megaton* and *megalopolis*, comes from the root **meg-*, which gives us English *much*, along with words like *major* and *majority* borrowed from Latin. Thus any word beginning with *mega-* is likely to involve the idea of greatness in size, in number, or something suggesting *much*. Spellings involving something like *-metr-*, as either a prefix or a suffix, may involve the idea of measurement, from Indo-European **me-*, as in *metric system, metronome, speedometer*, related to our word *meal* as in *mealtime*, something to eat at a point measured in time. Similar words, such as *metaphysics* and *metalinguistics* can involve the idea of beyond, from **me-*, which appears in English *mid* and *middle*, which are beyond the near. Such words may also involve *mater*, which as we have seen is related to *mother* and to *metropolis*, the mother city. In fact, a large proportion of the more useful prefixes and suffixes, from *anti-* to *vice-* have helpful cognates in English.

Native or Borrowed Words

A physician writing a prescription is likely to use borrowed words exclusively, and a scientist describing an experiment is likely to employ many terms wholly or in part from Latin and Greek. On the other hand, a small boy scribbling on the sidewalk what he believes to be naughty words is likely to use terms straight out of Indo-European, or words that found their way into the language centuries ago. A drill sergeant, yelling at his troops, is unlikely to adulterate his pure Old English vocabulary with much from a classical tongue. Of course none of these people is consciously preferring either native or borrowed words, but in a large way various categories of words have different uses, even categories determined by origin.

On the whole, in English native words are shorter and commoner than borrowed words. Many an English word is only the Indo-European root, however changed in shape. English *same* is Indo-European **sem-* or **som-*, with little change except in spelling, and *like* is Indo-European **lig-* with the final consonant unvoiced. Borrowed equivalents appear in such shapes as *similar, identical,* and *comparable,* the first of which is a cognate of *same*.

The Angles and the Saxons, both before and after they migrated to the island of Britain, had enjoyed a relatively stable culture, in which they found little occasion to coin new compounds to name new objects or concepts. After the Norman invasion of 1066, English ceased to be an official language; it was used mainly in the homes of the less educated and among workingmen and servants. So used, the language simplified even further. When culture developed in the later Middle Ages it was stimulated by influences from the more sophisticated Mediterranean peoples, and speakers of English borrowed foreign words to fill their new needs. When the study of writing developed they borrowed what was left of the Latin word *grammatica* and called the study grammar. They need not have done so; *grammatica* had been made up out of words meaning "the art of writing," and if the speakers of English had wanted to, they could as well have formed a compound, *word-use,* or they could have called the study simply writing—new uses can always be developed for old words. On the whole this was not the English practice; they borrowed foreign words for foreign things, and as a result English profits from what is probably the largest vocabulary ever developed anywhere.

Consider, for example, terms associated with grammar. Grammar as an aspect of speech is deeply rooted in the language and consequently changes slowly; the words through which English works, the words that reveal the grammar, are old and almost exclusively native. Words like *in, by, he, who, that, and,* and *but* are all native words. On the other hand, words like *sentence, adjectival, subjunctive, participle,* and *inflectional* are all borrowed. The concepts of grammar were imported from Latin; for a long time the only grammar taught was Latin or Greek grammar, and it was taught in Latinized language in the schools. The Anglo-Saxon *hierde* needed no grammatical terminology with which to herd his swine.

Thus, speaking broadly, English words sort themselves into two categories, with two sorts of uses, depending upon their origin. Native words have been lived with; they smack of homely affairs, eating and working, loving and hating, making a living. Borrowed words have been brought into the language because somebody felt a need for them, and this need was likely to be specialized—the creature needs were mainly taken care of by words already in the language. When new sorts of armor were imported from France, specialized French words came with the armor; when polyphonic music came in from Italy, it brought terms like *obligato* and *pianissimo.* Thus the terms that stir men's emotions are likely to be native; generalized terms and terms that promote precision are often borrowed. Native terms survived in the language because people needed them to live with; borrowed terms were imported into the language because somebody needed a precise term or a generalization that the native language had lost or had never developed.

A At this writing, two desk dictionaries, *Webster's New World Dictionary of the American Language* and *The American Heritage Dictionary of the English Language,* designated for convenience A and B, carry etymologies back to Indo-European. Below is material from these two dictionaries that will lead you to the Indo-European base and to related words. Work out the relationships among the words.

A **rhe·tor** (rĕt′ər, rē′tôr) *n.* [ME. *rethor* < L. *rhetor* < Gr. *rhētōr* < *eirein,* to speak: see WORD] **1.** a master or teacher of rhetoric **2.** an orator
rhet·o·ric (ret′ər ik) *n.* [ME. *rethorike* < OFr. or L.: OFr. *rethorique* < L. *rhetorica* < Gr. *rhētorikē* (*technē*), rhetorical (art) < *rhētōr,* orator: see prec.]

verb (vʉrb) *n.* [ME. *verbe* < OFr. < L. *verbum,* a WORD (used as transl. of Gr. *rhēma,* verb, orig., word)]

word (wʉrd) *n.* [ME. < OE., akin to G. *wort* < IE. *werdh-* (extension of base *wer-,* to speak, say), whence L. *verbum,* a word]

The first three entries (*rhetor, rhetoric, verb*); this dictionary gives the etymology in the language from which it was borrowed. It does not give the Indo-European root (in this dictionary called a base) but provides a cross reference to an etymology where the root will be found.

Indo-European root given for the native word, *word.* The final consonant can, or need not be considered part of the root.

B **rhe·tor** (rē′tôr′, -tər) *n. Obsolete.* **1.** A teacher of rhetoric. **2.** An orator. [Middle English, from Medieval Latin *rēthor, rhētor,* from Greek *rhētōr.* See wer-⁶ in Appendix.*]
rhet·o·ric (rĕt′ər-ĭk) *n. Abbr.* **rhet.**

[Middle English *rethorik,* from Old French *rethorique,* from Latin *rhētorica,* from Greek *rhētorikē* (*tekhnē*), "rhetorical (art)," from *rhētorikos,* rhetorical, from *rhētōr,* RHETOR.]

wer-⁶. To speak. **1.** Suffixed zero-grade form *wr̥-dho-* in Germanic *wurdam* in Old English *word,* word: WORD. **2.** Suffixed form *wer-dho-* in Latin *verbum,* word: VERB, VERVE; ADVERB, PROVERB. **3.** Suffixed form *wer-yo-* in Greek *eirein,* to say, speak: IRONY¹. **4.** Variant form *wrē-* in: **a.** suffixed form *wrē-mn̥* in Greek *rhēma,* word, verb: RHEMATIC; **b.** suffixed form *wrē-tor-* in Greek *rhētōr,* public speaker: RHETOR. [Pok. 6. *uer-* 1162.]

No root given in individual etymologies, but a cross reference to a root in the appendix leads the user to the root.

The appropriate entry in the appendix; it surveys the occurrence of descendants from the root as they appear in various languages.

Pok. is an abbreviation for Julius Pokorny, author of the standard etymological dictionary *Indogermanisches Etymologisches Worterbuch* (Bern, 1959).

You will note that these two dictionaries have different machinery for handling references to the Indo-European root and the modern words in English derived from it. On the basis of your experience with this set of words, what seem to be the advantages and the disadvantages of each?

B Until recently all etymological dictionaries were either inadequate or extremely difficult for anyone except language scholars to use. Now there are two good ones, *Klein's Comprehensive Etymological Dictionary of the English Language,* 2 vols. (Amsterdam, 1966), and *The Oxford Dictionary of English Etymology* (Oxford, 1966), which can be thought of in part as a supplement to the *Oxford English Dictionary,* which is too old to have modern etymologies. The first is more nearly comprehensive, the second more readily available and easier to use. The following are the portions of the ODEE that parallel the passages in exercise A.

rhetor rī·tɔɹ professor of rhetoric XIV; (professional) orator XVI. Late ME. *rethor* (later *rhetor*) – late L. *rethor,* var. of L. *rhētor* – Gr. *rhētōr,* f. **ᵷrā-* (as also in *rhêma* word), f. **wer-* (cf. VERB, WORD). So **rhetor**IC re·tərik art of using language for persuasion. XIV (Ch., Trevisa). Late ME. *ret(h)orique* – OF. *rethorique* (mod. *rhétorique*) – L. *rhētorica* (med.L *reth-*) – Gr. *rhētorikē,* sb. use (sc. *tekhnē* art). **rhetoric**AL rīto·rikəl. XV. f. L. *rhētōricus.* **rhetori·**CIAN XV (Lydg.). – OF.; earlier †*rethorien* XIV (Ch.) – OF. *rethorien.*

verb vɔɹb (gram.) part of speech serving to predicate. XIV (Wycl. Bible, Prologue). – O(F). *verbe* or L. *verbum* WORD. So **ve·rb**AL[1] dealing with words XV (Caxton); consisting of words, oral; pert. to a verb XVI; concerned with words only XVII. – (O)F. *verbal* or late L. *verbālis.* **verbatim** vɔɹbei·tim word by word. XV. medL.; cf. LITERATIM. **verbi**AGE vɔ·ɹbiidʒ excessive accumulation of words XVIII; wording XIX. – F. *verbiage,* f. †*verbeier* chatter, f. *verbe+ -eier* :– Rom. **-idiāre* :– Gr. *-ízein.* Cf. Pg. *verbiagem.* **verbo·**SE[1] wordy, prolix. XVII – L. *verbōsus.* **verbo·**SITY. XVI. – L.

word wɔɹd (coll. pl. and sg.) things or something said; report, tidings; divine communication; vocable. OE. *word* = OFris., OS. *word* (Du. *woord*), (O)HG. *wort,* ON. *orð,* Goth. *waurd* :– CGerm. **wordam* :– **wṛdho- *werdh-,* which is held to be based on **wer-,* repr. by Gr. ᵷéréō I shall say, L. *verbum* word (cf. VERB), Skr. *vrátam* command, law, vow, OPruss. *wirds* word, Lith. *vardas* name. Hence **wo·rd-**BOOK lexicon, dictionary. XVI (Florio); cf. G. *wörterbuch* (1631 in Kluge), Du. *woordenboek* (†*woord-*), Icel. *orðabók,* Sw. *ordbok,* Da. *ordbog.* **wo·rd**Y[1]. OE. *wordig.* ❡ For parallel IE. phonetics cf. BEARD, RED.

As it is an etymological dictionary, the ODEE gives more space to the histories of words than do either of the desk dictionaries quoted in exercise A. Do the dictionaries agree essentially for the information each provides? What does the ODEE provide that neither of the others has?

Now try combining the information in the three sets of citations with what you can find in your own desk dictionary or other dictionaries to which you have access. You should, for example, find developments like *verbatim* and *verbosity,* phrases like "take one at one's word," "speak a good word for," and compounds like *word-for-word.* Try to summarize your findings in a paper. If you survey everything you know by now you will need to write a composition of several thousand words. Your instructor may authorize you to restrict your subject, perhaps to the words that came into Modern English through direct descent, or to either the Latin or the Greek streams, to a survey of recent phrases that go back to *wer-*[6], or something of the sort.

C The following is a select list of Indo-European roots and some of the cognates that have descended from them. For almost any of these roots an industrious student could find hundreds of Modern English words—try the cognates of any of the words spelled *can,* for example. The root ideas are given in parentheses.

ar- art, arm, armada, armor, article, articulate (to join)

au- ear, auricle, auricular, auriculate, auscultation (to perceive)

aues- east, easter, aurora, aurum (to shine)

bhudh-/men- bottom, profound, foundation, fundament, funds (soil)

deigh- dough, duff, figure, effigy, lady (to knead)

deik- toe, digit, diction, token, teach (to point)

dekm- hundred, decade, century, cent, reckon, read, riddle (ten)

ed- eat, ate, edible, edibility, comestible, obese (to eat)

edont- tooth, teeth, dentist, dentistry, orthodontist, edentate (tooth)

gan(dh)- can (noun), canister, canasta, canal, channel (reed)

*gene-/*geno-* can (v), know, gnome, agnostic, could, uncouth, quaint, acquaintance, cognition, ignorant, connoisseur (to know)

glogh- gloss, glossary, glottal, epiglottis, gloze (thorn)

*kali-/*gel-* cold, cool, chill, gelid, gelatin, glacier, glace (cold)

kel- hall, hold, hull, hill, hole, hulk, conceal, color, Colorado (to cover)

kwon- hound, canine, cynic, canary, cynosure, kennel (dog)

*laub-/*lewp-* leaf, loft, lodge, lobby, lobbyist (peel off, bark roof)

leip- life, live, leave, liparoid, lipolytic (to endure)

leuq- light, luminous, lunar, Loki, de luxe, luxury, lucid (shine)

mel- meal, mill, malm, mollusk, mollify, Molinari (to grind)

oqw- eye, oculist, optical, ophthalmologist, ogle (to see)

pater- father, Pope, paternal, expatriate, padre, patron (pa-pa)

388

*ped-/*pod- foot, pedal, pew, pedestrian, gastropod (to go)

*penqwe- finger, quintet, five, Quinquagesima, quintessence, pentagon (five)

*pou- fowl, pullet, pauper, foal, fowler, puerile (small)

*pu- foul, putrid, pus, putrefaction, filth, defile (to stink)

*que- head, capitol, chapter, hump (to bend)

*(s)que- hide, hat, hood, hut, hoard, cuticle (to cut)

*rewos- room, rural, rustic, roister, ream, reamer (wide)

*seqw- say, see, seer, saga, saw (to see)

*slab- (from *leb-) sleep, labor, lapse, laboratory, elapse, collapse, elaboration, collaboration, relapse (to glide)

*wegh- way, vehicle, vehement, via, impervious, invoice, wain, wagon, convex, voyage, deviation, obvious (to go)

*wer- ward, ware, revere, guard, warden, warranty, guarantee, aware, guardian, reward, Ed, Teddy, disregard, wardrobe (to keep safe)

*wer-/*werbh- word, verb, verbal, verbatim, verve, verbosity, rhetoric, rhetorical (to say)

*werk- work, organ, playwright, wrought, erg, organize (to do)

Select three Indo-European bases and find twenty-five cognates derived from each. Once you have the root you will be led to modern words in your desk dictionary that will give you a start. For many of these roots an industrious student could find a thousand or more terms, counting obsolete uses, phrases, compounds, and the like. If you need additional references, the books cited in exercises A and B are useful. Very good for this sort of thing is Eric Partridge, *Origins*, 2nd ed. (New York, 1959). For older phrases the *Century Dictionary and Cyclopedia* is good, and for more recent phrases, the *New International Dictionary*, 3rd ed.

D As we have seen, most common words are native, but some borrowed words, like *faith*, became common early, and quite recently *facility* has grown in use. *Factor* is so common it has become jargonic. Perhaps you can guess why. Now examine the following words and divide them into two lists, one that you would guess to be native words, and one that you would guess to be borrowed. Then check the accuracy of your guess against a good dictionary, and try to account for any wrong guesses you made. On what basis were you guessing, and why did your guess prove to be unreliable, if it did? As you know by now, unless you can trace a word back through Old English (which your dictionary may call Anglo-Saxon) to Indo-European or at least to an intermediate language like Proto-Germanic, you cannot properly call it "native," but since roots for all these words may not be readily available to you, you can assume for this exercise that if the word was in Old English it is native. There are a few exceptions, early borrowings like *port* and *street*, but not many, not enough to invalidate your results in this exercise.

an, and, aggression, alembic, aria, as, ate, barbiturate, best, blaze, brain, brontosaurus, carve, church, churn, cook, common, council, cyclometer, demoralize, dog, earth, emphasize, enthymeme, expose, fat, father, filter-ability, flexion, for, game, give, glaciation, hand, habitual, hen, her, hypo-crite, in, interest, iota, it, king, know, labyrinth, land, like, language, lay, legislature, lung, man, manage, mimicry, mow, not, nominative, odorifer-ous, paternal, piano, pick, prosody, pure, read, refutation, revenge, ring, scissors, scorpion, she, smoke, snake, spectroscope, the, that, to, trans-cendental, translate, turquoise, up, uxorial, who, why, yacht

E The following are some of the more common prefixes from Latin and Greek used in Modern English:

ab- (abs-)	ex- (ec-)	pro-
ad- (ac-, af-,	extra-	proto-
ag-, al-, an-,	hyper-	pseudo-
ap-, ar-, as-,	in- (il-, im-, ir-)	re-
at-)	inter-	retro-
ambi- (ambo-)	intra-	se-
ante-	intro-	semi-
anti- (ant-)	mal-	sub- (suc-, suf-, sug-,
arch-	multi-	sum-, sup-, sur-,
bi-	neo-	sus-)
cata-	non-	super-
circum-	ob- (oc-, of-, op-)	supra-
com- (co-, col-,	para-	syn- (sy- syl-, sym-)
con-, cor-)	per-	trans-
contra-	peri-	tri-
de-	post-	uni-
di- (dis-)	pre-	vice-
ex- (e-, ef-)		

Be sure you know the use and meaning of each prefix, verifying in a good dictionary those about which you may be uncertain. Then choose five prefixes, and find at least ten words in which each of these occurs.

For more extensive lists of prefixes and suffixes, see Arthur Garfield Kennedy, *Current English* (Boston, 1935), pp. 337–45, or Jerome C. Hixson and I. Colodny, *Word Ways: A Study of Our Living Language* (New York, 1939).

WORD CHOICE

CHAPTER 20

The skillful writer constantly refines his choice of words.

Ford Madox Ford reports that when he heard of the death of Joseph Conrad, his long-time friend and collaborator, he saw again in his mind the two of them driving past "a ramshackle, commonplace farm building in an undistinguished country over slight hills on a flinty byroad," and heard Joseph Conrad saying, "Well, Ford, *mon vieux*, how would you render that field of wheat?" He goes on to recount that they had spent many hours through many years in that way, jolting through "a country of commonplace downlands," asking themselves how they would describe a field of wheat under the conditions of the moment. Should one say, "Fields of wheat that small winds ruffled into cat's paws"? No, that was too literary. But what ideas and what words should one use? Then there was that "ten-acre patch of blue-purple cabbage." What should one do about that?

Here we have the picture of two distinguished writers, spending great chunks of their lives asking each other what words to use to describe a field of wheat or a patch of cabbages. Quite surely they wrote well partly because they studied words and the power of words. Conrad said his purpose was "above all things to make you see," but he understood that before he could make anyone else see, he had to see. Unless a writer sees sharply, he cannot make others see sharply. Unless he hears vividly, he cannot make others hear. How does snow look when it falls in large flakes, widely spaced, in no wind? How do the brakes of a car sound when the driver jams them on suddenly to avoid a crash? What is the differ-

391

ence between the smell of roasting turkey and roasting goose? If one goes to his wardrobe in the dark and finds the particular garment he wants by feel, what in the texture of the cloth identifies it? How does your best friend walk?

To answer questions like these the student needs words and he needs to be able to discriminate among them. In chapter 19 we looked at words primarily as linguistic shapes—sounds and spellings—at the evolution of these shapes and at ways of increasing a vocabulary by understanding where words come from. In this chapter—and in chapter 27, the Glossary—we look at what words can do, at problems of selecting the word best suited for a purpose. For looking at words from either point of view, good dictionaries are likely to be the writer's best tools.

A vocabulary, a word-hoard, is not merely a collection of objects—even an Anglo-Saxon hoard of treasure was more. Some objects were more valuable than others; a warrior could do more with a fine sword than he could with a buckle, and he valued it more. He also had a different use for it. Similarly, some terms in a word-hoard can do more than others; words have different values and different uses. The dictionary not only records the shape of words, it provides information with which we can evaluate words and choose among them.

What Dictionaries Are For

Regrettably, dictionaries are not today so helpful as they might be, because most users of them do not know very precisely what they are good for. This is something of a paradox. Probably nowhere in the world have dictionaries been so extensively purchased, so widely admired, and so persistently consulted as they are in the United States today. Most Americans think they know what a wordbook is good for, and they consult "the dictionary," with a faith that is touching if not entirely justified. Often they try to use a dictionary for what it is not and for what it was never intended to be, and accordingly, they fail to get from it what they might.

More than two centuries ago, Dr. Samuel Johnson learned and recorded the purposes of a dictionary in the course of planning and editing his *Dictionary of the English Language* (1755). Before he began his project, he tried to obtain subscriptions for his book by promising that with it he would purify the language and fix it in this new-found purity. During the years he spent editing the volume, he educated himself. He became convinced that language always changes, that nobody can purify it, nobody can fix it, and nobody can determine what it will become. That may be unfortunate, as it may be unfortunate that all men are not kind and that no baby is born with educated brains, but Johnson was right. Most of his contemporaries thought that language should be and could be purified and fixed; many people still believe this. But the fact is that nobody, not an emperor, a gangster, a grammarian, a president, a lexicographer or anybody else, can successfully determine language; hence he cannot prescribe it. At best he can hope to describe it, and even that description will be inadequate and will not last—the language will go right on changing, even before the dictionary can be printed and adopted. It changes while the dictionary lies open before the expectant user.

Thus a lexicographer does not tell people how to use the language. He will not, because he knows that in honesty he cannot. A good lexicographer knows more about a language than do most people, although he cannot know everything; but in any event, only the user of the language can know what he wants to do with it. At best the lexicographer can hope to describe language, although he is entitled to infer that if he describes it well, people will know how to use it better than they might otherwise. Thus a dictionary editor does not prescribe language; he collects it, and by an instructive coincidence, the Indo-European root *leg-, from which the word lexicographer is constructed, means "to collect." That is, a maker of dictionaries reads and listens, and he records what he finds. He tries to learn how the language is used, in written and in oral form, and if communication through computers ever becomes subtle enough so that we can call computer signs a language, the lexicographer will need to ask how it is used in computer form. He recognizes that language can be employed more or less formally, more or less traditionally, and that it is shot through with the influences of dialect and usage. He studies the evidence he has collected; if he cannot understand all the evidence he calls in specialists, a doctor to explain medical terms, a jurist to clarify legal definitions. He views the evidence in light of the history of the language in question, and in the light of modern linguistics. He tries to analyze the results and to describe them, partly in written language, partly in conventionalized symbols, and he assembles all this information in readily accessible form. The result is what we call a dictionary.

What do these procedures mean for the user of the dictionary? Obviously they mean that whoever consults the dictionary should try to use it as its maker meant it to be used, as an instrument with which to understand the language, whether the person who has consulted the dictionary wishes to interpret an abstruse piece of writing, wants to say something more precisely than he might otherwise, or just likes to have fun with words. The lexicographer does not feel that he is a preacher, or a court of law, or God in His heaven. It is not his business to tell other people what they should be doing, not even what they should be doing about their language. He believes that his business is to describe the language as well as he can, and that if he can do that job well, he has earned the right to be content. If people insist upon misusing his book he cannot help it; he believes that he has been honest. He has tried to describe the language, hoping the description will be helpful to all sorts of people, but if the users will not employ a tool as it was meant to serve, that is their affair, even though also their loss.

How a Dictionary Is Made

A modern dictionary rests upon citations of specific uses of words, oral or written, but traditionally mostly written. Such citations are collected by the million, and in the great scholarly dictionaries, a portion of them are reprinted. This reprinting can become expensive and cumbersome. The *Oxford English Dictionary* endeavored to print citations for all uses of all words in the language, but the job became so monumental that the completed dictionary fills more than a dozen large volumes, and the editors had to cut it off arbitrarily at 1900 and propose supplements or sister dictionaries that will probably double the size. Obviously, a dictionary that must be convenient cannot reprint many citations.

Citations of actual uses of words, however, are behind the definitions in modern dictionaries. One recent desk dictionary, for example, gives the following as one definition for the word *scalp:* "[*Colloq.*] to buy and sell in order to make small, quick profits." The entry also includes a symbol indicating that the use is an Americanism. The editor who prepared that definition would probably have begun by reviewing earlier dictionaries, and these would have included the scholarly *Dictionary of American English* (1944). Some reader for that dictionary had noticed the following in *Harper's Magazine* for 1886:

> [The scalper buys] any quantity of grain that may be offered, sells it at an advance of 1/8th cent per bushel, thus scalps the market.

The dictionary reprinted this passage, along with further instances of the same use of *scalp* in 1897 and 1902. Accordingly, that dictionary defined "to scalp the market" as "to buy and sell grain or stocks, taking small profits quickly as the market fluctuates." The editors labeled the word *Colloq.*, presumably thereby responding to the indications in all three citations that the word was normally confined to the speech of a limited group and was unusual in its appearance in writing.

The editors of the desk dictionary in question would also have consulted *A Dictionary of Americanisms* (1951), which interprets somewhat differently the evidence of the earlier citations and of subsequent uses its readers have noticed. This dictionary suggests a broadening use of the term by including "to make a quick profit by buying and selling" as one definition under the general entry *scalp* and then adding "scalp the market" as a phrase. The editors of this specialized dictionary also dropped the label *Colloq.*, probably because they considered the earlier evidence of limits in usage inadequate or because their own research suggested that usage had changed. By entering the use as an Americanism they were observing that the earlier citations, and presumably those found by their own research staff, all recorded American uses and that readers for the *Oxford English Dictionary* had apparently found no instances of the use outside American English. Later, the editors of the desk dictionary referred to above could telescope the conclusions of the earlier lexicographers, confirmed by their own research.

This sequence of events suggests how lexicographers work. The editors of all three dictionaries were relying upon the known verified occurrences of the word; none of them presumes to go outside this evidence and make any expression of personal convictions. The first two sets of editors differed in minor ways in their interpretation of available material; no doubt several editors reviewed the entry for each book, and they may have argued as to whether there was or was not sufficient evidence to label the use *Colloq.*, but they had to decide one way or the other.

The editors of the desk dictionary had their own staff of readers, but apparently these produced no new evidence as to *scalp* in this use. They must have considered eliminating the entry; the word is no longer common in this specialized sense. The editors no doubt noticed that the *Century Dictionary* did not include the use; the compilers of that dictionary probably did not know it. The editors of many abridged dictionaries did not know it or had ignored it. The *New International*, 2nd ed., did have it, but included this use as part of a larger sense that comprises also selling tickets at an inflated price—this edition of the *New International* was published too early to make use of the findings of the dictionaries of Americanisms cited above. After whatever arguments, the editors of the desk dictionary decided to treat this, to rely upon the evidence brought out by the scholarly dictionaries of Americanisms, but greatly to reduce those entries. They saw no reason to

395

go outside the work of these previous lexicographers, but they needed to compress, and sometimes to make decisions, especially when their predecessors had disagreed. Accordingly, they used a conventional symbol to indicate that the use is an Americanism, reduced the definition by removing nonessentials, and cut all the citations—no doubt after studying them very carefully and trying, unsuccessfully, to find more. They accepted from one body of lexicographers the conclusion that *scalp* can be considered an independent word in this sense as well as part of the phrase "scalp the market," which they decided not to include, and they accepted the conclusion of the other body of lexicographers that the use should be labelled *Colloq.* (The editors of a rival dictionary had come to a similar conclusion but preferred the somewhat less restrictive term *informal.*)

A lexicographer is first of all a learned man, learned especially in language, and he is likely to have become a skillful editor. He is also a professional; he works in accordance with a set of principles and practices accepted in general by all modern practitioners of lexicography. He works by collecting evidence about language, studying this evidence objectively if possible, and by making careful, informed guesses when the evidence does not permit objectivity. The editors we have observed above were concerned with discovering the meaning and the social standing of a use; they did not need to consider spelling and pronunciation because those matters were handled elsewhere, but if the editors had suspected that *scalp* is pronounced differently as a term in finance than as a term in anatomy, they would have pursued the same technique. They would have endeavored with citations to learn how the word was spoken by those who used it. That is, lexicographers begin by determining what they believe the evidence to be. Then in editing they sift out what they trust will be most welcome to the prospective user of the book, and marshall it into a reference work, using conventional symbols for economy and endeavoring to write in a style at once factual, clear, and concise.

What a Dictionary Is Good For

A modern desk dictionary is likely to provide several sorts of information, including the following:

1. *An entry, that is a word, phrase, abbreviation, combining element, or the like.* This entry, usually printed in boldface type, provides a key for the user and a spelling. For most modern words, only one spelling is considered correct, but for some there is an American

usage, as *jail,* and a British usage, *gaol.* A lexicographer is likely to enter both and to identify them. For some words there are variant spellings not so restricted spatially, as with *traveler* and *traveller.* For such a word both forms are likely to occur as one entry, with one of them first. This order does not necessarily mean that one is "preferred" to the other — after all, one has to come first. The entry means, at a minimum, only that the editors find that both spellings are in common, reputable use; of course, if the editors of an American book put *traveler* before *traveller* they may be suggesting that the first use is more common in the United States, the second more common in England. With a sequence like *catalog* and *catalogue* they may be recognizing that *catalogue* was formerly the only accepted form, but that *catalog* seems to be becoming the commoner practice. Or they may mean only that in a sequence, one must come before the other.

For the lexicographer the entry raises the question: What is a word? Is *fast* one word because of its spelling, or four words because it can be any of at least four parts of speech, or some other number? The *Century* had seven entries for *fast;* some dictionaries have one. Is *fasting* a separate word, or a form of *fast*? Fortunately, such questions need not bother users of dictionaries much; usually the editor has planned his book so that the user has only to look up a spelling, and he will be led to the use he wants.

One more problem involved in entries is important for the user of the dictionary, although mainly he is unaware of it. If he looks up a word and finds it, he does not ask himself how the word got there. But somebody had to decide that each word, or a particular use of a word would or would not be treated. English includes millions of named uses; no dictionary has included all of them, and probably none ever will. Most dictionaries can afford, in cost and convenience, to enter but a small part of them. But which ones? Thus the lexicographer labors over his word list, deciding which shapes and which uses he will include. If he does his job well, the user is likely to find what he wants; if not, the user may be disappointed but may never know why. Anyone comparing two dictionaries will do well to check the word lists carefully.

2. *Pronunciation.* Early in an entry, most frequently immediately after it and commonly within parentheses, the entry word will be transcribed into some system of phonetic symbols. These symbols may approximate those in the International Phonetic Alphabet, although most dictionaries use a system worked out by the editors of that dictionary and reproduced at the bottom of alternate pages. Somewhere, most frequently in the introduction, this system will be explained.

Here variant pronunciations become a problem. A brief word

like *orange* is said to have a dozen common pronunciations, and a word like *charivaree* can be pronounced with two, three, or four syllables. Obviously, in a desk dictionary, the editor cannot include all possible pronunciations, not even all possible acceptable pronunciations. He has to choose; he may select pronunciations in one dialect—in England, often the speech of the court. One set of lexicographers concluded that the dialect of an educated person in Chicago was as near to central as they could hope to find, and they used that. Others have been selective, trying to judge the spread of pronunciation, word by word. Whatever the lexicographer elects to present as the pronunciations, he means, as he does with his spellings, that this form is acceptable. He may mean nothing more than that. If he gives the pronunciations of tomato as /təmetə/ and /t'mato/ he does not mean to imply that the first is preferred to the second or that other pronunciations like /t'metə/ and /tʊmatə/ are wrong. He means only that the two he has given are acceptable, and since he had to choose only very few he provided those that he thought might be most helpful.

3. *Grammatical information.* Next is likely to appear a symbol like *n.* for noun, or *v.t.* for verb, transitive. Once more, the lexicographer is trying to be helpful, and is somewhat embarrassed because he knows that his statement may appear more authoritative than he means it to be. He knows that a traditional grammarian, a functional grammarian, a structuralist, a transformationalist, and a tagmemist mean different things by a designation like *noun*, and that some grammarians reject such terms entirely. He knows, also, that the language is changing; if he enters *orbit* as a noun and a verb he is not saying it can never become an adjective, or even possibly an adverb. But he does know that words can be used in some ways and not in others, that they have what is sometimes called "privilege of occurrence." He knows, also, that this privilege of occurrence tells us something about the word, that it can fill one sort of slot and not another, that its use becomes involved in meaning. Thus he tries to use a set of grammatical symbols that he hopes most users will recognize and find usable. He is saying that a word can have a certain privilege of occurrence with a designated meaning, and he trusts his user will not assume he means more than that. He is not saying the word can have no other use and no other meaning.

4. *Etymology.* All but elementary dictionaries include some etymology, and as we have seen in chapter 19, some may have etymologies going back to the earliest known shapes of words. In many dictionaries the etymology may appear in square brackets, after the grammatical designation, and usually after only one of various related words. Some dictionaries have the etymology last,

hoping thus not to confuse inexperienced users, or to impede those who refuse to be bothered with matters like word origins, which they may deem impractical.

5. *Usage.* Most dictionaries do something about usage. Many use usage labels, like *slang, obs., U.S. dial.,* and the like; if the word has more than one use, the label is likely to appear immediately before the definition, since various uses of a word may command various social standings. For example, *scalp,* mentioned above, is restricted; it may be colloquial, and it might even become slang in a sense like "scalp the market," but it is surely standard as a name for the skinlike covering of the skull. The treatment of usage becomes involved in the problem of usage; both are discussed in chapter 27.

6. *Definitions.* Here we are at the heart of the dictionary. Most words have several uses; some, like *get,* may have dozens. Defining these uses, both in the sense of setting limits to them and describing the impact of the word within these limits, becomes the most difficult job for the lexicographer and, usually, the most useful service for those who consult his volume. In many dictionaries, senses are labeled by numbers, and subdivisions of these meanings may be designated by letters. Whatever the system, the whole represents a sort of chart of the spread of meaning as the lexicographer has conceived it.

7. *Synonyms.* For many entries, the last section is either a list of synonyms (and possibly antonyms) discriminated from one another, or a cross reference to such a list that appears under another entry. There are also specialized synonym books, which fall generally into two categories: one sort, which may be called a dictionary of synonyms, is intended to distinguish in detail among the more common synonyms; the other sort, commonly called a thesaurus, is intended to suggest synonyms, on the theory that a writer cannot think of a word but would know what to do with it if he could recall it. Some books try to do more or less of both.

Semantic Change

We have seen that a word, or any other linguistic unit, can be looked at in at least two ways. It is a shape, something that can be written or spoken; we have seen that these shapes mainly descend within the language from an ancient parent, or they are borrowed from other languages. We have observed, also, that a word can have use. It can have grammatical impact, as we observed in studying sentence structure. It can have semantic use, also; it can mean. We have yet to inquire what we mean by meaning, but we might notice first that whatever meaning is, and however words manage to achieve it, it occurs in groups of words that have some relationship to the families of language shapes.

Let us see how sample words got what we call their meaning. Recently *backlog* has grown rapidly; manufacturers have backlogs of orders, judges have backlogs of cases, jobbers have backlogs of goods. But a century ago, apparently, nobody used the word in this way; a backlog was a device for radiant heating. It was so called because it was put at the back of a large fireplace, with the lighter wood, including the forestick, in front of it so that the flames would make the front surface of the backlog glow and radiate heat. (The curious reader will find a description of such a fire in Whittier's *Snowbound.*) But the great backlog might burn for days, and perhaps for this reason became a figurative indication of something in reserve.

Neither did the parts of this word mean what they mean in *backlog*. The old Norse word *lag* did not mean wood; it is related to our verb *to lie*, from Indo-European **legh-*, meaning "to lie down," and thus a log is the result, *the lying thing*. That is, the *lag* or *log* meant the fallen tree after it was lying on the ground, and then the trunk of a fallen tree in any position. Nor has *back* always meant back. In Old English, *baec* approximately meant the side away from the face or front of the human body, and thus anything opposite the front could become the back — but not always, for the backbone of a quadruped is at the top, and correspondingly the back of a handsaw is at the top in sawing. Once *back* had developed the meaning of opposite to the front, it acquired all sorts of other uses; to *back up* is to go toward the rear, but to *back somebody up* is to support him, presumably from the rear. Any good modern dictionary is likely to have columns involving *back*, from *back and fill* to *backyard*.

As the word *back* was lived with, it grew to fit human needs. Having by generalization acquired the general force of *opposite-front* or *to-the-rear*, it became specialized again in a great variety of words and phrases like *backstroke, backhanded, backorder;* and by more figures of speech a bumptious kind of person became a *backslapper* and an old-fashioned person was *backnumberish*. The sorts of mental processes involved in these developments are too numerous to examine here, but as we saw in chapter 19, words grow as they do partly because they reflect the way the human mind works.

Such reflections of man and society can work through a whole family of words, represented in many languages. Consider the descendants of the Indo-European root **derew-*, which meant firm or hard. This root descended into Old English as *treow*, our word *tree,* which used to mean wood as well as a standing tree. It also became the name for things made out of tree in the sense of wood; that is, Old English *treg* became our word *tray,* and Old English *troh* became our word *trough.* It also became Old English *treowe,* our word *true,* and *trimian,* to make firm, which gives us modern *trim.* These uses may have descended from the idea in the Indo-European root, or they may have developed as derived ideas associated with wood and trees.

Meanwhile, the same root descended into other languages. Old Norse developed the word that we borrowed as *trust,* very much as we developed *true.* Latin had a word from **derew-* that we write as *durus,* meaning hard; before the day of metals, wood was considered hard. Figuratively, *durus* gives us words like *obdurate,* meaning stubborn; Scotch *dour,* meaning hard, unbending, severe; and, through French, *duress,* meaning hardship. It presumably is related, also, to Latin *durare,* meaning to last, which gives us dozens of words like *endure* and *durable.* In Greek, *drus* became the word for an oak tree, *hamadryad* the designation of a deity that dwelt in a tree; modern developments include plants like *philodendron* and *rhododendron.* The root appears also in Gaelic *druid,* perhaps influenced by borrowing, and in many other languages as words not borrowed into English, like Russian *derevo, drevo,* a tree. Thus words are always associated with some kind of use, and this use will descend from an earlier meaning, but as men live with the word the meaning may change so much that the earlier meaning becomes obscured or even reversed. A philodendron is a plant, but not characterized by hardness; truth can be an abstraction, and to endure is something one does. Some meanings have strayed even / further; *ravel* and *unravel* are now almost synonyms, and a *nice* girl used to be a foolish one.

THE MEANING OF MEANING: WORD CHOICE
20a

We have used the word *meaning* because we needed some way to designate the power of words to do things to and for people, although strictly speaking no word has meaning as a physical object can have length. The bars of metal in the Bureau of Standards, which determine our inches and feet, keep the same length at a given temperature, no matter who measures them, so long as the measuring is accurately done, but no words are kept at a controlled temperature in the Bureau of Standards. Words exist only in people's minds, and all minds are different. No word has a "meaning" that it inevitably calls up in everyone.

20a   **W**

Revise, choosing words more accurate for their context, making diction more precise. (For confusions among particular words, see chapter 27, Glossary.)

ORIGINAL	REVISION
The capture of the ridge had seemed an inhuman feat. [*Confusion with* humanly impossible *or* superhuman *may account for the inaccuracy.*]	Capturing the ridge had seemed impossible.
The inheritance brought them only transitive pleasure.	The inheritance brought them only transitory pleasure.
The critic's statement inferred that he had plagiarized.	The critic's statement implied that he had plagiarized.
When he entered, her face turned a livid red.	When he entered, her face turned a vivid red.

Theoretically Humpty Dumpty is justified in telling Alice, "When *I* use a word, it means just what I choose it to mean— neither more nor less." No authority can keep him from using the word *glory*, as he does, to mean "there's a nice knock-down argument for you." Practically, however, Humpty is not communicating much. Mrs. Malaprop, a character in Sheridan's *The Rivals*, made herself famous and added the word *malapropism* to the language by misusing words she did not understand. When she complimented herself on a "nice derangement of epitaphs" and said that someone was "headstrong as an allegory on the banks of the Nile," she certainly did not mean what her listeners understood by *derangement, epitaphs,* or *allegory.* Like Humpty, Mrs. Malaprop could indulge her whims if she wished; words have no mystical connection with a particular "meaning." But communication is possible because at any time in history by common agreement people associate certain words with certain thoughts. We can communicate because we agree, closely enough for practical purposes, to let certain words symbolize certain ideas. Writers who are ignorant of the agreements, or careless in paying attention to them, who do not choose words with precision, risk inaccurate communication.

People can agree about meaning because words relate to things in the real world and are, relatively speaking, common and enduring, but the use and choice of words is complex because words are related to things through various human minds. A word is a symbol a human being uses to reveal his idea about something.

Referent   Thought   Word

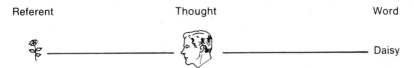

A writer or speaker can use *daisy* as a symbol to express his thought about a thing, a particular flower growing in a meadow, a referent. Speakers of English, by general agreement, use this symbol when they think of this particular kind of flower. The symbol would not work if the writer were thinking of a four-footed animal that brays or of a carved representation of George Washington. Neither would it work if he were writing in French or German. Conversely, any users of the language, readers or listeners, could interpret this symbol similarly.

Word   Thought   Referent

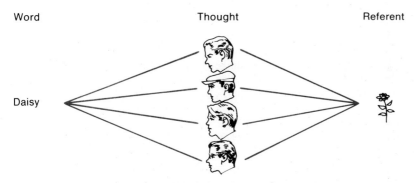

Daisy

Furthermore, a writer may have various thoughts about a referent he sees growing in a meadow, and he may choose any one of a number of words quite different from *daisy*. See illustration on page 404.

Each of these words—like many others—has the same referent, but each conveys a slightly different thought about the referent. *Plant* indicates that the writer is distinguishing the referent less precisely than does *flower; posy* suggests something about the background and attitude of the writer; *Bellis perennis, white weed,* and *table decoration* indicate special attitudes toward the referent.

As these differences illustrate, the writer constantly faces the problem of choosing words that will do precisely what he wants them to do. Word choice is not easy, but use of the exact word often

Referent   Thought   Word

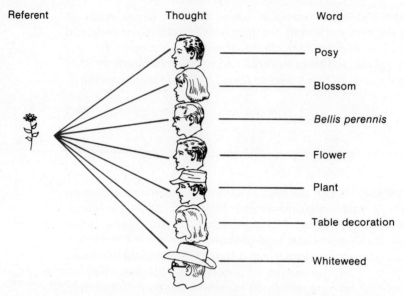

Posy

Blossom

Bellis perennis

Flower

Plant

Table decoration

Whiteweed

distinguishes good writing from mediocre. Almost any piece of good prose, such as the following, will illustrate:

> For Cooper was distressed by the new American world he found and bitterly resented many of its changes. He felt that America had retrogressed a century in these seven years, or perhaps he had stayed away too long, for he remembered Jefferson's saying that Americans might find themselves aliens if they spent more than five years out of the country. He had gone abroad in the days of the stagecoach, and the railroads were running on his return, while the scholarly John Quincy Adams had given place to Jackson and the piping times of ultra-republicanism. He was not prepared for the tawdry vulgarity that assailed him in the New York streets, or the flaring red of the bricks and green of the blinds, and this "rainbow capital" seemed to him a mean provincial town that could hardly compare with the second-rate cities of Europe. The scramble for money depressed him, and the general self-complacency, as if the "perfection of the people" had really been achieved, the mania for change and speculation, the "gulpers" in the dining-rooms, the pigs that ran wild in the gutters and the rowdy press. For the yellow journals of the eighteen-thirties abounded in violent epithets, "offal," "garbage," "liar" and "bilious braggart," and Cooper himself was presently styled a "spotted caitiff" and a "leprous wretch," a "tainted hand," an assassin and a jackass. The most respectable editors, Bryant, for instance, assaulted one another on the streets. Cooper was disconcerted too by the coldness of the ordinary American manner, in contrast to the warmth and cordiality he had known in France, the lack of aesthetic sensibility, the timidity and wariness, so different from the freedom and frankness

he had known of old. For when he referred to the bad pavements and the poor lighting of the town, his friends led him aside and begged him to be careful. It was unpatriotic to criticize American things. It was disloyal to suggest that the Bay of Naples could be mentioned in the same breath with the harbour of New York. It was shocking to compare the Alps with the Rockies. Yet, for all the bragging one heard in New York, there was little independence of mind, and England still did most of the thinking for the country.

VAN WYCK BROOKS, *The World of Washington Irving*

Study of this passage reveals that certain words do a great deal. Some of the vividness of the picture James Fenimore Cooper found on his return grows from details, the pigs in the New York gutters, the author of "Thanatopsis" assaulting a fellow editor, but part of it grows from Brooks' choice of words. The country had "retrogressed a century" since the "days of the stagecoach." Modifiers make precise distinctions: "*piping* times," "*tawdry* vulgarity," "*flaring* red," or "*rowdy* press." Brooks uses words out of the day to picture the day, the "gulpers" in the dining rooms, and epithets for Cooper like "leprous wretch." One might notice the variety of words Brooks uses to indicate different degrees of disturbance in Cooper; sometimes he is "depressed," sometimes "disconcerted," and he "bitterly resented" the changes. One might notice, also, the impact of the word *led* in the passage, "his friends led him aside and begged him to be careful," and the nice distinction among *unpatriotic*, *disloyal*, and *shocking*.

The effectiveness of the diction in the Brooks passage depends on a number of distinctions governing word choice—distinctions between different symbolic and figurative uses of words, between concrete and abstract words, between denotation and connotation, between contexts in which words appear.

Symbols and Word Choice

Modern philosophers, developing a theory of symbolic transformation, suggest that the symbol was the tool with which man built civilization, the device with which he made himself human. Man, living in a complicated and seemingly confused world, was able to reduce his universe to something like order by using symbols. Symbols, which could attach to thoughts as well as to physical phenomena, enabled man to grasp relationships, to see wholes. Man is a symbol-making animal; by his ability to deal in symbols he became unlike most other creatures, which seem not able to use symbols, but only to respond to signs, although recent research suggests that chimpanzees, and perhaps other primates, can use symbols.

The discovery of symbols made language possible. We have already noticed that words are symbols, that a sequence of letters can stand for a thought about a flower and things associated with a flower, but the process which created language continues to operate, and words, acting as symbols, readily develop new symbolic power. Take, for example, a favorite remark among stockbrokers, "The bulls make money and the bears make money, but the pigs seldom do." Taken in the sense that we might call "literal," a bull meaning a male bovine and a bear a large ursine quadruped, the sentence makes no sense; neither of these makes money. But, of course, both words are used here as symbols for types of investors: a bull buys stocks hoping to profit from a quick rise in their value, and a bear sells stocks, hoping to buy them before the delivery date at a lower price. Metaphorically the words have developed symbolic abilities that have become so crystallized that they appear in any good modern dictionary as meanings. *Pig* is also a symbol, and in the sentence above we can guess readily what it means, but in this sense, a buyer who endeavors to make as much profit as possible, the word will not be found in dictionaries. More than a century ago the word became a derogatory term among criminals for a police officer, especially for a police informer. The use did not survive, and somewhat later a *pig* was a sluttish woman. Recently the term has been revived as a contemptuous term for a policeman; the use apparently started among black militants, but it is now becoming so common that it may lose its symbolic force, since people who may pick up the term respect and value the police. That is, man's ability as a symbolmaker persists; man readily extends words to new symbolic implications and understands complex symbolic uses. Writers, taking advantage of man's continuing ability to make and unmake symbols, must be sensitive to shifts in symbolic values.

Specifically, the symbolic power of words permits the writer to be both concrete and general, specific and abstract, at the same time. He can choose a specific detail that has the vividness of the concrete, but one that has general symbolic overtones. In conversation we rely on symbolic associations even though the symbols have become trite. We use *whistlestop* instead of describing abstractly a provincial town; we speak of a person who would kick small dogs or would poison wells. Often, of course, such specific comments are accompanied by more general ones, but the well-selected specific detail may give the desired impression more vividly and convincingly—perhaps even more accurately—than the general description. Katherine Brush, in introducing a character, mentions two specific details but makes no general statement about the person:

406

Concrete

> Miss Levin was the checkroom girl. She had dark-at-the-roots blonde hair and slender hips, upon which, in moments of leisure she wore her hands, like buckles of ivory loosely attached.
>
> *Night Club*

Somerset Maugham makes a general comment about a room he is describing, then illustrates with two specific details that become symbols:

> It was a room designed not to live in but for purposes of prestige, and it had a musty, melancholy air. A suite of stamped plush was arranged neatly round the walls, and from the middle of the ceiling, protected from the flies by yellow tissue paper, hung a gilt chandelier.
> "Rain"

ABSTRACT AND CONCRETE WORDS **20b**

Sketching the referent of the word *daisy* is relatively easy, and the resulting picture may also portray the referent of the word *flower,* but a picture of the referent behind the "full" meaning of the word *flower* would be more difficult. It would have to include not only daisies but also irises and begonias, the blooms on thistles, the bloom stage in a field of corn, in fact everything in the writer's experience that made up the idea he was expressing by the word. Or consider drawing a picture of the referent behind the word *beauty.* The picture of the daisy might be a part, but hundreds of other bits from the writer's experience would be necessary, and a picture would become virtually impossible.

Obviously *flower* is more general than *daisy,* and *beauty* is more general than *flower. Beauty* can also be said to be *abstract,* whereas *daisy* is *concrete.* Roughly, one can say that abstract words refer to generalities or to ideas, and that concrete words refer to things or objects. Or, in terms of the discussion above, concrete words stand for a thought about a referent that can be pictured or specified; abstract words go back to referents so complex or general that they cannot be visualized. These statements, however, require two qualifications. First, *abstract* and *concrete* are relative terms, like *general* and *specific* (see chapter 3). Compare the following:

There was *something* on the table.

There was a *creature* on the table.

There was a *tarantula* on the table.

Creature is more concrete than *something, tarantula* more concrete than *creature.* The ideas become more specific; the words become

20b   Concrete

Revise by making diction more concrete and thus more precise.

ABSTRACT	MORE CONCRETE
When we were in some fighting it was hard to know what was going on because so many things were happening that usually you did not know much about it until after it was over. You were excited, and though maybe you would know the things that were occurring, it was hard afterward to know just what had happened, especially around you. STUDENT THEME [*The theme suffers from a lack of detail reflected in concrete diction.*]	Who know the conflicts, hand to hand—the many conflicts in the dark, those shadowy-tangled, flashing moonbeamed woods, the writhing groups and squads, the cries, the din, the cracking guns and pistols, the distant cannon, the cheers and calls and threats and awful music of the oaths, the indescribable mix; the officers' orders, persuasions, encouragements; the devils fully roused in human hearts; the strong shout, *Charge, men, charge;* the flash of the naked sword, and rolling flame and smoke?—Walt Whitman's diary, slightly repunctuated.
The abnormal condition within Hamlet's mind is a governing factor that is the foremost force in molding his character traits.	The turmoil in Hamlet's mind altered his character. [*This may not be true, but it approximates what the student apparently meant to say.*]

more concrete and increase in exactness and suggestiveness as they do so. Second, just as the general develops out of the specific, abstract expressions grow from more concrete ones. *Color* stands for a thought that would be hard to express if we had only more concrete terms like *red, yellow, blue, green.*

Consider the following sentence proposed by George Orwell to illustrate how some writers might translate a passage of the Bible:

Objective consideration of contemporary phenomena compels the conclusion that success or failure in competitive activities exhibits no tendency to be commensurate with innate capacity, but that a considerable element of the unpredictable must invariably be taken into account.

Concrete

Although the sentence exaggerates deliberately, it suggests how abstractions can obscure ideas. Compare the passage from Ecclesiastes that Orwell has "translated":

> I returned, and saw under the sun, that the race is not to the swift, nor the battle to the strong, neither yet bread to the wise, nor yet riches to men of understanding, nor yet favour to men of skill; but time and chance happeneth to them all.

Instead of one general statement, the original uses five specific examples; instead of abstractions like *consideration, phenomena, conclusion, success,* and *failure,* the original uses more concrete words like *race, battle, bread,* and *riches.* Almost always, clear and accurate writing uses concrete words whenever possible.

Almost certain to make writing muddy are words that have risen to sudden popularity and have been favored with such promiscuous use that their meanings have almost disappeared. In a sentence like "They decided to evaluate the situation at all levels," *situation* is vague in its abstractness, but *levels* is even less precise. Interestingly, other catchall words or phrases might be substituted with very little change in meaning and almost no improvement in communication—"in all phases" or "on all facets" or "from all aspects." The term *jargon* is frequently used to characterize diction that relies too heavily on overworked abstraction, especially when used needlessly; "in an intoxicated condition" is neither clearer nor fancier than *intoxicated* or even *drunk;* "of an unpredictable nature" has no advantages over *unpredictable;* "He studied in the area of philosophy" says no more than "he studied philosophy," unless the phrase is intended to suggest that he explored only the outskirts of the subject. See *Jargon* in the Glossary, chapter 27. A list of words to look on with suspicion might include *angle, area, aspect, breakdown, circumstances, deal, cool, groovy, claim* (verb), *picture, point, facet, factor, setup, situation, phase, basic, regard* (noun), *fundamental, force, rate* (verb), *hassle, worthwhile, unique, outstanding, viable, put over, put across, overall.*

DENOTATION AND CONNOTATION: SLANTING 20c

Roughly speaking, a word's communication of a thought about a referent is the word's denotation, what is sometimes called its "dictionary meaning." *Flower* and *table decoration,* therefore, have different denotations; but *flower* and *posy* have a common denotation. Still, no botanist today would write that "the

---

20c   # Slant

Avoid colored, prejudicial, or "slanted" terms.

ORIGINAL

In high school there were some radicals who always stabbed any new worthwhile project in the back just because they were rats at heart.
[*Apparently, the writer is trying to discredit by calling names, but he is mainly discrediting himself.*]

My mother is a perfect angel with a saintly face and the most perfect disposition in the world.
[*Words like* angel *and* saintly *have some emotional force, but are vague enough to be unconvincing.*]

REVISION

There was one faction in our high school that tried to block any change that my group tried to institute.
[*The attitude of the writer has changed, and relatively objective words have replaced colored words.*]

Mother is seldom cross, never angry without good reason, and always helpful; years of smiling have left little wrinkles at the corners of her mouth.
[*Concrete terms clarify the passage and strengthen the appeal.*]

---

begonia bears monecius posies"; he would feel that the word *posy* is unsuited to scientific description. On the other hand, one might wish to suggest that certain wallpaper was old-fashioned by saying, "It was all cluttered up with pink posies." That is, each of these words can do something more than point to a particular thought. This power of a word to do more than designate, to make emotional and interpretive suggestions, is the word's *connotation*. Connotation is an essential part of the meaning of a word, to be distinguished from denotation only in analysis.

Connotation is always individual. To a garden lover, the word *flower* may suggest hours of pleasure in the sunshine, a sense of pervading joy, or even ecstasy. To someone else it may suggest bad taste as reflected in plastic decorations in a cheap restaurant, or if one has been ill from mimosa, it may even suggest nausea. But to a considerable degree, even though connotation is personal, most people share much of the connotative power of a word, for most of us have somewhat similar heritages and experiences. The word *home* connotes something different for each of us, but most people share feelings about the word, and would distinguish them from other feelings associated with *house*. Lately the word *drug* has developed connotations for many young people that is foreign to their parents, but even so the term has connotations shared by portions of the population, if more than one set of connotations. Thus, to a degree, the emotional qualities of words can be used for communication, and the connotative power of words is so great that most good writers make conscious use of it.

In general, the connotations of words serve to emphasize characteristics of a referent or to reveal attitudes toward it. *Statesman* and *politician* may describe the same person, refer to the same referent.

Referent   Thought   Word

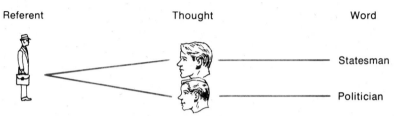

The thoughts expressed by the words differ, however; the words have become associated with emotional suggestions so that *statesman* emphasizes wisdom, dignity, vision, and integrity, and *politician,* especially in American use, suggests intrigue, time-serving, and self-seeking. Through their connotations, the words present different views of the referent. Connotational meanings, therefore, are exploited especially in any writing or speaking that seeks to persuade, to move, or to stimulate emotion.

Concern about propaganda and analysis of propaganda have made our society alert to the emotional qualities of words, especially as used in politics or advertising. Compare the following statements, which describe the same incident:

> Senator A ranted interminably this afternoon in a bigoted attack on the new save-the-schools budget.
>
> Senator A delivered a full and detailed address this afternoon in a spirited criticism of the governor's give-away budget.

In their emotional content the words in the first are clearly "slanted" or "loaded" against the senator; words in the second seek to move the reader to approve the speech. To suggest that "emotional" words should not be used is absurd, but the writer should be aware of their limitations and their weaknesses. From neither of the statements above does the reader know what Senator A did. The connotations of the words outweigh their denotations. Many similar words in English, especially words like *freedom, communist, radical, liberal, fascist, relevant, militant,* or *civil liberties,* have developed such varied connotations that they can be used only with care and skill if the writer is to avoid distortion. Furthermore, misleading use of the emotional power of words is as false as any other kind of verbal lie because the connotations of a word are part of it. The writer who intentionally distorts the truth through his choice of "loaded" or "slanted" words should be challenged on his integrity rather than his skill with language.

FIGURATIVE LANGUAGE: METAPHOR

20d

Irresponsible exploitation of connotations can distort truth, but skillful management of emotional meanings can make language more precise, more interesting, more intense. The importance of connotations can be seen especially in figurative language, in a device like the metaphor. Metaphor, or comparison in language, is more than embellishment; it is part of language itself. We use metaphors constantly in conversation ("He ran like crazy; he is a little devil"). Words develop through metaphors; we speak of the *hands* of the clock, the *foot* of the bed, the *head* of the household, the *legs* of a chair. Sails *belly,* and crowds *thunder* applause as the *shell shoots* across the *line.* We no longer think of the italicized words as figures of speech, but they developed as metaphors, and words are developing in this manner constantly. Metaphor, then, is a device by which connotations of words provide precise and vivid meanings. Consider the following relatively elaborate comparison from *Romeo and Juliet:*

> This bud of love, by summer's ripening breath,
> May prove a beauteous flower when next we meet.

The metaphor is complex, but essentially it uses the word *flower* to express the referent usually denoted by *love.*

Referent   Thought   Word

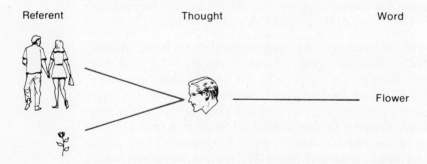

Flower

By using the word *flower* rather than the word *love,* Shakespeare emphasizes parts of both the connotational and denotational meanings of love. He makes us think of the "flowerlike" significance of love, its ability to grow, its beauty, its relation with time. The metaphor, in its context, allows the writer to exploit the emotional meanings of the words.

GUIDE TO REVISION

20d   **Fig**

Control metaphorical writing to produce only the desired effects.

CLEAR BUT PEDESTRIAN

The long mountains came down to the abrupt coast, and you could see them rather mixed up, running every which way. Some were angular, and some were rounded, and they all looked sad and depressing. Back from the shore where they were high the peaks were all snow-covered, and even nearer there were patches of snow and glaciers on them.

METAPHORICAL

These long mountains . . . lie, one after another, like corpses, with their toes up, and you pass by them, . . . and see their noses, tipped by cloud or snow, high in behind, with one corpse occasionally lying on another, and a skull or a thigh-bone chucked about, and hundreds of glaciers and snow-patches hanging to them, as though it was a winter battlefield.

WORTHINGTON C. FORD,
Letters of Henry Adams

ORIGINAL

A creative person who has no political crystallization, not merely cuts the production end of his work, but loses a vital gut that is part of the social continuum.
[*Doubtless the man who published this to advertise an obscure magazine thought he was both profound and witty.*]

He was always getting on band wagons, going off in all directions, and ending up clear out in left field.

We keep clipping the wool off the goose that lays the golden eggs, and instead of getting on the beam we pump her dry.

REVISION

A creative artist who ignores contemporary politics limits himself as a creator and to a degree cuts himself off from society.
[*This is prosaic, perhaps, but not silly. The artist is no longer whacking off his production while disemboweling himself and undergoing crystallization.*]

He is impetuous.
[*At best the figures are trite; mixed they become ridiculous.*]

Taking excessive profits inevitably destroys the source of those profits.

Words affect, and are affected by, the words they accompany. The writer needs to choose his words with care, selecting so that in both denotation and connotation they are appropriate in their contexts. Consider, for example, the following sentences:

> My *love* is like a red, red rose.
>
> The *love* of money is the root of all evil.
>
> Greater *love* hath no man than this, that a man lay down his life for his friends.
>
> Friendship is *Love* without his wings.
>
> God is *love*.
>
> The students announced a *love*-in.

The word *love* appears in each sentence, but the connotations and even the denotations differ. The context, the company the word keeps, indicates its meaning.

The writer must choose his words with their contexts in mind. The lists of discriminative synonyms in dictionaries suggest how words fit different contexts (look up, for example, *joke*, *wit*, or *wise*). Even synonyms cannot be changed at random; for example, dictionaries list *exonerate* as a synonym for *clear*. Substituting *exonerate* would sharpen meaning in a sentence like "The attorney hoped to clear the ex-convict," but it would not serve in a sentence like "Pam cleared the dishes from the table" or "The pole-vaulter could not clear twelve feet."

ECONOMICAL WORD CHOICE   20e

English works best when used efficiently. People in dreadful need of communication can usually make themselves understood in few words. "Help!" "Fire!" "Murder!" say more than "I am in need of assistance," "There is a conflagration," and "A person is being illegally dispatched." Of course complicated ideas and fine distinctions require elaborate treatment; they cannot be considered in few words, but the fewer the better, so long as the expression is adequate. Good writing results from a plenitude of ideas and an economy of words, not from a desert of ideas and a flood of vocabulary. Most writers, especially most beginning writers, should throw out words, and even well-constructed sentences may improve with the removal of nonessential or redundant words. The following will bear more than normal attention.

1. *Cutting deadwood.* Good writers resolutely cut out the words doing no work. Notice that if the italicized words are omitted, the following sentences are clearer and sharper.

> *It happened that* she was elected *to the position of* secretary *and this was* [of] the oldest club *that existed* in the city.

> Although he had always considered his sister *to be of the* awkward *type,* he found her *to be* a good dancer.

2. *Direct expressions.* Often shorter, more direct routes to meaning can be discovered. Notice, for example, the substitutions suggested in brackets for the italicized words in the following sentences.

> Meg's tears *had the effect of making* [made] Gordon regret *the accusation that he made hastily* [his hasty accusation].

> *By the time the end of the month rolled around* [By the end of the month] *it seemed to us a certainty* [we knew] that our first business venture would *be a success* [succeed].

GUIDE TO REVISION

20e   **Wordy**

Revise for economy, eliminating redundancy and repetition.

WORDY

Although the story is in the supernatural class, Hawthorne manages to put over his point and show the effects on a person when he is confronted with the fact that everyone contains a certain amount of evil in his physical make-up.

CONCISE

Hawthorne uses the supernatural to suggest that evil appears in everyone.

[The original version was cluttered; with the verbiage cleared away, the writer can make the sentence direct and precise.]

WORDY

But if you get right down to the facts in the case, we cannot reorient this tract of real estate, nor can we determine what disposition is fated to be made in the future of this acreage fresh from God's hand, and last but not least we cannot render a decision as to whether or not this section of the earth's surface is to be employed for purposes other than divine.

CONCISE

But in a larger sense, we cannot dedicate—we cannot consecrate—we cannot hallow this ground.

ABRAHAM LINCOLN, *Gettysburg Address*

[The first version is an obvious parody of Lincoln's famous sentence, but it illustrates how useless words obscure rather than clarify.]

A well-chosen verb or adjective can say as much as a wordy clause.

3. *Economy in modifiers.* Modifiers tend to decrease the impact of the other modifiers. Words like *very, really, surely, actually, merely, simply, great,* and *real* tend to accumulate in careless composition. Consider whether the modifiers italicized in the following sentence should be omitted.

> As I crept *hesitantly* out of the *dark,* dingy, *grimy* hotel and felt the *blazing,* withering sun on my back I was *very* sure I did not *really* want to *actually* spend a month in the city.

Often the effect of modifiers can be embodied in telling nouns or verbs. *Liar,* for most purposes, says everything in "a person given by nature or habit to disseminating untruths;" *charge* or *accuse* says more than "lodge a protest against."

Brief writing is not necessarily good writing; expression in a complicated world must usually be detailed, and details require words, many of them. Even publishers, who have to pay printing bills, often advise authors to "write it out," but granted that the writer uses space enough to express himself, the fewer words the better. Notice the following:

> Spring comes to the land with pale, green shoots and swelling buds; it brings to the sea a great increase in the number of simple, one-celled plants of microscopic size, the diatoms. Perhaps the currents bring down to the mackerel some awareness of the flourishing vegetation of the upper waters, of the rich pasture for hordes of crustaceans that browse in the diatom meadows and in their turn fill the waters with clouds of their goblin-headed young. Soon fishes of many kinds will be moving through the spring sea, to feed on the teeming life of the surface and to bring forth their own young.
>
> RACHEL L. CARSON, *Under the Sea Wind*

This is good writing, not because it is brief, but because it is economical. Carson is saying something more than that the mackerel, after hibernating off the continental shelf, mysteriously wake up every spring; she is fitting the annual migration of the mackerel into the impelling cycle of the seasons; explanation requires detail, and details require words. The student might try to remove one word without damaging the effect. In the last line, for instance, "teeming life" could be reduced to *life,* but the account would suffer. Note how much is implied in a passage like "hordes of crustaceans that browse in the diatom meadows." Word economy is not sparing words; it is putting them to work.

Words may have meanings that will make sense in only one "direction." It makes sense to say "Jewels have an attraction for Irene" or "Jewels attract Irene," but *attraction* will not

GUIDE TO REVISION

20f   **Dir**

Revise, substituting more accurate choices for words used to point in a "false direction."

ORIGINAL	REVISION
The Elizabethan audience had a great fascination for wars and duels.	Wars and duels fascinated the Elizabethan audience.
Once action is put forth the problems become disintegrated; therefore, let us build up our weaknesses.	Prompt action will solve many problems; therefore let us overcome our weaknesses.
Necessary financial reimbursements sent to the above address will receive my prompt attention.	I shall promptly pay any bills sent to my address.

work in the opposite direction, "Irene has an attraction for jewels," unless the writer intends the unlikely meaning that Irene somehow draws jewels to her. Consider the following sentence:

An enemy of the prairie dog never manages to approach the "town" unawares.

The writer is probably thinking of the fact that the citizens of the "town" will not be unaware, but in the sentence the word turns in another direction to modify *enemy* and convey an unintended meaning. Compare:

No enemy of the prairie dog can approach the "town" undetected.

The following sentence shifts direction in another way:

I have a very inadequate feeling when I think of writing about this book.

An "inadequate feeling" is probably possible, but probably not what was intended here. The writer probably meant to say:

> I feel inadequate when I think of writing about this book.

FOR STUDY AND WRITING

A On the following pages are entries from five recently edited American desk dictionaries. They are labeled A through E, for convenience; A and B are the same dictionaries so designated in chapter 19.

A **read·y** (red′ē) *adj.* **read′i·er, read′i·est** [ME. *redie* < OE. *ræde*, ready, prepared (for riding), akin to *ridan*, to ride, G. *bereit*, ready, ON. *greithr*, prepared, Goth. *garaiths*, arranged: for IE. base see RIDE] **1.** prepared or equipped to act or be used immediately *[ready to go, ready for occupancy]* **2.** unhesitant; willing *[a ready worker]* **3.** *a)* likely or liable immediately *[ready to cry]* *b)* apt; inclined *[always ready to blame others]* **4.** clever and skillful mentally or physically; dexterous *[a ready wit]* **5.** done or made without delay; prompt *[a ready reply]* **6.** convenient or handy to use; available immediately *[ready cash]* **7.** [Obs.] at hand; present: a response to a roll call —*vt.* **read′ied, read′y·ing** to get or make ready; prepare (often used reflexively) —*n.* [Colloq.] ready money; cash at hand (usually with *the*) —*SYN.* see QUICK —**at the ready** in a position or state of being prepared for immediate use *[to hold a gun at the ready]* —**make ready 1.** to prepare; get in order **2.** to dress

- Entry, followed by pronunciation.
- Grammatical designation.
- Comparison of adjective.
- Etymology, including Indo-European base.
- Example of use.
- Uses designated by arabic numerals, sometimes with subdivisions indicated by small letters.
- Usage label within square brackets.
- Other grammatical uses.
- Cross reference to synonyms.
- Phrases.
- Phrase having more than one use.

Webster's New World Dictionary of the American Language, Second College Edition (1970)

B **read·y** (rĕd′ē) *adj.* **-ier, -iest. 1.** Prepared or available for service or action. **2.** Mentally disposed; willing: *He was ready to believe them.* **3.** Liable or about to do something. Used with an infinitive: *ready to leave.* **4.** Prompt in apprehending or reacting: *a ready intelligence; a ready response.* **5.** Available: *ready money.* —**at the ready.** Designating a rifle in position for aiming and firing. —*tr.v.* **readied, readying, readies.** To cause to be ready. [Middle English *redy,* Old English *ræde.* See **reidh-** in Appendix.*]

- Fewer definitions than in A; what accounts for the difference.
- Some definitions cover same area, but have different emphasis; e.g., 2.
- Definition 4 seems to fuse 4 and 5 of A.
- B does not recognize verb or noun.
- B admits only one phrase; A has two uses for second phrase.
- B has reference to IE root in appendix.

The American Heritage Dictionary of the English Language (1969)

Examine the entries, using the marginal notes, and then write a paper comparing the entries, discussing them from different points of view as suggested by the notes.

C

read·y (red′ē), *adj.*, read·i·er, read·i·est, *v.*, read·ied, read·y·ing, *n.*, *interj.* —*adj.* **1.** completely prepared, in fit condition, or immediately available for action or use. **2.** willing or not hesitant: *ready to forgive.* **3.** prompt or quick in perceiving, comprehending, speaking, writing, etc. **4.** proceeding from or showing such quickness: *a ready reply.* **5.** prompt or quick in action, performance, manifestation, etc.: *a keen mind and ready wit.* **6.** inclined; disposed; apt: *too ready to criticize others.* **7.** in such a condition as to be imminent; likely at any moment: *a tree ready to fall.* **8.** immediately available for use: *ready money.* **9.** present or convenient. **10. make ready, a.** to bring to a state of readiness or completion; prepare. **b.** *Print.* to prepare and adjust a press for printing. —*v.t.* **11.** to make ready; prepare. **12. ready about!** *Naut.* prepare to tack! —*n.* **13. the ready, a.** *Informal.* ready money; cash. **b.** the condition or position of being ready for use: *to bring a rifle to the ready.* —*interj.* **14.** (in calling the start of a race) be prepared to start: *Ready! Set! Go!* [ME *redy*, early ME *rædig* = OE *ræde* prompt + *-ig* -Y¹] —Syn. **1.** fitted, fit, set. **2.** agreeable, glad, happy. **3.** alert, acute, sharp, keen. —Ant. **1.** unfit.

Survey of grammatical uses.
Largest number of uses marked with designation.
Indication of specification in use 3.
Fewer but longer examples than in A.
Some uses not recognized in other four dictionaries.
Includes synonyms and antonym.

The Random House Dictionary of the English Language (1968)

D

read·y (red′ē) *adj.* read·i·er, read·i·est **1.** Prepared for use or action. **2.** Prepared in mind; willing. **3.** Likely or liable: with *to: ready* to sink. **4.** Quick to act, follow, occur, or appear; prompt. **5.** Immediately available or at hand; convenient; handy. **6.** Designating the standard position in which a rifle is held just before aiming. **7.** Quick to perceive or understand; alert; facile: *a ready wit.* **8.** *Obs.* Here; present: used in answering a roll call. — *n.* **1.** The state of being ready. **2.** The position in which a rifle is held before aiming. **3.** *Informal* Cash: with *the.* — *v.t.* read·ied, read·y·ing To make ready; prepare. [ME < OE *ræde, qeræde + ig*, suffix of adverbs]

Different approach to defining; more use of one-word synonyms, few examples; no breakdown within uses; definitions brief but succinct.
No phrases; contrast treatment with those dictionaries that do recognize phrases.
Use of "with to," "with the."

Standard College Dictionary (1963)

E

¹ready \′red-ē\ *adj* [ME *redy*; akin to OHG *reiti* ready, Goth ga*raiths* arrayed, Gk *arariskein* to fit — more at ARM] **1 :** prepared mentally or physically for some experience or action **2 a** (1) **:** willingly disposed **:** INCLINED (2) **:** likely to do something indicated **b :** spontaneously prompt **3 :** notably dexterous, adroit, or skilled **4 :** immediately available **syn** see QUICK
²ready *vt* **:** to make ready
³ready *n* **:** the state of being ready; *esp* **:** preparation of a gun for immediate aiming and firing

Etymology more nearly like those in A and B.
Recognizes relationships within areas of meaning; e.g., 2.
Provides separate entries for verb, noun.

Webster's Seventh New Collegiate Dictionary (1971)

Close comparison of such entries as those above will do much to reveal the whole problem of meaning. For example, compare 4 and 5 under A with 4 in B. Both sets of editors have endeavored to cover the same area, which A considers two uses; B recognizes this duality by giving two sorts of examples, but makes no distinction in essential meaning. There is also a difference in the way the editors look at this use; B emphasizes the promptness; A the mental or physical state that leads to promptness.

B In judging a dictionary, the buyer or user should be alert to the word list. Does the dictionary treat a relatively rare word like *zebek* or *Zeitgeist?* Has it caught new uses of old words, such as those now used in discussions of ecology? One ready test is to note the phrases and compounds recognized in the dictionary, which older dictionaries tended to neglect. Following is the list of entries for compounds with *ready* in the five dictionaries excerpted above:

A	B	C	D	E
readymade (2 uses)	ready-made	ready-made	ready-made (3 uses)	ready box
ready-mix	ready-witted	ready-mix (2 uses)	ready-mix	ready-made (3 uses)
ready-to-wear	(1 phrase in entry)	ready room	ready money	ready room
ready-witted		ready-to-wear	ready-to-wear	ready-to-wear
			ready-witted	ready-witted
(3 phrases in entry)		(2 phrases in entry)		

Compare the lists; some dictionaries have more than others, and some have what would seem to be a better selection than the others.

C Most persons are concerned with usage, but dictionaries vary in their treatment of it. Some limit themselves to a few usage labels, like *slang, colloquial,* or *nonstandard.* Within limits this practice is defensible; a usage label gives the reader some warning, and usage is so complex that any adequate statement requires more space than most dictionary makers can afford. The method is obviously inadequate, however; usage is so varied and subtle that the state of any word cannot be described in a single, arbitrary label, and usage may change rapidly. Many dictionaries now in use still say that *teen-age* is either slang or colloquial, although most students of language would say that it is now part of standard American speech.

The following is some of the evidence concerning *myself* when used in the sense "They invited Mary and myself." Of the five dictionaries treated in the exercises above, A and E do not treat this use; C says that the use is "considered nonstandard"; D treats it as "an emphatic form of *me*" and labels it "informal." Dictionary B has what the editors call a Usage Panel, made up of a hundred selected people, to whom doubtful locutions were referred. The entry in that dictionary includes the following:

> *Usage:* The use of *myself* (for *me*) in compound objects, as in *He asked John and myself,* is condemned by 95 per cent of the Usage Panel (Gilbert Highet: "a prissy evasion of *me*"; Walter "Red" Smith: "the refuge of idiots taught early that *me* is a dirty word"). Also strongly condemned is the use of *myself* (for *I*) in subjects, as in *Mr. Jones and myself are undecided.*

Some dictionaries have relied in part upon citations to suggest

420

usage. One of these, the *New International Dictionary of the English Language,* 3rd ed., treats this usage as follows:

> (3) for emphasis instead of nonreflexive *me* as object of a preposition or direct or indirect object of a verb ⟨my income supports my wife and myself⟩

Nothing is said that suggests that this usage is in any way suspect. Since in the same dictionary other words are limited, either by usage label or by inference from the sort of citations given, we are probably entitled to assume that the editors of this dictionary meant to suggest no restrictions on the use of *myself* in this sense. The following is one of the uses of *dig: New International*, 3rd ed.:

> **6** slang a: to listen to or look at; pay attention to ⟨dig that fancy hat⟩ b: UNDERSTAND, APPRECIATE ⟨what I don't dig over there is the British money—Jimmy Durante⟩

This use is labeled as slang and the use is suggested in a familiar remark and in a quotation from a well-loved comedian. For words in better standing a more authoritative person is likely to be cited. Somewhat similarly, no usage label is given for *OK,* but the citations are suggestive of conversation: "OK, Doctor, I'll let you know," quoted from John Hersey, and "He gets the OK of the Production Code censors," quoted from Joseph Wechsberg.

More extensive discussions of *myself* can be found in dictionaries of usage. The famous volume was H. W. Fowler's *Dictionary of Modern English Usage;* as revised by Margaret Nicholson under the title *A Dictionary of American-English Usage* this work condemns the locution without question, as follows: "WRONG : *one of the party & myself.*" The same work, as revised by Sir Ernest Gowers, is somewhat more permissive; he suggests that such constructions "are best avoided." Bergen and Cornelia Evans, writing in *A Dictionary of Contemporary American Usage,* are much more detailed, as follows:

> But *myself* is also used in place of *I* or *me* in sentences where it does not reflect the subject of the verb. Some of these uses are more acceptable than others.
>
> *Myself* may always be used where the formal rules of grammar require *I* but *me* is the traditionally preferred form. That is, *myself* may be used after a linking verb, as in *the guests were myself and Alyse;* after *than, as* or *but,* as in *no man was ever better disposed, or worse qualified, for such an undertaking than myself;* and in an absolute construction, as in *Miss Wordsworth and myself being in the rear.* . . . This use of *myself* is established beyond question, in speech and in literature.
>
> *Myself* may also be used in place of *me* when it is part of a compound object, as in *he saw neither myself nor any other object in the street.* When *myself* is placed first, as it is in this example, the construction has an old-fashioned tone, but when it is the last element, as in *they invited my sister and myself,* it is normal spoken English today. It is literary English in either position.

As to "Mrs. Washington and myself adopted the two youngest children" the authors remark only that "it is now old-fashioned and is condemned by many grammarians."

The following is from Margaret M. Bryant, *Current American Usage: How Americans Say It and Write It* (New York, 1962).

Summary: Myself is most often employed as a reflexive pronoun or as an intensive in standard English, but it has a number of other standard uses: 1) as an emphatic member of a compound subject or object; 2) as a subjective complement; 3) in comparison; 4) in absolute construction. The same conclusions apply to the other persons of the reflexive pronouns: yourself, himself, herself, etc.

Myself is familiar as a reflexive pronoun (or direct object), as in "I hurt *myself*" and as an intensive (or subject appositive), as in "I *myself* did it" and "I did it *myself*." However, it has a number of other established uses in standard English, according to two extensive studies of modern prose and speech (Cherney, R. Thomas).

Data: 1. As the emphatic member of a compound subject or object. Except in poetry ("*Myself* will to my darling be/Both law and impulse"— Wordsworth), *myself* is rarely used as the simple subject in place of *I*, but the emphatic form is used as part of a compound subject, especially in informal conversational English. It has been employed in this way since the Middle English period, as Chaucer's *Canterbury Tales* testify: "Ther was also a Reve and a Millere,/. . . A maunciple, and *myself* . . ." The locution is frequent in Shakespeare ("My father and my uncle and *myself*/ Did give him that same royalty he wears" (*I Henry IV*, IV, iii, 54–55). Citations may also be given from Benjamin Franklin, Ralph Waldo Emerson, and Nathaniel Hawthorne, but more recent illustrations are: "After the frames are on the beach another fellow and *myself* ought to carry them and stack them" (E. B. White, *Harper's,* Dec., 1941, 105); "Why have Walter Hampden, Victor Jory, Ernest Truex, June Duprez, Richard Waring, Philip Bourneuf, Margaret Webster and *myself* . . . banded together and signed up . . . ?" (Eva Le Gallienne, *The New York Times,* July 21, 1946, Sec. II, 1). One commonly hears statements like: "The gang, John, and *myself* are going home" or "My wife or *myself* will attend to the matter."

Myself also occurs in a compound object, in an enumeration, not occupying first place. Two investigators (Hook, Pooley) of contemporary prose found two such usages, similar to "He invited Jane and *myself* to the play" and "Are you going to call Pat, Jane, and *myself* before you go?" *Myself,* of course, is firmly established as a reflexive object ("I cut *myself*"), an indirect object ("I bought *myself* a new bag"), and the object of a preposition ("This scene between Johnny and *myself* will explain everything"), but as a sole object of a verb, except in the reflexive sense, it is not acceptable English, according to the findings of the above-mentioned investigations.

2. As a subjective complement (predicate nominative). This construction is a common one, as in "I am (not) *myself* today." It is also used in a series, thus: "The members of the . . . force were Ronnie Green, . . . Bill Moss . . . and *myself*" (George X. Sand, *Ford Times,* Jan., 1952, 2); or in a compound subjective complement: "The other two are Mr. Stein and *myself,* and we . . . are the 'conventional' or 'traditional' prosodists" (John Crowe Ransom, *Kenyon Review,* Summer, 1956, 460).

3. In comparison. In informal English, one hears *myself* after *than* and *as:* "It was not easy for as poor a typist as *myself*"; "A force greater than *myself* had picked me up and was disposing of me" (Whittaker Chambers, *Witness,* 1952, p. 282); "They are . . . quite as capable as *myself* in answering questions" (Louis Bromfield, *From My Experience,* 1955, p. 51).

4. In absolute constructions. Examples of this kind are not frequent, according to one study already cited (Cherney), but they occur: "A number of ranchers here, *myself* included . . ." (*Wall Street Journal,* Jan. 14, 1955, 11).

The same conclusions apply to the other persons of the reflexive and intensive pronouns (*yourself, himself, herself,* etc.), but *hisself* and *theirselves.* forms of *himself* and *themselves,* are nonstandard usage.

Other evidence: Barnhart, Files; Bryant, *EJ, XLVII* (Feb., 1958), 98; Burnham, *AS,* 25 (Dec., 1950), 264–67; Hall, 175–77; Marckwardt and Walcott, 37, 71–72; *OED;* Pooley, *TEU,* 156–59; *AS,* 7 (June, 1932), 368–70; *Word Study,* 16 (Mar., 1941), 1.

Clearly, these statements vary greatly in content and in method, in the sort of evidence on which the various authors and editors rely. Nicholson says without qualification that the locution is wrong; she does not indicate how she comes to this conclusion. The editors of the *American Heritage* dictionary have taken the percentage of their panel, 95 per cent of whom condemned the locution, and they have added some comments. By inference, we probably must assume that the editors of the *New International,* 3rd ed., did not object; Bergen and Cornelia Evans say flatly that the use is "normal spoken English today." Bryant finds the use common in English for more than five hundred years. Insofar as you can determine the bases on which these persons make their decisions, how do they differ?

Now make a similar comparison. Select one of the following words, or another word whose usage interests you, look it up in at least five places, and compare the results. The dictionaries cited in this chapter are possibilities, along with dictionaries of usage like those by Fowler, Bryant, and the Evanses.

ain't, aggravate, aren't (as in "aren't I"), belly, colossal, complected, cute, dandy (as an adjective), dumb (for stupid), enthuse, finalize, guts, guy (as a noun), irregardless, less (with plural noun as in "less men"), loan (as a verb), raise (to bring up or rear a child), tummy, type (as in "a new type car")

D Consider the problem of pronunciation. Of the five dictionaries quoted above, A gives the pronunciation of *real* as either (rēəl) or (rēl), thus recognizing that the word can be pronounced with a pure vowel or a vowel plus a glide so noticeable that the whole becomes almost a diphthong. Of the remaining dictionaries, B, C, and D essentially agree, but E divides the word into two syllables and gives only the pronunciation with a diphthong, although it recognizes two possible diphthongs. Look up the pronunciations recorded for the following words in at least five dictionaries and compare the results:

1. aunt   3. laboratory   5. orange
2. glacier   4. literature   6. park

E Recalling that words have changed their meanings, look up five meanings for each of the following words, and mark them G (for generalization), S (for specialization), F (for figure of speech), CE (for cause to effect or effect to cause), or O (for other), depending on how the meaning seems to have developed:

1. bank   4. hand   7. pipe
2. chair   5. home   8. run
3. general   6. man   9. under

F Each of the sentences below is followed by words that can be synonyms for the italicized words in the sentence. Indicate which could be substituted in the sentence and explain changes in meaning that would result.

1. Her mother *pressed* her to stop using drugs. (*exhorted, urged, commanded, begged, importuned, stimulated, influenced, provoked*)

2. The general was not willing to pay the *price* of victory. (*value, charge, cost, expense, worth*)

3. Sharon felt no *fear* as she faced the microphone. (*dismay, alarm, horror, anxiety, dread*)

4. The president did not have enough *power* to enforce the rules. (*potency, puissance, strength, energy, force*)

5. Her *pride* would not allow her to dress as the other girls in the house did. (*vanity, haughtiness, superciliousness, egotism, vainglory*)

6. *Examination* of the evidence showed that the jury had been wrong. (*inquiry, inquisition, scrutiny, investigation, proposition*)

7. The judge had no *sympathy* for lawbreakers. (*pity, commiseration, condolence, tenderness, agreement*)

8. His devices were so *transparent* that nobody was deceived. (*translucent, lucid, diaphanous, limpid, luminous*)

9. The entire *company* joined in the song. (*group, throng, assemblage, flock, circle, audience, congregation, sorority*)

10. Many members of the audience were *moved* to tears. (*incited, prompted, impelled, instigated, actuated*)

G The figures of speech in the following sentences vary in complexity. Study each one in terms of the referent-thought-word relationship discussed in 20a. Then decide as specifically as you can which parts of the referent are emphasized or changed by using words metaphorically.

1. The moon was a ghostly galleon. . . . ALFRED NOYES

2. This man was hunting about the hotel lobby like a starved dog that has forgotten where he has buried a bone. O. HENRY

3. A wit's a feather, and a chief a rod;
   An honest man's the noblest work of God. ALEXANDER POPE

4. An honest God is the noblest work of man. SAMUEL BUTLER

5. A pun is not bound by the laws which limit nice wit. It is a pistol let off at the ear; not a feather to tickle the intellect. CHARLES LAMB

6.   Like our shadows,
   Our wishes lengthen as our sun declines. ALEXANDER POPE

7. I wonder why anybody wanted to wing an old woman in the leg. HILDA LAWRENCE

8. So 'tis not her the bee devours,
   It is a pretty maze of flowers;
   It is the rose that bleeds when he
   Nibbles his nice phlebotomy. JOHN CLEVELAND

9. All of Stratford, in fact, suggests powdered history—add hot water and stir and you have a delicious, nourishing Shakespeare. MARGARET HALSEY

10. Our two souls, therefore, which are one,
    Though I must go, endure not yet
    A breach, but an expansion
    Like gold to airy thinness beat. JOHN DONNE

H This exercise requires that you have various dictionaries available. At least one from each numbered group is desirable: (1) *The Oxford Dictionary of English Etymology, Klein's Comprehensive Etymological Dictionary of the English Language,* or Eric Partridge, *Origins;* (2) *A New English Dictionary on Historical Principles,* also known as the *Oxford English Dictionary,* or (much less desirable) *The Oxford Universal Dictionary on Historical Principles;* (3) *The Century Dictionary and Cyclopedia* (1889–1897, usually printed in eight to ten volumes; *not* the later one-volume abridgment); (4) *Webster's New International Dictionary,* 2nd ed.; (5) the same, 3rd ed.; (6) *A Dictionary of Americanisms* or *A Dictionary of American English;* (7) Harold Wentworth and Stuart Berg Flexner, *A Dictionary of American Slang,* or Lester V. Berrey and Melvin Ban den Bark, *The American Thesaurus of Slang.* If none of the dictionaries in group 1 is available, substitute dictionary A or B mentioned above, preferably both.

    Select one of the words from the following list and look it up in a dictionary of the seven different sorts. Then try to decide which dictionaries would be necessary if you were to write the history of the word from its appearance in Indo-European and its developments throughout the history of English to modern American slang. In some of the dictionaries you will need to be alert to the importance of cross-references:

1. check	**3.** flood	**5.** point	**7.** sweet
2. day	**4.** land	**6.** seven	**8.** white

STYLE:
TONE AND
POINT OF VIEW

CHAPTER 21

Style grows as the writer grows, as he learns to know his subject, to control his point of view, and to fill the needs of his audience.

Since the dawn of sophisticated culture, men have pondered style in writing; here are some of their observations:

A good style must, first of all, be clear. . . . It must be appropriate.

A good style must have an air of novelty, while concealing its art.

Style is the man himself.

He that will write well in any tongue . . . must speak as the common people do, but think as the wise men do.

Let your matter run before your words.

A man's style is as much a part of him as his face, his figure, or the rhythm of his pulse.

All styles are good save the boresome kind.

Style is the physiognomy of the mind.

There is no way of writing well and also writing easily.

I confess to you I love a nobility and amplitude of style, provided it never sweeps beyond its subject.

The secret of the style of the great Greek and Roman authors is that it is the perfection of good sense.

A man's style in any art should be like his dress — it should attract as little attention as possible.

I hate a style . . . that slides along like an eel, and never rises to what one can call an inequality.

The turgid style of Johnson, the purple glare of Gibbon, and even the studied and thickset metaphors of Junius are all equally unnatural, and should not be admitted.

The quotations suggest that style is engaging to discuss but hard to define precisely, or even to describe usefully. Many thinkers have written brilliantly about it, but few have said much that is at once succinct and helpful to a writer, particularly to a beginning writer. Is style "the man himself," as much part of a man "as his face," or is it "the physiognomy of the mind"? If so, is it nothing that can be acquired, except by making oneself over? Or is style something that can be learned, and if so, is it "the perfection of good sense," or should it avoid anything that can be called "a purple glare" while cultivating "an air of novelty" and "concealing its art"? Neither the philosophers nor the writers agree, nor has insight increased much with the centuries—the first two quotations above are of Aristotle—but there must be some truth in all these statements, and they are not entirely antithetical. A good reconciliation is that of Edward Gibbon: "The style of an author should be the image of his mind, but the choice and command of language is the fruit of exercise." That is, even though style may be an image of the mind, a writer can improve the image, and there are ways of learning to do this.

In a broad way, then, style is the character of a piece of writing. It is everything from cast of mind to command of language, from the organization and development of material to the drafting of sentences and the building of paragraphs. It is, in short, all things that have been the subjects of the previous chapter of this book—and of some yet to come—so that this chapter can be thought of as a summary, a wrapping-up of chapters 1–20.

Style as the Man

Within limits, Arthur Schopenhauer was surely right when he observed that "Style is the physiognomy of the mind," and although the pronouncement should not be taken too literally, either as a figure of speech or a limiting definition, it emphasizes the central characteristic of a good style: it has something to say. Fundamental in style are content, matter, meaning, information; obviously, to some degree, style is the man. For this reason, many intelligent, mentally alert, well-educated people write interestingly, even brilliantly, without ever having studied language or composition formally. The habits of mind that produce clear thinking also promote a good writing style. Many a scientist writes well, not so much because he has studied writing as because he has studied bugs or atoms. For the student, therefore, the preceding chapters of this book are almost all fundamental to the cultivation of a good style, because they are concerned mainly with the handling of content—finding a theme idea, collecting information to develop it, thinking logically about it, and so on. But some scientists who know much about bugs or atoms also write abominably. Style must be something more than "the man himself"; clumsy writers are not necessarily clumsy people, and if *clumsy* is to a degree a sliding middle term in this sentence, the fact remains that writing has its own qualities, that good writers are not necessarily good men, or vice versa.

A good style requires knowledge of a subject; it also requires knowledge of language—what it is, how it works, how it can be used. Style is the man, but a good style is the wise man using words and sentences so that they reveal him faithfully. A writer as a person has his character, but he also has what rhetoricians sometimes call his "voice," his way of expressing himself as a writer.

Style and Reading

A writing style develops, of course, in many ways, but especially from reading. Elizabethan writers like John Lyly acquired much of their ornate styles from reading Latin; nineteenth-century writers often reveal their early reading of the Bible. Probably the best single thing a student can do to improve his writing is to read. In fact, he can profitably read writers whom he admires and make a conscious attempt to learn from them, analyzing their sentences, their diction, their tone. Writers often learn by direct imitation, learning what they can from another writer and then going on to create their own styles. Chaucer, for instance, as a young man admired the French poets of his day and imitated them until he could do as well as they in their own manner—in fact, the French poets like Machaud whom he imitated are now mainly remembered because they influenced Chaucer. Then he found out about the great Italians of his time, Boccaccio and Petrarch, and imitated them. But he did not become truly himself until he had outgrown both his French and Italian models and had begun to write in his own style. Robert Louis Stevenson describes how he "played the sedulous ape"; that is, he imitated writer after writer, deliberately, until he had mastered their ways of writing. "That," Stevenson concludes, "is the way to learn to write . . . . Before he can tell what cadences he truly prefers, the student should have tried all that are possible; before he can choose and preserve a fitting key of words, he should long have practiced the literary scales."

"Perhaps," Stevenson goes on, "I hear someone cry out: But this is not the way to be original! It is not; nor is there any way but to be born so." Originality is a virtue much admired in writing, but a student cannot write originally by imitating what seems clever in some other writer. Trying to make characters talk like those of Damon Runyon or Hemingway will not in itself produce originality, nor will attempts to reproduce the superficial characteristics of an unusual style — to omit periods or capital letters, to write in incomplete sentences, to affect nonstandard diction. Originality is not mere novelty or trickery. Especially unimpressive are old favorites of student writing such as the character sketch of "my best friend" that turns out in the end to be a description of a dog or a horse, or the theme that spends five hundred words telling why the writer could not find a topic, or the narrative that ends with the revelation "and then I woke up." Most students, however, are born with originality, at least with individuality. The originality emerges in writing when the student thinks and learns enough about his topic to make the ideas he presents his own. Tricks and devices are likely to be less original than clearly conceived material presented with sincerity, directness, and simplicity.

A good style, then, emerges primarily as the writer reads and listens discerningly, develops and controls his thoughts, learns standard patterns for handling ideas in sentences and larger units of composition, and cultivates a vocabulary that will permit him to clothe his thoughts in adequate words. Efforts to develop a style mechanically or artificially almost always fail. The writer can, however, profitably focus attention on characteristics of writing particularly identified with style — on what may be called the writer's "voice," as it is revealed in tone and point of view.

The Writer's Voice

Theoretically at least, a writer is always acting, playing a role. The voice through which he communicates with his reader is, in varying degrees, one he assumes for the occasion. The writer of fiction, indeed, may assume a role quite different from the part he plays in real life, telling his story in the words of a narrator from a different position in society or a different period in history or even a different planet. J. D. Salinger wrote *The Catcher in the Rye* in the words of a teen-ager; Herman Melville adopted the voice of the sailor Ishmael to narrate *Moby-Dick;* William Faulkner in many of his stories used the voice of an itinerant sewing-machine salesman. The writer of expository prose is less obviously an actor; he is not working to create a character as his narrator. But to a degree at least he also plays a role as he writes, varying his voice according to his purposes and his audience, wearing one mask to write for a group of small children and another for the readers of a scientific journal.

The following passages illustrate rather obviously some of the different voices writers may adopt for different subjects and different audiences.

> The art of yesteryear comes vibrantly alive in the magnificent collection of Old Fashioned decorator decanters. Original hand-blown glass has become a prized collector's item, its direct and honest beauty bringing a classic charm to any setting. Washed by the light from a window the clear, liquid topaz, deep cobalt blue and limpid seagreen glass glows with a warm internal beauty. Among the designs in this collection are the Benjamin Franklin decanter, the Liberty Bell, Medicine Bottle, the Dolphin jug and nine more just as famous. Limited editions of these decanters sell for up to $25.00 or more, and the 12 in this collection represent the most precious designs in the history of American glass making. A superb decorating collection, you'll want to order several sets as special gifts.
>
> *Advertisement*

As soon as he hits the slightly pretentious archaism of *yesteryear* and the mildly romantic exaggeration of *vibrantly alive* the reader recognizes the carefully enthusiastic, confidential, soothing note that frequently appears in advertising copy. For the audience of the "first magazine for women," the writer apparently assumed that he would sell more bottles at $3.98 a dozen appealing to potential glass collectors as fellow enthusiasts adjectivally sharing with the reader the "warm internal beauty" of the "limpid seagreen glass."

The following passage, prepared for a different audience for different purposes, suggests a quite different voice.

> Academic institutions exist for the transmission of knowledge, the pursuit of truth, the development of students, and the general well-being of society. Free inquiry and free expression are indispensable to the attainment of these goals. As members of the academic community, students should be encouraged to develop the capacity for critical judgment and to engage in a sustained and independent search for truth. Institutional procedures for achieving these purposes may vary from campus to campus, but the minimal standards of academic freedom of students outlined below are essential to any community of scholars.
>
> AMERICAN ASSOCIATION OF UNIVERSITY PROFESSORS,
> *Joint Statement on Rights and Freedom of Students*

The voice here—formal, careful, proper, objective—characterized the composition of a number of serious writers collaborating on committee prose, prose that suggests no personality at all, not even the affected personality of the advertisement.

The following passage also deals with a serious subject, but the writer speaks with a different sort of voice.

> In ten years of journalism I have covered more conventions than I care to remember. Podiatrists, theosophists, Professional Budget Finance dentists, oyster farmers, mathematicians, truckers, dry cleaners, stamp collectors, Esperantists, nudists and newspaper editors—I have seen them all, together, in vast assemblies, sloughing through the wall-to-wall of a thousand hotel lobbies (the nudists excepted) in their shimmering grey-metal suits and Nicey Short collar white shirts with white Plasti-Coat name cards on their chests, and I have sat through their speeches and seminars (the nudists included) and attentively endured ear baths such as you wouldn't believe. . . .
>
> TOM WOLFE, *Pause, Now, and Consider Some Tentative Conclusions About the Meaning of this Mass Perversion Called Porno-Violence: What It Is and Where It Comes From and Who Put the Hair on the Walls*

For his *Esquire* audience Wolfe plays the role of an informal, almost chatty reporter, using contractions, working for humor in the list of conventions and the joke on nudists, working for freshness in the diction—perhaps without total success in his metaphor "ear baths." The writer here is obviously avoiding any hint of the sweetness that pervades the advertisement above, but curiously, the voice he adopts has something in common with that of the advertisement as it presses for familiarity.

In the following the writer plays the role of himself.

> In the exclusive set (no diphtheria cases allowed) in which I travel, I am known as a heel in the matter of parlor games. I will drink with them, wrassle with them and, now and again, leer at ladies, but when they bring out the bundles of pencils and the pads of paper and start putting down all the things they can think of beginning with "W," or enumerating each other's bad qualities on a scale of 1–100 (no hard-feeling results, mind you—just life-long enmity), I tiptoe noisily out of the room and say: "The hell with you."
>
> ROBERT BENCHLEY, "Ladies' Wild"

Although the writer speaks autobiographically, he is adopting a voice for the particular rhetorical occasion, assuming a particular character to introduce his anecdotes on parlor games and having this character speak in a conversational manner. How closely the character of the sketch resembles the real Robert Benchley is irrelevant.

431

Examples of this sort could be easily multiplied; theoretically the writer uses a slightly different voice for every writing situation — every subject and every audience. Very much as stock characters develop in the theatre, however, certain kinds of writing voices become stereotyped, and the writer may be tempted to select a voice by imitating a familiar sound. Role playing of this sort, by attempting to assume an attitude because it has succeeded, produces a good deal of bad writing, partly because a kind of dishonesty shows.

The linguistic role playing of the writer who adopts various voices for various composing efforts need be neither hypocritical nor insincere. The voice is part of what might be called the rhetorical stance a writer assumes as he undertakes a creative project. This stance includes the attitude he will assume toward his audience and toward his subject matter, the point of view from which he will consider his material, and the voice through which he will speak. The writer of expository prose is usually seeking the voice that will express his feelings and opinions as honestly and sincerely as possible. He may be trying to sound "natural"; but writing is a creative act, and even when the writer is seeking only to express his own personality, he adopts a tone and takes a point of view — he speaks through a voice. Style can be thought of as those characteristics of writing that reveal the voice of the writer, his individuality.

Parodies provide a ready means of studying style as an expression of a voice, since parodies are verbal caricatures that criticize a style by exaggerating, often to absurdity, some of its qualities. Of the following paragraphs, the first provides an example of a distinctive, though not necessarily distinguished, modern style, and the second is a critical parody of it.

> . . . They rushed down the street together, digging everything in the early way they had, which later became so much sadder and perceptive and blank. But then they danced down the streets like dingle-dodies, and I shambled after as I've been doing all my life after people who interest me, because the only people for me are the mad ones, the ones who are mad to live, mad to talk, mad to be saved, desirous of everything at the same time, the ones who never yawn or say a commonplace thing, but burn, burn, burn like fabulous yellow roman candles exploding like spiders across the stars and in the middle you see the blue centerlight pop and everybody goes "awww." What did they call such young people in Goethe's Germany? Wanting dearly to learn how to write like Carlo, the first thing you know, Dean was attacking him with a great amorous soul such as only a con-man can have. "Now, Carlo, let *me* speak — here's what *I'm* saying . . ." I didn't see them for about two weeks, during

432

which time they cemented their relationship to fiendish allday-allnight-talk proportions.

JACK KEROUAC, On the Road

I was just thinking around in my sad backyard, looking at those little drab careless starshape clumps of crabgrass and beautiful chunks of some old bicycle crying out without words of the American Noon and half a newspaper with an ad about a lotion for people with dry skins and dry souls, when my mother opened our frantic banging screendoor and shouted, "Gogi Himmelman's here." She might have shouted the Archangel Gabriel was here, or Captain Easy or Baron Charlus in Proust's great book: Gogi Himmelman of the tattered old greenasgrass knickers and wild teeth and the vastiest, most vortical, most insatiable wonderfilled eyes I have ever known. "Let's go, Lee," he sang out, and I could see he looked sadder than ever, his nose rubbed raw by a cheap handkerchief and a dreary Bandaid unravelling off his thumb. "I know the WAY!" That was Gogi's inimitable unintellectual method of putting it that he was on fire with the esoteric paradoxical mood. I said, "I'm going, Mom," and she said "O.K.," and when I looked back at her hesitant in the pearly mystical UnitedStateshome light I felt absolutely sad, thinking of all the times she had vacuumed the same carpets.

JOHN UPDIKE, On the Sidewalk

This style does not follow the advice of Samuel Butler, quoted above, that a style should "attract as little attention as possible." The tricks are so obtrusive that parody is relatively easy. But the parody reveals, by what it selects to ridicule, characteristics of Kerouac's style.

The parody, even though it does not refer specifically to the paragraph of the original, concentrates on the subject matter — the preoccupation of the original with "madness" for life or a "great amorous soul." But the parody also makes fun of the attitude of the original toward this abstract subject matter, its tone. By exaggerating at the same time the excessive enthusiasm of discussion and the triviality of what is discussed, the parody implies that the tone is inappropriate. In the absurdity of the "beautiful chunks of some old bicycle crying out without words of the American Noon" the parody indicates that the facts of the original do not justify the frenzied manner in which they are described. In small details, the parody catches the rhythm of the original and picks up characteristics of style — tricks like the compounded adjectives, the self-conscious images, the pretentious and vague literary allusions.

Aspects of style can seldom be separated from one another. Sentence structure, paragraph patterns, diction, are all elements of style; a style is the particular combination of choices among these elements made by a writer. But the choices are governed especially by what has been called the writer's stance, the position he takes for a particular writing task. The writer moves out of himself, communicating through a voice, adopting a tone and a point of view.

Tone: Attitude Toward Material and Audience

Tone, though a useful term, is almost as difficult to define as *style*. It is metaphorical in its meanings, used in reference to all the arts but basically connected with sound. That is, the tone of a paragraph has much the same importance as the tone of voice in which something is spoken. "Yes," spoken in different tones, can have differing effects—questioning, doubting, hesitating, acknowledging, affirming. In the same way, a composition has different effects, expresses different attitudes, depending upon its style. *Tone* is used here to refer to the quality of a piece of writing that reveals the writer's attitude toward his subject matter and toward his audience.

Compare the following passages from two student themes, written about the same central idea—that some types of advertising should be discontinued.

The general public has great faith in communications media. People tend to believe what they see and hear on television and what they read in newspapers and magazines. Advertising, therefore, that makes false claims about the values of a product or the consequences of failing to use it may cause real hardship and may eventually even harm the standing of a company.

The current campaign, for instance, to exaggerate the horrors of underarm perspiration or oily hair seems calculated to produce some kind of shift in social values. . . .

"Don't you want to kiss me again?" Gullible asked, quickly chewing her breath mint to get at the little drop of something it contained.

"I can't," he said. "That no-wetness stuff you use dries me up so much it cracks my lips." He turned away, slipped on her newly-waxed floor, fell down, and broke his neck.

"I used the wrong floor wax," she said. "If I'd used the new, shinier, harder, more glasslike plastic kind, he'd have zoomed right out the front door and the police wouldn't find the body here."

She heard a noise from the bathroom. She and her roommate, Janet Boobtubery, had taken one of those apartments they had seen on television in which, if you open the medicine cabinet you look

434

into the neighbor's bathroom. They thought it would be a nice way to meet men. But the couple next door were two elderly ladies, who had learned from the tube that women need iron more than men, and were spending their final years trying to get frisky eating pet food. Janet, looking through the medicine cabinet, had seen a jar of something she thought might make her hair lustrously manageable. But it was the cream the old ladies used for dentures, the kind the manufacturers said would never let go. It never did. Janet put some on her hair, accidentally bumped her head on the medicine cabinet, and was still dangling there. . . .

The first theme is serious and objective, an attempt to make a reasoned, logical statement; the second is ironic, exaggerated; it employs ridicule, reducing to absurdity the kind of advertising its author resents. The themes differ in *tone*—that is, in the attitude the writer takes toward his material and toward his reader.

Since tone reflects attitudes, it can vary almost infinitely. Compare, for example, the following brief passages on the same general topic—the weather.

What happens in this particular case—and it accounts for half our winter days—is simply that the cool ground of the wintry continent chills this moist, warm air mass—chills it just a little, not enough to change its fundamental character, and not all the way up into its upper levels, but in its bottommost layer and that only just enough to make it condense out some of its abundant moisture in the form of visible clouds; it is quite similar to the effect of a cold window pane on the air of a well-heated, comfortable room—there is wetness and cooling right at the window, but the bulk of the room's air is not affected.

WOLFGANG LANGEWIESCHE, *What Makes the Weather*

And spring? Ah! there is no spring in the Delta, no sense of refreshment and renewal in things. One is plunged out of winter into: wax effigy of a summer too hot to breathe. But here, at least, in Alexandria, the sea-breaths save us from the tideless weight of summer nothingness, creeping over the bar among the warships, to flutter the striped awnings of the cafés upon the Grande Corniche.

LAWRENCE DURRELL, *Balthazar*

Clearly the pieces differ in tone. Partly, of course, the differences grow from the content, but the content, the selection of materials, is determined partly by the writer's attitude. The first is informal and familiar, but its tone is mainly objective; its purpose is to inform the reader of facts. The second is concerned more to convey an impression, a "feeling" about the day, and its style and tone are different, more "poetic," more dependent on images.

Precise description of the varieties of tone is almost impossible. The writer may approach his material and his audience seriously, or he may adopt a joking or whimsical manner or both. He may promote confidence with a judicial calm, or he may stimulate action with eager enthusiasm. He may be objective, formal, informal, ironic, jovial, confidential, flattering, wheedling, belligerent, conciliatory. Aristotle describes tragedy as written in "lofty language," and the impact of poetic drama depends greatly on the formalized, nonconversational quality of verse. An encyclopedia article normally attempts an impersonal tone. The following are only a few of the more obvious approaches that may determine tone:

1. *Objective.* A telephone directory or a compilation of statutes reveals little of the opinions or prejudices of its writer, but it has tone; that is, it assumes an objective, noncommittal attitude toward its material and its readers. Many other types of writing approach a similar tone, offering material as impartially as possible. Scientific works, textbooks, histories, newspaper accounts, factual magazine articles, or informative bulletins are likely to be primarily objective in tone.

2. *Formal.* Serious writing often, though not always, promotes a formal author-reader relationship, when the author assumes in his writing a dignity and decorum dictated more by literary tradition than by the habits of ordinary speech. Consider the following selection from Emerson's essay "Self-Reliance":

> Trust thyself: every heart vibrates to that iron string. Accept the place the divine providence has found for you, the society of your contemporaries, the connection of events. Great men have always done so, and confided themselves childlike to the genius of their age, betraying their perception that the absolutely trustworthy was seated at their heart, working through their hands, predominating in all their being.

The tone of planned, formal expression appears in the vocabulary, in the patterned, balanced rhythm, in the elevated manner. The tone suits Emerson's subject and purposes; a similar manner would be embarrassingly inappropriate for a student theme pleading for softer seats in the gymnasium.

3. *Informal.* Much modern writing gains the allegiance of the reader by an intimate, genial manner. Charles Lamb's essay "Old China" establishes an informal tone at once:

> I have an almost feminine partiality for old china. When I go to see a great house, I inquire for the china-closet and next for the picture-gallery. I cannot defend the order of preference, but by saying that we have all some taste or other, of too ancient a date to admit of our remembering distinctly that it was an acquired one.

Lamb chats with his reader, observing neither forms nor ceremony. His essay may have a serious purpose, but it remains friendly, informal.

4. *Emphatic, enthusiastic.* Especially in fiction, writers may heighten style and overstate for emphasis. Observe an emotional scene in Charles Dickens' *Bleak House:*

> I saw before me, lying on the step, the mother of the dead child. She lay there, with one arm creeping round a bar of the iron gate, and seeming to embrace it. She lay there, who had so lately spoken to my mother. She lay there, a distressed, a sheltered, senseless creature.

The context may justify the highly rhetorical, figurative style, although out of context the passage sounds inflated. Such a tone conveys emotion, but unjustified, it rings false.

5. *Understated.* A different tone permeates Norman Mailer's account of a death in *The Naked and the Dead:*

> Abruptly he heard the mortars again, and then right after it a machine gun firing nearby. A couple of grenades exploded with the loud empty sound that paper bags make when they burst. He thought for an instant, "There's some soldiers after them Japs with the mortar." Then he heard the terrible siren of the mortar shell coming down on him. He pirouetted in a little circle, and threw himself to the ground. Perhaps he felt the explosion before a piece of shrapnel tore his brain in half.

In contrast to the heightened style of Dickens, the passage from Mailer treats a death with almost exaggerated restraint, using colloquial language, emphasizing facts rather than describing emotions. Many modern writers, especially, use understatement, letting the facts rather than the style convey the desired emotion.

6. *Ironic.* Compare the following passage from *The Pickwick Papers* with the passage from *Bleak House* quoted above.

> Rising rage and extreme bewilderment had swelled the noble breast of Mr. Pickwick, almost to the bursting of his waistcoat, during the delivery of the above defiance. He stood transfixed to the spot, gazing on vacancy. The closing of the door recalled him to himself. He rushed forward with fury in his looks, and fire in his eye.

437

The two passages by Dickens differ in tone. In *Bleak House* the tone is dramatic and tense, in keeping with the narrator's discovery of the dead mother. In *The Pickwick Papers* the scene shows a humorous character reacting to a belligerent little doctor who has just said, "I would have pulled your nose, sir." The incident is dramatic but not tragic, and the tone is ironic. That is, the reader understands from the context that he is not to interpret words literally — that the breast of Mr. Pickwick is more "noble" in size than in courage, that the "fury" in Mr. Pickwick's looks or the "fire in his eye" is more ludicrous than frightening. Irony may vary from this sort of tolerably subtle whimsy to bitter sarcasm. It may be the tone of a sentence like a young man's "Aren't you afraid we'll be early?" to a girl who has kept him waiting in the dormitory hall until the play is half over. It may be the tone of an entire essay like Swift's famous "Modest Proposal," suggesting that if Irish children are to be starved they had as well be butchered. Writing may be ironic whenever a statement in its context suggests a sense different from — often opposite to — its literal meaning.

The possible variations on these or other approaches are infinite; good writing requires a tone appropriate to the writer, his material, and the reader. Usually what seems most "natural" to the writer works best. Some variety in style and tone is inevitable, even desirable, but in general a writer should adopt a tone suited to his subject and maintain it. A writer or speaker may assume an easy, conversational manner to introduce his subject and become more terse, more dramatic, more persuasive as he moves into the body of his composition. A conclusion may differ somewhat in tone from the evidence that has preceded it. A violent shift in tone may be deliberate and striking, but skillful writers generally avoid sharp shifts of tone, and they never shift tone without good reason.

APPROPRIATENESS OF STYLE AND TONE 21a

A writer adjusts his style and tone to be appropriate both to his subject and to his audience — to the circumstances in which he is writing. The style of a columnist ridiculing the foibles of bargain-hunting shoppers differs from that of a sociologist trying to explain why a juvenile delinquent may kill for fun. An editorial writer for a college newspaper may discuss student membership on faculty committees as a serious requirement of a democratic society, or he may take an ironic approach, ridiculing the administration's fear of student influence; a writer for the audience of a metropolitan paper is more likely to treat the subject lightly. Neither writer, however, would be likely to comment humorously on a large-scale violation of a national border that carried threats of war. An economist would use quite different approaches in a paper prepared for a learned society analyzing the financial structure of a beach community, in a report to a corporation on the same community as a site for a shopping center, and in a letter to his wife suggesting that the community would be a pleasant place for a vacation. Situations and purposes for writing vary so much that any "rules" for appropriateness are dubious, but the following observations may be useful to the student writer.

1. *Suitability.* Creative writing may reflect only the author's sense for significance, but most expository and argumentative writing must be suited to the audience. Much writing, most newspaper writing, for example, should be understandable by all adults. The writer of popular works should avoid rare words and complex constructions, and even in semipopular writing he should explain any terms not in common use. But popular writing is not the only kind of useful writing. Most good writing for children will bore intelligent adults. Conversely, a theoretical physicist would be justifiably irked if, in reading a learned paper on his speciality, he was constantly interrupted by explanations of matters familiar to every graduate of Physics 1 — but not to every layman. Good professional music criticism may baffle even a learned reader who does not know music; much good philosophy written for philosophers will inevitably be unreadable for many of us. Most writing should be guided by the audience for which it is intended; usually, student writing is directed toward a semipopular audience, but the student should learn, also, to do more specialized writing upon occasion. Many college students are preparing for careers in which their most important writing will be specialized or technical.

2. *Maturity and taste.* The student writer needs to remove himself far enough from his subject matter to view it objectively, with perspective. The student whose theme describes with a straight face the glories of winning a first prize at a 4-H fair — "the most important moment of my life" — may be unintentionally humorous.

3. *Sincerity and simplicity.* Conscious efforts to adopt a style usually fail. They sound insincere, affected, or merely pompous. The kind of sports writing, for example, that relies on calling a baseball a pill or the old apple is likely to sound false and weary, not clever and racy. The theme that tries to be impressive by referring to Shakespeare as the bard or the swan of Avon is likely to sound trite and juvenile. Sinclair Lewis in *Babbitt* burlesques the affected high style of some society-page prose:

21a **Tone**

*Adapt tone to the material and the audience and avoid
unwarranted shifts in tone.*

ORIGINAL

Why must students go on gulping down rehashed lectures, which were dull fifty years ago? Why should young adults suffer through the harangues of profs who have never learned to teach, whatever they may know about the love life of the frog? Why are students never listened to? I ask you, must all courses be irrelevant?

Our committee decided that so far as learned (?) pronouncements from self-constituted experts (?) are concerned, we had had it, and . . . .

[*The tone of neither paragraph is well suited to serious discussion, and the attitude of the writer shifts unaccountably. The attempted humor of the second paragraph is not more convincing than the bombast of the first.*]

Graduation from high school is a very important event, often shaping much of a person's future career in life. It is a time of commencement, not of ending. But it also is a time when a person realizes the importance of the hard struggle that has carried him successfully through four years of heartbreaks and triumphs. When those wonderful words of congratulation ring out after the awarding of diplomas, every graduate knows a thrill that he will never forget. It is truly a wonderful moment.

[*The tone of overstatement and high seriousness is not justified by the occasion, and the passage does more to reveal the immaturity of the writer than to convince a reader.*]

REVISION

Our committee considered the abuses cited by various students — that many professors repeated dull lectures, now long out of date; that some lecturers were more concerned with their specialities than with the needs of their students, that the reasonable complaints brought by students were seldom listened to, and that many courses were not relevant to modern needs. We decided that the first steps toward reform might come from a questionnaire that would permit students to evaluate faculty members . . . .

[*The writer, by speaking with a different, less petulant voice, establishes himself as a person worthy of attention, and the consistency of his restrained tone gives his ideas more chance for acceptance.*]

To the high school graduate, commencement may seem the most important event in life. The parade in white dresses and blue suits or caps and gowns, the music with all the ringing discords of which a nervous school orchestra is capable, the grim, freshly scrubbed faces, the earnest platitudes of the student orations, all convince the graduate that this is the real turning point of his life. He leaves certain that he will never forget a moment of what has occurred, and a year later he may actually remember something of it.

[*A lighter tone, with factual details replacing the overstatement, leads to a less naïve paragraph. Other approaches would have been possible.*]

When the light of day next os-mosed through our hero's case-ment it discovered the would-be Romeo and mighty guzzler with a disturbance in that portion of his anatomy known as the cranium that was so perceptible that it resembled nothing so much as the activities of a jackhammer. In short, he was, to use the vernacular, hanging over.

[*Some readers may find this mildly amusing the first time through, but a discerning person is likely to resent a cheap attempt to show off.*]

Jeffrey was half awake with the pain throbbing in his temples. He fought his way under the covers, but he could not escape the sense of smothering. He tried with his right hand to block off the sunlight from the window, but he could not get things quite right. His head kept pounding, and his eyes hurt. He struggled up, dizzy and blinking.

[*The revision is not funny, but it does not sound affected, and it says much more than did the original.*]

'Twixt the original and Oriental decorations, the strange and deli-cious food, and the personalities both of the distinguished guests, the charming hostess and the noted host, never has Zenith seen a more recherche affair than the Ceylon dinner-dance given last evening by Mr. and Mrs. Charles McKelvey to Sir Gerald Doak. Methought as we—fortunate one!—were privileged to view that fairy and foreign scene, nothing at Monte Carlo or the choicest ambassadorial sets of foreign capitals could be more lovely. It is not for nothing that Zenith is in matters social rapidly becoming known as the choosiest inland city in the country.

For a sample of a style that is perhaps more subtly bad than society-page prose, consider the following from a contemporary mystery novel:

The black gabardine suit she wore instead of the electric-blue gown seemed to have been stroked to her form by a sensitive young sculptor who fell in love with his creation and let his sensual imagina-tion run wild. She walked toward him with slow grace, and he saw the tautness that made her red mouth seem completely imperious, in the firm mold that some mistake for courage.

And for a moment he was trapped again, like a small boy looking at the grandest, most sparkling and magnificent red wagon he has ever seen. She was the chrome and polished enamel, the speed and the powerful promise of the low-slung car shining through the win-dow from the plush interior of the showroom.

WILLIAM L. ROHDE, *Murder on the Line*

The effort in the writing shows; neither the prose nor the lady is as seductive as the writer apparently intended; the description does not ring true.

For most purposes the student writer does best to write sin-cerely, naturally, simply, directly.

4. *Objectivity and emotion.* Directness and sincerity become a virtue of style and tone especially when the writer tries to convey emotion. As in life buckets of tears do not measure the depth of grief, so in writing multiple superlatives do not reveal sincerity of emotion. If emotion is there, it will be conveyed best by a straight and objective presentation. Writing that tries to milk more emotion than the facts warrant is *sentimental*—false in its emotion.

5. *Humor.* Humor usually profits from a straight face. Notice, for example, the style of the following brief excerpt from James Thurber's reminiscences:

> One day General Littlefield picked our company out of the whole regiment and tried to get it mixed up by putting it through one movement after another as fast as we could execute them: squads right, squads left, squads on right into line, squads right about, squads left front into line, etc. In about three minutes one hundred and nine men were marching in one direction and I was marching away from them at an angle of forty-five degrees, all alone. "Company, halt!" shouted General Littlefield. "That man is the only man who has it right!" I was made a corporal for my achievement.
>
> *My Life and Hard Times*

The writer lets the humor grow from the facts. Intended humor may fail because the writer relies on overworked tricks—stale quips or slang intended to suggest a blasé style, attempts at exaggerated, thesaurus-inspired wit ("In elucidating that toothsome phenomenon characterized among the ranks of the intelligentsia as granulated cow. . ."), or irony with a question mark to explain the joke ("The instructor started his clever? lecture"). These devices can be, and have been, successfully used, but they usually amuse the writer more than the reader.

POINT OF VIEW   **21b**

Compare the following passages describing the same scene from the reign of terror that followed the French Revolution:

> The call to plunder was received with enthusiasm, and in the morning of the 25th of February a troop of women marched to the Seine and, after boarding the vessels that contained cargoes of soap, helped themselves liberally to all they required at a price fixed by themselves, that is to say, for almost nothing. Since no notice was taken of these proceedings, a far larger crowd collected at dawn of the following day and set forth on a marauding expedition to the shops. From no less than 1200 grocers the people carried off every-

21b **PV**

*Revise to maintain a point of view preserving
consistency in place, time, and person.*

ORIGINAL

   From my corner I could see the
long platform of the subway station
stretching dimly beside the tracks.
A girl clicked through the turnstile
and sat at once on the bench beyond the change booth. The street
was empty and quiet. For a moment
there was no rumble of trains, no
sound of voices—a frightening
silence.

   [*The third sentence shifts the point of
view by making the reader change the
position he has assumed to imagine the
scene.*]

   The play begins with a scene on
the castle walls of Elsinore. Horatio,
a friend of Hamlet, met the soldiers
who were on watch and learned
from them about the ghost that had
appeared. Then as the soldiers were
talking, the ghost, dressed in full
armor, appeared again.

   [*The writer, as he proceeds, perhaps begins to think of his experience in
reading or seeing the play rather than
the play itself. After one sentence he
changes tense.*]

   If you want your campfire to be
both safe and useful, you have to
build it carefully. You have to begin by selecting a good place for
the fire. One should be sure that
there are no trees within ten feet
of the site and that all leaves and
brush have been cleared away.

   [*The writer begins with* you *as his
subject but shifts in the third sentence
to* one, *for no apparent reason.*]

REVISION

   From my corner I could see the
long platform of the subway station
stretching dimly beside the tracks.
A girl clicked through the turnstile
and sat immediately on the bench
beyond the change booth. For a
moment there was no rumble of
trains, no sound from the street
above, no voice—a frightening silence.

   [*The revision retains the detail of
the original, but presents it from the
point of view already established.*]

   The play begins with a scene on
the castle walls of Elsinore. Horatio,
a friend of Hamlet, meets the soldiers who are on watch and learns
from them about the ghost that has
appeared. Then as the soldiers are
talking, the ghost, dressed in full
armor, appears again.

   [*The revision consistently considers
the play as a piece of literature still in
existence that can therefore be referred
to in present time.*]

   If you want your campfire to be
both safe and useful, you must build
it carefully. Begin by selecting a
good place for the fire. You should
be sure that there are no trees within
ten feet of the site and that all
leaves and brush have been cleared
away.

   [*Changing* one *to* you *keeps the
point of view consistent. The writer
might, of course, have used* one *and he
instead of* you.]

thing on which they could lay their hands — oil, sugar, candles, coffee, brandy — at first without paying, then, overcome with remorse, at the price they themselves thought proper.

NESTA H. WEBSTER, *The French Revolution*

And now from six o'clock, this Monday morning, one perceives the Bakers' Queues unusually expanded, angrily agitating themselves. Not the Baker alone, but two Section Commissioners to help him, manage with difficulty the daily distribution of loaves. Softspoken, assiduous, in the early candle-light, are Baker and Commissioners: and yet the pale chill February sunrise discloses an unpromising scene. Indignant Female Patriots, partly supplied with bread, rush now to the shops, declaring they will have groceries. Groceries enough: sugar-barrels, rolled forth into the street, Patriot Citoyennes weighing it out at a just rate of elevenpence a pound; likewise coffee-chests, soap-chests, nay cinnamon and clove-chests, with *aqua-vitae* and other forms of alcohol, — at a just rate, which some do not pay; the palefaced Grocer silently wringing his hands!

THOMAS CARLYLE, *The French Revolution*

The passages differ in various ways, but perhaps most obviously in point of view — that is, in the position in space and time from which the writer looks on his subject. The first writer assumes that she is looking back on events of the past, describing them objectively. The second pretends that he is on the scene as the events happen and asks the reader to join him in watching the events as they occur. As part of his rhetorical stance, the writer adopts a point of view in space and in time and also in the person he assumes himself to be, in the voice he adopts; usually he needs to maintain this position consistently throughout his composition.

The writer of a treatise on philosophy may not need to worry much about the position in space he assumes. In a description, however, and in some other expository composition, location may be important. The writer of a description needs to decide where he is in relation to the scene he is describing. He may, of course, pretend simply that he is located in some spot of heavenly omniscience from which he can describe everything. For a sharper sense of reality, he may pretend to stand in a specific place, from which he can logically describe only what would be within his range of vision.

A position in time is necessary in any kind of writing, and maintaining it consistently can be difficult, requiring the writer's constant attention as well as care in the tense of verbs. In a narration the writer is likely either to assume that he is looking back from the present, as in Webster's paragraph on the French Revolution above, or to pretend that he is recording events as they occur, as in Carlyle's paragraph. An expository composition, such

444

as a term paper on Shakespeare, may involve a variety of times such as those implied in the following:

1. Shakespeare *was* thirty-eight years old when the first edition of *Hamlet* appeared in London.

2. He *had earned* a reputation as one of the leading dramatists of his day.

3. *Hamlet has been discussed* and *criticized* more than any of the other plays.

4. It *is* a favorite on the modern stage.

5. In the play Hamlet *is faced* with a decision.

6. Ironically the only course consistent with Hamlet's character and satisfactory to the audience *leads* to disaster.

The first sentence indicates the basic attitude of the writer; he is in the present writing of events in the past. The second mentions what has occurred *before* the past time of the first. The third concerns what has occurred continuously and indefinitely in the past. The last three treat the play as it exists at the time the writer is discussing it.

There is a story that Harold Ross, long the editor of *The New Yorker,* had a favorite criticism of a cartoon: "Who's talking?" He would demand that the artist open the speaker's mouth wider or otherwise indicate who was responsible for the words in the caption. The writer may have more trouble than the cartoonist in showing who's talking, but he has to do it. Usually the writer uses the third-person approach for objectivity: "Student government requires," "The new teacher entered." He may want to assume a more personal relationship and describe events or facts in the first person as he saw them: "I observed student government," "My new teacher saw me." He may, although it is out of fashion except in some newspapers, avoid *I* by using the editorial *we,* a device for shifting the responsibility for a statement by suggesting that the entire newspaper accepts it: "We believe that student government requires." In a slightly different sense, *we* is often used — as it is in passages in this text — to indicate people in general: "We use pronouns to stand for nouns," or more particularly, the author and his audience: "We have had occasion earlier to notice." In a narrative the writer may speak objectively but recount events from the point of view of a main character: "George soon discovered that student government requires." The possibilities are numerous; the writer should be consistent enough to keep the reader from confusion.

A Following are two paragraphs, the first a selection from a novel and the second a selection from a parody of the style of the novelist. Write a discussion of the parody as a representation or criticism of the novelist's style. Is the parody fair? What specific qualities of the novelist's style does the parody exaggerate?

1. Sight of the old gilt clock had made Arthur Winner think of his father — indeed, the room was full of such mementos. A little-disturbed museum, its collection, informal and unassuming, preserved evidences of that many-sided mind, of the grasp and scope of interests, of perceptions so unobtrusive as to be nearly private, of quiet amusements and quiet enjoyments. Seeking Arthur Winner Senior's monument, you could look around you. You could ask yourself, for example, how many lawyers — or, to give the point proper force, how many small-town lawyers, born and brought up in a fairly-to-be-called rural county seat like Brocton — would, fifty or more years ago, have had the interest — let alone, the taste, the eye — to pick over, unaffected by then current ideas of what was fine or beautiful, of what was rare or valuable, the then next thing to junk — the secondhand, the old-fashioned, the discarded — and select, exchanging a few dollars for them, exactly the items that the antique trade (at that time hardly born) was going to look on as prizes half a century later. Would you guess one in a thousand, or one in ten thousand?

   JAMES GOULD COZZENS, *By Love Possessed*

2. Author Winner sat serenely contemplating his novel. His legs, not ill-formed for his years, yet concealing the faint cyanic marbling of incipient varicosity under grey socks of the finest lisle, were crossed. He was settled in the fine, solidly-built, cannily (yet never parsimoniously, never niggardly) bargained-for chair that had been his father's, a chair that Author Winner himself was only beginning to think that, in the fullness of time, hope he reasonably might that he would be able (be possessed of the breadth and the depth) to fill. Hitching up the trousers that had been made for his father (tailored from a fabric woven to endure, with a hundred and sixty threads to the inch), he felt a twinge of the sciatica that had been his father's and had come down to him through the jeans. Author Winner was grateful for any resemblance; his father had been a man of unusual qualities; loyal, helpful, friendly, courteous, kind, obedient, cheerful, thrifty, brave, clean and reverent; in the simplest of terms: a man of *dharma*.

   FELICIA LAMPORT, "James Gould Cozzens by Henry James Cozened"

B Following are selections from varied types of prose, some modern, some earlier. Describe what seems to you the "stance" of the writer of each, the point of view and the tone; then discuss how the tone is revealed in each paragraph. Since the passages are taken from their contexts, you may wish to check your judgment by consulting the whole works.

1. Although I had been baffled in my attempts to learn the origin of the Feast of Calabashes, yet it seemed very plain to me that it was principally, if not wholly, of a religious nature. As a religious solemnity, however, it had not at all corresponded with the horrible descriptions of Polynesian worship which we have received in some published narratives, and especially in those accounts of the evangelized islands with which the missionaries have favoured us. Did not the sacred character of these persons render the purity of their intentions unquestionable, I should certainly be led to suppose that they had exaggerated the evils of Paganism, in order to enhance the merits of their own disinterested labours.

HERMAN MELVILLE, *Typee,* chap. xxiv

2. In taking up the clue of an inquiry, not intermitted for nearly ten years, it may be well to do as a traveller would, who had to recommence an interrupted journey in a guideless country; and, ascending, as it were, some little hill beside our road, note how far we have already advanced, and what pleasantest ways we may choose for further progress.

JOHN RUSKIN, *Modern Painters*

3. Of recent years there has been a noticeable decline of swearing and foul language in England; and this, except at centres of industrial depression, shows every sign of continuing indefinitely, until a new shock to our national nervous system — such as war, pestilence, revolution, fire from Heaven, or whatever you please — revives the habit of swearing, together with that of praying. Taking advantage of the lull, I propose to make a short enquiry into the nature and necessity of foul language: a difficult theme and one seldom treated with detachment.

ROBERT GRAVES, "Lars Porsena"

4. "And who is this? Is this my old nurse?" said the child, regarding with a radiant smile a figure coming in.

Yes, yes. No other stranger would have shed those tears at sight of him, and called him her dear boy, her pretty boy, her own poor blighted child. No other woman would have stooped down by his bed, and taken up his wasted hand, and put it to her lips and breast, as one who had some right to fondle it. No other woman would have so forgotten everybody there but him and Floy, and been so full of tenderness and pity.

CHARLES DICKENS, *Dombey and Son,* chap. xvi

5. The King? There he was. Beefeaters were before the august box; the Marquis of Steyne (Lord of the Powder Closet) and other great officers of state were behind the chair on which he sate. *He* sate — florid of face, portly of person, covered with orders, and in a rich curling head of hair. How we sang, God save him! How the house rocked and shouted with that magnificent music. How they cheered, and cried, and waved handkerchiefs. Ladies wept; mothers clasped their children; some fainted with emotion. People were suffocated in the pit, shrieks and groans rising up amidst the writhing and shouting mass there of his people who were, and indeed showed themselves almost to be, ready to die for him. Yes we saw him. Fate cannot deprive us of *that* . . . that we saw George the Good, the Magnificent, the Great.

WILLIAM MAKEPEACE THACKERAY, *Vanity Fair,* chap. xlviii

447

6. I suppose you could call it a frame. But it wasn't like no frame that was ever pulled before. They's been plenty where one guy was paid to lay down. This is the first I heard of where a guy had to be bribed to win. And it's the first where a bird was bribed and didn't know it.

RING LARDNER, "A Frame-up"

7. John B. Smith takes the stand.
   Q. Mr. Smith, are you familiar with the clichés used in football?
   A. Naturally, as a football fan. . . .
   Q. Mr. Smith, as an expert, what lesson do you draw from the game of football?
   A. Life is a game of football, Mr. Sullivan, and we the players. Some of us are elusive quarterbacks, some of us are only cheer leaders. Some of us are coaches and some of us are old grads, slightly the worse for wear, up in the stands. Some of us thump the people in front of us on the head in our excitement, some of us are the people who always get thumped. But the important thing to remember is—Play the game!
   Q. How true!

FRANK SULLIVAN, "Football Is King"

8. Animals talk to each other, of course. There can be no question about that; but I suppose there are very few people who can understand them. I never knew but one man who could. I knew he could, however, because he told me so himself. He was a middle-aged, simple-hearted miner who had lived in a lonely corner of California, among the woods and mountains, a good many years, and had studied the ways of his only neighbors, the beasts and the birds, until he believed he could accurately translate any remark which they made.

MARK TWAIN, "Jim Baker's Blue-Jay Yarn"

9. It is true to nature, although it be expressed in a figurative form, that a mother is both the morning and the evening star of life. The light of her eye is always the first to rise, and often the last to set upon man's day of trial. She wields a power more decisive far than syllogisms in argument, or courts of last appeal in authority. Nay, in cases not a few, where there has been no fear of God before the eyes of the young —where His love has been unfelt and His law outraged, a mother's affection or her tremulous tenderness has held transgressors by the heart-strings, and been the means of leading them back to virtue and to God.

T. L. HAINES and L. W. YAGGY, The Royal Path of Life

C Revise the following passages so that the point of view is consistent:

1. A person who wants to get something out of his classes must do more than simply the required work. You can often get a degree by doing just the minimum, but you cannot get an education that way.

2. At the beginning of the play Romeo was very much in love with Rosalind. He seemed almost amusing as a lovesick youth. Then he meets Juliet, and at once he is madly in love with her. The sudden change was not convincing to me.

3. No matter how carefully one plans, you can always count on forgetting something.

4. The six main streets of the town spread out like spokes of a huge wheel, whose hub was the courthouse circle where I walked. I started toward Grand Avenue, which runs north, and could see traffic lights flashing for eight or ten blocks up Grand. As I stopped to look into the window of a book store with a display suggesting that it specialized in office supplies more than in books, several girls passed me and went into a place farther down the block, that had a sign reading "Discotheque." They were dressed like hippies, with long, straggly hair and lots of beads. While the door was open the beat of rock music filled the street. A rock combo was writhing and stamping on a low platform. The girls looked around for partners, and I considered going in, but instead sauntered west toward Grand Avenue.

5. When I first read the story I thought Hemingway was interested mostly in the two killers who come into the restaurant and inquire about Ole. They were revealed through their clipped speech and their attempts to bully the boys in the diner. Most of the story seems to concern them. Nick did not speak very often.

6. If you expect people to take you seriously, you must take time to think about what you say. It is not enough to speak with conviction or pound the table with enthusiasm. One must know what he is trying to do and have a plan for doing it.

7. After he ate the soup and finished the huge salad, he began to regain his cheerfulness.

8. *Huckleberry Finn* is more than a children's book. Huck, of course, is interesting to children. He was always doing something exciting. I can remember still how interested I was when I first read the book. But the novel has ideas in it that appeal also to an adult mind.

D In the nineteenth century, two contemporaries wrote philosophies of clothes. One, ecstatic, philosophical, and violent, was the work of Thomas Carlyle. The other, moral, pedantic, doctrinaire, was an editorial by Louis A. Godey, editor of *Godey's Lady's Book*. The "paragraph" below has been made by mixing selections from these two accounts. Naturally, the tones of the two are quite different. Judging by the tone, try to sort out the sentences so that you get two consistent accounts. The sentences occur in the same order they had in the original versions. The following might be used as a topic sentence for the selections from Carlyle: "Man's earthly interests are all hooked and buttoned together, and held up, by Clothes." The following would serve as a topic sentence for the passages from Godey: "The Bible, as our readers well know, is the standard of authority by which we test the right or the wrong of ideas and usages; nor can we comprehend the full import of clothing or its advantages unless we look at the evil results that follow neglect of or disobedience to this law of necessity for the human race, ever since 'the Lord God clothed' the first man and woman before sending them out of Eden."

[1] Clothing has nine distinct phases of teaching the philosophy of its usefulness. [2] It gives covering, comfort, comeliness; it marks cus-

449

tom, condition, character, and civilization; it symbolizes Redemption through Christ, and the holiness of the saints in Heaven. [3] Society sails through the Infinitude on cloth, as on a Faust's mantle. [4] Strange enough, it strikes me, is this same fact of there being Tailors and tailored. [5] The Horse I ride has his own whole fell; the noble creature is his own sempster, and weaver, and spinner. [6] A clothing of rags symbolizes wretchedness, wickedness, ignorance, imposture, or imbecility. [7] While I—good Heaven—have thatched myself over with the dead fleeces of sheep, the bark of vegetables, the entrails of worms, the hides of oxen and seals, the felt of furred beasts. [8] Nakedness is savagery, or shameless sin, or extreme misery. [9] Heathenism has no darker shadow on its God-forsaken horizon than the half nude millions on millions of its worshipers; until these people are clothed, neither China nor India can become Christian countries. [10] Day after Day I must thatch myself anew; day after day this despicable thatch must lose some film of its thickness, till by degree the whole has been brushed thither, and I, the dust-making, patent Rag-grinder, get new material to grind on. O subter-brutish! vile! most vile! [11] Wherever Christian civilization prevails, as in Europe and America, dirt and disorder in a household or in dress are proofs of ill-conditioned or ill-trained people. [12] For have not I too a compact all-enclosing Skin, whiter or dingier? Am I a botched mass of tailors' and cobblers' shreds, then; or a tightly-articulated, homogeneous little Figure, automatic, alive? [13] The dress must be decent before we can have confidence in the character of any person. [14] For my own part, these considerations, of our Clothes-thatch, and how, reaching inwards even to our heart of hearts, it tailorizes and demoralizes us, fill me with a certain horror at myself, and mankind. [15] We feel and judge thus intuitively, because the instincts of humanity tell us that without decent clothing there cannot be real delicacy of feeling or true dignity of mind, unless the 'miserable' suffers from the sins of others. [16] And this does not weaken the force of our moral of dress—that there is or has been wrong doing wherever we see people badly or indecently clothed. [17] There is something great in the moment when a man first strips himself of adventitious wrappings; and sees indeed that he is naked, and, as Swift has it, 'a forked straddling animal with bandy legs'; yet also a Spirit and unutterable Mystery of Mysteries.

E Biblical scholars recognize that the Old Testament we know is made up of several older versions edited into one by breaking up the earlier accounts and running them together. Two of these versions are called *P* and *JE*, *P* standing for a version supposed to have been the Priests' Code, and *JE* for a more popular account combining two versions, in one of which the Lord is called Javeh, and in the other Elohim. Thus, whatever the reason for the Bible's appearing in this form, many of the Old Testament stories are told twice, and naturally the style differs in the two versions. For example, here are two accounts of early days in the Garden of Eden in the King James Bible, but with modern punctuation and paragraphing. The first is from *JE*.

Now, the serpent was more subtil than any beast of the field which the Lord God had made, and he said unto the woman, "Yea, God hath said, 'Ye shall not eat of every tree of the garden?'"

> And the woman said unto the serpent, "We may eat of the fruit of the trees of the garden, but of the fruit of the tree which is in the midst of the garden, God hath said, 'Ye shall not eat of it, neither shall ye touch it, lest ye die.'"
> And the serpent said unto the woman, "Ye shall not surely die."

Now try to describe this passage. For what sort of reader does it seem to be intended? What is the content? How would you characterize the style? Next, study the following passage from *P.*

> This is the book of the generations of Adam. In the day that God created man, in the likeness of God made he him, male and female created he them; and blessed them, and called their name Adam, in the day when they were created. And Adam lived an hundred and thirty years, and begat a son in his own likeness, after his image, and called his name Seth. And the days of Adam after he had begotten Seth were eight hundred years, and he begat sons and daughters.

Now try to describe the audience, the content, and the style of this passage and contrast it with that from *JE.*

The following is a continuous passage from chapter 11 of Genesis, which contains material from both *P* and *JE.* Identify the passages from each and determine where the break or breaks come. Enumerate as many differences in style as you can with which you distinguish the two versions.

> And the whole earth was of one language, and of one speech, and it came to pass, as they journeyed from the east, that they found a plain in the land of Shinar, and they dwelt there.
> And they said one to another, "Go to, let us make brick, and burn them thoroughly," and they had brick for stone, and slime they had for mortar. And they said, "Go to, let us build us a city and a tower, whose top may reach unto heaven, and let us make us a name lest we be scattered abroad upon the face of the whole earth."
> And the Lord came down to see the city and the tower, which the children of men had builded, and the Lord said, "Behold, the people is one, and they have all one language, and this they begin to do. And now nothing will be restrained from them, which they have imagined to do. Go to! Let us go down and there confound their language, that they may not understand one another's speech."
> So the Lord scattered them abroad from thence upon the face of all the earth, and they left off to build the city. Therefore is the name of it called Babel, because the Lord did there confound the language of all the earth, and from thence did the Lord scatter them abroad upon the face of all the earth.
> These are the generations of Shem: Shem was an hundred years old, and begat Arphaxad two years after the flood. And Shem lived after he begat Arphaxad five hundred years, and begat sons and daughters. And Arphaxad lived five and thirty years, and begat Salah, and Arphaxad lived after he begat Salah four hundred and three years, and begat sons and daughters.

451

If you wish to check the accuracy of your guess, the break comes between the ninth and tenth verses in the King James numbering. If you care to pursue this study and make a more elaborate distinction between the styles of *P* and *JE,* the following include suitable passages in the King James numbering; the Douay Version differs slightly: Genesis 5:1–28 *(P)*; 5:29 *(JE)*; 5:30–32 *(P)*; 6:1–8 *(JE)*; 6:9–22 *(P)*; 7:1–5 *(JE)*; 7:6 *(P)*; 7:7–24 *(JE)*; 8:1–5 *(P)*; 8:6–12 *(JE)*; 8:13–20 *(P)*; 8:21–22 *(JE)*; 9:1–17 *(P)*; 9:18–27 *(JE)*; 9:28–29, 10:1–7 *(P)*; 10:8–19 *(JE)*; 10:20 *(P)*; 10:21 *(JE)*; 10:22–23 *(P)*; 10:24–30 *(JE)*; 10:31–32 *(P)*.

DISCUSSION, EXAMINATIONS, IMPROMPTU WRITING

CHAPTER 22

Impromptu composition requires special focus on an immediate topic.

The principles we have been considering in this book apply in various ways to many different sorts of writing — to poems and plays as well as to technical reports and newspaper editorials. For students they apply most immediately to classroom activities, in which students constantly find themselves required to explain what they know — to participate in a discussion, to answer examination questions, to write an impromptu theme, to discuss a poem or a film, to report the results of a library investigation. All of these types of writing develop most readily through combinations of the general and the specific. Even a brief comment in class is more convincing if it states a proposition clearly and supports this generalization with specific evidence, if it points toward a main topic or toward an instructor's question.

Discussion

Discussion can be thought of as cooperative communication, in which two or more people work together to comment on a topic. It differs from a speech or an essay because more than one person participates, and each speaker from time to time responds to a commitment somebody else has made. Commonly it progresses as a sequence of questions and answers.

Questions are useful in a discussion to keep talk going. In a class discussion both students and instructor can use questions to clarify and to direct, but some kinds of questions are more useful to discussion than others. A question requiring only a brief, factual answer — "How many lines in a sonnet?" — may allow an instructor to check a student's preparation or a student to get a bit of information; but it may end rather than stimulate a discussion. Such a question might be followed by another, however, from either a student or the teacher, that could start more talk — for example, "What are the advantages of writing in a form that limits you to fourteen lines? Aren't some ideas more or less than fourteen lines long?" The second question may be loaded, including something of the questioner's opinion in it, but it opens the way for further comment. Questions in a discussion may call for opinion and interpretation — "Does that poem of Rod McKuen say more to young people than older ones?" or "What kind of man is Willy Loman in *Death of a Salesman?*" A class discussion is intended to illuminate a subject by exposing it to a variety of ideas, and questions should be directed to that end. Some questions merely delay progress, including those that are muddy in their phrasing or are desperate attempts to convince the instructor of the student's interest.

Questions may be more comment than question. In the most famous recorded discussions, the dialogues of Plato, the basis of the "Socratic method," Socrates asks questions that embody his own view and require only that his listener agree or disagree. But usually an answer is more enlightening than a question and harder to produce. The key to fruitful participation in discussion is to develop comments in the ways suggested earlier, by generalizing clearly and by using specific details and illustrations as support. Discussion succeeds when the participants develop careful answers to questions and respond to other comments by explaining any disagreement they may have or by adding any support that may occur to them.

Television interviews, like those conducted on *Meet the Press*, illustrate how questions and comments can be skillfully handled. For example, Anthony Quinn, a widely experienced American actor, was asked how he would distinguish between American and British dramatic interpreters. He replied that he thought that Shakespeare had phrased the distinction in the line "To be, or not to be, that is the question." He then went on to explain. The best British actors, he said, like John Gielgud and Lawrence Olivier, were the product of exacting training. They had learned to act, at least in part to project character and emotion without entirely participating in either. Their training and their art had led them not to try "to be" the person in whose role they were cast, but to create the impression of this person by using the techniques they

454

had learned. On the other hand, he pointed out, no such rigorous training for actors exists in America, and hence an American actor does try to be the person he portrays. Quinn illustrated from his own experience. He had been cast in the part of Quasimodo in *The Hunchback of Notre Dame,* and had tried so hard to comprehend what being a monster would be like that his face and body had become contorted. Doctors had to labor with him to get him back to his normal self.

Quinn's answer shaped itself into the pattern of a standard expository paragraph. Playing on the well-known line from Shakespeare, he opened with a topic sentence that committed him to explain the special meaning he was giving *to be.* He thus provided a basis for organizing his comment in two parts. He first discussed British acting, showing how British trained actors do not try "to be." He then turned to American actors, explaining why they do try "to be" and illustrating with a striking example from his experience. Quinn had undoubtedly thought often before about the topic, probably had answered the specific question before. The student in a class discussion is likely to be neither as experienced in extemporaneous speaking as Quinn nor as lucky in getting a question he has already thought about. But he can work toward the kind of organized and developed comment Quinn produced.

The Examination Paper

The question-answer procedure becomes more formal in the examination, which is intended not as an exchange of ideas but as an opportunity for a student to reveal the knowledge he has acquired and his understanding of its significance. There is some justification in the student complaint about examinations that "They don't want to know what you know, but what you don't know"; but generally examinations are thought of positively, and the student's best approach is to try to use them to express his views as well as he can.

Oral examinations have some advantages because they proceed much like discussions and both the questioner and the student can direct comments toward subjects about which the student can talk. In a good oral examination the questioner is likely to explore until he finds a subject that the student seems to know about and then to press the student to develop the subject as far as he can. The student can respond by admitting frankly when he has no information—bluffing seldom works—and then framing careful and well-developed answers when he has something to say.

In colleges, written examinations are most common, and they take many forms. Most types, however, even the various short-answer ones, are designed to do more than test memory. Statements to be marked *true* or *false,* questions requiring a choice from among a number of alternative suggestions, or questions with blanks to be filled all allow the student to handle ideas in the ways this book has been suggesting. Questions that require some kind of free response—ranging from those that ask for a one-sentence definition to those that specify a topic for an extended essay—challenge the student most directly to display his writing ability.

Preparing for Examinations

An answer to an examination question, like any other kind of writing, works best after some kind of prewriting, some preparation. The examination paper is different, however, since it is impromptu and since the writer almost always is under pressure to work fast. Preparation for an examination is therefore especially important. In one sense this preparation occurs over the entire period of the course, and a few frantic hours of black coffee and borrowed notes will not substitute for eight weeks of attention. Nevertheless some systematic review, planning for writing, can be helpful.

1. *Learning Facts.* Education is not merely learning facts; history is not knowing dates and literature is not associating works with their authors. Knowledge of facts is not the end of a course of study, but it is usually a necessary preliminary to the more important ends. Thinking and understanding are thinking and understanding about something.

A good examination question is not likely to request merely a recitation of facts, but a good answer to any question will need facts to support and develop its statements. The difference between a C or D answer and an A answer may reflect the amount of information the writer can supply to bolster his arguments. More particularly, a good answer requires plenty of precisely chosen detail, but to select just the right details the student must have a variety to choose from.

Merely reading a textbook or a set of notes over and over, hoping to remember enough from the exposure to get by, is not an efficient way of learning. The student is much more likely to remember if he thinks of facts in groups, as they relate to subjects.

456

For example, if he is studying the history of the English language, he can make his information manageable by fitting together historical events that influenced the development of English. He will already remember the date 1066 for the Norman invasion of England, and he can make a start toward remembering other influences by relating them to this, working back in time to the Scandinavian invasions of England or to St. Augustine and the introduction of Continental Christianity in 597, or working ahead to the Renaissance. Or the student reviewing a physics course can remember formulas better if he groups, for example, those relating to electricity and if he thinks of them as meaning something, not just as numbers or letters.

2. *Relating Facts.* This procedure for learning facts implies relating facts, and the student preparing wisely for an examination thinks about how one set of facts may be compared with another, about the significance of facts. In a sense, he tries to anticipate the questions he will be asked—not by trying to psychoanalyze his instructor or by collecting guesses from other students, but by trying to pick out the important topics that have been considered in the course and to think about what can be said about them. For any course many specific questions are possible, but the number of general subjects likely to be stressed is limited. If the course has included a series of essays on the military draft as a means of maintaining a peacetime army, the student can anticipate certain types of questions: comparing the views of one essay with those of another; discussing, with examples from the essays, the advantages or disadvantages of a conscription system or a volunteer army; analyzing the logic of one or more of the essays. In a course in history the student can anticipate questions that ask him to analyze causes, to trace the development of an institution like the Supreme Court or the British parliament, or to evaluate the influence of religion or of revolutionary writing during a particular period in history. Very often lecture notes, the textbook, and exercises or questions in a textbook suggest ways of organizing ideas and information.

The anecdote concerning Anthony Quinn, related above, suggests a good technique for review. The student should ask himself the best questions he can think of and draft oral answers. He should start with a carefully thought-out topic sentence and develop it with concrete evidence. If he finds he does not have the evidence, he knows what to review. This device will tend both to direct his study and help to fix key material where it will be readily at hand—and he may even find that he has use in an examination for the paragraph he has already composed in his mind.

A few commonsense, practical considerations are worth mentioning because under the pressures of time they are often forgotten. The most obvious is to check directions carefully—to observe any specifications on the form the answer is to take, such as a limitation on length; to note whether any choice among questions is allowed; to be aware of all the parts of a question. Usually the student does well to scan the entire examination before writing anything and to allot time for answering each question, allowing a few minutes after finishing for checking.

The most obvious advice is to read the question carefully. Short-answer questions depend primarily on careful reading, seeing all the implications of a false-true question or weighing carefully the relative accuracy of multiple-choice alternatives, of which more than one may come near to the best answer. For questions requiring essay answers careful reading is the first step in planning an answer.

A question specifies the kind of statement of a main idea, the kind of committing statement, that should direct the answer. Particularly because of limits on time, therefore, the student should start an answer by directing it precisely as the question prescribes, paying attention to qualifications in the question. If a question reads "What were the political reactions to Lincoln's Emancipation Proclamation of 1863?" the answer should not ignore the qualification in the word *political*. A survey of events leading to the proclamation, a discussion of the effects of the proclamation on slaves in the South, or speculation about Lincoln's humanitarian motives would not be relevant to the main point of the question. An answer should also be developed with strict attention to the differences between introductory words like *how, why, what,* and *when* and phrases like "the reasons for," "the purposes of," and "the effects of." If a question reads "Why did the movement for racial equality become especially prominent in the 1960's?" an answer is not adequate if it becomes a plea for tolerance or a set of examples to show that inequalities still exist. When the question is not phrased as a question, the verb that carries the main predication of the sentence needs particular attention. Verbs like the following appear regularly in questions phrased as directions, and the success of an answer may depend on the writer's ability to interpret their meaning accurately: *explain, discuss, comment on, describe, narrate, construct, reconstruct, trace, defend, analyze, outline, compare, contrast, develop, argue, justify, illustrate, cite evidence for, list, name, review, define, identify, clarify.* Following are samples of different types of questions and suggestions about how they might be analyzed.

1. *Describe the procedures required for amending the Constitution of the United States.*

The question is precise, requiring only an organized presentation of information. A good answer might begin with a summary statement: "The Constitution of the United States provides for amendments through a process of action by the legislature and ratification by the various states." It might then be organized in two parts, the first listing in chronological order the steps required for taking an amendment through the Congress and the second outlining the procedures and requirements for ratification by the states.

2. *Did the New Deal of the 1930's effect any changes in the fundamental structure of American government?*

A question of this sort might technically be answered with a simple *yes* or *no*, but obviously if such a question appears in an essay examination it implies that the answer not only express an opinion but justify it. Often, as in this case, there is no right or wrong answer. Here the answer turns on an interpretation of "fundamental structure." A *yes* answer would need to describe the specific changes that occurred as a result of New Deal policies, indicating the sense in which the writer considers the changes fundamental. A *no* answer might discuss various New Deal policies and argue that they had no lasting effect on the structure of the government. And a *yes–no* answer might also work, showing the kinds of changes the New Deal policies made and explaining the senses in which the changes were and were not "fundamental."

3. *Discuss George Orwell's* 1984 *as a comment on the importance of freedom of speech.*

The question restricts the answer to a single aspect of the satire in Orwell's novel, but it suggests an answer that generalizes about the criticism in the book and then illustrates with detail. The answer might begin with a statement like "Orwell's *1984* emphasizes the importance of freedom of speech by presenting the absence of free discussion as one of the notable instruments of tyranny in his imaginary totalitarian world." The answer could then describe in detail some of the manifestations of restrictions on free speech in the world of the novel—the development of Newspeak, the uses of censorship to mold opinion, and the ultimate loss of the ability to think independently because of the regulations on expression of ideas.

4. *Compare and contrast attitudes toward war in Heller's* Catch-22 *with those in Hemingway's* A Farewell to Arms.

The question requires comparison and thus suggests an answer divided into two parts. The writer might discuss attitudes toward war in one novel and then the other, or he might prefer a division on the basis of points of difference or similarity, with the attitudes in each novel discussed for each topic. A generalization might open the discussion and provide a basis for unifying it — for example, "Although they describe two different wars, *Catch-22* and *A Farewell to Arms* both look at war realistically; but whereas Hemingway's novel implies an underlying respect for war, Heller's satirical approach suggests something nearer tolerant contempt." After a general opening comment the student could describe passages from each novel illustrating his initial contention. Questions requiring comparisons appear frequently on examinations in many subjects — comparison of two literary characters, of two economic theories, of two ways of solving a mathematical problem, of two paintings of a similar subject. The word *compare* implies noticing both similarities and differences, but since some people insist that comparison excludes contrast many instructors, like the one who drafted the question above, discourage misunderstanding by using both words.

5. *The character Fortinbras is sometimes omitted in productions of* Hamlet. *Does his omission in any way weaken the play? Discuss any importance he may have in the presentation of central themes of the play.*

This longer question requires pulling together a number of bits of information and some interpretations of the play. The question provides a focus and a limitation — on the character of Fortinbras. It also requires some consideration of basic themes of the play and of the character of Hamlet. The answer, again, might begin with a generalization — for example, "Fortinbras serves as a foil to Hamlet, a representation of what he is not but might have been, and therefore is important to the play in helping to define Hamlet's character and in developing themes of the play." The answer could proceed by illustrating different parts of this generalization — citing scenes or incidents in which Fortinbras presents a contrast to Hamlet and then supporting the contention that this contrast contributes to characterization and to expression of themes. A question of this sort is usually intended to give the student a chance to show that he can do original thinking and can organize his thoughts. He will do well to rise to the opportunity.

6. *"Without aid from Europe the colonists would never have been successful in the American Revolution." Discuss this statement.*

Questions written around a quotation are usually intended to stimulate speculation or even disputation. Usually there is no "right" answer and no need for the answer to take a single side or attitude. An answer to the question above might consider arguments both to support and to contradict the statement. The answer might lead the student to describe as precisely as possible what aid the colonists did receive from Europe, to explain how that aid affected their cause, and to suggest what might have occurred had there been no such assistance. A question of this sort has inevitably been chosen with care; the student should read it with unusual attention.

Writing Essay Answers and Impromptu Themes

Many examination questions are like the samples above, but others are not, and each examination question becomes a particular exercise in impromptu writing. All impromptu compositions, however, whether of examination answers or impromptu themes, which are common classroom exercises, present some special problems. They must be written in a limited time, usually with not much leisure for thinking about the specific question or topic, and without much time for revision or rewriting. The student may spend too many minutes developing a relatively minor point, one not central to the main question or topic, leaving insufficient time for the main subject. The student may be tempted to pick the first familiar-sounding words in a question and start writing. Such a student, writing an examination in American history and crammed with information about the Revolutionary War, may face a question like "How significantly did the American Tories affect the progress of the Revolutionary War?" He notices hastily that the question involves the war, on which he has been concentrating his review, and launches into a chronological account of campaigns and strategies. Later he is surprised to discover that his answer was unsuccessful because it was not directed to the point of the question.

Even for impromptu writing a few minutes spent in preliminary planning are not wasted. If the topic for an impromptu theme is announced in advance, the student can prepare a rough outline and think about specific illustrations he may use, keeping his plan in mind as he writes. For unannounced questions or topics, rough notes for a plan jotted in the margin or on scratch paper may speed and improve the writing. Since impromptu writing does not allow time for elaborate planning or complex organization, a scheme working from a unifying statement of a main idea and illustrating it specifically usually works best. And one practical help for framing a topic statement for an essay answer is to begin—at least in thinking about the answer—with a statement using the exact words of the question. An answer to the question "What were the major characteristics of Surrealist art?" might begin "The major characteristics of Surrealist art were . . . ." As in most writing, the devel-

461

opment that follows the statement of the main idea works best when it includes specific illustrations and examples. In timed examinations the student should always reserve time enough to correct spelling and punctuation errors and to make minor revisions.

FOR STUDY AND WRITING

A Following is a short excerpt from a television interview on *Meet the Press,* November 15, 1970, with Lord Clark, who had recently completed a television series and a book, *Civilisation.* Study the excerpt and then answer the questions following it.

[1] MR. SPIVAK: Lord Clark, you say in your book *Civilisation,* and I quote, "One must concede that the future does not look very bright." Upon what then do you base your feeling that we are not entering a new period of barbarism?

LORD CLARK: On my experience of the young people in provincial universities in England. That may not be a wide enough ground to base an opinion on, but I see a lot of them. I'm the chancellor of the university. I make it my business to meet all the young people I can. They are extremely bright-minded; they learn very difficult courses. They have open minds, and I think they are probably as intelligent and as aware of the arts and of the importance of civilization as any generation has been.

[2] MR. SPIVAK: Yet you finished the book by writing, and again I quote, "One may be optimistic but one can't exactly be joyful at the prospect before us" for the future of civilization. Isn't that hedging your bet? Aren't you being pessimistically optimistic or optimistically pessimistic?

LORD CLARK: That is exactly how I feel. I feel that the young people are very bright and intelligent, and there is a lot of hope to be found there.

On the other hand, I think that the crushing weight of mechanization, to mention only one of the things that are bringing us down, may in the end prove stronger than any group of young people can be.

[3] MR. SPIVAK: You also say that you cannot define civilization in abstract terms, but you think you can recognize it when you see it. What are some of the signs by which you recognize our civilization today?

LORD CLARK: That isn't so hot because in fact the visible signs today are not very reassuring. I can't say I recognize very great signs of civilization in modern painting and modern sculpture. That may just be because I am getting old. I don't even recognize it in the greater part of what you might call current international architecture, which seems to me very monotonous and very much the same all over the world, and lacking in a sense of scale and proportion. So, insofar as I have committed myself to saying I recognize civilization by looking at Notre Dame or the Place de la Concorde or whatever it may be, I must say, no, what I see now doesn't reassure me very much.

[4] MR. SPIVAK: Aren't those the symbols — the signs of civilization? Those aren't the things that make our civilization, are they? Aren't there other things and men that make our civilization, and aren't those the final signs —

LORD CLARK: Yes, of course, there are. That I have overplayed, and it is a very proper criticism of the whole series that law and philosophy and many other aspects of human activity don't get enough of a show. The reason for that is perfectly simple. This was a television performance, and the people had to look at something.

Every now and then of course I got stuck with a subject which I had to mention, like the growth of the free economy, the banking economy in Holland, and I had to think of some trick so that people would still have something to look at. That is why I went around the canals in Holland on a boat.

1. Discuss the connections between the four questions. To what extent are they framed to move the discussion in a sequence of related topics?

2. Does Lord Clark answer all the questions directly? Consider especially the answer to the third question.

3. How fully are Lord Clark's answers developed? Mention one or two specific details that he uses as illustrations.

4. What is the general attitude toward the future of civilization expressed by Lord Clark in these answers?

5. Think of a possible fifth question to follow the last question of the selection.

B Following are a number of possible questions that might appear in essay examinations on various subjects. You will probably not have information to produce full answers to most of them, but for each write a comment, similar to the comments above, indicating what the question requires of an answer, how you might approach an answer, what kinds of information a good answer would require.

1. What is the doctrine of laissez faire in economics?

2. Compare attitudes toward life expressed in Browning's "Rabbi Ben Ezra" and FitzGerald's translation of *The Rubáiyat of Omar Khayyám.*

3. What evidence is there that racial differences do not affect intelligence?

4. Describe one difference between the basic philosophical principles of Plato and Aristotle.

5. Outline the procedures for extracting the square root of a number.

6. In what ways does Shakespeare's *The Tempest* conform to the classical dramatic unities?

7. What are the most important characteristics of a sonata?

8. Can the principles of Mendel's law be applied to heredity in human beings?

9. How did attitudes of the national government of the United States during the period following the Civil War retard the development of the South?

463

10. Is there any evidence that television programs have an influence on the behavior of children under six years of age?

11. According to the advocates of the system, what are the advantages of using the International Teaching Alphabet in the teaching of reading?

12. Describe innovations in composition that appeared in paintings of the Italian Renaissance.

13. What is the relation of the sentence "Good fences make good neighbors" to the main theme of Robert Frost's poem "Mending Wall"?

14. In what respects could Arthur Miller's play *The Price* be said to fit Aristotle's analysis of tragedy?

15. How important was federal legislation to the progress of the Civil Rights movement in the 1960's?

C Frame three questions that you think might be asked in courses you are taking. Then write an answer to one of them.

WRITING ABOUT
LITERATURE

CHAPTER 23

Critical writing develops general observations about a literary
work with specific details from the work itself.

Writing and reading are so intimately connected that one inevitably
involves the other; accordingly, study of composition usually
includes some attention to literature. Literature provides ready
illustrations of rhetorical principles. A sonnet shows how form and
organization can work; a good poem illustrates precision and economy in diction; a short story or novel may demonstrate the value
of direct sentence patterns. Thus writing about literature has
double value for a study of writing; it encourages analysis of the
kinds of techniques the student himself is learning, and it provides
interesting and manageable subject matter. People like to talk
about the books they have read or the films they have seen.

Discussions of literature may take many forms — casual comments about the exciting episodes in a novel or the unusual costumes in a movie, blurbs on a book jacket intended mainly to
promote sales, informative summaries in a newspaper book review,
essays that use the work of literature only as a starting point for
an independent comment on some related subject, book-length
analyses of the works of a writer or of a literary genre. Literary
criticism may be primarily subjective, attempting to describe the
feelings and insights of the reader; or it may be primarily objective,
attempting to analyze the work, to show how it is constructed and
how it achieves its effects. It may attempt to evaluate, although deciding that a work is good or bad is not an essential requirement of
literary criticism. It may discuss the themes of a novel and their
relation to contemporary social problems, may concentrate on

details of a poem's diction and prosody, may emphasize the staging of a play, or may relate a work to the life of its author or consider its place in literary history.

Partly because of the diversity of literary criticism and the knowledge it demands of a critic, to a student a paper about literature may seem a formidable assignment—after all, most serious literary criticism depends on wide reading and extended study of the development of literature. Faced with a multiplicity of opportunities, the young writer may miss all of them by turning to one of two extremes—either attempting so little that his paper is insignificant or attempting so much that he cannot cope with it.

The most frequent example of the first extreme is the paper that becomes only a paraphrase or a summary of events:

> *Othello* is a very interesting play. In the beginning two men who do not like Othello, Iago and Roderigo, are talking, and Iago says that he is unhappy because he has not got a promotion. Then they go to Brabantio's house and wake him up to tell him that his daughter has run away with Othello. Brabantio goes out looking for Othello, finds him, and accuses him of bewitching his daughter. . . .

A good summary is not easy, and frequently a summary of the plot of a story or of a scene or a paraphrase of a poem may be a useful part of a paper. A summary may also be a useful exercise for a writer in preparing a paper. But the paper that does nothing but retell a story adds little to the story itself. People are interested in reading about literature because comparing their experience with that of others may give them new insights or fuller appreciation. A simple summary adds very little.

At the other extreme the student writer may attempt a project so ambitious that he finds himself relying on broad generalizations, critical clichés, and the opinions of other critics. For example, he decides to write on "The Significance of *Othello* in the Development of Tragedy." He has read some other tragedies, but not many; he finds a book on the history of tragedy that helps him somewhat, but he lacks background to make full use of it. He quotes from the book, but the quotations do not ring true in the paper because they do not relate closely enough to the writer's own views and experience. He can make general statements about the development of tragedy by relying on his reference book, but he cannot illustrate them. This kind of paper may sound like a parody of literary criticism, echoing phrases and lacking substance. At its worst, such a paper becomes emptily pretentious, tending to assert as if it were a discovery that Shakespeare was "a master of the art of depicting characters" or that his plays "reveal a deep insight into human nature."

This chapter does not attempt a discussion of the complex techniques of literary criticism, but it suggests one way in which the student can write about literature without being trivial and without exceeding the bounds of his knowledge. Our suggestion is that the student deal primarily with the work itself but that he focus his discussion on some set of characteristics of the work. That is, we are suggesting that a theme about literature can be developed with the same general procedures suggested in this book for any expository writing—by settling on a central idea and developing it with information from the story or poem or play being criticized.

Following are some of the kinds of considerations that may produce ideas for writing about literature. Obviously not all possibilities are included, and the topics are not mutually exclusive. They are suggested as different ways of focusing or unifying discussion, not as ways of limiting it. Thus a paper centering on the themes of a story may well include analysis of the characters as they contribute to the expression of the theme, or a paper on characterization may include discussion of imagery as it distinguishes characters.

Meaning: Theme

Although Archibald MacLeish in "Ars Poetica" says that "A poem should not mean/But be," most works of literature mean in some way, and sometimes a worthwhile paper explains what or how they mean. At its simplest such a paper is explication, telling what words and sentences say and imply. A Shakespeare sonnet, for example, might warrant a line-by-line interpretation. Discussion of the meaning of a ballad like "Edward" or "Lord Randal" might comment on the story that is implied by the poem but not directly told:

> "Lord Randal" does not tell a story, does not use the methods of narrative, but a story is obviously behind it. Lord Randal is poisoned and about to die. We are not told how or why or by whom he was poisoned, but when he tells his mother that he had his dinner with his true-love and that she gave him "eels boiled in broth," we make an obvious connection. We are not told anything about the mother's feelings for his true-love, but the mother's quick suspicion makes us confident that the two were not totally compatible. The poem progresses with a series of hints about the narrative it implies. . . .

This explanation of one version of the ballad is only part of a longer discussion, but treatment of imagery and the emotional force of the poem are unified about this explanation. Sometimes a discussion of meaning requires examining the background of a story or poem. A paper on Stephen Crane's *Red Badge of Courage*, for instance, might explain scenes of the novel by providing information about military tactics during the Civil War, or it might illuminate the scene in which the hero's arm is amputated by describing surgical techniques of the period. An explanation of George Meredith's sonnet "Lucifer in Starlight," might include the information presupposed by the poem about the myth of Lucifer, the archangel who rebelled against God and was thrown out of heaven. On the basis of such background the paper could explain how Meredith's poem develops the myth.

A discussion of meaning in a literary work, however, may expand to treat its themes. A theme may be defined as what the literary work says about its subject. That is, the theme is not just a general subject—charity, or integrity, or war—it is what the work says or suggests about that subject, that charity may be a disguise for hypocrisy or that war is humiliating to those who participate in it. A theme may be directly stated, with the story clearly devoted to illustrating it. Or it may be implied. A work may have no obviously expressible theme, or it may have several. Usually the theme is complex enough so that a single sentence expresses it only inadequately.

Reading, obviously, should not become a hunt for a message or a moral. A story or poem does not necessarily attempt any high-sounding observations about life. But almost any literary work tends to extend its implications, to stretch the reader's vision. Nathaniel Hawthorne's *Scarlet Letter* is essentially a story about a portion of the lives of a few characters, but inevitably the problems of an individual like Hester Prynne suggest similar problems as they apply to women in general and ultimately stimulate us to think about broader problems. The novel makes a number of comments on human behavior: that a guilty conscience can destroy a human being, that rigid and arbitrary codes of behavior can do more harm than good, that Puritanism was partly based on hypocrisy, that hate can destroy as surely as guilt. These are not necessarily *the* themes of the novel, but they represent the kind of thematic statement that might serve as the central idea for a paper on the novel. A student might use a statement like one of these as his main idea and then discuss various aspects of the novel—characterization, point of view, setting, or handling of dialogue—as they illustrate or clarify this main concept.

A paper on themes in Andrew Marvell's poem "To His Coy Mistress" might begin thus:

Marvell's "To His Coy Mistress" is most obviously a plea for seduction, like many other poems of its time developing the theme that, since life is short, one should live for the moment. The dramatic speaker develops logical arguments to convince the lady that her coyness is a crime, to urge "Now let us sport us while we may."

In the first section of the poem he describes with amusing exaggeration the leisurely course their love might take if they had "world enough, and time." He would spend a hundred years praising her eyes, "Two hundred to adore each breast:/But thirty thousand to the rest." In the second section. . . .

As the poem develops, however, broader implications of the theme emerge, and the poet seems to be exploiting the fairly conventional argument to make observations on time and its effects on life. The first section speculates about a kind of timeless state, extending both before and after the present—he would love "ten years before the Flood." In the second section he returns to reality, hearing "Time's wingèd chariot" and seeing "deserts of vast eternity" ahead. And then in the third section. . . .

The paper could be filled out with details from the poem supporting further the observations about themes.

Voice: Point of View and Tone

The writer's voice, as indicated in chapter 21, is especially important in any sort of creative writing, and generalizations about point of view and tone often provide a focus for a paper about literature. For example, Browning's "My Last Duchess" is presented in the words of a dramatic speaker, the Duke of Ferrara, speaking as if he were observing events as they occur. Although he is discussing the inadequacies of his most recent duchess with an emissary arranging for his marriage with his next, the reader is interested also in what he reveals about his own character. A paper focusing on the voice in the poem might move in any of several directions. It might imply a generalization like "Browning's 'My Last Duchess' develops dramatic irony because the reader interprets the words of the speaker in more than their literal sense." The paper could employ examples from the poem illustrating how the duke reveals more than he intends. Or the paper might begin with a statement like "Told from any other point of view Browning's 'My Last Duchess' would have turned out to be a quite different poem." The essay could then speculate about the effect the poem would have if told by an omniscient observer looking back at the events or told by the emissary from the prospective new duchess or by one of the servants.

Analysis of fiction can also focus on point of view and tone. Sherwood Anderson's story "I'm a Fool" begins as follows:

> It was a hard jolt for me, one of the most bitterest I ever had to face. And it all came about through my own foolishness, too. Even yet sometimes, when I think of it, I want to cry or swear or kick myself.

Almost immediately the reader can form an impression of the narrator, also the protagonist in the story. A paper might show how the reader's interests and sympathy are influenced by the use of a first-person narrator. Point of view may also provide focus for a study of a novel; a paper, for instance, dealing with the point of view of Joseph Conrad's *Victory* might show how the novelist uses as first-person narrator an outside observer, who is able to report on the other characters almost as an omniscient narrator. The paper might show how the use of the first person provides a feeling of intimacy but how the novelist, by keeping the narrator free from involvement in the story, is able also to examine events through the eyes of several characters.

Characterization

Since literature is usually about people, a discussion of characters or of characterization provides one ready way to organize a critical paper. Dozens of books and articles attempt to analyze *Hamlet* by describing the main character or by discussing Shakespeare's methods of revealing him. Criticisms of the novels of Dickens frequently focus on the characters, pointing out, for example, the differences between the rounded portrait of David Copperfield and the more limited sketches of flat characters like Mr. Micawber or Mrs. Gummidge. Following is the beginning of a description of Juliet in *Romeo and Juliet:*

> The first thing to mark about Juliet, for everything else depends on it, is that she is, to our thinking, a child. Whether she is Shakespeare's fourteen or Brooke's sixteen makes little difference; she is meant to be just about as young as she can be; and her actual age is trebly stressed. Her tragedy is a child's tragedy; half its poignancy would be gone otherwise. Her bold innocence is a child's, her simple trust in her nurse; her passionate rage at the news of Tybalt's death is easily pardonable in a child, her terrors when she takes the potion are doubly dreadful as childish terrors. The cant saying that no ac-

470

tress can play Juliet till she is too old to look her should therefore go the way of all parroted nonsense. A Juliet must have both the look and the spirit of a girl of from fourteen to sixteen, and any further sophistication—or, worse, a mature assumption of innocence—will be the part's ruin. One must not compare her, either, to the modern girl approaching independence, knowing enough to think she knows more, ready to disbelieve half she is told. Life to Juliet, as she glimpsed it around her, was half jungle in its savagery, half fairy tale; and its rarer gifts were fever to the blood. A most precocious young woman from our point of view, no doubt; but the narrower and intenser life of her time ripened emotion early.

HARLEY GRANVILLE-BARKER, *Prefaces to Shakespeare*

The passage begins with a general opinion about Juliet—that she is a child—and illustrates this thesis with incidents from the play and arguments. It is the beginning of a longer discussion of her character, which traces the events of the play as she motivates them and as they affect her.

An author can reveal his characters in several ways, depending on his medium. In a novel or story he may describe the character directly, sometimes at length, sometimes with careful details about experience, sometimes with a view of how the character's mind works. In a script for a play or film such direct description is limited to stage directions, but the dramatist has the advantage of an actor who becomes the character. A director can, in fact, establish certain broad outlines of characterization almost at once by the character's appearance—most obvious in conventions like the moustache of the melodrama villain or the white hat of the hero in the Western movie. In any work of literature the author most frequently reveals a character through what he says and does. Browning in "My Last Duchess" never describes the duke of Ferrara, but the duke reveals his arrogance and pride and cruelty through his choice of words; he resents that the duchess ranked his "gift of a nine-hundred-years-old name/With anybody's gift," and he points out carefully that he chooses "never to stoop." In Conrad's *Victory* the character of Schomberg is established by his cruelty to the girl Lena. The author also can present one character by recording how others react to him or what they say about him, and the reader interprets these reactions in the light of his understanding of all the characters. When Polonius reports that Hamlet is mad for love, the reader weighs this pronouncement against what he already knows about both Hamlet and Polonius—especially the evidence he has seen that Polonius' insights are not always wise.

A theme about literature, then, can discuss the ways in which the author reveals his characters, considering how much he depends on direct description or how much he tells us of their appearance. Such a paper might distinguish whether some characters are included only to make a particular point in the plot, whether some seem stock characters more reminiscent of other novels than of the world, whether some seem to exist mainly to illustrate a theme or idea. In some plays, for example, characters do not have names and they are called Man or Woman to emphasize that they represent people generally. In some novels names characterize — Squire Allworthy or Mr. Gradgrind or Becky Sharp.

More commonly, papers treating characterization analyze a character, using details from the work to show what kind of person he is. This type of characterization presents some hazard, because it may tempt the writer to forget that he is describing a literary character and not a real person. If he does not remember that the character exists only in the work in which he appears, the critic may wander into endless speculation about matters neither mentioned nor implied in the work and therefore not susceptible to supported presentation — whether Walter Mitty divorced his wife two years after the end of the story, what kind of prenatal influences might have hardened Lady Macbeth. A commonplace expression of praise in student papers — that "the characters are so true to life" — is applicable only figuratively. Literature interprets life, illumines life, but literature is not life.

Effective character studies, however, can be written, analyzing a character as he appears in a poem or story or drama and describing his part in the entire work. A paper on James Thurber's "The Secret Life of Walter Mitty" might begin as follows, starting with three sentences expressing a thesis:

> Viewed from one direction, Walter Mitty, the main character of Thurber's short story, is only comic, an object for derision, an almost pathetic slave to self-deception. From another direction, he is a common man's hero, ascending into a world of heroism and aspiration, while combating the forces of suburban conventionality represented by his wife. The juxtaposition of the two views makes the story an example of genuine humor, in which an element of seriousness lies just beneath the surface of the fun.
>
> The comedy in the story grows partly from the incongruity between the henpecked Mitty in the car and the television hero of the Mitty fantasies. In real life Mitty doesn't need his gloves, but puts them on and expresses his individuality only by taking them off when his wife has left. He protests that he doesn't need overshoes, but he buys them. In his daydreams he is Dr. Mitty, the authority on streptothricosis, or Captain Mitty waiting to get that ammunition dump.
>
> But while we laugh at Mitty's posturing, we are also on his side, pleased in an amused way at his triumph over his wife. . . .

The sketch could go on developing its second point with illustrations from the story and building further the analysis of Mitty's character.

Conflict and Plot

In fiction and drama the characters are usually involved in conflicts, and the pattern in which these conflicts move to a conclusion constitutes the plot of the work. A play or a novel usually includes several conflicts, often of different sorts—for example, between two characters or groups of characters, between a character and forces of his environment, or between ideas or motives or pressures within a character. *Hamlet* develops a series of complex conflicts—among the most obvious those between Hamlet and the king, between Hamlet and his mother, between Hamlet and Laertes, between Hamlet and the tradition of revenge, and within Hamlet's mind between his feeling of obligation to follow the ghost's command and his reluctance to act. Analysis of all the conflicts and interlinking plots in a novel like *War and Peace* would require an extended essay.

A paper on William Faulkner's story "Spotted Horses" might focus on the point of view, on the results of having the story narrated by the sewing-machine salesman who observes the events, or on the character of Flem Snopes, who is behind the sale of the wild horses; but it might also focus on conflicts of the story, developing about a discussion of one main conflict:

> Faulkner's "Spotted Horses" describes a series of conflicts between characters—between Flem Snopes and Henry Armstid, between Flem and Mrs. Armstid, between the Armstids and the Texas man—but the central conflict is between Flem and the entire community, which he manages to cheat and dominate. Although the story is primarily humorous, its development of this central conflict makes an ironic comment on the power of unprincipled shrewdness to exploit ignorance and misdirected pride.
>
> Flem Snopes is clever and extremely skillful at anticipating the reactions of his fellow townsmen. He sponsors the sale of mustangs. . . .

The analysis could characterize Flem and others and describe the way in which Flem wins his advantage, but it could gain unity by keeping attention on what it selects as the central conflict of the story.

A great variety of topics can grow from examinations of the way in which a work of literature is constructed, from the way the writer uses conventions of his form. A paper may concentrate on a story's use of its setting or atmosphere:

> In "The Fall of the House of Usher" Poe uses the setting, the bleak, decaying Usher mansion, almost as a character. The crumbling walls of the house seem as alive as the disintegrating psyche of Roderick Usher that they symbolize.

Or a discussion of a play might center on the way the dramatist handles the necessary exposition:

> In the first scene of *Hedda Gabler* Ibsen gives the audience all the information it needs about the past lives of the characters through Miss Tesman's visit and her conversation with her son and Berta, the maid.

The paper could develop by citing specific examples of the kinds of information that emerge in these opening conversations.

Poetry, especially, since it depends heavily on conventions and techniques, is often discussed in terms of its prosody—its rhythm, meter, rhyme, and other sound patterns. The following brief selection from a discussion of sound effects in Francis Mahoney's poem "The Bells of Shandon" indicates one direction for a paper based on poetic techniques:

> . . . The poet establishes a pattern of *feminine rimes* . . .—perhaps from some vague notion of achieving melodious effects suitable to a poem on the music of the bells. But very soon we see that the feminine rimes have become as merciless a taskmaster to the poet as the meter. The poet gives us such rimes as: *wild would*, with *childhood; Shandon*, with *grand on; Mole in*, with *tolling;* and finally such an absurdity as *Moscow*, with *kiosk O*. Such rimes as these, which have the effect of having been consciously striven for and violently forced, tend to give a comic effect. But such an effect is not intended here. It is the effect which is shown by the rimes in Byron's *Don Juan* or in many of the plays of Gilbert and Sullivan; but the effect in such a work as the present is entirely inappropriate. In this poem, the ludicrous effect is completely at variance with the solemnity of tone which the poet apparently wants to secure.
>
> CLEANTH BROOKS and ROBERT PENN WARREN, *Understanding Poetry*, 1st ed.

The passage uses specific illustrations to demonstrate an opinion about the effect of the poet's handling of rhyme.

Many other kinds of papers might develop about the sound patterns of a poem. A discussion of Browning's "My Last Duchess" might consider the way in which the poet handles iambic pentameter couplets, making such frequent use of run-on lines and rhythmic variations that the reader is sometimes hardly aware that the poem is rhymed. Sometimes a line-by-line analysis of versification can be informative, marking accents and considering the effects of regularity of rhythm or variations from regularity. For any poem that follows a set pattern the critic may wish to show how the poem fits its form, to describe the rhyme scheme and meter, to show how the ideas are distributed in the various parts of the pattern.

A discussion of a play or film may emphasize influences of the staging or direction. A discussion of a television drama might criticize its reliance on stock movie devices, like the horseback chase through the mountains or the runaway coach, or might praise it for the skillful use of the camera to emphasize details of the plot. A paper on a Shakespeare play might consider the advantages and disadvantages of a bare stage, of modern or period costuming, of stylized or natural acting. A paper might focus on the effects of the conventionalized staging for Thornton Wilder's *Our Town.* It might center on the use of music to complement the action of the play or the use of various kinds of sound effects — the rain in Somerset Maugham's *Rain* or the drums in Eugene O'Neill's *Emperor Jones.*

Language and Literature

Metaphors and other figures of speech can provide unusually attractive approaches to literature. Figurative language has particular importance as the author strives for precision in his communication of both meaning and emotion. A number of modern studies of Shakespeare isolate images in the plays and reveal how the images reinforce themes of the play — for example, how the characterization of Macbeth is sharpened by the recurring metaphors picturing him in clothes too large for him. An analysis of a poem may explain metaphors and trace the connections between them. A paper on one seventeenth-century poem might begin:

> Robert Herrick's "Corinna's Going A-Maying" turns about an ironic contrast that grows from the poet's use of metaphor. In a kind of cheerful blasphemy Herrick couches his plea for the seduction of the lady in terms of religious ceremony.

In the first stanza the birds have said matins and "sung their thankful hymns," and the poem urges Corinna out to celebrate May Day because "'tis sin,/Nay, profanation, to keep in."

The paper could continue tracing the religious metaphors as they occur through the poem.

Related to figurative language are the author's uses of devices like allegory and symbolism; allegory, in fact, is sometimes called extended metaphor. In the most obvious type of allegory, abstractions like Knowledge or Good Fellowship become characters in the work. Allegories may be highly complex, as in Edmund Spenser's *Faery Queene*, with characters representing more than one idea and perhaps also various historical figures, with enough uncertainties that readers and critics still argue about identifications.

We have already observed (see 20d) that language is symbolic, that words are symbols for thoughts. As symbols, therefore, words are more versatile than signs, which establish one-to-one connections. For example, as natural signs, a patch of green grass in the desert is a sign of water and a cloud a sign of rain; as arbitrary signs, a cross stands for Christianity and a flag for a country. Symbols differ because they do not apply directly to phenomena but to thoughts about them. In literature symbolism involves not only the use of words as symbols but also the use of objects, persons, actions, or phenomena in such ways that they have significance beyond themselves. In Hawthorne's *The Scarlet Letter*, for example, the letter *A* that Hester Prynne wears on her breast becomes a central symbol. In one sense the letter serves as a sign, standing almost literally for Hester's sin, adultery. As the novel progresses, however, the letter makes broader and more complex suggestions as a symbol of Hester's feelings of guilt and also of the newfound strength of character that grows from Hester's suffering and courage. When Hester removes the letter, the reader can sense her feelings of lightness and release; when she embroiders the letter, the reader recognizes her growing pride and self-reliance. Thus Hawthorne's symbol becomes more varied and subtle as the book progresses, but even so his use of the device is relatively simple compared with the symbolic complexity found in the novels of James Joyce and Thomas Mann and in the poems of William Butler Yeats and Dylan Thomas.

In drama symbols are often physical objects or actions on the stage or screen. In *Hedda Gabler*, for example, Thea's hair becomes symbolic of the relationship between Hedda and Thea, not only of Hedda's envy of Thea, but also of her feelings of guilt about her. We learn in the play how Hedda, whose hair is "not particularly abundant," has pulled Thea's hair and once threatened to burn it. In the play Hedda strokes Thea's hair in one central scene in which she is envious of Thea, and then strokes her hair again at the very end of the play as she goes off to her death. Films are especially suited to the use of visual symbols because the camera can readily emphasize or even exaggerate them. A paper on a film might focus on a central symbol:

> In Orson Wells's *Citizen Kane* the rosebud symbol contributes both to suspense in the plot and to the characterization of Kane.
> The picture of the rosebud is introduced. . . .

The paper could trace the uses of the symbol in the film, and then discuss the implications of the symbol as they suggest Kane's yearning for some kind of contentment he cannot identify but that seems to be connected with the innocence of childhood by the symbolic rosebud.

Comparison and Contrast

Any of the topics suggested above might be varied by using it in a comparison—between two characters, for example, or between two treatments of a similar theme, or between two methods of handling the exposition in a play. Themes of comparison frequently produce incisive and enlightening criticism, but they work best if they are limited to particular aspects of the work going beyond general observations about similarities or differences in two works. A paper comparing a novel or play with a film based on it, for example, is likely to succeed if it can focus on a central basis for the comparison. A paper might work, for instance, by developing the following:

> The film version of Shakespeare's *Henry V* has advantages over the play on the legitimate stage because of the wide range of the camera.

The paper could cite instances—the battle scenes, for example—in which the film medium allows effects impossible on a stage. Comparison may be useful in describing a character; a scholar, observing that Romeo has been called "an early study for Hamlet," remarks that the statement is "true enough to be misleading," and continues as follows:

The many ideas that go to make up Hamlet will have seeded themselves from time to time in Shakespeare's imagination, sprouting a little, their full fruition delayed till the dominant idea ripened. We can find traits of Hamlet in Romeo, in Richard II, in Jaques, in less likely habitations. But Romeo is not a younger Hamlet in love, though Hamlet in love may seem a disillusioned Romeo. The very likeness, moreover, is largely superficial, is a common likeness to many young men, who take life desperately seriously, some with reason, some without. The study of him is not plain sailing. If Hamlet's melancholy is of the soul, Romeo's was something of a pose; and there is Shakespeare's own present convention to account for, of word-spinning and thought-spinning, in which he cast much of the play, through which he broke more and more while he wrote it; there are, besides, the abundant remains of Brooke's Romeus.

HARLEY GRANVILLE-BARKER, *Prefaces to Shakespeare*

This passage, which begins a fairly extensive discussion of Romeo's character, clarifies the writer's interpretation of Romeo by contrasting him with Hamlet.

The topics suggested above represent only a small selection of the kinds of writing about literature that may be undertaken. Especially if the writer has some background in literary studies or is able to undertake some research into literary questions, dozens of other ways of discussing literature become available. A paper may, for example, relate a work to a literary type or genre — *Hamlet* or Arthur Miller's *Death of a Salesman* as tragedies, *Gulliver's Travels* as satire. A paper may consider relations between a work and the society it reflects — the depression and John Steinbeck's *Grapes of Wrath*, *The Red Badge of Courage* as a discussion of the War Between the States. A paper may consider various ways in which a work is a part of literary history — Alexander Pope's *Rape of the Lock* and eighteenth-century ideas of the epic, influences of Christopher Marlowe on the plays of Shakespeare, Milton's "Lycidas" as an expression of the pastoral tradition. For themes of this sort, however, as well as for those based exclusively on the work itself, the writer needs primarily to focus his attention on a central idea and to provide adequate specific support for his generalizations.

Research for Writing on Literature

Most serious writing, except what grows from personal experience — and even some of that — requires something resembling research, and writing about literature is no exception. Some study, although intended to lead eventually to enlarged critical understanding, is occupied almost exclusively with research. For example, the medievalist John Matthews Manly conceived the idea that Chaucer, in creating the Canterbury pilgrims, was using as his originals well-known figures of the day, whom any contemporary would have recognized. In the resulting study, Manly's purpose was that of a literary critic; he wanted to promote our understanding of Chaucer as a poet. We see Chaucer somewhat differently if we believe he was describing an acquaintance, was imitating a character in an earlier work, or was generating a personality from his imagination. But Manly's methods had to be almost exclusively those of research; the problem was this: could he find, among Chaucer's contemporaries, figures who resembled the pilgrims in such specific detail that we must believe that the poet reported and did not much invent? The answer, if it was to be found, would appear in local records and not much in Chaucer's own writings.

Manly spent months working in the British Museum and elsewhere; undergraduates are not usually in a position to undertake such studies, but even for the papers suggested above, which grow mainly out of a literary work itself, the student is likely to need some reference work. Obviously, Herman Melville knew things about whales that he would not have learned in any forecastle or in a whale boat, and even for a study of the White Whale as symbol a critic would want to canvass what Melville knew about whales and where he got his information. Melville was extremely productive in the decade prior to 1852, but published little during the next forty years. Even if a critic is interested only in the literary quality of Melville's work, he will still want to know why a creative artist produced so erratically. Was he ill? Did his wife discourage him? Was he too busy earning a living? Was he depressed by the reception of his books? Had he run out of ideas? Some reading in Melville's biography, in his letters, and in the reviews of the day might provide answers. Even if a critic wants to say little more than that Melville's poetry has been unduly ignored at the expense of his prose, he will do well to check to see whether this is one of the clichés in Melville criticism or whether it is something approaching a discovery.

A student may wish to clarify the subject matter of a work, turning to literary history or to conventional reference works to do so. When did Shakespeare write *Hamlet* and where and when was the play first produced? Which of the lines in the plays commonly attributed to Shakespeare did he write and which seem to result from corruptions or to reflect interpolations by other hands? Such questions of text and canon can usually be studied with some objectivity. Even questions like the influence of Old Norse on the writings of Emerson permit somewhat objective research; what references are there in Emerson's published works, in his letters and journals, in recorded conversations with friends? Which languages could he read? What translations were available to him? Which books did Emerson have in his library and what volumes did he borrow? Whom did he meet when he went to England? Research may also reveal the influence or the reputation of a work. How many copies of *War and Peace* have been printed? Into what languages has it been translated? How was the book reviewed on its appearance? What have critics had to say about it more recently? Such questions can be approached as research projects, and even when introduced into a paper having critical purposes they permit focusing on an appropriately limited topic.

Thus research in literature is much like research in other areas. The materials differ with the subject, but approaches and methods are similar, whether the subject is a political party or a poem. Major problems in research and research writing are considered in chapter 24.

FOR STUDY AND WRITING

A Study the following poem, "The Flea" by John Donne, and answer the questions following it.

> Mark but this flea, and mark in this,
> How little that which thou deny'st me is;
> It sucked me first, and now sucks thee,
> And in this flea our two bloods mingled be;
> Thou know'st that this cannot be said
> A sin, nor shame, nor loss of maidenhead;
>   Yet this enjoys before it woo,
>   And pampered swells with one blood made of two,
>   And this, alas, is more than we would do.
>
> Oh stay, three lives in one flea spare,
> Where we almost, yea, more than married are.
> This flea is you and I, and this
> Our marriage bed, and marriage temple is;
> Though parents grudge, and you, w' are met,
> And cloistered in these living walls of jet.
>   Though use make you apt to kill me,
>   Let not to that, self-murder added be,
>   And sacrilege, three sins in killing three.
>
> Cruel and sudden, hast thou since
> Purpled thy nail in blood of innocence?
> Wherein could this flea guilty be,
> Except in that drop which it sucked from thee?
> Yet thou triumph'st and say'st that thou

480

Find'st not thyself, nor me the weaker now;
   'Tis true, then learn how false fears be:
   Just so much honor, when thou yield'st to me,
   Will waste, as this flea's death took life from thee.

1. What is the dramatic situation in the poem; who is talking to whom?
2. Describe the metrical pattern of the poem. Are there variations on the pattern?
3. Trace the logic of the speaker's argument.
4. Discuss the tone of the poem. How serious is it?
5. What is the main theme of the poem? How significant is it?

After considering the questions above, frame three sentences about the poem that might serve to introduce a paper about it or paragraphs in a paper about it.

B Select any of the excerpts from possible papers on literature in the discussions above and complete it, studying the work it discusses and adding generalizations and details to complete the discussion.

C Read a recent novel, preferably one so recent that you have as yet seen no reviews of it. Check back through the present chapter, refreshing your memory of the various sorts of literary studies. Select five approaches that would be suitable for the novel you have read, and write a theme sentence for each. Then select one of these approaches and write a brief critique of five hundred to a thousand words.

THE INVESTIGATIVE
PAPER

CHAPTER 24

A research or investigative report requires evaluation of evidence,
objective writing, and careful documentation.

The modern world, perhaps particularly the modern American world, relies upon objective information. Theoretically, of course, nothing can be known objectively; most information must filter through human brains, and man is a notoriously inexact creature. Even an electronic measuring device will show variations. But a complex society requires reliable information, and if information cannot be absolutely reliable, we need to make it as reliable as we can. Fortunately, with the proper tools and techniques, man has learned to observe and report with a high degree of objectivity. The use of language and of the mind in connection with investigative study warrants special attention, for research writing presents its own characteristic rhetorical problems.

Investigative methods are particularly the business of people in college. Most of what colleges teach has been discovered by the same means that have become standard in research; and to understand the past, to grasp the world in which he lives, the student needs to appreciate research, the tool with which others have learned what he is now learning. Moreover, much college activity requires knowledge of basic research procedures—whether the student is working in a laboratory, evaluating historical evidence in textbooks, or observing and ordering psychological or sociological phenomena. The student needs research skill to continue his own education.

Likewise, he must deal with objective reports if he is to participate in the affairs of the world. Investigation is the basis of most serious intellectual activity, not only in the arts, in the sciences, and in the learned professions, but also in commerce, technology, government, and education. The lawyer preparing a brief works through previous judgments, using indexes and summaries, and applies the information he collects to his particular case. The sales manager proposing a new campaign investigates past records of his own company, campaigns of other companies, and general economic and sociological conditions, isolating material that will help him plan his own project and predict its results. Techniques vary with materials and the purpose of the investigation, but the essential process behind much of the world's activity is research of a sort—acquiring knowledge about a subject and applying it to new circumstances.

Writing, as we have seen, varies with the author, the subject, and the audience. In research writing the author is likely to keep himself out of the report, as much as he reasonably can, and to express himself by revealing the nature of the subject and by ministering to the needs of his audience. He endeavors to limit himself to the evidence, and the amount of the evidence and the degree of particularity with which he presents it will be dictated largely by his audience. Consider an ecologist concerned with the fact that pink shrimp will become extinct where the temperature of the water changes only a few degrees. Explaining this phenomenon to his small daughter he would limit himself to determinable facts, but he would omit some of the detail and all of the scientific technicalities, and perhaps concentrate on the plight of the baby shrimp that cannot feed and grow if they are too warm or not quite warm enough. Testifying before a Senate committee concerned with the impact of atomic power stations on marine life he would be more comprehensive; although he would still be concerned with objective fact, he would eliminate as much technical terminology as he could and would supply only limited documentation. Reading a paper to a convention of his fellow biologists he would not hesitate to be technical, would provide the most minute detail, along with elaborate documentation, and might restrict himself to a limited problem—for example, to the functioning of the female sex organs at certain temperatures. That is, the writer of an objective report always strives to work within the facts, but the degree of his objectivity and the extent of the material he presents vary with his subject and his audience.

Particularly useful for study and practice is the research article. Much reliable detail appears first in this form. A scientist, or some other investigator using controlled methods, sets out to explore a subject, or he believes he has encountered an important idea. He works at it for days, weeks, months, even years. Eventually, if his research is successful, he embodies his findings in an essay-like statement, usually at first a rather brief piece, an article or a monograph, which, if he happens to be a candidate for a degree, is called a thesis or a dissertation. This article or monograph is not intended for popular or even semipopular consumption; it is addressed to the author's fellow scholars. It may be accepted at once as clearly a reliable and important contribution to knowledge, or it may be fought over by other scholars for years in reviews, in rival articles, in seminars and at conventions, but eventually it will either be discredited or accepted as part of the recognized body of learned information. The contents that have survived what has been called "the cockpit of learning" will now find their way into scholarly books, into textbooks, and general or specialized reference works.

Inevitably, this ideal pattern will show variations; research commissioned by the armed forces may remain classified for many years, and just now techniques are being developed to store new information in data processing machines without the formality of printing, but on the whole this is the common sequence: research, publication, criticism of the research, which criticism leads eventually to more popular publication. For example, at this writing, the theories of stratificational grammar are exciting students of language. The idea was conceived by a Dane, Hjelmslev, and published in a monograph; it was picked up by M. A. K. Halliday in England and by Sydney M. Lamb in this country. Lamb and his students published several articles about it; then in 1962 Lamb produced what he called an "interim document," and in 1966 a monograph, *Outline of Stratificational Grammar*, in which the diagram of a sentence is characterized as "highly tentative." Meanwhile, reviews and articles continue to appear, but to date nobody has presumed to publish anything like a supposedly comprehensive statement about stratificational grammar or to base a textbook upon it.

Exhaustive original research is likely to require more practice and more time than are available to the student in a basic course in composition. Thus the sort of paper described below, even though it requires many of the procedures of research, is often called a library or investigative paper. As a project in serious investigation and objective reporting, however, the investigative paper can be a revealing and engaging writing experience.

Choosing a Subject for Investigation

A subject for research should have at least these four qualifications: it should be within the range of the student's capabilities; it should be conducive to objective treatment; it should be chosen with a view to the limitations of the library and other sources of information, and it should be sufficiently restricted to permit detailed work. For the beginning student, the first of these limitations will exclude many technical subjects, since the specialized knowledge required even to read the available publications may require years of preparation. The study of an American Indian language would require a knowledge of phonetic and phonemic structural analysis; discussing the nature of matter would require a knowledge of both higher mathematics and atomic physics. Many aspects of most subjects, however, can be studied by any literate person.

A research paper should be objective, and objectivity requires rigid restriction of the subject. Objectivity, as we have seen, represents an ideal, not an achievable reality, but the writer can endeavor to be objective, and some subjects are more amenable to objective treatment than are others. "Why I Believe the Republican Is the Best Party" is not a likely subject for research. The writer is not prepared to be objective; he has already made up his mind. Neither is he likely to provide much evidence; psychologists may some day have evidence on how political opinions are formed, but the writer is probably not prepared to study the topic in an objective way.

Consider another proposed topic: "Why I Am Opposed to Segregation in Ghetto Schools." The subject is unsuitable because it cannot be treated objectively. On the other hand, much has been printed on the general problem of segregation, and the writer could find a workable topic within it, such as "The Ungraded School as a Partial Answer to Segregation," that would be approachable through objective investigation. The subject may still be too broad, but it could be restricted; and particularly if the writer can collect firsthand information on the effects of ungraded schools in ghettos, he may produce a paper of considerable value.

The third qualification, that adequate material be available, will not be important for most subjects, provided the student has a good library at his disposal. The holdings in well-established libraries are so great that the beginning student, although he may at first have difficulty locating the most useful material, will soon find himself buried in information and wondering how he can reduce his subject further. Libraries in small or new colleges, however, may be inadequate, and may force the student to abandon an otherwise promising subject, and some libraries, especially in institutions with a technical or professional bias, may be so restricted that the general collection of books is inadequate. Some subjects carry their own restrictions; research reports developed by a business house may be kept from competitors, and rare manuscripts or old newspaper files may not be available for general use. On the other hand, the student may wish to take advantage of special materials locally available. He might, for example, write the history of his home town, using materials collected in the state historical society, or he might write the biography of a figure prominent in his community, using local newspaper files.

RESTRICTING RESEARCH SUBJECTS 24a

We observed in chapter 1 that the author always faces the problem of restricting his subject, that development becomes possible only within restrictions. In preparing an investigative paper the need for isolating and delimiting the subject

GUIDE TO REVISION

24a	R Subj

Restrict the subject so that it can be adequately treated in the time and space available. For general principles of restricting a subject by analysis, see 5a.

ORIGINAL

1. The History of My Family
2. The Problem of Protest
3. The Dilemma of the Railroads
4. The Development of a Pollution-free Power Unit
5. Tom Wolfe as an Observer of the American Scene

[*All these subjects are much too large, and each could be restricted in any of several ways, especially by limiting the time, areas, groups, and people involved.*]

REVISION

For (1) time and space might suffice if pushed far enough. In addition, for (2), the research worker might want to ask if a particular pattern of revolt appeared at a given time and place. For (3), types would be natural; the problems of the commuter train differ from those of the transcontinental and feeder lines. A process, like the chemistry of combustion may be important for (4). For restricting a literary subject see chapter 23.

becomes acute; the choice of an over-inclusive subject both magnifies the investigator's task and minimizes his chances for a significant report. On most subjects available information abounds, and the student who proposes a topic like "The Westward Movement in America" or "The Development of Aviation" faces months of reading. Furthermore, if he were to collect the necessary information, he would need a volume or two to do it justice; what he could put into a college research paper would probably turn out to be a kind of outline—generalities without support. The solution is to narrow the scope of the paper until it can be investigated practically and discussed fully.

The process of restricting a subject may continue even into the final draft of the paper as the writer sees more and more clearly where to focus attention. He may not realize the breadth of his subject until he starts compiling a bibliography and doing some reading. Preliminary restriction of a subject is necessary, however, before the writer can even start intelligently to collect a bibliography.

Subjects can be restricted in many ways. For example, most subjects must be restricted in both time and space; the history of the world is a good subject for a reference book but not for research. Nobody in one lifetime could do so much original work. Other common means of restricting subjects include the selection of results or causes, of trends, of streams of influence, of processes, of groups, or types. One piece of research may be concerned with establishing the actuality of a supposed fact, and another may collect and evaluate opinions. Often, once the research worker is able to ask pertinent questions about his subject, the best means of restricting a topic become obvious.

The Trial Bibliography

An early step in any investigation is the preparation of a trial or working bibliography. It provides the writer with a preliminary knowledge of his subject so that he can restrict his project intelligently and can plan his reading. Incidentally, it records information that the writer will need later for his documentation and for his final bibliography.

The trial bibliography includes all the books, articles, pamphlets, and other documents that the writer can locate through the conventional sources—library catalogs, periodical indexes, checklists, and bibliographies printed in standard reference tools (see chapter 4). As the writer works with his subject, he will continue to accumulate references—for example, items that he finds in the footnotes of works he is reading—but his trial bibliography should contain everything he can locate through general reference works and specialized bibliographies.

To illustrate both procedures for compiling a working bibliography and also the way in which the process can contribute to a topic, we might assume that a writer has decided to prepare an investigative paper on some aspect of road building. He begins generally, looking up *roads, transportation,* and *road building* in several encyclopedias. He discovers that modern methods of building roads have developed in the last two centuries, and he then looks up social histories, like Traill's *Social England*, and books on transportation. In some of these he finds extensive bibliographies and bibliographical footnotes, and he makes cards for these. On one of them he notes that when Josiah Wedgwood's dishes became popular all over Europe, Wedgwood built private roads, because the public roads were so bad that he had to pack his dishes on muleback, and when packs slipped off mules, that was the end of the dishes. The writer becomes interested and tries to find out all he can about Wedgwood and his ware. In the *Dictionary of National Biography* he finds biographies of Wedgwood and bibliographical suggestions for further investigation. He discovers an elaborate series of British local histories, called the *Victoria County Histories*, and he surmises that the county history for Wedgwood's shire will tell him something about the roads of the area and probably refer to more detailed studies that will include Wedgwood's roads. By now the writer is well on his way to locating the material for an investigative paper on the manner in which ornamental vases contributed to the revolution in road building. From now on he has only to use reference works intelligently and faithfully.

Two things the investigator should avoid. He should not begin by asking the librarian, "Is there anything in the library on building roads?" Any good library contains hundreds, thousands of works on building roads, but the librarian does not have time to prepare a list of them. That is the investigator's job, not the librarian's. Similarly, the investigator should not try to get his work done for him by writing an authority for information; he should not write the county engineer, "Please tell me all you know about building roads." Most of what an investigator wants to know is in published form; his job is to find it.

Bibliography Cards

As soon as the investigator begins locating items that may be pertinent to his subject, he should start compiling his bibliography. And he should work systematically, to avoid errors and to avoid having to repeat his work. The following are generally accepted procedures:

> Record bibliographical items on uniform small cards or slips of paper; three-by-five-inch cards are customary.
>
> Record only one item on each card, so that the cards can be readily rearranged and works that prove to be irrelevant can be removed from the list.

488

Keep cards for irrelevant items, noting on them that they have been checked; this precaution will prevent wasting time checking the same item more than once.

Record the bibliographical information in accordance with the style described below.

A library card and the bibliography card that results from it look like this:

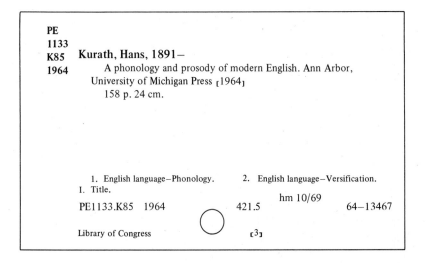

```
PE
1133
K85    Kurath, Hans, 1891–
1964        A phonology and prosody of modern English. Ann Arbor,
            University of Michigan Press ₍1964₎
                158 p. 24 cm.



            1. English language–Phonology.    2. English language–Versification.
        I. Title.
                                                      hm 10/69
        PE1133.K85   1964                  421.5                    64–13467

        Library of Congress                          ₍3₎
```

The name of the author is reversed, as it was on the catalog card, and for the same reason, so that the card can be filed for ready reference. The whole card should be checked, but especially the author's name—printing it in block capitals may save misreading. If the writer mistakes *Kurath* for *Kuralt* or *Kaplan*, he may cause himself endless trouble. The title is underlined to avoid confusing it with anything else, and all the details of publication are taken so as to identify the particular edition. The lowered brackets around the date on the library card indicate that this number does not appear on the title page, but was assumed from the copyright date; for bibliographies in which all details are scrupulously preserved such a date should be enclosed within square brackets, but most styles do not require this distinction. For his convenience, although this material will probably not appear in a finished bibliography, the writer does well to include the call number and some indication of what use the book may be to him—

this last may have to be added after the writer can consult the book itself. A bibliography card for a pamphlet is likely to be much like that for a book, since the pamphlet is likely to be identified as a single publication.

If the bibliography card represents a magazine article as listed in a periodical index, there are likely to be abbreviations to be expanded, and the items to be recorded will be somewhat different. Following is a reproduction from *Reader's Guide to Periodical Literature:*

> GRAND CANYON
> Grand Canyon by helicopter. B. Thomas.
>   il Travel 133:46-50 Je '70
> Heck of a hole in the ground. il Newsweek
>   75:23 Je 22 '70
> Trees on the rim; photographs. P. D. Dun-
>   can. Am For 76:12-15 Jl '70
> GRAND CANYON NATIONAL PARK
> Moods of the North Rim: Grand Canyon Na-
>   tional Park. J. Fain. il Nat Parks & Con
>   Mag 44:4-7 My '70

A bibliography card for the first entry would look like the following:

```
THOMAS, B.

    "Grand Canyon by Helicopter,"

  Travel,  133 (1970), 46-50.

                (Illustrations;

                apparently no

                bibliog.)
```

The name of the author has been put first for filing. This index does not include given names of authors for works entered by subject; in a research paper, however, the author's name should be given as it appears on the work itself. Accordingly, when the research worker examines the article he should check it against his card, adding the full name and correcting any other omissions, while being alert to possible errors. The title of the article is enclosed in quotation marks and the name of the periodical underlined. If the title is abbreviated in the index — as it is in the third item or under GRAND CANYON above—the full name can be found in a list of abbreviations somewhere in the volume; again, since these may have been somewhat skeletonized, the research worker should check for accuracy and completeness when he consults the article itself. The next number is the volume, followed by the year in parentheses, followed by the inclusive pages. The month is not necessary, since the periodical is paged consecutively; for the next item in the *Reader's Guide* the date would be necessary, since *Newsweek* is paged by individual issues. The research worker can add a note for himself if he wishes—the *il* means *illustration(s)*—and he will probably want to add the library call number later.

Bibliography cards have specific uses. In the preparation of a research paper they guide the writer in the second step of the process—which begins as soon as reference sources have been checked to compile a trial bibliography—the collection of material and the taking of notes (see chapter 4). Bibliography cards should be distinguished from note cards, which have a different use; but they are useful in the preparation of note cards because note cards can identify the sources of material with short titles or even key numbers, referring to the bibliography cards for full information. Bibliography cards can provide a record of the items the writer has checked and those still to consult. As he works the writer can turn to the bibliography cards for information—the spelling of an author's name or a date of publication. Eventually, when he prepares documentation for his paper, whether in a bibliography or in footnotes, the writer turns to his bibliography cards for the detailed information.

Documentation

Characteristically, the research report is documented; that is, the information in the paper is supported by references to its sources, usually in footnotes or in parenthetical references to a bibliography. The writer of an investigative paper needs to indicate what kind of evidence supports his conclusions—whether to strengthen his case by appealing to authority or to place responsibility for an opinion where it belongs. He needs to assist the reader who wants to check sources in more detail or wants to explore the subject further. In general, documentation is needed for the following data.

1. *The source of a significant quotation.* In carefully documented writing, any direct quotation used as evidence should be identified. Material quoted for embellishment need not be identi-

fied in a footnote. For instance, suppose a writer begins a discussion as follows:

> "In the beginning was the word"; whether or not we now accept this statement literally, words have been at the beginning of many ideas, and hence they have been at the beginnings of what grew out of the ideas.

The quotation from the New Testament does not require a footnote. Most readers would recognize it, and in any event it is only a stylistic device. If, however, the passage were used as evidence of the Greek veneration of language, it should carry a footnote.

2. *The source of information not sufficiently familiar so that most readers would know it or be able to find it readily.* The date of Shakespeare's death or the name of the twenty-fifth president of the United States needs no footnote; anyone who does not take the writer's word for such details can find them in dozens of reference works. All major assertions in a serious discussion, however, should be supported by documentation.

3. *Controversial matter and opposing views.* Any serious investigation is likely to lead the writer into fields where opinions differ. Whether he takes sides or not, the writer should be sure that both sides are represented in footnote references.

4. *Details or statistics that would interrupt the paper.* Statistics, figures, tables, or other supplementary data are sometimes placed in footnotes, where they are available for reference but do not interrupt the progress of the discussion. With discretion, details too good to miss but not quite on the subject may be added in footnotes. Additional evidence intended for the unusually skeptical critic may be placed in footnotes.

All systems of documentation have the same purpose, to identify a source precisely and to lead quickly and accurately to the passage in question. The means, however, vary, and all publications either develop their own style sheets, which include style in documentation, or they adopt one already developed. In general, two systems are in use. The system here described relies primarily on footnotes in a numbered sequence; the first footnote carries the bibliographical details that identify the source and it also specifies the appropriate point in the source, usually by including the page or inclusive pages. Subsequent references to this work include the author's last name, enough more information to identify the work if the author's last name is not sufficient, and the page or pages. This is the traditional system, still used for most writing in humanistic and historical subjects; it is flexible enough to accommodate large bodies of highly varied material. When used in a dissertation or a thesis, it customarily is accompanied by a bibliography, but the footnote system is itself so adequate that few scholarly journals relying upon it now wish bibliographies for articles, and even long scholarly works running to several volumes may not require bibliographies.

The second system uses no footnotes, but relies upon a bibliography and parenthetical notes within the text. By this system, a reference to page 141 of the Kurath volume cited above would appear in a line of type as follows:

> Monosyllables may carry full stress (Kurath, 1964, 141), but receive half stress. . . .

That is, the reader is referred to *Kurath* in the alphabetized bibliography, to the work listed there which was published in 1964, and to page 141. This system has virtues that have commended it to many scientists. It is economical; no space is required for footnotes, and notes in the text are brief. Since a scientific paper is likely to be read by few scholars, most of whom know one another and will even remember in which year significant works were published, the reader is not likely to have to refer frequently to the bibliography. For the humanities it is less satisfactory; a work that ranges over various areas and stretches of time is likely to rest upon a bibliography so varied that even a mature scholar would find himself flipping back and forth to the bibliography, and unless there are many references to the same work the saving is not great anyhow. Some journals skeletonize even further, numbering items in the bibliography, so that a note looks like the following: (83, 145). This system is very economical, but it encourages error, and errors in figures are difficult to detect. Some journals use a combination of the methods, with full bibliographical details given in a footnote for the first reference, notes within the text referring to the bibliography thereafter. Fortunately, anyone familiar with either style or a combination of them can readily adapt to another; the essence of documentation appears through the handling of sources, not through the details of the citation.

FOOTNOTE FORM   **24b**

Footnotes are keyed to the text by reference numbers. A superior numeral—a number slightly raised—appears in the text, immediately after the quotation or the material to be documented and after all punctuation except the dash. References are numbered consecutively throughout a paper, with arabic

24b

Fn

Revise so that footnotes conform to the prescribed style sheet.

ORIGINAL

Markwart, Albert H. Introduction to English Lang. published in 1942 by Oxford U. Press, page 143

[*The author has either not prepared his original note carefully or he has not checked his work. Nor has he followed style. In the column to the right the footnote is styled according to the* MLA *Style Sheet.*]

REVISION

Albert H. Marckwardt, *Introduction to the English Language* (New York, Oxford Univ. Press, 1942), p. 143.

[*The author confused the style for bibliography and footnotes, neglected to italicize the title, omitted the place of publication, did not repeat the title exactly, and was careless in spelling, punctuation, and styling.*]

numerals without punctuation, and in books through a minimum of a chapter. Numbers are not repeated within a paper or chapter, even though the reference may be to the same book or article. Asterisks and printer's symbols are rarely used except for special purposes. In the Modern Language Association style, which is described in the following pages, footnotes are accumulated and typed on a separate sheet of paper; this is the system most convenient for the printer, who uses a size of type for footnotes that is different from the type in the body of the text. For a term paper the instructor may require that footnotes be ruled into the text, with a rule above and below each note, or accumulated at the bottoms of pages or at the end of the paper. In papers not being prepared for publication footnotes are usually typed single spaced. Even if footnotes are placed at the bottom of pages, they are numbered consecutively for the whole work; the printed pages would not correspond to the typed pages, and the resulting changes in numbers can lead to various sorts of confusion.

The footnote may provide supplementary information of various sorts, but more often it simply cites a work from which information has been taken. This kind of citation is styled to read as though it were an abbreviated sentence, generally punctuated like a sentence, with some parts implied by punctuation and other conventional signals. Thus a footnote referring to Kurath's volume could read like this:

494

[76] Hans Kurath, *A Phonology and Prosody of Modern English* (Ann Arbor: Univ. of Michigan Press, 1964), p. 118.

The footnote is a skeletonized way of suggesting something like the following: "[This quotation appears in] Hans Kurath ['s book], *A Phonology and Prosody of Modern English,* [which was published in] Ann Arbor [by the] Univ [ersity] of Michigan Press [in] 1964, [on] p [age] 118."

Most modern publications carry at least the routine bibliographical information adequate for this kind of footnote reference, but some do not, especially local, occasional, or fugitive items. If the conventional information is incomplete, but can be discovered, the writer should include it within square brackets. If he cannot find it he can insert abbreviations in the appropriate place; *n.d.* indicates no date, *n.p.* no publisher, and *n. pag.* no pagination. The research worker should avoid occasions to cite unpublished material; the reader has no way of checking the source. If unpublished manuscripts are mentioned, a footnote can be used to explain where the originals are to be found; if a writer has occasion to refer to information in a private conversation, an unpublished interview, notes taken from a lecture, and the like, acknowledgment can be made in the text; a footnote is usually unnecessary.

A form like the above is the most common for a reference to a single published volume; but publications—books, series of books, periodicals—appear in such variety that many alternatives are necessary. A style sheet even approaching completeness would be only confusing in a book like this one. Extensive style sheets are available in the *Manual of Style* published by the University of Chicago Press and the *Style Manual of the United States Government Printing Office,* both of which are frequently revised. The summaries below should serve for most references.

Books: Footnote Form

The nearest to a standard bibliographical style for literature and some other subjects is that adopted by the Modern Language Association and embodied in the *MLA Style Sheet,* 2nd ed., to which the student may refer for items not provided for in the simplified description below. With slight alterations the system will serve for most humanistic studies. More extensive variations are required to adapt the system to styles used in many of the sciences; see pp. 524, 525.

For the first footnote reference to a book the following describes a pattern entry:

1. Author. The name of the author or authors appears first, followed by a comma, and in normal order, *not* reversed as though for alphabetizing. The name usually should be copied exactly as it appears on the title page; however, names appearing in an unusual or shortened form may be expanded, the expansion enclosed within square brackets. If an author uses only his first initial, expansion is especially useful; modern library catalogs are so extensive that finding the proper J. Smith can be an exhausting chore. *Special cases:* If a book has more than three authors, standard form is to use the name of the first author, followed by "and others" or "et al."

2. Title. Second is the title, copied exactly from the title page, not from the spine or cover of the book, underlined in script or typing to represent italics in type. It should be included entire unless it is very long; almost no recent books have titles long enough to warrant reduction. If the title immediately precedes material enclosed within parentheses, it is followed by no punctuation; if matter not in parentheses follows it, the title is separated from that material by a comma. *Special cases:* If the book has a half title, that should be included, underlined and separated from the main title by a colon. If the citation refers to something printed as a separate work in a book — an essay in an anthology for example — this title should appear in roman, within quotation marks, before the title of the book. That is, sequence is then as follows: quotation marks, title of essay in roman type, comma, quotation marks, title of book in italics. See also Briefer Pieces: Footnote Form. If there is a title within a title, it should be in roman type, not italics, as in *The* Arabian Nights *in American Literature.*

3. Editor or translator. Normally, the name of an editor or translator appears after the title; it is preceded immediately by "ed." or "trans." This sequence is preceded by a comma; it is followed by a comma if more material intervenes between it and parentheses, but if matter within parentheses follows, there is no punctuation after the name of the editor or translator. *Special case:* If the book is being cited for something written by the editor or translator, his name comes first, followed by a comma, followed by "ed." or "trans.", followed by the title of the work, followed by a comma, followed by the word "by," followed by the author's name.

4. Edition. If the edition being used is not the first, the number should be mentioned in the form "2nd ed." "3rd ed." "4th ed." and so forth. Indication of the edition is preceded by a comma and followed by a comma unless the next portion of the footnote is enclosed within parentheses.

5. *Series.* Some important works appear in series with titles like *Stanford Studies in Language and Literature.* If the book being cited is part of such a series, the series title should be included, in roman, preceded by a comma and followed by the number of the work in the series, in arabic numerals, followed by a comma unless the next portion of the footnote appears in parentheses. *Special case:* Some series, especially those for some European universities, are very complex. This material can be included as it appears on the title page or translated into English.

6. *Volumes.* If the work consists of more than one volume, and the reference is to the entire set, the number of volumes is included with a form like "4 vols." The indication of volumes is preceded by a comma and is usually followed by matter in parentheses. *Special case:* For citation from a particular volume of a set containing several volumes, see 8 below.

7. *Place, publisher, date.* These items are enclosed within parentheses, with a colon between the place of publication and the publisher and a comma between the publisher and the date. The name of the publisher may be shortened; "The Macmillan Company" can appear "Macmillan." *Special cases:* If a volume is published over a period of years, the citation should be inclusive, as in "1961–68." If a work is not yet completely published, the entry is left open, as in "1971–,". If a work is listed as published in several cities, usually the first is sufficient. If a work has been reprinted and the research worker is using the reprint, the bibliographical details above should be preceded by the date of the original edition, semicolon, and "rpt." The older MLA style discouraged the use of publishers' names, and many styles still omit them, especially for books out of copyright. If no publisher is named, a comma follows the place of publication.

8. *Page reference.* The last item, unless reference is made to an entire work, concerns the page or other specific portion of the work cited. Standard sequence is as follows: a comma after a parenthesis, "p." for one page or "pp." for more than one page, the number or numbers of pages in arabic, closed with a period. If the reference is to a passage in a work of more than one volume, the abbreviations "p." and "pp." are not used, but the volume appears in roman numerals followed by the page indication in arabic numerals as in "II, 21–29." *Special cases:* If the reference is to tabular or illustrative material, an appropriate designation replaces the page number, as in "fig. 3." If the reference is to a footnote, this indication is added to the page references, as in "89, n. 2."

Sample Footnotes: Books

The following sample footnotes indicate how the principles listed above may be applied to some frequently encountered kinds of books.

1. *A book in a single volume with a single author:*

[1] Albert C. Baugh, *A History of the English Language,* 2nd ed. (New York: Appleton, 1957), pp. 49–50.

When the first edition is not used, the number of the edition is indicated. Notice that all details on the title page of a book need not be recorded. The title page of this volume identifies Baugh as the Felix E. Schelling Memorial Professor of English, University of Pennsylvania; this need not be recorded. It also records the publisher as Appleton-Century-Crofts, Inc.; some styles require that this name be preserved exactly, but most styles, including the MLA, allow skeletonizing the name of the publisher.

[2] *A History of the English Language,* 2nd ed. (New York: Appleton, 1957), pp. 49–50.

When the author's full name is given in the text, and even if the title is also given this form is used in the footnote.

2. *A work in more than one volume:*

[3] René Wellek, *A History of Modern Criticism: 1750–1950* (New Haven: Yale Univ. Press, 1955–), IV, 371.

For a work in several volumes, the volume is indicated in roman numerals, but no abbreviation is used for the word *page(s)*. Works issued in more than one volume may be issued in more than one year. The entry above is called an open entry, indicating that the final volume has not yet appeared. If the final volume appears in 1972, the dates of publication will thereafter be recorded as 1955–1972. The title page of Wellek's book lists two cities as places of publication, but only one is cited in the footnote, the one in which the book originated.

3. *A reprint of an older edition:*

[4] C[live] S. Lewis, *The Allegory of Love: A Study in Medieval Tradition* (1936; rpt. New York: Galaxy–Oxford Univ. Press, 1958), pp. 224–36.

To cite a reprint, the date of the first publication is used, followed by publication data for the volume actually consulted; the footnote above indicates that the book was published in 1936 but the citation refers to the 1958 Galaxy edition by Oxford University Press. The footnote records a subtitle of the book, separated from the main title by a colon but marked for italics. The author's name is expanded from its form on the title page, with the first name completed in brackets.

4. *An edition:*

⁵Geoffrey Chaucer, *The Works of Geoffrey Chaucer*, ed. F. N. Robinson, 2nd ed. (Boston: Houghton Mifflin, 1957), p. 457.

Usually an edition is cited under the name of the author being edited, but it may be cited under the name of the editor, especially if the reference is to the editorial apparatus.

⁶F[red] N[orris] Robinson, ed., *The Works of Geoffrey Chaucer*, 2nd ed. (Boston: Houghton Mifflin, 1953), pp. xxxiv–xxxv.

5. *A translation:*

⁷Vladimir Nabokov, *King, Queen, Knave*, trans. Dmitri Nabokov (New York: McGraw-Hill, 1968), p. 16.

6. *A book in a series:*

⁸Ruth Wallerstein, *Richard Crashaw: A Study in Style and Poetic Development*, Univ. of Wisconsin Studies in Lang. and Lit., No. 37 (Madison: Univ. of Wisconsin Press, 1935), p. 52.

The data on the series is included after the title, not in italics, and is followed by information on publication.

7. *A book by two or more authors:*

⁹Wilmarth H. Starr, Mary P. Thompson, and Donald D. Walsh, eds., *Modern Foreign Languages and the Academically Talented Student* (Washington: National Education Association, and New York: MLA, 1960), p. 88.

If this item had only two authors or editors, the citation would begin as follows: Wilmarth H. Starr and Mary P. Thompson. If there were four or more authors or editors, the following style could be used: Wilmarth H. Starr, *et al.*, meaning "and others."

Notice that the book also has two publishers, both of which are mentioned.

    8. *Works prepared by a corporate author:*

    [10] President's Commission on Higher Education, *Higher Education for American Democracy* (Washington, D.C.: GPO, 1947), I, 26.

Books prepared by an agency or other group may be listed under the name of the agency, as above, or under the title, followed by *by* and the name of the agency. An abbreviation is used for Government Printing Office.

    9. *Anonymous works:*

    [11] *The Home Mechanic's Handbook: An Encyclopedia of Tools, Materials, Methods, and Directions* (New York: Van Nostrand, 1945) p. 237.

An anonymous work, especially a reference book, is listed by title.

    10. *Standard reference works — dictionaries, encyclopedias:*

    [12] *Webster's New International Dictionary of the English Language,* 2nd ed., under *onomastic.*

For standard reference works publication data need not be included; if there has been more than one edition, however, the cited edition should be identified. In a work arranged alphabetically, like a dictionary, no page number is necessary; but if the alphabetical entry would not be obvious, it should be indicated:

    [13] *Encyclopaedia Britannica,* 14th ed., under "Jonson, Ben."

    [14] Edward Sapir, "Language," *Encyclopaedia of the Social Sciences* (New York: Macmillan, 1933).

A signed article in an encylopedia or other standard work should be cited under the author's name and treated like a periodical article (see below). If the article is signed with initials that are identified in a list somewhere in the encyclopedia, the name can be completed in brackets: E[dward] S[apir].

    11. *A work cited from a secondary source:*

    [15] Thomas Campbell, *Essays on English Poetry* (London, 1848), p. 39; cited in Albert C. Baugh, *A History of the English Language,* 2nd ed. (New York: Appleton, 1957), p. 224.

When a writer wants to refer to material not available to him but quoted in a secondary work, he should include data on both the original source and the work he is using.

For briefer pieces, for articles in periodicals, essays in collections, pieces in anthologies, and the like, the following describes standard entries:

1. Name. The author's name is reproduced as for a book, the name taken from the article itself, not from a bibliography, which may use an abbreviated form.

2. Title. The title, complete, should be taken from the original; it is enclosed within quotation marks and followed by a comma, not underlined.

3. Name of periodical. The name of the periodical follows, in full, underlined for italic type, followed by a comma. *Special case:* A few periodicals have been issued in more than one series; for such journals the series indication — for example "N. S." for "New Series" — follows the comma after the name of the periodical. Some styles allow the use of standard abbreviations for specified periodicals, *PMLA, TLS,* etc.

4. Volume number. The volume number in arabic is preceded by a comma, and is usually followed by matter in parentheses. *Special cases:* Formerly, the volume number was given in roman numerals and some style sheets still require this distinction. If the periodical is not paged consecutively by volumes, the number of the issue should be included; style is: volume number, comma, the abbreviation "No.", followed by the issue number in arabic.

5. Date. After the indication of the volume or the volume plus the number, the year is enclosed within parentheses, preceded by no punctuation but followed by a comma. *Special cases:* For weekly news magazines and reviews and for newspapers an acceptable form is the day, followed by no punctuation, the month, followed by no punctuation, the year, followed by a comma, but the whole *not* enclosed within parentheses. If the periodical is not paged by volumes and has no numbers, it can be identified by date or season as in (Spring, 1971), both season and year in parentheses.

6. Pages. The page number or numbers in arabic, preceded by a comma and followed by a period, close the entry. If the volume number has not been included, the page reference is preceded by "p." or "pp." *Special cases:* For newspapers the column indication should be added to the page indication, as in "p. 26, col. 3." Large newspapers may also require indication of parts, sections, and the like; these should appear in the order from the largest groupings to the smallest.

The following samples indicate some frequent applications of the principles above to articles and parts of longer works.

1. *An article in a journal paged consecutively through a volume:*

[16]Bill Thomas, "Grand Canyon by Helicopter," *Travel,* 133 (1970), 49.

Since paging is consecutive through the annual volume, no identification of the individual issue is needed. This is the most common type of periodical citation, and variations on it can be inferred from the samples for books above—for example, for articles having more than one author, or for an anonymous article.

2. *An article in a journal with each issue separately paged:*

[17]Rodney Fox, "Attacked by a Killer Shark!" *The Reader's Digest,* 87, No. 520 (1965), 51–52.

The footnote identifies the issue by number, since each number is separately paged. If the journal does not distinguish volumes, it is identified by number only:

[18]W. M. Frohock, "The Idea of the Picaresque," *Yearbook of Comparative and General Literature,* No. 16 (1967), 47–49.

If the journal does not label either volume or number, it is identified by the season of its publication:

[19]Ann Barton, "Victorian Business Woman," *The Countryman,* Winter, 1965, p. 419.

An issue of a periodical frequently published, like a weekly magazine, can be identified by date only:

[20]Hollis Alpert, "But Who Wrote the Movie?" *Saturday Review,* 26 Dec. 1970, p. 9.

3. *An article from a newspaper with a complex organization:*

[21]Walter Kerr, "Two That Try To Break the Rules—and Fail," *New York Times,* 27 Dec. 1970, Sec. 2, p.1, col. 1; p.5, col. 3.

For most newspaper citations this form can be simplified; it thus becomes essentially like that for a weekly magazine, except that reference to the column is added to that for the page.

4. *A signed review:*

[22]Geoffrey Wolff, rev. of *Military Men*, by Ward Just, *Newsweek*, 28 Dec. 1970, p. 62.

5. *An unsigned review:*

[23]"Social Anthropology and the Study of the Classics," rev. of *Myth*, by G. S. Kirk, *Times Literary Supplement*, No. 3572 (1970), p. 2, col. 4.

6. *A chapter or selection from a book entirely by one author:*

[24]Tom Wolfe, "A Sunday Kind of Love," in *The Kandy-Kolored Tangerine-Flake Streamline Baby* (New York: Farrar Straus, 1964), p. 290.

The footnote combines the form for an article and a book, using the word *in* to clarify the relationship between them.

7. *A work in a collection:*

[25]John Dewey, "Does Human Nature Change?" in *Confrontations: Readings for Composition*, ed. James K. Bowen (Glenview, Ill.: Scott Foresman, 1969), p. 195.

Footnote references to anthologies, especially to textbooks, are avoided in a manuscript to be published, partly because libraries do not regularly collect textbooks and reference to them may be difficult. The writer should go to the original if possible and cite that, but for student papers citations from anthologies are usually permitted for convenience.

8. *A citation from a secondary source:*

[26]Ernest Tuveson, "Space, Deity, and the 'Natural Sublime,'" *Modern Language Quarterly*, 12 (1951), 20–38; cited in W. Ross Winterowd, *Rhetoric: A Synthesis*, (New York: Holt, Rinehart and Winston, 1969), pp. 49–50.

The original article is recent enough that it could probably be located, but if it is unavailable the citation in the secondary source could be used.

Subsequent References

The examples above serve for only the first footnote citation of each work. Thereafter a simplified form is used, identification of an item plus necessary volume and page references. If only one work by an author is cited, either a book or an article, the author's name will suffice:

[27] Lewis, p. 98.

If more than one work by the same author is cited, a simplified title should be added to the last name:

[28] Nabokov, *King*, p. 267.

The footnote presumes that another of Nabokov's works is being cited elsewhere. For anonymous works a skeletonized title is used:

[29] *Mechanic's Handbook*, p. 343.

Formerly, citations after the first were handled with references like *ibid.* and *op. cit.* This method is now but little recommended; for details see Abbreviations and Conventions, below.

Parenthetical Documentation

Some style sheets do not sanction parenthetical documentation within the text, but many journals, including *PMLA*, the *Publications of the Modern Language Association*, permit limited parenthetical documentation, especially when references are not extensive enough to clutter the text and not so complicated that they become confusing. The following suggests style:

> Albert C. Baugh in *A History of the English Language*, 2nd ed. (New York, Appleton, 1957), p. 138, observes that William the Conqueror never learned English, but that some writs were issued in his name, composed in English and addressed to recipients some of whom probably could not "have read the writ themselves in any language" (p. 144).

Parenthetical documentation is common in discussions devoted mainly or exclusively to a literary work or the works of a single writer. The following sentence occurs in an article discussing Emily Brontë's *Wuthering Heights*.

> Joseph is ever calling everyone else a "nowt," a nothing, denying everyone a place (except in hell) in his scheme of things: "Bud yah're a nowt . . . like yer mother afore ye!" (p. 22); "marred, wearisome nowt" (p. 122); "good fur nowt, slatternly witch" (p. 78); "nasty, ill nowt" (p. 251).

The edition being cited has been identified in a previous footnote. If the notes had referred to an edition of an author's works printed in several volumes the parenthetical citations would have appeared as follows: (*Works,* I, 27), (*Works,* II, 89).

References to a play or a long poem are almost always handled parenthetically. A quotation from a play, for example, can be cited by a parenthetical reference to act, scene, and line (*Caesar* III. i. 47); because of the many editions a page reference would be less useful. If the play is identified in the text, indication of the place is sufficient (III. iv. 19–21). References to long poems can refer to parts and lines (*Iliad* V. 33); references to the Bible cite book, chapter, and verse (John 3:16) and the version used if necessary (DV; John 3:16).

BIBLIOGRAPHY FORM   **24c**

A bibliography of the principal works consulted, including all those cited in the paper, is customarily appended to a long documented composition, to an academic thesis or disserta-

GUIDE TO REVISION

24c   **Bibliog**

Revise the bibliography to conform to a standard style.

ORIGINAL

R. J. Kaufman, *Richard Brome: Caroline Playwright,* (New York, Columbia)
[*Errors, possibly through confusion with footnote form, include failure to reverse the author's name, failure to italicize the subtitle, nonstandard punctuation, and omission of the date.*]

Larry L. King, *Blowing My Mind at Harvard* in Harper's Vol. 241, 1445 (1970)
[*Errors include confusion of italics and quotation marks, failure to reverse the author's name for alphabetizing, and omission of pages.*]

REVISION

Kaufmann, R. J[ames]. *Richard Brome: Caroline Playwright.* New York: Columbia Univ. Press, 1961.
[*Spelling of the author's name is corrected, periods separate main sections of the entry, and the name of the publisher is completed.*]

King, Larry L. "Blowing My Mind at Harvard." *Harper's,* 241, No. 1445 (1970), 95–105.
[*Quotation marks identify the article title and italics the journal. Since issues are paged separately, volume and number are specified.*]

tion, and to works using a system with parenthetical short references to the bibliography. Usually the items in a bibliography are listed in alphabetical order according to the last names of authors, the first word of the title after *a* or *the* if there is no author, or the name of an issuing agency if something like a government bureau issues an anonymous work. An anonymous work can be alphabetized under *Anon.,* but this system becomes cumbersome for a study involving many anonymous pieces. When more than one work by the same author is listed, the works are frequently arranged in chronological order according to dates of publication. Sometimes, for special purposes, an entire bibliography is arranged chronologically. A long bibliography may include one list for books and another for periodicals, or it may be subdivided to reveal different aspects of the subject of the paper.

The bibliography is compiled from the cards of the working bibliography, supplemented by additional titles that have been collected during the progress of the paper, and follows the style prescribed above for bibliography cards. That is, the two items listed above on bibliography cards would appear in the bibliography as:

> Kurath, Hans. *A Phonology and Prosody of Modern English.* Ann Arbor: University of Michigan Press, 1964.
>
> Thomas, Bill. "Grand Canyon by Helicopter." *Travel,* 133 (1970), 46–50.

The style for most bibliographic entries can be inferred from the samples of footnote form given above. A comparison of the two forms may be helpful.

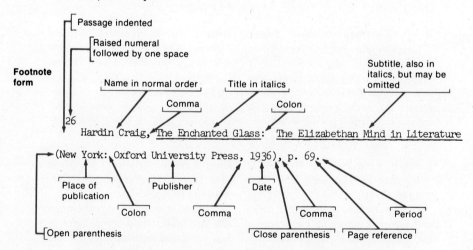

Note: For inclusive pages, reference is pp. 69–72. For work of more than one volume, style is I, 82.

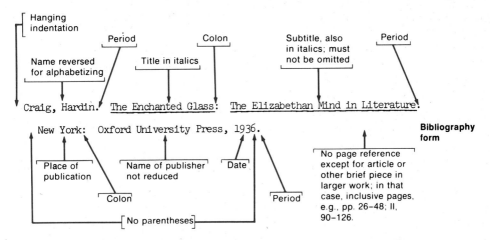

Note: In both forms mention of an editor not treated as author follows the title; for a book of more than one volume, mention of the number of volumes appears before the data on publication.

Sample Bibliography Entries

The following illustrate how some of the works styled above for footnotes would appear in the bibliography:

Baugh, Albert C. *A History of the English Language.* 2nd ed. New York: Appleton, 1957.

Chaucer, Geoffrey. *The Works of Geoffrey Chaucer.* Ed. F[red] N[orris] Robinson. 2nd ed. Boston: Houghton Mifflin, 1957.

Fox, Rodney. "Attacked by a Killer Shark!" *The Reader's Digest,* 87, No. 520 (1965), 47–54.

The Home Mechanic's Handbook: An Encyclopedia of Tools, Materials, Methods, and Directions. New York: Van Nostrand, 1945.

Lewis, C[live] S. *The Allegory of Love: A Study in Medieval Tradition.* 1936; rpt. New York: Galaxy–Oxford Univ. Press, 1958.

Sapir, Edward. "Language." *Encyclopaedia of the Social Sciences.* New York: Macmillan, 1933.

Wolfe, Tom. "A Sunday Kind of Love." *The Kandy-Kolored Tangerine-Flake Streamline Baby.* New York: Farrar Straus, 1964.

Abbreviations and Conventions

Abbreviations are used more freely in conventionalized sections like footnotes and bibliographies than in straight text, but some abbreviations formerly common in footnotes are now not much used, notably *ibid.*, meaning in the same place, *op. cit*, in the work cited, *loc. cit.* in the place cited, and *ff.* and *et seq.*, meaning following. In most instances served by abbreviations like *ibid.* the parenthetical note described above is both more economical and more convenient for the reader. For occasions in which a parenthetical note will not suffice, an abbreviated note like the following is more revealing and almost as economical: Wellek, *History*, III, 67. Formerly, bibliographical explanations, including abbreviations, were mostly in Latin, but the practice of using English is growing. Even if the Latin is used, modern practice permits dispensing with italics. A list of these symbols can be quite long (see *MLA Style Sheet*, 2nd. ed., pp. 28–29), but for most purposes, those in the following list will suffice:

p., pp. — page, pages.

l., ll. — line, lines.

v., vv. — verse, verses.

vol., vols. — volume, volumes.

no., nos. — number, numbers.

cf. — compare.

n. — note, footnote.

supra — above; preferred to *ante;* the English is now often preferred.

infra — below; preferred to *post;* the English is now often preferred.

c. — copyright; used when the date of a copyright is known but the date of publication is not.

c., ca. — circa, about; used in approximate dates (ca. 1888).

ff., et seq. — and following; used to complete a citation to pages; not the best practice — inclusive page reference (pp. 86–93) is preferable.

passim — at intervals through the work or pages cited.

sic — thus; may be used after an obvious error in a quotation to indicate that the error was in the original; best used sparingly; when inserted in a quotation, should be enclosed in brackets.

n.d. — no date.

n.p. — no publisher.

n. pag. — no pagination.

ed. — editor, edited, edition.

trans. — translated by, translation.

rev. — revised.

508

Graphs, tables, and other illustrations or tabulated inserts are imperative for many technical papers, and much complicated material is best shown in visual or tabular form. The writer should always consider whether a table or an illustration will not make his meaning clearer. Inserts of this sort should usually be labeled for ready reference in the text. Use *plate* to refer to a full page (Plate IX), *figure* for an illustration in the text (Figure 8), and *table* for a tabular or graphic arrangement (Table 3).

Style in the Investigative Paper

Research writing is usually directed to a relatively limited audience, to persons already interested in the subject. It does not follow, however, that research writing should be dull. The editors of the *MLA Style Sheet*, 2nd ed., remark:

> Readability is a prime consideration of scholarly writing. American scholarship over the past quarter century has moved away from fact gathering for its own sake and a system of annotation virtually independent of the text. Prose is more pleasant to read if it does not require one to jump constantly to the foot of the page or to the back of the book. Every effort should be made to make the text self-sufficient, to make the annotations unobtrusive, and to consolidate footnote references. Yet scholarship will continue to differ from the personal essay in that its facts and inferences are fully documented. Successful scholarly writing achieves that most difficult feat of blending maximum interest and readability with maximum accuracy and evidence. In presenting his documentation economically the writer must depend upon the perception of his reader.

Thus research writing is objective writing having its own characteristics; it utilizes objective techniques and is subject to dangers that should be particularly avoided. The student should review particularly the discussions above of taking notes, respecting intellectual honesty, and organizing longer papers (chapter 4). In addition, some matters mentioned earlier will warrant more detailed attention here.

The handling of materials in any research report should be objective and relatively impartial, and the style should reflect this objectivity. If the writer has opinions to express, he should label his opinions clearly. Research reports mainly employ the third person, although good practice now allows the use of the first person to avoid excessive use of the passive voice where circumstances require some discussion of the author and what he did—for instance, in describing how equipment was set up, or why an investigation was conducted in a certain way—but a research report should be couched in generally objective terms.

The reader of any difficult or controversial report wants always to know whether the author is sure he is right, whether his evidence is sound. But writers cannot always be sure; they do not always have adequate evidence. Thus, the writer should make clear what he knows certainly and why; he should appropriately alert his reader to the uncertainty involved in qualified assertions, those he has made because the evidence is extremely good, although inconclusive; and he should identify any observations that are guesses that he has made just because they are his best guesses, subject to revision. Keeping the reader constantly aware of the writer's own estimate of the conclusiveness of his statements is not easy, and it can become cumbersome, although it need not be. Part of the secret of a good objective style grows from learning to keep the reader informed, unobtrusively, of the writer's own estimate of his material. The devices for doing this are legion, too numerous to be detailed here, but the beginning writer will do well to study competent pieces of serious writing, in magazines like *Harper's* and *The Atlantic*, for instance, and in scholarly and scientific journals.

Another problem bothers almost every beginning research worker: what should he do when the authorities disagree? They do disagree. Most important problems cannot be settled certainly and finally, and even for minor questions the evidence is often contradictory. If the writer finds no reason for preferring one of his disagreeing sources, he can present the evidence on all sides and cite all authorities in his footnotes. If he thinks one argument is better than the others, he can present it and then cite opposing evidence in the text or in a footnote. Even if he is sure that one side is right, he should cite opposing opinions in footnotes.

Since evaluating evidence and dealing with inconsistencies are parts of the same problem, they may appropriately be considered together. Notice the following, an excerpt from a popular discussion of American English.

That this meaning of the word *lumber* was brought to America is evident from its survival in some local dialects as well as from a good deal of early legislation. The *Boston Records* for 1663 show that the inhabitants were cautioned to "take care that noe wood, logges, timber, stonnes, or any *other* lumber be layed upon the flatte to the annoyance of any vesseles," and a similar law was passed in 1701 against encumbering any street, lane, or alley. Certainly in a pioneer community with building going on constantly, cut timber would inevitably be piled in the streets from time to time, and the circumstance that this was so often the offending impediment seems to have led to a specific association of *lumber* with cut or milled wood, in contrast to uncut logs or possibly standing trees, as is suggested by the report of Sir Edmond Andros, written in 1678: "The Comodit999yes of the Country to ye westward are wheat . . . pipe staves, timber, lumber & horses."

ALBERT H. MARCKWARDT, American English

Since the book was intended for popular reading, Marckwardt did not provide footnotes, but the passage indicates that documentation is essentially a quality written into the prose itself, a characteristic of style to which the footnotes are only an important appendage. Exact documentation was not possible, because without footnotes Marckwardt's sentences would have become too cluttered with details if he had provided all bibliographic information, but the essential documentation is there. The writer quotes his sources exactly, and he gives enough evidence of source so that we are convinced he is founding his observations upon carefully selected fact, and we are even provided with rough citations. Marckwardt mentions these sources urbanely, making no great to-do about them; but any examination of his terminology will reveal that he is constantly assessing his evidence and making us quietly aware of when he feels confident and when he is making a plausible guess. He starts by saying that the existence of "this meaning" of *lumber* in America "is evident," and he indicates that he has two sorts of evidence, survival in dialects and early legislation. He then cites two specific instances in which building materials cluttering up streets or the waterfront were called "lumber"; here he makes flat assertions, but he is very careful as to what he asserts. He says the "inhabitants were cautioned," and he apparently assumes we will presume that the caution was needed. He points out that the caution might well be needed in a pioneer community. So much for his background; he is now ready for his main conclusion, the reason for his paragraph—how did a word that meant something like *rubbish* come to mean "cut or milled logs"? He believes he has the answer, but the answer is only inferred; he has no direct, reliable evidence for it, and accordingly he makes his proposal, but cautiously: "The circumstance . . . seems to have led to a specific association. . . ." He has some collateral evidence, but this also is not conclusive, and accordingly he uses the phrase "as is suggested." That is, though Marckwardt does not in this passage have the advantage of being able to use footnotes, he has written the essence of his documentation and his estimate of the worth of his evidence into the text itself; this is sound practice, even when the writer is addressing readers who welcome footnotes.

Compare Marckwardt's passage with the following from a documented history of the English language (footnote numbers have been changed to avoid confusion):

According to the same chronicler[1] William the Conqueror made an effort himself at the age of forty-three to learn English, that he might understand and render justice in the disputes between his subjects, but his energies were too completely absorbed by his many other activities to enable him to make much progress. There is nothing improbable in the statement. Certainly the assertion of a fourteenth century writer[2] that the Conqueror considered how he might destroy the 'Saxon' tongue in order that English and French might speak the same language seems little less than silly in view of the king's efforts to promote the belief that he was the authentic successor of the Old English kings and in the light of his use of English alongside of Latin, to the exclusion of French, in his charters. His youngest son, Henry I, may have known some English, though we must give up the pretty story of his interpreting the English words in a charter to the monks of Colchester.[3] If later kings for a time seem to have been ignorant of the language,[4] their lack of acquaintance with it is not to be attributed to any fixed purpose. In the period with which we are at the moment concerned — the period up to 1200 — the attitude of the king and the upper classes toward the English language may be characterized as one of simple indifference. They did not cultivate English — which is not the same as saying that they had no acquaintance with it — because their activities in England did not necessitate it and their constant concern with continental affairs made French for them much more useful.

ALBERT C. BAUGH, *A History of the English Language*

[1]Ordericus Vitalis, ed. Prevost, II, 215.

[2]Robert Holkot, on the authority of John Selden, *Eadmeri Monarchi Cantuariensis Historiae Novorum siue sui Saeculi Libri VI* (London, 1623), p. 189.

[3]The story was considered authentic by so critical a student as J. Horace Round ("Henry I as an English Scholar," *Academy*, Sept. 13, 1884, p. 168), but the charter has since been proved by J. Armitage Robinson to be a forgery. Cf. C. W. David, "The Claim of King Henry I to Be Called Learned," *Anniversary Essays in Medieval History by Students of Charles Homer Haskins* (Boston, 1929), pp. 45–56.

[4]We do not know whether William Rufus and Stephen knew English. Henry II understood it although he apparently did not speak it (see below, p. 144). Richard I was thoroughly French; his whole stay in England amounted to only a few months. He probably knew no English. Concerning John's knowledge of English we have no evidence. As Freeman remarks (*Norman Conquest*, II. 128), the royal family at this time is frequently the least English in England and is not to be used as a norm for judging the diffusion of the two languages.

We may note some similarities and some differences between Marckwardt's and Baugh's paragraphs. In general, they read very much alike. Marckwardt has no footnotes, and Baugh's treatment can be read without them. Both paragraphs read smoothly; like Marckwardt, Baugh can keep his reader constantly aware of where his evidence comes from and how much he, as a scholar, trusts it. He is constantly evaluating this evidence; he is aware that chroniclers have varied in statements about William the Conqueror and his attitude toward English. He notices the testimony of one chronicler that William at forty-three tried to learn English and he observes that "there is nothing improbable in the statement," but recognizing that chroniclers are not always reliable, he makes no commitment himself. He records but declines to accept the opinion of another writer, partly because the person lived long after William, partly because William's own actions seem to belie the statement. He rejects out of hand a legend concerning William's son; the chronicle reporting it has been proved a forgery. As for the knowledge of English possessed by other twelfth-century figures, he offers his own guess as "simple indifference." He does not labor his uncertainty; he does not say, "Of course this is just an opinion, and every man is entitled to his own opinion, but I have read a good many chronicles and scholarly studies, and I have tried hard to produce a fair answer, and for what it is worth, this is my best estimate." He implies all this, however, when he says "the attitude . . . may be characterized. . . ." That is, scholarly writing that carries footnotes is much like scholarly writing that has no footnotes; it should be clear, orderly, well balanced, factual, judicial, and urbane, and the reader should be able to follow it with or without the footnotes.

On the other hand, footnotes provide the scholarly writer distinct advantages; observe how Baugh exploits them. He can, of course, be more precise; he can cite works exactly, giving the edition, the volume, and the page; he can quote long titles intact, can cite more than one source for a fact, and all this without interrupting the flow of his prose. He can save space and the reader's time by banishing some details to the footnotes. For example, he rejects the story of Henry I besting the monks of Colchester in a few words because he can provide the details in the footnote. He has examined the evidence and has found it so convincing that he need not equivocate; if the reader is not content to trust Baugh as a scholar, he probably will be convinced when he reads the footnote; if not, he has the references and can pursue the question. Baugh does not need to defend his position in the text; but Marckwardt, having no footnotes, presumably would not have felt he could be so cavalier. What about those people who had read the story of Henry I in some old history book and had believed it all their lives? Doubtless, without footnotes, the writer would have felt he had to interrupt his account to explain why he doubted this story; the footnote permits the writer to make his decision and get on with pertinent parts of the discussion.

Somewhat different is the last footnote, because it allows Baugh to introduce material that, without footnotes, he would probably have omitted as a digression. Some writers use footnotes even more extensively for this purpose than does Baugh; Van Wyck Brooks, for example, in a charming series of books on early America, uses footnotes to provide quantities of engaging supplementary information. This sort of thing can be carried too far; and the more scholarly style sheets tend to deprecate it.

Samples of Investigative Papers

Following are samples from investigative papers: a page of a student paper as it would look when typewritten, the opening pages of another paper of the sort commonly required in composition courses, and a brief paper from a professional journal that illustrates a different system of documentation.

The sample page is from a student paper, "A Yet Unexorcised Ghost," by James Assuras. It illustrates the typing style that accumulates footnotes at the bottom of each page. It also illustrates the use of parenthetical references to locate a quotation from a play with the edition used identified in a footnote. The quotations and footnotes are single-spaced, although in a manuscript being submitted for publication they would be double-spaced.

Agnes Arnold's "Young Man on a Horse" began as a paper written from a "controlled research" pamphlet, a collection of source materials on the Battle of Gettysburg; but as it expanded it required library investigation, and footnote references are to original sources. Pamphlets of this sort, designed to provide information for student papers, are used in many composition courses, and the sample papers illustrate how evidence from a research pamphlet can be handled and annotated and also how the pamphlets can become the basis for further research in a library.

The third brief paper, "On the Nutritional Value of Cannibalism," was written by Andrew P. Vayda and was published in *American Anthropologist*, 72, No. 6 (1970). It illustrates one version of the style for documentation described above and used for much scientific research, in which brief parenthetical references refer to items in a bibliography.

Page from "A Yet Unexorcised Ghost"

The critics apparently do not agree, and so far as I have been able to discover, they have produced five different sorts of answers, some of which subdivide into alternate answers. He [the Ghost] may have been, as he purported to be, King Hamlet's soul,

> Doom'd for a certain term to walk the night,
> And for the day confined to fast in fires,
> Till the foul crimes done in my days of nature
> Are burnt and purged away.   (Hamlet, I, v, 9-13)[1]

Even so, was he a Roman Catholic soul in Purgatory, or a Church of England soul?[2] Granted that he is the soul of a deceased king, is he on a personal mission of revenge, of kingly justice, or is he the emissary of some higher power who has sent him to intervene in affairs of state?[3] The Ghost may be a devil,[4] as Hamlet himself recognizes:

> The spirit I have seen
> May be the devil: and the devil hath power
> To assume a pleasing shape; (II, ii, 627-29)

---

[1] I employ here, and throughout, the spelling and line numbering in The Complete Works of Shakespeare, ed. Hardin Craig (Chicago, Scott Foresman, 1951).

[2] The distinction is extensively drawn in Lily B. Campbell, Shakespeare's Tragic Heroes: Slaves of Passion (1930; rpt. New York, Barnes & Noble, 1952), p. 121.

[3] The latter interpretation has been presented in I. J. Semper, "The Ghost in Hamlet," The Catholic World, 162, (1946), 313.

[4] Robert H. West, "King Hamlet's Ambiguous Ghost," PMLA, 70 (1955), 1107-17.

by

Agnes Arnold

It was the third day at Gettysburg, midafternoon. Major General George E. Pickett's rebel-yelling Confederates had stormed Cemetery Ridge, and were boiling over a stone wall and a rail fence which had provided some protection to Brigadier General Alexander S. Webb's troops, holding the Union center. If they succeeded, if the charging men in gray could stay there, if they could establish a front around the clump of trees to which they had marched across open fields, the Union forces would be split, the Army of the Potomac cracked and faced with disruption or extinction. Nothing adequate for defense would stand between General Robert E. Lee and his undefeated Army of Northern Virginia and the populous Northern cities, Philadelphia, New York, Boston. If Pickett's men had stayed on Cemetery Ridge, Lee could quite probably have dictated, from either New York or Philadelphia, the terms on which the United States of America was to become two countries rather than one.

A half hour later, the decimated remnants of Pickett's men who "had moved across that field of death as a battalion marches forward in line of battle upon drill"[1] were fleeing, those who could run or crawl. Perhaps the most dramatic account of what turned the tide is that of Frank Aretas Haskell, a young Wisconsin civilian turned lieutenant, writing to his brother, H. M. Haskell.[2] Lieutenant Haskell was returning from an attempt to deliver a message when he stopped to view what he called the "tremendous" conflict, and observed that there was "no wavering in all our line." His account continues,

> Wondering how long the Rebel ranks, deep though they were, could stand our sheltered volleys, I had come near my destination, when — great heaven! were my senses mad? The larger portion of Webb's brigade — my God, it was true — there by the group of trees and the angles of the wall, was breaking from the cover of their works, and without orders or reason, with no hand lifted to check them, was falling back, a fear-stricken flock of confusion! The fate of Gettysburg hung upon a spider's single thread.[3]

Haskell goes on to tell how "a great magnificent passion" overcame him as he saw how "the damned red flags of the rebellion began to thicken and flaunt along the wall," and he dashed to stem "the tide of rabbits," commanding them to face about and fight, and

[1] George E. Pickett, *Soldier of the South: General Pickett's Letters to his Wife,* ed. Arthur Crew Inman (Boston: Houghton Mifflin, 1928), p. 70.

[2] *The Battle of Gettysburg* (Wisconsin History Commission, November, 1908), pp. 112–130.

[3] *Battle,* p. 119.

COMMENT

Arnold uses an extensive introduction. Usually, such a long introduction would be quite inappropriate in a paper of moderate length, but her approach may be justified because it provides a dramatic opening to a semipopular presentation and at the same time allows her to introduce material that is to prove useful in the body of her paper.

The author is not yet ready to state her main idea, but she is centering attention on the central figure.

The first quotation in the paragraph, since it is less than a sentence long, is run in and enclosed in quotation marks. The second, longer quotation is indented without quotation marks; in a class paper the long quotation would be single-spaced.

Miss Arnold was instructed to accumulate footnotes at the bottom of each page.

The first footnote illustrates standard form for an edited work. Since this is the only work by Pickett cited in the paper, it can be referred to in subsequent footnotes by the author's name plus the page reference; see footnote 11.

Footnote 3 uses a short form of the title cited in footnote 2. The writer might also have used an abbreviation here, making the footnote *Ibid.,* p. 119, but the use of the short title is now common practice.

517

beating with his sword on their "unpatriotic backs." Soon General Webb came sweating up on foot and "did all that one could to repair the breach," but his men were "falling fast." The Confederate flags "were accumulating at the wall every moment" now, and Webb had only three small regiments with which to oppose them. "Oh, where is Gibbon? where is Hancock?[4]—some general—anybody with the power and the will to support that wasting, melting line?"

Haskell had no troops under him, but he was aide to General Gibbon,[5] and thus had a sort of derived authority, so long as nobody asked questions. He set about trying to find help. The most copious body of reinforcements would have been the First Army Corps, which had not as yet been engaged, commanded by Major General Abner Doubleday, but Haskell concluded that Doubleday was "too far and too slow," and he recalled, also, "on another occasion I had begged him to send his idle regiment to support another line battling with thrice its numbers, and this 'Old Sumpter Hero' had declined."[6] What about Hall?—Colonel Norman J. Hall, of the Seventh Michigan Infantry, commanding the third brigade, was stationed immediately to Webb's left.[7] His men had been under heavy attack, but "the fire was constantly diminishing now in his front."[8] Haskell located Hall, sword in hand, who agreed to "move my brigade at once," and soon five regiments were marching to the rescue of Webb's three. But this was not enough—how about Harrow? Brigadier General William Harrow was in command of the whole second division, and in addition—although Haskell did not know this at the time—he was now in command of the entire Second Army Corps, since both Hancock and Gibbon had been severely wounded. Harrow could not be found, presumably because he had gone back to headquarters to relieve Hancock and Gibbon, but Haskell did not stand on ceremony. He managed to get men from the Nineteenth Maine, the Fifteenth Massachusetts, the First Minnesota, and the Thirty-second New York Militia to follow him, and "all that I could find I took over to the right at the *double quick*." Arrived he saw that the Union troops had been pushed well up the ridge, that in their confused milling they were suffering terribly from the Confederate troops firing from the wall from which Webb's regiments had fled. Haskell endeavored to organize a charge on the wall, but with some difficulties, as his description reveals:

[4] *Battle*, pp. 119–22. Major General Winfield S. Hancock was in command of the Second Army Corps, of which Brigadier General John Gibbon was second in command, and in direct command of the second division; Webb commanded the second brigade within this division. Generals Hancock and Gibbon were thus Webb's immediate superiors, as well as Haskell's.

[5] *The War of the Rebellion: A Compilation of the Official Records of the Union and Confederate Armies*, series 1, (Washington, D.C.: GPO, 1889), 27, part 1, 418. Hereafter cited as *Records*.

[6] *Battle*, p. 122.

[7] *Records*, pp. 374 and 439.

[8] *Battle*, p. 124.

518

COMMENT

How much should a writer quote? Arnold has elected to quote verbatim the description of the flight from the wall, partly because it is a dramatic scene dramatically recorded, but also because some of the later discussion is to hinge on this scene. She could, of course, have gone on quoting, but the whole passage would run to several hundred words, and much of it is not germane to her eventual purpose. Accordingly, she gives her own running account, but she inserts within it words, phrases, whole sentences from the original that preserve the flavor of Haskell's account, although she has reduced the original by about 90 per cent. One might notice that Miss Arnold is identifying all sources within the text of the article, but making no great to-do of her documentation. The identification is started unostentatiously in the sentence on p. 516 beginning "Lieutenant Haskell was" by inserting the words "what he called the 'tremendous' conflict." No citation is necessary here because we get to it in the next sentence, and the two passages are related by "His account continues." After the quoted passage no further citation is necessary, because "Haskell goes on to tell" lets us know that the remaining details come from the next page or two.

If Arnold were here trying to make a parade of her knowledge, she could seed this passage with footnotes, but she wisely restricts them to the quotations that involve a change of page reference.

Arnold continues to keep the story dramatic by quoting bits from Haskell's account, but moves the story rapidly by relying mainly on her own summary. This procedure is the more appropriate because the essay depends in part on what Haskell did, how much of a hero he was; and since the writer's case is to hinge in part on the validity of Haskell's account as against Webb's official report, details are necessary but are best in Haskell's words. She could, of course, have reproduced Haskell's entire letter, but long undigested accounts are not usually so useful as more succinct versions with brief quoted passages.

The observation that Haskell was to learn only later why he could not find Harrow might have been relegated to a footnote, as could that about Hancock and Gibbon having been wounded. But on the whole the text should be readable without the footnotes, and apparently the author felt that her audience would want to know this much about Haskell's dilemma and the reasons for it.

Footnote 4 is informational; we need to know who these officers are. The author has worked out their relationships by studying various reports in her sources.

Footnote 5 provides an example of a reference to a complicated title. Titles of this sort are not common, but they are relatively more common in scholarly and scientific writing than in most prose, and they are sometimes complicated enough so that they do not fit into a standard style. When in doubt the writer should give enough bibliographic details to identify the specific volume certainly.

My "Forward to the wall" is answered by the Rebel counter-command, "Steady men!" and the wave swings back. . . . These men of Pennsylvania, on the soil of their own homesteads, the first and only to flee the wall, must be the first to storm it. "Major — *lead* your men over the crest, they will follow." "By the tactics I understand my place is in the rear of the men." "Your pardon, sir; I see *your* place is in the rear of the men. I thought you were fit to lead."[9]

Under Haskell's urging, a color-sergeant dashed toward the wall and was shot down, but others followed him, gained the wall, breached it, and soon Pickett's charge was thrown back. The battle was won, and although nobody knew it yet, the issue of the war was determined.

Such was the high tide of the Confederacy as Haskell professed to have seen it, but his part in saving the day at Gettysburg for the Union forces found no reflection in the report of General Webb, whose troops he had relieved. On the surface, Webb's report appears to be brief, factual, and reliable. His command suffered in the bombardment, he reports, and then sustained the brunt of Pickett's charge. He continues,

> The Sixty-ninth Pennsylvania Volunteers and most of the Seventy-first Pennsylvania Volunteers, even after the enemy were in their rear, held their position. . . . but the enemy would probably have succeeded in piercing our lines had not Colonel Hall advanced with several of his regiments to my support. . . . The conduct of this brigade was most satisfactory. Officers and men did their whole duty. . . . I saw none retire from the fence.[10]

Webb makes no mention of Haskell.

One cannot help wondering why. Was Haskell so in love with his own Homeric account of the battle that he grossly distorted it? His being able to hear the commanders on both sides of the fighting above the thundering of thousands of men firing at each other rather suggests that he may have imagined some of what he reported. Was he handsomely making himself a hero for the family back home? Did he have an exalted notion of himself? Or did Webb deliberately suppress any mention of Haskell? He did mention Hall, but Hall was a general, and obviously protocol required mentioning superior officers; was Haskell's performance sufficiently routine for a lieutenant so that it did not warrant individual notice? Or did Webb have some reason for belittling Haskell's assistance? After all, if we are to accept Haskell's account, he saved Webb's forces from defeat and probably from destruction; he may well have saved the day for the Union forces, and he quite probably saved Webb himself from death or capture. Webb may have had both psychological and professional reasons for preferring to ignore Haskell's services.

[9] *Battle*, 129–30. I have not been able to identify this major. The major did, however, have some reason for remaining at the rear, since troops were constantly being disrupted by the loss of their officers, who were prime targets. For example, Pickett retired with only one field officer unhurt; he lists seven colonels and nine lieutenant colonels killed or seriously wounded — Pickett, p. 71.

[10] *Records*, p. 428.

Again Arnold has elected to quote a considerable passage, partly because it will prove germane to the central idea of the paper. One might notice the way she introduces this passage, keeping attention on what Haskell is doing and identifying the quotation with the phrase, "as his description reveals."

Here the writer encounters a somewhat different problem. As will appear below, she has become convinced that Webb was a liar, even though he may have been a sort of white liar, trying to protect the reputation of his troops, and his manner of doing this may have made him look rather less trustworthy than, in fact, he was.

Now the author is ready to state her main idea. It is announced by the topic sentence, beginning "One cannot help wondering why," which directs the reader's attention to the main problem of the paper, although not too belligerently. The author makes her point and lets us know where the article is going without saying "I shall now endeavor to prove to you. . . ."

Footnote 9, like footnote 4, illustrates how footnotes can be used to present information that would be useful to a reader intending to pursue the subject of the paper in detail, although it is not essential to the main narrative and might break continuity if included in the text.

Closer examination of the available documents may cast some light on these questions. First we might notice that at least two details in Webb's report are suspect. He says, as we have seen, that "officers and men did their whole duty," and "I saw no one retire from the fence." The first of these statements cannot be true; Captain Davis, reporting for the Sixty-ninth Pennsylvanians, was doubtless making the best of the situation when he wrote, "our troops, with few exceptions, met them bravely,"[11] and Colonel Smith, reporting for the Seventy-first, mentioned that a captain and a private, "are under sentence of court martial," an admission which surely suggests they had done something less than their duty. Webb's other observation is even more suspect; when he says, "I saw no one retire," he must be deliberately using language to deceive. Possibly he did not see them; Haskell says the general arrived after "the larger portion of Webb's brigade" had fled. In the smoke of battle he may not have seen them, or he may have been appropriately bringing up the Seventy-second Pennsylvania, which had been held in reserve; he may have told the truth when he said he did not *see* them, but he certainly knew they had retired. If he did not know it, he must have been one of few men in both armies who remained in ignorance; Union commanders on both sides of him reported the retirement as one of the routine details of the battle, and Confederates, both in Pickett's charge and out of it, recorded the Union retirement.[12] Webb must have colored his account to protect the reputation of his men, and quite possibly of himself.

If so, one may raise the question, also, as to whether Webb did not gloss over some of Haskell's exploit for similar reasons. We know that Webb was not in all details a reliable reporter; was Haskell? Here we might consider at least two sorts of evidence: what corroborative evidence does Haskell's report receive from the reports of other observers, and how reliable does Haskell seem to be, particularly when he is dealing with his own achievements? As for the first, a modern reader of the contemporary reports gains the impression that a large part of the Union army was recounting Haskell's exploits, and if so, the information must have come to Webb's attention, for the general's report is dated more than a week after the battle,[13] whether or not he noticed Haskell in the fighting. . . .

[11]*Records*, p. 431.

[12]Particularly convincing is the highly circumstantial account in a personal letter from a Confederate officer. He records that "Armisted's men rushed across the wall and pursued the enemy . . . we pushed up to the wall, and could almost see the Yankee gunners leaving their places and running in our lines for safety"—Charles E. Loehr, "The Old First Virginia at Gettysburg," *Southern Historical Society Papers*, 32 (1904), 35. One might notice also Hall's description of the battle lines at this point, which shows Webb's troops drawn well back from both the stone wall and the rail fence (*Records*, pp. 437–41). Hancock's official report recorded that "the most of that part of Webb's brigade posted here abandoned their position"; presumably he had received Webb's report when he made his (*Records*, p. 374).

[13]*Records*, p. 428.

After a paragraph that presents us with the alternatives, a paragraph that becomes, in effect, a topic sentence for the whole paper, the writer makes clear how the article is to be organized.

Here the author faces a common problem — what should one do when the evidence is contradictory? Actually, there is almost always some contradictory evidence, even on such matters as when a person like Shakespeare was born. For many of these questions the evidence has been sifted, and readers are given results of the sifting of evidence; whereas the writer is now faced with the problem of doing the sifting. Did Webb's men run, or did they not? In this case the decision is easy: Webb's superior said they retired, even after receiving Webb's report; his fellow officers said the men retired; the attacking Confederates said the same thing, and so did people who wrote letters and had no notion that they were giving evidence. They were just telling their friends what happened. Only Webb seems to have tried to suggest that his men did not retire, and he does this in such a way that one suspects he is twisting words to tell the literal truth while telling what amounts to a lie. Accordingly, the writer says confidently that Webb's men did retire, and addresses herself to the crucial problem of whether it is possible that Webb did not know this.

The author has now established her first point, that Webb was not above distorting evidence if he had good reason to do so. But that he distorted evidence to protect his men does not establish that he distorted evidence to belittle Haskell. Here we need more direct testimony, and the author recognizes that we have evidence of two sorts: (1) Webb is not an entirely reliable witness, but is Haskell any better? and (2) do the reports of other witnesses confirm Haskell's account of himself in any entirely convincing way? Since the second is more objective, she starts with that, reviewing the testimony, or lack of it, in the reports of officer after officer who either mentions Haskell or would have been in a position to see what he did.

On the Nutritional Value of Cannibalism

Andrew P. Vayda

Columbia University

Accepted for publication 6 March 1970.

While duly appreciative of Garn and Block's attempt (*AA* 72:106) to calculate the amount of protein available from the flesh of a 50 kg man, I regard as extremely misleading their suggestion that a group has to "consume its own number in a year" for cannibalism to be of nutritional value. Although it may be, as Garn and Block argue, that "regular" people-eating is without much nutritional significance, "irregular" people-eating, which may well be the more common mode of cannibalism, still needs to be considered in terms of its satisfaction of nutritional requirements. In this connection, I suggested some years ago (Vayda 1960a:70–72 and 1960b) that human flesh, while not a regular item of the diet of the Maoris of New Zealand, was nutritionally important to Maori warriors on distant expeditions against other tribes, for it was precisely on these expeditions that food supplies were likely to be short. More recently, Rappaport (1967:84–87) has indicated that pork, while not a regular item of the diet of the Maring people of New Guinea, may nevertheless be of critical nutritional importance when consumed in irregularly occurring ritual contexts that correspond to stress situations. Specifically, Rappaport has noted that the consumption of the flesh of sacrificial animals by individuals suffering from illness or injury or otherwise undergoing stress is probably important for counteracting the stress-induced increase in these individuals' catabolization of protein, for the negative nitrogen balance resulting from this increase, if not offset by the ingestion of high-quality proteins, may impair the healing of wounds and the production of antibodies and have other physically harmful consequences for people, like the Marings, whose protein intake has been marginal, even if adequate for everyday activities in the absence of illness or injury or other appreciable stress. The question of whether the consumption of human flesh might function in the same or a similar way—perhaps especially among people who are on low-protein diets and without ready access to such animals as cattle or pigs as sacrificial items and sources of high-quality proteins—has hardly been asked. Yet just such questions about irregularly occurring anthropophagy must be answered—with whatever appropriate quantifications are feasible—before firm conclusions about the role of nutrition in the practice of cannibalism can be made.

References Cited

Garn, Stanley M., and Walter D. Block
    1970 The limited nutritional value of cannibalism, American Anthropologist 72:106.

Rappaport, Roy A.
1967   Pigs for the ancestors: ritual in the ecology of a New Guinea people. New Haven: Yale University Press.

Vayda, A. P.
1960a Maori warfare. Polynesian Society Maori Monographs, 2. Wellington: Polynesian Society.

1960b Maori women and Maori cannibalism. Man 60:70–71.

COMMENT

This short paper illustrates a type of documentation now used in many scientific journals; by this system, brief parenthetical references within the text refer to a bibliography appended to the paper.

The first reference—*AA* 72:106—identifies by citing the journal, abbreviated, the volume and the page; the authors are mentioned in the text. The second—Vayda 1960a:70–72 and 1960b—names the author and distinguishes his two works by their date and, since they both appeared in the same year, *a* and *b*. The third reference—1967:84–87—requires only the year and pages since the author is specified in the text and only one of his works is cited.

The bibliography contains essentially the same information as the kind of bibliography suggested in this chapter for class papers, but the form is modified to accommodate the reference system; the author is put in a separate line, and the date appears after his name to provide identification of the particular work.

A Research attempts to find answers to questions, and one good way to find a topic for a research paper is to pick a question and start looking for an answer to it. Select one of the following questions—or a question of your own approved by your instructor—and do enough preliminary investigation in the library to suggest to you the scope of the problem involved and the availability of material. Prepare three bibliography cards for items pertinent to the question. Then write a brief statement of your preliminary assessment of what would be involved in finding an answer or partial answer to your question.

1. What is the evidence for the existence of "Unidentified Flying Objects"?
2. What caused President Harding's death?
3. Was Mary Queen of Scots guilty of conspiring against Elizabeth?
4. Can bees distinguish colors?
5. What sort of law man was Wyatt Earp?
6. Was Lizzie Borden insane?
7. Is the ballad "Frankie and Johnnie" based on a real event?
8. How did the Egyptians build their pyramids?
9. Do ants fight wars?
10. What is the origin of the legend that a toad has a jewel in its head?
11. What was the evidence presented to justify burning Joan of Arc at the stake?
12. What did Noah Webster think about spelling?
13. Did Adolph Hitler die in Berlin?
14. Has atomic testing had any effect on weather?
15. Has fallout from atomic testing had any effect on animal or plant life?
16. Was there a shot from a sniper before the National Guard opened fire on students at Kent State in 1970?
17. What was the critical reception in 1970 of the rock opera *Jesus Christ Superstar*?
18. Did Columbus discover America?
19. Did Washington chop down a cherry tree?
20. How closely did Davy Crockett resemble the legends about him?
21. Is cancer becoming a young person's disease?
22. What was the Teapot Dome Scandal?
23. What was the role of H. L. Mencken in the Scopes trial?
24. How much scientific evidence is there for the existence of extrasensory perception?
25. How accurate historically is Shakespeare's portrait of Richard III?

B Using the style recommended above and information from sample footnotes, correct the following as bibliography entries.

1. Dmitri Nabokov translator of *King, Queen, Knave* by Vladimir Nabokov, published by McGraw-Hill in New York in 1968.
2. *Richard Crashaw:* A Study in Style and Poetic Development by Wallerstein, Ruth, (Madison, Wisconsin Pr., 1935) No. 37 of University of Wis. Studies in Lang. and Lit.
3. Starr, Wilmarth H., Mary P. Thompson, and Donald D. Walsh, eds. Modern Foreign Languages and the Academically Talented Student, published in New York by MLA and in Washington by National Education Association (1960).
4. W. M. Frohock, The Idea of the Picaresque. Published in No. 15 of the Yearbook of Comparative and General Literature. 1967. Pages 45–54
5. Alpert, H. *But Who Wrote the Movie?* "Saturday Review" 26 Dec. 1970, pp. 7–14.
6. Rev. of "Military Men" by Ward Just, reviewed by Geoffrey Wolff in Newsweek for 28 Dec. 1970 (pages 62–63).

C Prepare a sequence of footnotes for references in the following order to the works in B above.

Nabokov, p. 18; Nabokov, p. 39; Alpert, p. 9; Frohock, p. 49; Nabokov, p. 77; Wallerstein, p. 91; Alpert, p. 11.

THE WRITING SYSTEM: PUNCTUATION

CHAPTER 25

Punctuation can enforce meaning and reveal grammatical structure.

All languages are systems, or systems of systems, and most systems — including the means of writing English — are in part conventional, embodying old customs, enshrined in tradition that has become ordered and arbitrary, so that the reason behind a practice may be obscured in the rule that prescribes it. Of this confusion, Lewis Carroll, author of *Alice's Adventures in Wonderland,* was quite aware, as the following passage suggests:

> At this moment the King, who had been for some time busily writing in his note-book, called out "Silence!" and read out from his book "Rule Forty-two. All Persons more than a mile high to leave the court."
>
> Everybody looked at Alice.
>
> "I'm not a mile high," said Alice.
>
> "You are," said the King.
>
> "Nearly two miles high," added the Queen.
>
> "Well, I sha'n't go, at any rate," said Alice: "besides, that's not a regular rule: you invented it just now."
>
> "It's the oldest rule in the book," said the King.

Even the "oldest rule in the book," however, may have behind it good sense and good logic, provided it reflects the winnowed experience of long practice and thus becomes what Alice thought of as a "regular rule." A writer can learn a convention more easily and apply it more aptly if he understands the logic behind it, but even a rule that smacks of the mental processes of the King of

528

Hearts may have its uses. It may clarify a convention, and conventions simplify life. Anyone in this country who consistently drives on the left-hand side of the road will not stay long out of jail, a hospital, or the morgue. Anyone who drives on the right-hand side in England is in similar danger. A writer who fails to follow certain conventions, though he may be physically safe, is in danger of being misunderstood.

Some conventions in the English writing system scarcely call for elucidation here. Almost any child born in an English-speaking country knows that writing goes from left to right and from top to bottom, although in some languages writing starts in the lower right-hand corner and in others alternate lines run in opposite directions. Anyone who writes a language using the Roman alphabet knows that if a line rises on the left-hand side of a circle, the letter is a *b*, but if it rises on the right-hand side, the letter is a *d*. Some conventions, however, are complex, and customs may differ for special purposes. Publishers and publications have style sheets which prescribe their practices in manuscript form, punctuation, capitalization, and even spelling, considering many details of style too specialized for inclusion in the discussion of principles such as those treated in chapters 25–26. For details of style, *A Manual of Style*, prepared by the staff of the University of Chicago Press and frequently revised, has been standard practically since the first edition appeared in 1906. Also useful is John Benbow, *Manuscript and Proof* (New York, 1943), the manual for the American Oxford University Press.

PUNCTUATION   25

One writing convention, punctuation, is mainly concerned with the identification of sentences and with revealing structure and relationships within sentences. It is closely related to pitch, stress, and rhythm in speech, since the modulations of the voice and bodily gesture do for oral speech what punctuation is intended to do for written language. Punctuation also reveals meaning, since meaning alters with structure. Consider the following:

Open fire; at noon our own troops will be out of range.
Open fire at noon; our own troops will be out of range.

If she plans to be married, before she is twelve she should have started a hope chest.
If she plans to be married before she is twelve, she should have started a hope chest.

---

25   **P**

*Revise punctuation according to the principles and
conventions described in this chapter.*

ORIGINAL

On January, 11, 1971 I had my
sixteenth birthday, and passed my
driving test but my parents did not
let me drive the car alone for another year.

REVISION

On January 11, 1961, I had my
sixteenth birthday and passed my
driving test, but my parents did not
let me drive the car alone for another year.

However, it may be the responsibility is entirely our own.
However it may be, the responsibility is entirely our own.

The doctor said he was depressed and humanity was disappointed.
The doctor said he was depressed, and humanity was disappointed.

The American soldiers who had been hiding in the old barn were all
killed.
The American soldiers, who had been hiding in the old barn, were
all killed.

Turn the heat on, Willie.
Turn the heat on Willie.

Styles in Punctuation

As late as the eighteenth century English punctuation was
primarily rhetorical; that is, marks or "points" were directions for
speaking, indicating pauses. In Modern English, punctuation has
become more codified, working largely in a set of relatively consistent practices intended to clarify meaning in writing and to
help mark the grammatical structure of the sentence. The writer
follows principles that make punctuation marks emphasize sentence patterns—but since pauses and pitch changes in speech also
clarify grammatical patterns, pauses and punctuation marks may
coincide. Thus the student may get help with punctuation problems by considering how an expression would be pronounced.
For example, the question of whether to put commas around a
modifier can often be decided by considering how the sentence
would be pronounced to convey the intended meaning. Consider: **530**

The two student senators [,] who had been arguing for an expanded athletic program [,] voted against intercollegiate athletics
for women.

The writer thinking of the *who*-clause as restrictive would pronounce the sentence with no significant pause after *senators* and
with rising inflection on *program;* he would use no commas in the
sentence. The writer thinking of the clause as nonrestrictive would
in speaking pause after *senators* and *program* and would tend to
raise the pitch of his voice on the first syllable of *senators* and lower
it on the last syllable of *program.* He would use commas before and
after the clause to signal its nonrestrictive meaning.

Even though practices in punctuation are less arbitrary today
than they were when they depended greatly on the whim of the
writer or even the convenience of the printer, fashions still vary —
from writer to writer, country to country, and time to time. Some
writers use a comma whenever its inclusion might clarify; others
punctuate more lightly, omitting marks whenever they can without obvious danger of being misunderstood. Some newspapers
insist on a comma before the *and* in a series, some do not; book
publishers generally use it. Books printed in England commonly
have no period after *Mr;* books printed in America do. Since writing is as flexible as it is, and human minds are as various and variable as they are, punctuation practice is not likely to be completely
stable, but punctuation of standard English expository prose is
sufficiently standardized to make clear punctuation relatively
easy.

Punctuation and the Sentence Pattern

With some understanding of how punctuation works, and
of the meaning of punctuation marks, the student can mark his
writing with little trouble. To begin with, he needs to observe that
punctuation is mainly confined to the four following general uses,
most of them designed to help the reader focus attention on the
main sentence pattern.

1. *Division.* Punctuation marks the ends of main sentence
patterns — of sentences or of independent clauses in sentences. The
period, question mark, and exclamation mark, with different
meanings, indicate the ends of complete sentences. The semicolon,
and sometimes the colon or dash or comma, indicate secondary
breaks between independent clauses within the sentence.

2. *Continuity.* Punctuation tends to preserve the flow from subject to verb to complement by setting apart any elements that interrupt the thought of the pattern—nonrestrictive modifiers, parenthetical expressions, and the like. Usually the comma is used for such purposes, although semicolons, dashes, and parentheses sometimes mark sharper separations.

3. *Coordination.* Punctuation separates coordinate elements not sufficiently separated by function words. Usually commas are sufficient for such separation, but sometimes a semicolon is used.

4. *Convention.* Punctuation has conventional uses—to clarify statistical material, to mark bibliographic materials, to identify quotations, and so on. Most of these uses have been established by custom and are mechanical habits or traditions to be learned.

Punctuation Marks

Uses of the various marks of punctuation are discussed below; in general, the values of the marks are as follows:

.   The *period* marks the ends of sentences not to be distinguished as questions or exclamations (see 25a). It has also a few conventional uses, mainly to mark abbreviations.

?   The *question mark* (interrogation point) is used at the end of a direct question—not an indirect one (see 25a).

!   The *exclamation mark* is used at the end of a complete or incomplete sentence to indicate strong emotion or feeling (see 25a).

:   The *colon* has mainly conventional uses, especially to introduce formal lists (see 25i); it sometimes separates independent clauses (see 25b).

;   The *semicolon* mainly separates independent clauses, although it sometimes separates items in series (see 25b and 25d).

,   The *comma* is the most common punctuation mark in English, with a wide variety of uses (see especially 25c–25h).

—   The *dash,* made with two hyphens on the typewriter, sometimes marks sharp breaks between clauses and sometimes sets off parenthetical material more sharply than a comma would (see 25j).

" "   *Quotation marks* enclose direct quotations, phrases and sentences reproduced as spoken or written. They also have various conventional uses to indicate special usages and distinctions (see 25j).

( )   *Parentheses* have mainly conventional uses, but they also sometimes mark material to be sharply set apart within the sentence (see 25k).

[ ]   *Brackets* mainly have conventional uses to set off inserted materials. Since standard typewriters usually do not have brackets, brackets should be inserted by hand in typed material or made with the diagonal and underlining bars (see 25k).

. . .   The *ellipsis,* three periods, marks an omission, usually from quoted matter (see 25a).

END PUNCTUATION, PERIOD FAULT **25a**

End punctuation—usually a period, but sometimes a question mark or an exclamation point—marks the end of a sentence, but as we have seen, a sentence is not one thing. It may be more or less than what was long called "a complete thought." It frequently embodies an SVC pattern along with subsidiary structures that accompany the basic pattern. It may preserve only part of the basic pattern (see chapter 12), or it may comprise a combination of such patterns (see chapter 15). Most sentence-like sequences close with a period. There are two exceptions: most direct questions are terminated with the question mark, also called an interrogation point, and exclamatory matter may be suggested by an exclamation point. Use of a period to mark an expression not a sentence, sometimes called the *period fault,* usually reveals a basic error in sentence structure, the use of an inappropriate sentence fragment (see chapter 12). Usually, also, the *run-together* or *fused* sentence grows from more serious trouble than mere lack of a period (see 25b).

The following six uses of end punctuation are also common in Modern English:

1. *Indirect question.* The period is used after an indirect question, in which the question is not phrased verbatim but is part of a statement.

I asked her, "Will you go?" (*Direct question*)
I asked her if she would go. (*Indirect question*)

2. *Exclamation.* The exclamation mark indicates emotion or feeling. It is seldom used except in reporting conversation, particularly after interjections like *Ouch!* and *Murder!* Some beginning writers endeavor to liven their compositions with exclamation marks. This device seldom works—any prose so feeble that it must be propped up with punctuation had best be revised. Modern practice is to use the exclamation mark sparingly.

25a   **P1**

Revise so that end punctuation emphasizes the basic pattern of the sentence, not a fragment of it.

ORIGINAL	REVISION
He finally acknowledged that all people have an equal right to decent housing. Which was what I had been saying all along.	He finally acknowledged that all people have an equal right to decent housing, which was what I had been saying all along.
[*Special circumstances might justify the unusual punctuation, but normally parts of the basic sentence pattern, or close modifiers of it, are best not segregated with end punctuation.*]	[*With a comma replacing the first period the flow of the sentence is preserved, and when the end punctuation does appear it emphasizes the whole structure.*]
By Sunday I could stand no more, and I said, "Aren't you ever going to leave."	By Sunday I could stand no more, and I said, "Aren't you ever going to leave?"
[*Even though the whole sentence makes a predication, the question should be marked with a question mark.*]	
The question was whether Morgan would attack the center or make the long detour around Old Baldy and attack on the flank?	(1) The question was whether Morgan would attack the center or make the long detour around Old Baldy and attack on the flank.
[*The indirect question should be followed by a period. If the question were put directly, it would be followed by a question mark.*]	(2) The question was this: would Morgan attack the center, or would he make the long detour around Old Baldy and attack on the flank?
"Help," she screamed. "My dress, in the cogs."	"Help!" she screamed. "My dress! In the cogs!"
[*A girl being dragged into power machinery may be excited enough to warrant exclamation marks.*]	[*The revision does not bolster weak prose; it makes clear at once the drama of the sentences.*]

3. *Abbreviation.*   In American usage the period appears after most abbreviations: P.M., Mr., pp., Ave., St., U.S.A., *ibid.*, A.D. Any good dictionary will include abbreviations in the word list or in a special section (see also 26j).

The period is not used after letters standing for some widely used phrases which become cumbersome if written out: HUD, ZIP, POW, AFL-CIO, ICBM, ESP; after letters that represent scholarly or technical journals: PMLA, CA, MLR; after letters of radio stations: KLRB, WUISB, KATO; after MS (plural, MSS) for *manuscript;* certain unions and associations: WAA, AEF, CIO.

4. *Ellipsis.*   Three consecutive periods (. . .) make a punctuation mark known as the ellipsis, inserted in the place of material omitted from a quotation. When the omission comes after a completed sentence or completes a sentence, the period needed to mark the end of the sentence is retained. In such instances, therefore, four consecutive periods appear. The sign of ellipsis can be used also to mark any kind of gap in an original being reproduced.

ORIGINAL

Genius is the activity which repairs the decays of things, whether wholly or partly of a material and finite kind. Nature, through all her kingdoms, insures herself.
                    RALPH WALDO EMERSON

QUOTATION WITH OMISSIONS

Genius is the activity which repairs the decays of things. . . . Nature . . . insures herself.
                    RALPH WALDO EMERSON
[*The four periods mark both the omission and the end of a sentence.*]

5. *Question within sentence.*   The question mark is occasionally used after inserted interrogative material.

> Anyone who loves his country—and who does not?—will answer a call to duty.

The question mark is used, sometimes in parentheses, to indicate that a fact, especially a date, is approximate or questionable.

> *The Play of the Weather* (1533?) continues the convention. John Heywood, 1497(?)–1580(?), wrote the play.

Used as an attempted witticism or to mark sarcasm, the question mark is out of fashion and likely to appear amateurish.

> The next motion showed how wise (?) [*better omitted*] the committee was.

6. *Question as request.*   A request or command that for politeness is phrased as a question may conclude with either a question mark or a period.

> Will you please sign and return the enclosed voucher? *or* . . . voucher.   **535**

Independent clauses, independent sentence patterns, are usually punctuated in one of three ways:

They are treated as separate sentences (see 25a).

Within a sentence, they are separated by a semicolon.

GUIDE TO REVISION

25b

P2, RT, CS

Revise to correct run-together sentence or to remove a comma fault; consider redrafting the sentence.

ORIGINAL

The children tore the stuffed stockings from the mantel then they crept quickly back to bed.

[*The clauses can be made separate sentences, or separated with a semicolon (1); one clause can be subordinated (2); or one subject can be removed and the verb in the clause made part of a compound verb (3).*]

The two boys cleared away the brush, then they pitched their tent and spread out their blankets.

[*The comma does not indicate a large enough break to signal the beginning of a new statement. The sentence can be revised by supplying a semicolon (1), by making one element dependent (2), or by constructing a single clause (3).*]

He had been, he said, a most unconscionable time dying, however he hoped they would excuse it.

[*A conjunctive adverb (however, moreover, therefore, then, hence) is a modifier and does not obviate the need for a semicolon to separate the clauses.*]

REVISION

(1) The children tore the stuffed stockings from the mantel; then they crept quickly back to bed.

(2) After the children had torn the stuffed stockings from the mantel, they crept quickly back to bed.

(3) The children tore the stuffed stockings from the mantel and then crept quickly back to bed.

(1) The two boys cleared away the brush; then they pitched their tent and spread out their blankets.

(2) After they had cleared away the brush, the two boys pitched their tent and spread out their blankets.

(3) The two boys cleared away the brush, pitched their tent, and spread out their blankets.

(1) He had been, he said, a most unconscionable time dying; however, he hoped that they would excuse it.

(2) He had been, he said, a most unconscionable time dying; he hoped, however, that they would excuse it.

> We always like those who admire us; we do not always like those whom we admire.

> Man is certainly stark mad; he cannot make a worm, and yet he will be making gods by dozens.

Within a sentence, they are joined by a coordinating conjunction (*and, but, for, or, nor, yet, so*) with a comma preceding it (see 25c).

> Statesmen are not only liable to give an account of what they say or do in public, *but* there is a busy inquiry made into their very meals, beds, marriages, and every other sportive or serious action.

Notice that the semicolon is used when the second clause is introduced by a conjunctive adverb, a connective like *hence, then, therefore, however, nevertheless, in fact,* or *moreover.*

> I do not have a taste for caviar; however, I should like to be able to afford to develop one.

For the position of the conjunctive adverb, see 16d.

Besides these three main methods of punctuating independent clauses, two other methods are standard, although less frequently used. Short, closely related clauses, especially when they appear in series, are sometimes separated by only a comma.

> The rain falls constantly, the river continues to rise.

> The camera rolls back, the boom moves out, the water ripples gently, and the only one now to make a move outside the lighted circle is the man with the little fog can and the fan.

Occasionally, a colon separates independent clauses when the second clause specifies or exemplifies the idea of the first (see 25i).

A sentence in which independent clauses are joined without punctuation is sometimes called a *run-together* or *fused* sentence. Use of a comma between clauses when a semicolon or period is needed is sometimes called a *comma fault* or *comma splice.* The error usually involves more serious troubles than punctuation; it is a symptom that sentence patterns do not adequately relate ideas. Correction requires more than addition of a semicolon; it requires rewriting, often reducing one independent clause to a subordinate element.

PUNCTUATION BEFORE COORDINATING CONJUNCTIONS   **25c**

Even when independent clauses have a coordinating conjunction (*and, but, for, or, nor, yet, so*) linking them, they are separated by a comma, which signals a new clause rather than a compound complement or verb. Notice that in the following sentence the reader would momentarily misunderstand if the comma were omitted.

GUIDE TO REVISION

25c   **P3**

Revise to provide adequate punctuation between coordinating clauses joined by a conjunction.

ORIGINAL	REVISION
Jack had been brought up on golf and tennis did not interest him. [*The writer can supply a comma (1), or make one clause dependent (2).*]	(1) Jack had been brought up on golf, and tennis did not interest him. (2) Since Jack had been brought up on golf, tennis did not interest him.
Men have sworn at one another from earliest times, according to a Chinese classic on profanity, and to abstain from this natural exercise of the tongue is unhealthful but since elaborate swearing requires high intellectual ability, the ordinary swearer is cautioned to consider moderation. [*Complicated clauses, containing commas within them, are joined here without punctuation.*]	Men have sworn at one another from earliest times, according to a Chinese classic on profanity, and to abstain from this natural exercise of the tongue is unhealthful; but since elaborate swearing requires high intellectual ability, the ordinary swearer is cautioned to consider moderation. [*A semicolon is needed to point out the major division of the sentence.*]

She fed all the peanuts to the elephant, and the monkey had to be satisfied with popcorn.

Without the comma the reader would miss the structure of the sentence until he came to the second verb, thinking momentarily that the monkey had shared the peanuts. On the other hand, the comma is not usual unless the conjunction introduces a clause; if it joins two verbs or complements the pattern is usually clear without punctuation (see 25m).

Jack spent his mornings playing golf and his afternoons swimming.   **538**

When long or complex clauses containing commas are joined, a semicolon may be needed in addition to a coordinating conjunction to mark the main division in the sentence.

> Although the police had been ordered to keep everyone out of the building, they paid little attention to the back doors; and long before the rally was scheduled to begin, the big hall was packed with students.

PUNCTUATION IN A SERIES   **25d**

Commas separate words, phrases, dependent clauses, and sometimes very brief independent clauses (see 25b) when they are coordinated in a series of three or more.

> She announced that she was staying in bed until noon, that she was not cooking lunch for anybody, and that she would decide later about dinner.

Some newspapers do not require a comma before *and* ("lettuce, endive and celery"), but most publishers and writers of standard English prefer the comma before *and* ("lettuce, endive, and celery") on the ground that the omission of the comma is occasionally confusing.

> Their menu includes the following: veal steak, roast beef, pork chops, ham and eggs.
>
> She purchased the following: veal, beef, pork, ham, and eggs.

In the first sentence the reader may be uncertain whether or not the eggs are fried with the ham.

If all the items in a series are joined by connectives, no punctuation is needed "lettuce and endive and celery."

A combination like "bread and butter" within a series is treated as one element of the series.

Consecutive modifiers that tend to modify individually rather than to combine as a composite modifier form a series and are usually separated by commas. Compare:

> The streetcar had badly constructed, old-fashioned seats.
>
> The streetcar had grimy cane seats.

In the first, the adjectives seem to modify *seats* independently. As a rough test, insert the word *and* between them and see if the con-

25d   **P4**

Revise so as to clarify relationships within a series.

ORIGINAL

REVISION

We distinguished highways, roads, trails, streets and alleys.
[*Acceptable in some informal writing; usually not preferred in standard English.*]

We distinguished highways, roads, trails, streets, and alleys.

She bought a secondhand, fur coat.
[*Secondhand and fur do not modify separately.*]

She bought a secondhand fur coat.

The only available room was a dirty, vermin-infested, sleeping porch.
[*Dirty and vermin-infested modify in series, but sleeping is not part of the series.*]

The only available room was a dirty, vermin-infested sleeping porch.
[*Only the two items in series are separated; each of them modifies sleeping porch.*]

I canned dozens of gleaming many-colored jars of fruit.
[*The modifiers are in series; and could sensibly be put between them.*]

I canned dozens of gleaming, many-colored jars of fruit.
[*A comma should separate the items of the series.*]

The Council included the following representatives: President John A. Rickert, administration, Professor George P. Barrows, faculty, Avery Warren, student council, and Janice Worley, W. A. A.
[*The commas alone do not adequately distinguish the two sorts of words in the series.*]

The Council included the following representatives: President John A Rickert, administration; Professor George P. Barrows, faculty; Avery Warren, student council; and Janice Worley, W. A. A.
[*With semicolons to distinguish the main divisions, relationships within the series become clear.*]

struction still produces a familiar pattern. If it does, as in "badly constructed and old-fashioned seats," the modifiers are probably in series. In the second, however, *grimy* seems to modify all that follows it; the modifiers do not work independently in a series. "Grimy and cane seats" does not fill a familiar pattern for modifiers. As another rough test, reverse the order of the modifiers.

Those in series can be logically reversed, "old-fashioned badly constructed seats"; those not in series cannot, "cane grimy seats."

Numerals and common adjectives of size, color, and age seldom appear in series: "twenty-four scrawny blackbirds"; "two little girls"; "a spry old man"; a pretty little girl."

The semicolon may substitute for the comma to divide items in a series or list when the items are complicated and contain punctuation within them.

ORIGINAL

She told me that, in view of my prejudices, my poor health, and my interests, I would never be happy as a teacher, that I would find myself, at the end of a day, exhausted from policing dozens of squirming children, and that I would find my evenings, during which I hoped to practice music, given over to school plays, the school band and orchestra, and playing command canasta with the superintendent's wife.

[*Since the sentence is long and involved, and broken only by commas, the reader has difficulty seeing at once the organization.*]

REVISION

She told me that, in view of my prejudices, my poor health, and my interests, I never would be happy as a teacher; that I would find myself, at the end of the day, exhausted from policing dozens of squirming children; and that I would find my evenings, during which I hoped to practice music, given over to school plays, the school band and orchestra, and playing command canasta with the superintendent's wife.

[*Semicolons separate the three dependent clauses and mark the main divisions of the sentence.*]

PUNCTUATION OF NONRESTRICTIVE OR PARENTHETICAL MODIFIERS **25e**

When modifiers limit closely, especially when they supply the information that identifies or distinguishes subject or complement, they are called restrictive and are not set off by punctuation. Modifiers not essential to the subject-verb-complement combination, which supply incidental information (as this clause does), are called *nonrestrictive,* and must be set off by punctuation. Compare:

All the children who were in the front row received ice cream.

All the children, who were in the front row, received ice cream.

First, read the two sentences aloud. As we read the first, we raise the pitch of the voice on *row* and tend to pause after it. As we read

25e   **P5**

Revise to set off nonrestrictive or parenthetical matter.

ORIGINAL

I bought the material, that Mother had picked out.
[*The modifier identifies or defines the material; it is restrictive.*]

That evening which has always seemed the most terrifying of my life the dining room ceiling fell on us.
[*The modifier is not essential; it adds incidental information and is nonrestrictive.*]

My grandmother, who still had a powerful voice went to the door and shouted.
[*The subject,* grandmother, *is separated from the verb, and the modifier is not set off.*]

We started running for the express station which was still several blocks ahead.
[*The punctuation is accurate only if the clause identifies one station of at least two.*]

Politicians, generally speaking consider the desires of their constituents.
[*The expression must have punctuation both before and after.*]

The discussion is, indeed, silly.
[*The punctuation is not wrong, but it probably sets off the modifier more than necessary.*]

Aunt Agnes dyed her hair, painted her eyelashes, and plucked her brows although she always wore shoe-length dresses.
[*The* although-*clause had better be set off with a comma.*]

REVISION

I bought the material that Mother had picked out.
[*The restrictive use of the modifier is clear without punctuation.*]

That evening, which has always seemed the most terrifying of my life, the dining room ceiling fell on us.
[*The nonrestrictive modifier must be punctuated to set it apart from the main parts of the sentence.*]

My grandmother, who still had a powerful voice, went to the door and shouted.
[*Commas should appear both before and after the nonrestrictive modifier.*]

We started running for the express station, which was still several blocks ahead.
[*In most contexts, the clause would be nonrestrictive.*]

Politicians, generally speaking, consider the desires of their constituents.

The discussion is indeed silly.
[*Probably the writer intends* indeed *to modify* silly *only, not to be parenthetical.*]

Aunt Agnes dyed her hair, painted her eyelashes, and plucked her brows, although she always wore shoe-length dresses.

the second, we raise pitch on the main syllable of *children,* drop it on *row,* and pause after both *children* and *row.* That is, we distinguish restrictive and nonrestrictive in speech by intonation. We can tell which are nonrestrictive by thinking how they sound, and the punctuation helps us see how they should sound. The punctuation in writing reveals the meaning as the sound patterns do in speech. Both the sound and the punctuation show that the first sentence suggests that, of all of the children, only certain lucky ones, those in the front row, were treated; "who were in the front row," without commas, is read as restrictive. It restricts or limits *children* to the group it names, specifies certain children, but the second sentence says that all the children received ice cream. The clause is nonrestrictive, as the commas indicate.

Sometimes, as in the sentences above, modifiers can be interpreted as either restrictive or nonrestrictive, but usually the modifiers make sense with only one kind of punctuation. A nonrestrictive modifier can be recognized because it can be dropped out of the sentence without distortion of the main meaning.

The old house, badly out of repair, was hard to sell.

Omission of "badly out of repair" would not change the central idea of the sentence. But compare:

An old house badly out of repair may be no bargain.

"Badly out of repair" is required as part of the subject; it cannot be omitted without shifting the meaning. Punctuation on only one side of a nonrestrictive modifier is especially confusing because it separates essential parts of the main sentence pattern.

Following are some of the types of modifiers that are commonly nonrestrictive and therefore require commas:

1. *Appositive modifiers:*

My brother, chairman of the board, opposed the stock issue.

"Chairman of the board" adds incidental information but is not essential to the subject-verb-complement pattern. Sometimes, however, an appositive does restrict the subject and is not separated.

My brother John is chairman of the board.

John specifies which brother, restricts *brother.* The use of commas in such sentences is difficult to reduce to inclusive rules, but the inclusion or omission of punctuation tells the reader something of the writer's intent.

2. *Verbal modifiers:*

The catcher, having played twelve innings, was glad to be taken from the game.

3. *Adjectives following the words they modify:*

The three books, dirty and charred, were all he saved from the fire.

4. *Parenthetical expressions:*

He decided, however, not to throw the pie.
The cape, as the illustration shows, reaches nearly to the ground.

General modifiers of the sentence like *of course, for example, that is, however, indeed, therefore,* and *in conclusion* need punctuation to separate them from the main pattern of the sentence unless they modify restrictively. Parenthetical expressions that interrupt sharply or dramatically or that are not grammatically a part of the sentence are sometimes set off by dashes (see 25k) or parentheses (see 25l).

5. *Final qualifying clauses:*

Fools cause as much damage as criminals, although they are seldom punished.

Qualifying clauses, especially those beginning with *although,* are often nonrestrictive even when they follow the main clause. When they are nonrestrictive, they are usually set off by a comma; when they are restrictive, they are not punctuated. Even clauses beginning with *because* or *since* may be nonrestrictive following the verb:

"Did you go to the picnic?" "I went, because I had to."

The modifying clause supplies additional information, not that required to answer the question. Notice again that intonation supplies a practical clue; when the word before the modifier would be accented in speech and followed by a fairly clear pause, the sentence is likely to require a comma to indicate that the modifier is nonrestrictive. When no special accent falls on the word before the modifier and the main stress of the sentence is on the verb of the modifying clause, the modifier is probably restrictive.

544

Introductory modifying clauses and other long or complicated modifiers are set off from the rest of the sentence by commas. The punctuation is especially necessary, even with a

GUIDE TO REVISION

25f   **P6**

Revise punctuation to clarify an introductory modifier.

ORIGINAL

Before we had finished eating the salad and the fish were snatched away from us.
[*A comma would prevent momentary misunderstanding.*]

By daylight, we could find our way.
[*The comma does no harm, but the introductory modifier is short.*]

In the morning light filtered through the chinks in the ceiling.
[*Even though the modifier is short, the comma is needed to prevent misunderstanding.*]

Accordingly I resigned.
[*Though brief, the introductory element is set off in meaning and would be set off orally.*]

REVISION

Before we had finished eating, the salad and the fish were snatched away from us.
[*The comma marks the end of the modifier.*]

By daylight we could find our way.
[*The comma is unnecessary.*]

In the morning, light filtered through the chinks in the ceiling.
[*The comma separates the two words, which might otherwise be linked by their meanings.*]

Accordingly, I resigned.
[*The comma is preferable.*]

short modifier, if the reader might otherwise have difficulty identifying the point at which the modifier stops. Often introductory modifiers are like restrictive and nonrestrictive modifiers in that the intonation intended provides a clue to punctuation. Consider:

Meanwhile the dog ate our dinner.

Spoken, the sentence would probably carry a sharp rise in pitch on the first syllable of *meanwhile* and a pause after the word; a comma after *meanwhile* would enforce this intention.

The comma has a number of conventional uses to separate parts of geographical, temporal, or metrical material — anything that takes a statistical form — and parts of a grammatical structure that may otherwise be confusing.

GUIDE TO REVISION

25g	**P7**

Use commas to separate or to combine statistical material.

ORIGINAL

Mary was born January 4, 1952 in Chicago, at 1227 Second Avenue.

He cleared the bar at six feet four inches.

REVISION

Mary was born January 4, 1952, in Chicago, at 1227 Second Avenue.

He cleared the bar at six feet, four inches.

1. *Dates.* In general, commas are used between elements of a date. When a year is part of a date, it usually has commas both before and after it. Parts of a single element, such as the name of a month and the figure indicating the day, are not separated. With abbreviations both a period and comma may be required.

They arrived by train at 10 A.M., Monday, January 9, 1967.
Tuesday night, July 6, 1820, the debate began.

In some styles, commas are omitted in brief indications of date: "In March, 1972, she. . . ." or "In March 1972 she. . . ." In the style used by the Armed Forces, and becoming increasingly popular generally, the day precedes the month and no comma is necessary: "11 August 1916."

2. *Addresses.* Elements of addresses are similarly separated. When more than one element appears in an address, the last element is followed by a comma, unless the address is itself a separate unit, as in the address of a letter. Parts of elements, such as a street number and the name of the street following it, along with some code numbers, such as those in Zip Code, are not separated.

He gave 1162 West Avenue, Cleveland, Ohio 44100, as his address.

3. *Other statistics.*   Commas separate parts of measurements, divisions of a whole, and other statistical details. The last element of a series of divisions, like parts of a book, is usually separated from what follows, but the last part of a series constituting a measurement is usually not.

He was six feet, eight inches tall.

The sentence appears on page 11, line 28, of the new book.

She must enter in Act III, scene 2, before the music begins.

COMMAS TO CLARIFY CONSTRUCTIONS   **25h**

Occasional structures, not readily classified, become confusing because of omissions, an unusual juxtaposition of words, and the like. If the sentence cannot be clarified through

GUIDE TO REVISION

25h   **P8**

Insert a comma to clarify the construction.

ORIGINAL

I told him to speak out out of turn if necessary.
[*The unusual repetition of* out *becomes confusing without special punctuation.*]

He looked up the words he had intended to say formed only by his lips.
[*The sentence can be understood, but the reader's familiarity with the idea of looking up words leads to momentary confusion.*]

An hour of lecture presumes two hours of preparation, an hour of laboratory none.
[*Presumes is assumed between* laboratory *and* none.]

REVISION

I told him to speak out, out of turn if necessary.
[*With a comma to separate the second* out *from the first the structure and the meaning become clear.*]

He looked up, the words he had intended to say formed only by his lips.
[*The inserted comma emphasizes that* words *is not the object of* look up.]

An hour of lecture presumes two hours of preparation, an hour of laboratory, none.
[*The comma makes the structure clear.*]

revision, or if the writer has good reason not to revise the construction, the passage should be so punctuated that its meaning is clear. Usually the insertion of a comma will give the reader the necessary clue. Pope's famous dictum, punctuated as Pope did not write it, "Whatever is is right," would be at least momentarily disturbing. With a comma inserted, the meaning is clear: "Whatever is, is right."

PUNCTUATION WITH QUOTATIONS   **25i**

Quotation marks are relatively recent punctuation symbols, but partly because of their varied history they now serve a variety of purposes. The word *quote*, related to our *quota*, is etymologically associated with the idea of numbering, and early "quotes" were indications of chapter numbers. The word *quote* meant also to cite or to call attention to; and partly because many passages to which marginal attention was directed were bits out of famous writers, the word *quotation* developed the meaning now common, that is, written or spoken matter repeated verbatim. Modern uses of quotation marks, and other devices for directing special attention to a passage, reflect the various meanings of *quote* as they have been applied during recent centuries.

Various writing systems employ various conventions to identify matter singled out for special attention. In American English a quoted passage may be preceded by two raised and inverted commas and followed by two apostrophes. In British practice only one inverted comma and one apostrophe are used. Particularly in recent decades, words and passages that would formerly have been placed within quotation marks are frequently underlined in script and set in italic type when printed. At present, styles vary; for more on the vexed question of which passages should or should not be enclosed within quotation marks see chapter 24, especially 24b, 26h, and the Glossary, chapter 27, under *italics*.

Conventions concerning the punctuation of quoted material include the following:

1. *Direct quotations.* Words reported as conversation or words previously written or spoken are enclosed in double quotation marks.

"Get out," she said.

After his service in Vietnam, he agreed that "the paths of glory lead but to the grave."

25i   # P9, Quot

Provide punctuation appropriate to the quotation in its context.

ORIGINAL

I am sorry, she said, but those weeds you are lying in are poison ivy.
[*Material quoted directly should be set off by quotation marks.*]

Shaw pretended to believe that all man's civilization is founded on his cowardice, on his abject tameness, which he calls respectability.
[*The latter part of the sentence is quoted directly.*]

I told "her she ought to stop wasting her time."
[*The quotation is not direct; the direct quotation was something like "You'd better stop wasting your time."*]

She said I was in a hassle and that I had blown my top.
[*Hassle* and blown my top *are quotations from the character's manner of speech.*]

The old garden had been taken over by heather aster, the poverty weed.
[*Without quotation marks,* poverty weed *is taken as merely an alternative name.*]

An upright contraption, known as a "moon box", was used to show an artificial moon on the stage.
[*The comma always goes inside the closing quotation mark.*]

"Are you afraid of the dark"? the child asked.
[*Since the question mark punctuates the quoted material, it belongs inside the closing quotation mark.*]

REVISION

"I am sorry," she said, "but those weeds you are lying in are poison ivy."

Shaw pretended to believe that all man's civilization "is founded on his cowardice, on his abject tameness, which he calls respectability."
[*The quoted matter has been placed within quotation marks.*]

I told her she ought to stop wasting her time.
[*The quotation marks have been removed, since an indirect quotation is not enclosed.*]

She said I was in a "hassle" and that I had "blown my top."
[*The characteristic words have been enclosed within quotation marks.*]

The old garden had been taken over by heather aster, the "poverty weed."
[*Quotation marks might be used to show that the name is quoted from local speech.*]

An upright contraption, known as a "moon box," was used to show an artificial moon on the stage.

"Are you afraid of the dark?" the child asked.

Even a three- or four-word phrase taken directly from a source is distinguished by quotation marks (see chapter 24).

> Mencken quipped that the Kinsey Report proved only that men lie about their adventures in love and that "pedagogues are singularly naïve and credulous creatures."

2. *Special usages.* The concept of quotation is sometimes extended to call attention to a way of saying something or to include short expressions that quote speech from a special level of usage and from a particular country, region, social class, or person.

> It was then the fashion for popular music groups to describe themselves as "Neanderthals," "zanies," or something else unpleasant.

The quotation marks are used because a quotation from some other speaking group is implied. Quotation marks are no longer generally used as indiscriminate apologies for slang or colloquial English. In most instances, the slang should be used without apology if it is appropriate and omitted if it is not.

3. *Indirect quotations.* Indirect quotations are not placed within quotation marks, but a few words within an indirect quotation may be quoted directly. Compare:

> DIRECT: In his quiet way, he said, "I am excessively annoyed with the hoodlums next door."

> INDIRECT: In his quiet way, he said that he was "excessively annoyed" with the hoodlums next door.

4. *Words out of context.* Quotation marks may be used to indicate that a word is used as a word, but italics increasingly serve this purpose (see 26h and *Glossary,* chapter 27).

> The noun "boy" is the subject.

5. *Titles.* Quotation marks distinguish titles in two special circumstances: (1) when mechanical limitations, such as those in typesetting for a newspaper, make italics impractical; and (2) when a short work is to be distinguished from the larger work that contains it (see 24b, 26h).

> Robert Frost's "Mending Wall" appears in *Poetry of America.*

6. *Quotations within quotations.* In American practice, single quotation marks enclose a quotation within a quotation.

> The witness said, "I was just opening the door when I heard her scream, 'Drop that!'"

7. *Introductions to quotations.* When an expression like "he said" introduces a quotation, it is separated from the quotation by a comma.

I said, "I have always hated Pomeranians."

Sometimes a formal introduction to a quotation is followed by a colon, but the comma is not used before an indirect quotation.

I said that I had always hated Pomeranians.

8. *Position of quotation marks.* Quotation marks appear before and after the quoted material. When a quotation runs for more than one paragraph, the mark of quotation begins every paragraph but closes only the last one. Long quotations may be printed without quotation marks, in smaller type and indented; in typescript, the passage is indented and typed single-spaced.

9. *Quotation marks and other marks.* The position of a quotation mark in relation to other punctuation used with it is determined partly by logic and partly by arbitrary convention. Commas and periods are always placed inside quotation marks. All other punctuation marks are inside if they punctuate only the quoted words, outside if they punctuate an entire sentence containing a quotation.

The rafters used a long handspike, which they called a "picaroon."
He asked me to open the "boot"; I did not understand.
"Are you ready?" I asked.
Do you know who said that "life is but an empty dream"?

THE COLON   **25j**

The colon once functioned as a stop, like a semicolon, but it has become mainly a mark of anticipation, presenting whatever follows it. It resembles in force the sign of equality in mathematics; that is, whatever comes before the sign is in at least one sense equal to what comes after it. Its major uses are the following:

1. *Series.* It is most frequently used to precede a series that has already been introduced by a completed statement, often containing the word *following* or *follows.*

25j   **P10, :**

*Use the colon for its specialized purposes, not as the
equivalent of a semicolon.*

ORIGINAL

REVISION

The common silk dress goods are:
raw silk, taffeta, crepe de chine,
shantung, pongee, silk chiffon, silk
organdy, satin, and silk velvet.
[*The list is a complement and should
not be separated from the verb it completes.*]

The common silk dress goods are
raw silk, taffeta, crepe de chine,
shantung, pongee, silk chiffon, silk
organdy, satin, and silk velvet.
[*The colon that breaks the continuity
of the subject–verb–complement pattern
is omitted.*]

In high school I competed in the
principal girls' sports, that is: in
hockey, swimming, and basketball.
[*The colon properly introduces a formal series; here* hockey, swimming,
and basketball *are in apposition with*
sports.]

In high school I competed in the
principal girls' sports, that is, in
hockey, swimming, and basketball.
[*The meaning is at once clear with a
comma, and accordingly the lighter
punctuation is preferable.*]

Almost everybody tries to come
to Washington: everybody com-
plains about the weather after he
gets here.
[*The colon is no longer used as the
rough equivalent of a semicolon.*]

Almost everybody tries to come
to Washington; everybody com-
plains about the weather after he
gets here.

The common silk dress goods are the following: raw silk, taffeta,
crepe de chine, shantung, pongee, silk chiffon, silk organdy, satin,
and silk velvet.

I found that there were four kinds of girls in college: those who
came to get married, those who came to get an education, those who
came because their parents made them, and those who came because they did not know what else to do.

The colon is not needed, however, when the series immediately
follows the verb as a group of complements.

2. *Independent clauses.* The colon is occasionally used between independent clauses when the second part of the sentence
has been introduced in the first.

Two events occurred that spring to make Marie less happy in her
new home: the mangy cat that had been her companion was hit by a

car, and the low spot near the garage that became a fine mud puddle after every shower was filled and leveled.

The colon is unusual in this use, however, unless the second part of the sentence clearly repeats or clarifies the first.

3. *Conventional uses.* The colon also has certain conventional uses, notably after the formal address of a letter, in statements of time, and in citations from the Bible.

Dear Sir: 8:35 P.M. Genesis 5:1–3

THE DASH **25k**

The dash (–), made with two hyphens on the typewriter and typed with no space on either side, is used to mark sudden breaks in the flow of a sentence. It stops the reader abruptly,

GUIDE TO REVISION

25k **P11, Dash**

Consider dashes as means of marking breaks in sense or in structure.

ORIGINAL

These discoveries,—evolution, relativity, and now atomic fission,—have given us a new conception of the world.

[*The comma is not necessary with the dash.*]

Knowing only the most elementary principles of chemistry—I should never have attempted the experiment alone—However—I set up the equipment—and got out the necessary materials—not knowing how explosive they were—especially in combination—

[*This is a jumble because the writer has not punctuated.*]

REVISION

These discoveries—evolution, relativity, and now atomic fission—have given us a new conception of the world.

Knowing only the most elementary principles of chemistry, I should never have attempted the experiment alone. However, I set up the equipment and got out the necessary materials, not knowing how explosive they were, especially in combination.

[*The dashes have been replaced by standard punctuation.*]

a little like an open closet door bumped into in the dark. Dashes are useful and versatile punctuation marks, but they should be used with care and restraint. Most commonly they have the following uses.

1. *Emphasis.* A dash may emphasize a sharp break or change in thought. Usually this occurs within a sentence, where the dash serves to separate the different elements.

> If he has any decency he will come and apologize—but has he any decency?

2. *Interruption.* A dash may mark a dramatic or striking interruption or set off parenthetical material (see 25e) when the writer desires a sharper separation than commas signify. Parentheses usually set off an insertion not grammatically part of the sentence (see 25l).

> The new queen of the senior ball—and she was fully aware of her royalty—swept into the room.

The dash is especially useful if the modifier has internal punctuation.

> Often had he recalled, in Asia, the drowsy verdant opulence of his home—those willow-fringed streamlets and grazing cattle, the smell of hay, the flowery lanes.

3. *Summation.* One English sentence pattern used occasionally lists a long series of subjects or modifiers followed by a dash and usually by a pronoun or other word summarizing the list.

> A brown, crusty turkey, fluffy mashed potatoes, jars of jam, pickles and olives, and mince and pumpkin pies—all these and more appeared before Linda, as if she were in a dream.

4. *Introduction.* The dash is sometimes used between clauses when one clause introduces another, or it may introduce a list, less formally than a colon (see 25j).

> Of the thoughts that flashed through my mind one persisted—if I screamed the children would wake up.
>
> He bought samples of all the common silk dress goods—raw silk, taffeta, crepe de chine, shantung, pongee, silk chiffon, silk organdy, satin, and silk velvet.

5. *Convention.* The dash has various conventional uses. It may be used before a citation at the end of a quotation.

Nothing endures, nothing is precise and certain (except the mind of a pedant).

—H. G. WELLS, *A Modern Utopia*

It is used also in various kinds of informal tabular arrangements.

Humanities—fine arts, literature, language, philosophy.
Social sciences—history, political science, sociology, economics.

In current usage, other punctuation marks are avoided with a dash.

Writers too indolent to decide what they wish to say, and thus how to punctuate, sometimes try to save themselves trouble by using dashes for everything, hoping that the reader will do the thinking that the writer should have done. The device seldom works.

PARENTHESES AND BRACKETS **251**

Parentheses enclose inserted material that does not fit into the grammatical structure of the sentence and that adds incidental information. In this book, for example, parentheses punctuate cross-references or examples inserted into sentences. They can also enclose sentences or passages irrelevant to the main discussion.

The statue bears this inscription: "To our bountiful lady, Margarita Fernandez." (Señora Fernandez was an Indian woman who married a Spaniard and at his death inherited his mining wealth.) It is an outstanding example of Spanish Baroque.

Parentheses have various special uses such as enclosing numbers or letters in an enumeration.

He cited reasons as follows: (1) no student had been allowed in the building in the past; (2) furniture was not well enough built to stand student use; and (3) students had adequate facilities without new quarters.

Punctuation goes inside the parentheses when it punctuates only the parenthetical materials, outside when it punctuates the whole passage. Parentheses are generally used only in pairs, but single parentheses have some formal uses, notably after each of a series of numbers, to separate them from adjacent text.

25l   **P12**

Make appropriate use of parentheses or brackets.

ORIGINAL	REVISION
He distinguished between the members of the family *Juniperus, Juniperus communis, Juniperus virginiana,* and the like, and the plants resembling juniper, such as retem, *Retama raetam.*	He distinguished between the members of the family *Juniperus* (*Juniperus communis, Juniperus virginiana,* and the like) and the plants resembling juniper, such as retem (*Retama raetam*).
[*The words separated by commas seem at first to be words in a series.*]	[*Parentheses clarify the sentence.*]
To write you need a sharp pencil and a quick mind (the first of which can be easily acquired).	To write you need a sharp pencil and a quick mind, the first of which can be easily acquired.
[*Clauses within a sentence are usually sufficiently set off with commas.*]	[*The comma is sufficient; for a sharper break, a dash would be preferable to parentheses.*]
We hold these truths to be *self-evident* (the italics, of course, are mine), that all men are created equal. . . .	We hold these truths to be *self-evident* [the italics, of course, are mine], that all men are created equal. . . .
[*The parentheses imply that the inserted matter was part of the original and was there in parentheses.*]	[*The inserted matter has been enclosed within square brackets.*]

Brackets are used to enclose matter inserted into a direct quotation, and within parentheses, to avoid the confusion of parentheses within parentheses. They may also be used for various typographical purposes. In the Guides to Revision in this book, brackets enclose comments on examples.

INAPPROPRIATE OR EXCESSIVE PUNCTUATION   **25m**

Punctuation is intended to clarify; sprinkled indiscriminately through writing, especially when it separates closely related sentence elements, punctuation distracts or obscures. The mistaken notion that any pause in speech warrants a comma in writing is responsible for some excessive punctuation.

And some inappropriate commas are the result of misunderstanding or misapplication of general principles of punctuation. Some of the more frequent sorts of redundant punctuation are the following:

1. *Separation of main sentence parts.* Punctuation that separates subject from verb or verb from complement may be especially misleading. Compare the following:

ORIGINAL	REVISION
Every book on the shelf, had been damaged by water.	Every book on the shelf had been damaged by water.

The unnecessary comma in the original separates subject from verb. A comma on one side of a modifying clause has the same effect.

GUIDE TO REVISION

25m   **P13, No P**

Remove excessive or misleading punctuation.

ORIGINAL	REVISION
The girl who had bought the high-heeled shoes, came wobbling back into the store. [*The comma on one side of the modifying clause separates subject from verb.*]	The girl who had bought the high-heeled shoes came wobbling back into the store. [*The modifier is restrictive, and no punctuation is needed.*]
My father, and John ran up the walk, and threw their arms around us.	My father and John ran up the walk and threw their arms around us.
Mary was afraid, that someone else would wear a pirate costume.	Mary was afraid that someone else would wear a pirate costume.
Of course, I looked in the drawer for the flashlight; but someone had taken it. [*The semicolon is acceptable, but the sentence would be clear with a comma.*]	Of course, I looked in the drawer for the flashlight, but someone had taken it.

ORIGINAL	REVISION
The lamp that Wilbur had made from discarded copper tubing, won a prize.	The lamp that Wilbur had made from discarded copper tubing won a prize.

The modifying clause is clearly restrictive, and no comma is needed, even though in speech there would be a slight pause after *tubing*.

2. *Unnecessary comma with* and. The practice of using a comma before *and* in a series or between independent clauses should not be distorted into the notion that a comma always precedes *and*.

ORIGINAL	REVISION
Louise finally emptied the drawer on to the bed, and found what she was looking for.	Louise finally emptied the drawer on to the bed and found what she was looking for.

The comma does not obscure, but it is unnecessary unless the writer wants to suggest a pause before *and*.

3. *Unnecessary comma before final clause.* Perhaps because final clauses may modify nonrestrictively and hence may be set off by commas, students sometimes precede a clause used as a complement or restrictive modifier with a comma.

ORIGINAL	REVISION
Everybody knew, that Dorothy would be elected on the first ballot.	Everybody knew that Dorothy would be elected on the first ballot.

The comma separates verb from complement.

FOR STUDY AND WRITING

A Supply appropriate punctuation and capitalization in the following sentences. The meaning may change with various sorts of punctuation.

1. I said rats if they are eating the cake I don't want any of it

2. One avocado did not ripen I don't know why the other one did

3. A certain truck carries the following signs this truck stops for a red light or a red head backs up 25 feet for a blonde and courtesy is our motto

4. He was playing left end you say so you say he was playing left end is that it

5. He was the worst dean I ever heard of with the alumni his putting the whole Sigma Nu house on probation is still a favorite story

6. Two times two are four four times four are fifteen no four fours are sixteen or are they or is it is

7. So you think you're pretty good do you feel like taking off your glasses and settling this outside

8. The following have registered thus far Alice Melarkey Los Angeles Muriel Jones St. Louis Florence O'Brien Seattle Florence Schmidt Syracuse and Helen Adney Atlanta

9. A number of changes account for the movement of beef raising into the southeast wornout cotton lands heavily cropped for years will no longer raise a high-production crop successfully and meanwhile Texas ranchers finding they have insufficient pastures in this the driest year in a decade are glad to acquire additional grazing land in the eastern gulf states

10. Joseph Joubert is credited with the following some men find their sole activity in repose others their sole repose in activity

B The sentences below could be corrected by supplying adequate punctuation, but most of them would be improved by revision. Correct each by changing punctuation; then revise each by making one of the independent clauses dependent and compare the results.

1. The clerk opened the bank door at the time he did so the three robbers pushed their way into the bank.

2. The team lost the final game of the tournament, for this reason June cried herself to sleep that night.

3. My sister was beautiful and talented however she did not win a trip to Atlantic City.

4. The wounded were evacuated by helicopter, they could not do this if antiaircraft fire was heavy, however.

5. I finished washing all the dinner dishes then Laura said she thought we might mop and wax the kitchen floor.

6. It was cold and rainy outside, however, the house was warm and dry.

7. I was in the hospital during the time I was there I fell in love with the head nurse.

8. I never learned the multiplication tables for this reason I have always been slow at mathematics.

C Punctuate the following sentences, paying particular attention to punctuation of nonrestrictive and parenthetical modifiers.

1. Gladys who was the only daughter of a steel manufacturer used to make me angry and jealous showing off her new clothes.

2. She is the girl who won the 4-H scholarship.

3. After one hour saturate the curls with neutralizer for bleached, dyed, or overdry hair see instructions on the front of the folder.

4. What we called the "coasting hill" a long grade that wound past the cemetery and down through the school yard unfortunately crossed Lake Street at the intersection by the feed and grain store a crossing that was much used by farmers on Saturday our only coasting day.

5. The sorority that my mother favored was the only one that showed me any attention.

6. In our school Beeson County High School most of the students were interested in sports especially basketball and accordingly you did not ask whether a boy had anything in his head but only whether he was tall enough to hold his head six feet in the air.

7. Then she started talking about a tepidarium whatever that is.

8. The atoll a coral reef that barely broke the water was nothing to turn to for protection particularly in stormy weather.

9. The tailored suit which I had brought home with me from Hadley's Bazaar a department store in New York City hung on me like a Hindu robe but everybody admired the outfit I had made a simple little dress devised out of some coarse basket-weave that Aunt Lilly gave me.

10. That summer I was employed as assistant to the playground director in Jordan Park the same park in which the previous summer I had refused to take part in the group games.

D Supply the missing punctuation in the sentences below, and correct inappropriate punctuation; where two marks of punctuation are required, be sure you put them in the proper order. Some sentences are well punctuated as they stand.

1. I turned and ran toward the subway station, — or thought I did, for it was snowing so that I could not see, — then I bumped into someone.

2. Janice (a quiet girl who went out little) was eager to have dates.

3. Inside I saw: a cat, some kittens, and an old white-haired woman.

4.   . . . the play's the thing
Wherein I'll catch the *conscience* the italics are mine of the king.

5. Maximilian had three courses before him he could try to become a genuine ruler of the Mexicans for the Mexicans; he could take his scraps of a French army and flee; or he could go on living in indolent luxury, which would probably be ended by a firing squad.

6. "The so-called Dixiecrats [dissident southern Democrats] hoped by this move to gain the balance of power."

7. Alice — the scrawniest little girl in our block — was growing up to be a beauty.

8. To distinguish the types of furniture, note the following: bamboo grows in sections and is hollow; rattan, a much stronger material, grows solid.

9. They had something they called a "booby-hutch," which was defined as "a carriage body put upon sleigh runners."

10. "They the Pueblo Indians make a kind of bread called guayave which the white people call a 'hornet's nest.'

E Insert the correct punctuation in the following:

When I was in Cuernavaca Mexico on a vacation trip in July 1966 I heard a story of what became of one of Rivera's murals It seems that the proprietor of a fashionable restaurant ordered his walls decorated Since I do not wish to be libelous let us say that the restaurant was at 268 Morales Avenue which it was not The proprietor a small ingratiating excitable man considered various muralists interviewing them from the time he arose at 10 a m until he went to bed at 2 a m Finally he settled upon Rivera who was known to be fashionable with certain groups especially the foreigners The mural finished he awaited the approval of the dignified people in the town Members of the important old families who were eager to view the newest monument to local progress responded to his invitation They came in holiday mood and looked they left enraged They had seen their own faces painted upon the bodies of gangsters robbers cutthroats and quacks with small ceremony and no delay at all they rendered their artistic judgment If those pictures stayed up the most important people would stay out What to do The proprietor loved his murals for they had cost him much money he loved his business for it had brought him much money So he paced the floor which was new and only partly paid for and tore at his trim carefully waxed mustache At that he had an idea and with deft strokes painted bushy whiskers sprightly goatees and respectable muttonchops upon the faces of the abused citizens Should he not reason that whiskers that would render a mayor unrecognizable would also make him genial and as a result might he not be expected to eat the restaurant beefsteak But the device that the proprietor's mustache inspired was more ingenious than successful The outraged citizens were more outraged than ever not only had the proprietor insulted them by calling them bandits but he had further and doubly insulted them by implying that they grew bad beards As for Rivera he threatened to shoot the proprietor for desecrating art Torn between art and the artist between his patrons and their patronage the bedeviled proprietor saved at once his sanity and his business by having the whole room replastered.

MECHANICS: MANUSCRIPT FORM, SPELLING, CAPITALIZATION, PRINTING PRACTICES

CHAPTER 26

Accurate composition requires the ability to use writing conventions quickly and consistently.

We have seen that punctuation is a relatively orderly system, mainly concerned with revealing grammar in the sentence. Other conventions, most of which do not fall into a system, are both broader and narrower in application; some concern the entire composition, but many are restricted in application to individual words. Some have good logic behind them, but many are conventional only— although they may be none the less important for that—and some, although arbitrary, have revealing history behind them.

MANUSCRIPT FORM   26a

Manuscripts must be clear and they should be attractive. Individual publications, newspapers, or college classes have special requirements for preparation of a paper, but any manuscript, whether submitted for publication, presented as a business report, or prepared to fill a class assignment, should be neat, standard in appearance, and conventional in spelling, capitalization, syllabification, and use of italics, abbreviations, and numbers.

The following rules are standard and fit the requirements of almost any publisher or reader:

1. Typewrite in black or write in black or blue-black ink on standard size (8½ × 11-inch) paper, unruled for typing, and ruled for

handwriting with standard measure ruling, not the narrow ruling sometimes used for notebook paper.

2. Write on only one side of the paper; having to flip loose papers irritates a reader or editor, and in a manuscript of any length can lead to various confusions.

3. Double-space between lines of a typewritten manuscript. Most editors refuse to look at unsolicited copy that is not double- or triple-spaced. Keep typewriter type clean and use a well-inked ribbon.

4. Make handwriting legible, distinguishing clearly between capital and small letters.

5. Leave generous margins on all sides of the paper — at least an inch and a half at the top and the left and an inch at the right and the bottom.

6. Indent about half an inch for each new paragraph — five spaces on the typewriter. In typing, leave one space after internal punctuation, two spaces after end punctuation.

7. Proofread all written work carefully; the reader sees what you wrote, not what you meant to write.

Manuscripts submitted for publication usually carry a notation like the following in the upper right-hand corner of the first page:

> My Years in Jail
> John Doe
> 13 Skidrow Street
> About 92,000 words

GUIDE TO REVISION

26a   **M**

Check requirements for standard manuscript form and revise your manuscript accordingly.

ORIGINAL

Most Universities now include Students on all important Comittees. Some however seem not to have learned from bitter experiance

[*The writer probably knows better; he has been careless.*]

REVISION

Most universities now include students on all important committees. Some, however, seem not to have learned from bitter experience.

[*Errors in punctuation, spelling, and capitalization have been corrected.*]

Instructors specify requirements for papers submitted in class. Often brief papers are folded lengthwise and endorsed on what would be the front cover if the paper were a book. Longer papers are usually left flat, with information on the outside page. For class papers a notation like the following may be required:

Mary Edmonton
English 101, Sec. 24
Theme VI
October 10, 1966
Professor John Hancock

The Spelling System

Among the conventions that apply to individual words, spelling constitutes a system, and although it is not consistent, English spelling is more orderly than many users suppose and more orderly than it may at first appear. Part of the confusion springs from the alphabet, a precious heritage and a handy tool even though it has inadequacies, some of which have grown into it. The learned men who worked out a way of writing spoken English adapted the Latin alphabet to the purpose, but the Latin alphabet was not entirely adequate for English. The Roman writing system had come west from early Semites, who had so few vowel sounds in their spoken language that, for economy, they did not mark them and hence had no symbols for vowels. The Greeks, who transmitted the Semitic writing system, converted a few symbols for consonants into symbols for vowels, but they never converted enough, and the Romans added only a few more. Accordingly, the Latin alphabet, which could not record all the sounds in Latin, was still less adequate for English, which has sounds not in Latin.

Some adaptations helped. A Latin symbol that looked like u was carved on stone with straight lines, so that two letters, *U* and *V*, were available to English. Doubled, this symbol gave yet another, *W*, called *double-U* in English and the equivalent of *double-V* in German. A straight vertical line became both *i* and *j*. Similarly, when Latin provided no symbols for the initial sounds of words like *think*, *she*, and *chip*, digraphs or combinations of two letters *th*, *sh*, and *ch* were used to stand for the single sounds. In spite of such helps, however, we have too few letters for all the English sounds.

Furthermore, changes in English have complicated and confused the writing system. Old and Middle English existed in various dialects, which survived irregularly. *Girl, pearl,* and *world* now all contain the same sound, but they are spelled differently because they were once pronounced differently and the letters reflect the

564

earlier sounds. *Meet* and *meat* were once pronounced differently and therefore spelled differently: the sounds have now fallen together while the spellings remain distinct. Old English had a sound rather like *khkhkh*, which was later written *gh;* the sound disappeared from the language, but the letters that designated it persist in words like *through* or *rough.* Similarly, many sounds written with the letter *g* disappeared—becoming first vowels, then parts of diphthongs, then nothing—but they have left spellings with *i* or *y,* as in *maid, day,* and *said.*

A major confusion comes from our extensive borrowing of foreign words, introduced without much change in spelling. Thus we spell one term *fait accompli* because it comes from French, another *blitzkrieg* because it was German, another *sputnik* because we have transliterated it from Russian. From French we have adopted *c* as a spelling for the sound of *s,* while keeping it in its English use as the equivalent of *k.* Meanwhile, we picked up more equivalents of Old English *c,* so that, although we have generally too few letters, we squander symbols writing this sound as *c, ck, k, ch, qu, que,* and, in combination, *x.* Since more than two thirds of the words in most dictionaries have been borrowed from some language with sounds and spellings different from those in English, and since we have never systematically overhauled our system, spelling is far from regular.

In spite of the confusions we have inherited, however, the English writing system is far from chaotic. Medieval scribes had no universal spelling rules, but they recognized some principles, two of which can be observed in the phrase "spelling rules" itself. *Spelling* has two *l's* to indicate that the preceding *e* stands for a short vowel sound, and *rules* has an extra *e* to indicate the long pronunciation for *u.* Thousands of modern words have similar spellings because we have inherited the words and the principles from medieval scribes. In fact, modern systematic analyses of English indicate that more than 80 per cent of English words are spelled according to discernible principles.

Spelling and the Sound System

In an ideal spelling system, every phoneme—every working sound unit—would have a single symbol to represent it in writing. That is, every sound that for users of a language causes a difference in meaning would be represented by a different letter or some other mark. Because languages constantly change, this kind of correspondence—one phoneme, one symbol—is seldom realized, although a few languages, like Finnish, with relatively new writing systems, approximate it. English does not have such correspondence. Most speakers of English employ about thirty-five phonemes, twenty-four consonants and eleven vowels, although linguists vary classifications slightly. The English alphabet has only twenty-six letters. English writing does not distinguish the consonant sounds in the middle of *ether* and *either*, although these sounds are phonemes, distinguishing meaning. Neither does it distinguish the vowels in *bow*, as in *rainbow*, and *bow*, indicating the prow of a boat. Furthermore, using different symbols for the same phoneme suggests a nonexistent difference between the second *bow* and *bough*.

Most of the time, however, English spelling presents no such difficulties. Take the word *melt;* practically speaking, it could be spelled only as it is. The first letter, *m*, indicates only the phoneme /m/, the sound created when the air column vibrates through the nose and the lips are closed. Similarly, *l* and *t* are used almost exclusively for /l/ and /t/, and these phonemes are usually expressed by no other symbols. The exceptions are few; *l* is still written in some words like *balk, chalk,* and *would,* although the pronunciation survives in but few dialects; in a few words the sound /t/ is written *th* as in *thyme.* The letter *e* has many uses, but when it appears with no following vowel and in a word of one syllable, it commonly represents only one phoneme, the sound familiar in words like *get, met,* or *let.* Nearly half the phonemes of the language are spelled consistently with a single letter.

A few symbols and sounds are slightly complicated. Some symbols work in pairs to represent one sound; they are called "digraphs." *Ch* as a pair of letters working together represents a sound in *chug* and *much,* and it is about the only way you can represent this sound, although, especially in proper names, it may represent a sound more commonly spelled with *sh,* as in *Chicago* and *Charlotte.* Similarly, *ng* represents one sound and practically speaking only one sound; *ph* working as a unit represents one sound, although the same sound can be spelled *f.* The confusions here are not many, however, and can be readily learned; the sound /f/ can be written in more than one way, as *f, ff,* and *ph,* and even *gh* in *enough,* but the last two spellings are rare.

Even the complicated sounds can be broken down to make some sense. Take one of the worst, as it appears in *fish, fission, complexion, initiate, chaise, schwa, censure, conscious,* and some others. The commonest spelling is *sh,* and it is commonest because this was the spelling that represented the sound in native English words—*wish, dish, she, ship.* Since these words come from Old English they are usually short, common words. The other spellings are mostly in borrowed words, but they, too, fall into patterns. Many come from Latin, using a *ti* spelling—*condition, situation, negation, vitiate.* These words tend to be long, abstract, and rather formal. The spelling with *ch* usually comes from French or through French — even *Chicago,* although it was an Indian word, comes to us in a French spelling. *Sch* is the German spelling. Most other spellings — and they are few — represent some kind of softening or eliding of an older sound; for example, *fission* comes from a form of Latin *fissio,* where the two *s*'s represented a long or repeated sound, but the sound shortened and became more slack in English, which has a sound pattern different from Latin, while the old spelling remained.

The hardest sounds, of course, are vowels. Eleven or twelve different vowel sounds occur commonly in English, plus some combinations of sounds or diphthongs, and these are spelled with only six letters, *a, e, i, o, u, y.* Furthermore, these letters are not used consistently for the same phonemes. The letter *e,* for example, perhaps the most versatile of all, can appear in *get, greet, great, river, ride, covey, sieve, receive, complete, aye, new, changes, decay, unique,* and many others, with sounds and without them. Still, the common uses are few and can be understood historically. We have already seen that English borrowed the Latin short *e* and used the letter for the same sound in English that it had in Latin, in words like *get.* If scribes feared the reader might not know the sound was short, they doubled a following consonant, as in *getting.* They also borrowed the same vowel long, as in our word *street,* from Latin *sternere,* and although this sound has changed in English, the change need not concern us here. If an early scribe wanted the reader to know that the vowel was long, he added a second vowel, as in *street, speech;* or he might add another *e* after a following consonant, as in *ride, compete.* Thus, some *e*'s have always been silent; others have become silent or nearly so, mainly because stress moved away from a stressed vowel. For example, *government* formerly had considerable stress on the last syllable, so that the vowel in *-ment* was pronounced about like the *e* in *get.* Now, however, the stress is on the first syllable, and the vowel in the last syllable has been reduced to a schwa, a very slack, colorless vowel like the first syllable of *about,* or to nothing. Meanwhile, the sound that was once represented by *-er-* has fallen out completely in some dialects, so that many people, and cultured people at that, pronounce *government* as though it were spelled *guvmnt.* Thus, although *e* as a spelling is complicated, it mainly represents the short sound in *spell,* the long sound in *meet,* the neutral schwa in *decay,* or a silent letter of which some were used to mark preceding long vowels. All these appear in patterns well known to all literate users of English.

The linguistic phenomenon by which a word once pronounced something like *go-ver-na-ment* is reduced to *guv-mnt* is called syncopation, leaving out something. It happens regularly in language and complicates spelling as pronunciations change while spelling

567

remains constant. Thus a student who writes *airfiel* for *airfield, in-trest* for *interest, exackly* for *exactly,* or *recanize* for *recognize* is probably producing a fairly accurate representation of what he usually says. Since syncopation is normal, we cannot expect to cure such spelling errors by sounding out every letter in pronunciation; words like *phthisicky* or *colonel,* to mention only obvious examples, would cause trouble. We can recognize that the writing system differs from the oral system, and that it often reflects pronunciations of an early date, but that the sound system may help us understand the system of writing symbols. We can profit, for example, from the practices mentioned above, whereby the final *e* signals that an earlier vowel is long, and a doubled consonant that it is short. Knowledge of these practices distinguishes *dine* from *din* and *diner* from *dinner.* A student aware of these tendencies of the writing system would probably not misspell *getting, combine, helpful, referring, occurring, excellence, permitted, riding, Britannica, ninety, arguing, during* and similar words frequently missed.

ANALYZING SPELLING PROBLEMS 26b

Spelling ability is not necessarily an index to intelligence or education, but certainly the person who spells inaccurately works under a handicap. He is likely to be considered uneducated by anyone who catches him in errors, and he is likely to be limited in his writing, as he relies on simple but sometimes colorless words in order to be safe in his spelling. Some people are so eye-minded that they learn to spell unconsciously. By the time they have seen a word spelled correctly several times, they know it. Others have to work at spelling, not because they are slow or stupid but because their minds happen not to work in the way that records spelling automatically. But fortunately almost any intelligent person can learn to spell reasonably well if he will work at it. A "bad" speller is usually only a person who does not spell without learning, who has never been properly taught, or who has never tried hard enough to learn, and in an orderly way.

A student who has reached college and still has spelling difficulties can probably progress best by analyzing his errors and working systematically on the basis of his analysis. To begin, he needs to find out which words he misspells and, if possible, why he misspells them. He should first make a list of all words he has to look up in the dictionary in order to verify their spellings and of all words he misspells in his writing, indicating any repeated errors. The lists should be drawn from as much of the student's normal writing as possible. For diagnostic purposes, the lists should record the actual misspellings but should also include a correction of each error. Diagnosis is likely to reveal that any student's errors tend to be primarily of the same sorts — for instance, that he is careless, that he does not know the conventional letters for English sounds, or that he misspells the same few words over and over. He may find that he consistently makes several types of errors. From his list, however, he can discover which of the following kinds of common difficulties he needs to work at most.

1. *Habitual misspelling.*   A student whose list includes mainly repeated mistakes in words like *receive, too, their, separate,* or *loose* for *lose* has a relatively easy problem. He has never learned the small number of common words with difficult spellings. He needs to memorize spellings of these difficult words, perhaps using a list like that in E of "For Study and Writing" at the end of this chapter.

2. *Carelessness.*   If a list reveals that a student has spelled a book title four different ways in one paper, has omitted the final *e*

GUIDE TO REVISION

26b   **Sp**

Correct the misspelling, considering whether it suggests a fundamental spelling problem or violates a common spelling rule (see pp. 572–73).

ORIGINAL

REVISION

occured, refering, counsellor, begining, equiped, equippment
    [*A final consonant in an accented syllable with a short vowel usually doubles before an ending beginning with a vowel.*]

occurred, referring, counselor, beginning, equipped, equipment
    [*It usually does not double when the syllable is unaccented or before an ending beginning with a consonant.*]

ninty, lonly, guideance, leisurly
    [*Final silent* e *is usually retained before an ending beginning with a consonant.*]

ninety, lonely, guidance, leisurely
    [*It is dropped before an ending beginning with a vowel or to avoid an awkward sequence of letters.*]

trys, happyest, appliing, applys
    [*Final* y *usually changes to* i *before an ending beginning with a vowel.*]

tries, happiest, applying, applies
    [*When the ending begins with* i, *the* y *does not change.*]

beleive, decieve, frieght
    [*To indicate the sound of* e, i *usually precedes* e *except after* c.]

believe, deceive, freight
    [*When the combination represents the sound of* a, *it is* ei.]

in writing *inane*, and has spelled *Eliot* correctly once but incorrectly twice, the student obviously needs to start being more careful. He may not have known the spelling of the title, but he could have looked it up and spelled it consistently. Even if the slips on *inane* and *Eliot* got through a first writing, they should have been caught in revision.

3. *Errors in recording sounds.* In a rough way, spelling records sound patterns, though not always obviously or consistently. The student who finds his lists including errors like *Scananavian* for *Scandinavian, athelete* for *athlete, preform* for *perform, tradegy* for *tragedy, prejudice* for *prejudiced, thing* for *think, quanity* for *quantity, cause* for *because, refered* for *referred,* or *wend* for *went* is having trouble with sounds and their spellings. He can correct many of his errors by learning more precise pronunciations—*pronunciation* rather than *pronounciation,* for example. He should study the English sound system and learn which letters are used for which sounds.

4. *Confusion of similar words.* Words cause trouble when they have the same sound but different meanings—*sight, site,* and *cite; to, too,* and *two; rite, write, right,* and *wright; led* and *lead.* The cure for errors with such groups is to look up these homonyms in a dictionary and learn enough about them to keep them separate. The confusion of *of* for *have* (as in "He would *of* done it") is doubtless encouraged by pronunciation, since in many dialects *'ve*, the abbreviation of *have*, is pronounced like *of*. Words not pronounced identically but spelled similarly are confusing, especially if the difference in spelling involves only a transposition or doubling of a letter. The following frequently cause trouble: *angle, angel; casual, causal; chose, choose; lose, loose; desert, dessert; canvas, canvass; accept, except; affect, effect; principle, principal.*

5. *Errors from analogy or etymology.* Spelling by analogy or etymology can be very helpful, but analogies may lead a writer astray, especially if they rest upon false assumptions. One of the more common misspellings is *definate* for *definite,* probably because of the large number of English words ending in *-ate.* The misspellings like *pronounciation* and *renounciation* result from the analogy with the corresponding verbs. The spelling *primative* is probably influenced by the more common *primary.* The frequent misspellings *Britian* and *villian* are probably made by false analogy with many English words having *i* and *a* in this sequence, as in *Parisian, gentian, Martian.* Even very accomplished spellers will make occasional errors of this sort, but awareness of the problem helps to solve it, and thorough acquaintance with the word will cure personal difficulties.

6. *Confusion with prefixes and suffixes.* Numerous words cause

trouble because they include a syllable, often a prefix or a suffix, that can be spelled in several ways or that differs but slightly from another syllable. Thus, *-ible* is confused with *-able,* and *-ents* with *-ence.* Is it *indistinguished* or *undistinguished, indistinguishable* or *undistinguishable?* Differences in meaning and use offer some help. The suffixes *-ents* and *-ants* are plurals, as in *residents* and *attendants; -ence* and *-ance* are evidences of an abstract noun, as in *residence* and *attendance.* Latin prefixes and suffixes tend to be used with Latin words, Anglo-Saxon affixes with Anglo-Saxon words. Thus we have *unable,* since both *un-* and *-able* come from Anglo-Saxon, against *indigestible,* since *in-, digest,* and *-ible* are Latin, but the rule is by no means consistent, as the confusion mentioned above in connection with words related to *distinguish* will illustrate. Frequently, *-able* follows words that are complete as they stand, whereas *-ible* follows syllables having no meaning without the suffix (*acceptable, marketable,* but *terrible*), even though a silent *e* has been dropped from the word (*drivable*). Some tendencies can be observed, also, in the letters that suffixes follow, but many students find learning the words easier than learning the tendencies and the exceptions. For what the tendencies may be worth, here are the most common: *-able* usually follows hard *g* or *c* (*applicable*), *i* or *y* in the root word (*justifiable*); *-able* is common in words having a long *a* in a related word (*irritate,* and hence, *irritable*). The suffix *-ible* usually follows soft *c* or *g* (*tangible*), *miss* or *ns* (*sensible*); if the suffix can replace *-ion* in another word, without change of adjacent letters, *-ible* is usual (*perfection,* and hence, *perfectible*). The ending *-ar* is much less common than *-er* or *-or* (*grammar, calendar,* and a few others); *-er* is usual among words coming from Anglo-Saxon if the *-er* indicates a person's temporary or permanent occupation (*teacher, walker*); *-or* is the common ending, especially in words from Latin (*doctor, governor, motor*). Among the prefixes warranting unusual attention are the following:

per–	(meaning *through* as in *perfect,* carried through to the end)	pre–	(meaning *before* as in *prerequisite, predecessor*)
anti–	(meaning *against* as in *antitoxin, anti-Russian*)	ante–	(meaning *before* as in *antebellum, anterior*)
di–	(meaning *twice* as in *dibase, digraph*)	de–	(meaning *from, concerning,* or *down* as in *depart, define, descend*)

The endings *-cede, -ceed,* and *-sede* cause some confusion. The regular form in English is *-cede* (*concede, precede, recede*). The exceptions can be easily learned; one word ends *-sede* (*supersede*), and three end *-ceed* (*exceed, succeed, proceed,* but not *procedure*).

In modern English, especially American English, all unaccented vowels tend to lose their quality and become a schwa, the sound of the vowel in *the* when *the* is not pronounced like *thee*. Thus, for many American speakers the vowel in the final syllable of *resident* and *attendant* has the same sound, which is the same sound they use for the next to the last vowel sound in *accommodate*. Since one sound is here serving for *e, a,* and *o* (and it can serve, also, for *i, u, y,* and a number of others) phonetics will not help much directly. Indirectly, even in these special problems, however, recognition of the differences between the oral and the written systems of communication help make spelling easier to learn. The spelling of *resident,* for example, can be inferred from *residential,* where the *e* retains its pronunciation because it has kept the stress.

Spelling Rules

Although most rules for spelling English words have exceptions, a few of them apply consistently enough to be worth remembering.

1. *Double consonants, double vowels, final silent* e. In general, (1) consonants are doubled only after short vowels; (2) silent *e, o, a, i,* or *y* marks a preceding long vowel. The first part of the rule is complicated by the fact that some consonants are never doubled (*q, v, j, h, w, x*); others are seldom doubled except before an ending (*b, d, g, m, n, r, t*). Some consonants are usually doubled but not always (*f, l, s, c* [double *c* is spelled *ck*]). Thus, we spell *cuff, hill, spell, hack, hiss,* but *bed, dog, man, cur, get.* The second part of the rule involves various means of indicating a long vowel (*hoed, hose, speak, cede, read, day, maid*) and the fact that these same indications of a long vowel sometimes stand for a short vowel (*head, dead*). As usual, there are exceptions (*add, axe*).

A final consonant in an accented syllable having a short vowel is regularly doubled before an ending beginning with a vowel (*forgot, forgotten; omit, omitting; hug, hugged; slur, slurred*); in unaccented syllables the consonant is not doubled (*counsel, counseled; benefit, benefited*). Alternate forms (*traveller, travelling*) often occur but are discouraged in American spelling, which avoids unnecessary doubling. If the vowel in the syllable is long, a following consonant is not doubled (*ride, riding; eat, eaten*).

Final silent *e* is usually retained before an ending beginning with a consonant (*bore, boredom; love, lovely*) and dropped before an ending beginning with a vowel (*hate, hating; cure, curable*). Most exceptions fall into patterns. If the final *e* is preceded by a vowel, it is usually dropped regardless, to avoid an awkward sequence of letters (*true, truly; argue, argument*). It may be dropped if it might

572

lead to mispronunciation when retained (*whole, wholly*). If the final *e* is used to indicate that a preceding *c* or *g* has the soft sound, that is, if it occurs before *a, o,* or *u,* it is retained (*notice, noticeable; courage, courageous*). In the United States, however, *judgment* is preferred to *judgement,* since the *d* is sufficient indication that the *g* is soft.

2. *Combinations of* y *with endings.*   A final *y* regularly changes to *i* before an ending beginning with a vowel (*ally, allies; cry, cries; lucky, luckier*). Exceptions mostly stem from obvious reasons. If *y* is preceded by a vowel, it usually is not changed (*monkey, monkeys; destroy, destroyer*). If the ending begins with *i,* the preceding *y* is not changed (*fly, flying, flies; fry, frying, fries*). Proper nouns ending in *y* add *s* with no other change (*two Marys, all the family of Frys*).

3. *Combinations of* i *and* e.   When *i* and *e* are combined to indicate the sound of *e,* the old rhyme reminds us "Put *i* before *e*/ Except after *c.*" Thus we spell *relieve,* but *receive.* Among exceptions, the more common can be kept in mind by remembering the following sentence: "At his *leisure* the *sheik* will *inveigle* and *seize* the *weird* words *either* and *neither.*" The standard spelling is *ei* when the symbol represents the sound of *a,* as in *weigh, neighbor.* In a few words having other sounds, *e* precedes *i,* as in *height, foreign, sovereign.*

CAPITALS

26c

Whether or not we call capitalization a problem in spelling, capitals do help us to identify words. The radio announcer who says, "We shall now listen to an angel recording," seems to be predicting a miracle if we assume he is thinking of a lower-case angel, but if he is thinking of an upper-case angel— "We shall now listen to an Angel recording"—he is merely announcing a record of a particular brand.

Capital, or upper-case, letters were early introduced into the writing system, and they have always marked something important. In medieval manuscripts a big illuminated letter may open a chapter—*capital* and *chapter* are both related to the word *head.* In modern writing capitals still mark some kind of special significance. Following are their most important uses:

1. *Sentence capitals.*   The first word of a sentence begins with a capital. When a sentence is quoted within another sentence, it is also capitalized; but when a quotation is divided by an introductory expression, the second part is capitalized only if it is a complete sentence.

Mr. Wilde replied, "There is no sin except stupidity."

"A cynic," said Mr. Wilde, "is a man who knows the price of everything and the value of nothing."

26c   Cap, lc

Correct dubious capitalization and consider whether the example reflects inadequate grasp of a fundamental principle.

ORIGINAL

During my Second Year in High School, I took American Literature, European History, Mathematics, french, and Home Economics, and a new course entitled social problems.

[*Terms like* high school *and* literature *are not proper nouns, even though the writer is thinking of only one school and one literature.*]

I went to the Library and read a copy of the Library.

[*The first* library *is not a proper noun; the second names a magazine and follows the rule for titles (see 26j).*]

In the Autumn the ducks move South from Canada, and hunting is good in some parts of the west.

[*Names of the seasons are not capitalized.*]

REVISION

During my second year in high school, I took American literature, European history, mathematics, French, and home economics, and a new course entitled Social Problems.

[*Social Problems is capitalized because it is a title given to a course, not a description of the material in the course.*]

I went to the library and read a copy of *The Library.*

[*The revised form makes clear the nature of each* library.]

In the autumn the ducks move south from Canada, and hunting is good in some parts of the West.

[*Directions as such are not capitalized, but a direction is capitalized as a name.*]

2. *Poetry.* Traditionally each line of a poem begins with a capital, although much poetry, especially recent poetry, does not follow the convention.

3. *Proper names.* Proper names, abbreviations of proper names, and words derived from proper names are usually capitalized—names of people, places, languages, institutions, months, days of the week, historical events, etc.

World War I, Episcopal Church, Latin, the Declaration of Independence, Goucher College, the Midwest, the U.S. Navy

The names of the seasons are not capitalized, and names for points of the compass are capitalized only when they name a region.

They went west in the summer of 1869 because they had grown tired of the East and of Eastern traditions.

Names of relatives are capitalized when used like the person's name but not when used as common nouns.

My sister wanted Mother to give up her job.

4. *Initials and abbreviations.*   See 26i.

5. *References to deity.*   Nouns referring to deity are regularly capitalized; pronouns referring to Christian deities usually are, but usage varies. Pronouns referring to pagan deities are not capitalized.

Jesus, Savior, the Holy Spirit, He gave His only begotten Son, Jupiter, Aphrodite

6. *Titles.*   The principal words of titles begin with capitals (see 26j).

7. *I, O.*   *I* as a pronoun and *O* as an exclamation are capitalized.

The major problems concerning capitalization turn on the question, when is a noun a proper noun? Superficially, the answer is easy: a proper noun is a name. But when does a noun become a name? The definition gives some trouble, not because the main distinctions involved in it are illogical, but because they are subtle enough to require clear thinking. For instance, Mrs. Hardy has a son, whom she names Thomas. Obviously, *Thomas Hardy* is a proper noun, the given name of a particular person. Thomas Hardy writes some novels set in southwestern England near an imaginary town called Casterbridge. *Casterbridge*, also, is a proper noun. But suppose that a tourist wishes to visit the scenes of these novels, does he visit the Hardy Country or the Hardy country? Similarly, a river is named for Henry Hudson. Is it the Hudson River or the Hudson river? Does it flow through the Hudson River Valley or the Hudson River valley? There is a women's college on the bank of this river; is the president the President of Vassar College, since there is only one such president at a time, or the president of Vassar College, since presidents are of common occurrence? Are the subjects taught in this institution American literature or American Literature, History of the Americas or history of the Americas?

The confusions arise in several ways, but partly because every object on earth exists as an individual. Every pebble on the beach is a separate pebble, but one stone becomes the basis of a proper noun only if it is given a name, Plymouth Rock, for instance. On this basis one can answer the questions in the previous paragraph. The area described in Hardy's novels is the Hardy country, because there is no definite, designated area that has been officially so named, as there is an area officially named Connecticut. For the same reasons, it is Hudson River, but Hudson River valley. The president of Vassar College is president, not President, unless she should sign herself, with her title, which then becomes Mary E. Smith, President of Vassar College. The subjects taught are American literature and history of the Americas, but if these subjects become titles of specific courses, then as titles they would be written American Literature and History of the Americas. The question is not whether the noun is the name of an individual object, being, sort, area, or anything else, but whether the noun is a name given to a particular unit, not shared by other units of its sort.

Words derived from names and closely associated with them are usually capitalized. *American* derives from the name *America*, and although there are many Americans the word is capitalized. On the other hand, proper nouns that have become common nouns are not capitalized. In the early nineteenth century, sample forms for the British army were made out with the name *Thomas Atkins*. Eventually Tommy Atkins became the colloquial name for a British soldier; now *tommy* has become a common noun. Similarly, a Victrola was a trade name of an instrument manufactured by the Victor Company, but the instruments became so common that any record player was called a *victrola*. Salad dressing made of oil and vinegar is called French dressing, because French cooks developed and popularized it and Americans borrowed it from France, but since tossed salads continue to be popular, *French dressing* may yet become *french dressing*. *Chinaware* comes from China, but we no longer capitalize *china* in this sense. We capitalize *Sardinia*, because it is the name of an island, but not *sardines*, associated with it; we capitalize *Sargasso Sea* but not *sargassum*, the name for the weed that floats in the sea, although sargassum belongs to the genus *Sargassum*, capitalized because it is a name. Thus proper nouns can become common nouns and common nouns proper nouns, in some uses but not in others. If the writer is uncertain, he should consult a good dictionary.

COMPOUNDS, HYPHENS 26d

When two words are used together to have a single meaning, they tend to combine in spelling, either as a single word or as a hyphenated word. The following examples illustrate how spelling differences signal differences in meaning:

The redcap wore a red cap.

The old stylebook was an old-style book.

The fairyland lady rented a room and became a fairy landlady.

He threw a big brown stone at the big brownstone.

GUIDE TO REVISION

26d   **Hy**

Hyphenate, join, or leave as separate words in accordance with modern practice, consulting a good dictionary if necessary.

ORIGINAL   REVISION

The car sank hub deep in the re-   The car sank hub-deep in the re-
cently-graded road.   cently graded road.
[*Recently, which modifies graded,*   [*Hub-deep is hyphenated; two words*
should not be hyphenated.]   *join to form a modifier.*]

Our slow baked bread has been   Our slow-baked bread has been
slowly-baked.   slowly baked.

The alloy is rust, weather, and   The alloy is rust-, weather-, and
heat-resistant.   heat-resistant.
[*Alternatives preferably include the*
hyphen with each alternative.]

Notice that in speech we distinguish the uses by stress; we stress the first syllable of *redcap,* but *cap* in *red cap;* we stress *stone* the first time it is used in the fourth example but stress the first syllable of *brownstone.* Often we can see a kind of logical need behind the development of compounds. Presumably the black board in the front of a schoolroom was identified by its color so long that it naturally became a blackboard to distinguish it from any black board that happened to be around. But often no logic of any sort is observable. One can rationalize that *post office* has remained two words because there is no other meaning from which it has to be distinguished; but what of *courthouse?* There are, actually, no consistent principles for spelling compounds, but several tendencies in practice are general enough to be useful.

1. *Compound adjectives and verbs.*   When two words function as an adjective or a verb with a single meaning, they are regularly hyphenated.

577

He was only six feet tall, but he made a seven-foot jump.

One twentieth-century innovation was the pay-as-you-go tax plan.

We hot-roll all the metal and double-rivet the joints.

Macbeth was not caught red-handed, but he had a red hand.

Unless a compound adjective is formed from a word that has already become a single noun (*backhanded*), it is almost always hyphenated.

When the first of two modifiers modifies the second, however, the modifiers are not hyphenated, especially if the first is an *-ly* adverb.

The widely advertised camera took poor pictures.

The wide-lens camera was easy to operate.

2. *Compound nouns.* With nouns consisting of components, however, practices are much less consistent, and a dictionary is often necessary.

When the second word of a compound noun is stressed, the compound is seldom written as a single word (*high water, club steak, back road* but *headwaiter*).

Compound nouns are hyphenated only in special circumstances — especially when the first word of the compound is a possessive (*Dutchman's-breeches*), when the two words indicate parts of a joint idea with neither modifying (*secretary-treasurer*), and when a noun is joined to a word like *out* or *up* (*fade-out, slip-on*, but compare *fallout, breakdown, markup*, and *countdown* or *count-down*).

Compound nouns stressed on the first word follow no consistent pattern, except that they tend to combine with continuing use, especially if there is possibility of a confusion of meaning with a noncombined pair of words (*highway, limestone, mailman, mailboat, iceman, coalbin, gasman;* but compare *garbage man, mail car, ice pick, coal oil, gas mask*).

3. *Alternatives.* If there are alternatives for the first element of a hyphenated compound, each of the alternatives may have a hyphen (*eight- and ten-paddle canoes, lower- and middle-income housing*).

4. *Prefixes.* Typically prefixes like *mis-, non-, dis-, anti-,* and *pre-* join words with no separation, but in a few circumstances hyphens are common. Hyphens sometimes separate a prefix ending with a vowel from a word beginning with the same vowel (*pre-eminent, semi-independent, re-elected*, but *co-ordinate* or *coordinate*). Hyphens separate some other prefixes as well: (a) *ex-* when it means "former" (*ex-president*), (b) a prefix with a proper noun (*anti-Nazi*), (c) most compounds with *self-* (*self-defense, self-taught*, but *selfsame*),

578

(d) a prefix that leads to a combination that might be confused with another word (*re-cover* to distinguish from *recover*).

5. *Numbers.* Compound numbers from twenty-one to ninety-nine are hyphenated. A fraction used as a modifier is hyphenated unless one element of it is already a hyphenated compound. Fractions used as nouns are usually not hyphenated.

> *twenty-seven* cattle, nine hundred and *ninety-nine*, a *four-fifths* majority, *four fifths* of the class, a *three-sixteenths* drill

Hyphens are used to join the figures in inclusive dates (*1790–92, 1850–1900*) and to join inclusive figures when these appear in tabular form (*500–1,000, 10,001–10,025*).

PLURALS   **26e**

English vocabulary is made up mainly of (1) native words that have come from Old English, and (2) words borrowed from other languages. Roughly speaking, a piece of writing

GUIDE TO REVISION

26e   **Pl, Sing**

Use the standard plural form, distinguishing between plurals and possessives, and if necessary consulting a dictionary for rare forms.

ORIGINAL	REVISION
High over our heads we saw dozen's of vapor trail's from the plane's. [*The apostrophe is used with possessives, but not with regular plurals.*]	High over our heads we saw dozens of vapor trails from the planes.
Be sure to dot your is and cross your ts. [*Numbers, letters, symbols, figures, and words out of context form the plural with 's.*]	Be sure to dot your *i*'s and cross your *t*'s. [*Notice also that italics show that the letters are used out of context.*]
Mrs. Appleby brought all the little Applebies with her.	Mrs. Appleby brought all the little Applebys with her.

is likely to contain about equal quantities of each, a fact of interest for spelling. Although Old English formed plurals in a variety of ways, most such nouns were reduced eventually to a single system, so that native words generally form their plurals by adding *s* or *es*. To form regular plurals, add *s* if the sign of the plural is not pronounced as a separate syllable (*boy, boys; regulation, regulations*); after a consonant, if the sign of the plural is pronounced as a separate syllable, add *es* (*grass, grasses; class, classes*); if the singular ends in *e*, add *s* (*house, houses; bridge, bridges*).

Some few nouns were not regularized in Middle English and retain archaic forms (*ox, oxen; deer, deer; brother, brothers* or *brethren; child, children*). For such words, consult a good dictionary. Words ending in *o* formerly regularly added *es* (*tomato, tomatoes; Negro, Negroes*), but words recently borrowed usually have only the *-s* ending in the plural (*radio, radios; banjo, banjos*). Thus words ending in *o* do not follow a reliable rule; exceptions must be learned. For nouns ending in *y*, see 26b. In nouns having a final *f* or an *f* before a final silent *e*, the *f* is often changed to *v* before the sign of the plural (*wife, wives; loaf, loaves*), but there are many exceptions (*sheriff, sheriffs; belief, beliefs*).

Words borrowed from other languages offer special problems. English speakers tend to change words slowly, to keep a word relatively long in the form in which it has been borrowed. Eventually, if the word becomes common, it becomes Anglicized with a normalized plural. The change does not greatly affect the plurals of words from German, French, and Spanish, most of which form plurals with *-s*, but words from Latin and Greek are somewhat complicated because they may retain endings from the complicated classical declensional systems. Latin words ending in *um* usually form the plural by changing the *um* to *a* (*datum, data; agendum, agenda*); *us* is changed to *i* (*focus, foci; cactus, cacti*); *a* is changed to *ae* (*alumna, alumnae*). Foreign words eventually acquire a plural form by analogy with English; that is, the plural ends in *s* or *es*. Thus, for a time, there are two current forms; *focuses* is now more common that *foci*. Sometimes foreign plurals are not recognized for what they are, and are treated like singulars. Thus one hears "This data is unreliable," although *data* is plural and *is* is singular; and one hears "The committee made up its agendas," although *agenda* is already plural without the *s*. Eventually these blunders may become standard speech (our accepted plural *children* results from a similar blunder), but foreign forms are usually retained in writing.

Numbers, letters, and symbols become plural with the addition of *'s* ("two 2's;" "a row of x's"). Sometimes apostrophes are also used in the plurals of words spoken of as objects (if's and and's), but the current tendency is to form these plurals without the apostrophe ("pros and cons"; "but me no buts"). These are the only plural forms that use the apostrophe.

NUMBERS

26f

Numbers that can be expressed in two words are spelled in standard writing; thus, all numbers one hundred or below are usually spelled. Exceptions to this rule are frequently made in the interests of simplicity and clarity. If, for example, several numbers are used in a passage and some of them are large, all of them are written in figures.

GUIDE TO REVISION

26f

Num

Unless otherwise prescribed in your style sheet, spell all numbers that can be written in two words, except in a sequence having numbers including at least one that cannot be so expressed; in such a sequence, write all numbers as numerals.

ORIGINAL	REVISION
1938 is remembered in our valley as the snowy year. [*A figure should not begin a sentence.*]	In our valley, we remember 1938 as the snowy year. [*The sentence is rearranged to avoid the initial figure.*]
The 4 of us moved into a little garden cottage at sixty-two Longfellow Avenue.	The four of us moved into a little garden cottage at 62 Longfellow Avenue.
He called out the following numbers: ten, sixty-four, a hundred, 256, 11,822.	He called out the following numbers: 10, 64, 100, 256, 11,822.

On a western highway, one passes through towns marked on the map with populations from zero up. For instance, traveling east on Highway 80, one leaves the San Francisco–Oakland metropolitan area, population 2,942,000, passes through Sacramento, 750,800; Verdi, 356; Mill City, 72; and Toy and Dad Lees, 0, since the Lees have moved.

Some style sheets, including those of many newspapers, prescribe figures for all numbers above ten.

Figures are regularly used in certain standard contexts: for street and room or apartment numbers in addresses (1238 Ralston Street, 14 West Twenty-third Street); to designate portions of a book (chapter 10, page 371); for dates (January 10, 1838), and for decimals and percentages when using words would become complicated (3.1416, 57%).

Figures are not used to begin a sentence, and numbers are not written both as figures and as words, except in legal documents. For hyphenation in numbers see 26d.

APOSTROPHES, POSSESSIVES, CONTRACTIONS   26g

The apostrophe developed as a mark to indicate omissions, and it remains a useful spelling device to distinguish a few words in the language, such as *who's* from *whose*. In its main use, to indicate possessive forms, the apostrophe is perhaps an anachronism. The use developed from a curious blunder. Renaissance grammarians supposed that a form like *the kingis book*, an alternate medieval form for *the kinges book*, should actually read *the king, his book*. They assumed that an *h* had been omitted and used an apostrophe to mark the omission. They were wrong, but the apostrophe has been adopted to signal the possessive in writing, even though in speech the possessive is distinguished by its position before a noun. Following are the main conventions governing the use of the apostrophe.

1. *Possessives.* The apostrophe is used as a sign of the possessive or genitive case.

For singular nouns and indefinite pronouns and for a few plural nouns whose possessive form is pronounced with an added *s* or *z* sound, the possessive is spelled by adding an apostrophe and *s: Paul's temper, the cat's tail, anybody's opinion, the people's choice, all men's fate.*

For plural nouns ending in *s* the possessive is spelled by adding only an apostrophe: *the soldiers' rifles, the schoolgirls' idol, the horses' collars.*

Nouns of specification in time, space, quantity, or value follow conventions for the apostrophe in the possessive, even though the genitive carries no meaning of possession: *an hour's walk, a quarter's worth, at their wits' end.*

Singular nouns, especially proper names of more than one syllable, that end with an *s, sh,* or *z* sound may be spelled in the possessive with only an apostrophe, to avoid an awkward series of sounds: *Xerxes' army, Velasquez' painting, for conscience' sake, Frances's* or *Frances' earring, Keats's* or *Keats' poems.*

Apos, Poss, Cont

In compounds and phrases, the last element takes the possessive form: *mother-in-law's visit, anyone else's rights, the King of England's crown.*

GUIDE TO REVISION

26g　　　　　**Apos, Poss, Cont**

Revise, using apostrophes accurately to mark possessives or omissions and using contractions consistently.

ORIGINAL

When June went to North State Teacher's College for a years work, she found that the warm winds' there made her hair curl.
[*The apostrophe should be omitted from the proper name.*]

The Jones's dog chased the Macks's cat.
[*The sense indicates that plural possessives are required.*]

Youre supposed to pick it up by the back of it's neck.
[*The contraction* you're *requires an apostrophe; the possessive pronoun* its *does not.*]

The first spectographic tests weren't directed toward detecting amino acids.
[*Contractions are avoided in formal writing and in the more serious sorts of informal prose.*]

The play does not adequately prepare the reader for the climax, and therefore the main scene isn't convincing.
[*The inconsistency with contractions* —does not *and* isn't— *suggests a shift in style.*]

REVISION

When June went to North State Teachers College for a year's work, she found that the warm winds there made her hair curl.
[*Year's, a noun of specification, requires the apostrophe;* winds, *a plural, does not.*]

The Joneses' dog chased the Macks' cat.
[*The apostrophe after the regular plural forms the plural possessive.*]

(1) You're supposed to pick it up by the back of its neck.
(2) You are supposed to pick it up by the back of its neck.

The first spectographic tests were not directed toward detecting amino acids.

The play does not adequately prepare the reader for the climax, and therefore the main scene is not convincing.
[*The general tone of the sentence seems serious enough that contractions are probably inappropriate.*]

In expressions showing joint possession, only the last element takes the sign of the possessive: *Germany, France, and England's position; John and Robert's fight.* A possessive form for each of two or more coordinated nouns indicates individual possession: *Harry and Bert's bicycle* (they own it together), *Harry's and Bert's troubles* (each has troubles of his own).

The double possessive, in which both the apostrophe or a possessive pronoun and *of* are used, is idiomatic in English: *a friend of my father's, a cousin of Ann's, a book of his.*

The apostrophe is often omitted in proper names that have become established: *North State Teachers College, Clayton County Old Folks Home.*

Pronouns, including the possessive forms ending *s* and *se—his, hers, its, ours, yours, theirs,* and *whose*—are used as possessives and do not have apostrophes.

2. *Contractions.* The apostrophe is used to indicate the omission of one or more letters or figures in contractions: *can't, isn't, o'clock, the gold rush of '49.* The apostrophe is especially important to mark a few contractions readily confused with possessive forms of pronouns not requiring apostrophes. Notice the following pairs:

CONTRACTIONS	POSSESSIVE PRONOUNS
it's (it is)	its (The cat carried its kittens.)
they're (they are)	their (They ate their lunch.)
you're (you are)	your (Mind your manners.)
who's (who is)	whose (Whose little boy are you?)

Since they are primarily devices of speech, contractions like *I've* and *don't* are not appropriate in formal writing and are usually avoided in serious informal composition, partly because of the difficulty of using them consistently.

3. *Plurals.* Apostrophes usually are used to form plurals of letters, symbols, and words mentioned as words: *the 1920's, A's* (see 26e).

4. *Dialect.* The apostrophe is used to indicate omissions in reports of dialectal speech.

"I rec'leck how y'r paw come courtin' like 'twar yestiday," she said.

Overuse of the apostrophe to record dialect, however, only clutters the page and confuses the reader. Writers usually mark only noticeable omissions in order to suggest pronunciation and do not attempt to record all variations.

Writing systems have generally made use of two styles of letters, those drawn for relatively formal purposes, and those written rapidly in a free-flowing hand. When written letters

GUIDE TO REVISION

26h **Ital**

Underline to indicate italic type in accordance with modern practice.

ORIGINAL	REVISION
Soon, very soon, we shall start for *sunny California,* hoping to have the *time of our lives.* [*Overuse of italics for emphasis destroys the emphasis.*]	Soon, very soon, we shall start for sunny California, hoping to have the time of our lives.
After Professor Lovejoy's lecture, it became "de rigueur" to have read "The Road to Xanadu." [*Italics are preferable.*]	After Professor Lovejoy's lecture, it became *de rigueur* to have read *The Road to Xanadu.*
Man is the subject of the sentence. [*Italics should point to* man, *used out of context.*]	*Man* is the subject of the sentence.

became the basis of printed letters, both styles were imitated; the formal letters, called *roman,* were made upright, and the informal letters, made slanting, were called *italic.* Both styles were long used for display purposes, but now they are being standardized, and the difference between them provides the writer with a good means of distinguishing some uses. In general, roman type is used as body type, the main type in which a book or magazine is printed; italic type is used for special purposes. The following are the most common.

1. *Emphasis.* Italics may be used for emphasis or contrast, as in "The President's spokesman—*not* the President himself—said you acted like a nincompoop." This device can readily be overworked, and good writers use it only sparingly, many not at all.

2. *Foreign terms.* Italics are used for foreign terms not yet Anglicized, as *savoir-vivre, Weltschmerz.*

3. *Words out of context.* Increasingly, italics are used for words out of context, that is, words used for themselves, not for their meaning or use in the sentence.

Hamlet is a noun; etymologically, *hamlet* means a little enclosed place.

Formerly, words used out of context were placed within quotation marks, and this practice is still acceptable in many style books, but italic type is becoming the standard means of indicating that a word is employed for itself, not for its meaning.

4. *Titles.* Increasingly, also, italic type is used for titles (see 26j). For the more complicated citations required in footnotes and bibliographies see 24b and 24c.

ABBREVIATIONS

26i

In general, abbreviations are avoided in writing, except in footnotes, bibliographies, formal lists, compilations of statistics, tables, addresses, and the like. There are a few exceptions: common forms of address when used with proper names (*Mr., Mrs., Messrs., Dr., Jr., Sr., Ph.D., LL.D., D.D., S.J.;* but not *Rev., Sen., Gov., Prof.,* or *Pres.* in formal writing); times of day (*4:00* p.m. or *4:00* P.M.); *Before Christ* and *Anno Domini* when used with a date (B.C., A.D.); a few common standard abbreviations when used in informal, technical, or business writing (*cf., e.g., no., etc.*); some government agencies (*NLRB, OPA, ICC, OEO*). Except in footnotes, bibliographies, addresses, tables, and the like, the following are spelled out: names of states and countries (*California, United States*); details of publication (*volume, page, chapter*); addresses (*street, avenue, road*); months and days of the week (*December, Sunday*); business terms (*company, manufactured*); and other words not specifically excepted (*Christmas, mountain, fort, saint*).

Contractions (*don't, aren't*) are inappropriate in formal writing.

Characters or symbols used for *and* are not acceptable in standard writing.

In formal writing the titles *Reverand* and *Honorable* are considered adjectives, are preceded by *the,* and followed by a designation like *Mr.* (*the Honorable Miss Charlotte Prism*). When a name with a title like *Sir* or *Lady* is shortened to one name, the first name is used; Sir Winston Churchill is Sir Winston.

The abbreviation *A.D.* precedes the date, and *B.C.* follows it.

26i   **Ab**

Use abbreviations only in accordance with standard practice.

ORIGINAL

The pol. sci. assign. for Mon. is something about the U.N. meeting in N.Y.

Rev. McIntosh was in charge of the service.
[*The abbreviation is used only in newspaper writing and some informal writing.*]

Rome endured from 390 b.c., when it was sacked by the Celts, until 410 a.d., when it was sacked by the Germans.

REVISION

The political science assignment for Monday concerns the United Nations meeting in New York.

(1) The Reverend Mr. McIntosh was in charge of the service.
(2) The Reverend Ira J. McIntosh was in charge of the service.
[*Formally, two styles are acceptable.*]

Rome endured from 390 B.C., when it was sacked by the Celts, until A.D. 410, when it was sacked by the Germans.

TITLES   **26j**

The title of a brief theme or other piece of student writing should be centered on the first page, separated from the body of the composition by a blank line if handwritten, and by at least four spaces if typed. Principal words, usually all except articles and short connectives, are capitalized, but a title at the head of a manuscript is not underlined or enclosed in quotation marks. Titles of long manuscripts are placed on a separate title page.

When a title appears within a manuscript, it should have capital letters to begin all words except short prepositions, conjunctions, and articles, and should be distinguished as a title either by underlining to indicate italics (see 26h) or by quotation marks. Practices vary, however, in handling different sorts of titles. Older practice was to use quotation marks for all titles; newspapers still tend not to use italics because they complicate typesetting. More recently publishers have preferred italics for titles of longer works and sometimes also for titles of poems and other short pieces. The following statement from *The MLA Style Sheet* describes a widely accepted procedure for handling titles.

<table>
<tr><td>

26j

</td><td>

Title

</td></tr>
</table>

Use standard form for a title.

ORIGINAL	REVISION
"Confrontation on the Campus" [*Except for titles within titles quotation marks and italics are not used in titles as they appear on manuscripts.*]	Confrontation on the Campus [*The first letters of all words are capitalized in titles except articles, conjunctions, and prepositions.*]
People will say we're in Love is one of the most popular songs from Oklahoma!	"People Will Say We're in Love" is one of the most popular songs from *Oklahoma!*
Robinson's poem Mr. Flood's Party appeared in the volume "Avon's Harvest," and was reprinted in COLLECTED POEMS.	Robinson's poem "Mr. Flood's Party" appeared in the volume *Avon's Harvest* and was reprinted in *Collected Poems.*

Enclose in quotation marks (do not underline) titles of articles, essays, short stories, short poems, songs, chapters and sections of books, and unpublished works such as dissertations. Underline titles of published books, plays, long poems, pamphlets, periodicals, operas, movies, and classical works (except books of the Bible). The above conventions do not apply to names of series or societies or editions; leave them in roman, without quotes.

For titles in footnotes and bibliographies, see 24b and 24c.

WORD DIVISION   26k

      A somewhat uneven right-hand margin is preferable to numerous divided words, or words incorrectly divided. In copy to be printed, hyphenation is uncommonly inconvenient, since the printer may not be sure whether the hyphen marks only the end of a line, or the end of a line that breaks a hyphenated word. When necessary, however, words may be divided between syllables. Syllabification is complicated. In general, it follows pronunciation, and consonants attach to the vowels following them (*pa-per, re-gard*); two consonants that represent two sounds go one with each syllable (*mis-ter, har-dy;* but *soph-o-more*); prefixes and suffixes remain syllables by themselves (*ach-ing, ex-alt*), unless modern pronunciation has obscured a suffix (*chil-dren*). Double consonants are separated unless they are the ending of a word with a suffix (*rat-tle, swim-ming,* but *miss-ing*). Words of one syllable cannot be divided. Words should not be divided so that a single letter appears on either line. There are more rules and many exceptions; unless the writer is certain he should consult a good dictionary. When a word is divided, the hyphen appears at the end of the first line, not at the beginning of the second.

GUIDE TO REVISION

26k	**Div**

Divide words in accordance with standard practice, consulting a dictionary in doubtful cases.

ORIGINAL

If the division is doub -tful, consult a dictionary.

REVISION

If the division is doubt- ful consult a dictionary.

FOR STUDY AND WRITING

A Correct mechanics in the following, noting any uses that would be acceptable in informal writing but inappropriate in formal writing.

I've just purchased in a 2nd hand book store a copy of *Appleton's Guide to the United States* for eighteen ninety-two. It's full of entrancing old things, but since for the past 8 or 10 years our Family has gone every Summer to the Adirondack mts., I was particularly interested in the description of those mts. The eds. point out that this section 30 yrs ago "was known even by name only to a few hunters, trappers, and lumbermen," but they're now able to give a detailed description of it. They correctly locate the area between L. Champlain and L. George on the East, and the St. Lawrence R. on the w. They also identify Mt. Marcy as the tallest mt. in the area, giving the measurement as five thousand three hundred thirty-four feet. They concede that this pk. is not so high as the Black Mts. of N.C., nor the White Mts. of N. Hampshire, but they point out that they're interspersed by more than 1000 lakes, the largest of which are more than 20 mls. long. These lakes're said to be infested with Trout weighing 20 lb. or more. Hunting was also A-1; for instance, the hunter could take woodcock from Sept. 1st to April thirtieth, & the fine for shooting game out of Season seems to have been only $25, which by our standards wasn't very high. The Publication also gave instrs. that a "lady's outfit" should include "a short walking-dress, with Turkish drawers fastened tightly with a band at the ankle." Travel in the area was apparently done by boats, built a few ft. long, carried by the guides on their shoulders from lake to lake and from river to river.

B Correct the faulty use or omission of italics, quotation marks, and capitals in the following:

Among the curiosities of literature and thought is the career of Lord Monboddo, a Scottish *baronet,* author of a book called Of the Origin and Progress of Language. He believed that human speech came from the speech of animals, and imported an *orangoutang* into scotland, assuming that the animal represented *the infantine state of our species.* The *chimp,* as the animal was called, was presumably a representative of "Pongo pygmaeus" or Simia satyris. Lord Monboddo taught the animal to play the flute, after a fashion, but in Monboddo's words, he *never learned to speak.* The lord patiently tried to teach the animal to say "hungry" and "eat," but without success. The learned Journals of the day, periodicals like the Quarterly Review and Blackwood's Edinburgh Magazine, ridiculed poor Monboddo, publishing articles with titles like Misguided Jurist and *This Monkey Business.* Not until long after the publication of Darwin's Descent of Man did students of modern thought realize that Lord Monboddo had been ahead of his day. Among the milder satirists of the radical jurist was Thomas Love Peacock, who made genial fun of Monboddo and his Orangoutang by inserting into his book Melancourt, a satirical novelette, a certain sir Oran Haut-ton, whose name was of course a pun upon the french haut-ton, that is, high-toned.

C In the following paragraph, identify the specified forms to fill the blanks:

_____ [plural of *beekeeper*] have long been intrigued by their _____ [possessive plural of *bee*] peculiar habits. A _____ [possessive singular of *beekeeper*] year allows him some _____ [form of *month* indicating extent] leisure, when he is likely to wonder what a _____ [possessive singular of *bee*] mind is like, and spend long _____ [plural of *evening*] reading _____ [possessive singular of *Maeterlinck*] description of the social organization of the _____ [plural form of *bee* in the possessive with *of*] and _____ [possessive singular of *Fabre*] Entymology, available in _____ [possessive singular of *Mattos*] translation. Maeterlinck, alone, provides a long _____ [singular form of *evening* indicating extent] reading, or for that matter, several _____ [plural form of *evening* indicating extent] reading, and raises curious questions. Why, for instance, with _____ [possessive singular of *it*] reputation for industry, does a bee spend time on a sunny afternoon in what is called "play," when this time is _____ [appropriate possessive singular of *it*] for the using? The beekeeper was likely to answer, "Why, indeed? _____ [contraction of *they are*] strange _____ [plural of *creature*] and _____ [contraction of *there is*] no accounting for _____ [possessive of *they*] doings." But _____ [plural of *scientist*] work differently. The _____ [possessive singular of *scientist*] method requires the collection and study of _____ [plural of *datum*]; that is, in the case of the _____ [plural form of *bee* for the possessive with *of*], studying them when they are supposed to be at play. On any warm afternoon they can be observed before the hive in a sort of dance in the air, making figures like _____ [plural of *s*] and _____ [plural of *z*]. The beekeeper had assumed a few bees had become tired of industry, and danced around a little to feel better, but the _____ [possessive plural of *scientist*] _____ [plural of *record*] showed that these _____ [plural of *bee*] were returning workers, laden with honey, who with a series of _____ [plural of *signal*] were informing their fellow workers where they got the honey. In short, the supposed "play" is the _____ [possessive singular of *bee*] way of giving directions, what might be called *The* _____ [possessive plural of *honeybee,* form suitable for a title] *Daily Market News.*

D In the passage below italicized words include several compounds. Which should be (1) combined into a single word, (2) hyphenated, or (3) left as they are? For each, decide whether the current form can be determined by the rule or must be sought in a dictionary.

During the war in *Indo China*, a young *helicopter pilot* found himself in a *base hospital* and also in a *semi rigid plaster cast*. He was *thirty one* years old, *brim full* of energy, was *naturally curious*, and had a *ghetto born* horror of waste. He contemplated his cast with a *sadly jaundiced eye*. It was a *hand made* cast, intended to restrict his *inter costal* muscles, and it was *nicely calculated* to hold the *spinal column* while at the same time there was space enough to allow *abdomino thoracic* movement. In fact, by contracting his stomach muscles, he could enjoy a *side glimpse* of his own navel. There was enough space, he decided, to allow him to insert a *hen's egg*. He ordered a raw egg for his *mid morning* lunch, and proceeded to transform his cast into the equivalent of a *setting hen,* an *incubator cast,* if you will. That is, he tucked the egg under his cast, and it fitted nicely into his navel so long as he kept his *stomach muscles* contracted. But he was not a *mother hen* by nature. After *one day's* care, he relaxed and smashed the egg. He *back ordered* the egg, however, and was heard to remark, "I'll *mother hen* one of those things if I have to stay here until I've grown a *hen's nest* in my beard." Three weeks later he *hatched out* a little, downy, *baby chick*. He might, of course, have become a *duck incubator,* too, or started a *turkey flock,* even a whole *barn yard,* but he remembered that *turkey eggs* require a *five or six week* period, and he did not have room on his bed for a *duck pond*.

E Dean Thomas Clark Pollock of New York University made an extensive summary of college spelling, for which he used nearly 600 reports from college teachers, listing 31,375 spelling errors, which included 4,482 different misspellings. Two salient facts emerge from this study: most words are misspelled very seldom, and most of the misspellings occur with relatively few words. More than a third of all the words were misspelled only once, but the 27 words misspelled more than 100 times each accounted for 5,097 misspellings; that is, less than 1 per cent of the words were involved in more than 16 per cent of the errors. Similarly, the 417 words misspelled more than 20 times accounted for more than half the misspellings. The moral of all this is that most young people who have trouble with spelling have their trouble with relatively few words, and learning to spell correctly may be easier than they think.

Following are the 308 word groups that account for 20 or more misspellings on Dean Pollock's list, printed in the order of the frequency with which the words were misspelled. They warrant careful study.

their
they're
there

two
too
to

receive
receiving

exist
existence
existent

occur
occurred
occurring
occurrence

definite
definitely
define

separate
separation

believe
belief

occasion

lose
losing

write
writing
writer

description
describe

benefit
benefited
beneficial

precede

referring

success
succeed
succession

its
it's

privilege

environment

personal
personnel

than
then

principle
principal

choose
chose
choice

perform
performance

similar

professor
profession

necessary
unnecessary

began
begin
beginner
beginning

control
controlled
controlling

argument
arguing

proceed
procedure

achieve
achievement

controversy
controversial

all right

possess

possession

psychology
psychoanalysis
psychopathic
psychosomatic

analyze
analysis

equipped
equipment

affect
affective

rhythm

tries
tried

weather
whether

forty
fourth

criticism
criticize

apparent

sense

conscious

studying

varies
various

category

embarrass

excellent
excellence

grammar
grammatically

repetition

consistent
consistency

prevalent

intelligence
intelligent

realize
really

led

loneliness
lonely

prefer
preferred

surprise

explanation

fascinate

immediate
immediately

interpretation
interpret

thorough

useful
useless
using

noticeable
noticing

probably

imagine
imaginary
imagination

marriage
prejudice

disastrous

passed
past

acquire

busy
business

Negro
Negroes

among

height

interest

origin
original

conscience
conscientious

accommodate

comparative

decision
decided

experience

prominent

pursue

shining

practical

woman

acquaint
acquaintance

exaggerate

incident
incidentally

effect

government
governor

prepare

recommend

appear
appearance

convenience
convenient

mere

opinion

possible

ridicule
ridiculous

summary
summed

attended
attendant
attendance

coming

difference
different

hero
heroine
heroic
heroes

opportunity

paid

quiet

villain

accept
acceptance

acceptable
accepting

dominant

predominant

foreign
foreigners

independent
independence

particular

technique

transferred

discipline
disciple

humor
humorist
humorous

quantity

accident
accidentally

character
characteristic
characterized

hypocrisy
hypocrite

operate

planned

pleasant

athlete
athletic

challenge

fundamental
fundamentally

liveliest
livelihood
liveliness
lives

philosophy

speech

sponsor

unusual
usually

across

aggressive

article

disappoint

suppose
curiosity
curious
desirability
desire
knowledge
ninety
undoubtedly
optimism
permanent
relieve
religion
together
you're
familiar
suppress
where
whose
author
authority
authoritative
basis
basically
before
conceive
conceivable
consider
considerably
continuous
dependent
extremely
finally
satire
careless
careful
condemn
maintenance
parallel
permit
weird
efficient
efficiency
friendliness
friend

fulfill
piece
temperament
carrying
carried
carries
carrier
happiness
response
further
laboratory
oppose
opponent
propaganda
propagate
therefore
hindrance
approach
approaches
physical
advice
advise
entertain
influential
influence
significance
exercise
involve
leisure
leisurely
sergeant
subtle
Britain
Britannica
completely
dealt
divide
excitable
favorite
interrupt
perceive
persistent
reminisce
suspense

amount
approximate
curriculum
disease
especially
fallacy
financier
financially
meant
politician
political
relative
scene
sophomore
guarantee
guaranteed
huge
indispensable
laid
length
lengthening
mathematics
remember
seize
several
substantial
tendency
whole
accompanying
accompanies
accompanied
accompaniment
hear
here
luxury
moral
morale
morally
phase
playwright
represent
schedule
source
capital

594

capitalism

certain

certainly

chief

counselor

counsel

council

divine

fictitious

primitive

regard

roommate

story

stories

strength

accustom

forward

pertain

safety

satisfy

satisfied

sentence

theory

theories

tremendous

vacuum

view

accomplish

arouse

arousing

despair

guidance

guiding

ignorance

ignorant

magnificent

magnificence

narrative

obstacle

shepherd

simply

simple

straight

synonymous

themselves

them

amateur

attack

attitude

boundary

clothes

expense

fantasy

fantasies

intellect

irrelevant

laborer

laboriously

labor

later

license

medieval

naturally

noble

peace

sacrifice

strict

symbol

actually

actuality

actual

adolescence

adolescent

against

appreciate

appreciation

experiment

field

hungry

hungrily

hunger

interfere

interference

likeness

likely

likelihood

magazine

maneuver

mechanics

medicine

medical

miniature

mischief

omit

persuade

those

thought

tragedy

yield

GLOSSARY OF
USAGE
AND TERMS

CHAPTER 27

Use determines language and use readily crystallizes into usage.

The writer constantly makes choices; rhetoric may be described as a study of linguistic choices—of the bases and effects of selecting among various possible ways of putting ideas. Grammar contributes to this kind of study of writing, since its function is to describe the constructions. This book has been concerned with grammar as it illumines techniques and problems of writing. A study of usage—of the customary environments, the social limitations, the special effects of various expressions—also contributes to a study of writing. This book has been concerned with usage as it helps determine the effect of the expressions the writer chooses—in questions of reference and agreement, for example. Special problems of usage, however, and a number of grammatical terms have not been pertinent to preceding discussions; they are collected in the following pages for ready reference.

Varieties of Usage: Dialect

The more English spreads throughout the world, the more varied it becomes. In spite of the standardizing influences of modern communication media, the English of India, of Yorkshire, of Nebraska, and of West Australia differ considerably—in pronunciation, in idiom, in vocabulary. Expressions like "pure English," or "the Queen's English," or even "correct" English have never meant much, and they mean less today, but, meanwhile, the ability to deal with usage has become, if anything, more important. As Americans place more reliance, both economic and social, on education and attach more importance to the use of language as evidence of education, usage plays an ever larger part in people's lives. Usage can be understood, and appropriate usage can be cultivated, partly on the basis of the modern concept of dialect.

Dialect was formerly understood about as one of the characters in George Eliot's *Adam Bede* conceived it:

> They're cur'ous talkers i' this country, sir; the gentry's hard work to hunderstand 'em. I was brought up among the gentry, sir, an' got the turn o' their tongue when I was a bye. Why, what do you think the folks about here say for 'heven't you?'—the gentry, you know, says 'heven't you'—well, the people about here says 'hanna yey.' It's what they call the 'dileck' as is spoke hereabout, sir. That's what I've heard Squire Donnithorne say many a time; 'it's the dileck,' says he.

That is, to George Eliot's speaker a "dileck" was English "as is spoke hereabout." But we recognize that the speaker also used a dialect, and we can conclude further that Squire Donnithorne spoke a dialect, although probably neither he nor the man proud of having been "brought up among the gentry" would have called it that. They probably thought of a dialect as something to be ashamed of, although it is not. Everybody speaks a dialect, or several dialects, inevitably; in fact, languages cannot be used except through dialects. Everybody speaks as he does because of the circumstances to which he was born, how and where he lived, what he has done and who he has known, and somewhat because of what he has or has not done to police his language use. From a linguistic point of view one dialect is as good as another; if a dialect did not serve the needs of some people it could not exist. No doubt a herdsman's "hanna yey" served him as well as the squire's "heven't you," considering the life that each of them lived. Of course dialects are not equally useful; they are not equally fashionable, equally suited to all times and places. Presumably the squire could have passed as a gentleman and a substantial person wherever he might go, whereas the herdsman with his "hanna yey" would have been branded at once as unschooled. Thus people born to an unfashionable dialect may wish to cultivate a more fashionable manner of speech, and even people who are not aware of a general dialectal handicap may wish to prefer a standard locution different from the one they inherited.

Variations in language habits, in usage, can be classified in many ways, most of them overlapping; the following are some of the more notable.

1. *Geographic dialects.* The term *dialect* is used to describe any kind of subdivision—any discernible variant—of a language,

but it is especially associated with particular usages common to a region or area. Thus, in America we may speak loosely of a southern dialect or a New England dialect, and linguistic geographers, investigating precisely, can discover dialectal differences within these areas, such as those that characterize various sorts of speech within a state like Texas. Differences in pronunciation—the vowels in *cow* or *either* or *can't*—and in vocabulary—*poke, sack, bag; skillet, frying pan, spider; earthworm, fishworm, angleworm*—are especially remarkable.

2. *Cultural levels.* Differences in usage related to social and cultural relationships may be obvious but complex and hard to specify—for example, the distinction between the language of the educated and the uneducated. Thus, "she don't know English" might be called uneducated, "she doesn't know English" educated. A similar widely used classification distinguishes standard from nonstandard English. Standard English is the language used by educated people, the language that commands respect and esteem, that provides social and professional status. Nonstandard, sometimes called vulgate, characteristic of the uneducated, is in social disrepute, like bad table manners; *ain't* and most double negatives are labeled nonstandard. Other kinds of cultural distinctions may be specialized—the cant of criminals or hobos, the slang of musicians, the shoptalk of psychiatrists. Social attitudes also prompt people to label some expressions—not very consistently—as obscene or affected or in poor taste.

Distinctions based on cultural or social levels are difficult to establish, partly because cultural levels in our society are not sharply defined and partly because culture, society, and language are constantly changing. *Ain't* was once in good standing. A quarter of a century ago almost every editor excoriated *contact* as a verb; now the same editors may use the word without a second thought. Is *teen-age* now standard or educated English? One highly respected dictionary does not recognize it at all, and under its unhyphenated spelling gives only a British word meaning "brushwood used for fences and hedges." Meanwhile, other dictionaries enter it as both a noun and a modifier and do not suggest anything wrong with it. In England the word *bloody* is in bad odor, taboo in polite mixed company; in America it means only that something has blood on it.

3. *Functional varieties.* Probably more important, though less likely to stimulate popular controversy, are variations in usage to suit different purposes and different kinds of situations. That is, varieties may be distinguished within standard English. No one of these is "better" than the others, but one may be more appropriate. For example, contractions (*won't, aren't*) are certainly standard English; they are appropriate in speech and some informal writing

598

but not in formal writing. Three functional varieties are commonly distinguished, although they are only approximations. Formal English has the advantage of wide currency and permanent value; it is used in serious writing—in serious books, quality magazines, official statements. Informal English is more popular, more familiar, employing some devices generally associated with speech, common in newspapers and magazines and many books directed to a wide public. Colloquial English is the language of speech, of familiar conversation, but it may also appear in personal letters or other writing intended to be conversational in tone.

Usage and "Correctness"

The complexity of such variations in language and the uncertainties of linguists in trying to categorize them contribute to the emotionalism that tends to develop around disputes on usage. Faced with the prospect of alternatives in language, usually reasonable people may react violently, either lamenting the seeming chaos and urging that some authority should set us right, or refusing to recognize the reality of variations and aggressively defending their own attitudes on the prepositional purity of *like* or the evils of the split infinitive. In reality, of course, arguments about what is "correct" are likely to be futile. The kinds of variations in language mentioned above, and others like them, are facts; they exist, whether we like it or not. They exist because users of a language change it, adapting it to fit their changing and increasing needs. Immutable standards of "correctness," therefore, even though they might be convenient, are impractical.

It does not follow that usage makes no difference, that anything goes. Usage makes a great deal of difference, but decisions on usage, unfortunately, require more than discovering a rule and following it. Selection among varying usages, like any rhetorical selection, requires the writer to try to anticipate results. Facts about usage—the company an expression usually keeps, the attitudes various kinds of people have toward it, even the emotional reactions it is likely to arouse—are the data, the information, on which the writer acts. He decides to say "I did it" rather than "I done it" because the expressions have different associations, and he wants one set of associations or does not want the other. He can anticipate the effects of each, and he makes his choice accordingly. He would have more trouble deciding whether to say "Two and two is four" or "Two and two are four." Both versions are common; usage is divided. The writer can only use his best judgment in the light of what he knows about expressions among which he must choose; the more he knows about language, the more appropriate his choices are likely to be.

Writers and speakers, of course, do not think of all alternatives each time they utter a sentence and then consciously choose among them. They write and speak by habit. The practical problem for most students is to develop facility in standard English, especially in the sort of standard English appropriate for formal or some informal writing. This kind of English may not always be familiar, but it is necessary for the serious business of the world, and any student hoping to exert influence on affairs must command it. He needs to use standard English not because other people use it, or because someone has made a rule — any more than a carpenter cuts a board with a saw because other carpenters do or because someone has made a rule about saws. The carpenter uses the saw because it works better than a breadknife. Standard English is necessary because it works better for serious purposes. The following list, therefore, sets forth some common usage problems that should be understood by anyone competent with standard English. (For disputed uses, we have generally relied upon *Current American Usage*, ed. Margaret M. Bryant [New York: Funk and Wagnalls, 1962].) Included also are a few grammatical and rhetorical terms that have not been discussed in the text and that may be useful. Entries for such terms or for subjects discussed begin with capital letters, entries for words for which usage is considered with lower-case letters. For usages and terms discussed in the text but not included here, consult the Index.

a, an The indefinite article (see *Articles*). Sound determines the spelling. *A* is used before words beginning with a consonant sound, even when a sound like /y/ is spelled with *e* or *u* (*a person, a history, a unit, a European*). *An* is used before words beginning with a vowel sound or a silent *h* (*an elbow, an hour*). Contemporary usage prefers *a* before a pronounced *h*, although *an historian* sometimes still appears.

above In common use as both a modifier and a noun, but often felt to be too formal for informal use:

FORMAL: In view of the *above*. . . . The *above* conclusions. . . .

Absolute construction Usually composed of a verbal with its subject expressed, an absolute construction functions as a sentence modifier (see 16e).

She rode down the highway, *her hair flying in the wind.*

accept, except To accept is to receive; to except is to exclude.

600

He decided to *accept* the bribe. They agreed to *except* the contro-versial paragraphs of the motion.

Except is also a function word to indicate an exception.

They all quit *except* Duncan.

Accusative case   See *Objective case.*

Active voice   See *Voice.*

actually   Like *really,* frequently overworked as a broad intensifier.

A.D.   Abbreviation of *anno Domini,* "in the year of (our) Lord," used for dates after the birth of Christ when dates A.D. and B.C. could be confused. Being Latin, it preferably precedes the date (A.D. 43).

ad   Informal shortening of *advertisement,* not appropriate in for-mal English.

adapt, adept, adopt   To adapt is to adjust, to make suitable. *Adept* means "skilled, proficient." To adopt is to accept or to take as one's own.

The children *adapted* their habits to their new home. She is *adept* at typing. The resolution was *adopted.* He *adopted* the mannerisms of his teacher.

Adjective   Modifiers of nouns and pronouns are called adjec-tives; for confusion with adverb forms, see 16b and *Adverb;* see also *Comparison of modifiers.*

Adverbs   Modifiers of verbs or modifiers are classed as adverbs. For confusion of adverb and adjective forms, see 16b. The follow-ing statements describe some characteristics of adverbs and their relation to adjective forms; see also *Adjective; Comparison of modi-fiers.*

1. Most single-word adverbs end in *-ly.* Not all adverbs can be so distinguished, but most adverbs were formed by the addition of the word *like* to some other word, usually an adjective. When combinations such as *stormy-like* and *handsome-like* were short-ened, they became *stormily* and *handsomely.* We now make ad-verbs by adding *-ly* to almost any modifier. A few adjectives have been formed by adding *-ly* to a noun (*homely, leisurely*).

2. Some adverbs existed in Anglo-Saxon and have survived in their early form; thus the ending *-ly* was not necessary to make ad-verbs of them (*well, however, down, ahead*).

3. A few words function as either adverbs or adjectives (*better, early, fast, much, more, late*).

4. A few words function informally or colloquially as either adverbs or adjectives, even though *-ly* adverb forms exist and are usually preferred in formal writing or speaking (*cheap* or *cheaply, close* or *closely, deep* or *deeply, even* or *evenly, loud* or *loudly, slow* or *slowly, tight* or *tightly*). Compare:

It was a *slow* train. Go *slow* in this zone. You should proceed *slowly* with the reorganization.

5. A few words are frequently confused because of similarities in spelling and meaning.

Adjectives	Adverbs
good (kind, agreeable, satisfactory)	*well* (satisfactorily, in a pleasing or desirable manner)
well (fortunate, fitting or proper, in good health)	
real (authentic, genuine)	*really* (actually, in a real manner)
sure (firm, secure, dependable)	*surely* (certainly)
some (in an indefinite amount)	*somewhat* (to a certain extent or degree)

advise, advice   The first is the verb, the second the noun.

I *advise* you to listen to his *advice.*

adviser, advisor   Both spellings are in current use; the *-er* spelling is perhaps more usual.

affect, effect   *Affect* is a verb meaning "influence." *Effect* is usually a noun meaning "result," but it may be a verb meaning "cause" or "bring about."

The weather does not *affect* her disposition. The weather has no *effect* on her disposition. The envoys tried to *effect* a compromise.

agenda   In Latin, a plural, meaning "things to be done," with a singular, *agendum.* The word has come in English to mean "a list of things to be done" and has developed its own English plural, *agendas.*

aggravate   Used in formal English to mean "intensify" or "make worse." Used informally in the sense of *annoy* or *provoke.*

INFORMAL: The children *aggravated* her.

FORMAL: The children *annoyed* her.

FORMAL: The new ointment only *aggravated* the disease.

agree   Idiomatically we agree *with* a person, *to* a proposal, *in* principle, *on* a course of action.

alibi   Formally used only in the legal sense, an indication that a defendant was elsewhere at the time of a crime; informally, "an excuse."

all (of)   Constructions with *all of* followed by a noun can often be made more concise by omission of the *of*. Usually *of* is retained between *all* and a pronoun.

> He could not bribe *all of* them with *all* the money in the world.

all right, alright   *Alright* is a common and plausible misspelling for *all right* but is not accepted in standard usage.

already, all ready   *Already* is a single modifier meaning "before some specified time." In *all ready*, *all* modifies separately.

> The team was *already* on the field. They were *all ready* for the kickoff.

all the farther (further)   Common colloquially; *as far as* is standard.

alumnus, alumna   An alumnus is a male graduate; *alumni*, the plural of *alumnus*, is usually used for groups including both males and females. An alumna is a female graduate; *alumnae* is the plural form of *alumna*. The contraction, *alum*, is not acceptable in standard English. The possible Anglicized plurals, *alumnuses* and *alumnas*, are nonstandard.

among, between   The formal distinction that *between* is used of two and *among* of more than two has not been rigidly observed, at least informally.

> The men divided the reward *between* Bob and me. The book records differences *among* [or *between*] synonyms.

amount, number   *Amount* indicates a sum or total mass or bulk. *Number* refers to a group of which individual parts can be counted; it is a collective noun, singular when designating a unit, plural when designating individuals.

> A *number* of friends were in the lobby. The *number* of his crimes is astounding. A large *amount* of wheat has been stored.

Analysis, analytic   In grammar, analysis is the principle by which relationships within the sentence are revealed by the position of words and by the use of relationship words. English makes great use of analysis in its grammar; thus *to the good girls* is grammatical, but *girls good the to* is not. Analytic grammatical principles are also called distributive. For analysis in rhetoric, see 5a.

603

and which, and who Standard only when the following clause is coordinate with a previous clause introduced by *which* or *who*.

> NONSTANDARD: That was the first car I owned, *and which* I expected to cut down for a racer.

> STANDARD: The car, which was the first I ever owned *and which* I expected to cut down for a racer, was. . . .

angle Currently popular in a number of colloquial expressions, rapidly becoming trite; see 20b.

> COLLOQUIAL: He knows all the *angles.* What's the *angle* on this?

Antecedent A word or construction to which a pronoun or pronominal modifier refers is called its antecedent (see 17e).

anxious Formerly restricted in meaning to "apprehensive," "worried"; still sometimes suspect formally in the newer sense of "eager."

> FORMAL: He was eager [not *anxious*] to enter the game.

anybody, any body; anyone, any one Combine the words to make the pronoun form; separate if the first portion is a modifier.

> *Anybody* may come. *Any body* in the burning ruins. . . .
> *Anyone* could do that. *Any one* infraction of the rule. . . .

any more Standard when used negatively.

> STANDARD: They do not live here *any more.*

> COLLOQUIAL: Deans are more tolerant *any more.*

anyways Prefer *anyway* or *anyhow.*

anywheres Nonstandard; omit the *s.*

apt See *liable.*

area Overused, usually redundantly, to refer to a subject or discipline.

> He was a student *in* [not *in the area of*] agriculture.

around Informal when used for *about.*

> There were *about* [not *around*] a thousand people present.

Articles   *A, an,* and *the* function as determiners to point out nouns (see *a, an; the*).

The, called the *definite article,* often refers to something previously mentioned.

> One evening Father remarked casually that we might soon go to see Niagara Falls. Thereafter, for days, all conversations led inevitably to a discussion of what we would do when we went to see *the* Falls.

The often identifies a particular object from others in its class. Compare:

> He lost his eye in *an* accident. He lost his eye in *the* accident I was telling you about.

The can replace a personal pronoun referring to part of the body.

> Take the bow in *your* left hand and the bowstring in *your* right. Take the bow in *the* left hand and the bowstring in *the* right.

Since *the* usually implies a reference to something previously mentioned, its use to introduce a noun new to the context may be confusing.

> When we first entered the park, it seemed almost deserted. *A* [not *The*] man was sitting alone on a bench, and a pigeon pecked at a paper cup.

The suggests that the man had been introduced previously. *The* has some special uses, as in "*the* man in the street," meaning the average person, and some generalized uses: "Take *the* ball in the left hand."

The indefinite articles *a* and *an* have developed from the word *one* and retain some of their earlier meaning. Usually they have the force of *any.*

Many noun expressions, including terms for common phenomena, may require no article. Plural nouns including all members of a class usually require no article.

> When *morning* came, *daylight* seeped through the venetian blinds.
> On the whole, *Americans* like *dogs, cats,* and *children.*

Abstract and general nouns usually require no article.

> *The history* of your town is part of the study of *history.*
> *Evening* came down and soon we could see thousands of *stars. The night* was clear and bright.

as   Not standard as a substitute for *that* to introduce a noun clause.

> *I am not sure that I* believe you [not *I do not know as I.* . .].

As is often imprecise when it is used as a subordinating conjunction indicating cause; in "As we were sitting on the beach, we had a good view of the race," *as* could mean "while," "when," "because," or "since." The more precise function word is usually preferable. For confusion of *like* and *as,* see *like.*

as (so) long as   Both are common except in expressions involving time or space (see *not* . . . *as*).

> The table is *as* (not *so*) *long as* the desk.

as to   Especially at the beginning of a sentence *as to* is standard English to emphasize or point out.

> *As to* the recommendations, the less said, the better.

As to is usually awkward as a substitute for *about* or *of:*

> He spoke to me *about* [not *as to*] the nomination. He doubted *whether* [not *as to whether*] he should make any promises.

aspect   Overused; see *Jargon.*

at   Redundant in questions with *where* (see *where at*).

athletics   Plural in form, but often considered singular in number.

auto   No longer much used as a colloquial shortening of *automobile; car* is a more common short form.

awful, awfully   Overworked as vague intensives: *awfully good, awfully bad.* Since the words are overused, their effectiveness is blunted. In formal English *awful* means "awe-inspiring."

bad   When used as subject complement, sometimes confused with the adverb *badly* (see 16b).

> She felt *bad* [not *badly*] all day.

B.C.   Abbreviation of *before Christ,* used to mark dates that could be confused with dates in the Christian era. It appears after the date (52 B.C.).

be   The verb *be* or *to be* is made up of forms from several older verbs, and is thus irregular. It has the following forms: infinitive, *to be;* gerund and present participle, *being;* past participle, *been;* first person present in singular, *am;* second person present, *are* (*art*, used with *thou*, is archaic); third person present singular, *is* (*be* is preferred in relatively formal writing for the subjunctive or imperative: *if that be true; be thou me*); first and third person past singular, *was;* second person past singular and all past plurals, *were. Were* is also used in the subjunctive and conditional moods; see *Mood*.

because Standard to introduce a modifier, not a noun clause (see 13c).

> The reason I ride the elevator is *that* [rather than *because*] I am lazy.
> I ride the elevator *because* I am lazy.

being as, beings as Nonstandard usage for *since* or *because*.

> *Because* [not *being as*] I lived here, I know what I am doing.

beside, besides *Beside* is used as a preposition, meaning "by the side of." *Besides* may be an adverb or preposition, meaning "in addition" or "except."

> He had to sit *beside* the teacher. It was too late to go to the dance, and *besides* I was tired.

between See *among*.

blame Some writers still insist that formally at least "He blamed me for it" must be used rather than "He blamed it on me," but the latter is used widely in educated speech and in some writing. "He put the blame on me" is not.

blond, blonde The feminine ending *e* of the French word is sometimes retained, with *blonde* used to refer to women; but *blond* is currently used for both sexes, and any distinction is disappearing.

broke Used to mean "out of money," *broke* is not used formally; *financially embarrassed* as a substitute is trite and affected.

bunch Overused to mean "group."

> *A group* [not *a bunch*] of students. . . . *A large amount* [not *a bunch*] of material. . . .

burst, bust Standard principal parts are *burst, burst, burst. Bust* or *busted* in the sense of "burst" is nonstandard as is *busted* in the sense of "bankrupt."

but On the theory that *but* is a preposition when it means "except," many writers have insisted that any pronoun immediately following it must appear in the objective case, but the nominative is widely used, especially as part of the subject.

Nobody but *me* (or *I*) saw the crash.

but, hardly, only, scarcely Negative words are not used in standard English with another negative (see *Double negative*).

> He *had* [not *didn't have*] but one alternative. He *knew* [not *didn't know*] only one answer. I *hardly* [not *don't hardly*] think so.

but that, but what *But that,* and especially *but what,* have been condemned as redundant when used for *that* as a conjunction or as a relative pronoun, and even as nonstandard, but both are reputably used, as in the following from the New York *Times:* "There is little doubt but what Mr. Baruch's venture. . . ." Most careful writers, however, avoid the constructions.

can, may In formal English, *may* refers to permission (*Mother, may I go swimming?*) and *can* to ability (*I can swim across the pool*). Informally, *can* is commonly used for both meanings, and even formally *can* sometimes refers to permission to distinguish from *may* referring to possibility:

> I *can* [I have permission to] go swimming. *I may* [possibly I shall] go swimming.

Cant The term has had a various history and many uses, all of them suggesting nonstandard language of some sort. Related to the modern word *chant,* it once referred mainly to the whining tone used by beggars and to their slang. The most common modern use is that defined by Bergen and Cornelia Evans in *A Dictionary of American Usage* as "stock phrases full of pretentious high-mindedness or pseudo-profundity, repeated mechanically because they are fashionable, without being genuine expressions of sentiment." Thus cant might be briefly defined as uncommonly pretentious jargon. See *Jargon, journalese.*

can't help but, can't hardly A double negative (see *but, hardly, only, scarcely*).

> I *cannot help believing* [not *cannot help but believe*] she is honest.

case Overworked in expressions like "in this case" or "in the case of"; see *Jargon.*

Case As a grammatical concept, case is the way in which nouns and noun substitutes work. Ancestors of English made extensive use of case, and the various cases were revealed by inflectional endings. Most of these endings have now been lost, and their functions have been absorbed by other grammatical devices. The ideas

608

expressed by *at* and *to* in "at the street corner" and "to the campus" would formerly have been expressed by case endings. In the sentence "The coach gave Chuck a chance" we know that *Chuck* is the indirect object, *chance* the direct object because of their positions. Modern English has only two cases in the noun, genitive or possessive (see *Possessive case*) and a general case used for all other purposes. Some of the ancient case system is preserved in various pronouns (see *Pronoun*).

censor, censure, censer   To censor is to examine, especially to examine printed matter for possible objections. To censure is to reprimand or to condemn. A censer is a receptacle for incense, especially one used in religious ceremonies.

> Half the story was *censored*. The students condemned their treasurer in a vote of *censure*. Choirboys carried the *censers*.

certain   Redundant in expressions like "this certain person" or "in that certain instance." *Particular* is preferable where *certain* could be ambiguous, meaning either *some* or *reliable* (*certain examples*).

circumstances   Currently misused and overused in jargonic writing; use a more exact expression.

> He was *in great difficulty* [not *in very difficult circumstances*].

cite, sight, site   To cite is to refer to. *Sight* means "view" or "spectacle." A site is a location.

> He *cited* an old legal document. The mountains below were a beautiful *sight*. We visited the *site* of the new building.

claim   Overused as a blanket term; see *Jargon*.

Clause   In the older grammatical statement, any construction that could have been a sentence if it stood alone was called a clause if it was incorporated into a sentence. That is, a clause was any construction including a subject and predicate, the kind of construction that in this book is called an SVC. Structural linguistics designates most verbal constructions as clauses, even though they do not contain finite verbs. Transformational grammar makes little use of the concept of the clause, but all kernel sentences and many transforms could be clauses. See chapter 12.

Clichés   See *Trite expressions*.

Collective noun   A collective noun indicates more than one (*a committee of citizens, an army of ants*). For agreement involving collective nouns, see 17g.

609

Colloquial Derived from the Latin verb meaning "speak," *colloquial* refers to the functional variety of standard English mainly appropriate to conversation. The label is sometimes confused with *localism*, to which it is unrelated, and is sometimes mistakenly thought to designate nonstandard usages. It marks an expression appropriate in conversation but not in formal and some informal writing.

Comparison of modifiers We recognize three degrees of modifiers, as follows: positive, implying no comparison (*fast car, beautifully landscaped*); comparative, implying that one exceeds another ("The boulevard is a faster street than the highway and is more beautifully landscaped."); and the superlative, which implies the highest degree, at least within certain limitations ("The boulevard is the fastest road out of town, and the most beautifully landscaped").

Modifiers are compared in two ways.

	Positive	Comparative	Superlative
SHORT ADJECTIVES:	red	redder	reddest
	short	shorter	shortest
	greedy	greedier	greediest
	homely	homelier	homeliest
LONG ADJECTIVES:	beautiful	more beautiful	most beautiful
	superficial	more superficial	most superficial
ADVERBS:	slow	slower	slowest
	rapidly	more rapidly	most rapidly
	beautifully	more beautifully	most beautifully
	superficially	more superficially	most superficially

Short adjectives (all adjectives of one syllable and most adjectives of two syllables) and a few adverbs (especially those not ending in *-ly*) are compared by adding *-er* in the comparative and *-est* in the superlative. All long adjectives and most adverbs are compared by preceding the positive form with *more* and *most*. Adjectives of two syllables can be compared either way, and the distinctions are too subtle to be described by rule. The same person might say "He is *stupider* than an ox" but write "I never saw a *more stupid boy.*"

A few modifiers retain irregular forms.

Positive	Comparative	Superlative
good	better	best
well	better	best
bad	worse	worst
little	less	least
much	more	most

610

many	more	most
far	farther	farthest
far	further	furthest

complected   A popular equivalent of *complexioned* in phrases like *dark-* or *light-complected;* generally considered dialectal or colloquial.

> She was *light complexioned* [not *light complected*].

Complete sentence   A sentence used to be defined as "a complete thought," although no thought is complete, even though explained through a whole book. A sentence is often called complete if it has a subject, a verb, and a complement if one is needed (see chapter 12).

Conjunction   Conjunctions serve generally to reinforce coordination and subordination, the two main processes whereby the SVC pattern expands or develops. Theoretically, a *coordinating conjunction* joins like or equal or coordinate elements, joining either complete patterns or parts of patterns. A *subordinating conjunction* functions only with complete sentence patterns, joining a dependent clause to another element. Although distinctions between the types of conjunction are not always logical, *and, but, for, or,* and *nor,* and often *so* and *yet* are conventionally recognized as coordinating conjunctions; they may join independent clauses or other sentence elements in parallel construction.

> I jumped into the car without trouble, *but* Mary slammed the door on her fingers.
>
> Although it was Sunday *and* although I knew I ought to get up for church, I turned over to take another nap.
>
> The pavement was icy *and* treacherous from a night of raining *and* freezing.

Historically, conjunctions mostly had uses other than joining, and many of them have retained other functions. The ancestor of *but* meant "outside" or "from the outside," and *but* is now widely used to mean "except," functioning like a preposition ("none *but* the brave"; "all *but* me"), or even like a pronoun. *And* formerly meant something like *next;* now it can function essentially like a relative, as in "Spare the rod *and* spoil the child," in which *and* has the force of *if* applied to the clause preceding it, and it can replace *to,* as in "Try *and* stop me."

Subordinating conjunctions, also called *relative conjunctions* and *relatives,* signal a subordinate or dependent clause. Subordinating conjunctions need to be chosen with care to define relationships precisely (see 17c).

611

Although [not *while*] Father did not approve of alcoholic beverages, he always had some in the house for guests. *Because* [*since* might be misleading] she was only a little girl, my sister was not allowed to sit at the table.

For the similar function of conjunctive adverbs, see *Conjunctive adverb.* For the distinction between subordinating conjunctions and relative pronouns, see *Relative pronoun.*

Conjunctive adverb Like coordinating conjunctions, conjunctive adverbs connect parallel clauses but at the same time modify within a clause. Observe the following:

She was in no mood to take advice. I was angry, *however*, and I told her what I thought of her leaving the party.

The adverb *however* links the sentence to a preceding sentence. Other conjunctive adverbs are *thus, then, nevertheless, nonetheless, moreover, likewise, similarly, also, furthermore, consequently, therefore, hence,* and *besides.*

Conjunctive adverbs are punctuated like modifiers, not like coordinating conjunctions. Within a clause a conjunctive adverb is treated like a modifier outside its normal order and separated by commas ("The next day, *however*, we found the lost ball"); at the opening of a clause that does not begin a sentence it is preceded by a semicolon ("She left; *however*, she soon came back"). The impact of a conjunctive adverb may alter with its position; at the beginning of a clause or sentence a word like *however* tends to modify the whole SVC pattern; within a clause it tends to modify the preceding word or phrase.

conscience, conscious *Conscience* is a noun referring to a sense of rightness. *Conscious* is an adjective meaning "awake" or "aware" or "active mentally."

Let your *conscience* be your guide. I was not *conscious* of his fear.

contact Overworked as a verb synonym for *talk with, telephone, ask about, advise, inform, query, write to, call upon.*

continue on Redundant as a verb with a separable suffix; omit *on.*

Contractions Like other colloquial locutions, contractions are standard for intimate or nonchalant relationships. They have developed because they are convenient aids to speech, easy to pronounce, but they are not appropriate to formal writing (see *don't; its, it's*).

FORMAL: We *do not* [not *don't*] as yet have accurate relative heights for the tallest mountains, partly because mountaineers *have not* [not *haven't*] agreed on a uniform method of measurement.

could of   Sometimes, because of its sound, mistakenly written for *could have.*

He *could have* [not *could of*] looked up the word in the dictionary.

council, counsel, consul   *Council* means "advisory board" or "group." *Counsel* means "advice" or, especially in law, "the man who gives advice." A consul is a government official.

He was elected to the administrative *council.* The dean's *counsel* always made sense. He was American *consul* in Brazil.

couple   Nonstandard as a modifier meaning "two" or "about two"; sometimes used informally followed by *of* (*a couple of people*).

I gave him *two* [rather than *a couple*] dollars.

cute   Overworked colloquially as a vague way of expressing approval.

He was an *attractive* [or *charming* or *pleasant* or *handsome* rather than *cute*] boy.

Dangling construction   Subordinate constructions not readily and certainly linked to a major portion of the SVC pattern are said to dangle; see 16e.

data   Originally the plural form of Latin *datum*, often considered singular in colloquial usage but still plural in formal English. *Strata* and *phenomena* are plurals of the same sort. The Anglicized plural *datas* is not standard.

FORMAL: *These* [not *this*] data confirm [not *confirms*] the theory.

date   A useful neologism, now generally considered standard, meaning "appointment" or "to make an appointment," or "the person with whom an appointment is made," especially if the appointment is social and with a person of the opposite sex. *Current American Usage* says it "occurs in informal standard writing, especially that dealing with teen-agers and their social relationships."

613

deal Currently overworked as a vague slang term for any transaction or arrangement or situation. A more specific term is preferable. *A Great deal of* is loosely used as an equivalent of *many* or *much*.

definite, definitely Overworked as vague intensifiers in expressions like "a definitely fine party."

Dependent clause See *Subordinate clause*.

Determiner Articles (*a, an, the*) and some other words like numerals (*forty*, in "forty old golf balls") are now often called determiners rather than modifiers or adjectives.

different from, different than *From* is idiomatic when a preposition is required; *than* introduces a clause.

Direct object Transitive verbs require objects, of which the most common is the direct object; in "Karen likes pizza," *pizza* is a direct object (see chapter 12).

disregardless Nonstandard; use *regardless*.

do An extremely useful verb sometimes carelessly used in idioms in which it cannot function (see 17f).

Everyone has an ambition he wants to *fulfill* [rather than *do*].

Do sometimes functions as an intensifier: "He may be stupid, but he does have good manners." Like any device for emphasis, this one is easily overworked; "I do so want you to be my friend," suggests the conversation of schoolgirls in Victorian novels.

don't Contraction of *do not*, common in conversation but in writing not standard after *it, he, she,* or a singular noun.

It *does not* [or *doesn't* in conversation, not *don't*] seem wise.

Double negative Although a double negative is conceived in many languages as a device for enforcing the negative sense, two negatives are generally disapproved in standard Modern English. The older assumption, that "two negatives make a positive," borrowed from mathematics, seems not to apply to the way speakers of English think of grammar, but the locution remains unfashionable.

We *did* [not *didn't do*] nothing wrong. We did not see *anybody* [not *nobody*] on the pier.

Two negatives are used in the same statement in English to give varying emphasis to a positive idea.

It was *not impossible* to see their meaning. I was *not* totally *unimpressed*.

614

Double negatives are used in various other conventional ways, and some have even become strongly emphatic: "Don't think he isn't a good quarterback!"

doubt   *Doubt that* implies a negative; *doubt whether* (informally *doubt if*) assumes that there is room for doubt.

> I *doubt that* he will come [presumably he will not]. I *doubt whether* he will come [probably he will not, but he may].

due to   Like *owing to* or *on account of, due to* is originally an adjective modifier ("The delay was due to the icy roads"). Its use adverbially is not generally accepted as standard English, although it has long been common in introductory adverbial phrases ("Due to unavoidable circumstances, the delivery has been delayed"). *Because of* is the preferable adverbial idiom.

> *Because of* [not *due to*] the icy roads, the bus was late.

each and every   Used in legal documents and common in officialese, but redundant and needlessly pompous for most uses.

each other, one another   Some careful writers distinguish, using *each other* to refer to only two and *one another* to refer to more than two.

effect   See *affect, effect*.

either, neither   Usually singular in number (see 17g and ff.) and used to designate one of two, not one of more than two (see also *each other*).

> *Any* [not *either*] of the three books has the information.

enthuse   Colloquial but overworked for *be enthusiastic* or *make enthusiastic*.

equally as   A wordy confusion of *as good as* and *equally*.

> My cake was *as good as* Sue's. The cakes were *equally* [not *equally as*] good.

etc.   Abbreviation for *et cetera* meaning "and so forth" or "and the like," appropriate only when statistics or lists justify abbreviations. *And etc.* is redundant; *et* means "and."

everybody, everyone   Historically, these words are the equivalent of *every individual,* relying on the earlier use of *body* as a synonym for *person,* as in "If a body meet a body, comin' thro' the rye." Thus traditionally the words are singulars and require singular verbs

615

and reference words—*his* rather than *their* is the approved possessive. Actually, in modern usage both words are most frequently
used with plural force (*Everybody came*), and hence plural verbs and
reference words are common in conversation and in some informal writing.

> FORMAL: *Everybody* considers *his* own best interests.

Every one is usually followed by *of* ("Every one of them is guilty").

exactly   Currently popular as a meaningless word. The person
who asks "Exactly what is poetry?" probably does not want to be
told "exactly," even if he could be.

except   See *accept*.

expect   Colloquial in the sense of "suppose" or "suspect."

> I *suppose* [not *expect*] that his paper is finished.

Expletive construction   Expletive constructions employ an expletive to fill the subject slot in the sentence pattern (see 14a).

extra   Nonstandard in the sense of "unusually."

> The coffee was *unusually* [not *extra*] good.

fact, the fact that   Often overused as a roundabout way of saying
that.

> He was aware *that* [not *of the fact that*] everybody disliked his plan.

factor   An overused blanket term; see *Jargon*.

famed   Used for *famous* or *well known*, *famed* usually suggests journalese or amateur writing.

farther, further   A distinction, not universally made, prefers *farther* as the comparative form of *far* in expressions involving space,
and *further* to mean "in addition." Modern dictionaries recognize
the interchangeable use of the two words.

feature   Used to mean "emphasize" or "give prominence to," *feature* is becoming standard usage, but the word has been so overworked in this sense by press agents that it bears watching. In
expressions like "Can you feature that?" the word is not standard.

fellow   Colloquial when used as a synonym for *man, friend, person*.

fewer, less   *Fewer* is used in distinctions involving numbers, of
individual items, *less* in relation to value, degree, or quantity.

> There were *fewer* than ten students. The receipts were *less* than the
> expenditures.

616

field   Overworked and often redundant when used to refer to a realm of knowledge or subject; see *Jargon*.

> He was an expert *in* [not *in the field of*] chemistry.

figure   Colloquial for *think, expect, suppose, conclude, believe*.

> I did not *expect* [not *figure*] the course to be difficult.

fine   Nonstandard as an adverb.

> She sang *well* [not *fine* or *just fine*].

fix   In standard English a verb meaning "make fast" and, more recently, "repair." The word is nonstandard as a noun meaning "predicament" and as a verb meaning "intend" or "prepare" ("I was fixing to go"). It has many colloquial uses, most of them less precise than alternatives — for example:

> She was *fixing* breakfast. She was getting *fixed* up for the party. The alderman *fixed* his traffic ticket. She wanted me to *fix* her hair.

folks   Colloquial for *people* or *relatives*.

Form   The word *form* can be confusing in modern grammar, since it has been used differently by the newer and older grammarians. In the older terminology *form* designated the makeup of a locution, its spelling or pronunciation. Thus *sang* and *sung* would be forms of *sing*. Many grammarians now use *form* to designate anything that differs from other linguistic units; *sing, sang,* and *sung* are three different forms (see *Form class*).

Form class   A term used in some modern grammatical statements to designate a set of words that can appear in the same position or slot in a given construction. Thus, all the words that could appear in the blank in constructions like *The _____ walked* belong to the same form class, have *privilege of occurrence* (which see) in the same position. Obviously many individual words belong to more than one form class. Major form classes are roughly equivalent to parts of speech.

formally, formerly   *Formally* means "in a formal manner"; *formerly* means "previously."

> We had to dress *formally* for the party. She was *formerly* a singer.

Functional shift   In English many words shift readily from one use or function in a sentence to another. *Cow* is regularly classified as a noun, but consider the following:

617

The principal thought he could *cow* the rebellious students. The road to the old mine was little more than a *cow* path.

In the first sentence *cow* is a verb, in the second a modifier. The word *fast* can function in several ways. ("It was a fast trip." "We fast during Lent." "He ran fast." "They broke their fast Sunday.")

funny Overused and imprecise as a synonym for *strange, odd, unusual, perplexed.* A more exact word is preferable.

Generative grammar A generative grammar is one that attempts to formulate the rules whereby sentences can be created in oral or written language. In Modern English, the most extensively studied generative grammar is called transformational or transform grammar (which see).

Genitive case See *Possessive case.*

Gerund A verb form having some nominal use and having at least one unit ending in *-ing.* The gerund has active and passive uses, with a form for each: active ("*Proving* his thesis was impossible"); passive ("I questioned his *having proved* his thesis"). For the form of the pronoun to be used with the gerund, see *Possessive with gerund.*

get, got Useful verbs and the basis of many standard idioms, but also used in many colloquial and slang expressions. ("The song gets me." "The pain got him in the back." "Better get wise.") Used to mean "must" or "ought to," *got* is colloquial and usually redundant.

We *must* [or *have to,* not *have got to*] finish by evening.

good An adjective, not to be confused with *well,* the corresponding adverb.

The car runs *well* [not *good* or *pretty good*].

good and Nonstandard as an intensive.

He was *very* [not *good and*] angry.

gotten Alternative form for *got* as past participle for the verb *get.*

guess Dictionaries record *guess* in the sense of "believe," "suppose," "think," but some writers restrict it to colloquial usage.

Hackneyed expressions See *Trite expressions.*

had of Nonstandard for *had* (see also *could of*).

I wish he *had* [not *had of*] told me.

618

had ought, didn't ought, hadn't ought   Nonstandard redundant forms for *ought* or *should*.

> He *ought not* [or *should not*, not *hadn't ought to*] say that.

hang   Principal parts of the verb are *hang, hung, hung*, but to refer to death by hanging, they are *hang, hanged, hanged* in formal English.

> We *hung* the new picture. The murderer was *hanged.*

hardly   See *but, hardly, only, scarcely.*

he or she   The combination is not usual as an equivalent for *one. He,* alone, is usually preferred.

healthful, healthy   A distinction gradually breaking down restricts *healthful* to mean "conducive to health" and *healthy* to mean "possessing health."

heap, heaps   Not common in standard written English in the sense of "a great deal."

heighth   Common misspelling for *height.*

hisself   Nonstandard for *himself.*

honorable   Used as a title of respect, mainly for people holding a political office. It is usually preceded by *the* and used only with a full name (*The Honorable John H. Jones* or *The Honorable Mr. Jones,* not *Honorable Jones* or *the Hon. Jones*).

however   Conjunctive adverbs, most frequently *however,* tend to modify a whole predication if they appear initially in a clause, but thereafter to modify the preceding word or structure; see *Conjunctive adverb.*

human   Originally an adjective, *human* is now often used as a noun meaning "human being."

IC cut   Structural linguistics works in part by what are called IC cuts (Immediate Constituent cuts). By this procedure, a piece of language is cut into its immediate constituents, the parts that comprise it (see p. 241).

idea   A handy word that careless writers readily overuse. A more exact word is often preferable.

> My *purpose* [not my *idea*] is to become a nurse. The *theme* [not the *idea*] of the book is that crime never pays.

Idiom   Idiom is the result of custom in language. Usually it is logical, though not always; but to use the language a writer must learn idioms, whether or not they are logical. Many native speakers have learned most idioms unconsciously, but writers with poor linguistic backgrounds have trouble. Furthermore, many idioms have become common only in nonstandard English. Some are listed here; others can be found in a good dictionary.

if, whether   *If* implies uncertainty; *whether* implies an alternative.

> *If* he will trust me, I shall tell him. I shall tell him, *whether* or not he believes me.

If is not used with *regardless.*

> *Even though* [not *regardless if*] he is a doctor. . . .

imply, infer   To imply is to suggest a meaning; to infer is to draw a conclusion from evidence.

> The attorney *implied* that the witness was lying. The jury *inferred* that the attorney was trying to discredit the witness.

in, into   *In* implies rest or motion within a restricted area; *into* is preferable to indicate motion from the outside to the inside.

> She lives *in* town. We drove *into* town.

in back of   Redundant; prefer *behind.*

in regards to   Nonstandard; use *in regard to.*

Incomplete sentence   Sentences are not easy to define (see *Complete sentence*), and to write them one need not be able to define them, but the term is often used for sentences left carelessly incomplete (see 12a).

Independent clause   Any structure that could be a sentence and is incorporated into a sentence without being made subordinate is called an independent clause. All clauses not subordinated are conceived to be independent; see *Subordinate clause* and chapter 12.

Indirect object   An object complement (see chapter 12), usually in sentences involving asking, telling, giving, and the like, specifying what receives the direct object.

> Tam gave his nag [indirect object] a dig [direct object] in the ribs. She told him [indirect object] the truth [direct object].

Indirect question   Indirect questions usually convert a direct question into a noun clause complement, frequently introduced by *whether.* For punctuation of indirect questions, see 25a.

DIRECT: Mrs. Howard asked, "Are the others ready?"
INDIRECT: Mrs. Howard asked whether the others were ready.

Using the reversed pattern (VSC) in an indirect construction is not standard in written English.

He asked *whether I was* [not *was I*] coming.

For verbs in indirect questions, see *Tense*.

individual Originally an adjective, *individual* is loosely used, and often overused, as a synonym for person. As a noun, the word is best used to emphasize the singleness or separateness of an item or person.

Students are not merely names in a card file; they are *individuals*.

infer See *imply*.

inferior than Nonstandard; use *inferior to.*

Infinitive A basic verb form, the form in which verbs are entered in dictionaries and other formal lists. Infinitives can also appear in sentences, as nominal terms ("*To tell* the truth was his only purpose"), as parts of verbs with or without the signal *to* (*will* tell, *want* to tell), and in predicate structures in which the infinitive form can be described equally well as part of a verb or the complement of the verb, as in the sentence implied above, "I want to tell you." Six infinitive forms are relatively common in English:

	Active	Passive	Progressive active
PRESENT:	to lose	to be lost	to be losing
PAST:	to have lost	to have been lost	to have been losing

Inflection Inflection is the grammatical principle through which relations within the sentence are revealed by a change of form in a locution. Thus *sings, sang,* and *sung* are inflected forms of the verb *sing; he, his,* and *him* are inflected forms of the third person singular masculine personal pronoun. Languages that are ancestors of English made much use of inflection; Modern English grammar uses it but little; see 17g.

ingenious, ingenuous *Ingenious* means "having or giving evidence of resourceful intelligence." It can be used of either persons (*an ingenious strategist*) or things (*an ingenious device*). *Ingenuous* means "naïvely frank." It is used only of persons and of things closely associated with them (*an ingenuous proposal*).

inside of Redundant as a compound preposition; omit *of.*

621

Intensifier Words like *very,* and sometimes words like *deeply* ("I am very sorry;" "He is deeply concerned"), which are often called adverbs, are now increasingly called intensifiers, since they intensify but do not much modify.

invite A verb. Not acceptable as a substitute for *invitation.*

> I asked Joe for an *invitation* [not an *invite*] to the dance.

irregardless Nonstandard; use *regardless.*

it Although sometimes convenient, usually to be avoided in impersonal constructions, especially in locutions like "It says in the book . . . ," in which *it* seems to have an antecedent but does not (see 17e).

its, it's *Its* is the possessive form of *it. It's* is the contraction of *it is.*

it's me, it is I "It's me" is common informally; in written form, except in recording conversation, "It is I" is standard.

Jargon, journalese Jargon is vague writing using blanket terms (see 20b), but it is notable in that the writer of jargon uses more words than he needs, apparently pleased with himself because the large, pompous words fill so many pages. He is not concerned with making the words say much. The writer of jargon says "the field of mathematics" rather than *mathematics,* "difficult in character or nature" rather than *difficult,* "in an intoxicated condition" rather than *drunk.* Favorite words of the jargon fancier include *case, factor, character, circumstances, conditions, situation, picture, line, persuasion, level, variety, degree, type, outstanding, worthwhile.*

> JARGONIC: In the case of Jim, it was apparent that his condition was of a serious nature.
>
> REVISION: Jim was seriously ill.
>
> JARGONIC: There were several instances where Hamlet could have put the quietus on the king, but he failed to come through because the situations were not applicable to the circumstances in his case.
>
> REVISION: On several occasions Hamlet could have taken revenge, but he wanted to kill Claudius in some act that would assure the king's going to hell.

A particular sort of jargonic writing has long been known as journalese because it reveals the flamboyant, careless superficiality characteristic of cheap journalism, though not of good newspaper writing. Avoid it by refusing to use words just to make an impression, by thinking clearly, and by endeavoring to say exactly what you think.

JOURNALESE: A new edition of State University hoopsters is slated
to make its debut Saturday night to lift the curtain on
the current hardwood season.

REVISION: State University's basketball team will play its first
game of the season Saturday night.

Juncture   In phonemic analysis, *juncture* is the term for a pause
and all that goes with it. Sets of symbols to reveal juncture are not
standard at this writing, but one common system uses cross or
plus juncture /+/ or nothing between words, bar juncture /|/ to
indicate breaks often marked in punctuation by a comma, double
bar /‖/ or sustained /−/ juncture for important breaks within a
sentence, and double cross /#/ or terminal juncture to close a sentence. Some systems use rising, horizontal, and falling lines. Junc-
tures are suprasegmental phonemes, and thus indications of
juncture are placed within slant lines, which are used to mark
phonemes.

Kernel sentence   In transformational grammar a kernel sentence
is a basic pattern from which all structures can be derived. In the
present volume such structures are said to fit the SVC pattern.

kind, sort   Singular words, which formally can be modified only
by singular demonstrative adjectives, *this* or *that*. Plural forms,
those kinds or *these sorts*, are used, and colloquially *kind* and *sort* are
commonly treated as if they were plural (*these kind*).

kind of, kind of a   Colloquial as the equivalent of *somewhat, rather*.

lay   For confusion of forms of *lay* and *lie*, see *lie*.

lead, led   *Lead* is the present tense of the verb. Because of the
identical pronunciation, the past tense, *led*, is often misspelled *lead*,
the name of the metal.

He *led* [not *lead*] the horse to water.

less   See *fewer*.

let, leave   Both are common in a few idioms ("*leave* [or *let*] it
alone"), but in other idioms, especially when the verb carries a
sense of permission, *let* is standard.

Let [not *leave*] them stay. *Let us* [or *let's* not *leave us*] go soon.

liable, apt, likely   Interchangeable informally, but often distinguished in careful writing.

She is not *likely* [rather than *liable* or *apt*] to tell her teacher.

Strictly, *liable* means "responsible for" or "subject to."

623

He is *liable* for the damage he caused.

Apt means "has an aptitude for."

Marie is an *apt* pupil.

lie, lay Three pairs of similar verbs have been so thoroughly confused in dialect and nonstandard usage, and even in literate conversation, that many people have trouble distinguishing between them in meaning and spelling, particularly in their uses with separable suffixes. See also *rise-raise* and *sit-set*.
    Lie (*lay, lain*), intransitive, but usually modified or combined with a suffix like *down*, indicates that the subject occupies a position.

> The book *lies* on the table. The book *lay* on the table yesterday. The book *has lain* on the table in the past.

Lay (*laid, laid*), transitive except for a few special uses ("The hens lay well;" "Lay on, Macduff"), means *place* or *put* and now appears mainly in a variety of special contexts (see a dictionary).

> He *lays* brick in his spare time. The men *laid* their plans carefully. The soldiers *have laid* down their arms.

like, as In formal written English *like* is used only as a preposition ("He ran like a deer"), and *as* and *as if* are conjunctions ("He ran as if he had seen a ghost"). Informally, however, the distinction is disappearing ("He looks like he could use some sleep"). The confusion has perhaps aggravated a tendency to overcorrection, misusing *as* as a preposition ("He ran as a deer"). Sometimes the distinction is useful to specify meanings; compare "He slipped into the house as a thief" and "He slipped into the house like a thief" or "He cried as a baby" and "He cried like a baby." In general, college writing requires limiting the words to their formal functions.

> *As* [not *like*] I said, the meeting is canceled.

line Jargonic or slang or redundant in certain current uses.

> He sells books [not *Selling books is his line*]. I want to buy something *similar to* [not *along the lines of*] the dress in the window. He was *deceiving her* [not *handing her a line*].

literally An antonym, not a synonym, of *figuratively*. The student who wrote "I was literally dead when I got in" did not say what he probably meant.

624

loan Now generally accepted as a synonym of *lend;* many careful writers, however, use *loan* only as a noun and prefer *lend* as a verb.

locate Provincial as a synonym for *remember* or *take up residence.*

lot(s) of Colloquial as a synonym for *many.*

love Imprecise and sometimes affected as a synonym for *like.*

mad Colloquial in the sense of "angry." Use *angry* or a more exact word like *vexed, furious, annoyed.*

Malapropism A slip in word choice. Mrs. Malaprop, a character in Sheridan's *The Rivals* built a sort of notoriety for herself, and added a word to the English vocabulary, by misusing words she did not understand. When she complimented herself on a "nice derangement of epitaphs" and accused someone of being as "head-strong as an allegory on the banks of the Nile," she certainly did not mean to say *derangement, epitaph,* or *allegory.*

Mass noun A mass noun refers to a quantity ("a bushel of corn," "a portfolio of stocks") but is singular in form and in use. That is, it requires a singular verb unless it is itself plural ("bushel . . . was;" "bushels . . . were").

math Clipped form of *mathematics,* not appropriate in formal writing.

may An auxiliary verb, past tense *might,* expressing possibility or likelihood or permission (see also *can, may*).

> It *may* rain tomorrow. The application *may* be considered this week.

Merged verbs See *Verb sets.*

might of Use *might have* (see *could of*).

mighty As a synonym for *very,* not acceptable in formal English, although common in speech in certain areas.

> She was a *very* [not *mighty*] pretty girl.

Mood English verbs can express mood: the indicative mood states a fact, the interrogative asks a question, the imperative issues a command, the conditional marks conditions, the subjunctive expresses uncertainty, supposition, or desire. Usually auxiliary verbs indicate mood; most special forms have disappeared, but a few special subjunctive forms survive in formal usage at least, mainly in the following situations: (1) in main clauses to express a wish ("The Lord be with you"); (2) in *if*-clauses expressing a so-called "condition contrary to fact," that is, a supposition that is impossible or thought to be improbable ("If I were he, I would quit"); (3) in *that*-clauses expressing a wish, command, or request ("The major ordered that the prisoners be held for interrogation"). In formal uses the present subjunctive is sometimes used in *if*-clauses that are not contrary to fact ("If these data be verifiable, the hypothesis becomes untenable").

The special forms for the subjunctive that survive are two: (1) the third person present subjunctive singular does not have the ending -*s* or -*es* (indicative, *he proves;* subjunctive, *if he prove*); (2) for the verb *to be*, the present singular subjunctive form is *be*, the past singular subjunctive form *were*.

> If my brother *were* [not *was*] here, you would behave. If I *were* [not *was*] you, I would tell the truth. If I *had known* [not *would have known*] you were coming, I would have cleaned the house.

moral, morale   *Moral* is a modifier, concerning the preference of right over wrong; *morale* is a noun suggesting good spirits and a healthy attitude.

> George Washington was a *moral* man. The victory improved the soldier's *morale*.

more than one   Logically plural, sanctioned by custom as singular except when the meaning clearly requires a plural verb.

> *More than one* man is eager to marry her. If there are *more than one* apiece, they should be divided equally.

Morpheme   A morpheme is a working unit of language. A morpheme may be the same as a word; *boy* is a word, and it is also a morpheme, written in phonemics /bɔi/. *Boys*, however, is two morphemes, since the sound represented by -*s* in spelling and by /z/ in phonemics is a working unit of the language, indicating plural.

most   Nonstandard as a synonym for *almost*.

> I am home *almost* [not *most*] every evening.

muchly   Nonstandard; use *much*.

must   Currently overworked as a noun.

myself   Perhaps to avoid choosing between *I* and *me*, or from a sense of modesty, some speakers use the reflexive rather than the personal pronoun, but the form is not standard in formal writing.

> Henry and *I* [not *myself*] decided to remodel the boat. They invited Anne and *me* [not *myself*] to the luncheon.

626

nature   Jargonic in certain current wordy expressions; see *Jargon*.

    The job was *difficult* [not *of a difficult nature*].

neither   Used of two; see *either*.
neither . . . nor   Used as correlatives.

    She could *neither* set up her experiment *nor* [not *or*] conduct it.

nice   Colloquial as a synonym for *affable, agreeable, amiable, congenial, considerate*, and so on through the alphabet. Prefer a more exact word. Carefully used, *nice* means "precise," "exact," "discriminating."
nice and   Colloquial as an intensive.

    The coffee was *pleasantly* [not *nice and*] hot.

Nominative case   See *Subjective case*.

none   As a subject, *none* takes a singular or plural verb depending upon the meaning intended.

not . . . as   Some writers on usage have objected to this construction. They prefer "He is *not so* [rather than *not as*] dull as his younger brother." Either construction is now generally considered acceptable.

Noun   The older definition was that a noun is "the name of a person, place, or thing." This statement is too loose for close grammatical analysis; is *red*, which is the name of a thing, a noun or an adjective? *Running* could be called an action word and *perseverance* a quality, but they may work like nouns. Modern students prefer to say that a noun is the sort of word that can serve as a subject, or that a noun is the kind of word that can serve as head word in a construction like "the little old man," or that a noun is the kind of word that takes *-s* or *-es* in the plural. There are some exceptions (*child, children; deer, deer*); see *Proper noun*.

Noun as modifier   English words adapt readily to different functions (see *Functional shift*), and words that are usually nouns often modify (*rock garden, city jail, Sunday supper*). Excessive conversion, however, can muddy prose:

    He applied to *the office of the committee for price stabilization* [rather than *the price stabilization committee office*]. He organized his theme *so that it had an introduction, development, and a conclusion* [rather than *according to the introduction, development, conclusion method*].   **627**

Noun clause See *Clause.*

Noun phrase The term *noun phrase* is used in at least two ways in English grammatical discussion. In the older use, a noun phrase was one of the types of prepositional or verbal phrase, as in "I have heard of the book." Older grammarians called "of the book" a noun phrase, object of the verb, although many more recent grammarians would make *of* part of the verb. In transformational grammar, and in some structural analysis, a noun phrase is any group of words having a noun as head word; thus "a very lively little pup" is a noun phrase. It can be abbreviated N or NP.

nowheres Nonstandard; omit the *s.*

Object The word *object* is variously used, sometimes to identify the direct object, sometimes to indicate any word or words that complete a transitive verb (see chapter 12).

Objective case, object case The objective case is presumably used for direct objects ("I detest him"), for indirect objects ("I told her the facts"), for other sorts of complements that do not refer to the subject ("They called it Boston"), and for objects of prepositions ("beside her"), but it can now be recognized by form only in certain pronouns; see *Pronoun.*

Objective complement A complement (see chapter 12), after the direct object, that provides another name for the object or otherwise amplifies the object.

> The devil wanted to make Tam's *wife* [direct object] a *widow* [objective complement].

of Confused with *have.* See *could of, might of.*

off of, off from Redundant and nonstandard; use *off.*

on Sometimes redundant with dates.

> I shall see you *Tuesday* (rather than *on Tuesday*).

on the part of Often a clumsy equivalent of *by;* see *part.*

one Used in English in impersonal constructions, although it sometimes seems stiffly formal. It may be replaced by *he,* and *one's* by *his,* for a second reference.

only For the position of *only,* see 16d.

-orama, -orium Faddish suffixes overused in various advertising coinages: *seafoodorama, lubritorium* (for a filling station).

out of Prefer *out* ("out the door"; not "out of the door").

628

outside of Redundant as a compound preposition ("outside the barn," not "outside of the barn"). *Outside of* is colloquial in the sense of "except."

> He failed all his examinations *except that in chemistry* [not *outside of chemistry*].

outstanding Overworked; see *Jargon.*

over with Colloquial as a synonym for *done, finished with, ended, completed.*

overall Useful as a synonym for *general,* but currently overused; accurately used in a phrase like "the overall length"; see *Jargon.*

part, on the part of Often used in wordy writing.

> WORDY: There was some objection, *on the part of* the administration, to the moral tone of the skits.
>
> REVISED: The administration objected to the moral tone of the skits.

Participle Participles are verbals, that is, they are verb forms, although they tend to function as adjectives. In English they include two sorts of distinctive forms, present participles ending *-ing* ("the running girls") and past participles, of which many end in *-t, -d,* or *-ed* (*spoilt meat, bared fangs, studied insult*). A few preserve older forms (*sung, written, gone, taught*). They can be used as parts of verbs ("I am writing," "I have written," "I am amazed"), and as modifiers ("an amazing affair," "a written page"). Participles are difficult to identify as parts of speech, presumably because they have started as verbs but have developed other privileges of occurrence. In the sentence "The lecturer continued, talking very rapidly," the form *talking* would seem to be verbal. In the sentence "The circus bought a talking dog," *talking* would seem to be an adjective; the dog need not have been talking when he was purchased, *talking* being merely a classification to be contrasted with *hunting* or *performing.* Compare "He heard the dog talking." In the sentence "The lecturer continued talking," *talking* might be defended as any of several parts of speech, and this confusion is common. In the example above, how do we know that *amazed* in the sentence "I was amazed" is not an adjective, rather than part of a passive verb?

Parts of speech Traditionally words of the language are classified—on a variety of bases—into parts of speech: nouns, pronouns, verbs, adjectives, adverbs, prepositions, conjunctions, particles including interjections. This classification, derived from Latin

629

grammar, has been criticized by modern linguists as inconsistent and inadequate, and some grammarians have substituted *form classes*, based on formal distinctions rather than meaning or function. Modern grammars, although modifying definitions, still use the traditional terms for parts of speech but recognize the limited uses of the classifications, especially because English words move so readily from one use in the sentence to another (see *Functional shift*).

party Not usually acceptable in composition as a synonym for *person;* used in legal papers ("party of the first part") and by telephone operators ("I have your party on the line").

Passive voice see *Voice.*

past, passed *Past* is the modifier or complement, *passed* the verb form.

> His troubles were *past.* She had *passed* all the tests.

per-, pre-, pro- Three prefixes, borrowed from Latin, that are readily confused. Etymologically, they are related to such English words as *fare, far,* and *for,* and they share in some of the meanings preserved also in their English cousins. *Per-* means "through," as in *percolate* and *perforate,* preserving the idea of movement as in *fare.* *Pre-* means "before," as in *pre-Columbian, pre-eminent,* preserving the idea suggesting *before* in *far.* *Pro-* means "for" or "forth," as in *projectile, pro-administration,* observable in the expression "being *for* somebody or something."

Personal pronoun See *Pronoun.*

phase Often jargonic; see *Jargon.*

phenomena Plural; the singular is *phenomenon* (compare *data*).

phone Informal; in formal composition use *telephone. Phone up* is colloquial; formally use *telephone, call on the telephone;* less formally, *call up.*

Phoneme A phoneme is the smallest linguistic unit recognized by the users of a language. Phonemes are either segmental or suprasegmental; the suprasegmental comprise the oral pattern of sentences, the pitch, tone, and juncture. The segmental phonemes are those that can be broken up; these are the sounds often associated with letters. Thus the phoneme /t/ comprises the sounds usually symbolized by the letter *t*. In English, /t/ and /d/ are two phonemes, although they are only one in some languages. In English /r/ is one phoneme, but in Spanish sounds associated with the spelling *r* comprise more than one phoneme because different sounds distinguish one word from another. To distinguish phonemes from letters and from sounds in phonetics, they are put within slant lines.

Phonemics The system of recording language in phonemes.

Phonetics The study of linguistic sound, and also the system of recording language by using standardized symbols for sounds. Phoneticians usually use IPA (the International Phonetic Alphabet). Phonetic symbols are enclosed within square brackets [a].

Phrase A phrase is a group of words working together for a grammatical use. The older grammar recognized mainly prepositional, verbal, and verb phrases (see *Prepositional phrase; Verb phrase*). More recent grammarians recognize as a phrase any combination of words clustering on a head word (see *Phrase structure*).

Phrase structure In transformational and structural grammars, phrase structure is the study of groups of words that work together. The commonest phrases are noun phrases (abbreviated NP) and verb phrases (abbreviated VP).

picture Currently overused in expressions like "I gave them the whole picture." More specific writing provides the cure: "I told them why I needed five dollars." See *Jargon*.

piece Nonstandard in the sense "a short distance."

Pitch Pitch in language is the highness or lowness with which a segmental phoneme or phonetic unit is uttered. Pitch is sometimes indicated by a sequence of numbers, 1–3 or 1–4, with the lowest number the lowest pitch, the highest number the highest pitch. Pitch can also be indicated by a line that rises and falls. The following is a common pitch pattern for some American English sentences:

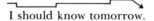

I should know tomorrow.

plan on Redundant and colloquial in some uses ("plan to go," not "plan on going"; "plan to see," not "plan on seeing").

plenty Not acceptable as an intensive (*excellent*, not *plenty good*).

point Overworked as a blanket word; see *Jargon*.

He had many admirable *characteristics* [not *points*].

poorly Used in some dialects, not in formal writing, in the sense "in poor health."

Possessive before gerund By analogy with the classical languages, many style sheets require that a gerund be preceded by the genitive, and *Current American Usage* records that "in written formal English" nominals "almost always occur in the genitive before a gerund." Practically, a distinction in precise meaning can sometimes be obtained by using the possessive of a noun or pronoun to modify a verbal noun or gerund. Compare:

> He saw *Alfred* [or *him*] drinking sloe gin. He disapproved of *Alfred's* [or *his*] drinking.

In the first, the whole expression, "Alfred drinking sloe gin," tells what he saw; in the second it is the drinking that is disapproved and it is identified as Alfred's.

> The principal was not amused by *their* [not *them*] playing poker in class. I was surprised by my *father's* [not *father*] believing in ghosts.

Possessive case   The possessive case, also called the genitive case, reveals possession ("Mary's hair") and various other relationships ("our representative," "the people's choice"). It appears in many pronouns (see *Pronoun*) and commonly in nouns, where it usually requires a phrasal form ("of father," "of Father's") or an apostrophe ("the boy's, the boys' "); see 26g.

Postponed subject   Through the device of an expletive (*there* or *it*) the subject of a sentence can be "postponed" so that it appears after the verb (see 14a).

Predicate   In general, the predicate comprises all the sentence not the subject or closely related to it. In English sentences it usually follows the subject and makes a predication about the subject; that is, it completes the subject–verb–complement pattern. It may consist only of a verb, as in "Birds sing," but it usually comprises a verb and a complement, and whatever other words go with these. The concept of the predicate is not much used in either structural or transformational grammar, although in actuality the predicate would usually be the constituent to the right of the first IC cut, or the VP in $S \longrightarrow NP + VP$.

prejudice   A noun, not to be confused with *prejudiced*, a modifier.

> He was *prejudiced* [not *prejudice*] against John.

Prepositions   Prepositions include words like *in*, *inside*, and *by* in some of their uses and are involved in prepositional sequences like "by means of" and "in accordance with." They function only within the basic sentence, joining a noun or noun substitute to some part of a sentence. The preposition and the noun following it constitute a *prepositional phrase*, which can function as almost any sentence element, usually as a modifier; for idiomatic use of prepositions,

632

see 17d. Some words, mostly identical in form with prepositions, are best thought of as modifiers or parts of verbs; they are the second element in terms like *get up, get out, get over, get by,* and *get off.* Some of these particles are adverbial in force; *out* in "put the cat out" can appropriately be called an adverb, but the same form in "put the runner out" can be well described — although not inevitably — as part of the verb. Whatever these particles are to be called, they are scarcely prepositions, and hence the old copybook rule that a sentence should not end with a preposition does not apply — the rule presumably grew from the etymology of the word *preposition.* Such forms often occur best at the end of clauses or sentences, and good writers have so used them for centuries. See *Verb sets.*

presence The noun form corresponding to *to be present* ("The chairman requests your presence on the platform"); to be distinguished from *presents,* plural of *present.*

principal, principle The two words should be distinguished. *Principal* can be a modifier meaning "first in importance" ("I answered his principal objections"), or a noun naming somebody or something first in importance ("a high school principal," "the principals in the fight"). *Principle* is always a noun.

> The law of the conservation of matter formulates a fundamental *principle* in physics. Machiavelli has been accused of having no *principles.*

Principal parts From the principal parts, most forms of most verbs can be derived. For many hundreds of years all English verbs have been made on the pattern *fire, fired, fired, walk, walked, walked.* These are often called weak verbs. Older verbs, if they have not been changed to follow the pattern of the weak verbs, may retain a variety of older patterns and thus seem to be irregular. Of these so-called strong verbs, the following are most likely to give trouble.

Infinitive	Past	Participle
awake	awaked, awoke	awaked
be	was, were	been
bear	bore	borne
begin	began	begun
blow	blew	blown
break	broke	broken
burst	burst	burst
catch	caught	caught
choose	chose	chosen

633

Infinitive	Past	Participle
cling	clung	clung
come	came	come
dive	dived, dove	dived
do	did	done
drag	dragged	dragged
draw	drew	drawn
drink	drank	drunk
eat	ate	eaten
fall	fell	fallen
give	gave	given
go	went	gone
grow	grew	grown
have	had	had
know	knew	known
lay	laid	laid
lead	led	led
lend	lent	lent
lie	lay	lain
lose	lost	lost
pay	paid	paid
prove	proved	proved, proven
put	put	put
ride	rode	ridden
rise	rose	risen
run	ran	run
see	saw	seen
set	set	set
shine	shone	shone
sit	sat	sat
speak	spoke	spoken
steal	stole	stolen
swim	swam	swum
swing	swung	swung
take	took	taken
teach	taught	taught
throw	threw	thrown
wake	woke, waked	woke, waked
wear	wore	worn

Standard English requires use of these principal parts:

I must have *broken* [not *broke*] my glasses. By noon we had finished the digging and *begun* [not *began*] to pour the concrete.

Privilege of occurrence This term refers to the uses to which an expression can appropriately be put. For example, *the* has privilege of occurrence before *student*, but not, unless it is part of another structure, after *student*. That is, *the student* is a grammatical structure, but *student the* is not. Roughly speaking *privilege of occurrence* from a structural point of view describes the nature of what is often called a part of speech. Thus, *carbon* and *campus*, when used as nouns, have similar privileges of occurrence.

prof Slang when used as a common noun ("I like the course but not the prof"). Acceptable in journalistic and informal writing as an abbreviation with a full name (*Prof. George B. Sanders*, but *Professor Sanders*). Best formal style requires that *professor* be written out in all titles.

Pronoun, types and forms Pronouns function as nouns, but take their meaning from their antecedents, the expressions to which they refer (see *Antecedent*). Several types of words are classified as pronouns, and many of them preserve case distinctions (see *Case*), which indicate how they are used. Because form changes to indicate case are not characteristic of modern English, various problems in usage of pronoun forms have developed. For usage problems other than those considered below, see also *myself; what; who; whom; whose; Possessive before gerund*.

    1. *Personal pronouns* have case distinctions as follows: Subjective or nominative case, used for subjects and for complements referring to subjects after linking verbs; objective or dative-accusative case, used for various sorts of objects, including objects of prepositions, and for subjects and objects of most verbals; and possessive or genitive case, referring to various personal relationships, including possession.

	First Person	Second Person	Third Person
SUBJECTIVE			
SINGULAR:	I	you	he, she, it
PLURAL:	we	you	they
OBJECTIVE			
SINGULAR:	me	you	him, her, it
PLURAL:	us	you	them
POSSESSIVE			
SINGULAR:	my, mine	your, yours	his, her, hers, its
PLURAL:	our, ours	your, yours	their, theirs

The second possessive forms are used as subjects or complements, most frequently as subject complements ("The book is mine").

    In standard English subjective forms are always used as subjects of a sentence or clause:

    Jim and *I* [not *me*] made the first team. I told them that *he* [not *him*] and Nancy could divide the lunch.

To test usage with a double subject, drop out the noun; one would not say "Me made the team." *I* and *we* are customarily last in a sequence, other pronouns first:

> *Evelyn and I* [not *I and Evelyn*] won the doubles.

In formal written English, subjective forms are still used for a pronoun complement following a linking verb ("It was I who finally spoke"; "the real victim is she"). The subject–verb–object pattern is so prevalent, however, that users of English tend to prefer the objective form whenever it appears after the verb. Informally, "It's me" or "The real fools are us" is common.

Related is the use of a personal pronoun after *than* or *as* in a comparison. Formally, subjective forms are preferred, on the theory that the pronoun is the subject of a shortened clause ("She is older than I [am]"; "I am as well qualified as she [is]"). Here also, pressures of usual word order make the objective forms common informally.

Standard usage of objective forms is consistent. The objective case is used for objects of verbs, for objects of prepositions, and for subjects or objects of most verbals. Self-consciousness about the forms, a tendency to overcorrect, and perhaps some notion that *I* is more elegant than *me* produce frequent infelicities with pronouns in objective positions. Nominatives used like the alternatives in the following sentences have the extra disadvantage of sounding pretentious or affected.

> He told my wife and *me* [not *I*] that the tickets were ready.
> We never liked the Broadnicks, neither *her* [not *she*] nor her husband.
> Just between you and *me* [not *I*], no hair ever got that color naturally.
> The manager promised *us* [not *we*] girls the new apartment.
> The man sitting in front of John and *me* [not *I*] kept his hat on.

2. *Relative pronouns* introduce subordinate clauses but also refer to antecedents and function in noun positions in the sentence. In "Grandmother, *who* wore spit curls to her dying day, arrived looking like a squid," *who* introduces the modifying clause but also refers to *Grandmother* and serves as subject in its clause. The other relative pronouns, *which* and *that*, keep the same form in all cases, although *whose* is sometimes used for the possessive of *which*. *Who* and *whoever* are used to refer to persons and sometimes animals, *which* for inanimate objects, and *that* for either. Some writers prefer *that* to introduce a restrictive clause and *who* or *which* for a nonrestrictive clause. See also *who, whom, whose.*

636

3. *Interrogative pronouns* signal questions; they include *what* and the forms used as relative pronouns.

> *Who* is he? *Whom* do you see? *Whose* book is it?

4. *Intensive pronouns* and *reflexive pronouns* have forms developed from personal pronouns: *myself, yourself, himself, herself, itself, ourselves, yourselves, themselves* (not *theirselves*). Their names distinguish only their use; intensive pronouns emphasize; reflexive pronouns redirect the predication to the subject. Compare:

> INTENSIVE: I cut the rope *myself.*
>
> REFLEXIVE: I cut *myself.*

Some intensive or reflexive forms, especially *myself*, are growing in popularity as objective forms in the predicate, apparently because the user fears that *me* may be wrong or assumes that *myself* is more modest. The practice is especially common in combinations ("They invited Doris and myself"), but most style sheets still prescribe the objective in formal writing.

5. Indefinite pronouns (words like *anyone, everyone, anybody, everybody, anything, everything, each, any,* and *all*) and *demonstrative pronouns* (*this, that, these, those, such*) do not change form to show their use in their clauses. They are pronouns when they function as substantives; often the same words are modifiers. Compare:

> PRONOUN: *Any* of you may taste the jam.
>
> MODIFIER: *Any* person here may taste the jam.
>
> PRONOUN: *That* is the man I saw through the window.
>
> MODIFIER: I saw *that* man through the window.

For agreement with indefinite pronouns, see 17g.

Proper noun   In general a proper noun is a name; in "Spot caught a rabbit; he has a black spot on his back," *Spot* is a proper noun, *spot* is not. Proper nouns are capitalized (see 26c).

proved, proven   *Proved* is the only form having historical foundation, but *proven* is also commonly accepted. The verb *prove* is often used carelessly of statements that are not proved; often *suggest, imply,* or *indicate* would be more accurate.

providing   In older usage, not admitted as a synonym of *provided,* a conjunction meaning "on the condition"; common in modern usage.

put across   Blanket term for *explain, prove, demonstrate, expound, argue, make clear, establish,* and the like (see *Jargon*).

quite Generally accepted, although often unnecessary, in the sense of "entirely" ("quite dead," "frozen quite to the bottom"); colloquial in the sense "somewhat," "rather" ("quite cold," "quite a big job").

raise For confusion of forms of *rise* and *raise*, see *rise*. *Raise* is now generally accepted as a synonym of *rear* in the sense "bring to maturity," but many writers prefer *rear* when referring to human beings.

rate Currently overused and misused; slang in some usages ("He does not rate with us").

re In the sense of "about," used for formal purposes only in legal documents and skeletonized commercial writing.

real Colloquial as an intensive ("It was a real nice clambake"). Use *really*, *very*, or a word expressive enough so that it needs no intensive.

really A useful word frequently overused and misused so that it clutters sentences; see *Jargon*.

INEFFECTUAL: He had been *really* traveling.

REVISED: He was gasping for breath because he had been running.

REDUNDANT: It was *really* true.

REVISED: It was true.

reason is because See *because* and 13c.

reason why Usually redundant ("The reason why I like to swim. . . ."); omit *why*.

reckon Dialectal and inexact as a synonym for *believe, suppose, assume*.

Redundancy Excess words, especially those that double the meaning of neighboring words, are called redundant, and are usually the result of careless repetition or of inadequate knowledge of the full meanings of the words used. "Repeat again," "continue on," "return back," and "diametrically opposite" are common examples of redundancy.

REDUNDANT: He was the first originator of the theory that we all now unanimously accept that understanding should be substituted in the place of punishment.

REVISION: He originated the theory, now unanimously accepted, that understanding should replace punishment. [The following of the original are redundant: *first, originator; all, unanimously; substituted, in the place of.*]

REDUNDANT: In this modern day and age of the present, one can never return back to the old methods of home industry of earlier times.

REVISION: One cannot return to old methods of home industry.

regard, regards   Often overused; see *Jargon*. *Regards* is nonstandard in constructions like *in regards to.*

Relative   Also called relative conjunction, subordinating conjunction; see *Conjunction.*

Relative pronoun   *who, whoever, whom, whomever, whose, whosever, which, that;* see *Pronoun* and *who, whom.* Relative pronouns can be distinguished from relative or subordinating conjunctions by the fact of their having grammatical use within their own clauses, usually as subject or object.

PRONOUN: He said *that* was right.

CONJUNCTION: He said *that* I had a good point.

Repetition   Repetition is often an effective device for emphasis, and it is often necessary. Repetition of a key word, for example, is preferable to the use of ostentatious synonyms. A paper on Shakespeare is bound to repeat words like *drama* or *play* or *Shakespeare,* and to avoid repeating the author's name with clichés like "the Bard" or "the Swan of Avon" is more obvious than the repetition. Careless repetition, however, particularly of easily noticed expressions, makes writing wordy and amateurish. Moreover, repetition of words is often a symptom of some fundamental weakness—of inadequate subordination, for example (see chapter 16).

REPETITIOUS: *Users* of the library often *use* little care in handling books.

REVISION: Users of the library often are careless in handling books.

REPETITIOUS: He announced *that* if anyone wanted to argue *that* he should wait until the next meeting.

REVISION: He announced that if anyone wanted to argue he should wait until the next meeting.

respectfully, respectively   *Respectfully* means "in a respectful manner" ("respectfully submitted"); *respectively* means "in the specified order," "severally" ("The balloons were identified as 4b, 5a, and 2g, respectively").

Retained object In some passive constructions, the word that would serve as direct object in the equivalent active sentence is retained as object of the passive verb.

> svc: The president awarded him [indirect object] the *medal* [direct object].

> PASSIVE: *He* [from indirect object] was awarded the *medal* [retained object] by the president.

reverend Used in standard English with the first name or initials of the person described or with the title Mr. (see 26j); in formal usage preceded by *the*.

> The Reverend William Dimity, The Reverend W. L. Dimity, The Reverend Mr. Dimity

Rhetorical question A question used for emphatic effect, implying agreement with the speaker ("Who would condone shooting a helpless old woman?"). The device can be overly dramatic and is readily overused.

right Informal as an intensive in expressions like "right away"; prefer *immediately, at once, promptly,* etc. A localism in the sense of "very."

> It was a *very* [not *right*] good fight.

right on In the sense of perfect or excellent, nonstandard at this writing, but growing in acceptance.

rise, raise The two verbs are frequently confused. *Rise (rose, risen),* intransitive, often combined with suffixes like *up,* indicates that the subject moves.

> He *rises* before dawn. He *rose* before dawn yesterday. He *has never risen* before dawn in his life.

Raise (raised, raised), usually transitive (but "John opened the betting, and Tom raised"), indicates that the subject acts on something, making it rise or appear.

> He *raises* his hand when he wants to talk. The committee *raised* a new issue. His salary *has* not *been raised* for a year.

said Pseudo-legal affectation as a modifier; if necessary, use *this, that, these,* and the like.

> Having rejected *the motion* [not *said motion*], the committee adjourned.

same   As a pronoun used with *in*, *same* is sometimes useful in legal documents, but sounds affected in most writing.

> Having made his bed he must lie *in it* [not *in same*].

scarcely   Not to be used with another negative (see *Double negative*).

> There *was scarcely* [not *was not scarcely*] any butter.

seem   A useful word, often misused or overused, especially as a qualification in constructions like "it would *seem* that."

> The evidence *suggests* [not *would seem to suggest*] that Shakespeare was once a schoolmaster.

seldom ever   Redundant; omit *ever*.

Separable verb   See *Verb sets.*

set   For confusion of forms of *sit* and *set*, see *sit.*

set-up   Slang in the sense of "an easy victory," and currently overused in jargonic writing to mean anything related to organization, condition, or circumstances ("I liked the new set-up"); see *Jargon.*

shall, will   The verbs *shall* and *will* are troublesome because they have a troubled background. In Old English *shall* and *will* were not signs of the future; the word for *shall* meant "ought to" and the word for *will* meant "willing to," "to be about to." These meanings have been preserved in *should*, which implies obligation, and *would*, which implies willingness. But *shall* and *will* became indications of the future, just as words with the same meaning today ("I am about to go"; "I have to go") are becoming future forms. For hundreds of years little effort was made to distinguish between *shall* and *will* as auxiliaries, and users of English apparently never have had any deep-rooted feeling for a distinction between them — a fact that may account for the distinction's being difficult. In the eighteenth century, a popular grammarian laid down rules for the use of *shall* and *will*, and most handbooks of usage since then have repeated his rules — though a few have turned them exactly backward. At present, most people, especially in America, pay little attention to these rules. Partly because contractions (*I'll, we'll*) are so common in speech, *will* is used in all persons in most informal situations. A few people, however, attach great importance to the arbitrary distinction between the words, and the following rule is still observed in some formal English.

> In the first person, use *shall* to denote simple futurity, *will* to denote determination and purpose; in the second and third persons, use *will* to denote simple futurity, *shall* to denote determination and purpose.

641

In general, *should* and *would* also follow this rule, except when the use would interfere with the basic meaning of these two words, *should* implying duty, *would* implying willingness.

> I *shall* consider each of the arguments. I predict that the people *will* reject the offer.

shape Colloquial in the sense of "condition," "manner."

> She was *well trained* [not *in good shape*] for the tournament.

should For distinctions between *should* and *would*, see *shall, will*.

should of Mistaken form of *should have;* see *could of*.

show Slang as a synonym for *chance, opportunity;* colloquial as a synonym for *moving picture, play*.

show up Not standard in either the sense "arrive" ("Jim did not show up") or the sense "expose" ("He is no gentleman, and Mary showed him up.")

sic See p. 508.

sign up, sign up for, sign up with Not acceptable in formal English.

Signal words See chapter 17.

sit, set The two verbs are frequently confused. *Sit* (*sat, sat*), intransitive except for a few uses, especially with suffixes like *out* or *with* ("She sat out the dance; she sits a horse gracefully"), indicates that the subject occupies a place or seat or is in a sitting position.

> He *sits* by the window. He *sat* by the window last week. He *has sat* there for a year.

Set (*set, set*), transitive except for a few uses ("The sun sets in the west; the hens are setting"), means *place* or *put*, often varied in combinations with words like *off, up, by*.

> He *sets* the lamp on the table. They *set up* the new organization yesterday. Finally they *have set out* on their journey.

situated Often used redundantly.

> The house was *in* [not *situated in*] the tenement district.

situation Wordy and jargonic in expressions like "the team had a fourth-down situation." See *Jargon*.

size Not generally accepted as a modifier ("this size of dress," not "this size dress").

642

Slang   Slang develops variously, notably because we like to play with words. We put old words to new uses or coin new expressions, largely for the sake of novelty or cleverness. The results vary. Occasionally a slang expression fills a genuine need, persists, and is accepted as part of the language. Often it is accepted by limited groups and remains current in nonstandard or standard colloquial use. Usually it has quick popularity and then disappears. Using slang—especially if you make it up yourself—can be amusing, and the result vivid, but for two reasons slang is limited in its usefulness. First, it is usually known to so few people, in such a restricted group geographically or socially, and for so short a time, that it can be used for only the most local and ephemeral purposes. Second, much slang is so general that it means almost nothing. The user of slang often does not know what he wishes to say, and the listener to slang does not know what, if anything, has been said.

> SLANG: It's okay by all of us if the dean of women wants to throw the book at us, but she better have the straight dope before she makes her move.
>
> STANDARD: None of us will object if the dean of women enforces the rules, but she should learn the facts before acting.

Slot   This term has been popularized through modern grammars to indicate a position in a sentence pattern that can be filled by an appropriate word or words. For example, a sentence will have a subject slot and a verb slot, which can be filled by words or groups of words having the appropriate privilege of occurrence.

so   Avoid the excessive use of *so* to join independent clauses (see 16a).

so as   Not to be confused with *so that* (see 17c).

so long as   See *as long as.*

some   Not standard to indicate vague approval.

> It was *an exciting* [not *some*] game.

somebody's else   The sign of the possessive appears on the last word (see 26g). Use *somebody else's.*

sometime, some time   One word in the sense "occasion," "some other time"; two words in the sense "a period of time."

> Come up to see me *sometime.* The repairs will require *some time.*

somewhat of   *Somewhat* is most commonly an adverb ("They were somewhat slow"); *somewhat of* is not a standard idiom.

643

somewheres   Nonstandard. Omit the *s*.

sort   See *kind*.

sort of, sort of a   Both are clumsy and colloquial as modifiers.

> I was *rather* [not *sort of*] tired. He was *an amateur* [not *sort of a*] plumber.

speak, speech   The difference between the vowels in the verb *speak* and the noun *speech* is fruitful of spelling errors.

state   Currently misused as a loose equivalent of *say, remark, observe, declare*. Carefully used, *to state* means "to declare in a formal statement." See *Jargon*.

> The board *stated* that the coach's contract would not be renewed. The coach *said* [not *stated*] that practice would be postponed until four-thirty.

stationary, stationery   *Stationary* is a modifier meaning "not movable" or "not moving"; *stationery* is a noun meaning "writing materials." They can be distinguished by remembering that l*ett*ers are written with station*e*ry.

Stress   Stress in phonemics refers to the force or tenseness with which segmental phonemes are uttered. Stress is part of the pattern of the sentence, of the suprasegmental phonemes. Stress is often indicated by the following system of symbols: no symbol, light stress; / ˆ /, moderate stress; / ` /, relatively heavy stress; / ´ /, very heavy stress.

Subject   In all grammars of modern English, the subject, under whatever terminology, is an important part of the sentence. In "Planes fly," the subject is *planes*. Often, the subject is the first word or group of words that by its nature could be a subject (see 13a).

Subjective case, nominative case   The subjective case is used for subjects and for complements referring to the subject. It can no longer be recognized in the form of nouns; for the subjective case in pronouns, see *Pronoun*.

Subordinate clause   A subordinate or dependent clause is one that is made subordinate to an independent clause or to a part of a clause. Modifying clauses function as adjectives ("Joan is the only girl who got an A") or adverbs ("Smile when you say that"). Noun clauses may be classified as subordinate ("Whoever dissents should raise his right hand").

Subordinating conjunction   See *Conjunction*.

Substantive   Any nominal word or construction may be called a substantive; see *Noun; Noun clause; Noun phrase; Pronoun; Verbal; Verb phrase.*

such   Overused as a vague intensive (see 15c).

>   It was *a very* [not *such a*] warm day.

suit, suite   *Suit,* the commoner word, can be either a verb ("Suit yourself") or a noun ("a tailor-made suit"). *Suite,* only a noun, has several specialized uses.

>   The ambassador and his *suite* occupied a *suite* of rooms.

suspicion   A noun, not appropriately used to supplant the excellent verb *suspect.*

sure   Colloquial as an intensive.

>   He was *certainly angry* [not *sure sore*].

take and   Redundant and nonstandard in most uses.

>   He *whacked* [not *took and whacked*] down the hornet's nest.

take sick   A regionalism not generally accepted in formal English; prefer *become ill* or *sick* or a more exact expression.

Tense   English has developed verb forms and combinations of verbs to indicate subtle variations in tense or time. These are not always consistent with traditional names for tenses; the so-called simple present, *I prove,* for instance, usually indicates a customary action ("I go to class at eight") or future action ("I begin classes next week"). Native speakers, however, have little trouble distinguishing the forms; troubles with tense usually occur because the writer shifts his point of view (see 21b). This should remain consistent, and when two or more times are distinguished within the sentence, the forms of verbs should reveal the order of events. In general the relationship of the tenses can be suggested by a formula like the following:

	The past perfect forms	are to	the other past forms
as	the past forms	are to	the present forms
as	the present forms and the future perfect forms	are to	the other future forms.

This works out somewhat as follows:

> When the boss *had come* [past perfect form] I *received* [past form] my pay.

> At noon, if the boss *has come* [past form] I *receive* [customary present form] my pay.

> By noon, the boss *will have come* [future perfect form], and I *shall receive* [future form] my pay.

> By noon, if the boss *comes* [present form], I *shall receive* [future form] my pay.

When a direct quotation is reported as an indirect question, the word order shifts and the time is sometimes pushed back.

> DIRECT: "You *were* wrong," he said.
> INDIRECT: He said I *had been* wrong.

Patterns are not consistent; in the following the tense does not change:

> DIRECT: He asked, "Was Caroline on time?"
> INDIRECT: He asked whether Caroline was on time.

The tense of a verbal is determined by the relationship of the time of the action of the verbal to the time of the action of the main verb. The present verbal is most common and is used when the verbal and the main verb refer to action at the same time.

> We expected him *to burn* the papers.

Both verb and verbal refer to the past; the verbal is therefore present in form.

> *Smiling* at his discomfort, she looks at the photographs.

Verb and verbal both refer to the present and both forms are present. The present form is also used sometimes with a function word like *after* to suggest action preceding that of the main verb.

> After *smiling* at his discomfort, she closed the photograph album.

The past forms regularly indicate action previous to the time of the main verb.

> We expected him *to have burned* the papers. *Having smiled* at his discomfort, she closed the photograph album.

646

The burning and the smiling preceded the expecting and the closing. The simple past participle often describes a state of affairs
caused previously but existing at the same time as that of the main
action.

> *Reconciled*, he continued to praise the photographs.

terrible, terribly   Overused and misused; colloquial as general intensives ("She is a terribly sweet girl") and as blanket words signifying anything unpleasant ("I had been vaccinated and felt terrible"). See *Jargon*.

terrific   Recently misused and overused as a general synonym for
large, impressive, dramatic, significant, dexterous, or *important,* it can
now scarcely be used in its standard meaning, "causing terror."

that   Like *who* and *which, that* is often unnecessary to introduce a
clause (*Everybody knew* [*that*] *he had failed*). Omission is confusing,
however, when it causes temporary misreading:

> Mr. Chamberlain *forgot that the umbrella* [not *forgot the umbrella*] had
> been torn.

For reference of *that,* see 17e.

that there   Nonstandard; omit *there.*

that, which   Both *that* and *which* are used as relative pronouns (see
Pronoun, 3). *That* is the oldest of the relatives and can be used to
refer to either persons or things; *which* does not refer to persons.
A recent distinction, perhaps prescribed in an attempt at neatness,
specifies *that* to introduce restrictive clauses and *which* and *who* to
introduce nonrestrictive clauses. The distinction has never been
common, even in formal writing, but many writers distinguish
between *that* and *which* on this basis.

the   The definite article (see *Article*).

their, there, they're   Commonly confused in spelling. *There,* which
can be remembered by its similarity to *where,* means "in that place"
("Lie there, Nipper"). *Their* is the possessive of *they. They're,* the
contraction of *they are,* is not acceptable in formal composition.

these   Should be avoided as a substitute for *the* (see *this*).

these kind, these sort   See *kind.*

they   For the colloquial use of *they* to refer to people or society,
see 17e.

this   Like *the, this* as a determiner indicates that the noun it precedes has been previously mentioned.

> On our way home from Sunday School, *a* [not *this*] man came up to
> me and took my hand, and then *he* [not *this fellow*] said. . . .

For reference of *this*, see 17e; for *this* as a symptom of inadequate subordination, see 16a.

this here   Nonstandard; omit *here.*

tho   A variant spelling of *though* not perferred for formal composition.

those   Avoid *those* as an intensive with no reference.

> He looked back fondly on *his* [not *those*] old college days.

thusly   Affected or nonstandard for *thus.*

to, too, two   Distinguish the function word *to* ("to the game," "learn to read") from the adverb *too* ("too sick," "too hot"), and the numeral *two* ("two seats on the aisle").

toward, towards   Alternative forms; *toward* is more common in the United States.

trait   Redundant in *character trait;* use *trait* or *characteristic.*

Transformation   In transformational grammar, the deep structure of a sentence becomes the surface structure through transformations. "Astrid was chased by a bear" can be considered a transformation of "A bear chased Astrid." "Red dress" can be considered a transformation of "The dress is red." See chapter 12.

Transformational grammar, transform grammar   Transformational grammar is a generative grammar, in that it endeavors to provide rules by which sentences are generated. See chapter 12.

Trite expressions, clichés   Many expressions in English cannot stand popularity. Idioms, of course, and standard expressions appear over and over without losing their effectiveness, but slang or other attempts at cleverness or vividness emerge after overuse with as little vigor as any other stale joke. Metaphors that do not enter the language as new words often become trite. The writer who first referred to a wife as a "ball and chain" may have been amusing on the comic-strip level; the thousandth person who imitated him was not amusing on any level. Expressions that have been so tarnished by time that their charm, and often even their meaning, is gone are called trite or hackneyed expressions or clichés. Trite expressions are dangerous partly because they paralyze the mind. As ready-made channels for thought they invite the ideas of the writer, who can then cease thinking. An editorial writer commented in a discussion of academic freedom in a university:

> Any teacher who disagrees with his dean's academic views is not
> playing on the team and should turn in his suit.

The "team" metaphor was worn out long ago, but the writer fell into the set pattern so easily that he failed to analyze his own remarks. The convenience of the trite expression led him into an argument by false analogy (see 10b).

TRITE: When war first reared its ugly head, John Q. Public took it in his stride and played ball.

REVISION: Faced with war, we did what had to be done.

TRITE: In our day and age, in this great country of ours, progress has taken place by leaps and bounds.

REVISION: America has progressed.

try and *Try to* is preferred in standard English.

type In formal English, *type* is a noun or verb, although colloquially it is often an adjective ("a ranch-type house").

This type of research [not *this type research*] yields results.

unique For the use of *unique*, see 16c.

up Useful in verb sets (see *Verb set*), *up* can frequently be separated from the verb, but often the sense is clearer and the construction smoother if *up* is kept close to the verb.

AWKWARD: He made his mind up.

REVISED: He made up his mind.

Upside-down modification A minor modifier allowed to usurp part or all of the basic sentence is said to involve upside-down modification. Special circumstances might justify a sentence like "She was getting ready to cross on a red light when a man wearing rather old clothes mugged her," but for most purposes some of the modifiers should be subordinated or removed.

The *d* is elided in speech but not omitted in writing.

We *used to* [not *use to*] go to the beach every summer.

used to could Nonstandard for "used to be able."

Verb See chapter 12. For problems with forms of verbs see *lie, lay; Mood; Principal parts; rise, raise; sit, set; shall, will; Tense; Voice.*

Verb phrase In the older grammar, a verb phrase was any combination of words serving as a verb. Thus *has gone* and *will go* were verb phrases. In transformational grammar the word is used in larger senses; it can be used to indicate the verb and all that goes

649

with it, and is thus equivalent to the word *predicate*, or it can be used to indicate the verb and its modifiers, but not the complement.

Verbal Formed from verbs, verbals retain some verb functions but serve primarily as nouns or modifiers or parts of complex verbs (see *Gerund; Infinitive; Participle*). Verbals cannot serve as finite or complete verbs (see 12a). For tense of verbals, see *Tense*.

Verb set Verb sets, also called merged verbs, separable verbs, and verb-adverb combinations are verbs made from a standard verb form plus a participle, such as *step up*, *wind down*, and *look over* (see pp. 250–51). Many are involved in colloquial or slang expressions such as *beef up, cop out,* and *beg off,* but some are standard and may even have no synonyms. In general they can be recognized since the meaning of either of the combination is somewhat different from the meaning of either of its parts or of the two taken together. *To step up* may mean "to step up," but more frequently it means "to increase," not "to step," and the increase need not take place in steps. A grammarian might have difficulty distinguishing some verb sets from a verb plus a modifier. In "He was put out by the reply," the term *put out,* although colloquial, is certainly a verb set, but in "She put out the light" the decision might be difficult. This distinction, fortunately, the writer need not make.

very The most useful intensive, but since it is usually only an intensive, with relatively little meaning, it is as likely to weaken writing as to strengthen it. Most good writers use *very* sparingly. Older practice was to forbid the use of *very* before a past participle without an intervening *much* (*very much pleased,* not *very pleased*). The distinction is still maintained in some formal writing.

Voice A distinction in verb forms between the active, in which the subject of the verb is the actor, and the passive, in which the subject of the verb receives the action. The passive employs a form of *to be* as an auxiliary and a reversed sequence of the SVC pattern, so that the complement appears first and the subject last, if at all. ("He was arrested by the narcotics squad.") Passive constructions may be difficult to distinguish from equations using linking verbs; in the example above, "He was hooked on heroin," the combination *was hooked* can be thought of as the passive form of the active verb *hook,* or as the linking verb *was* plus the adjective *hooked,* which was formed as a past participle but may now be thought of as an adjective (see *Participle.*) For specific uses of the passive, see 14b.

wait on Except in the sense of "serve," *wait for* is idiomatic.

We have been waiting *for* [not *on*] you to arrive.

want for   In most constructions, omit the *for*.

> I *want* [not *want for*] you to meet her.

ways   Colloquial for *way* in the sense "a distance."

> It was a long *way* [not *ways*] to the road.

we   The editorial *we, we* used for *I* or to stand for a newspaper, is generally confined to journalistic writing; *we* is common as an impersonal subject meaning "people in general," or "the writer and the reader."

weather   Frequently confused in spelling with *whether* ("I asked him whether or not we could depend upon fair weather").

well   An adjective in the sense "in good health," "cured" ("The patient is now recovered and is quite well"); an adverb corresponding to the adjective *good,* but not to be confused with it (see 16b).

> She played her part *well* [not *good*]. The blueprints look *good* [not *well*].

what   Nonstandard as a relative pronoun.

> I liked the places *that* [not *what*] he recommended.

What all occurs in some dialects ("What all they do I have to do"), but *all* is redundant.

when   Avoid the *when*-clause in a definition (see 13c).

where   Nonstandard or colloquial when substituted for *that*.

> I noticed in the paper *that* Senator Jones is a candidate for re-election [not *I see by the paper* where *Senator Jones is up for re-election*].

where at   In most constructions, omit the *at*.

> Where is he? [not *Where at is he?* or *Where is he at?*]

whether   See *if*.

which   For *which* after *and*, see *and which*; for the use of *which* to refer to human beings, see *Pronoun*; for *which* and *that*, see *that, which*.

while   In Old English, *while* (spelled *hwil*) meant a period of time, as it still does in a phrase like "in a short while," and most subsequent meanings preserve the idea of time. For centuries *while* was most commonly used as a relative conjunction to indicate that the time in the subordinate clause is the same as that in the main clause ("While I broil the chops, you might set the table"). Presumably this use developed a concessive conjunction, the equivalent of *although* ("While Father disapproved of the damage an off-road vehicle might do to the ecology, he hated to deprive us of having a good time"). Read with the traditional meaning of *while,* that the one action took place while the other took place—and presumably only at that time—the sentence is confusing and even nonsensical. Recently, another use has appeared, in which *while* serves as a coordinating conjunction, the equivalent of *and* ("Jenkins will run in the relay, while he also competes in the javelin"). This sentence, likewise, will be nonsense to many careful readers, although such uses are now common in sports writing and in some other areas. Of course there is nothing wrong with a word developing new uses; they do it all the time, but these last two can be ambiguous and even ridiculous; consequently, most careful writers avoid them.

who, whom Logically, relative and interrogative pronouns take their form from their use in their clause—*who* for a subject or subject complement, *whom* for an object. When the words occur out of the usual subject–verb–complement order, however, users of the language do not always make the case distinction. Compare:

> I asked him *who* he thought he was hitting. I asked him *whom* he thought he was hitting.

In these sentences the pronoun functions as object of *was hitting;* formal written usage would require *whom*. Since the pronoun is the first word in its clause, however, in the subject position, speakers tend to use *who,* the subject form. Formal writing might require:

> *Whom* did Tom invite? *Whom* do you see? I don't know *whom* he is taking to the party.

In nonformal situations *who* is common in such sentences. *Whom* is used consistently when the pronoun immediately follows a preposition.

> I wasn't sure to *whom* [not *who*] I was speaking.

Concern for correctness with such pronouns often causes exaggerated deference to *whom* and becomes more disturbing than informal neglect for the case distinction. Notice the following:

Who [not *whom*] does he think he is? I met the girl *who* [not *whom*] everyone said would win the beauty contest. I asked him *who* [not *whom*] he was.

who's   The contraction of *who is.*

whose   English no longer has a possessive form for *which. Whose,* the possessive of *who,* is now regularly used to avoid the often cumbersome *of which,* even though *who* is usually restricted to reference to people.

I do not like a ring *whose setting* [compare *the setting of which*] reminds me of snakes.

will   For the distinction from *shall,* see *shall, will.*

wire   Informal for either *telegram* or *telegraph.*

wise   Currently in vogue and overused as an informal suffix for almost everything ("The meal was good tastewise"). Often the uses sound as absurd as this example.

without   Nonstandard as a substitute for *unless.*

I will not stay *unless* [not *without*] you raise my wages.

wood, woods   In the United States either is acceptable as a synonym of *forest.*

worst kind, worst way   Not acceptable in the sense "very much."

worthwhile   Overused blanket word (see *Jargon*).

would have   Often awkward.

If they *had* [not *would have*] done that. . . .

would of   Mistaken form of *would have* (see *could of*).

you   To be used with caution in impersonal constructions (see 17g).

you-all   Informal Southern form as the plural of *you;* not acceptable for formal composition.

FOR STUDY AND WRITING

A In the following sentences supply the proper form of the appropriate verb and explain your choice.

> **1.** He had been (*lie, lay*) on his back for three weeks, and he was so weak that he could not (*rise, raise*) his hand.

2. The coat still (*lie, lay*) where we had left it in the morning.

3. When the peasants finally (*rise, raise*) in rebellion, issues that had (*lie, lay*) dormant for years assumed new importance.

4. After I had eaten, I (*lie, lay*) down on the couch and (*sit, set*) the book on the stand in front of me.

5. All the children (*lie, lay*) in the tall grass watching the ducks (*rise, raise*) into the air and head south.

6. The pitcher should be (*sit, set*) wherever you (*sit, set*) it this morning.

7. They let the injured man (*lie, lay*) in the middle of the highway until the ambulance arrived.

8. (*Lie, lay*) the slices of eggplant in a dish, (*lie, lay*) a weight on them, and allow them to (*sit, set*) there overnight.

9. He had (*lie, lay*) emphasis on this fact, that the land (*lie, lay*) adjacent to the river.

10. He (*lie, lay*) a wager that the billfold would be found (*lie, lay*) on the dresser.

B For each blank in the following sentences select an appropriate form of the verb in parentheses:

1. When I _____ (*eat*) my lunch, I took a short nap.

2. While I was looking in the closet for my windbreaker, part of the ceiling _____ (*fall*) down.

3. Since you say you can see in the dark so well, why _____ you _____ (*stumble*)?

4. While I _____ (*set*) the table, you might boil some water.

5. Before you screw down the lid, be sure you _____ (*check*) the safety valve.

6. You _____ (*prove*) the theorem before you could have proved the corollary.

7. Mother told me that strange men _____ (*be*) not to be trusted.

8. When Uncle Oliver came to dinner he always _____ (*bring*) us oranges.

C For each blank in the following sentences select an appropriate form of the verb in parentheses:

1. If it _____ (*be*) noon, I would go right now.

2. If the plant _____ (*be*) sitting on the piano, it must have left a mark in the dust.

3. If only Father _____ (*be*) here!

4. If anybody _____ (*save*) him, Dr. Worley would be the man.

5. If your father _____ (*be*) not carrying a gun, I would think him a religious man.

6. Rosalie, I often wish you _____ (*be*) smarter than you are.

7. Quentin, I often wish you _____ (*act*) smarter than you do.

654

8. Children, _____ (*can*) you not keep from squabbling if you would try?

9. If those children _____ (*can*) keep from squabbling, I would let them play together.

10. If I _____ (*be*) you, I would take it back and get my money.

D In the following sentences, select the appropriate forms of the verbal and explain the reason for your choice:

1. I was ashamed (to lose, to be losing, to have been losing) the game for our team.

2. I was glad (to receive, to have received) your invitation.

3. It was the largest audience ever (to convene, to have convened) in Severing Hall.

4. When you get into the boat be sure (to fasten, to have fastened) your life belt.

5. The stairs are steep; be sure (to hold, to have held) the guard rail.

6. Father came along just when I was about (to be arrested, to have been arrested).

7. If they were not doing their algebra, they ought (to be doing, to have been doing) it.

8. Those who were about (to die, to have died) took a glance at each other.

E Choose the appropriate pronoun form in the following sentences, and give the reason for your choice.

1. Everybody thought Uncle Angus was stingy, but he left (we, us) girls a beautiful house.

2. The bartender told my cousin and (I, me) that we should go get a few years older.

3. Ask the patrolman (who, whom) he thinks he is arresting.

4. The quarrel between my sister and (I, me, myself) began when I was a child.

5. Mother promised a glass of lemonade to (whoever, whomever) could get back from the store first.

6. I cannot help wondering (who, whom) he thinks he is.

7. Aunt Amy asked Ethel and (I, me, myself) out for the weekend.

8. He was afraid to ask (who, whom) would be playing the piano accompaniment.

9. We heard voices coming over the water, and we knew it was (they, them).

10. The trouble between my roommate and (I, me) all began when she joined the women's liberation movement.

11. (Who, whom) do you expect to find buried under the cellar steps?

12. You may nominate (whoever, whomever) you please.

13. Harry kept complaining about the rain, but after a while we agreed that (he, him) and (I, me) would start out.

14. When Father cooks, nobody feels sorry for (he, his, him) sweating over a hot stove.

15. (Who, whom) do you think will be the new basketball coach?

F Discuss the suitability of the italicized expressions in the following sentences for (a) campus conversation, (b) informal composition, and (c) formal composition.

1. Whatever you want, she is *liable* to want something *of a different nature,* like *movieing* while you want to *rap with some cat.*

2. *Like I said,* my *girl-friend* knows so little about football she *thinks* "clipping" is charging ten *bucks* for seats in the end zone.

3. A *stolid,* bald-headed gentleman was *staring* at me as though he thought he was *acquainted with* me, but was not *quite* certain.

4. *Here's* the *deal,* and you can *take it from me, it's a dilly.*

5. *Irregardless* of my mother's warnings, I decided to *date* him.

6. I was so *enthused I figured I'd contact 'em first off.*

7. I *suggest* the *inclusion* of this *data* on the *agendas.*

8. *A great number of* onlookers *blamed* the accident *on* Jim.

9. Maybe it's *okay lecturewise,* but *man,* I don't *dig* it.

10. He was *right on,* but I *suspicioned* he might *split.*

G Substitute fresher, more expressive terms for the trite expressions in the sentences below. You may find that you must use more revealing words than those in the original, since trite expressions can become nearly meaningless.

1. Crime never pays and true Americanism requires that we stamp it out, each and every time a crime wave raises its ugly head in this great and glorious land of ours.

2. And last but not least, in advertising you have to sell yourself; that is, to make it short and sweet, you have to hit the market smack on the nose.

3. With her hair a sable cloud about her face, her peaches-and-cream complexion, her ruby lips, and her eyes like stars, she was as pretty as a picture.

4. Martha was a perfect baby, as happy as the day is long.

5. The wily southpaw zipped a fast one over the corner, and the old speed king had done it again. You can't hit 'em if you can't see 'em.

6. The last examination had put me out like a light, and accordingly, although I was down in the dumps—it was blue Monday for me—I determined to burn the midnight oil.

7. We would willingly point with pride at the progress onward and upward in this land of the free; we have no inclination to drag a red herring across the trail to becloud the issue; but any lover of government

of the people, by the people, for the people must view with alarm the state of the nation in this day and age, and unless we go back to the principles of the founding fathers, we are in grave danger of having our cherished liberties gone with the wind.

8. He took the unwelcome news like a man. He became sober as a judge, but I knew he was true as steel, all wool and a yard wide, and that he would snap out of it.

9. He was tall, dark, and handsome, with lean flanks and piercing eyes, always smelling faintly of good English tobacco and well-oiled leather, every inch a man's man.

10. It appears like the Washington moguls believe this VIP is incapable of fending for himself lest he misses the boat entirely. Hence we get this ostentatious parade of potentates who hope to literally boost their nominee into office by finagling us native sons of the West into swallowing their platform—hook, line, and sinker—which would for fair kill the goose that laid the golden egg.

H Remove redundant words and phrases from the following:

1. Adley's design was the most unique among all those submitted.

2. Formerly in the olden days there was no free popular education available to all without charge.

3. It was the consensus of opinion that the statements were directly antithetical.

4. While the nations work against one another, the presence of war is constantly at hand.

5. We hold diametrically opposite views on most questions.

6. My mother, she thought I ought to go to the cheaper college, but the differences in cost were infinitesimally small.

7. The way this story was written made it seem to make me feel that it could really have actually happened to me.

8. A girl should be able to make a living in her special particular line.

9. In spite of all the illegal crimes he had committed, the leader of the gang went entirely scot-free.

10. It is the one and only unique sacred white Burmese camel in the United States.

I The passages below are wordy, many of them because they contain jargon. Rewrite them, making the sense clear in good English, if the passage suggests any sense. Some sentences may mean almost nothing, for blanket terms characteristically fill space with words, not with meaning. If a sentence has no discoverable meaning, write a sentence which says what you imagine the writer may have intended to say.

1. In this day and age the problem of drinking intoxicating beverages has had a much freer scope in recent years than was the case at an earlier period in time.

2. The person in search of worthwhile science fiction material can find the basic circumstances at every facet of modern literature.

3. Some critics commented on his lecture to the highest degree.

4. Everybody should be capable of practicing in some line of work. Being able to support yourself is very important in this respect.

5. Although this may not be the over-all case, it does include the majority of advertisements, and the factors in the movement are to the extreme.

6. Reading—the anesthetic of a tired mind; the broadening of one's educational frame of reference; the opening of new and unfound fields of thought; a must in everyone's life.

7. The big day rolled around, but Hamlet, who had the inclination for abruptness of action, curbed his burning desires, and therefore slowness of action resulted.

8. I told her that if she wouldn't get on the beam and stop blowing up the insignificant factors in the case she had better get out of the picture.

9. Though the evidence in the case seems to be that the crisis has passed and the Giants are over the hump of the slump that cost them great gobs of ground in the pennant chase, the Giant high command did not permit the chinks in the Giant armor turned up by the losing skid to go unnoticed. Quietly, behind the scenes, they are attempting to mend their fences, and you may be sure they will leave no stone unturned in their effort to batten down the hatches.

10. Another advantage of the cow is her ability to relax, and humans would be better off if they had this fundamental feature.

INDEX